please return

# A Reader in Sociology:
# Christian Perspectives

# A Reader in Sociology: Christian Perspectives

Charles P. De Santo
Calvin Redekop
William L. Smith-Hinds

*Editors*

HERALD PRESS
Scottdale, Pennsylvania
Kitchener, Ontario
1980

Library of Congress Cataloging in Publication Data

Main entry under title:
A reader in sociology.

  Includes bibliographies and index.
  1. Sociology, Christian—Addresses, essays,
lectures. 2. Sociology—Addresses, essays, lectures.
I. De Santo, Charles, II. Redekop, Calvin Wall,
1925- III. Smith-Hinds, William L., 1938-
BT738.R38      261.8      79-22381
ISBN 0-8361-1221-0

A READER IN SOCIOLOGY: CHRISTIAN PERSPECTIVES
Copyright © 1980 by Herald Press, Scottdale, Pa. 15683
  Published simultaneously in Canada by Herald Press,
  Kitchener, Ont. N2G 4M5
Library of Congress Catalog Card Number: 79-22381
International Standard Book Number: 0-8361-1221-0
Printed in the United States of America
Design: Alice B. Shetler

15 14 13 12 11 10 9 8 7 6 5 4 3 2 1

To Paul M. Schrock
for his encouragement and support
in bringing this reader
together.

# CONTENTS

# III. SOCIOLOGICAL THEORY: A CHRISTIAN APPROACH

# TO THE STUDENT

The purpose of this book, *A Reader in Sociology: Christian Perspectives*, is to stimulate Christian college students to think about the various topics in introduction to sociology courses from a Christian point of view. By way of introduction, we would like to suggest some reasons why an introduction to sociology course ought to be examined from a Christian perspective.

## Sociology and Values

Christian college students ought to think carefully about the values that are promoted in sociology courses. Ideally, some say sociology is value-free, but in practice sociologists, like anyone else, make value judgments and ethical statements.

### Sociology Is a Science, but . . .

Most sociologists would agree that sociology is a science. In sociology the scientific method is used to examine human group behavior. Human behavior is examined in order to understand it, to make predictions about it, and perhaps even to discover ways of control or liberation. The only values needed in this kind of effort are those required by the scientific method, such as commitments to honesty and to the examination of all relevant evidence. Sociology provides no basis for speculating about what ought to be in human behavior or about how persons ought to behave. Nevertheless, sociology instructors, like politicians, the clergy, reformers, and all of us, will invariably make value judgments and ethical statements.

Clearly, then, when sociology instructors begin to make value judgments, such as "busing is good because it gives ghetto children a chance for a better education," they have ceased being sociologists and become "preachers" or "reformers." Of course, they may be able to draw upon sociological studies that support the conclusion that children bused to suburbia do better academically, but when they begin to advocate action programs, they are speaking as non-sociologists. No one, not even sociologists, can be wholly scientific and value-free. Therefore, we Christians ought to bring our philosophical and religious perspective to bear on the sociological process and the interpretations of research findings and suggestions for their use.

## The Sociological Method

A Christian college student ought to think carefully about the sociological method. Sociologists follow several methodological principles in their search for knowledge of human behavior. From time to time, each of these principles may have advantages or limitations from a Christian point of view. Consider the following examples.

### The Empirical Method Is Only One Approach

Consider empiricism. Sociology is an empirical science. It deals only with things that can be measured by the five senses, things in the natural world. A fact, to sociologists, must be, directly or indirectly, visible, audible and/or tangible. Sociologists do not deal with the supernatural world, although they can study beliefs about the supernatural world and how such beliefs are related to human behavioral patterns. For purposes of research, sociologists follow the principle that only things which are empirically verifiable are their province or legitimate field of study. Sociologists, as sociologists, are not supposed to make any judgments about matters of the supernatural world and matters of faith, although many do. Similarly, sociologists who are Christians follow the principle of empiricism too, although some would argue that sociology, is intrinsically value laden. Many, however, also believe that the research findings ought to be used to effect changes which reflect a Christian perspective. This is a major reason why sociologists who are also Christians have contributed to this anthology.

The contributors to this *Reader* are persons who would agree that sociology should be objective, empirical, but many would suggest that sociologists thus far have unduly limited the dimensions of what they include in empirical. Some sociologists, notably Father Andrew Greeley and George Hillery, Jr., think that the spiritual dimension needs to be given more recognition and attention in sociological thought and research, since it is indeed a vital part of the human experience.

*The Questioning Spirit Is Essential to "Doing" Sociology*
Consider the questioning spirit in sociology. Sociology, like all sciences, by its very nature must persist in questioning. Sociologists must have freedom to ask "why?" repeatedly—about every- and anything. Because sociologists persist in subjecting everything, even so-called sacred things, to scrutiny, John P. Williams tells of one evangelical seminary where the sociology instructor is called the "professor of worldliness" by the students and some of his colleagues. One of the problems a Christian sociologist faces, says Father Andrew Greeley, is that often the church equates the sociologist's research findings with the sociologist's personal beliefs, much to his dismay. The Christian sociologist, nevertheless, must ask why anyway, and he or she must be free to examine all things—from why men and women visit porno shops, to why they go to prayer meetings. Why men go to Rotary Club meetings more religiously than to church. Why evangelical colleges feel the need to place greater restrictions on Christian students than secular colleges place on their students. Why Christians are just as class conscious as non-Christians. (Calvin Redekop and Donald Kraybill both speak to the subject of stratification and class distinctions from a Christian perspective.) Why Christians defer to the rich and powerful in the Christian church, just like people in secular institutions. Nothing is "sacred" and excluded from the sociologist's scalpel.

*Sociological Research Is Open-ended and Conclusions Are Tentative*
Consider the tentativeness of sociological research findings. Conclusions from research findings in sociology are tentative. Not all the evidence is in yet. Generalizations and theories may be modified in the light of further thought or new evidence on the matter. Furthermore, sociological research findings present only a partial view of human behavior. Human beings are finite, not infinite. They are limited in knowledge and ability. Therefore, while sociologists are studying primary groups, they are not studying social institutions. While they are studying the unionization of workers, they are not researching the bureaucratic organization of corporations. What is more important,

while they are sociologizing, they are not psychologizing, philosophizing, or (to coin a neologism), biologizing. This brings to mind the *Hindu Fable of the Elephant*. A blind person holding the elephant's tail certainly does not have the whole elephant in hand. In view of the limitations of the sociological perspective, like any other perspective, a little "epistemological humility" may help keep sociologists from taking themselves too seriously. Sociologists make their work public because they realize the tentativeness of all thought and research findings. It is only in the give and take, in the dialogue with other colleagues in the discipline that a more accurate analysis and a fuller understanding are achieved.

### Relativity Should Be Judged by the Scriptures

Consider the principle of relativity in social life. (See William Hasker's article on "Cultural relativity".) Sociologists follow the principle that patterns of culture such as values, norms, beliefs, and symbols are relative. In other words, particular values, norms, beliefs, and symbols are meaningful only within specific cultural contexts. We Christians acknowledge that values, norms, beliefs, or symbols vary from one society to another. We maintain, however, that certain basic Christian values, norms, beliefs, or symbols are not relative, but absolute. Of course, no society's way of life is 100 percent Christian. Christians hold fast to Christ, but are cautious about everything else, including many so-called Christian values, norms, beliefs, or symbols that often turn out to be non-Christian upon closer scrutiny. Much of what passes for Christian values, norms, beliefs, or symbols are often nothing more than "middle-class American patterns of culture," or "American pagan patterns of culture." For example, many of us in the church determine an individual's worth by how much material wealth he has or we identify "wholesomeness" with stylish permanent press clothes, and deodorized, cologned, and perfumed youth! The basic biblical way of life cannot be identified with either the American evangelical lifestyle that is heavily influenced by Madison Avenue, or with the lifestyle of the Hutterites, to mention one group, who have withdrawn from the mainstream of our society. The Christian way of life and American middle-class way of life are not identical.

The study of sociology can be a liberating experience. One learns through studying sociology to employ many helpful concepts when viewing society or a given problem within society—one learns to sit where they sit (Ezekiel 3:15) and see that "things are seldom what they appear to be" (R. Heddendorf). It is seldom that one will meet a Christian who has a true sociological perspective who is provincial or dogmatic about nonessentials. The Christian, therefore, brings all cultures under the scrutiny of the Word of God. The non-Christian actually goes through a similar process—he evaluates things in the light of his own philosophical or religious system.

## Assumptions in Sociology
*There Are a Variety of Schools of Thought in Sociology*
Christian college students ought to think carefully about assumptions in sociology. Sociologists, like people in other disciplines, make assumptions or take for granted certain beliefs about human nature, society, the relationship between society and the individual, and social change. Of course, there are several schools of thought in sociology, each with differing assumptions. Nowadays, the most prominent schools of thought in the U.S.A. seem to be conflict theory, structural-functionalism, and symbolic interaction. These are usually discussed in standard textbooks. We shall comment briefly on assumptions in some of these schools of thought.

An important assumption about society usually concerns which of the social institutions is considered the most influential. Conflict theorists assume that economic life is the driving force in society. Accordingly, other institutions such as family, religion, polity, and education simply reflect changes that take place in the economic sphere. The political institution, for example, is seen as the executive committee for business. In addition, many conflict theorists take a dim view of the religious institution because they see it as resisting change and blinding people to needed improvements in social life. In contrast to this view, Max Weber, one of the founding fathers of modern sociology, while acknowledging that the economic life is often a foundation of social life, contended that the religious may also become particularly influential at times. In his famous book, *The Protestant Ethic and the Spirit of Capitalism,* he argued that religious ideas influenced the development of capitalist ideas and helped give rise to the capitalist economy.

From a Christian perspective, all models of society used by sociologists may have some relevance, yet none is completely accurate or true. Margaret Poloma and Stan Gaede, in an attempt to come up with a Christian model, have synthesized the conflict and functionalist models of society. Yet even they would admit that their thinking is tentative and incomplete. The Christian's main concern with any model is whether or not the model squares realistically with Christian conceptions of human nature and needs, and with Christian responsibility for the wellbeing of human beings and society.

### The Nature of Man Is Important

Consider assumptions about human nature. Conceptions about human nature are inseparably linked to models of society. Sociologists tend to view human beings as *amoral* at birth. As they mature physically and socially through interaction with others, their personality develops. Sociologists also tend to see human beings as being molded by significant others and by group and institutional pressures. While not denying human freedom, they consider the destiny of human beings to be largely at the mercy of forces outside individuals. Christians would not deny that we often are victims of such outside forces; however, they would place a greater responsibility on individuals for their destiny. Christians begin with the faith assumption of the fall of human beings in Adam. Then, as G. K. Chesterton observed long ago, the faith assumption that human beings are basically sinful and self-centered is perhaps one of the easiest assumptions to support empirically. Human beings do have freedom of choice, howbeit the range of choice is often extremely limited, especially for people in Third World countries on the verge of starvation, or for deprived people living in slums in modern metropoles. Those of us who live in relative affluence in democracies, however, ought not to permit the forces operating in the world to squeeze us into their mold.

### Christians Insist That More Than the Structure Needs Changing

Consider assumptions about the relationship between society and the individual. Many sociologists tend to blame the "system" and/or the "social structure" for the ills of society. Sociologists who are Christian would see the solutions for societal problems coming from at least two different sources. First, individuals must be reconciled to God through faith in Jesus Christ. This reconciliation will produce attitudinal and motivational changes in them, changes which in turn will affect their attitudes towards both themselves and others. They will not only begin to accept responsibility for themselves, but also for others— beginning with their own family. They will not only be at peace with themselves, but will begin to work for harmonious relationships with others. Second, individuals' attitudes will change towards social structures they regard as unjust. They will join forces with those inside and outside the Christian community who work for a more equitable distribution of freedom, opportunities, goods, and power. They will work to change the system, insofar as it is oppressive, whether it be a free enterprise, a socialist, or a totalitarian system.

### Change Is Constant— Not Necessarily Bad or Good

Sociologists may also have differing assumptions about social change—for example, whether social life is improving, decaying, or going in circles. Change is constant. Even in small, traditional, and isolated communities or *Gemeinschaft* communities, as Tönnies called them, or in societies held together by what Durkheim called *mechanical solidarity*, that is, those with a simple division of labor where people are bound together by a common faith and family ties, there is social change. It is just slower and more difficult to perceive in the short run. Change in itself is not necessarily "bad" or "good." Generally, if it is beneficial to a particular group, they consider it good. On the other hand, if it poses a threat to their well-being or prosperity, they view it as bad. Perhaps there is no progress without change, but not all change is progress. Therefore, although Christians must be open to change, they must evaluate it critically and be selective about what they accept. Only those changes which are beneficial to the individual and to society in the long run ought to be endorsed and supported. Think of the environmental problems we face today because we accepted many changes prematurely!

### Growth Occurs Through Change

The concepts of development and change ought to be applied to one's faith also. As Christians we subscribe to basic Christian doctrines or beliefs and hold that they do not change; they are absolutes. These absolutes include the belief that God exists, that Jesus Christ is Savior and Lord, that God indwells the believer by his Holy Spirit, that we ought to be obedient and responsible servants of God, and that God's nature and will for our life are revealed in the Bible. But how we perceive these basic doctrines and others ought to change as we grow in general knowledge, Christian knowledge and understanding, and as we mature chronologically and socially through interaction with others. It is either growth or atrophy. Hopefully, Christian college students will choose growth which necessitates change.

## The Christian Faith and Sociology

The main point of these brief remarks is that sociological concepts, generalizations, theories, and research findings must all be examined and interpreted from a Christian point of view. One does not have to speak long with other persons to realize that their presuppositions or assumptions influence their thinking. Furthermore, while they should not, they may even influence the objectivity and honesty with which they conduct research. We are referring not only to the quality of their research, but also to the areas they may avoid. For example, why is so little research done on the relationship between Christian conversion and alcoholism, drug abuse, delinquency, and/or crime? Is there possibly an unwillingness on the part of sociologists to consider the religious factor as a viable one for rehabilitation? Is there an anti-Christian bias?

After the research is completed, what does one do with the research findings? What policy decisions does one make? The decision-makers' philosophical and/or religious beliefs also come into play at this point. The Christian frame of reference is the Scriptures and the person of Jesus Christ. "Love the Lord your God with all your heart . . . soul . . . mind, and strength" and "Love your neighbor as you love yourself" (Mark 12:30, 31). "Do for others just what you want them to do for you" (Luke 6:31, TEV). These become the basis for policy and decision making for the Christian—on a personal, a corporate, a political and a social level. Manifest and latent consequences of proposed policy decisions are both considered—long range, as well as short range. Peter Uhlenberg and Bee-Lan Wang, writing on the population explosion, do a good job of raising questions about what the Christian response ought to be to the plight of millions. It is at this point, where presuppositions influence decisions about research findings and what is to be done with them, that Christian values are unique and relevant. The contributors to this anthology do just that—use Christian principles in their sociological analysis and interpretation.

## The Unity in Diversity of the Contributors

The Christian scholars who have written the articles in this anthology all share a common commitment to Jesus Christ as Lord. Beyond that, each one is a unique individual who has found God in Christ and seeks to serve him in a denomination or Christian community of his or her choice. Students will encounter a diversity of approaches to sociology and to the faith. Not all express themselves the same way. Roman Catholic Christians will express their faith differently from Presbyterians or United Methodists. No attempt has been made by the editors to force any kind of conformity in mode of expression—that would be an abridgement of academic and religious freedom. We want this *Reader* to reflect the diversity of opinions within both sociology and the Christian faith. We believe that to have a true learning experience one must encounter new ideas and fresh approaches. Students will encounter them in this *Reader*.

Each article is a complete chapter in itself, dealing with a specific topic. It is not a duplication of an introductory text, but it is intended to supplement it. These articles deal with specific issues or problems one would encounter in a standard textbook, but in this *Reader* the authors have related them to the Christian faith. At the end of each article there is a list of discussion questions for the student's personal consideration and/or for use in classroom discussion. In most cases references are attached. Since the book is designed as a collateral text, students are referred to their introductory textbook for a basic overview of sociology and for a basic bibliography.

It is our hope that by reading and discussing these articles students will develop a habit of thinking about sociology analytically and critically from a Christian perspective. It is hoped that they will ask "So what?" "What does this have to do with me and my personal Christian life?" "What responsibility does this lay on me?" By doing so, students will find the serious study of sociology can be a means of Christian growth (see John P. Williams, Jr.'s, article). After all, we are our brother's keeper. We are to be neighbors to those in need—whether they be poor and destitute in need of the basic necessities of life, or rich and affluent in need of learning how to live responsibly in a community.

# PART I
# INTRODUCTION

# INTRODUCTION

If you are a curious person who is concerned about what makes people, groups, organizations, and even nations tick, you will enjoy the study of sociology. It is a discipline that puts its nose into everything from where and what really influences a congressman, to what factors in the social environment contribute to adolescent delinquency. Sociologists investigate every facet of life within society. They are concerned with what holds society together, as well as what pulls it apart.

Sociologists not only describe and analyze what factors contribute to the population explosion in the Third World, but what factors account for zero population growth in many highly industrialized nations in the East and West. They are also interested in making generalizations, as a result of research, that will enable them to predict future behavior of individuals and groups. Sociological research is employed by all types of organizations with a wide diversity of philosophical, political, and religious persuasions. The John Birch Society and the Communist Party, the American Cancer Society and the Tobacco Industry, and the A.F.L./C.I.O. and the American Association of Manufacturers all either employ or utilize the fruits of sociological research.

While the legitimate researcher is honest and objective in carrying out his task and reporting his findings, we cannot always be sure that those who utilize the research are pure in their motives. But we are concerned in this first section with the *why: how,* and *where.* Why study sociology? How to go about it? Where does Christianity figure into it? The basic introductory text your instructor is using, the assigned readings, and class lectures will cover the traditional material.

In this reader on Christian perspectives in sociology, various scholars from colleges and universities challenge you to think about the relevance of a Christian approach to the study of sociology. In your other readings you will encounter Marxist and humanist sociologists. We challenge you with a Christian approach.

In Part I John P. Williams, Jr., discusses why you should study sociology, and some things a Christian should be aware of as he studies. William L. Smith-Hinds explores the various ways of knowing—of pursuing truth. Then Brenden F. J. Furnish discusses the scientific method, calls attention to some of its limitations, and some of the dilemmas it presents to Christians. Statistics is one of the tools used by researchers, and Gordon S. Bonham briefly presents the various ways statistics are used in research. Finally, John M. Mecartney provides the student not only with an excellent model of sociological research, but demonstrates that upward (financial) mobility does not necessarily mean that a clergyman/Christian will be unconcerned with the poor. Although there are many other variables that influence ones attitude towards the poor, Mecartney suggests that riches need not be a millstone about one's neck.

# 1
# Why Should a Christian Study Sociology?

*John P. Williams, Jr.*

She had grown up in a devout family. They took her to church twice on Sundays, to midweek services, and to any special meetings the church might hold. She had been raised on family devotions twice a day—once in the morning and once in the evening. She believed that it was important to read her Bible and to pray regularly, as well as witness to others about Jesus. Her family supported missionaries and tithed faithfully. In her religious circles, it was common to refer to Sunday as the "Lord's Day," to pastors as "men of God," to church work as "kingdom business," to tithe money as "the Lord's money," and to Christian development as "spiritual growth."

She was a lovely young woman in so many ways—poised, alert, conscientious, and trustworthy. But she was encountering quite a problem early in her college career. She was a student in the introductory sociology class I taught. One afternoon she remained after class to talk with me about things that were troubling her.

Her problem, as it turned out, was that she could not see why the study of sociology should be an integral part of her preparation for "full-time Christian service" as a director of Christian education. She felt the Lord had called her to a career in which she could help people grow spiritually. In her mind, Bible study, theology, missions, church history, Christian education courses, and perhaps music and art (as they applied to Christian education) were vital to her career interests be-

**John P. Williams, Jr.**
*Associate Professor of Sociology*
*Marion College (Indiana)*

John Williams has research interests in the sociology of sport, the family, and religion. He has done studies of the Old Order Amish. He received an MA from the University of Akron, and the PhD from Iowa State University. Mr. Williams is a recorded minister in the Friends Church, and he has a special interest in the relationship between the Christian faith and sociology.

cause they helped develop "spiritual gifts." But sociology, the study of human relationships, seemed so unspiritual, if not downright secular. Sociology, she reasoned, might be able to give us some insight into people's behavior, but the Christian's real goal is to bring people into a right relationship with God. She was having a terrible time trying to study sociology. She just couldn't see how sociology would fit into the program designed to prepare her for Christian service.

This young woman is a composite of a number of students I have known over the past eight years as a teacher of sociology in an evangelical Christian college. Her tendency to dichotomize life into the sacred and the secular is shared by hosts of students who, though perhaps not preparing for "full-time Christian service," wonder if their studies really carry any Christian significance.

## Wholeness of Life in Christ

I understand how they feel, for I have fought some of the same battles. When I left seminary some years ago to take a college teaching position, a number of my friends expressed regrets that I had "decided not to go into the ministry." It took me some time to fully realize that any career (assuming it is decent, moral work) can be a calling in which we are Christ's ministers, whether through preaching, counseling, teaching, social work, research, business, industry, or homemaking. All our talents are to be invested for God's glory and the service of people.

I suspect most Christians lose sight, to one degree or another, of God's claims on the whole of life and thereby compartmentalize life into the sacred (made up of prayer, Bible study, God-consciousness, worship, private devotions, witnessing, and the like) and the secular (consisting of ordinary, day-to-day matters such as meals, study, sleep, work, interpersonal relationships, recreation, paying taxes). In such a double-minded state, it is no surprise that sociology, the study of human interaction, seems so worldly and unspiritual. Most of us are ambivalent like many students and some faculty at a prominent evangelical seminary I visited recently. Although they joked about it, there were also some serious reasons why they nicknamed the seminary's sociology instructor, "Professor of Worldliness."

In contrast to our compartmentalized approach to life, the simple, startling assumption of the Christian Scriptures is that all of life is sacred. Whatever we are doing, we should be serving the Lord. "And whatever you do," exhorts Paul, "in word or deed, do everything in the

name of the Lord Jesus, giving thanks to God the Father through him"
(Colossians 3:17).

The wide gap we have allowed to develop between the ostensibly
sacred and secular parts of life is basically a result of placing limitations
on God's sovereignty, as well as having a faith that is too narrow. Again
in Colossians, Paul describes the remarkable relevance of Jesus Christ
to all of life by declaring him to be both creator and sustainer of the
universe: "He [Christ] is the image of the invisible God, the first-born
of all creation, for in him all things were created, in heaven and earth,
visible and invisible, whether thrones or dominions or principalities or
authorities—all things were created through him and for him. He is
before all things, and *in him all things hold together*" (Colossians 1:15-
17, emphasis mine). The Bible teaches that our Lord Jesus Christ is the
unifying center of life; he holds everything together and gives the
world order, coherence, and meaning. "All things" includes not only
our relationship with God, but also the atom, molecules, the human
body, the planets, the galaxies, our minds, human relationships, communities, societies, and cultures. All life is held together by the same
Christ. Without him, everything would fall apart and become senseless.

Christians must begin to bridge the gap between the sacred and
the secular by, first, acknowledging Christ Jesus as Lord of *all* life and
truth. After all, all truth is his truth. Although for academic reasons we
identify aspects of life, labeling them as "theological," "psychological," or "sociological," they are all fragments of the total truth about
God, man, and the world which are all held together in him.

Thus, in a very real sense the young woman in the sociology class
should have been motivated to careful study of human interaction because it is part of God's truth. God's truth about the human condition
(for example, man's sinfulness, man's creation in God's image, or man's
interdependence with other men as in the concept of the "body of
Christ") has been revealed in the Bible. But much of the knowledge
about man's relationship with other men has been left for us to discover.

### Christian Incentives to Study Sociology

In an even more particular sense, God has given us several significant incentives to gain sociological knowledge—incentives that go beyond the general mandate to make him Lord of all life, valuing all truth
as God's truth. These special motivations to study sociology are rooted

deeply in man's nature and in God-given moral imperatives. We turn now to an examination of five biblically based reasons why Christians should study sociology.

### God's Design: Social Creatures

We should study sociology, first, *because God has designed us to be social creatures.* We were made to need other people and to be needed by them. At the very creation of human life, God made an observation about our sociability that rings just as true now as it did then. The Lord formed man from the dust of the ground. He gave man the garden of Eden, challenging him to work and he gave him freedom to eat of every tree except one. "Then the Lord God said, 'It is not good that the man should be alone; I will make him a helper fit for him" (Genesis 2:18). The Lord proceeded to form beasts of the field and birds of the air and bring them to the man for naming, " . . . but for the man there was not found a helper fit for him" (Genesis 2:20b). So the Lord made someone appreciably superior to the beasts, a creature like Adam himself. He made another person who would complement Adam and communicate with him.

It was Adam's need for companionship that led to Eve's creation. And when she was brought to Adam, the two persons were at last made complete. They found fulfillment in each other. "Therefore a man leaves his father and his mother and cleaves to his wife, and they become one flesh" (Genesis 2:24).

Solitary confinement in prison is one of the harshest punishments imposed on prisoners precisely because it hurts so much to be alone for prolonged periods of time. History is replete with accounts of people who devised ingenious ways to communicate with other people even when they were cut off physically from human presence. American prisoners in North Vietnam during the late 1960s and early 1970s tapped out signals to each other on the walls that separated them. The apostle Paul wrote many letters to individuals and churches from prison cells, even as he lamented his inability to be with them. He wrote, "I thank my God in all my rememberance of you . . . thankful for your partnership in the gospel. . . . For God is my witness, how I yearn for you all with the affection of Christ" (Philippians 1:3, 5a, 8). The apostle John communicated his solidarity with fellow Christians from his exiled home on the isle of Patmos: "I John, your brother, who share with you in Jesus the tribulation and the kingdom and the patient endurance, was on the island called Patmos on account of the word of God and the testimony of Jesus" (Revelation 1:9).

Our fundamental, God-given nature is social. To ignore this basic truth is to forget who we are, and how we are expected to live.

I remember a Sunday school chorus we used to sing when I was a youngster. The words were, "He is all I need, He is all I need, Jesus is all I need." I think the writer of that song was trying to say that Jesus is our ultimate help and supplier, but in saying that "Jesus is *all* I need," he overstated the case. He overlooked the way God meant for people to care for and minister to one another. After all, God was there with Adam in the Garden of Eden and if God was *all* Adam needed, why did the Lord comment that it was not good for the man to be alone? Why didn't the Lord just "snuggle up" closer to Adam and meet all his needs without the help of a mere mortal like Eve? The obvious answer is that God designed us to be social creatures, to relate to other people and to interact meaningfully with them as well as with himself.

Since we are created not only for God but also for other people, God is pleased when we take seriously our God-given social natures. Systematic sociological study of just how those social natures function is one way we can mature as Christians.

*God's Design: Socialized Creatures*

Second, we should study sociology *because God has designed us to become fully human only in relationship with other persons.* It may sound peculiar or strange to some to suggest that we are not fully human at birth, but consider the natural state of the human infant. He is born "unfinished," able only to eat, sleep, and excrete. He cannot talk, think noble thoughts about God, or emote in any complex fashion. The infant develops his human qualities through interactions with others.

Witness the young child who has been rejected, ignored, or cut off from normal human warmth. If he lives, he behaves more like an animal than a person. Physical retardation stems from physical deficiency or damage, but intellectual and social retardation is dullness that comes from an environment that lacks social stimulation and attention.

The Bible emphasizes that man is made in the image of God. In other words, man mirrors, however imperfectly, some of God's personal qualities. Thus, we are rational. God's communication with us is premised on our ability to comprehend meaningful discourse. The entire Bible is addressed to us on the assumption that we, unlike the animals, are capable of complex and abstract thought communicated through language symbols. We are choice-makers, responsible for our actions. We are relational, just as God is relational.

But notice that all of these abilities (and doubtless many more) which we associate with the image of God are *learned*. They are learned largely through contact with other people.

God has chosen human society as the means by which those fragile infants will, over a period of time through sustained human interaction, be nurtured from primitive potential to beautiful, complex, whole persons—able to walk, talk, care, share, and love. Few things are sadder to see than human potentials wasted because of child neglect, abuse or insufficient attention. Nor are there many things more beautiful to see than tiny promises of personality gradually blossoming into lovely human beings, complete with facility for relationships with other people and with God.

The incarnation gives us clues not only about the nature of God, but also about the true nature of man, for Jesus Christ was fully God and fully man. As a human being, the infant Jesus was dependent upon his parents. As a child and adolescent he was socialized through human interaction with others, as well as through communion with God. His manhood, likewise was the result of divine/human interaction. The gospels remind us that full personhood unfolds only as we relate to other people and learn from them what it means to think, act, and feel in truly human fashion. Perhaps Jesus, at some points in his life, was less dependent upon other people than we are due to his unique intimacy with the Father. Yet he, nonetheless, did experience a growth process. Clearly, he was not a pre-formed freak who uttered sentences at eight days of age or discerned all knowledge without study. The boy Jesus, it is said by Luke the physician, " . . . *increased* in wisdom and in stature, and in favor with God and man" (Luke 2:52b).

Socialization, the study of human relationships and their impact on the process of becoming fully human, is therefore an area of study that we should be greatly interested in.

### God's Design: Accountable Creatures

Third, we should study sociology *because God has designed us to exercise responsibility for other people and for society.*

Responsibility to God and to other persons is imbedded in our very natures. No matter how much we try to protest or squirm out of it, we are nevertheless accountable. The lesson in the tragedy of Cain and Abel is that we are not born into the world (or assigned to a college dorm) so that we might merely coexist with other people, sneering at their flaws and using them for our purposes. On the contrary, we are called by God himself to actually take responsibility for others. I am my brother's keeper, or even better, my brother's brother. What happens to him makes a difference to me. It does not matter if he is different from me, if he gets on my nerves, or even if he offends me. It is still my responsibility to do what I can to help him.

Consider Cain and Abel. One was a farmer, the other was a sheepherder. They got on each other's nerves. They were different. They offended each other. Cain became so intensely jealous of Abel that he murdered him in cold blood. The Lord asked Cain, "Where is Abel your brother?" Cain covered up with a lie and a self-serving cop-out: "I do not know; am I my brother's keeper?" (Genesis 4:9b). One can almost hear Cain mumbling under his breath, "Come now. Do you expect me to be responsible for *him*?"

The Lord's response to Cain, "What have you done? The voice of your brother's blood is crying to me from the ground" (Genesis 4:10b), and his swift punishment of Cain's horrible offense, combine to reinforce the lesson of personal responsibility.

Sometimes Christians offer a Cain-like cop-out saying, "I am just one person. I cannot be expected to exercise responsibility for other people, much less society. It is all I can do to keep myself together."

An honest reading of the Scriptures should dispel this myth of isolationism in several ways. First, we see God working through his people to shake Egypt to its foundations and restructure a society by liberating the Hebrew slaves. Second, we hear the prophets Amos and Hosea demanding high ethics in the home, the marketplace, and the places of worship. Third, we get a preview of God's judgment of the nations in Jesus' words: "Before him will be gathered all the nations, and he will separate them one from another as a shepherd separates the sheep from the goats. . . . Then the King will say. . . . 'Come, O blessed of my Father, inherit the kingdom prepared for you from the foundation of the world; for I was hungry and you gave me food, I was thirsty and you gave me drink, I was a stranger and you welcomed me, I was naked and you clothed me, I was sick and you visited me, I was in prison and you came to me.' Then the righteous will answer him, 'Lord,

when did we see thee hungry . . . or thirsty . . . a stranger . . . or naked
. . . (or) sick in prison?' . . . And the King will answer them, 'Truly, I
say to you, as you did it to one of the least of these my brethren, you did
it to me' " (Matthew 25:32-40).

Being responsible for each other means knowing where people
hurt and helping them, knowing how the social system works, how society changes, and how we can direct that change toward humane ends.
Sociology explores issues like these and thus can be an enormous help
in equipping us for responsible participation at both the interpersonal
and societal levels.

### God's Design: Just Creatures

Fourth, diligent study of sociology can help Christians *because
God has designed us to bring about justice in social relationships and
society as a whole.*

If God has designed us to be responsible for each other, then justice shapes the content of our responsibility. The word "justice" appears frequently in the Scriptures and signifies righteousness, honesty,
and fair dealing between people.

The prophet Micah provides one of the Bible's plainest statements
about what God expects of us: "He has showed you, O man, what is
good; and what does the Lord require of you but to do justice, and to
love kindness, and to walk humbly with your God?" (Micah 6:8).

Early in Hebrew history, God made clear his expectations for Abraham, whom he has chosen to bless with a great and mighty nation.
Though wickedness and exploitation of people abounded (notably in
Sodom and Gomorrah), the Lord remained steadfast in his requirements: " . . . for I have chosen him [Abraham], that he may charge his
children and his household after him to keep the way of the Lord by doing righteousness and justice; so that the Lord may bring to Abraham
what he has promised him" (Genesis 18:19).

Centuries after Abraham, the prophet of Amos, an unpretentious
shepherd and tree trimmer, bristled with righteous indignation over the
rampant injustice of the day; pregnant women were being "ripped up"
(1:13), the rich oppressed the poor, justice was sold to the highest bid-
der (2:6, 7), moneylenders took advantage of poor farmers who were
devastated by drought (4:7-9; 5:11), and the wealthy displayed callous
indifference towards the hungry (6:3-6). The Lord's response to such
atrocities was pointed, to say the least: "I hate, I despise your feasts,

and I take no delight in your solemn assemblies. . . . Take away from me the noise of your songs; to the melody of your harps I will not listen. But let justice roll down like waters, and righteousness like an everflowing stream'' (Amos 5:21, 23, 24).

John Perkins, a contemporary black Christian who directs a multifaceted ministry of evangelism and social action through the *Voice of Calvary* in Mendenhall, Mississippi, recently authored a book entitled *Let Justice Roll Down*. In it Perkins describes his struggle to survive in a racist society, his conversion to Christ while a young adult, and his subsequent work to bring justice and opportunity to black Americans, particularly those in Mississippi. For his efforts, Perkins received threats on his life, imprisonment, and beatings.

Through the grace of God, he has continued to carry on his work without succumbing to hatred or bitterness. One of Perkins' keenest disappointments, especially in the early days of his ministry, was that he found most Christians unwilling to help and often hostile towards his efforts to make society more just. Christians, reflected Perkins, need sociological insight coupled with biblical realism.

> There are times when the biggest need is for information rather than exhortation. We need to know more about what really goes on before we solidify our theoretical ideas about what a Christian ''ought'' or ''ought not'' do.
>
> Whether we admit it or not, our reading of biblical ethics is colored by our perceptions of the world around us. If we think there are only a few ''bad guys'' such as burglars and murderers, and that all the given political, legal and economic structures around us are basically okay, then we are bound to read our Bibles in a certain way. We will assume that it tells us to ''lay low,'' whether we are a part of the law or only under the law; that the person who speaks out is a rebellious agitator.
>
> But that assumption can be badly shaken up by a good look at what happens to many people who are simply crushed by, rather than helped by, these social structures and institutions we take for granted. If sin can exist at every level of government, and in every human institution, then also the call to biblical justice in every corner of society must be sounded by those who claim a God of justice as their Lord (Perkins, 1976: 195).

Sociological analysis of social power, social stratification (the structured inequality of society), the dynamics of prejudice and discrimination, and similar topics is one way Christians can examine injustice and explore ways to redress inequities. Just as in Amos' day, it is still more comfortable to ignore unpleasant realities than to face them. Yet God calls us to aggressively work for justice. We can do this by gaining knowledge of evil and then systematically working to eliminate it. Sociological study can help us become more knowledgeable pursuers of injustice.

### God's Design: Loving Creatures

Fifth, it is important for Christians to study sociology *because God has designed us to love our neighbor as ourselves.*

Sometimes we are tempted to see love of neighbor as an option— something we can always add onto life, if we so desire. A little like adding an extra gadget onto our new car if we feel we can afford it.

Jesus refused to split love for God from love for man. He insisted that they go together, or we have neither. When one of the scribes asked Jesus to summarize the law, the Master replied, " 'And you shall love the Lord your God with all your heart, and with all your soul, and with all your mind, and with all your strength.' The second is this, 'You shall love your neighbor as yourself.' There is no commandment greater than these" (Mark 12:30, 31).

Love is costly. And yet for the Christian it is standard and not optional. Popular wisdom has it that love is characterized by "cardiorespiratory" signs like heart palpitations, deep breathing, tingles, goosebumps, and euphoric dizziness. Jesus taught that love is deeper, willing the best for the other and working to make that best come true.

John discussed Christian love quite simply, clearly, and bluntly in his writings. He equated failure to love with paganism. "Here we have a clear indication as to who are the children of God and who are the children of the devil. The man who does not lead a good life is no son of God, nor is the man who fails to love his brother" (1 John 3:10, Phillips). He continues with the reminder that "the man without love for his brother is living in death already" (1 John 3:14b, Phillips) and adds the practical admonition, "But if any one has the world's goods and sees his brother in need, yet closes his heart against him, how does God's love abide in him? Little children, let us not love in word or speech but in deed and in truth" (1 John 3:17).

Obviously we cannot love every person to the same extent. Nor can we actively express our love to most of the world's four billion people. But we do have lots of neighbors whose lives we affect daily. In fact, our neighbor is *anyone* we can affect. God's design is for us to will the best for them and act in a way that will serve their needs. Sociology, through its illumination of human relationships, can shed light on other people's needs, teaching us more about how to love, help, and contribute to their well-being.

### Summary and Conclusions
As you might have guessed by now, my chat with the under-motivated sociology student I described at the beginning of this essay did not cover all the preceding points. But she made me think about why I teach sociology, how sociology can help us glorify God, and the link between doing God's will and doing good sociology.

Admittedly, sociology is not by any means the only branch of knowledge which can help us understand God's designs on our lives. No single academic discipline offers any more than a fragment of God's grand truth about himself, man, and the world. But we shall miss even the fragments unless we bring godly zeal to our pursuit of all truth, including sociological truth.

To be sure, our knowledge is imperfect as well as fragmentary. "For now we see through a glass, darkly; but then face to face: now I know in part; but then shall I know even as I am known" (1 Corinthians 13:12). But at least we can see through the glass, even though dimly. God wants his children to see all they can see, and to know all they can know through the cloudy glass.

So on with it. And may sociology give you clearer vision, keener sensitivity, and fuller knowledge to be all God wants you to be. For your sake. For others' sakes. And for God's sake.

### Discussion Questions
1. Do you sometimes catch yourself dividing life into sacred and secular compartments? What do you put into each? Is this sort of dichotomization common in your church and family background?
2. What motivates you to study? As you see it, how is God related to your intellectual growth and development? Is your view biblically sound?
3. How far into your life does the lordship of Jesus Christ reach? Church life? Devotional life? Home life? Dating and sex life? Intellectual life?
4. What do you consider to be Christian ministries? How does your view compare to the New Testament concept of ministry? (You

may want to locate passages where the words "minister," "ministered," or "ministering" are used.)

5. Do you agree that people very much need other people? Are there some people who do not need others? Have you ever been completely cut off from human contact for more than a few hours? How did it feel? (An interesting experiment would be to plan a one-to-two-day period of solitude and then discuss it with others who have done the same. However, exercise caution! Such an exercise can produce unhealthy strains and should not be continued if dangerous symptoms show up.)

6. Is it possible for a human infant to grow into a normal, healthy person without the aid of other people? In what ways are human babies more dependent on parents than animal babies are dependent on their parent(s)?

7. Speculate on how Jesus' childhood and adolescence might have been unique. How might they have been ordinary?

8. Have technological devices like the automobile and television contributed to a reduced sense of responsibility between persons? For whom do you feel responsible, to one degree or another? When was the last time you put yourself out for a friend? A stranger? How did Jesus demonstrate responsibility for others in specific ways?

9. What constitutes genuine love? How does your definition compare with the one given in 1 Corinthians 13?

10. As you examine the contents of your sociology textbook and/or course outline, is there any area of study listed which is unrelated to a Christian lifestyle? In which area do you believe you need most to grow in knowledge and application?

## References

Balswick, Jack and Dawn Ward
   1976 "The Nature of Man and Scientific Models of Society." *Journal of the American Scientific Affiliation* (December), pp. 181-185.
Bube, Richard
   1976 "The Philosophy and Practice of Science." *Journal of the American Scientific Affiliation* (September), pp. 127-132.
Evans, C. Stephen
   1977 *Preserving the Person.* Downers Grove, Ill.: InterVarsity Press, especially Chs. 5 and 11.
Heddendorf, Russell
   1972 "Some Presuppositions of a Christian Sociology." *Journal of the American Scientific Affiliation* (September), pp. 110-117.
   1976 "The Evolution of Social Evolution." *Journal of the American Scientific Affiliation* (December), pp. 110-115.

Lyon, David
    1976 *Christians and Sociology.* Downers Grove, Ill.: InterVarsity
        Press.
Moberg, David O.
    1962 *Inasmuch.* Grand Rapids, Mich.: Eerdmans.
    1977 *The Great Reversal.* Philadelphia: Lippincott.
Perkins, John
    1976 *Let Justice Roll Down.* Glendale, Calif.: Regal.
Scanzoni, John
    1972 "Sociology." *Christ and the Modern Mind* (edited by Robert
        W. Smith). Downers Grove, Ill.: InterVarsity Press.

# 2

# Sources of Knowledge

*William L. Smith-Hinds*

"What should I do with my life?" is undoubtedly one of the most important questions anyone can ask. Other questions are intimately related to this one; for example, "What should I choose for my life's occupation?" "Whom should I marry?" "Where should I live?"

People seek answers to these and other questions in all sorts of places. Some people take aptitude tests. Others read horoscopes looking for tips on work, romance, and leisure. Some people page through newspapers or the *Occupational Outlook Handbook* looking for occupations that are in highest demand, offer the best pay, and require the least preparation. Others turn to the Bible. Some take drugs, hoping for a high that will give them new insights into themselves and life. Others just play it by ear.

Interestingly, people who are excited about one source of knowledge often neglect others. Horoscope lovers probably neglect the Bible. Aptitude test lovers probably give little or no credence to horoscopes. More than that, quite often people relying on one source of knowledge are rather critical of other sources. Bible lovers denounce fortune-telling—whether from palms, crystal balls, or tarot cards—as satanic. Indeed, this sort of antagonism is found not only among average, everyday down-to-earth people, but especially among intellectuals and scholars. Some intellectuals think that many scientists are counting, measuring, and comparing facts of little real importance. This is often referred to as "dustbowl empiricism." Other intellectuals

**William L. Smith-Hinds**
*Assistant Professor of Sociology, Lock Haven State College*
With considerable experience in Latin America, including a diploma from the Seminario Biblico Latinoamericano, Mr. Smith-Hinds has done research and writing in Honduras. He has taught courses in racial and ethnic relations, sociological theory, as well as research methods. He earned an MA in sociology from Temple University, and is now a PhD candidate at the University of Notre Dame. Before coming to Lock Haven, Mr. Smith-Hinds taught at Messiah College (Pennsylvania) and part time at the University of Notre Dame. He is an ordained minister in the United Brethren in Christ Church.

think that many philosophers are dealing with abstractions that have nothing to do with everyday life. This is often referred to as "armchair speculation." Some Christians are convinced that such scientific theories as evolution are pure speculation. They feel that it is not a simple matter of a few missing links; rather the whole chain is missing, and there exist only a few links on which the whole theory is built. Evolutionary theory, to some Christian leaders, is a devil-inspired threat to the faith and they attack it vigorously, often through the mass media. Some scientists and philosophers are most critical of religious knowledge. For example, Bertrand Russell in his book, *Why I Am Not a Christian*, suggests that throughout history those with religious knowledge have done more harm than good. Some of these thinkers see religious knowledge as little more than superstitution doomed to disappear when people become scientifically and rationally enlightened. The conflict among intellectuals over sources of knowledge rages on. The debates and struggles between "creationists" and "evolutionists," which are interestingly discussed by Leakey and Lewin (1977), are examples of this.

These conflicting views are undoubtedly disconcerting to anyone who thinks carefully about this matter. Moreover, the hostilities probably serve to turn people away from knowledge they ought to be considering carefully. A different approach to sources of knowledge is needed. This paper is an attempt to formulate a more conciliatory approach, an approach that is informed by sociology and compatible with a Christian perspective.

## Successful Decision-Making Requires Knowledge
*Decision-Making Pervades Social Life*

Someone asks jokingly, "How do you eat an elephant?" The response is "One bite at a time." An analogous, though much more important question is, "How do you spend a lifetime?" The answer is "One decision at a time."

Decision-making is a basic fact of life. Whether one stops to think about the important questions of life or not, he must make decisions. Decisions must be made about such matters as what to wear, what to eat, how to use time, whether to ask for or accept a date, whether or not to take a course pass/fail, whether to read the Bible, whether to smoke marijuana, how to spend money, and so on. Some decisions, seeming of little importance, are made almost automatically. Other decisions that could have major consequences on life demand more careful thought. Some decisions involve few options. Other decisions are complicated by the very fact that there are so many possibilities. There is plenty of time to make some decisions; others must be made in a hurry. People have dreams, big dreams, but they make decisions which take them on detours, detours which at times last a lifetime. So, people may make decisions blindly, ignorantly, and fortuitously. But wise people realize that successful decision-making requires knowledge. Our guiding maxim ought to be: Seek relevant knowledge before making decisions.

### The Abundance of Knowledge

There is certainly no shortage of knowledge. People are continuously bombarded with knowledge from many sources—books, television, radio, newspapers, and letters. Moreover, people carry hundreds of bits of knowledge in their mind. They know names of relatives and friends, telephone numbers, multiplication tables, traffic laws, health tips, sketches of American history, ideas about the family, and norms of the economy. If we took an inventory of everything that each individual knows, we would undoubtedly be amazed. (We would also be amazed at what they did not know!)

Knowledge of particular topics may be superficial and elementary or profound and complex. It may have been learned a long time ago or only recently. It may have been learned deliberately and with great effort or almost unawares and easily. It may be integrated into a whole, or it may simply be a collection of bits and pieces of information. People undoubtedly think that most of their knowledge is true, but they would surely admit that some of it is fictitious. Finally, while much of it is useful in everyday life, some of it is certainly not.

### Doubts and Persuasion

People are always trying to share some of their knowledge with us, especially when they know that we are faced with a decision. They may offer a solution to a problem, or a medicine for a particular ailment, or directions for finding a store, or advice about a person we are dating, or news about where to find bargains. We, like anyone else, are usually quite receptive and trusting, or at least pretend to be. Occasionally, however, we challenge the truthfulness and/or usefulness of the knowledge offered us. Such challenges may range anywhere from mild skeptical facial expressions to highly emotional and vigorous outbursts.

Most people are unable to accept challenges to the truth and/or usefulness of their knowledge calmly. Quite often they react by attempting to persuade us that they are correct. To do so, they may resort, consciously or unconsciously, to any of several commonly used persuasion techniques (Robertson, 1977:529). For example, they may tell us that some prominent person said so. Or they may tell us that most normal people agree with them, thus implying that we are weird or "not with it" if we disagree. Or they may include in their defense only those details that strengthen their case. In other words, they may stack the evidence in their favor. Or they may call us names such as communist, atheist, bigot, radical, or backslider, thus putting us in a very notorious company. Finally, they may say that they had a personal experience that convinced them of the truthfulness and/or usefulness of their knowledge. They may say that they actually saw a UFO, or actually heard a dead person talk through a living person (O'Brien and Bauman, 1978:56-58, 60, 62-63), or saw a person healed instantly.

This is certainly not an exhaustive list of persuasion techniques. Many others are readily available, including raising the voice or asking sensitive questions in the presence of people who would be shocked were an honest answer given. Nevertheless, of all the persuasion techniques, the personal experience argument is perhaps the most persuasive. It is extremely difficult to deny the truthfulness and/or usefulness of knowledge based on personal experience. Of course, we may ask for additional information about the personal experience in an attempt to discredit it. Trial lawyers often ask witnesses for additional information in an attempt to weaken, discredit, or even destroy their testimony. Yet this may backfire. Additional information may actually strengthen, rather than weaken the person's claim to true and/or useful knowledge. The story of the blind man healed by Jesus is a good example of this (John 9). Religious leaders kept asking the blind man questions in an attempt to discredit Jesus and the miracle. All his responses, however, only served to authenticate both Jesus and the miracle.

Without a doubt, knowledge based on personal experience is extremely difficult to deny. What is significant, however, is that very little of the important knowledge we have and use every day in decision making is actually supported by, or originated in, personal experience. Tradition suggests that "experience is the best teacher," but it failed to add "especially someone else's experience." And so it is. For example, most people have never seen the germs they believe they are washing off their hands before meals. People who eat carrots, believing them to be good for the eyes, wear glasses. Furthermore, most people insist on holding on to certain beliefs, even though much evidence indicates that such beliefs may be false. For example, many Americans believe that lower-class youths are much more likely than middle-class youths to commit crimes, or that most people on welfare could work if they really wanted to. Research findings, official publications, and newspaper articles indicate that each of these beliefs may actually be false (Robertson, 1977:9). The bottom line is that most of our knowledge is based on "someone else's experience;" most of our knowledge is based on secondhand information. Some of it, in fact, is based on little more than hearsay.

Successful decision-making requires knowledge, but knowledge ought not be accepted or rejected indiscriminately. This is especially true today in the light of the rapid changes taking place in social life, in communication, and the growing influence of large organizations with their ubiquitous public relations activities (Postman and Weingartner, 1971:11-21). We must constantly improve our ability to critically evaluate the knowledge we encounter. Paul's comment is relevant here. He said,

> Do not scoff at those who prophesy, but test everything that is said to be sure it is true, and if it is, then accept it. Keep away from every kind of evil (1 Thessalonians 5:20-22, Living Bible).

While Paul was speaking specifically about prophesying or preaching, his advice applies equally well to knowledge from other sources.

## Life Is Larger Than Any Single Source of Knowledge
*A Secular Perspective*

Where does knowledge come from? Where do people obtain knowledge about vitamins, sex, God, politics, communists, or money? Most people acquire a great deal of their knowledge from other people—from parents, teachers, and friends. But where did other people acquire their knowledge? Unfortunately, it is usually impossible for us to trace knowledge back to its original source. What is more, few people have the time, ability, or interest to do so, although, theoretically, it is possible to do so. For centuries scholars have pondered this question of the ultimate sources of knowledge ("epistemology"). Needless to say, informed opinions on the matter differ widely.

Traditionally, scholars have tended to emphasize one or two sources of knowledge. I. M. Bochenski (1966) offers a lucid account of some scholarly opinion about sources of knowledge. For example, as a young man Bertrand Russell placed great emphasis on reason. It was at this time that he wrote his very influential book *Principia Mathematica* together with Alfred North Whitehead. Later in life, he came to place greater emphasis on science. In contrast to Russell, Benadetto Croce recognized two and only two sources of knowledge, namely, intuition and reason. Finally, and in contrast to both Russell and Croce, such existentialist philosophers as Sören Kierkegaard, Martin Heidegger, and Jean-Paul Sartre seem to emphasize intuition or insight to such an extent that they practically exclude other sources.

Discussions of, and disagreements over sources of knowledge persist to this day. Scholars continue to point out why some sources are superior or inferior to others. Nevertheless, there are scholars who take a more eclectic view and suggest that the three sources of knowledge mentioned above are important (Johnson, 1969; Kaplan, 1964; Levi, 1957). Earl S. Johnson, for example, clearly takes this position (1969:44-55). In answering the question "Where does knowledge come from?", he would respond, "From facts, logic, and imagination." These, of course, correspond to science, reason, and intuition, respectively. He restates his position by suggesting that human beings are knowing creatures. They hear, see, touch, smell, and taste; therefore, they use facts. Human beings are ordering or systematizing creatures, consequently, they use logic. Finally, human beings are passionate or feeling creatures and therefore use imagination.

One clear implication of all this is that we secure complete knowledge by utilizing different sources. The major source of knowledge in biology, sociology, chemistry, and other sciences is empirical facts. In philosophy and mathematics it is logic. And in the humanities—art, music, literature, and drama—it is imagination.

*A Christian Perspective*

In Christian perspective facts, logic, and imagination are certainly important sources of knowledge. However, in addition to being knowing, feeling, and ordering creatures, from a Christian perspective, persons are also spiritual beings. They are forever raising questions about such matters as the meaning and purpose of life, injustice, suffering, and death. Answers to such questions derived from facts, logic, and imagination abound, but they are usually unsatisfactory to many people. Therefore, human beings around the world have for centuries turned to *another* source of knowledge, namely, inspired revelation.

Scholars would undoubtedly grant some merit to inspiration as a source of knowledge. Many, however, insist that inspiration is one and the same as intuition, imagination, or insight. From a Christian perspective, of course, such a point of view is quite unacceptable. Any Christian agreeing that the divine inspiration of the biblical authors is the same thing as intuition or imagination is logically undermining his or her faith. If revelation were nothing more than a product of human imagination or intuition, then the Bible would be nothing more than a collection of human writings, interesting and even significant perhaps, but a human product nonetheless. Of course the Bible was written by human beings. Their life, experiences, and times played an extremely important role in shaping its content and these must certainly be taken seriously. Nevertheless, in Christian perspective, the Bible is significantly more than a human product. It is the message of God to human beings and this is precisely what is *most* important about it. In Christian perspective, the inspired revelation is a unique and important source of knowledge in its own right, and it must not be confused with other sources. This is the point the apostle Peter made when he wrote,

> First of all you must understand this, that no prophecy of scripture is a matter of one's own interpretation, because no prophecy ever came by the impulse of man, but men moved by the Holy Spirit spoke from God (2 Peter 1:20).

The bottom line is that in Christian perspective, there are *at least* four sources of knowledge, namely, facts, logic, imagination, and inspiration. Accordingly, there are at least four kinds of knowledge or, more precisely, four aspects to knowledge, if the unity of knowledge is accepted. These are: scientific, rational, intuitive, and revealed. Perhaps it is worth noting that this view diverges in several ways from the view commonly found in introduction to sociology books, though only one will be mentioned here. In most recent books (1977 to 1979) the word "knowledge" is reserved for scientific knowledge. Other knowledge not amenable to scientific inquiry is called "beliefs." At this point the discussion may seem like a quibble over words, but it is really calling attention to a major error that is passed on from textbook to textbook. Beliefs or ideas about what is true or false, real or unreal in the world exist in all disciplines, from theology to nuclear physics. Methods of verification, however, differ from discipline to discipline. The failure of writers to point this out clearly, often leaves readers with the impression that only scientific knowledge is reliable or trustworthy, and this is certainly not the case.

Needless to say, not only Christians accept revelation as a real, true, and important source of knowledge. Moslems, Jews, Mormons and others do, also. This raises the difficult question of relativism: how can we determine when revelation is true or false? On what basis can Christians say that the Bible is the special revelation from God and that other books are not? This is definitely too complex a problem to discuss here, but you ought to take a careful look at the article by William Hasker entitled "Cultural Relativity: A Christian Perspective" in this *Reader*. *Rumor of Angels* and the *Sacred Canopy*, two books by Peter L. Berger, may also prove helpful.

Obviously, in everyday life knowledge does not come labeled in neat packages. Most knowledge is all mixed together. One moment people use scientific knowledge, another moment they use intuitive knowledge. This is fine, except that people often use scientific knowledge in a "religious fashion," or rational knowledge in a "scientific fashion." This creates serious problems. Consequently, it is extremely important and most helpful to be able to distinguish knowledge from various sources. One way of doing so is to determine what kind of evidence is needed for verification. For example, how does a scientist test his knowledge to see if it is true or false? What about a believer or an artist or a philosopher? In other words, what is the final authority for each source of knowledge?

Ideally, the final authority for scientists is empirical facts. In science beliefs are true if, and only if, they represent things that can be seen, touched, tasted, smelled, or heard. Where this cannot be done with the naked eye (physically), instruments such as microscopes, telescopes, thermometers, or Rorschach tests are used. Historically, the invention of instruments and the discovery of new facts has often led to important scientific developments. Ideally for mathematicians, logicians, and philosophers the final authority is reason. Beliefs are true if, and only if, the arguments or "proofs," as mathematicians call them, are correct or convincing to other mathematicians, logicians, or philosophers. Many significant developments in these disciplines have been due to the formulation of new arguments or proofs, often formulated on the basis of new assumptions.

Ideally, for believers the final authority is revelation. For example, for Christians it is the revelation of God found in the Bible. Beliefs are true if, and only if, they are supported by the sacred Scriptures. Developments in the Christian faith have often been due to new interpretations of old and familiar passages.

Ideally, for artists, writers, and musicians, the final authority is the inner-most voice of the soul. Beliefs are true if, and only if, they receive this intuitive confirmation. Others may disagree with the colors, forms, or sounds, but the artist or musician, following the "inner light," works on confidently or even defiantly. It is no wonder that the value of some masterpieces was not appreciated until long after the master's death. Significant developments in these areas have often been due to new flashes of insight.

## The Unity of Knowledge

Many scholars probably believe in the unity of knowledge, that is, that somehow all knowledge fits together. This, however, is more hope than reality for most humans. In practice knowledge is like an enormous jigsaw puzzle, or perhaps several puzzles. All pieces are not available; nor do all available pieces fit together. Indeed, even within disciplines there are conflicts. To some people, knowledge from the various sources will always be irreconcilable—especially scientific and religious knowledge.

The situation, however, is not hopeless. There are points of contact at which knowledge from various sources actually become mutually supportive, at least for the time being. Consider astronomy. For a long time scientists accepted the "steady state theory" of the universe as the most plausible one around. According to this theory, which can be traced back to Aristotle, the universe was without beginning and would be without end. Clearly, this theory is incompatible with the biblical account of creation and the end of the world. Recently, in the light of new evidence, the "big bang theory" has come into prominence. According to this theory, the universe began in a tremendous explosion some 15 to 20 billion years ago and is expanding at incredible speeds. Logically, it would seem that the expansion may come to an end some day. For the time being, the big bang theory is more in harmony with the biblical account (*Time*, 1979:149, 150). Curiously, while many theologians are delighted about these developments in astronomy, astronomers are upset (Jastrow, 1978: 18-20, 24, 26, 29).

Consider another example. The word "alienation" has a long history in philosophy and the social sciences. Conflict theorists in sociology use the word in at least three ways. First, alienation may mean that people are separated from the fruits of their labor and, consequently, exploited. Second, alienation may mean that people are separated or isolated from each other. Each person pursues his individual interests, unaware of how his interests relate to those of the larger group or community. Finally, alienation may mean that people are estranged from themselves. They feel trapped doing things they would rather not do. They feel they are unable, or think they are unable, to change the situation. All of these meanings have traditionally been a part of the Christian concept of "sin." Of course Christians would add that one of the consequences of "sin" is separation from God. In Christian perspective, this separation of each individual from God is the root cause of other major social problems. It is only when individuals are reconciled to God that solutions to other problems are found. Interestingly, in conflict theory there is what might be called a "materialistic" analogy to the consequences of sin from a Christian perspective. Conflict theorists certainly insist that there is a separation between workers and owners, proletariats and capitalists. It is only when this situation is dealt with and resolved that other social problems can be solved.

There are other definitions of "alienation," for example that of Melvin Seeman (1959:783-791), yet the similarities between alienation and sin persist. It is no wonder that Bernard Ramm has said, "Alienation is modern man's word for sin" (1978:12, 13).

There are many more examples of points of contact. The interested reader can learn more of how historical and archaeological research and the Bible come together in *Evidence That Demands a Verdict* (Volumes I and II) by Josh McDowell.

What we have here is *not* a situation where religious knowledge explains only things that cannot be explained by knowledge from other sources. Neither is it a situation where religious knowledge is slowly eroding away, while knowledge from other sources—especially scientific knowledge—grows. Instead, religious knowledge actually comes together with other kinds of knowledge and, as a result, makes explanations more reliable and trustworthy. Of course, it would be beautiful if all knowledge were in harmony—if it all fitted together neatly. However, this is not the case. Therefore, difficulties must be dealt with in an honest, realistic, cooperative, and flexible manner. People must consider evidence from all sources as carefully as they consider evidence from their own favorite source. Perhaps in this way the points of contact may increase and more progress may be made toward the unity of knowledge.

## An Open Attitude Is Essential
*Dogmatists All*

Those critical of religion often call attention to the dogmatism of Christian believers and other religious people in general. Indeed, Christians are often dogmatic about certain things, at times more so than they ought to be. Nevertheless, this is *almost* a case of missing the log in one's eye, but seeing the straw in the neighbor's eye. Such critics tend to overlook the fact that scientists, philosophers, artists, etc., are also dogmatic about certain things.

Dogmatism refers to the strict or even stubborn adherence to certain principles and/or beliefs, even in the face of debatable evidence. In a sense it is the opposite of "openness." The dogmatist has made up his or her mind and does not even want to talk about it. The person who is open has made a decision, but he is also willing to consider new evidence and to think about it further.

There are at least two forms of dogmatisim; we shall call them (1) *methodological* dogmatism and (2) *content* dogmatism. Methodological dogmatism refers to a strict adherence to one method of verifying knowledge. Content dogmatism refers to the strict adherence to certain beliefs. Most scholars who are seriously engaged in their discipline are probably methodological domatists. For example, as was mentioned before, scientists require facts; Christian believers require the Word of God. Pragmatism is perhaps the greatest reason for a commitment to methodological dogmatism. Scholars committed to methodological dogmatism reap enormous rewards. It has led to a growth of knowledge in all areas, but especially in science. Methodological dogmatism is, however, a two-edged sword. On the one hand, its application has yielded enormous returns in knowledge. On the other hand, its application makes it impossible for scholars to deal with all aspects of reality. For example, from a scientific point of view it is impossible to deal with many questions concerning the soul, God, and heaven. Again, from a Christian point of view it is impossible to deal with many questions concerning anatomy, physiology, and the origin of physical differences among human populations. In fact, whenever scholars begin pontificating on topics outside their field, their remarks must be most critically evaluated.

Christians and other religious believers are probably more susceptible to content dogmatism. There are basic beliefs to which a person or a church must adhere to remain Christian, for example, those set forth in the Apostles' Creed. But there are many other debatable beliefs to which many Christians adhere just as strongly or rigidly. For example, some Christians believe that women should not serve as ministers, or that Christians should not go to see a movie, or that musical instruments should not be used in the church.

Yet while Christians may be more susceptible to content dogmatism, they are certainly not alone. Scientists, philosophers, artists, musicians, and others also adhere quite rigidly to certain beliefs about religion and life in general. For example, many insist that it is primitive to be religious, that God does not exist, that if he does he is not interested in human affairs, or that man is the measure of all things.

In this writer's opinion, an approach most compatible with the practice of sociology and a personal commitment to Jesus Christ would include

(1) a great deal of methodological dogmatism coupled with an acceptance of at least four ultimate sources of knowledge and an awareness of the strengths and weaknesses of each source,
(2) and as little content dogmatism as possible or as much openness as possible. Keep in mind, however, that 100 percent openness is probably impossible and, most of all, undesirable.

*Ups and Downs*

Any body of knowledge is important and can be kept alive as long as a group of people accept it and use it in their everyday life. Whether it is actually true or false is certainly significant, but makes little difference. Groups have been known to accept and live by beliefs considered false by most Americans, for example, the Flat Earth Research Society (*The New York Times*, March 26, 1979:A14). A group of people adhering to a particular body of knowledge may be politically powerful or weak. There tends to be a positive correlation between the political status of groups and the influence of the body of knowledge they adhere to. During the Middle Ages priests and other religious functionaries held powerful positions in Europe. Accordingly, religious knowledge was dominant over other forms of knowledge. Today in the United States scientists hold influential positions as advisers to policymakers in government and business and, accordingly, scientific knowledge is quite influential.

What does the future hold? In Iran it seems that just a short time ago scientists were most influential and scientific knowledge was in a favored position. In 1979 a charismatic religious leader became quite powerful and scientists are at least on the defensive. At least for the time being religious knowledge has become more influential. Of course such a drastic turn of events seems quite unlikely in the United States, and yet there is no certainty that scientific knowledge will maintain its hegemony indefinitely.

When it comes to knowledge, obviously, political power and truth are not synonymous. Historically, knowledge from various sources has had its ups and downs politically and this may continue to be the case. Nevertheless, a greater value must be placed on *truth* in knowledge, though power cannot be ignored.

### Interpretation and Experience

How is it possible for scientists to look at the same data and yet come up with conflicting conclusions? How can sociologists look at the same data and draw conflicting conclusions? How is it possible for Christians to read the same Bible and yet come up with conflicting views on similar topics? Some Christians believe "once saved, always saved." Others believe that Christ will come to earth again to rule over his kingdom for 1,000 years. Others deny that his return will usher in a kingdom of 1,000 years. Some Christians believe that there is an inherent contradiction between being a true believer and a follower of Jesus Christ—"the Prince of Peace"—and being a soldier. Other Christians consider it their duty to serve in the military forces if called.

One possible explanation is that Bible passages are not clear and lend themselves to varying interpretations. This, however, really fails to explain why such disagreements seem to last almost indefinitely.

Here is a different and perhaps more sociological explanation. It comes in two parts. First, knowledge from all sources has at least two sides to it, namely, (1) a theoretical or conceptual side and (2) a practical side, for lack of a better name. For example, in physical anthropology there are fossil remains—the practical side. Interpretations formulated on the basis of the fossil remains constitute the theoretical or conceptual side. Among Christians there is the Bible— the practical side. Interpretation of Bible passages constitute the theoretical or conceptual side. In addition to this, keep in mind that these interpretations are group, rather than individual, interpretations. For example, Presbyterians tend to believe in "eternal security," while Methodists tend not to believe in "eternal security." Or Mennonites tend to be pacificists but Presbyterians tend not to.

Second, most group interpretations are solidly grounded or rooted in group experience, whether historical or current. For example, in Latin America many ministers and priests faced with masses of people suffering from poverty, disease, unemployment, and injustice have formulated a theology of liberation. In other words, Christians faced with critical social problems often turn to the Word of God for answers and come up with interpretations which are then handed down in the church from generation to generation. Many of these interpretations are extremely creative and useful, and give descendants a legacy of which they are very proud and grateful. Occasionally, however, the interpretations are locally and temporally bound. Their original meaning and vitality are lost as they are passed on from generation to generation—they actually become a burden to people who must continue to carry them long after their usefulness has expired.

Why then the conficts? For scientists, theories are shaped by facts and experiences, especially group experiences. For Christians, interpretations are shaped by the Bible and experiences, especially group experiences. It should be apparent that as experiences differ, so will theories and interpretations—even if facts and the Bible remain the same.

## The Variety of Uses

Some scholars suggest that in historical perspective religious knowledge has done more harm than good. As evidence they cite such examples as the Inquisition, the prejudice and discrimination against Afro-Americans in the Bible Belt, and more recently, the mass suicide of the People's Temple in Guyana.

The sins of "the saints" are a difficult problem for Christians to deal with, yet there are some possible ways of doing so. A Christian may point out that many of the people who participated actively in such atrocities were not genuine believers who had a personal relationship with Jesus Christ. There is certainly some empirical support for this explanation. Note, for example, the differences found by Gordon W. Allport between persons with an intrinsic religious commitment and those with an extrinsic religious commitment (Greeley, 1972:206-213). People with an intrinsic religious commitment are committed to their religion as an end in itself; people with an extrinsic religious commitment are committed to their religion as a means to other ends. The latter tend to be more prejudiced than the former. Nevertheless, in view of the paucity of evidence, this explanation is really more of a hypothesis (and a hope) than an empirical generalization.

Another way to deal with the sins of "the saints" is to admit that Christians have done horrible things from time to time and to ask God for wisdom and strength to prevent the recurrence of such atrocities in the name of Jesus Christ.

Finally, what about other forms of knowledge? As the saying goes, people who live in glass houses ought not to throw stones. Other forms of knowledge have quite a record too. For example, scientific knowledge made possible the destruction of over 60,000 human beings in a flash in Nagasaki and Hiroshima. In addition, over 8 million human beings died in World War I and between 30 and 60 million in World War II.

Of course, scientific and religious knowledge has also been used in beneficial ways. Scientific knowledge has made possible a level of living unparalleled in history. Religious knowledge has enabled people to rise above themselves and turn dreams into realities. For example, take a look at the story in *Time* magazine on "Saints Among Us" (December 29, 1975:33-37). Much could also be said about rational and intuitive knowledge.

In summary, any kind of knowledge may be used in harmful or beneficial ways. Indeed, it may well be that the greater the knowledge available, the greater the potential to use it either for destruction and death or for abundant life. Human beings must make the choice.

### Discussion Questions

1. The word "knowledge" is not defined in the chapter. What is

"knowledge"? How does "knowledge" differ from "information" and "wisdom"?

2. In view of the abundance of knowledge available, is there any censorship? Is the presence or absence of censorship advantageous or disadvantageous to society?

3. In what ways do large organizations use knowledge in an attempt to influence our life? Is this advantageous or disadvantageous to society?

4. Does believing that divine inspiration is one and the same thing as intuition, imagination, or insight really undermine our faith? Explain.

5. Is it "ethnocentric" for Christians to believe that the Bible is the only true revelation or word of God? Explain.

6. What are some possible relationships between "knowledge" and "norms" and "values"?

7. Robert Jastrow states, "Theologians are delighted that the astronomical evidence leads to a biblical view of Genesis—but curiously, astronomers are upset." What are some of the implications of this situation?

8. What are some points on which scientific knowledge (for example, sociological knowledge) and religious knowledge seem to be in conflict?

9. Make a list of basic doctrines in your church. Has the Bible, or the historical and current experience of the church, been more important in the development of this doctrine?

10. Is it possible to be an outstanding scientist, philosopher, or artist (that is, one who produces original and creative work) and a committed Christian at the same time? Does a strong commitment to Jesus Christ predispose people to dogmatism and weaken their creative abilities? Explain.

## References

Bochenski, I. M.
    1966 *Contemporary European Philosophy, Philosophies of Matter, the Idea, Life, Essence, Existence and Being.* Berkeley and Los Angeles, Calif.: University of California Press.
Greeley, Andrew M.
    1972 *The Denominational Society, A Sociological Approach to Religion in America.* Glenview, Ill.: Scott, Foresman and Company.
    1979 "In the Beginning: God and Science." *Time* (February 5), pp. 149-150.
Jastrow, Robert
    1978 "Have Astronomers Found God?" *The New York Times Magazine*, Section 6 (June 25), pp. 18-20, 22, 24, 26, 29.

Johnson, Earl S.
1969 "Ways of Knowing." Carlton E. Beck and Jim A. Barak (Eds.), *The Study of Society*, Scranton, Pa.: International Textbook Company, pp. 44-55.

Kaplan, Abraham
1964 *The Conduct of Inquiry, Methodology for Behavioral Science*. San Francisco, Calif.: Chandler Publishing Company.

Leakey, Richard and Roger Lewin
1977 *Origins*. New York: E. P. Dutton.

Levi, Albert William
1957 *Varieties of Experience, An Introduction to Philosophy*. New York: The Ronald Press.

O'Brien, John and Edward Bauman
1978 "Accused of Murder by a Voice from the Grave." *Ebony*, 33 (June), pp. 56-58, 60, 62-63.

Postman, Neil and Charles Weingartner
1976 "Teaching as a Subversive Activity: Crap Detecting." Glen Gaviglio and David Raye (Eds.), *Society as It Is, A Reader*, 2nd Edition. New York: Macmillan, pp. 11-21.

Ramm, Bernard
1978 "One Doctrine We Can Prove." *Eternity*, 29 (June), pp. 12-13.

Robertson, Ian
1977 *Sociology*. New York: Worth Publishers.

Seeman, Melvin
1959 "On the Meaning of Alienation." *American Sociological Review*, 24 (December), pp. 783-791.
1979 "Still a Hoax to Flat-Earth Group". *The New York Times*, Section a (February 26), p. 14.

# 3
# The Scientific Approach to Social Research: Some Dilemmas for the Christian

*Brendan F. J. Furnish*

### The Scientific Orientation of Sociology

The view that sociology relies upon careful, objective, and systematic observation of social reality is widely accepted by almost all sociologists. The process of gathering information about social reality is known as social research. In general, there is widespread agreement in the discipline concerning the way research is accomplished. Most sociologists claim that they employ the scientific method as the basis for conducting a systematic, organized investigation of reality.

In the final analysis, science is essentially a particular way of acquiring knowledge about some kind of phenomenon. Now there are a variety of ways of acquiring knowledge about phenomena. For instance, we can "know" in an intuitive sense, and we can "know" in an experiential sense. Certainly the experience of Christian conversion involves the acquisition of a particular type of knowledge. The experience of the "new birth," however, is not necessarily something that lends itself to empirical verification.

The most important characteristic of science is the understanding that the practitioners follow a generally acknowledged and agreed upon set of rules of procedure. Most important to this scientific orienta-

**Brendan F. J. Furnish**
*Associate Professor of Sociology and Chairman of the Department*
*Westmont College*
Associate Professor Furnish received his MA from San Francisco State College, and he was granted the PhD in sociology from the University of Southern California. As a student he worked at Stanford on the Mark III accelerator in the Hansen Physics Laboratories. He began his teaching at Westmont in 1967. Although nondenominational in orientation, he is a member of the Conservative Baptist Church, and is chairman of the board of the Drug Abuse Prevention Center. He is presently writing several books, one dealing with the Easternization of Western Culture.

tion is the expectation that a scientist will rigorously *test* his or her knowledge. This is usually accomplished by the development of hypotheses which are carefully tested either by observation or experimentation.

To be sure, there is considerable debate about just how "objective" social research is (Webb, et al., 1966; Phillips, 1971; Lewis, 1975). In addition, much time has been spent arguing whether or not the data of sociology can be understood and dealt with in the same manner that data in the natural sciences are handled. This especially involves the tensions which have arisen between empirically and positivistically oriented sociologists and those who are inclined to take an existentialist approach to the acquisition of sociological knowledge, such as those who espouse ethnomethodology. Despite this difference in viewpoint, most sociologists feel that there is a high degree of correspondence between the "scientific approach" and sociological research methods.

## Scientists Make Assumptions, Too

When sociologists employ the scientific method, they accept specific assumptions about the world and the nature of reality. These assumptions form an important part of the "Game of Science" (McCain and Segal, 1973) and require that the scientist adopt a particular worldview. These primary assumptions of science are frequently exalted by terming them "postulates." The postulates of science require accepting these assumptions without proof if any useful communication is to occur. Indeed, these can be thought of as *faith* assumptions since they are unprovable philosophically speaking. In this regard, at least, science is analogous to the Christian faith, since we begin with basic assumptions, also. Herein is the first point of tension the Christian sociologist encounters, since some of these assumptions are not necessarily compatible with a Christian world-view or *weltanschauung*.

## Materialism and the Scientific Method

Science requires that the relationships and data used in the construction of hypotheses necessary for testing scientific knowledge must consist of things that can be observed. The sociologist is concerned with selecting variables that can be accounted for empirically, by one's senses. Thus, sociologists are interested in categories such as race, age, sex, education, income, etc. They would not attempt to measure "man's sinful tendencies," or try to scale the "fruits of the

Holy Spirit." They would not do this because such categories violate the materialistic assumption of science.

## Materialism and Reality

Several aspects of the postulate of materialism merit discussion. A fundamental belief of materialism is that the literal, physical world really exists. To the philosophically naive this appears to be a rather unnecessary and somewhat bizarre presupposition. However, philosophers such as Locke, Berkeley, Hume, and Kant have demonstrated the difficulty of proving the existence of the real world. Further, it is not difficult for a philosophical idealist to argue convincingly that the physical world does not exist. The Christian, however, has no real problem with this, since he accepts the witness of Scripture that "God created the world."

It should be observed that, historically, this assumption has long been a source of contention. The first- and second-century Gnostics generally tended to denigrate the reality of the material world. This particular heresy resulted in considerable trouble for the apostles and the early church fathers. Mary Baker Eddy revived this heresy in her development of Christian Science. In recent times, eastern religious thought, which is increasingly permeating western culture, has attempted to portray the material world as illusory.

The tension for the Christian obviously does not lie in believing in the existence of the real world, but in what many scientists feel must logically follow from this belief. Namely, that belief in the external world is based upon perceptions received through our physical senses. The non-Christian scientist then carries the argument a step further by asserting that there is simply no other way of knowing the world. Without agreement on this point, he argues, there can be no agreement about what is "knowable." Additionally, he presupposes that there are not, nor can there be, unknown forces that might prevent scientific investigation of particular phenomena. All knowledge is therefore derived from sensory impressions (cf., Lastrucci, 1967).

## "All"—Is Not Always ALL

The first problem with the strictly empirical approach is that it takes the "all," in "all knowledge," quite literally. For the Christian this is indeed a one-sided approach, since it discounts human spirituality. Believing that the material realm comprises all of reality leaves no room for the supernatural. For the Christian the above position is unacceptable because it would either involve giving up one's belief in the supernatural or compartmentalizing one's faith. Many Christians in the social sciences have done this—they have separated their role as social scientist from that of believer. Compartmentalizing faith from scientific research, can lead Christians into a kind of intellectual schizophrenia. This condition is worse than living with unresolved tensions that inevitably result from attempts to integrate faith and science.

### The Spiritual Is a Reality Also

The second problem for the Christian sociologist centers around the so-called "Postulate of Empiricism" mentioned earlier: i.e., the belief that we must assume that all knowledge is the result of sensory perception. This frequently places the Christian sociologist in a dilemma, since it implies that his peers will only accept an explanation for a particular phenomenon that is based upon empirically verifiable data. However, there are many times when the Christian realizes that there is a compelling spiritual explanation, not based on sensory perception, but on the operation of spiritual gifts, (e.g. spiritual discernment [1 Corinthians 12]).

For instance, this is often the case when one is doing research in the sociology of religion and studying the growth of certain cultic and occult organizations. One can collect data and give a satisfactory scientific explanation for the phenomenon. However, if the Christian sociologist adheres strictly to the empirical method, he will discover that he has left out *the* crucial explanatory variable because his scientific epistemology could not account for spiritual activities. Also, he might be fearful that his research will not be pusblished if he includes any spiritual explanations. He might even attempt to rationalize this by saying that spiritual matters would not be understood by nonbelievers anyway (1 Corinthians 2:14-16). Nevertheless, this remains a source of considerable frustration for some Christians involved in such work.

It is interesting to note that while many sociologists studiously attempt to keep their work "scientific" by carefully excluding the spiritual dimension, many, including portions of the scientific community, are becoming keenly interested in spiritual matters. For the most part, however, this interest is in the spiritual dimension outside of the Judeo-Christian tradition. Examples of this are becoming commonplace, such as articles about the integration of particle physics and

Eastern religion in scholarly physics journals (Capra, 1974; 1975; Postle, 1976); or the increasing concern about "spiritual" matters on the part of psychologists and psychiatrists, as issues of *Psychology Today* over the last few years will verify.

## The Naturalistic and Deterministic Elements of Science

As indicated thus far, the scientist gathers and organizes data both in order to be able to explain some particular phenomena, and in order to be able to predict the future occurrence of phenomena. This latter purpose is one of the goals of sociologists.

### Determinism—"It's All Fixed"

Despite a paucity of successful predictions, most sociologists tend to follow the deterministic outlook since it is also a necessary component of causality, which in turn is essential to scientific explanation. As a result, they hold that whatever happens does so of necessity and not by chance. It is further posited that events occur because of preceeding physical, social, or psychological events. This is a casual view which is occasionally referred to as "mechanistic." This is necessary if the sociologist is going to be able to make "if-then" statements.

All of this is tied to a fundamental postulate of science which claims that we must be able to consider the world about us as an ordered system. Explanation and prediction are based upon the notion of regularity. Whitehead has observed that this is a very basic assumption on which science is built, the "widespread, instinctive conviction in the existence in an order of things, and in an order of nature" (1960:9). An examination of this issue from a philosophical standpoint will demonstrate that it is quite impossible to prove the world to be an ordered and regular system. Thus, we must again accept these assumptions by faith. This is, in many respects, a rather astounding presupposition, since it puts so much faith in nature, per se.

### Regularity and Divine Intervention

The Christian finds nothing wrong with the notion of regularity. God is not a God of confusion. He organized the world in an orderly fashion. However, he has intervened in the course of history, and occasionally he has performed some unexpected and mighty act. While these violate the canons of regularity, they demonstrate his sovereignty over his creation. The acceptance of God's intervention in history is an essential basis of our faith. Likewise, we believe that he still does intervene and suspends the operation of the natural order which he created. Thus the Christian does not find the occurrence of miracles inexplicable. The scientist, however, who is completely committed to a naturalistic, materialistic world-view must either ignore such events or invent a suitable explanation, forcing the data to fit into his world-view.

Scientists have not always rejected the idea of God's intervention in his world. Merton has demonstrated that the pioneering scientists of the seventeenth century, who were largely of Puritan background, firmly believed that God was at work in his creation. As a result, they felt that the "study of Nature is to the greater glory of God and the good of Man" (1936:3). The development of a secular epistemology slowly displaced the primacy of God in science. As this took place scientists exchanged their understanding of the Creator/Maintainer for an impersonal and nebulous "force and order" in nature. This occurred despite the fact that the system is truly undecipherable if God is left out of account, since so much must either be assumed or left unanswered. Thus, the scientist may assume order and regularity while at the same time realizing that in nature itself, systems function in an entropic manner and, lacking inputs from without, all natural systems move from order to disorder and decay.

This has led to the development of a highly mechanistic view of humankind, perhaps best articulated by B. F. Skinner. The hollowness of this extreme position has generated an epistemological crisis which has been well described from a Christian standpoint by Schaeffer (1972), Alexander (1972) and Guinness (1973). This has also been a precipitating factor in the development of the mystical reaction now occurring in Western culture.

It should not be inferred from what has been stated thus far that all sociologists share this purely mechanistic orientation. One can argue that those who are involved in existential or phenomenological sociology, or for that matter, even those involved in structural-functional analysis, would reject the extreme mechanistic position described to this point (see Balswick and Ward, 1976). Nevertheless, researchers from these schools must develop either implicit or explicit hypotheses if they are to explain the phenomena they are dealing with. To be sure they may not work with specific quantitative indicators, but instead may deal with subjective, qualitative variables. The point is, however, that anyone interested in social research eventually must come to grips with the problem of constructing reliable, valid, explanatory, and (hopefully) predictive hypotheses. Also, they must develop an appropriate research design regarding the phenomenon under study. To do this requires addressing the epistemological issues which are being raised here.

*Naturalism, Man, and Determinism*

The sociological corollary of naturalism is that societies are ordered, regular, and predictable. Almost all sociologists believe this, with the exception of a rather small covey of "radical", existential sociologists (cf., Morris, 1975). The expectation of predictability and regularity in social behavior is the very element that makes sociology possible. It would be impossible to perform social research if individuals constantly acted in a capricious and unpredictable manner. All of this is predicated upon a very basic assumption concerning people. We must assume that people (and their organizations) are a part of the natural world. This permits individual and social behavior to be understood by scientific methods of study (cf., Lastrucci, 1967:39). A number of criticisms have been raised regarding the twin issues of naturalism and determinism in social research. Let us examine some that are especially germane to the Christian interested in social research.

First, there is the implication of unity between all of nature and humanity. Accordingly, people are of the same stuff as animals: there is little or no crucial difference. Thus, we find social and behavioral science researchers discussing man "the social animal." The important difference between the human and the ape is that the former somehow acquired an oral and written language and a culture which he can control and manipulate. Symptomatic of this are the efforts by some researchers, especially those in the behavioral sciences, to make extrapolations from their research on lower animals to the behavior of humans. Thus, some have attempted to extend Calhoun's (1962) studies on the effects of the overcrowding of mice, to problems in our cities. The end result is a glib discussion of the "behavioral sink" aspects of certain urban areas. Calhoun's study and conclusions are discussed and refuted by Freedman (1975). In a similar way Homans (1961) begins his theory of social exchange with a discussion of the behavior of pigeons. Finally, current interests in "sociobiology" contain strong elements of both naturalism and determinism.

From a methodological standpoint, there is a serious problem here with "external validity" (Campbell and Stanley, 1966). That is, it is simply not valid to generalize from research conclusions derived from one population sample to one that is completely different. For instance, one cannot assume that the sexual attitudes of male freshmen in the local community college are identical with those of all adult males in the United States. This appears fairly obvious, but "scientists" who should know better frequently make this error. Perhaps the most annoying instances of this involve psychiatrists who, on the basis of a few case studies of aberrant individuals generalize particular behaviors to an entire population. This is one of several fundamental problems with the behavioral "research" of Sigmund Freud. At any rate, scientists who generalize from the behaviors of rodents to the behaviors of people are guilty of committing this very fundamental research fallacy.

## Dualism vs. Monism

It seems to me, at any rate, that the bent toward naturalism has encouraged the development of a type of materialistic monism. The Christian, however, believes in the existence of both spirit and matter. He believes that he was created in the image and likeness of God. This means that the person is *not just* a body—he is a total unity of body, mind, soul, and spirit. However, the naturalistic, materialistic orientation would reject the reality of man's spiritual nature and, at best, remain agnostic about belief in the immortality of the soul. That is, since the soul cannot be measured by any type of quantitative or qualitative indicator, it cannot exist. Accordingly, this becomes a serious point of tension for the Christian since the scientific orientation demands that we ignore an important dimension of man. Interestingly enough, people appear to be shifting toward a greater concern with the "spiritual." Witness the growing concern with "holistic medicine," visitors from outer space, and all manner of strange paranormal activity.

We should not be particularly surprised by this turn of events. The Bible clearly teaches that physical human beings have both a soul and a spirit. Every culture has, until very recent times, acknowledged the spiritual element of existence through the development of some form of institutionalized ritual and religious practices. It is only lately that the purely materialistic, naturalistic approach, has attempted to ignore our spiritual nature. However, since the phenomenon of our spirituality is real, attempts to explain it away by invoking the scientific approach are to no avail. Thus our culture and its scientific disciplines (including sociology) are placed in a quandary. To accept the supernatural order as a real phenomena, operating separately from the materialistic order, would require a very painful reexamination of nature. Our definition of the reality of the supernatural, at least in Christian terms, would fly in the face of the conventional wisdom of our culture and would require a massive shift in the world-view of a great many people.

Some scientists have opted to resolve the dilemma by resorting to a kind of "scientism." That is, they do not attempt to separate the spiritual from the material. Instead, they treat both as components of the natural order. Essentially the approach holds that the existence of a phenomenon is sufficient to justify it as "scientific" data. Naturally, this raises some difficult epistemological and ontological problems in terms of the scientific orientation described thus far, especially in terms of the "postulate of empiricism." Some of those interested in the paranormal phenomena largely ignore these problems by claiming that "we simply do not know enough about these phenomena to quantify them at this time. However, given enough time, we will produce an adequate scientific explanation." Others involved in such "research" suggest that the definition of what we mean by sensory impressions will simply have to be expanded to include "senses" not now recognized. Again, this raises some very grave problems in terms of how one objectively tests such paranormal knowledge by the methods of science. Furthermore, this implies a very significant departure from the historical scientific position.

One startling aspect of this development is that interest in the paranormal has suddenly gained acceptance over the past few years. To be sure, J. B. Rhine began this type of "scientific investigation" with his studies of extrasensory perception at Duke University in 1930. However, most "orthodox" scientists either ignored Rhine or castigated his work as "pseudoscience." That this orientation would suddenly become acceptable "science" is indeed a fascinating phenomenon in and of itself. Some orthodox Christians are beginning to suggest that such an approach may lead to the frightening possibility of a spiritualized quasi science. On the one hand it may reject the existence of the Christian God as a superstitious and "unscientific" belief, or on the other hand it may welcome demonic forces not completely understood as natural phenomena (see Alexander and Fetcho, 1977:25-30).

Interestingly, C. S. Lewis anticipated such a state of affairs over thirty years ago. In his well-known book *The Screwtape Letters*, Lewis had his imaginary demon writing about the demons' existence and strategy. His words are amazingly prophetic in regard to the direction contemporary science appears to be moving.

> Our policy, for the moment, is to conceal ourselves. Of course this has not always been so. We are faced with a cruel dilemma. When the humans disbelieve in our existence we lose all the pleasing results of direct terrorism, and we make no magicians. On the other hand, when they believe in us, we cannot make them materialists and sceptics. At least not yet. I have great hopes that we shall learn in due time how to emotionalise and mythologise their science to such an extent that what is, in effect, a belief in us (though not under that name) will creep in while the human mind remains closed to belief in the Enemy [The Christian God]. The "Life Force," the worship of sex, and some aspects of Psychoanalysis may here prove useful. If once we can produce our perfect work—the Materialist Magician, the man, not using, but veritably worshipping, what he vaguely calls "Forces" while denying the existence of "spirits"—then the end of the war will be in sight (1973:32-33).

It appears indeed, that man has begun to "emotionalise and mythologise" science, as Lewis predicted.

### Freedom and Determinism

Next it is necessary to examine the problems created by determinism in science. This issue brings up the crucial problem of freedom, or for the Christian, what is commonly called "free will."

When we discuss naturalism and determinism we are brought back to the previously mentioned issue of mechanism in science. The mechanistic position is a logical outgrowth of the search for causation, which is necessary for scientific explanation and prediction. To the sociologist this means that an individual's behavior is entirely a product of social forces that act upon him determining his behavior. There are two significant Christian implications here for the Christian.

*Environmental Determinism—No, But . . .*

First, if people are purely products of their environment, then by modifying the environment we can modify people. This is implicit in much thought during the Enlightenment, and is probably best articulated by Marx's synthesis of Feuerbach's and Hegel's work. The idea was further solidified by the Darwinistic explanation of human origins, which some interpreted to mean that God was not involved in the creative process, and that creation was only an accident. Using this approach, some have redefined their conception of both God and man. If we are entirely a product of our environment, we are therefore beings who can largely determine our own destiny. We have within ourselves the power to be perfect; indeed, we can become godlike.

Thus, we can understand the attempt of much of the social and behavioral sciences, particularly in the applied areas, to modify the environment in order to produce better people. The Christian, likewise, has a moral obligation—indeed, a divine command—to improve the social and physical environment (Matthew 25:31-46; James 2:14-17). However, the Christian sociologist realizes that modifying the environment will not necessarily modify human behavior, not to mention "perfect" it. This is due to the fact that our perspective must also account for the presence of sin and evil, both personal and structural, in human beings and human social systems. Failure to understand the limitations of social determinism can lead to social engineering experiments which may, in the end, prove disastrous to personal freedom as we have known it in this country.

### What of "Free Will"?

The second implication of determinism has to do with whether or not people's actions are, in fact, determined by their environment. This is important to the Christian, since our notion of free will is at least partially contingent upon it. It is also important to the empirical sociologist since the notion of causation is predicated upon the notion of social determinism. This issue, more than any other, demonstrates the limitations of the scientific viewpoint in sociology. There are two distinct problem areas here. The first concerns the amount of existential freedom we actually possess as men and women, and the second has to do with whether or not we can actually use the mechanistic approach to give us valid descriptions and useful knowledge about people.

In regard to the first problem, we must ask ourselves whether or not the actions of people are so determined that men and women will relate to each other as predictable "objects." To be sure, there is a very high degree of standardization in human groups. This is the element which makes sociology both interesting and possible. Likewise, we know that nonconformity will meet with various sanctions which are designed to realign the recalcitrant group member. This does not, however, preclude the possibility of individual choice, which often becomes an issue when one has to make an ethical or moral decision. There are times when such a choice means that very severe social sanctions will be applied to the person who deviates from the path that the culture has chosen. Nonetheless, there are too many examples of people making such decisions, and willingly accepting the consequences, to simply ignore this phenomenon. Both past and contemporary Christian martyrs testify to the fact that we are not completely "prisoners of our society."

Moreover, to act as if we, as individuals, are completely determined is, as Berger has claimed, an act of "bad faith—a dishonest evasion of the agony of choice" (Berger, as quoted in Cuzzort, 1976:289. Incidentally, Cuzzort's treatment of Berger provides an excellent discussion of the issue of freedom and sociology). Accordingly, to imply that we are locked into deterministic social patterns is a myth that we willingly indulge in. While it might be painful, by a resolute act of the will we can free ourselves from past patterns of behavior. Thus, there is the possibility of choice and hence the idea of free will remains a viable concept.

### Can We Predict Individual Behavior?

The second problem in this area has to do with the usefulness of determinism in social research. While there are many aspects of people and their behavior that we can study, we must realize that the scientific description of human behavior is not sufficient in itself to account for the totality of their actions. This is because of the "unknown" and unpredictable element within humans, in addition to the existence of free will. The point is that scientific observation by itself is not sufficient to understand the whole person. We must realize the limitations of our approach anytime we begin to treat men or women as scientific objects. Failure to do so results in a gross perversion of personhood. Because people behave in a conscious, volitional manner, external observation does not enable one to know the complete person. This is one of the major issues between "scientific" sociologists and the existential, phenomenological sociologists.

More specifically, the question arises, are we so completely determined that our behavior is completely predictable (given enough information about us)? Perhaps a brief example will help answer this question. Suppose someone, after gathering exhaustive information about you as a person, were to tell you that you would become a thief at a certain time in your life. How would his prediction affect your future course of action? Would it provide a self-fulfilling prophecy that would lead you into a life of crime? Or would it instead engender a type of "reaction formation" which would cause you to completely avoid any appearance of such behavior? Either way, the conveying of this information to you would have some effect upon your choice of future action. On the one hand, you could choose to define your situation as criminal and you could become a criminal. On the other hand, you could choose to invalidate the prediction and studiously avoid a life of crime. In either case, his input to you would alter your conception of your situation and affect your future course of action.

Alexander provides some excellent insights relative to determinism in his book *Beyond Science*. He observes that,

> . . . it is difficult to see how any consistent claim to complete determinism could logically be upheld. If I am completely determined, and therefore not truly responsible for my thoughts, theories or actions, my coming to a conclusion about something must also be determined. But if I came to the conclusion that I am determined, then this conclusion must have also been determined. There is no particular reason therefore why I should value it as a conclusion more than any other conclusion. . . . These kinds of arguments have led many people to adopt a kind of schizophrenic existence in which intellectually they believe they are determined but in practice they behave according to their experience of feeling free (1972:55).

*Social Research Has Limitations, But . . .*

So there are apparently definite limits to strict determinism. This would also imply that there are some limitations to social research in general, and there are indeed. This does not, however, preclude in toto doing valid social research and making useful generalizations about human behavior; we need only remain aware of the limitations and restrictions of our scientific methods. Moreover our awareness of those limitations ought to make us somewhat humble about our research, since we know that we cannot make causal statements about the behavior of people with absolute certainty.

At this point the reader may well ask, "Since there are such limitations, why bother with this entire enterprise?" The answer is simple; we don't have many other options. Just as sociology provides a one-sided view of a particular phenomenon, and psychology (or anthropology, economics, etc.) provides another one-sided view of the same phenomenon, scientific research as a whole also presents a restricted viewpoint. However, it has proven to be a most useful viewpoint and has enabled us to gather a great deal of knowledge from a particular vista. We should not discard this approach merely because it has some inherent limitations.

## Attributes of Science

In addition to a set of assumptions, the social science researcher has a constellation of attributes that are essential to his role. These attributes include attitudes that he adopts. The most common of these are: skepticism, parsimony, ethical neutrality, the limited nature of scientific truth, and objectivity. We will consider each in turn. It should be observed that some of these attributes have come under considerable attack in the last few years and are being challenged by many scientists as well as nonscientists. As was the case with the scientific assumptions, some of the attributes provide tension points for the Christian involved in social research.

### Need for Healthy Skepticism

The first of the attributes is skepticism. The researcher should be skeptical, not just because he does not want to believe, but because it is the nature of science to "know," to question, and to require evidence. Skepticism—the questioning spirit—is especially appropriate in those areas for which there is little or no evidence. Thus, sociologists frequently are skeptical of "common sense" notions within the culture and have often challenged such assumptions. For example, social scientists have challenged and disproved the old commonsense notion that intelligence and race are related. Unfortunately, this notion continues to persist, even among some in the scientific community.

We tend to observe that sociologists are sometimes intensely skeptical of the Christian faith. This is largely because they claim that they cannot accept anything purely on "faith," but instead must have "hard" empirical evidence in order to believe in the existence of a phenomenon. Further, belief in the nonmaterial has been claimed to be nonrational from the standpoint of the scientific enterprise. This is unfortunate, particularly in view of our prior discussion, since science is grounded upon a series of unprovable faith assumptions. Further, for those who have taken the time to examine it carefully, Christianity is an exceedingly "rational" faith system which has stood the test of a very long period of critical scholarship.

We suspect that much of this type of skepticism is in part culturally determined. That is, at this time it is acceptable for some scientists to be skeptical of Christianity per se, while at the same time not necessarily skeptical of the spiritual realm in general. As was previously observed, some of these people are beginning to embrace other faith systems which Christians consider to be occult and demonic.

### Be Parsimonious, but Thorough

The second of the scientific attributes is parsimony. This has to do with the idea that a scientific explanation should be as simple as possible. It has its genesis in what has become known in philosophy as "Occam's Razor" (William of Occam claimed that "entities ought not be multiplied beyond necessity"). Therefore, if there are two explanations for a phenomenon, one will be rejected since only one, usually the simpler one, is sufficient for explaining the phenomenon.

Two aspects of tension for the Christian sociologist appear here. First, because of the demands of the scientific orientation and because of the implicit bias against Christianity previously alluded to, a materialistic, naturalistic explanation will always be accepted in lieu of an explanation based upon Christian supernaturalism. Second, this attribute tends to encourage the element of "reductionism" in sociology. This means that it appears simpler to explain a social phenomenon by focusing upon the individual rather than upon the group. The debate over the unit of analysis was clearly set forth by Durkheim many years ago when he argued for the primacy of the group as the sociological unit of analysis. Despite Durkheim's eloquent defense of this position, this still remains a strong point of contention in sociology. There is, incidentally, an analogous issue in American Christianity which tends to focus on individual sin and sanctification and seldom, if ever, on the structural and corporate elements of sin and sanctification (see Anthony Campolo's article "Politics and Principalities and Powers").

### Ethical Neutrality?

The third attribute to be discussed is ethical neutrality. This is a matter of heated controversy in contemporary sociology. Ethical neutrality makes the claim that the scientist *qua* scientist does not take a stand on matters of ethical, moral, political or religious preference in regard to his scientific research.

In sociology this area is closely related to the attribute and problem of objectivity, and has led to the development of supposedly "value free" social research. There are two basic elements to this. The first is concerned with the issue of whether or not a social researcher can prevent his own biases from influencing the outcomes and conclusions of his research. The second area has to do with whether or not a sociologist should make value judgments in regard to the propriety of performing certain types of research. That is, can the sociologist actually indulge in "pure science" and perform any type of social research; even if he knows that the research may be untimely or detrimental to the commonweal? Can or should one take the attitude, "I am acting as a scientist and I do not make judgments as to what will be done with my work: that is a matter for policymakers to decide"? This has been criticized by Gouldner (1964), who has called the notion of a value-free sociology "a myth." It may also be a tense area for Christian sociologists, particularly those who are aware of the limits of science. While a good sociologist must be honest, attempting to be value free in research, it is difficult to understand how an evangelical Christian could ever be ethically neutral in both his selection of research projects and/or his/her response as a private citizen. As a Christian he/she must take a stand. Furthermore, since there is so much interaction between faith, morals, and the political structure, it is hard to conceive of a Christian being ethically neutral.

### Research Findings Are Tentative-Limited

The fourth scientific attribute to be considered is the limited nature of scientific truth. This has to do with the nature of scientific truth. Science is thought of as self-correcting, in that yesterday's scientific knowledge is subject to modification, and perhaps negation, by the discoveries of today. Because of this, the "truth" of science tends to be transient and never permanent or absolute truth. Indeed, if scientific truth were to be thought of as absolutistic, there would be no further need of science.

Absolute truth is the hallmark of faith, it is not a characteristic of science. Unfortunately, many scientists, Christian and non-Christian alike, tend to forget the incomplete nature of scientific knowledge and treat scientific truth as absolute truth. This is especially a problem in the social sciences, where the ground is, so to speak, littered with discarded and outmoded theories. Failure to understand the temporal nature of scientific truth may be one of the reasons why so many people are turning away in disillusionment from science.

*Objectivity a Goal*

The fifth and final scientific attribute to be discussed is that of objectivity. Essentially, objectivity implies that the conclusions of scientific research are independent of the biases of the researcher. The goal of scientific objectivity is to utilize an impersonal type of procedure which is free of both subjective elements and the personal predilections of the scientist. For many years, scientific research was assumed to be synonymous with objective research; this belief is still maintained in many scientific circles.

Today, however, most sociologists acknowledge that it is impossible to conduct research that is truly "objective." This issue is similar to the problem of ethical neutrality. However, this time the situation deals with whether or not an investigator can hold his own biases and frames of reference so completely in abeyance that the gathering of research data and the interpretive conclusions of the research will not be affected in some idiosyncratic manner.

This takes two significant forms. The first has to do with the personal biases of the researcher. For example, one wonders how objective an investigator who does an observational study on male homosexual patterns in public rest rooms can be, particularly when, a few years after publishing the study, the author "comes out of the closet" and publicly announces his homosexuality?

Second, a more subtle form of nonobjectivity takes place in our necessary reliance upon models. This is because we cannot sense reality directly, but instead sense a representation of reality by means of an interpretive model. For instance, sociologists frequently discuss socioeconomic status, and the lay public has accepted this as a real entity. However, no one has ever sensed a status system per se (i.e., we have never seen, smelled, heard, felt, or tasted a status system). We believe it is there because we have indicators which fit our model, so we accept the model as true. The fact is that a model is a convenient fiction which helps us to interpret reality. A model is useful and valid only in so far as it reflects reality. When the writer of 1 Corinthians 13:12 says, "For now we see in a mirror dimly, but then face to face. Now I know in part; then I shall understand fully, even as I have been fully understood," he was not just speaking of our spiritual knowledge. He was also referring to the problem that finite man has understanding reality, which is largely understood by the use of models.

Each culture has its own unique models. Even our world-view is a type of model. In many ways this is also a problem of the sociology of knowledge, since the perception of reality varies from culture to culture. In terms of doing social research we should begin to see that our "objectivity" is filtered through a series of models and hence objectivity may have a strong situational component to it. This may severely limit the notion of objectivity in social research, especially in a cross-cultural sense.

## Summary and Conclusions

In this section we have briefly looked at a few of the usually unstated but widely accepted assumptions and attributes of science, especially as these apply to social research. We have also attempted to indicate some of the tension points and dilemmas that the Christian involved in social research may encounter.

In this discussion, science has been presented as a system which has limited claims to the acquisition of knowledge. It should not, however, be rejected out of hand merely because it has certain inherent limitations. For even with its limitations, social research has proven to be a most useful and indispensable means of acquiring certain types of knowledge. Nonetheless, because of these limitations, the social scientist must remain humble, realizing that there are other ways of perceiving truth as "Sources of Knowledge" (chapter 2 of this book) points out. Furthermore, there are areas of human existence that are beyond the ken of the social scientist.

Finally, the Christian should not avoid learning about science and the scientific method. Christians have a special obligation to be knowledgeable of both the scientific enterprise and the products of scientific research if they are to speak intelligently on social issues which call for moral and ethical judgments. Failure to do so is nothing less than irresponsible, something a Christian should never be.

## Discussion Questions

1. In what ways is science similar to religion?
2. Why should sociology be classified as a science? What limitations does it face that the "natural scientist" does not face?
3. Would it be possible for a sociologist to develop a questionnaire which would measure the amount of Christian charity (i.e. agape love) an individual might display? If so, how? If not, why not?
4. What is the meaning of the term mechanistic?
5. Why do we believe the world is an ordered system? How and why is this belief important to social research?
6. What problem (s) does the scientific belief in naturalism create for the Christian?
7. Why is determinism important to social research? What are the limiting factors of determinism?
8. Why do scientists tend to be skeptical? How would you attempt to convince a scientist that his/her skepticism in matters of the supernatural might be inconsistant with his/her scientific beliefs?
9. Contrast scientific truth with Christian truth. Is there a problem differentiating between the two? Should there be?
10. In what ways are the attributes of ethical neutrality and objectivism similar? Why are these attributes being challenged in science? What problems does the Christian have with these attributes?

## References

Alexander, Brooks and David Fetcho
  1977 *SCP Journal.* 1 (2), (August), pp. 25-30.
Alexander, Denis
  1972 *Beyond Science.* Philadelphia: A. J. Holman Co.
Balswick, Jack and Dawn Ward
  1976 "The Nature of Man and Scientific Models of Society." *Journal of the American Scientific Affiliation,* 28 (December), pp. 181-184.
Berger, Peter L., As quoted in Cuzzort, R. P & E. W. King
  1976 *Humanity and Modern Social Thought* (2nd edition). Hinsdale, Ill.: pp. 277-293.
Calhoun, J. B.
  1962 "Population Density and Social Pathology." *Scientific America,* 206, pp. 139-148.
Campbell, Donald and Julian C. Stanley
  1966 *Experimental and Quasi-Experimental Designs for Research.* Chicago: Rand McNally and Co.
Capra, Fritjof
  1974 "Bootstrap and Buddhism." *American Journal of Physics,* 42 (January), pp. 15-19.
  1975 *The Tao of Physics.* Boulder, Colo.: Shambhala Press.

Cuzzort, R. P. and E. W. King
1976 *Humanity and Modern Social Thought* (2nd ed.). Hinsdale, Ill.: The Dryden Press.

Freedman, Jonathan L.
1975 *Crowding and Behavior*. San Francisco: W. H. Freeman.

Gouldner, Alvin W.
1964 "Anti-Minotaur: The Myth of a Value-Free Sociology, in Irving Louis Horowitz (ed.). *The New Sociology*, New York: Oxford University Press, pp. 196-217.

Guinness, Os
1973 *The Dust of Death*. Downers Grove, Ill.: InterVarsity Press.

Homans, George Caspar
1961 *Social Behavior: Its Elementary Forms*, New York: Harcourt, Brace & World, Inc.

Horowitz, Irving Louis (ed.)
1967 *The Rise and Fall of Project Camelot*. Cambridge, Mass.: The MIT Press.

Lastrucci, Carlo L.
1967 *The Scientific Approach*. Cambridge, Mass.: Schenkman Publishing Co., Inc.

Lewis, C. S.
1973 *The Screwtape Letters*. New York: Macmillan.

Lewis, George H. (ed.)
1975 *Fist-Fights in the Kitchen*. Pacific Palisades, Calif.: Goodyear Publishing Co.

McCain, Garvin and Erwin M. Segal
1973 *The Game of Science* (2nd ed.). Monterey, Calif.: Brooks/Cole Publishing Co.

Merton, Robert K.
1936 "Puritanism, Pietism and Science." *Sociological Review*, 28 (January), pp. 1-30.

Morris, Monica B.
1975 " 'Creative Sociology': Conservative or Revolutionary." *The American Sociologist*, 10 (August), pp. 168-178.

Phillips, Derek L.
1971 *Knowledge from what?* Chicago: Rand McNally.

Postle, Denis
1976 *Fabric of the Universe*. New York: Crown Publishers, Inc.

Schaeffer, Francis A.
1972 *He Is There and He Is Not Silent*. Wheaton, Ill.: Tyndale House Publishers.

Webb, Eugene J., Donald T. Campbell, Richard D. Schwartz, and Lee Sechrest.
1966 *Unobtrusive Measures: Non-Reactive Research in the Social Sciences*. Chicago: Rand McNally Co.

Whithead, Alfred N.
1960 *Science in the Modern World*. New York: Mentor Books.

# 4

# What Meaning Has a Number?

*Gordon Scott Bonham*

Numbers are commonplace in American society. One class of numbers is called "statistics." The main function of statistics is to help the observer move from a subjective view of phenomena to an objective view, and to communicate that objective view with others. For example, an observer may notice that men are generally taller than women. He would like to find out if they really are taller, and if so, by how much. Statistics gives him a guideline on how to go about making such a test, and a way of presenting his findings so that someone else can understand and use them. The term "statistics" is often used to refer to both the process of measuring and the numbers used to summarize and communicate the results.

For the Christian, or any other person who has felt overwhelmed by statistics, or who has encountered statistics used in an effort to tear down beliefs or values, a few general statements may be helpful. Statistics are tools. What the tool does depends on the purpose of the user, how appropriate the tool is for the job, how sharp the tool is, and the skill of the user. The tool itself is neutral. There is a tendency for some to use statistics to attack or tear down some point of view or hypothesis rather than to support or build up a point of view. This is because statistics are better at disproving than they are at proving. It takes only one contradictory example to disprove, while it takes the absence of any contradictory example over a multitude of tests to prove.

Gordon Scott Bonham
*Survey Statistician, National Center for Health Statistics*
*U.S. Public Health Service*

Mr. Bonham worked as an architectural designer for several years before studying for the PhD in sociology at the University of Michigan. His research and publication interests include health, population, marriage, survey methodology, and cross-survey comparison. As an active Southern Baptist, he is Outreach Director and directs a children's choir, and has served as chairman of the board of deacons.

To understand statistics, we must know why one is using them. Statistics can probably be found to support or attack any argument or belief. Statistics have often been misused by people who are not interested in objective social research, but merely interested in sounding "scientific" as they try to sell a particular idea or product. However, properly used, statistics can help us understand our society and the needs of people, as well as suggest the most efficient ways to solve problems.

There are situations in which some statistical tools are inappropriate, and there are other situations in which no statistical tool is appropriate. Statistics are better used to measure, discuss, and test phenomena in the physical and social dimensions than they are for phenomena in the spiritual dimension. For example, there is no adequate measure of faith in God, although many have implicitly or explicitly tried to derive a measure. James suggested that the only way to measure a person's faith was by what the person does: "But some one will say, 'You have faith and I have works.' Show me your faith apart from your works, and I by my works will show you my faith" (James 2:18). However, James allowed for the possibility that there could be such a thing as faith without measurable works. He also refrained from saying that good works prove a man has faith.

The sharpness of the statistical tools is not a major problem. In most cases, the currently available statistical tools are more precise than the specifications or the measurements of the social phenomena to which they are applied. Probably more work is done in the field of statistics to relate the present tools to the inadequacies of the data than is done to develop new tools. The skill of the statistics user is often a problem.

Often, statistics are used crudely or improperly because the user does not have adequate knowledge or he is careless in his work. An uninformed audience allows poor use of statistics, having little basis for judging whether the statistics are used well or poorly.

The illustrations presented in the chapter are intended to familiarize the reader with a breadth of statistical usage and to give examples for particular points. The subject matter of the illustrations and many of the background details are not discussed because they do not directly relate to the point illustrated. Most of the numbers used are from published reports of the U.S. Bureau of the Census and the National Center for Health Statistics. The illustrations do not have a specifically

Christian focus for a number of reasons. The first is that many Christian focuses are not, and perhaps should not be, subject to statistical presentation or testing. Second, there is not a wide body of statistics with a specifically Christian focus. Third, the purpose of this chapter is to help the reader have a better understanding of what should be a neutral tool, and this suggests using neutral illustrations as much as possible.

## Questions and Answers—Which Comes First

Statistics are used in two entirely different ways. The first is in hypothesis testing. The second is in summarizing or describing a set of data for easier understanding and communication. Many times the two types of statistics, testing and summarizing, are used in conjunction with each other. However, they are distinct types and confusing them is one of the common misuses of statistics.

*Hypothesis Testing*

Using statistics in testing requires that a researcher make an explicit statement of what he expects to find prior to collecting or looking at any data. The explicit statement must be one that can be disproved. The hypothesis itself will give guidance about what information should be collected, how it should be collected, and how it should be analyzed after it is collected. Decisions must be made during the total process. The nature of each decision, and whether or not it is guided by statistical principles, determines how much faith can be placed in the research conclusions.

A researcher may have generally observed that "men are taller than women." This observation is subjective, however, and the researcher would like to objectively see if it is true. With the preceding hypothesis, however, measurement must be made wherever and whenever men and women exist. In addition, any single instance of a man being shorter than a woman will disprove the hypothesis. Perhaps a better and more testable hypothesis would be, "The average height of men at State University is greater than the average height of women at State University." This hypothesis requires that information on height be collected. It specifies that persons at State University are the ones to be measured. It also specifies that height will be averaged for each sex. Finally, it specifies that the hypothesis will be disproved and rejected if the men's average height is the same as or less than the women's average.

## Summarizing Data

Unlike testing statistics, summarizing statistics do not need any explicit hypothesis. The statistic that young adults were sick in bed an average of 4.1 days a year tests nothing. However, this statistic may be very useful for health planning. Even the statistics showing that young adult men are sick in bed 3.1 days a year, while young adult women are sick in bed 5.1 days a year does not test a hypothesis. Many hypotheses, however, could be supported by these findings. For example, one might infer that (1) women are in poorer health than men, (2) women are more likely than men to go to bed when they are sick, or (3) childbearing among women accounts for all the difference between them and men. But none of these hypotheses can be tested because they were not specified in advance of data collection or analysis. To interpret them as such would be a misuse of statistics. They can, however, suggest a hypothesis that could then be tested with other data.

Summary statistics are presented as if there were no hypothesis to which they related. Often, however, the researcher has an implicit hypothesis or bias. The reason for undertaking the analysis was to prove a particular point or to see if a hunch was worth following. There is no such thing as complete objectivity, and most scientists and statisticians will acknowledge their bias. Any interpretation of a statistic, therefore, should consider the possible bias of the researcher. For example, a poll conducted by one political party showing their candidate leading would probably be accepted with a degree of skepticism, while a poll conducted by the opposite party but showing the same candidate leading would not. The source of funding for the research gives one hint of possible bias. Another source of bias could be uncovered by asking who will benefit from the analysis and findings.

## Population or Sample?

The concepts of population and sample are intimately related to any hypothesis or summarization. These concepts have very general meanings but they also have specific meanings in the field of statistics.

## Population

A population is a group of people or things about which some information is desired or about which some statement applies. It is the universe under consideration. In the earlier hypothesis about the height of men and women, it was important to specify whether the population of interest was all people in the world who are, have, or will live, or whether the population is limited to State University at a particular point in time. Statistics for one population do not apply to any other population. The following are some examples of populations: persons in the United States in 1975, persons who voted in the last election, the 100 largest corporations as listed in a particular source, rural counties in South Carolina, and introductory sociology students who completed a questionnaire.

*Sample*

A sample is a part of the population so selected that it represents the population. Collecting information from a sample of the population can be done in less time, with less expense, with almost as much accuracy, and with as good or better quality as it could be done from drawing on the whole population. Most of the formal field of statistics deals with the probability that the sample reflects the population, and much of the work of a sociologist is inferring from a sample to the population of interest.

For a sample to reflect the population, it must be both unbiased and of sufficient size. For a sample to be unbiased, every person in the population must have the same initial probability of falling into the sample. Selecting a sample of students studying in the library at 10:00 p.m. on a Friday night would probably not produce an unbiased estimate of the grade-point average of all students. An unbiased sample would result from ordering all students by their ID numbers, randomly selecting one of the first 100 numbers, and systematically selecting every one-hundredth number thereafter to determine who should be interviewed.

The size of the sample is also important. The grade-point or academic achievement of one person randomly selected from the freshman class is not likely to reflect the average of the total class. An average based on ten students would be more accurate, and one based upon one hundred randomly selected students would probably be even more accurate. If the grade-point averages of different majors are to be compared, however, or if some major financial allocation was to be based upon the average, 100 students might not be enough. The size of the sample is determined by how detailed an analysis is desired and how precise the figures must be. Or to turn it around, the larger the sample, the more precisely the population characteristics can be measured. In addition, the characteristics can be analyzed in greater detail.

## Estimation

Any statistic or analysis directly relates to the population if measurement was made for each member of the population. If measurement was made for only a sample of the population, however, any statistic or analysis is only an estimate of the characteristic or relationship in the population. The *standard error* of the statistic shows how close the estimate is likely to be to the population value. Alternatively, it may show how far away the population value could be just due to the chance selection of the sample.

Sampling theory says that 95 times out of 100 the sample estimate will be within two standard errors on either side of the population value. For example, a dental survey found that 18.0 percent of the sampled white youths (12-17 years old) felt that their teeth needed straightening. The standard error for this statistic is 0.47 percentage points. It is therefore fairly certain that between 17.1 and 18.9 percent of the youths in the total United States at that time felt their teeth needed straightening ($18.00 \pm 0.94$). This could also be interpreted to mean that even though the actual felt need for orthodontic work in the population was 18.9 percent (or 17.1 percent), the estimate of 18.0 percent in this sample could be expected by chance.

## Probability

Statistical theory is based upon probability or chance. When a person flips a coin, there is a 0.5 probability that a head will show on the coin. If the person flips two coins, there is a certain probability (0.25) that two heads will show, but there is a greater probability that one head and one tail will show (0.50). If the person continues to flip, it would be expected that half of the coins would have a head showing and half of the coins would have a tail showing. However, no one would get too concerned if six out of ten flipped coins had a head showing. Nor would they get too concerned if seven out of ten coins had a head showing. But if a person flipped ten coins and all had a head showing, one would probably become suspicious of either the coins, or the way the person flipped them. How far away from the expected distribution of heads could the flipper get without someone rejecting the hypothesis that the coins and the flipper were unbiased? This example shows the basic principle of probability in statistics and the basis for making statistical tests. A certain figure or relationship is observed in the sample. What is the probability that the figure or relationship would be found in the sample if the true population figure was different, or if the relationship did not exist in the population? If that probability is small, generally 0.05 or less, we can reject the idea that the figure is different from the population figure or that the relationship does not exist in the population. There is always the chance that we could be wrong in our conclusion, but it is not very likely.

### Measurement

Measurement is important in determining the meaning of a statistic. Two properties of a good measurement are *reliability* and *validity*. A measure is reliable if someone else can use it with the same or similar population and achieve the same results. A measure is valid if it is really measuring what it purports to be measuring. A yardstick marked with inches and quarter-inches would be a reliable and valid way of measuring the height of people. Inches are standards that others could use, and two researchers measuring the same person would probably arrive at the same height within a quarter inch or so. However, the quarter-inch units of the yardstick would not be very reliable in measuring the heights of seeds. Likewise, feet and inches would not be a valid measure of "bigness" in a person since "bigness" also includes the concepts of mass and shape as well as height.

### Methods of Analysis

The methods of analyzing and summarizing data vary greatly. They are dependent on the purpose of the analysis, the type of measurement used, and the degree to which the data meet the required assumptions. Any of the methods can be used for either hypothesis testing or summarizing data. They can be used either for a whole population or for a sample. If a sample was used, however, greater concern must be placed on tests of statistical significance—tests to determine if a relationship observed in the sample could have occurred by chance, even if there were no actual relationship in the population.

### Numbers and Percentages

A statistical fact has very little sociological meaning by itself. However, when two statistical facts are compared, sociological analysis can begin. For example, a figure of 448,000 illegitimate births in 1975 does not have too much social meaning. However, comparing this number with 399,000 illegitimate births in 1970 shows that there has been an increase in illegitimate births during the five-year period. The figures together have social meaning and have interested legislators, religious groups, and family planning agencies.

One of the most common types of comparisons is the percentage. The percentage tells what part of a particular group or population possesses a characteristic. Mathematically, a percent = 100 (subgroup ÷ group). The subgroup must always be part of the group. This requirement is sometimes overlooked, with a prime example being the report that 50 percent of marriages end in divorce. This figure was derived from reports of 1,036,000 divorces compared to 2,153,000 marriages in 1975. However, the divorces in 1975 are not a subgroup of the marriages in 1975 (except for a few cases). Those couples divorcing in 1975 were married 1, 5, 10, 20, or even more years earlier. A proper use of percentages would be to say that a certain percent of the couples married in a particular year were divorced some number of years later. Demographers have made projections that 34-38 percent of the people born in the late forties (married about the late sixties) will have their marriages ended by divorce, if the present rates of divorce continue.

Another use of percents is the percentage increase or decrease in a figure over a period of time. The cost of a college education increased 70 percent between 1970 and 1976. Another way this could be stated is that the cost of college in 1976 was 170 percent of the cost in 1970. This type of increase says nothing about the actual amount of increase. A state supported school that cost $1,500 to attend in 1970 cost only $1,050 more to attend six years later, while a private school that cost $3,000 to attend in 1970 cost $2,100 more to attend six years later. The percentage increase says one thing, the absolute increase says another.

*Rates*

Rates can be used the same as percentages but to a different base (e.g., 10,000 rather than 100). They can also refer to a number of events divided by the population at risk of those events. A common rate of the later type is the crude birthrate. The crude birthrate is the number of births in a year per 1,000 persons living during that year. This rate is considered "crude" in that while it is a rate (persons living in a year are at risk of having a baby), it is only a select part of that population that is at actual risk—the female population approximately 15-44 years old. A more refined rate is the fertility rate which is the number of babies born in a year per 1,000 females 15-44 years old. As a subject is studied in greater depth, further refinements in a rate are often made.

### Ratios

Ratios are comparisons when one group is not a subgroup of another, or when a group is not subject to the risk of a particular event. A sex ratio of 95 indicates that there are 95 males in the population per 100 females. The sex ratio at birth in the United States is 105. It decreases to 100 at about age 23 and to 69 at ages 65 or older. This ratio can be used as an indicator of the higher mortality levels among males, and suggests differential probabilities of a man and a woman marrying (or remarrying) at various ages.

### Standardization

Standardization is used many times when comparison is made of two groups or populations which differ with respect to an important characteristic, but one which is not central to the analysis. For instance, 23 percent of white occupied apartments in 1960 were of poor quality, compared with 50 percent of black occupied apartments. Is this difference of 27 percent due to racial discrimination in housing? White families in general can pay more for rent and thus obtain better housing than can black families. Standardizing for the amount spent for rent, a variable not directly under investigation, accounts for 7 percent of the difference. The resulting 20 percent difference, after amounts paid for rent have been controlled, more closely approximates a measure of racial discrimination in housing.

### T-test

A t-test is one of the more common tests of statistical significance. It compares a sample value to a hypothesized population value or to another sample value. Mathematically, it is the difference between the two values divided by the standard error of the difference. The magnitude of the t-test statistic required for statistical significance varies with the number of observations in the sample. For a sample of 100 or more, a value of 2 is used as a rough rule of thumb for significance. This means if the difference is twice the standard error or more, the two values are statistically different.

In the dental survey, 18.0 percent of the white youths and 20.9 percent of the black youths felt they needed their teeth straightened. The standard errors of these figures are 0.47 and 1.44 percent respectively. The standard error of the difference is 1.5 percent, a weighted average of the two individual standard errors (standard error difference = $0.47^2 + 1.44^2 = 1.5$). The t-statistic is 1.9 {(20.9 - 1.80)/1.5} which is less than the 2.0 rule of thumb required. Therefore it must be concluded that the white and black percentages are not statistically different.

### The contingency table

One of the most common forms of data presentation and analysis is the two-way contingency table. In it there are two variables under consideration. In general there is an explicit or implicit hypothesis that one variable, the independent variable, has an effect on the other variable, the dependent variable. Percentages are often used, totaling to 100 percent for each category of the independent variable. In the example of Table 1, race is the independent variable that is considered to have an effect on the wantedness status of a pregnancy. When the columns sum to 100 percent (actual sums may be slightly different due to individual rounding of figures), comparisons are made across columns, or on the rows. Table 1 shows that a greater percentage of white babies (83.2) than black babies (58.9) were wanted by their mother just prior to being conceived. Conversely, a smaller percentage of white than black babies were unwanted by their mothers just prior to conception.

TABLE 1.  Percent of live births to mothers 15-44 years old in 1973 by whether or not the woman wanted the baby prior to conception, by race: United States.

| Baby wanted prior to conception | Race | |
|---|---|---|
| | White | Black |
| All conceptions | 100.0 | 100.0 |
| Wanted | 83.2 | 58.9 |
| Unwanted | 10.5 | 27.9 |
| Not determined | 6.2 | 13.2 |

More complex tables involve three or more variables. Tables may also contain frequencies, means, rates, etc., as well as percentages. In addition, tables may be used for summarizing data without any assumed causal relationship.

If a total population is represented in a contingency table, interpretation can be made directly. However, if a sample was used, it is important to test whether the associations between the dependent and independent variables could have occurred by chance. T-tests could be used to compare any two numbers, but there are measures of association for the statistical analysis of the total table. The most common of these is chi-square ($X^2$), but there are many others which are used. The purpose of any test is to determine whether or not the relationships between the variables in the table could have been due to chance even if there were no relationship in the population.

### Graphs

A graph is a visual presentation of data designed to highlight one or two major points. A bar graph, illustrated in Figure A, is a common type. The vertical scale shows the percentage of teenage population who are regular smokers. The various bars indicate the year of the data, and the age and sex of the population. The graph shows that smoking increases with age for both sexes and for each year of measurement. Smoking has increased over time for all age-groups of girls, but has been the same or declined for boys since 1970. By 1974, girls under 17 were more likely to be regular smokers than boys under 17, and the sex difference for 17-18 year olds had greatly narrowed since 1970.

### Life table

A life table is used to determine the average life expectancy of a person in the United States—71.9 years in 1974. This is a hypothetical figure which states that babies born in 1974 would live an average of about 72 years, if there were no changes during the next century in the proportion of persons dying at each single year of age. A life table takes the risks of different aged persons at one point in time and applies these risks to a hypothetical group as it ages over time. Although developed to analyze mortality, the principles of life table analysis can be applied to many different subjects. The estimated proportion of marriages that would end in divorce given in an earlier example used a life table approach. Marriages ending in divorce after x number of years of marriage was analogous to persons dying according to the mortality life table. The procedure could have yielded the average length—life expectancy—of a marriage if that figure was desired (with the proportion of marriages ending in widowhood and widowerhood taken into consideration).

FIGURE A. Teenagers Who Are Regular Smokers: 1968-1974

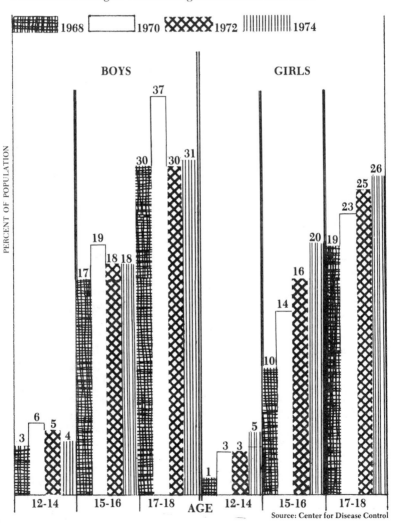

Source: Center for Disease Control

*Regression and Analysis of Variance*

Regression and analysis of variance are more complex statistical tools. Like any other statistical procedure, they make certain assumptions that must be acceptable for them to have meaning. In general, these procedures are used to answer one or both of the following questions. One, if any individual's rating on one variable is known, how well can that person's rating on a second variable be predicted? Two, how much of a change in the second variable is affected by a change in the first variable? For example, a person considering further education might want to know, "Is education really related to the salary a person makes?" And if it is, "How much higher salary can be expected with each additional year of school completed?" The earnings (EARN) of white males in 1974 were found to be significantly related to their education (EDUC), the prestige of their occupation (OCC), the number of hours worked (TIME), their years of experience (EXP), a decay in the value of their experience (DECAY), and a regional value if they lived in the South (SOUTH) (Farley, 1977). The regression equation was: EARN = 587 EDUC + 95 OCC + 1.76 TIME + 703 EXP - 13 DECAY - 862 SOUTH - 9,535. This equation indicates that each additional year of education increased the earnings of a white male by $587 per year. This amount is independent of the other variables included in the equation. Because education is related to occupation and years of experience, the total effect of education would usually be greater than $587 per year.

## Summary

A statistic is a number used to represent and summarize many events or objects. Statistics are also used to support or disprove a hypothesized relationship. In both cases, they may be used appropriately or inappropriately. The field of statistics gives guidance on how to use numbers and what they can and cannot represent. This chapter gives the student some insight into statistics and their use so that the student may interpret numbers in a more intelligent way. A person should be critical of any statistic or statement derived from a statistic. Below are some suggested questions to ask:

a. Was a hypothesis being tested or was data being summarized?

b. What is the population or group of reference?

c. Was the total population measured or was it sampled? If sampled, how was the sample selected?

d. How were the characteristics or concepts measured? Are they reliable and valid?

e. Was the form of analysis appropriate for the conclusions and the data?

f. Do the data support the conclusions, and how much confidence can be placed in the conclusions?

This chapter will not make the reader a skilled user of statistics, but it should help the reader better understand the tool. Jesus admonished his disciples, "Behold, I send you out as sheep in the midst of wolves: so be wise as serpents and innocent as doves" (Matthew 10:16). It is wise to have some knowledge of statistics. Statistics can be used by the Christian to help understand social relationships and to suggest ways for improving them. Statistical knowledge can also be used by a Christian to help counter destructive or improper use of the tools.

TABLE 2. Number of scientists by type of science and type of employer: U.S. 1974

| Employer in 1974 | Life scientists | Physical scientists | Environmental Scientists | Psychologists | Social Scientists |
|---|---|---|---|---|---|
| Educational institution | 29,651 | 26,380 | 5,832 | 17,010 | 20,677 |
| Federal government | 13,300 | 11,675 | 4,940 | 1,622 | 5,130 |
| Other government | 7,766 | 6,334 | 3,125 | 5,081 | 6,134 |
| Nonprofit organization | 2,799 | 4,989 | 502 | 3,704 | 3,101 |
| Industry or business | 15,415 | 61,187 | 11,603 | 3,500 | 7,272 |
| Self-employed | 379 | 618 | 1,839 | 1,722 | 740 |
| Military, not reported | 667 | 886 | 87 | 189 | 589 |
| Total employed | 69,979 | 112,069 | 27,929 | 32,827 | 43,643 |

## Discussion Questions

1. Telephone directories have been used from time to time to determine a sample, with every nth person being called or visited. What population would be represented by this type of sample? Would this be a biased sample of all persons living in a specified area, and if so, why?

2. How committed a person is and the nature of his/her Christian beliefs is related to many sociological phenomena. How would you measure the Christian religion and Christian commitment in order to have a reliable and valid measure?

3. Table 2 is a summary presentation of data. What hypotheses could be generated from it?

4. A favorite speculation is about the ability of the American family to survive as an institution. Statistics show the following:

    a. There are half as many divorces in a year as marriages.

    b. About 5 percent of persons above 40 have never married, and this percentage decreased between 1960 and 1975.

    c. In 1975, ⅔ of the women and ¾ of the men 35-54 were currently married, married once, and this figure is unchanged since 1960.

How should these different sets of data (all from agencies of the federal government) be explained, and do they support or disprove the hypothesis of a decline in the American family?

5. Data are available that show an increase over time in the number of illegitimate births. During the same time there has been a decrease in the number of all births, but an increase in the number of young women in the prime childbearing ages. With later marriages and more divorces, the number of unmarried young women has increased even faster than the numbers of all young women. What would be an appropriate rate or ratio to use in order to answer a question about whether illegitimacy is becoming a greater problem than it was in the past?

6. Why is it important to know who is funding research of a specific problem? E.g., cancer among workers in an asbestos plant.

7. Can one's values influence the way statistics are presented? Illustrate.

8. Why is it necessary to replicate research?

9. Can statistics be used to attack or support the Christian faith? How? Why or why not?

10. Why can't a Christian make ethical decisions on the basis of statistical finding?

### Reference

Farley, Reynolds
    1977 "Trends in Racial Inequalities: Have the Gains of the 1960's Disappeared in the 1970's?" *American Sociological Review*, 42 (April), pp. 189-208.

# 5

# The Relation of Social Mobility to Concern for the Poor: A Clergy Study

*John M. Mecartney*

A picture hanging on my office wall is Hoffman's "Jesus and the Rich Young Ruler." It is so realistic that one can almost hear Jesus saying to the richly dressed leader, "Sell all you have and give to the poor." Hoffman portrays the poor in the courtyard outside. Their rags are in sharp contrast to the rich man's garments. The artist reaches greater heights, however, when he shows the look of indecision on the face of the ruler. The ruler was involved in a very difficult decision. He was considering the meaning of downward financial mobility. The biblical story says that he rejected it. The man of wealth went away sorrowful because he had great possessions. The love of material wealth had kept him from following Jesus' way of life. In his case downward social mobility would have led to upward spiritual mobility.

Although there is no exact parallel between present-day ministers and the rich young ruler, the question can be raised as to the relation between the social mobility of clergy and an important indicator of the Christian spirit, concern for the poor. Are clergy who come to have less and less income likely to be more compassionate toward the less fortunate than their upwardly mobile colleagues? Or are the ministers who have above average increases in income most likely to be advocates for the poor? The findings of our study among Methodist clergy in

**John M. Mecartney**
*Associate Professor of Sociology*
*Mercy College of Detroit*

Mr. Mecartney has long been an activist in social concerns, including peace and civil rights organizations. At present he is a leader in the Democratic Socialist Organizing Committee. An ordained United Methodist, he served in churches for thirteen years before entering academia. In 1968 he received the PhD in sociology from Northwestern University and taught at Bluffton and Albion Colleges before coming to Mercy College.

Michigan shows the latter to be true. Ministers with the higher social mobility (income) tend to be the ones with the most concern for the poor.

The study of this interesting relationship was suggested to this writer by two professors at Garrett Theological Seminary, Dr. Murray Leiffer and Dr. Rockwell Smith. They suggested the idea of clergy mobility in relation to the question of poverty. The possibilities were seen, and the germ for a PhD dissertation was born. This chapter is dedicated to them.

### Usefulness

Many of the new sociologists who ask Lynd's question, "Knowledge for what?" abhor esoteric research on such subjects of irrelevancy as "The Wart on the Toe of King George I of England." Would our topic outlined above have any value for people?

In the first place there is always value in adding to knowledge even when its relevancy to life is not immediately understood. King George's wart—if he had one—might have had an influence on history. Knowledge that appears irrelevant today may be of great value to society tomorrow.

Second, there may be some interesting social applications if there is a relationship between mobility and outreach toward the poor. Does the continual and substantial raising of a minister's salary "spoil" him or her in Christian social witness? In some Roman Catholic orders the vow of poverty is taken. Does this state, in contrast to a person's previous financial condition, make him or her more helpful to the poor?

Third, although sociologists have long been interested in mobility, there has been a dearth of research about the concomitants of mobility (Mack *et al.*, 1957:2; Lipset and Bendix, 1959:73). Specifically a review of the literature on mobility has revealed no studies on clergy mobility and concern for the poor. Therefore, the subject might make a contribution to sociological knowledge.

Fourth, concern for the poor is one of the national objectives of not only the major church denominations—and some of the minor ones—but also of ecumenical agencies such as the National and World Council of Churches, and the National Association of Evangelicals. National leaders of our country have spoken about the "war on poverty" ever since President Kennedy was inspired by socialist Michael Harrington's book, *The Other America* (1963). A study of mobility and concern for the poor might be of some assistance in efforts to eliminate poverty, especially as this relationship applies to the professional group vitally concerned with values, the clergy.

## Concepts

*Upward Mobility*

Mobility has several meanings. The most common usage refers to movement from one geographical location or position to another. We are concerned here, however, with vertical, not horizontal, mobility. Sociologists have defined vertical or social mobility as "the process by which individuals move from one position to another in society—positions which by general consent have been given specific hierarchical values" (Lipset and Bendix, 1959:1-2). There are two types of social mobility. One involves the rise or fall in a person's status as compared with one's parent of the same sex when compared with a similar period in life. "The movement of people along a ranked dimension . . . may reflect changes in income or wealth from one year to the next or from one generation to the next" (Kriesberg, 1979: 43, 44). This is commonly called intergenerational mobility. The other type is intragenerational or career mobility. It has reference to changes in one's job status during a stated period of years.

Our study at first involved both types of social mobility. The intergenerational aspect, however, provided us with few differences between clergy since almost no clergy were downwardly mobile when compared with their father's occupation.

Concentration, therefore, was on career mobility. We limited our study to a specific period of years, 1957-1966. We measured mobility in terms of financial support for the clergy. This support included parsonage, utilities, travel, etc. While there are other ways of operationalizing career mobility, Allen (1955), in a study of the Methodist ministry, indicated that salary was the best indicator of ministerial status.

Since we needed at least three categories of mobility—as will soon be explained—the following procedure was used. Downward mobility was considered anything below the average (mean) raise for clergy in the 1957-1966 period. We needed to classify the upwardly mobile into sharply upwardly mobile and moderately upwardly mobile. While we could have made a break in the middle, we felt that sharp upward mobility should be a little higher. Therefore we considered those higher than one standard deviation above the mean to be sharply upwardly mobile. Those between the mean and one standard deviation above the mean would be designated as moderately upwardly mobile.

*Concern for "The Poor"*

Poverty can be defined in many ways. Official government financial categories in 1967 defined an urban family of four in a state of poverty if they had an income of less than $4,000 annually. In 1979 it was $6,700 (Parker, 1979:14).

Anthropologist Oscar Lewis has presented a definition of the "culture of poverty" associated with poverty. In our study, however, we decided not to give a definition of poverty to those clergy filling out the questionnaires. We would allow it to be self-defining. We felt that there would be a somewhat similar definition of poverty in the minds of most Methodist clergy in Michigan. On the other hand, if we had limited the definition of poverty to some specific category, such as income, the definition would have been too specific since many clergy do not know the exact incomes of people that they might consider in poverty.

Our study specifically involved "concern for the poor." It could also have made this term self-defining. The clergy could have been asked to what degree they were concerned with the poor. One can easily see, however, that subjective bias would enter in here. Therefore, certain objective questions were asked the clergy which we felt would test their concern for the poor.

To select the best questions we started with about fifty suggested by various people knowledgeable in the areas of poverty. Then using the Edwards' (1957) method of question selection two pretests were done, one with Methodist clergy in Wisconsin, and another with Methodist clergy in northern Indiana. This was done to eliminate all but the most useful questions. The final mixture included questions about both attitudes and behavior. Attitudes expressing concern for the poor were measured by agreement with the first two of these questions and disagreement with the third:

(1) Methodist ministers and laity should be trained for various roles in the war on poverty at the community level.
(2) The organizing of agricultural workers in the Mississippi delta and California is a proclamation of the church's concern for the downtrodden.
(3) It may sound hardhearted but the world would be a better

place if less help were given to the poor (who have shown themselves inferior), thus limiting their propagation.

Behavior was measured by asking how often the clergy mentioned the subjects of world poverty, national poverty, or local poverty in their sermons. (As might be expected there was more talk about poverty the farther it was from home. The poor at home tend to be "invisible" as Harrington (1963) has indicated.) Measured, too, were churchwide appeals involving the poor during the 1957-1966 period, as well as offerings taken for the poor. The degree of concern was also checked by the promotion given these offerings. Specific questions were also asked: "What does your church do directly in a material way for the poor in your community?" and "What projects do you support in your community which aid the poor?"

While there are ambiguities in any questionnaire, a traditional test of questionnaires, the Guttman Scalogram Analysis, indicated at least fair scalability on these questions which came through careful pretesting.

### Prejudice Studies and the Poor
Before formulating what is to be tested in a scientific study it is wise to review relevant literature on previous or similar studies. We have indicated earlier that there are no known studies on our specific subject. Prejudice, however, is akin to lack of concern for the poor. Dislike of racial and ethnic minorities would appear to be highly correlated with dislike of the poor.

Bettelheim and Janowitz in 1945 studied prejudice and mobility among World War II veterans. In 1964 they republished their findings with a survey of other literature on mobility and prejudice. These scholars claimed that the other studies generally supported their thesis that downward mobility was associated with more prejudice than upward mobility.° An author of one of the studies dissented about the interpretation of his study (Seeman 1966). He held that mobility aspira-

---

°These other studies of intergenerational mobility were Curtis, 1958; Greenblum and Pearlin, 1953; Silberstein and Seeman, 1959; Lenski, 1963; Pettigrew, 1959; and Tumin, 1958. The only career mobility study reviewed was material obtained by dissertation research by Leggett in 1962 which did not appear in his dissertation nor in his book in 1968.

tion rather than mobility itself was the significant factor in regard to prejudice. In other words, what was important to Seeman was whether people wanted to be upwardly mobile, not whether they were. Seeman held to his thesis though he did not find it to be true in Sweden—a culture different from that in the United States. To explore Seeman's thesis our study at first included aspiration for mobility as well as mobility. However, despite careful pretesting, the validity of the questions used did not pass the Guttman Scalogram Analysis test. There appeared to be other factors than mobility aspiration that were confusing the results. Therefore, we dropped mobility aspiration.

Despite certain defects in the Bettelheim and Janowitz study their work was the best done to date. (Tuch and Smith have now presented data generally supporting Bettelhcim and Janowitz's conclusions about upward mobility being associated with less prejudice than downward mobility. Tuch and Smith's study was intergenerational, however.) It therefore provided us with hypotheses which could be tested in our survey of Methodist ministers in Michigan when adapted to concern for the poor from prejudice. These researchers not only claimed that downward mobility led to more prejudice than upward mobility, but they also held that sharp upward mobility led to more prejudice than moderate upward mobility. The prejudice associated with sharp upward mobility, however, was less than that linked with downward mobility.

### Review of Theory

Before turning to the methods of our research it would be wise to examine various theories about the relation of social mobility to behavior. Ellis and Lane (1967) outlined three basic theories concerning social mobility and behavior. (1) Mobility may be due to certain conditions in a person's life. Mental strain, for example, might bring about mobility. (2) When a person senses that he or she is going to be upwardly or downwardly mobile, that person prepares himself or herself for the new status with only a little frustration. The new behavior is a compromise between that associated with the old status and that linked with the new status. These two theories have only limited support among sociologists. (3) Seminal sociologists such as Durkheim (1951) and Sorokin (1959) have held that mobility disrupts the lives of the mobile whether that mobility is upward or downward. Curtis (1958) held this effect from both upward and downward mobility is limited to close personal (or primary) relationships. In secondary relationships the disruption, which is a result of mobility, is limited to downward mobility. Mobility upward tends to give people a sense of well-being. The secondary relationship theory appears to apply more specifically to both prejudice and concern for the poor.

We therefore used this directional theory as revised by Curtis to apply to secondary relationships. However, we went farther and made another revision in relation to sharp upward mobility. We reasoned with Bettelheim and Janowitz that moderate upward mobility establishes a frame of mind which reflects satisfaction, but sharp upward mobility may be frightening and shaking. Can a person quickly go from a small church with low salary to a large church with high salary and take it in stride? A slow rise is the expected norm. But ministers who are rapidly promoted or experience little upward mobility experience frustration. This is especially true of those who are downwardly mobile. They usually experience feelings of frustration, depression, and alienation. Of course, these social-psychological theories could be upset by how seriously the clergy are committed to their Christian ethics. Christians do not necessarily believe that mobility is bad. As we said earlier, in the case of the rich young ruler, Jesus told him that downward mobility was necessary for his spiritual growth. In this study, however, we shall test the sociological factors, not the Christian ethical influence.

## Methods

After determining the subject and focus of a sociological study one should select a population on which to test hypotheses. With unlimited finances a national sample of all clergy would have been ideal. But no funding was available. Therefore, we confined ourselves to the clergy at hand in our denomination. Since we were then teaching at Albion College in Michigan, we studied Methodist ministers who were in the state for approximately ten years, 1957-1966. We included only full members of the two Michigan conferences with regular appointment.

One might reason that Michigan could be considered a sample of the Midwest or even the whole country, and either of Methodist clergy or of all clergy. However, because the sample was not random, it would be more accurate to limit the conclusions to the Methodist clergy in Michigan being studied. Also since these clergy were studied as a whole population, and not sampled, there would be no sampling error. All the differences would be significant, though there would be large and small differences as measured by percentages.

Since we were studying a whole population of Methodist clergy it was important to have a high return. Various pessimists predicted that the study would not find the cooperation of over half of the clergy. Special attention was therefore given to standard methods of obtaining returns for questionnaires.° A letter from Bishop Dwight Loder of the Michigan area (now in west Ohio) helped to legitimate the project. Then the questionnaire was sent. For those who did not return it, another questionnaire was sent. (We included with the questionnaire a letter from Dr. Charles Swan, a fellow sociologist/minister who was well known in Michigan. With only a couple of reminders, and with a number of other techniques still unused, an amazing 95 percent of usable questionnaires were returned. From these 224 statements of facts and feelings something definitely could be said about Methodist clergy in Michigan.

To increase the validity of the answers, all kinds of checks were made whenever possible. Conference records were consulted, indicating that sometimes clergy statements of their past income were in error by thousands of dollars. Validity was increased by promising anonymity. No names were on the questionnaires. Only a small number was placed on the top right of the sheet for purposes of inquiring about those who had not replied. No one knew the identity of the respondents except the researcher who was acquainted with very few Methodist ministers in Michigan.

Using the Bettelheim and Janowitz prejudice model, a major hypothesis was constructed to be tested along with three major hypotheses. We reasoned that the moderately upwardly mobile should have the most concern for the poor. The sharply upwardly mobile should have somewhat less and the downwardly mobile should have the least.

Our major hypothesis suggested that the moderately upwardly mobile would have more concern for the poor than those in the two other categories, the downwardly mobile and the sharply upwardly mobile.

The minor hypotheses tested were simple breakdowns of the major hypotheses. Clergy with moderate upward mobility would have more concern for the poor than those with downward mobility. The ministers

---

°These methods are included in Robin (1965), Mason *et al.* (1961), and Crotty (1966).

whose income did not keep up with the average raise would tend to have a less positive outlook on the poverty stricken than those whose income rose over the years in a moderate but above average fashion.

Also we hypothesized that those with moderate upward mobility would be more inclined toward the poor than those with sharp upward mobility.

Lastly, we felt that those who were sharply upwardly mobile would have more concern for the poor than those who were downwardly mobile. While there are frustrations for those who make fast headway up the ecclesiastical ladder, there are even more frustrations, resulting in less concern for the poor, among those who are downwardly mobile.

## Results

We found all the hypotheses confirmed except one. The exception was the second minor hypothesis. We thought that clergy who were moderately upwardly mobile would have more concern for the poor than those who were sharply upwardly mobile. In our study there appeared to be slightly more concern for the poor among the sharply upwardly mobile than among the moderately upwardly mobile. The clergy in the conference who had the fastest rise financially over the ten years studied were the strongest advocates for the poor.

With this reversal in our finding we see in our major hypothesis two elements working against each other. We had lumped together sharp upward mobility with downward mobility, to compare them with moderate upward mobility. We needed a revision comparing a simple category of upward mobility, including both sharp and moderate, with downward mobility. Apparently we were making things too complicated by following all the theories of Bettelheim and Janowitz. As would be expected, the simple comparison of upward with downward mobility resulted in the greatest differences in relation to concern for the poor. The findings are summarized in Table 3.

There are interesting speculations on our results. First, however, it might be worthwhile to look at an "intervening variable," a factor which confuses or throws more light on the research. Are younger men more concerned about the poor? Are they affected more or less by mobility than older clergy?

Table 1 on page 100 gives the age distribution of our 224 clergy, as well as the numbers and percentages in the high and low scoring cat-

TABLE 1

| Age Distribution of Methodist Ministers in Michigan and Scores on Their Concern for the Poor | | | | | | |
|---|---|---|---|---|---|---|
| Ages | | 30-39 | 40-49 | 50-59 | Over 60 | Total |
| Number | | 20 | 70 | 83 | 51 | 224 |
| Percentage | | 9% | 31% | 37% | 23% | 100% |
| Scores on Concern for the Poor | High | 12 | 37 | 44 | 22 | 115 |
| | Low | 8 | 33 | 39 | 29 | 109 |
| Percentages on Concern for the Poor | High | 60% | 53% | 53% | 43% | 51% |
| | Low | 40% | 47% | 47% | 57% | 49% |

egories in relation to concern for the poor. As might be expected the younger men (from 30-39) had more concern for the poor. Both middle range groups (40-49 and 50-59) were tied in relation to their outreach toward the poverty stricken. The men over sixty definitely had the least concern for the poor, with only about two thirds as many having high scores as among the young men. We can conclude that among clergy, as well as among the population in general, the older one grows, the less concerned he becomes for the poor.

But our problem here is not to look at the simple relationship of poverty and age, but to see how age changes the relationship in our hypotheses. The process of checking to see if a third factor changes the relationship between two other factors is called "holding constant" or "controlling for." Table 2 gives the data for the relation of upward and downward mobility to concern for the poor, not only for the total clergy, but also for each age grouping. The data for all the hypotheses are not given here but are summarized in Table 3. In Table 3 the differences in amount of concern for the poor between the various types of mobility are given in percentages. In column 5 of that table we find there was a 20 percent difference between upwardly and downwardly mobile clergy in relation to their concern for the poor. Since our theory held there would be more concern for the poor among the upwardly mobile than among downwardly mobile, we call that confirmed.

TABLE 2
**Testing the Major Hypotheses**

| Michigan Methodist clergy who have experienced moderate upward mobility demonstrate more concern for the poor than those who have experienced downward or sharp upward mobility | | | | | |
|---|---|---|---|---|---|
| | | | **MOBILITY** | | |
| | | | Moderate Up | Down or Sharp Up | Total |
| **TOTAL OF ALL AGES** | CONCERN FOR THE POOR | High | 43 (61%) | 72 (47%) | 115 |
| | | Low | 27 (39%) | 82 (53%) | 109 |
| | | | 70 | 154 | 224 |
| **AGE 30-39** | CONCERN FOR THE POOR | High | 5 (62%) | 7 (58%) | 12 |
| | | Low | 3 (38%) | 5 (42%) | 8 |
| | | | 8 | 12 | 20 |
| **AGE 40-49** | CONCERN FOR THE POOR | High | 16 (62%) | 21 (48%) | 37 |
| | | Low | 10 (38%) | 23 (52%) | 33 |
| | | | 26 | 44 | 70 |
| **AGE 50-59** | CONCERN FOR THE POOR | High | 18 (64%) | 26 (47%) | 44 |
| | | Low | 10 (36%) | 29 (53%) | 39 |
| | | | 28 | 55 | 83 |
| **AGE OVER 60** | CONCERN FOR THE POOR | High | 4 (50%) | 18 (42%) | 22 |
| | | Low | 4 (50%) | 25 (58%) | 29 |
| | | | 8 | 43 | 51 |

In the summary table on page 103 we call a hypothesis partially confirmed if the percentage differences are in the right direction but under 10 percent. Between 10 percent and 19 percent we call the hypothesis confirmed. At 20 percent or over we call it strongly confirmed. If there is no difference between the high and low scoring we say the hypothesis is rejected. It is reversed if the opposite of the hypothesis is seen in the data. A reversal with under 10 percent difference we call "slightly reversed," while over 10 percent is simply "reversed." There were two rejections also in all the totals and age groupings. Most of these data refuting our hypotheses came in the area suggesting that the sharply upwardly mobile have less concern for the poor than the moderately upwardly mobile. In examining Table 3 on page 103 we note that the key summary is in the "Added Information" section. (The reader will recall that sharp upward and downward mobility were working against each other in the major hypothesis.)

Especially interesting to note is the effect of age on each hypothesis. While the total group confirms strongly the association of concern for the poor with upward mobility, this does not seem to be the case among the young ministers. The two middle age groups have a strong association between upward mobility and concern for the poor, and the over-sixty group is at the partially confirmed level.

The surveying of the various hypotheses, except the one suggesting more concern among the sharply upwardly mobile than among the moderately upwardly mobile, indicates a similar pattern to our added information category. The total groups confirm the hypotheses. The middle age groups either confirm or strongly confirm all the hypotheses. The over-sixty group partially confirms the hypotheses. And they are close to confirmation. In the younger age group we find either partial confirmation with only a little difference, or a reversal in one category. This suggests more concern for the poor among the sharply upwardly mobile than for the downwardly mobile. Let us now discuss the significance of these findings.

### Discussion

As stated above, we held that concern for the poor had an inverse relationship to prejudice. In fact, lack of concern for the poor could indicate prejudice against the poor. We therefore used Bettelheim and Janowitz's model, along with Curtis' directional theory modified to accommodate Bettelheim and Janowitz's distinction between moderate and sharp upward mobility. Our research could be considered an attempt to replicate Bettelheim and Janowitz's study. They concluded that downward mobility was associated with more prejudice than upward mobility. Our study confirmed that. But their idea that sharp upward mobility would lead to more prejudice than moderate upward mobility was not confirmed.

It may be that there is a special case to be made for sharp upward mobility among the ministers. It could be that Methodist clergy do not receive high enough income, even if they are at the top of the scale within their denomination, to have substantial upward mobility, especially when compared with other professional groups and business. The

## TABLE 3

**Summary of Findings on Hypotheses and Percentage Differences with Direction in Regard to the Relationship of Concern for the Poor and Mobility of Michigan Methodist Clergy**

| GROUP | MAJOR HYPOTHESES More concern for the poor among moderate up than down and sharp up — Difference | More concern for the poor among moderate up than down — Difference | MINOR HYPOTHESES More concern for the poor among moderate up than sharp up — Difference | More concern for the poor among sharp up than down — Difference | ADDED INFORMATION More concern for the poor among up than down — Difference |
|---|---|---|---|---|---|
| Total | Confirmed 14% | Confirmed 19% | Slightly reversed 3% | Strongly confirmed 22% | Strongly confirmed 20% |
| 30-39 Age | Partially confirmed 4% | Partially confirmed 2% | Partially confirmed 5% | Slightly reversed 3% | Rejected 0% |
| 40-49 Age | Confirmed 14% | Strongly confirmed 24% | Partially confirmed 1% | Strongly confirmed 23% | Strongly confirmed 23% |
| 50-59 Age | Confirmed 17% | Strongly confirmed 21% | Reversed 19% | Strongly confirmed 40% | Strongly confirmed 25% |
| Over 60 | Partially confirmed 8% | Partially confirmed 9% | Rejected 0% | Partially confirmed 9% | Partially confirmed 9% |

mean increase for Methodist clergy in the ten years studied was $3,152, and the highest increase above the mean was around $3,000 more. Taking account of inflation, an increase of $6,000 could hardly be considered sharp upward mobility over ten compared with business and the professions. Therefore it may be that our study is not a repudiation of Bettelheim and Janowitz's sharp upward mobility theory at all.

We have earlier stated some of the socio-psychological reasons why clergy might find their concern for the poor diminishing as they become downwardly mobile. Insecurities might tend to lead them to seek scapegoats to explain their "failure" in a profit-oriented, capitalistic society. At least our data show that those who become poorer (or do not get ahead as fast as the average) do not usually have strong sympathy for the poor. Eugene Victor Debs, the most successful socialist candidate for president (1912), was not reflecting the feelings of the downwardly mobile in his classic quote: "As long as there is a lower class I am in it."

There is an alternative possibility that the association between mobility and concern for the poor is not a casual one. Mobility may not be a cause of concern for the poor. The relationship that exists may be established by a third factor influencing both mobility and concern for the poor. The falacious belief that correlation means causation has been illustrated for many years by the correlation between the rise and fall of alcohol consumption, and the rise and fall of ministers' salaries. Raises in ministers' salaries do not cause an increase in alcohol consumption. Rather it is the economic condition of the country that results in a rise or decline in both ministers' salaries and liquor consumption. In the area of our study it may be that clergy who include the social application of the gospel in their ministry are more successful. Their salaries naturally go up as they are appointed to the larger churches. They may not overtly strive to be upwardly mobile. It may be the unanticipated reward for faithful service.

Another factor might be at work also. The official stand of the Methodist Church has always been strongly oriented toward helping the poor. This was expressed in the early days of John Wesley. His followers went out not only to evangelize, but also to organize labor and cooperatives. In addition, they engaged in political action that later led toward democratic socialism in Britain. The various social creeds of the Methodist Church since 1907 indicate concern for the poor. Many bishops and district superintendents are oriented in this direction. It is possible that ministers who care most about the poor are among those promoted to larger churches.

Let us now examine the reasons for the age differences. Why is it that the middle-aged clergy from 40 to 59 seem to be more affected by mobility in relation to their concern for the poor than the younger men and the older men?

Dr. Rockwell Smith suggested the idea that the experience of the depression might have had an effect upon some ministers' attitudes toward mobility and poverty. The men in the 40-49 and 50-59 age categories in 1966 were in school, college, or seminary during the depression years. They knew poverty at a critical time in their lives. It made a lasting impression upon them and their future wives. They may, therefore, feel much more secure at being upwardly mobile than those who were not so impressed in this poverty period of U.S. history. On the other hand, the clergy over 60 began their ministries before the depression arrived. While it certainly did make an impression upon them, they probably were at a less impressionable time of their life. The younger clergy, on the other hand, knew little about the depression from personal encounter. They may not have acquired such a great need for economic security through mobility as those strongly influenced by the depression.

There is another possible explanation for the differential response of the various age-groups. The younger clergy have more concern for the poor without consideration of mobility. (See Table 1.) Their concern may be reflected also in a rejection of the social influence of mobility as they attempt to live their Christian ethics to the fullest. It may be that the teachings of Jesus concerning material things ("Take no thought what you shall eat, drink, wear ... ") is gaining new headway among the younger clergy. Perhaps they do not seek the richer material life.

It is fitting to conclude this article, which has been primarily sociological, with reference to social ethics. In fact these areas are becoming more related in current sociological conflict theory. It may be that sociology itself may be a "liberating" subject in that students can come to see the various social forces which indirectly or directly help to mold them. When people understand the social pressures on them they are more able to accept or reject them in light of their ethical stances. It may be that sociology may help Christians to become more Christian in their behavior.

## Discussion Questions

1. Read Matthew 19:16-23 or Mark 10:17-23. What did Jesus ask the rich man to do? Why? What would this do to his social mobility? What would it do for his spiritual life?

2. What usefulness might a study of the association between mobility and concern for the poor have?

3. What are the different types of mobility? Which is the focus of this study? How were downward, upward, and sharp upward mobility measured?

4. How was concern for the poor measured?

5. What other factor similar to concern for the poor had been previously researched? How was this factor used as a model for this study?

6. What methods were used to help assure validity in this research?

7. When the data were collected, which hypotheses were supported in relation to mobility and concern for the poor among Michigan Methodist clergy? Which hypothesis appeared to have contradictions within it? Why? What new information not in an original hypothesis was suggested?

8. What was the effect of age when it was controlled for or held constant? Did the conclusion for the total population hold for each of the four age groups? Explain.

9. If two things that vary are correlated or associated, why does this not necessarily mean one causes the other?

10. How can sociology be a "liberating" subject which allows Christians to practice their ethics to a fuller degree?

## References

Allen, Philip J.
  1955 "Childhood Backgrounds of Success in a Profession." *American Sociological Review*, 20 (April), pp. 186-190.

Bettelheim, Bruna and Morris Janowitz
  1950 *The Dynamics of Prejudice*. New York: American Jewish Committee.
  1964 *Social Change and Prejudice*. New York: Free Press of Glencoe.

Crotty, William J.
  1966 "The Utilization of Mail Questionnaires and the Problems of a Representative Return Rate." Western Political Science Quarterly, 19 (March), pp. 44-53.

Curtis, Richard F.
  1958 "Consequences of Occupational Mobility in a Metropolitan

Community." Unpublished PhD dissertation. University of Michigan.

Durkheim, Emile
1951 *Suicide: A Study in Sociology.* Glencoe, Ill.: Free Press (first published in France, 1897).

Edwards, Allen L.
1957 *Techniques of Attitude Scale Construction.* New York: Appleton-Century-Crofts.

Ellis, Robert A. and Clayton W. Lane
1967 "Social Mobility and Social Isolation: A Test of Sorokin's Dissociative Hypothesis." *American Sociological Review,* 32 (April), pp. 237-252.

Greenblum, Joseph and L. I. Pearlin
1953 "Verticle Mobility and Prejudice." Reinhold Bendix and Seymour Martin Lipset (eds.), *Class, Status, and Power.* Glencoe, Ill.: Free Press, pp. 480-491.

Harrington, Michael
1963 *The Other America.* Philadelphia: Penguin.

Kriesberg, Louis
1979 *Social Inequality.* Englewood Cliffs, N.J.: Prentice-Hall.

Leggett, John Carl
1962 "Working Class Consciousness in an Industrial Community." Unpublished PhD dissertation. University of Michigan.
1968 *Class, Race, and Labor.* New York: The Oxford University Press.

Lenski, Gerhard
1963 *The Religious Factor.* New York: Doubleday.

Lewis, Oscar
1961 *Children of Sanchez.* New York: Random House.

Lipset, Seymour Martin and Reinhold Bendix
*Social Mobility in Industrial Society.* Berkeley: University of California Press.

Mack, Raymond W., *et al.*
1957 *Social Mobility: Thirty Years of Research and Theory.* Syracuse: Syracuse University Press.

Mason, Ward, *et al.*
1961 "An Experimental Study of Factors Affecting Responses to a Mail Study of Beginning Teachers." *Public Opinion Quarterly,* 25 (Summer), pp. 296-299.

Mecartney, John Millard
1968 "The Relation of the Inter-Generational and Intra-Professional Mobility of Midwest Methodist Ministers to their Concern for the Poor." Unpublished PhD dissertation. Northwestern University.

Parker, Richard
1979 "Double-Entry Bookkeeping on Poverty." *Mother Jones,* 4 (August), pp. 13, 14.

Pettigrew, Thomas F.
   1959 "Regional Differences in Anti-Negro Prejudice." *Journal of Abnormal and Social Psychology*, 59 (July), pp. 28-36.
Robin, S. S.
   1965 "Procedures for Securing Returns to Mail Questionnaires." *Sociology and Social Research*, 50 (October), pp. 23-30.
Seeman, Melvin, *et al.*
   1966 "Social Mobility and Prejudice: A Swedish Replication." *Social Problems*, 14 (Fall), pp. 188-197.
Silberstein, Fred B. and Melvin Seeman
   1959 "Social Mobility and Prejudice." *American Journal of Sociology*, 65 (November), pp. 258-264.
Sorokin, Pitirim, A.
   1959 *Social and Cultural Mobility*. New York: Free Press.
Tuch, Steven A., and David L. Smith
   1979 "*Social Mobility and Prejudice: A Reexamination.*" A paper presented at the American Sociological Association, August, 1979 in Boston.
Tumin, Melvin
   1958 *Desegregation: Resistance and Readiness*. Princeton, N.J.: Princeton University Press.

# PART II

# THE SOCIOLOGICAL PERSPECTIVE AND THE CHRISTIAN

# THE SOCIOLOGICAL PERSPECTIVE AND THE CHRISTIAN

One of the unique attributes of human beings is that we can stand back, as it were, and look at ourselves. Hopefully, when we do this, we can sometimes laugh at ourselves because of our stupidity and shortsightedness. Too often we make hasty judgments about individuals and issues, only to realize that we neglected to consider many relevant variables. In every dispute or issue, there is not only your point of view and my point of view, but also many views neither of us has considered.

A good course in sociology should enable you to gain a sociological perspective on society. That is, it should enable you to stand off from society and, using the main concepts and insights gained from your course, look at problems and issues more fully. It was after the prophet Ezekiel (3:15) went into exile with the Jews and "sat where they sat" that he began to understand their plight. The sociological perspective should enable you to do that. Therefore, the sociologist can take nothing for granted. He must ask for, and demand, hard evidence before he will accept statements. Furthermore, when he accepts findings it is only on a tentative basis. All the evidence is not in, and he must keep an open mind about theories, models, analyses, and research findings.

The sociological perspective, then, is one of a detached observer and investigator. Peter Berger likens him to a "spy" (we might add, a double or multiple agent!). He uses whatever legitimate means are at his disposal to gather data for analysis so that he might "put the puzzle together." However important the sociological perspective may be, we must keep in mind that it is *only* one.

In the first chapter of this section Russell Heddendorf sets forth ten principles that will help you gain a sociological perspective. He offers a critique of some sociological principles, as well as some beliefs erroneously held by Christians. A healthy skepticism is important. David E. Carlson raises two important questions. He first asks if sociology can be Christian. Second, he asks if biblical principles can be harmonized with those of sociology and the role of the social worker. He helps us to see that truth is all of one piece, and that it finds its unity in Christ.

Andrew M. Greeley, in a candid essay, speaks about the basic compatibility that exists between Christian and sociological principles. Nevertheless, the Christian sociologist often meets with difficulties on two fronts. On the one hand, secular colleagues are often prejudiced against Christian sociologists, and on the other hand, the church is often unwilling to accept the Christian sociologist's findings. In spite of these difficulties, there is a vital role for the Christian sociologist to play within the discipline, as well as within the church.

Finally, George A. Hillery, Jr., argues for the legitimacy of a Christian perspective in sociology. He claims there is no really value-free sociology. Christians, like other sociologists, do operate from the basis of a select set of values. These values should influence the Christian sociologist in two ways. It should influence the way he does his research, and it should influence the areas he selects to research. More important, the Christian sociologist should place more emphasis on understanding *(verstehen)* the human situation and condition, than on predicting it.

There is much food for thought in Part II. Hopefully, it will enable you to begin to develop your own sociological perspective from a Christian point of view.

# 6

# Principles of a Christian Perspective in Sociology

*Russell Heddendorf*

Observing social life is something like taking a stroll through a forest. One encounters a host of diverse forms of life, some flourishing, some dying, and others completely lifeless. Few persons accurately interpret the condition of these forms of life without training in such matters. Consequently, the neophyte may experience poisoning by eating dangerous berries or by touching the wrong plants. He may also unwittingly cut down trees which have potential for bearing fruit, or plant things where there is little prospect for growth. It is with an attitude of stewardship, therefore, that one should seek to have a correct perspective on the forest or any diverse system one can observe in the physical or social world.

This same attitude of responsible stewardship should be employed by the Christian when approaching society in all of its diverse forms. Since we cannot expect someone to call our attention to discriminatory practices, we need to train ourselves to perceive them. Nor should we rely on an outsider as honest as the Apostle Paul to point out the corruption and divisions that exist within the church (1 Corinthians 1:10-12). If we are to be responsible for the social and spiritual welfare of those about us, we need a perception which is sociologically, as well as scripturally, sound.

Most persons readily confess an uneducated eye when hiking

**Russell Heddendorf**
*Professor of Sociology*
*Geneva College*

Mr. Heddendorf serves as an elder in the Reformed Presbyterian Church, Evangelical Synod. He received his PhD from the University of Pittsburgh. His special interests are the sociology of religion and social theory. He is on the steering committee of Christian Sociologists. Mr. Heddendorf taught at the City College of New York and several other colleges before going to Geneva College.

through the woods. Here is an unfamiliar environment, encountered infrequently, and seldom requiring an accurate interpretation of its secrets. Anyone other than an experienced botanist, then, may only guess at a tree's identity or the cause of its decay. But society demands of us more than that, for it is here that we live and have our being. The fact that we have fared well in this life may suggest an understanding of social life which is both accurate and responsible. This is, at best, a deceptive notion if it ignores the possibility that we have overlooked the corruption and illusions cluttering the path about us.

It would not be an exaggeration, then, to suggest that most of us are blind to the social world or, at best, nearsighted. Society provides numerous aids to help us grope through its shadows, but seldom has it provided all the light we need for complete understanding. The point is that society has a vested interest in shrouding its activities with deception and manipulation. In fact, the businessman and politician may be as guilty as the drug pusher or car thief. This claim should come as no surprise when we remember that men prefer darkness to light (John 3:19).

## Principles of a Sociological Perspective
### Society Is Not Always as It Appears

Thus, the first principle in developing a sociologically trained perception is this; do not assume that all is as it appears to be in society. If men love darkness rather than light it should come as no surprise to learn that deception and artificiality abound in social relations. Peter Berger, one sociologist who has provided much insight on this question, suggests that we should not take the world for granted. It is not always an "okay world." It must often be approached with caution. The Christian should have little trouble accepting this view if he recognizes the importance of the scriptural admonition to avoid belonging to the world (John 17:14).

Are we to assume, for example, that every man and woman registering together at a motel are married to each other (even if each wears a wedding band), or that a "friend" always has our best interests at heart? Our naivete may allow us to make such assumptions until a personal experience cautions us otherwise. We may also convince ourselves that a church congregation is alive and growing only to learn of dissatisfaction and a resultant schism. Too often the reality of the social world is experienced in these glaring ways.

*Society Is More Complex Than It Appears*

This problem of defining social reality suggests the importance of a second principle in the development of a sociological perception; society is more complex than it appears to be. Much of society is hidden from view simply because there is little effort to understand it. And we avoid such effort because we fear what might be found. Not understanding the close ties between some aspects of government and business and the underworld, the average citizen prefers to remain ignorant of such facts. There is a security in believing that governmental agencies are really as competent and honest as they are supposed to be.

Another false assumption often held is that good and evil are separate and readily identifiable as such. When separated into neat categories the social world is approached with confidence, even though it is misplaced. It is this sense of false security in the world as we believe it to exist which prevents an adventure into the real world. Few persons believed the events surrounding Watergate could have taken place, and even fewer could conceive of their full complexity. The challenge is to understand the facts as they exist and to accept them accordingly. But even more immediate is the challenge to perceive the little Watergates in the lives of all of us. The fact that we avoid such perceptions suggests that we are fearful of implicating ourselves.

Too many suburban areas, for example, that are fully aware of a drug abuse problem in their local high schools, refuse to admit that the problem exists. Corporately, there is a perceived unwillingness to deal with the problem even though it is recognized. The easiest solution is to deny the existence of the problem and hope that no one sees the apparent contradiction. On the individual level, the Apostle Paul could be more honest with himself as he perceived his moral problem, even though he felt incapable of coping with it (Romans 7:15-20). In both cases, the problem is one of responsibility as much as of perception.

But if Paul was incapable of handling his individual **sinfulness,** how much more helpless is modern man when faced with the moral problems of a world that staggers us with its complexity. There is no solution, of course, if we prefer to remain blind simply because of an apparent helplessness. The fallacy is assuming that we can wrestle alone against the world (Ephesians 6:10-13).

One is "copping out" if he turns from problems when responsible action is called for. Likewise, if we think a problem is unsolvable, this does not absolve us of our responsibility to try.

*Perception of Society Is Distorted When Simplified*

Indeed, misunderstanding can only lead to greater confusion. This fact reminds us of a third principle in the development of an informed sociological perception, namely: attempting to simplify our perception tends to distort it. It is one thing to ignore the problems of drug abuse in white communities but quite another to believe that all black communities have a high rate of drug abuse. Statistics on these matters would indicate that such simplistic assumptions are invalid, even if they do support our biased opinions.

Misperceptions of society, then, produce myths which can only contribute to the problem of complexity and increase the difficulty of seeing the truth in a social situation. Racial myths have developed simply because of a dichotomous view of the world which assigned "good" qualities to whites and "evil" qualities to blacks. Largely because of personal insecurity, persons prefer to think of themselves as superior to others. Instead of accepting the truth that God has created all persons equal, we distort this principle and cling to social myths.

*Society Is to Be Perceived as God Intended*

Here we find a fourth and critical principle. We are to perceive things in the social world as God intended them to be perceived. Having assigned a definition and purpose to creation, God expects man to use it as he intended. Environmental problems serve as a sharp reminder of our failure to assume our stewardship responsibilities in the physical world. But while we find the same kind of stewardship problem in the social world the issues are not as apparent, and solutions may be even more difficult to arrange.

For example, the Sabbath was set aside by God for rest from the earlier work of creation. While the truth of this fact may be readily accepted, it is not always observed in our daily lives. The complexity of modern life often involves us in work which is essential to the welfare of others. In fact, Christ himself testified to the impossibility of holding to a simplistic view of the Sabbath when faced with the responsibility of dealing with other problems. Nevertheless, he never denied the importance of the Sabbath and recognized the complexity inherent in the fulfillment of its meaning (Luke 13—14).

The problem, then, involves the proper use of God's creation, as well as the proper perception of it. The family, for instance, is not always recognized as a provision of God for the benefit of men and women, although anthropological data would support this contention. Numerous cases indicate that any society experiences problems when its family life is threatened. In other cases where a society has tried to maintain minimal family arrangements, men and women have sought for stronger family ties, especially when children are involved. But where there is not responsible use of the family as God intended, it is weakened and distorted in its social meaning. The simple rule which applies to all social phenomena is that our use of something is largely determined by our perception of it.

This rule can be illustrated with the example of church worship. Sociological studies clearly show that people use a church service for many purposes other than that for which it is intended. While most people probably attend church because they are seeking to worship God in some way, some may see it as a time to develop business contacts. Others may use it to achieve or display social status. Still others may take the opportunity it affords to catch up on community gossip. In many churches, there may be few parishioners who perceive a church service for the intended worship of God, and even fewer may use it as such. Unless we perceive the problem and resist its implications, we may become a part of the problem itself.

### We Are in the World and Yet Not of It

In fact, a fifth principle is this: we *are* in the world even if, in another sense, Christians ought not to identify with the world. The sociologist refers to the fact that we are socially located because we have some status in society. Whether bank president or skid row derelict, we avoid living alone and find some social circle to call our own. The friends and privileges found in this small world increase our security and give us a place in the larger society. All of us live in these small worlds and gain much comfort from them simply because they meet so many of our social needs.

But recognizing this fact, we must also be aware of the influence exerted on us by the world in which we are located. These groups are often hard taskmasters which demand of us at least as much as we receive from them. No athlete stays on a team unless his effort contributes to it. Celebrities often maintain their fame only at the expense of broken families. We may step from one world to another, but we cannot move completely outside of all of them. Ultimately, the demands must be faced and decisions made if we are to remain in a close and often tense relationship within these worlds.

There are several sociological traditions which take this problem of tension with the world seriously and offer suggestions for dealing with it. For example, conflict theory claims that direct opposition to social forces is the only way to resist the control of society. Based on Marxist presuppositions, the ultimate answer is found in violence and revolution which shatters the old social world and creates a new one. Varying forms of existentialism also exist which consider the world to be meaningless and devoid of any reality. They see such a world as an illusion or a deception, not to be taken seriously. If one cannot step out of the world, at least it is possible to laugh and be scornful of it.

The Christian recognizes that he should not permit the unethical systems of this world to squeeze him into their mold. Rather, he learns from Romans 12:2 that he is to be transformed by renewing his mind, and by perceiving the world from this new perspective. He is called by God to work for social justice and to help make all things new.

Of course this view is unique to Christianity since it assumes not only that God exists, but that he has a plan and a purpose for individuals, groups, associations, and nations. Furthermore, the Christian believes he can know God's will and cooperate with him in executing it. Nevertheless, the belief that mental attitude is critical in the development of a tension with the world is shared with classical sociological theory. These thinkers, who worked at the turn of the twentieth century, stressed the importance of the unconscious in the formation of action. What they had to say is still appropriate today and echoes many Christian presuppositions.

*Attitudes Form Actions and Not Vice Versa*

From these conclusions we may draw a sixth principle: our thoughts are to influence our actions and not vice versa. Some of the most important sociological studies have emphasized this truth in matters of economics, science, and racial discrimination. Those sociologists who have supported the opposing view, namely, that our values are formed by biologically or environmentally determined actions, usually present weak arguments because they view man as little more than an animal. In the final analysis, men are accountable for their actions because of their unique and creative consciousness as spiritual beings and they are to respond to those values revealed by God.

The point, then, is that we do make decisions and these decisions are influenced by the values underlying them. The question is whether these decisions will bring us to a place of conformity or tension with the world. Unless the mental attitude necessary to resist the world is present, we need to transform our thinking. What is needed is a recognition that there is a proper action which would be approved of by God in each particular situation. Only then can the Christian act with confidence.

Too often, however, we find it easier to act in another way and then justify it as preferable. In other words, our attitude approves of one form of behavior when it should be initiating a different form. The student who wants to do well on a test may decide that he ought to relax the night before a test rather than to study because he doesn't want to be tired the next day. In his opinion, he is properly motivated and it is not merely a case of justifying laziness. Furthermore, he may believe that it is an obvious decision which allowed for no other choice.

But the point is that the student did have a choice of studying or relaxing and having chosen the latter option, he manifests some preference. Since he could have no assurance that relaxation would produce a higher grade, some additional motive must have influenced his decision. Apparently, he valued relaxing more than studying and used the belief that it would produce a better grade to justify his behavior. In addition, he assumed that there was some necessary connection between relaxing and a higher examination grade.

### Social Ends Are Not Always Determined by Social Means

The fact that his latter assumption could be false leads us to a seventh principle: choice of means does not necessarily determine accomplishment of ends. As one sociologist has stated, there are "unanticipated consequences of purposive social action." As much as some action is designed to produce a particular end, failure to achieve that end might occur simply because man does not have control of his final objectives. The sociologist, Pitirim Sorokin, put the argument in more succinct terms: "man proposes but God disposes."

Even though modern man does not like the idea, he is always dogged by the possibility of failure. The fear haunts us— the belief that a person is responsible for failure, that he may be, in some way, inferior. To counteract this possibility, modern man is on an abiding quest to find means to guarantee success never realizing that such a guarantee is not possible. The decisions we make and the means we choose cannot, in the final analysis, determine our ends.

Does this fact suggest that decisions are meaningless and without purpose? Not at all. If decisions are not made for their effectiveness they can be made for their moral implications and the values they reflect. Witness the case of contraceptive devices. Unmarried couples rely on them in cohabitation because of their apparent effectiveness. The morality question is scarcely raised. And yet, contraceptives offer no guarantee that conception will not occur.

In contradistinction to modern thought, the scriptural principle always stresses the morality of an act or thought and not its effectiveness. Jesus tells us that the effectiveness of loving a neighbor is not as important as the morality of loving an enemy (Matthew 5:43, 44). What counts is not whether we may gain an objective but whether we may be obedient.

### Values Direct Perception of the World

This point brings us to an eighth principle: our values direct our perception of the world and our place in it. Actions are triggered by the attitudes we have toward them and the values on which they are based. The sociologist defines an attitude as "a tendency to act in a certain way in a given future situation." Accordingly, with this mind-set, we approach problems fully expecting to solve them. The assumption is that our attitudes do give birth to our actions.

The fact is, however, that attitudes are not always reliable predictors of behavior. Too many sociological studies have shown that last-minute circumstances may cause persons to change their behavior. Voting studies, for instance, demonstrate the unreliability of early forecasting of election results. As a voter comes under the pressure of different opinions he may radically change his original intentions and cast a very unpredictable ballot. Indeed, he may be quite unaware of the reason for the change or that it has even taken place.

Why is the voter, or any person for that matter, so fickle? For one thing, his values are often weak when focused on distant events. As an event approaches, the problems and questions loom larger than the promises and produce an apparent threat. Values are altered as the telescoping of time increases the problems inherent in the decision-making process. Ultimately, that action is often taken which maximizes immediate reward and minimizes immediate punishment, even though the original attitude suggested an opposing pattern of action.

In the real social world, then, people are motivated in a twofold way. First, there is a perception of a future event based on ultimate or ideal values. For example, the student knows he should study all weekend for a big test on Monday. Second, there is a perception of the situation which is usually more gratifying. That is, the student may decide to take in the rich program of campus events instead and plan to do better on the next test. Decisions reflect constantly shifting values even if we are not completely aware of their meaning for us. The apostle Paul experienced the same problem when he noted that he found himself doing what he did not want to do and not doing what he knew he should do (Romans 7:15-20). In the complex world of today we can only assume that Paul would encounter even greater problems of decision-making.

*We Live in a Secularized World*

Remembering that we are attempting to outline a Christian perspective for the sociological understanding of the world, we come to a ninth principle: we are living in a secularized world. For the sociologist this fact means that the Christian influence in the Western world has been largely replaced by other forces. The implications of this major shift in history are vast. But for our purposes here, we can concentrate on the fact that there has been a drastic change in personal motivation and commitment. Instead of seeking to please God, keeping in mind the idea of a final judgment and future rewards, we prefer to gratify ourselves, thinking of present pleasure and immediate rewards.

But it is important to note that this transition in thinking has not been complete. Many remnants of Christian influence remain in the value system of the Western world which is not ready to accept a full-blown secular hedonism. This is one of the major reasons why society becomes complex and is characterized by illusions; we employ religious and moral symbols to cover our basic selfishness and secularism. This deception, which is often unconscious, explains why many may attend church for personal reasons as noted earlier. Consequently, it is difficult to determine what is Christian and what is not, and what is truth and what is not.

Much of the problem of secularization, then, is that its influence is pervasive in society and has special implications for the individual. Secularism is not merely a charge to be leveled at those involved in picnics or shopping on Sunday morning. Nor can we point to secularism in the economic institution without recognizing its existence in the church as well. All of us encounter secularism and must deal with it honestly and responsibly.

As noted earlier, we do not live in a world in which we can draw a sharp dichotomy between good and evil. In fact, we are told quite clearly in Scripture that it is God's responsibility, not man's, to separate the wheat from the tares and the sheep from the goats (Matthew 13:24-30; 25:31-33). A problem invariably arises when we usurp God's role and begin to act as judge and jury prematurely. The security found in such a notion is false and becomes apparent when our efforts fail. Our own limitations become rather obvious when we attempt to solve the pressing social problems of our day.

*Social Problems Cannot Always Be Solved*

This point leads us to our tenth and final principle: we cannot always resolve social problems. This fact becomes more apparent when we realize that social problems are not separate and concrete social phenomena. Instead, they must be seen as deeply rooted in a society's values and attitudes. The problems of racial prejudice and discrimination, for example, have to be understood not only in terms of housing and jobs, but also in terms of a racial group's consciousness of itself and of other races as well. In a very real sense, the spiritual implication of every social problem lies below the surface. The question remains whether man has any direct control over such implications and their consequences. If not—and the argument for such a claim should be apparent by now—we cannot hope to solve our social problems.

It is a fallacy to assume that we can remedy social problems because as I mentioned earlier in our seventh principle, we cannot assume that we are going to accomplish our social objectives. In fact, the consequences may be worse than the original condition. One of the clearest historical illustrations of this fact is found in the case of Prohibition. With proper motives, well-meaning Christians sought to outlaw the consumption of alcoholic beverages in the United States. What was overlooked, however, was the fact that behavior is not changed by laws unless there is a comparable change in personal attitudes. Their motives may have been right, even though the action taken was inappropriate. Consequently, drinking became an illegal practice, but not an abandoned one. In fact the demand for bootleg liquor became so great that Prohibition stimulated the development of a new form of criminal behavior. Ultimately, it laid the groundwork for the formation of the underworld in contemporary American society.

But does this apparent inability to cope with urgent social problems mean that we are to remain helpless and unresponsive before them? Not at all, for help is to be provided not only because the Christian expects to remedy them, but because he is commanded to help the needy. If we cannot always know the proper instrument to use in dealing with social problems, we can at least cooperate with God by working with those constructive forces that seek for solutions. If we cannot solve problems, we can at least contribute to their amelioration.

But many would say, what is needed is major surgery, not a band-aid. It is true that many times the situation demands nothing less than a radical approach. The question remains whether, with all our human frailties and limitations, distinction can be made between the kind of remedy needed in one situation and that needed in another. It is quite possible that the conditions faced by the nation in the Sixties did, indeed, call for a radical approach. And while we can appreciate some of the positive and lasting effects produced by the violence and disruption, we must ask whether it was the best, or even the only, way. Certainly sociologists themselves are not convinced of the results. Civil rights laws were changed, but discrimination and prejudicial attitudes still persist. Urban problems were attacked, but slum conditions remain and even spread. The fact is that efforts at social change produced a painful and inevitable frustration for many reformers.

Looking to the future offers little solace simply because problems encountered then will probably be radically different from what we experience today. There is even good likelihood that the necessary approaches to these problems have not even been considered. In such a situation, what is radical today is obsolete tomorrow. Indebtedness, for example, was a radical solution to economic problems in a day when thrift was valued. But the current correlation of installment buying with divorce and family problems suggests that indebtedness may be a social problem today and unthinkable as a solution in the future.

The claims of futurologists notwithstanding, few predictions about the future of society can be made with any accuracy. It is quite possible that the traditional values of Christianity will be eroded even more, and that Christians may very well become an even smaller minority. The picture may not be unlike that experienced by the early church in the first century. There was then more of a responsive attitude among these church fathers than an activist spirit. Neither militant nor escapist in outlook, the church exhibited those qualities of patience and pacifism which God molded into victories.

God's provisions for man have not changed. They may be applied to the modern world as well as to the power of the Roman world. What has been added is a scientific knowledge responsive to the complexities of modern society and sensitive to the uniqueness of its problems. The need is for a balanced and integrated application of both sociological and spiritual understanding. Anything less would present a distorted and, at best, limited comprehension of society and its problems.

### Discussion Questions

1. What examples can you give of the "real world"?
2. What examples can you give of the "okay world"?
3. How might an attempt to simplify perception of marriage result in a distortion of its meaning?
4. How can we understand God's intention for the use of leisure?
5. How may "mind transformation" help a student to adjust to a university campus?
6. Explain why Principle Four influences Principle Six. Give an example.
7. How may our responsibility in social living be influenced by Principle Six?
8. What factors other than "last-minute circumstances" may prevent attitudes from giving rise to the expected actions?
9. Why may it be claimed that installment buying has become a social problem?
10. Are Christians in a minority in society today? (Consider principles one, four, and six.)

# 7
# Can Sociology Be Christian?

*David E. Carlson*

Christians can think Christianly about any subject or topic. Integration of academic subjects and Christianity is possible when one recognizes that in Christ are "hidden all the treasures of wisdom and knowledge" (Colossians 2:2, 3, NIV). One must not merely superimpose Christian doctrine over naturalistic thought. True integration is the product of a mind that is regenerated by and reconciled to Christ. That is, a mind supplied only with Christian truths falls short of integration because it is only another philosophical system without the energizing power of the Word of God. My first argument is that sociology can be Christian if one recognizes naturalistic academic subjects as basically secular religion. Second, I want to illustrate the process of integration by discussing the sociological and Christian views of society.

## Academic Subjects as a Religious Alternative to Christianity

All knowledge is essentially religious because it is based on beliefs. We begin our journey to factual information from a launching pad which remains basically unverifiable. These points of departure are professions of faith. They can be our gods.

The secular mind often ignores the truism that it is impossible to know unless we believe. The Christian mind understands this.

**David E. Carlson**
*Associate Professor of Sociology and Chairman of the Department*
*Trinity College, Deerfield, Illinois*

The author is an active member of the Evangelical Free Church, especially engaged in Christian education. Mr. Carlson has taught in seminary as well as college. In addition, he is codirector of a private Christian counseling agency. He earned his MA in sociology from Northern Illinois University, his MSW from the University of Chicago, and his BD from Trinity Evangelical Divinity School.

Augustine instructs, "Unless you believe you will not come to know. ... If you cannot understand, believe in order to understand" (Habrison, 1963:14). Another church father, Anselm also claims, "I believe so I may know" (Habrison, 1963:14).

An example of belief as the basis of knowledge is illustrated by the scientific enterprise. Science begins with the belief that the most reliable means of discovering knowledge is the scientific method. This method is used when a scientist develops a hypothesis (a statement describing the relationship between known and unknown facts) and then refuses to finalize his conclusions until sufficient evidence has been gathered. So what is labeled scientific knowledge is merely the result of gathering information through a method scientists believe to be reliable. When we examine the scientific means of discovering knowledge we find it is founded on a profession of faith. J. Ellul, a French Christian lawyer-sociologist, observes that science makes its claims of factual findings "in the name of god, the god of the scientific method. ... The god is false" (Zylstra, 1958:149).

Any academic subject which has faith in the absolute authority of sovereign reason makes an idol of man's intellect. When the search for knowledge leaves no room for God, the human mind "adores itself as being the ultimate source of truth and value" (Kooistra, 1963:46). Secular thinking merely gives "another form and a new name to the object of worship." When God is denatured, human reason and nature are deified (Matson, 1964:15).

Another way to illustrate the religious dimension of secular thinking is to question its limited view of reality. The secularist, whether he be scientific or humanistic in his orientation to the world, begins with the belief that all reality is natural. Essentially this denies the possibility of supernatural reality. While science supposedly takes a neutral position on the supernatural we see that it is not in accuality neutral. It is a religious belief that all reality is natural. The conception of an exclusively natural life becomes quite a mental or methodological abstraction for the Christian in the face of the transforming life in God (Sturzo, 1943:1).

So we see that any academic discipline can and does pose as a religious alternative to Christianity. It can lead the Christian into a subtle form of idolatry. This idolatry may take the form of believing in the god of the established fact. The temptation is to place all the data of experience exclusively on the natural plane when using science. "This is the heart of modern religion" (Ellul, 1967:37)—the world can only be reliably known through science. Its creed is, "Thou shalt not question the fact; the fact and truth are one."

The honest secular thinker remembers that facts are simply statements of results from research agreed upon by qualified scientists. He is suspicious of his own conclusions. He believes them *tentatively* because he knows he may have incorrect or incomplete data. The scientist, according to his own creed, does not take his findings as truth.

It seems then, that we must serve some "god" in the academic task. The question is: Which god will we serve? Is it the naturalist god of the fact or the God who transcends the natural because he created the natural? Man can be the slave of facts dominated by the material universe, or he can be the willing slave of the God who masters the material world and gives man the right to have dominion over the natural world.

## Can Sociology and Christianity Be Integrated?

If man cannot escape from a "god," then the choice is either to bow to the living God or to be idolatrous. While men have attempted to eliminate God or to put him outside of his world without permission to interfere—he has nonetheless interfered. Christ's incarnation testifies to that! God has not abandoned the world or left man as its master. In addition the Christian recognizes that "God does not introduce chance, accidental intervention, or arbitrary will . . . but only a factor already working in the laws of nature and back of them, whether seen there by natural science or not (Stuckenberg, 1895:29).

A Christian sociologist, therefore, believes that the natural and supernatural are intertwined in all social life. It is difficult to tell where the natural is at work without the supernatural. For it is in God that "we live and move and have our being" (Acts 17:28).

Integrating sociology and Christianity is rooted in the recognition that God is a transforming influx on the social scene. If we are to build an "integral sociology" we must do so by studying the social structure in light of the supernatural (Sturzo, 1943:7).

Some readers may get the impression from the argument thus far that sociology must cease to be a science if it is to become Christian. Not at all! Rather, the call is for sociologists and persons in all other disciplines to recognize that they cannot escape having a god. Once the metaphysical presuppositions of every academic enterprise are acknowledged to be faith statements there is a possibility of integration. Science then bows to worship the God who sustains all life and activity, rather than worship its methodology and conclusions. The door is open for the worship of the God who is a social-historical fact concretely existing in time and space without sacrificing science as a way of knowing God's natural revelation.

### The Process of Integration: The "Yes, but," Approach

But we are left with the question: How does a Christian begin to integrate a secular discipline with Christian doctrine? In the words of Harry Blamires, author of *The Christian Mind* (1963), "Christian thinkers may begin to integrate secular knowledge and sacred truth by going beyond the limited observations of the secularists."

He suggests, a "yes, but ..." approach. You have already been exposed to this "yes, but ..." approach in challenging the secularists' view of reality. Remember, the scientist believes that all reality is natural. I asked if the scientist could legitimately believe all reality is *only* natural? In asking this question, the secularist is pushed to acknowledge he has no basis for limiting reality only to the natural.

To use an example from sociology, the "yes, but ..." approach is useful when confronting the sociological generalization that man is a product of social forces. Yes, but ... is that all man is? Yes, but is man only the product of social forces? Yes, but does that mean man has no choices? Yes, but does that mean man is a victim of his social environment?

Another example from sociology illustrating the possibility of integration with Christianity is sociology's understanding that society is manufactured by man. The Christian sociologist, or any thinker for that matter, might respond: "Yes, but is that all society is? Yes, but didn't you just say man was the product of social forces? Now you are saying that man is really the producer of social forces which in turn shape him. Yes, but isn't society also the creation of God?"

The "yes, but ..." approach recognizes the element of truth (or error) in secular thinking. It focuses on the inherent myopic vision of naturalistic thought which ignores God. The Christian sociologist pushes his secular colleagues' thinking to look beyond the natural plane. Are you sure that is all there is?

Within the limited space of this article I'm going to turn the sociologist's view of society over and show that sociology's conception of society is incomplete in light of the biblical revelation. In no way am I implying we should or must reject the sociologist's insights. Rather, the Christian should expand and correct the sociological concepts whenever possible.

## A Christian View of Society: The Process of Integration

This is how I have begun to develop the sociologist's view of society beyond the secular framework. As I read the Scriptures, the idea of a Christian society is rooted in the hope Christ gave the world with his death and resurrection. He promised the establishment of a new heaven and new earth (Revelation 21:1), the coming of the kingdom (Matthew 4:17), and the building of a church (Matthew 16:18). We see that the whole earth groans for redemption (Romans 8:18-25).

The new society as expressed by God, as envisioned by the Old Testament prophets and experienced by the Israelites, is a society established on the basis of a covenantal relationship. The origin of this covenantal relationship is hinted at in God's promise to Noah that the rainbow is a sign that he would never destroy the world again through a flood. We see it more clearly when God approaches Abram, promising him a new nation (Genesis 12:2). Specifically, this covenantal relationship is given recognition by Abraham and his family through the symbol of circumcision. The rite of circumcision was instituted after God promised that he would be their God and that he would give him a son, Isaac, through which he would fulfill His promise (Genesis 17). Paul, in his capsule history speech at the synagogue of Antioch, reminded the Jews of this inheritance which is now fulfilled in Jesus (Acts 13:16-23; see also Exodus 3:6-8, 1 Kings 8:57, 58).

"The new society of Israel was brought into existence solely by God . . . an act as significant as creation" (Wright 1954:65). In a similar way, Christian society is a new society which God, not man, has created (Acts 13:16-23; 1 Peter 2:4-10). Notice here the admission to sociology that man has created a society which God judges to be in need of redemption.

Comparing the covenant with Israel to the establishment of Christ's society is a central theme in the New Testament record. Paul writes that before Christ the Gentiles "were utter strangers to God's chosen community, the Jews [with] . . . nothing to look forward to and no God to whom you could turn" (Ephesians 2:12, Phillips). The new social bond between people is Christ who replaces the old social bond determined by kinship, nationality, and culture. "The new community in Christ is a people knit together, not primarily by human structure of organization but instead by an inner mutuality of spirit provided by God in Christ (Wright, 1954:65; see Ephesians 2:19). Christian society is not bound together by rules and regulations or by customs and culture, but by a relationship to God. In the new society, of which today's Church is a manifestation, God transcends the present social organization so that relationships replace rules and community replaces commandments.

Christianity cuts across the conventional basis of cohesion and social bond. It supersedes the existing social stratification with an irresistable force bringing men together by a new value. "Spiritual affinity triumphed over the strongest bonds that hold men together" (Rauschenbusch, 1907:118). For example, Jesus called individuals to give up home, property, reputation, and life for his sake. This call to commitment cuts across all the commandments given by God himself except for the commandment to love him with all our heart, soul, and mind. Social bond is now the result of faith in a common Savior, Jesus Christ. It is he who makes us kin. "All of you who were baptized 'into' Christ have put on the family likeness of Christ. Gone is the distinction between Jew and Greek, slave and free man, male and female—you are all one in Christ Jesus!" (Galatians 3:28, Phillips).

While it is true that a Christian society has no ethnic or class distinctions, there remains on the temporal level division of labor. These differing jobs are referred to in Romans (chapter twelve) and First Corinthians (chapter twelve) as gifts from God. We see clearly developed the idea of society as an organism, versus the idea of society as an organization. The Christian society is the body of Christ—each person having his own function with no individual able to claim his role or position as more important than another's.

From a sociological perspective, this organism concept of society could be described as roles without hierarchal status. That is, each Christian has an ascribed role (a function given by God) to perform for the good of the body of Christ, but there is no role more or less important than another (1 Corinthians 12). Man has no achieved roles within the Christian society, i.e., he can do nothing through his own efforts. Our status (social position within the Christian community) is also ascribed, a gift by the grace of God. In light of the fact that there are no stratification differences in Christ (Galatians 3:28), the passages of

Scripture referring to the roles (expected behavior) of men, women, children, slaves, etc. appear to be *functional* and not valuational. That is, behavior necessary to maintain the social order in this world, but within the eternal frame of reference, carries no weight as to the worth of a person—either in God's eyes or in the eyes of fellow Christians.

The biblical ideal for a Christian society is one in which all support each other in a mutual pursuit for the smooth functioning of the body of Christ. There could be no real union except on this basis. Christians "aim at the social order which rests on a higher estimate of the ends of life. Men are the children of God and the attributes of God are love, goodness, wisdom, justice, forgiveness. If they were to satisfy their real desires they must try to act like God. . . . They must seek the kingdom of God first" (Scott, 1946:67).

Who is greatest in the Christian society? This is a question of an earthbound person whose mind has not been transformed by Christ. If the above discussion is true to the Word of God then there is only one who is great in the Christian society—the one to whom Christ gives witness—to God the Father. Status is a desire of the natural man. Rather than rejecting this desire to be better than others and to receive more recognition than others, Jesus reinterpreted "greatness" and used it to communicate an essential characteristic of the Christian society. Greatness, in the divine perspective, is not based on being served, or on wealth, or on birth, but on our service and ministry to others (Matthew 20:26).

In a similar vein, we see that members of a Christian society have different social characteristics, as well as a different set of priorities. Their values are distinct from the "natural" order of values. The Beatitudes in Matthew 5 illustrates this clearly. Neighborliness is defined according to a person's need, not on the basis of race or creed (Luke 10:29). Further, there is a passionate concern for others in recognition of service to Christ (Matthew 25:26). Recognition in the community is based on God's recognition, not man's (John 10:14). That is, God does the choosing and man responds to God. The Christian society is not built on chance or man's work.

A Christian society is one which is governed and directed by God. Christians reject the idea that society is wound up by a maker who has long disappeared from the scene to let the society run down and stop. Christians reject the idea that society developed only naturally and that if allowed to unfold freely, nature will ultimately iron out all of society's failures and faults. A Christian society is one whose builder and maker is God (Hebrews 11:10). As such it is an eternal society that is not subject to the life-death cycle of all temporal societies.

We must remember that the Christian society is a society of the future—one that is not commonly anticipated by earthbound man (1 Corinthians 2:9). To the Christian the eternal social order is above temporal and human relationships by virtue of the fact that it preceded them in time and was created by the Eternal One. The earthly order has its anchorage and point of focus in the divine society. "Its point of origin and pattern of progression descend from the divine to the human. As a kingdom of life this kingdom under God's rule has . . . long since had its inception; though it waits for its final consummation upon God's own future" (Petry, 1956:38).

In this regard, a Christian is not so much a creature of the past as a person who is molded by the future realization of his present hope. He is more than the product of past influences on him. Notice here the agreement with sociology that man is shaped by experiences and environment, *but* this is not all man is or has to be. His past and future are God's past and future—his perspective has been transformed to see beyond his accumulated past or future. This is not to deny the strong influence of history and social conditions on man's behavior and character. Rather it is a Christian way of affirming the reality of transcending time and space and its evil influence. A sociology based on any theology other than a Christian one could not incorporate this into its understanding of a world casually determined.

## Summary

I have attempted to show that a naturalistic-scientific view of the world is a religious belief system which implicitly denies the reality of the supernatural. I have also attempted to show that sociology can be Christian without interfering with the methodology of science. And lastly, I have demonstrated that "Christian sociology" pushes "natural sociology" beyond the temporal dimensions, showing that a Christian view of society: (1) is a living organism bonded together by Christ's death and resurrection, not merely man-made organization; (2) has no status-class distinctions based on sex, wealth, age, or ethnic origin—we all are one in Christ; (3) has division of labor based on God's gifts; (4) has its origin in God; (5) is made for the glory of God and the benefit of man; (6) is a temporal manifestation of what God has in mind; (7) has values which reverse the priorities of the world; and (8) is based on social service to one's fellowman—this service to others is equated with service to God himself.

## Discussion Questions

1. Discuss the definition of integration. Develop your own definition of integration, restating in your own words Professor Carlson's introduction.

2. How can presuppositions in sociology be "religious"? What are some ways we can avoid making sociology our religion?

3. Practice the "yes but" approach by first identifying sociological principles from your text, then rewrite the principle beyond the sociological perspective to include the biblical data.

4. Review the process of integration as illustrated by the discussion of the Christian society. Describe this process.

5. Can sociology and Christianity be integrated? Consider the reasons for integration. Why is this desirable? What difficulties arise if one neglects to integrate?

6. How can sociology continue to be sociology without it losing its uniqueness and distinctiveness when integrated with a Christian perpective? Consider how sociology contributes to correcting, informing, and modifying theology. What sociological concepts, principles, and findings challenge a limited Christian theology?

7. Discuss how man-made culture can be an instrument of God's grace. Consider the relationship between Christ and culture. You may want to use H. R. Neihbur, *Christ and Culture,* as a resource for this discussion.

8. Discuss Carlson's argument that in a Christian society "relationships replace rules and community replaces commandments." Consider the relationship of rules to relationships and community to commandments. What point do you believe Carlson is trying to make? Is his point biblical? How would you paraphrase his claim?

9. What happens to our Christian subcultural view of male and female relationships if we recognize Galatians 3:28 as truth? What changes will occur in our thinking, attitude, behaviors, and feelings toward those who are different from us? Consider the concept of ethnocentrism.

10. Who is greatest in the kingdom of God? What is the biblical view of ranking and stratification? What practical changes need to be made in our churches? What values challenged?

## References

Blamires, Harry
    1963 *The Christian Mind.* London: SPCK.

Ellul, Jacques
     1967 *The Presence of the Kingdom*. New York: Seabury.
Habrison, E.
     1956 *The Christian Scholar in the Age of Reformation*. New York:
          Scribner's.
Kooistra, R.
     1963 "*Facts and Values: A Christian Approach to Sociology.*" St.
          Catherines, Ont.: Christian Perspective Series.
Petry, Ray
     1956 *Christian Eschatology and Social Thought*. New York:
          Abingdon.
Rauschenbusch, Walter
     1907 *Christianity and the Social Crisis*. Chicago: Pilgrim.
Scott, E. F.
     1946 *Man and Society in the New Testament*. New York:
          Scribner's.
Stuckenberg, J.
     1895 *Christian Sociology*. Funk and Wagnalls.
Sturzo, Luigi
     1943 *The True Life-Sociology of the Super-Natural*. Catholic
          University Press.
Wright, G. E.
     1954 *The Biblical Doctrine of Man in Society*. London: SCM Press
          Ltd.
Zylstra, H.
     1958 *Testament of Vision*. Grand Rapids: Eerdmans, 1958.

# 8

# Scripture and Sociology/Social Work: Humpty-Dumpty Revisited

*David E. Carlson*

Have you ever tried to wipe up a broken egg? Recently I was helping my wife put away the groceries and I dropped an egg on our kitchen counter. What a slimy, slippery mess. My attempts to clean the egg off the counter would have made a great scene for a Laurel and Hardy movie. I got a dishcloth and pushed the egg from one side of the counter to the other side. Then I tried a spoon and cup. All you have to do is scoop the egg up with the spoon and pour it into the cup—right? Wrong! I pushed the egg and yolk around the counter top like a hockey player skating all alone toward an open net goal. I shot—ahh, goal—oh no—to my dismay the egg and yolk acted like a ball attached to a rubber band and paddle, bouncing back still attached to the spoon. Hey, wiping up an egg can't be this much trouble. But it was.

My thoughts drifted to a nursery rhyme—Humpty-Dumpty—and I took heart. Well, actually it was my way of coping with frustration and failure. You all know the social work principle, "when under stress, regress." So I recited the rhyme as a way of coping. "Humpty-Dumpty sat on a wall, Humpty-Dumpty had a great fall, all the kings horses and all the kings men couldn't put Humpty-Dumpty together again." I knew better than to try to put the egg together, that's a job for chickens, not horses and men. But how did they clean up the mess? Un-

**David E. Carlson**
*Associate Professor of Sociology and Chairman of the Department*
*Trinity College, Deerfield, Illinois*

The author is an active member of the Evangelical Free Church, especially engaged in Christian education. Mr. Carlson has taught in seminary as well as college. In addition, he is codirector of a private Christian counseling agency. He earned his MA in sociology from Northern Illinois University, his MSW from the University of Chicago, and his BD from Trinity Evangelical Divinity School.

fortunately, the nursery rhyme ends before it gives any practical suggestions on "what do you do with a broken egg?"

## Broken Eggs

Because of my experience with "broken eggs," I've been asked to write this article. Once upon a time I heard about yolks and whites. I didn't realize they were part of a product called an "egg." Much of my education has been like this. I didn't know that everything I was being taught actually fit together. I thought the subjects and ideas were separate like yolks and whites. Furthermore, I had little or no encouragement to try to put them together. In fact, as I recall it, many people actually discouraged me from seeing any positive relationship between sociology and social work or Christ and culture. As a sociology student, I was taught description and analysis was a sociologist's job while application and action belonged to another profession. The status of social work in the sociologist's eyes seemed a little lower than the janitors. As a fundamentalist Christian I was to be separated from culture—no drinking, dancing, card playing, movies, etc. But more subtly, and sometimes not so subtly, you and I may have been taught in our Christian subculture to abstain from reading or studying any thoughts or ideas taught by persons lacking the Christian stamp of approval. We may have been taught that teachings outside the church are suspect, if not outright dangerous.

When you and I attended school we found that God was unnecessary to explain, or account for, or to understand what was going on in the world, in our bodies, or in our society. God, for all practical purposes, did not exist. Oh, we used his name when pledging allegiance to the flag, but "God" was only another word like liberty, justice, republic. Who ever told us what these words meant? They were platitudes and clichés.

I remember the tension I felt at times between what I was taught in Sunday school and what I was taught in regular school. What a position to be in—to choose between what your parents and Sunday school teachers were teaching (they seemed so sure and spiritual) and what your regular school teachers were saying (they seemed so bright and knowledgeable).

But that tension is over for me now. I've rejected the view which says all knowledge is dangerous. I've also rejected the view which says God is unimportant in academic subjects. I've accepted the view that

Harry Blamires articulates so well in his book, *The Christian Mind* (1963). The "dominant evil of our time [is] the disintegration of human thought and experience into separate unrelated compartments." He argues that man and knowledge have been dismembered. In other words, Humpty-Dumpty has fallen, the egg is broken, human thought is alienated from God. All knowledge is seen to be natural with no supernatural component. Human thought is claimed to be unrelated to man as person. Thus, all knowledge is objective. In addition it is argued that human thought is segregated from nature. All knowledge is mechanical without purpose or moral. We can then ask, who cares? Where are all the kings horses and all the kings men now? Who is trying to put Humpty-Dumpty together again? Theodore Roszak, *Where the Wasteland Ends* (1972), argues that science has made us more ethnocentric. He claims, "However much science has revolutionized the life of the average man and woman, it has scarcely made (our) thinking less stubbornly ethnocentric than it was in the days of the paleolithic hunting camp" (1972:5).

I share Roszak's observation that we have developed in academia a "narrow cultural experience." He calls it the "mindscape of single vision." But single visioned culture is also characteristic of much so called Christian thinking. We have prepackaged our theological thinking into neat little categories—really put everything in a box. We have been told this is the way it is—it has been pre-thought, predigested, and neatly wrapped for us. So here we are as Christians taught to think categorically from two separate cultures, both somewhat antagonistic to or ignoring each other.

## Putting Humpty-Dumpty Together Again

Now what does all this have to do with sociology, social work, and the Scriptures? Very simply this. As Christians we have to be about the business of putting Humpty-Dumpty together again, i.e., building bridges between our Christianity, our ways of looking at man's social life, and our ways of helping man cope in a complex social world. It is about time we stop acting as if our view of the world (as Christians, as sociologists, as social workers, as academicians, etc.) is the only view. We have lost touch with the whole mosaic of wisdom and knowledge. We have behaved as if our culture is best, whether secular or sacred (ethnocentrism). We have lost touch with the reality of all truth being related. We are alienated, but we deny it. We act like ostriches with our head in the sand and exposing symbolically what we are. We are claiming there is Christ and culture, when we need to recognize that Christ is the Creator, Sustainer, Redeemer, and Lord of all knowledge and culture.

But what have we done in academics and in the helping professions? We have sought to emancipate our discipline from religion, when we needed only to emancipate social science from man-distorted and man-made theology. As social scientists we have tried to free our discipline from politics, when we needed only to acknowledge our ethnocentrism. We have tried to escape from ideology, when we should have become conscious of our finite views.

And as Christian thinkers, are we less guilty of furthering the alienation between Christianity and culture? No. Instead of welcoming the scientific perspective as a Christian community we have been threatened out of our minds. Instead of listening to the criticisms and perspectives, we counter attacked. Instead of acknowledging that the Scriptures do not teach us everything about everything, we became more dogmatic. Walter Kaiser, professor at Trinity Evangelical Divinity School expresses my position well. He wrote this in an article entitled "Unity," in *Trinity Today* (1972): "Knowledge is all one piece: every created being, reality or truth belongs to her maker: there can be no alien or 'worldly' truths to frighten, disarm and upset the Christian. Therefore, one of the Christian's highest callings is to reclaim for her Lord everything that rightfully belongs to Him. And in addition, it is to challenge every admixture of dilution of what is 'true, honest, just, pure, lovely and of good report' " (Phillippians 4:8).

### Integration: A Definition and Three Illustrations

I have been arguing for the integration of all knowledge. By integration I mean the thoughtful, planned bringing together of sociology, social work, and Scripture (distinct and separate components of reality and truth) in the recognition of their common relatedness and gestalt, without loss of the component's uniqueness and individuality and without ignoring conflict, paradox, or error.

The possibility of integration can be illustrated in the following three ways. First is the example of Christ's incarnation—the bringing together and joining of God and man, spirit and body, infinite and finite, sacred and secular. Second, marriage provides an example of integration—the bringing together of man and woman, two bodies, two minds, two different personalities, two different composites of experiences. And third, integration can be illustrated through the concept of the Church as Christ's body—each member unique, different, having a separate job but part of a larger oneness.

Some Christians, as well as academicians, are afraid integration will result in Christianity swallowing up sociology/social work or vice versa. This certainly is a possibility but this is not integration. To support my position I quote from an article by J. Gresham Machen (1912). "There are two objections to our solution of the problem. If you bring culture and Christianity thus into close union—in the *first* place, will not Christianity destroy culture? Must not art and science be independent in order to flourish? We answer that it all depends upon the nature of their dependence. Subjection to any external authority or even to any human authority would be fatal to art and science. *But subjection to God is entirely different.* Dedication of human powers to God is found, as a matter of fact, not to lessen but to heighten them. God gave those powers. He understands them well enough not bunglingly to destroy his own gifts. In the *second* place, will not culture destroy Christianity? Is it not far easier to be an earnest Christian if you confine your attention to the Bible and do not risk being led astray by the thought of the world? We answer, of course it is easier. Shut yourself up in an intellectual monastery, do not disturb yourself with the thoughts of unregenerate men, and of course you will find it easier to be a Christian, just as it is easier to be a good soldier in comfortable winter quarters than it is on the field of battle. You save your own soul—but the Lord's enemies remain in possession of the field."

Integration can be pictured as illustrated by this diagram.

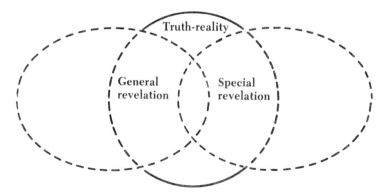

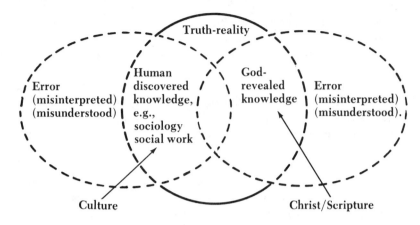

So integration to me is more than a Christian perspective or viewpoint toward sociology/social work. Integration must lead to putting divergent perspectives together into some meaningfully interacting whole. Christianity and sociology/social work must become part of a larger picture of reality. I think this can be accomplished at several different levels.

## Integrative levels

### The Historical Level

First of all, the *historical* dimension would be one way of bringing Christianity, sociology, and social work together. To aid you in this process I would suggest three paperbacks. Keith-Lucas, *The Church and Social Welfare* (1962); D. Moberg, *Inasmuch* (1965); and Moberg's newer book, *The Great Reversal* (1972). These authors argue that historic Christianity has always been in the forefront of social concern and action.

### The Philosophical Level

A second level at which integration can take place between Christianity, sociology, and social work is the *philosophical*. Every discipline has presuppositions. In social work we value the dignity and worth of man, the belief in man's capacity for self-determination and the possibility for change/growth. As a social work student in a secular graduate school I came to grips with the fact that there was little or no discussion of man's spiritual nature. And yet the atmosphere was not hostile to religious views. One might say there was a spirit of toleration for what one believed, with the injunction that one does not proselytize. Missionary activities and social work were to be separated. In a sense this philosophical position is sound, but in another sense it is quite limited. Religious people have a habit of trying to evangelize when they should be helping with an everyday concern; e.g., James reminds us that it does no good to say to the needy, "God bless you!" when we should give food, clothes, and shelter (2:14-17). The Bible also taught me that people's difficulties often have a spiritual dimension, but we must also be ready to look at the social, familial, emotional, economic side to their problems.

A further illustration of integration at the philosophical level came for me when I struggled with the idea of "man's self-determination." As a Christian this value at first bothered me because in my religious subculture I was socialized to believe man was totally dependent on God. These two ideas did not seem to be compatible. But I have come to see that self-determination can be viewed as man's capacity to choose and manage his everyday life, and it does not necessarily imply he can be, through his own efforts, victorious over his sinful nature.

*The Methodological Level*

A third level of integration involves *methodology.* In theology we *know* through special revelation and exegesis of the Scriptures. In sociology we *know* through research and experimentation. In social work we *know* through clinical experience, the rehabilitative processes, and exploration. Each way of knowing is unique and different. They produce different information. But we can bring together these different pieces of data and facts because we know they all belong to the Lord.

Different methodologies of helping people are currently at the root of much writing and discussion about "Christian counseling." To some writers Christian counseling is a confronting style which I choose to label prophetic. It is a direct approach of telling people what their problem is and how to solve it. Support for this position is gleaned from selected biblical illustrations which involve a confronting-prophetic style. The argument of this school of thought is that the Bible teaches only one way of counseling and that way is like preaching. While I'm sympathetic with those who desire to derive their methodology of helping from biblical data, I find their approach to be based on a bias that I cannot share. That is, they assume that the Bible is the sole source of teaching us ways to relate to people therapeutically. Now none of these people would use the Bible as a textbook for learning to build a house, caring for deteriorating teeth, or performing surgery. But when it comes to counseling, they hold the Bible up as the sole text.

My view of Scripture is this—it is God's revelation to man, telling man about God's creation, intentions, and redemption. It is like a letter telling man he is loved and it communicates clearly his need for salvation from sin. By no stretch of the imagination do I see God's Holy Word to be the sole source of knowledge about any subject—including God himself. Remember my chart showing the relationship between special revelation and general revelation? Consider also Paul's comments in Romans as well as David's in the Psalms which tell us that nature declares the handiwork of God (Romans 1:19-20; Psalm 19:1).

I am not against prophetic counseling. But I am against saying prophetic counseling is the only method approved by God. Another method of counseling which I think is also biblically based, but is selectively ignored by the prophetic counselors, is what I label priestly counseling. This is a supportive listening confessional, exploring, affirming relationship in which the social worker helps the person express his feelings and choose his own ways of coping with a difficult situation. My point is that those two approaches do not have to be used in isolation, or at the exclusion of the other method. (See Carlson, 1976, for a fuller treatment of this issue.)

### The Meaning Level

A further dimension to integration between Scripture, sociology, and social work is the level of *meaning*. As Christians we are concerned with ultimate meanings—eternal value, worth, and purpose. In sociology and social work our primary concern is with immediate meanings—their importance to person, friends, community, society, as well as their limited consequences for personality development. These two different levels of meaning need not clash. They can work together. As a Christian therapist my theology encourages me to look beyond today, to ask what difference it makes if you help this family through this crisis. And ringing loud and clear the message comes back from my theology: remember "inasmuch as ye have done it unto one of the least of these my brethren, ye have done it unto me" (Matthew 25:40). My theology also tells me that the sins of the fathers are visited on the second and third generation; and I'm glad to be part of the redemptive process which will have beneficial effects on the family life of my client's children's children.

## *The Motivational Level*

And lastly, integration between Christianity, sociology, and social work can take place at the level of *motivation*. In sociology we are motivated to know, to predict, and to control. In social work we are motivated to improve society, to help people function at their optimal level. To Christianity, those motives are really no problem. The Apostle Paul, tells us, "Whatsoever ye do in word or deed, do all in the name of the Lord Jesus, giving thanks to God and the Father" (Colossians 3:17).

Oh, incidentally, what do you do with a broken egg? Well it is pretty easy to clean up a broken egg if you mix the yolk and the white together. Let us not *divorce* Christianity from social work. But let us *distinguish* between Christianity and culture in recognition of the effects of sin on man's understanding and thoughts, and in recognition of how they are parts of a larger reality. As Christians, let us continually remind ourselves that Christ is the Creator, Sustainer, Redeemer, and Reconciler of all things—including sociology and social work "In whom are hid all the treasures of wisdom and knowledge" (Colossians 1:14, 17, 18, 20; 2:2, 3).

## Discussion Questions

1. Compare your education with the description of Carlson's early education. How is your experience similar? Different?

2. What do you believe to be the relationship between sociology, social work, and Christianity? On what basis do you hold your beliefs? Does Carlson challenge your views? How?

3. What is the Christian's relationship to man-made culture? Should we be afraid to expose our minds to nonbiblical thinking? Why? Why not? Notice that Carlson does not confuse *non*-biblical with *un*-biblical.

4. Discuss the Christian subculture's level of ethnocentrism. How can the Christian be broadminded and liberally educated and remain biblically committed?

5. Why should we as Christians try to put Humpty-Dumpty together again? What are the advantages?

6. Carlson criticizes secular education and professions as rejecting

of religion. Why is this attempt to emancipate the disciplines from religion unnecessary?

7. Consider the process of integration as reclaiming all thoughts, information, and knowledge that rightfully belongs to the Lord. How does this include nonbiblical data?

8. Discuss Carlson's definition of integration. Study this definition through the use of the charts, visualizing the integrative relationships between sociology, social work, and Scripture.

9. Discuss Machen's quotation in which he argues for Christians to take possession of academic and professional fields.

10. Observe the 5 levels of integration suggested by Carlson. Begin to practice integration by considering one sociological illustration principle for each of the five levels. What levels would you add to Carlson's list?

# References

Blamires, H.
  1963 *The Christian Mind*. London: SPCK.
Carlson, D.
  1976 "Jesus' Style of Relating: The Search for a Biblical View of Counseling" *Journal of Psychology and Theology*, Summer.
Kaiser, W.
  1972 "Unity" Trinity Today. *Trinity Evangelical Divinity School.*
Keith-Lucas, A.
  1962 *The Church and Social Welfare*. Chapel Hill.
Machen, G.
  1912 Address on "The Scientific Preparation of Minister" (September 20). Princeton Theological Seminary.
Moberg, D. O.
  1965 *Inasmuch*. Grand Rapids: Eerdmans.
Roszak, T.
  1972 *Where the Wasteland Ends*. New York: Doubleday.

# 9

# The Christian as Sociologist

*Andrew M. Greeley*

I propose to organize my comments on the vocation of the Christian sociologist around a number of assertions. These assertions can be taken as a "model" in that they vary in "ideal type" sense. It is a tool for looking at reality and not an empirically documented description of reality.

*No Conflicts Between Christianity and Sociology*
   1. *There are no necessary conflicts between the craft of sociology as it is practiced in the United States (and the Free World) and a Christian religious commitment.* American sociology has never purported to have metaphysical or theological competence. It has bracketed the question of the nature of the ultimate reality with an agnostic shrug of its shoulders, stating that there is nothing in either its data or its social theory which enables its sociology to make any judgment about the nature of ultimate reality. In principle, the sociologist says, it is a matter of indifference to the profession whether a scholar is religious or not. As a private person, the sociologist may well be skeptical of the believer (most of them are, I think). There is, however, nothing in his empirical evidence or his theoretical perspectives that enables him *as a sociologist* to either refute or—wonder of wonders—possibly confirm the existence of a "transcendent" reality in terms of sociological evidence.
   The "God hypothesis" is neither verifiable nor falsifiable. There

**Andrew M. Greeley**
*Professor of Sociology, University of Arizona*
*Director for the Study of American Pluralism*
*National Opinion Research Center*

Professor Greeley has been very active in the American ethnicity and pluralism dialogue. He has written and spoken extensively on the topic of American Catholicism, American Protestantism, and pluralism in general. He has been deeply involved in the academic community, as well as the larger community and national scene. Mr. Greeley is an ordained priest in the Roman Catholic Church.

may be, of course, other evidence in other realms of discourse that can verify it or falsify it, but sociology as such does not purport to be able to make judgments about such form of discourse (though it does claim the right to study the social context in which such discourse is used).

The sociologist will concede that his Christian colleague may well choose certain topics for research, have certain predispositions toward findings, and may have certain insights because of his religious stand. But in theory, at any rate, the secular sociologist would be forced to admit that everybody has presuppositions, commitments, proclivities, inclinations, and basic assumptions. The Christian sociologist, in this respect, is no different from anyone else. The secularist would also assume that the Christian sociologist would not permit his religious commitment to lead him to falsify data, to suppress findings, do hasty analysis, or report unsubstantiated assertions. In principle, again, there is nothing in the Christian commitment that would lead one to succumb to this temptation to do unscientific, unscholarly, and unprofessional work. The temptation, incidentally, is often much stronger than many sociologists, Christian or not, are willing to admit.

Furthermore, the mainstream of American sociology does not purport to be able to arrive at wise or moral social policy merely from its evidence and from its theory. Sociologists, like all other human beings, have their political and policy predispositions. They may even collect data to establish the "non-irrationality" of their policy recommendations. For example, children of working mothers do not seem to have any more problems than the children of nonworking mothers. But ordinarily the feminist sociologist would not conclude that the evidence proves that women must work, or even that there is no effect on the children of working mothers. All she would conclude is that her research has found no such effect. Thus, while some sociologists may well use their evidence to support social policies which a Christian would find distasteful or even immoral, in theory the responsible mainstream American sociologist would not attempt to derive ethical principles from empirical research.

The position stated here is, I think, a fair summary of how most American sociologists conceive of their profession. It is a "modified value free" approach to empirical science. It does not assume that the scholar is free of values or that his values will not affect what he does. The assumption, rather, is that the scholar can effectively distinguish between his values and his evidence, and between his role as a data collecting, theory-forming person and a social or moral policy-recommending person.

The Christian sociologist will find two dissenting positions. One inside his own community believes that all scholarly efforts ought to be directed at sustaining the gospel message. The other, outside his community and inside the profession, believes that scholarly research ought to be directed to the service of some overarching ideological world view which approaches social research with metaphysical, political, and policy assumptions that are beyond question. In its New Left manifestation, this ideological approach to social research was quite popular among young scholars in the sixties and early seventies, and may even be in control of some academic departments in the country. The Christian will have no trouble recognizing the ideological sociologist. In temperament, style, and rigidity, he is very much like the most narrow, dogmatic, and doctrinaire Christian sociologist from an ecclesial community. Given half a chance, both of these folks set up inquisitions to eliminate dissent.

But most American sociologists are committed to a modified value-free position. They realize how difficult it is for a person to sustain the balance and nuance that such a position requires. In principle, then, the sociologist who is a Christian is welcome in the profession. But in practice, as we will see in the next two assertions, he has problems, not merely from the doctrinaire left in his profession but also from the doctrinaire right in his ecclesiastical community.

### The Sociologist Profession Often Anti-Christian

2. *The sociological profession—as distinct from the sociological craft—is pervasively and often ignorantly anti-Christian.* Hence, the Christian sociologist will almost always find himself in a difficult position if he is plying his craft outside of a distinctly Christian environment. However much in theory he may be tolerant of someone else's "presuppositions," many an American sociologist finds it very difficult not to be prejudiced against a professed Christian. The origins of this anti-Christian and antireligious bias are hard to specify. The research evidence shows that sociology is particularly likely to recruit the alienated, the angry, and the antagonistic. With such people, organized religion of any sort is a convenient inkblot. Despite the fact that he is a student of institutions, and that he himself is very concerned about his own institutional affiliation, often in the core of his personality the so-

ciologist is anti-institutional. And there is no institution easier to hate, or so it seems to him, than the religious institutions. Many times it would appear that the antireligious sociologist comes from a very harsh and religious background himself, and he equates all religions with his own childhood experience (quite independently of any empirical evidence, of course).

Protestantism is equated with the most literal and punitive sort of fundamentalism, and is thought of as fundamentally anti-Semitic. Catholicism is blamed for the nineteenth-century pogroms in Poland and for Irish kids beating up Jewish kids in schoolyards in Boston and New York in the 1930s. I once asked a Jewish colleague who was complaining to me about what Poles did to his grandmother whether there wasn't some sort of statute of limitations. I suggested that he pursue the scholarly literature on the relations between Mosaic Poles and Christian Poles (as they call themselves) and the various Polish freedom movements of the early nineteenth century. But his anger at what my people had done to his people did not permit him to take a scholarly approach to the question.

It will also be argued that there are some presuppositions that are incompatible with scholarly research. One professor at the University of Chicago said that he could no more vote for a practicing Catholic in the sociology department than he could for a member of the Communist Party, because both of them had commitments that made it impossible for them to do objective scholarship. The man is still in the sociology department and still saying the same thing, and a considerable number of his colleagues agree with him. Although, I wish to emphasize, that by no means all agree with him. Such convictions illustrate the highest form of bigotry because they display an appalling ignorance of the nature of religious commitment, as well as the kind of commitment that any human being has, since all have presuppositions.

Nevertheless, the Christian sociologist, if he is moving in the profession outside of the Christian context, is going to encounter endless skepticism about his objectivity. Indeed, he may find himself in a Kafka-like situation where he simply cannot prove his objectivity or his scholarly skills because he is defined on a priori grounds as incapable of such skills. No matter how good your work is, it will still be judged inadequate. You ask why it is inadequate, and you are answered not by serious criticism of the work itself, but by the assertion that since you are a committed Christian you cannot possibly do good work.

Sometimes this prejudice may hide behind elaborate rationalizations and justifications, but the raw bigotry is still there obvious for all to see. (Once Professor Edward Shils said to the Hyde Park *Voices* newspaper, "Some of my best friends are Roman Catholics.") The knowledge that one is a victim of bigotry is not likely to be much consolation to the Christian sociologist. One must try harder, like Avis; one must be twice as good and, even then, it is often not good enough. And discrimination against one is anything but objectionable. As my colleague, James Coleman, remarked once, "There are two kinds of people it is legitimate to hate if you're a sociologist—Catholics and Southerners." He could have added "and publicly committed Christians."

In 1977, the American Sociological Association did a complex and elaborate study of the condition of "minorities" in its membership—blacks, Hispanics, American Indians, Asian Americans. The authors of the report pompously informed the profession that these groups altogether formed almost 20 percent of the population. But nary a word was said about another minority group, Roman Catholics, who are 25 percent of the population, who are substantially underrepresented in sociology, and who have been consistently discriminated against in the discipline. But then, as a colleague once said, "Women and blacks are underrepresented because of discrimination; Catholics are underrepresented because their religion interferes with their doing solid scholarly work." *Sic stat thesis*, as we used to say in the mother tongue.

The Christian sociologist, then, will find the profession about as friendly as the red suburbs of Paris were to the priest workers, or as cannibalistic tribes were to missionaries. He should consider himself fortunate that at least he's not going to get boiled alive.

*Church Community Often Hostile to Sociology*

3. *The Christian sociologist can also count on misunderstanding, opposition, and hostility from within his ecclesiastical community.* Substantial numbers of Christians are not willing to accept even the modified value-free position described under the first assertion, in part at least, because their intelligence is not flexible enough to comprehend it. Virtually every time I report a finding about the Catholic laymen's attitudes toward abortion or birth control, I am favored with a stack of long letters from people attacking my Christian commitment. They argue that even if 99 percent of the Catholics in the country approve of abortion under some circumstances, or practice birth control,

these activities are still "sinful." I have long since given up trying to respond to such correspondence. If I tried to tell them that all I am doing is reporting the facts of the situation, and not approving of them, and that they should argue with those who hold these opinions and not with me, they would not get the message. It is inconceivable to such correspondents that one can report the finding without accepting it oneself. They think that you are opposed to the teaching of the church if you find that other people aren't following that teaching. Whatever the ecclesial structure of a Christian sociologist's own community, he will inevitably encounter such a mentality—though the rhetoric within such a mentality will vary. For example, if one substitutes gospel for teaching authority, the substance of the criticism is the same.

Second, ecclesiastical bureaucracies (of whatever sort) do not like bad news. Since there are few "saints," and not very many more totally committed Christians, any empirical research is likely to look like bad news. Ecclesiastical bureaucracies react to bad news the same way kings did—they slew the herald who brought the news on the assumption that he who brought the bad news caused it. The Christian sociologist's work necessarily will be a challenge to take the "head in the sand" posture normally assumed by ecclesiastical bureaucracies. Bureaucrats, like all ostriches, do not like to be disturbed. Since they generally do not have available competent sociological expertise to respond intelligently, they turn to personal assaults on the integrity, faith, and loyalty of the sociologist. The final putdown comes when the bureaucrat wraps himself in his full robes, adjusts his phylacteries, and solemnly intones "faith (or morality or whatever) is not achieved by public opinion surveys"—the implication obviously being that this is what the sociologist is obviously suggesting.

Religious scholars of other disciplines inside ecclesial communities, particularly nonempirical ones like theology, are also often affronted by the sociologist's empiricism. He will be read long lectures on the dangers of philosophical empiricism, though he is not a philosophical empiricist, and the model the lecturer has in mind is a caricature of how the sociologist actually works. As one astute clergyman at a confrontation between social scientists, (mostly Americans), and theologians, (mostly German or German influenced), said, "It was a classic confrontation between German idealists and American empiricists. By definition, the empiricists have to listen and the idealists don't, so the empiricists lost."

The battle cry, "Sociologists to the lions," has not been heard in the last month or two among the ecclesial communities, but the Christian sociologist should be wary. There are a lot of folks in the churches who would like to feed the lions.

### Roots of Sociology Are Religions

4. *The roots of sociology are profoundly religious.* Few within the profession would deny that Durkheim and Weber have played the role of holy founding fathers. Indeed the best sociological article begins with footnote references to one or the other and, if possible, both (like most theoretical references, of course, these are dug up after the research has been done). It is no coincidence that the *Protestant Ethic and the Spirit of Capitalism* and the *Elementary Forms of the Religious Life* are two of the most important sociology books ever written—and both books are concerned with religion. Durkheim deals with religion as community; Weber with religion as meaning. Both see the religious impulse as central to social structure and culture. Religious sensitivity and insight ought to be especially important tools for the sociological imagination, if indeed we are the offspring of Durkheim and Weber. It is not necessary for the sociologist to be religious (neither of the holy founding fathers themselves apparently were), but it is necessary that he have religious sensitivity. While it is surely the case that some nonreligious persons are religiously sensitive, it is also true that a substantial number of those who purport to be religious are religiously insensitive. But the committed sociologist who is also a committed religionist has, potentially at any rate, some strong assets to bring to social research and theory construction. For all the ritualistic quotations of the *Protestant Ethic* and the *Elementary Forms*, the profession has made relatively little progress since the time of the founding fathers in clarifying the nature of the relationship between religion and society. This is not true of our sister discipline, anthropology, where remarkable progress has been made.

We therefore have a paradox, in that while sociology as a profession took its origins from the study of religion and its most quoted theorists were fascinated by religion, presently it is staffed to a considerable extent by religiously insensitive people who are either uninterested in or incapable of taking seriously the role of religion in the human condition. One does not want to make the case that the Christian sociologist must be a sociologist of religion. Some should be;

others should not be. In any event, the Holy Spirit should be left free to move scholars to do that which they do best (normally that is in the subject of their greatest interest). But if religion permeates human life (which Weber and Durkheim took as a given, although many, if not most, contemporary American sociologists vigorously deny it), then a sensitivity to the "religious factor" ought to be useful in every subdiscipline within the sociological profession.

The non-Christian sociologist may resent the Christian's presence in the profession. His fellow Christians outside the profession may also resent his presence in it. The Christian sociologist can afford to smile and utter modestly, perhaps under his breath, what the late Cardinal Cushing proclaimed at the 1945 CIO convention (back in the days when the CIO was considered a radical working class organization): "I'm here because I belong here."

*Sociology of Religion an Impoverished Field*

5. *Even though contemporary sociology arose from the concerns of Weber and Durkheim about religion, the sociology of religion is perhaps the most impoverished subfield in the discipline.* One needs only to peruse the mindless empiricism and the undisciplined theorizing in such journals as the *Journal for the Scientific Study of Religion* to see that the subprofession has not attracted the best minds, the most creative skills, or the most powerful sociological imaginations. Even though courses in the sociology of religion are popular whenever they are offered, many graduate departments, particularly the most prestigious ones, rarely offer courses in the sociology of religion. Furthermore, few have sociologists of religion in their senior faculty. Graduate students are not slow to get the point. The sociological study of religion does not have that much prestige. If you are both bright and ambitious, stay away from it. The profession is suffering somewhat from its past sins in this respect: With the precipitate decline of graduate school enrollment and the somewhat slower erosion of undergraduate school enrollment, sociologists now must scramble for undergraduate students or face budget cuts. Since the sociology of religion attracts undergraduates, there has been (one should excuse the expression) an unholy scramble for people who can teach courses in the sociology of religion and get along moderately well with undergraduates.

Much of the research in the sociology of religion is in the tradition of Charles Y. Glock, limited to unimaginative questions, measuring acceptance of doctrinal propositions, ethical imperatives, and devotional practice. The theoretical concerns usually are so simpleminded as to be embarrassing. For example, they have dealt with a naive secularization theory which purports to show several things: (1) an evolutionary progress away from religion, (2) attempts to revive the Protestant ethic (most systematically in Gerhard Lenski's anti-Catholic book, *The Religious Factor*), (3) ever more complex elaborations of church sect typologies (one article had sixty-four cells, many of which were filled by no religious organization that humankind has ever known), and (4) a naive Marxism which attempts to show either that religion is the opiate of the poor or the tool of oppression by the rich (heads I win, tails you lose).

*In fact,* there is little connection in American society between social class and religious behavior. All the major denominations have sects as well as church structures. Furthermore, there seems to be little change in basic beliefs, such as, acceptance of the divinity of God or life after death (70 percent in the early and the middle thirties, when the question was first asked, and still 70 percent; 70 percent for those under thirty who attended graduate school, and 70 percent for those over fifty who have not gone to college).

Some sociologists of religion, most notably Charles Luckmann (1967) and Peter Berger (1969), have attempted more elaborate and sophisticated theoretical perspectives.[*] In addition, one empirical sociologist, my colleague William McCready, in a breakthrough work, has demonstrated the utility of a socialization model of religion. He sees religion as learned behavior. You learn it from someone, most notably your parents and your spouse. A measure of the success of McCready's approach is that he can easily explain more than half the variance in religious behavior, while other perspectives are hard put to deal with 10 percent of the variance.

The most useful and insightful approach to the sociology of religion has been developed by the anthropologist, Clifford Geertz, a student of Talcott Parsons, and an interpreter of both Parsons and Weber (though, in my judgment, his work is intellectually superior to that of both of his distinguished predecessors). Geertz's definition of religion as a unique meaning system which purports to deal with the

---

[*]Peter L. Berger, *Rumor of Angels*. New York: Irvington, 1969; and Charles Luckmann, *The Invisible Religion*. New York: Macmillan, 1967.

basic tragedies and complexities of human life has extraordinary possibilities for empirical research, possibilities which rarely have been pursued. Geertz is often uncited in books on the sociology of religion. Much better to ask questions about infant baptism and about literal belief in hellfire a la Charles Y. Glock. (McCready and I have, however, made one such attempt. See *Ultimate Values of the American Population*. Los Angeles, Sage Press, 1977.)

There is then relatively little in the sociology of religion that is likely to make the empirical study of religion a respectable preoccupation with the larger profession. You can do it if you want to, but people will think you are strange if you do. Anyway, you'll be taken much more seriously as a sociologist of religion if you happen to be an agnostic. Biased? Of course not!

### *The Christian Sociologist Bears Witness*

6. *In addition to religious sensitivity, there is another potential contribution the Christian sociologist can make to his profession.* Because he is a member of an ecclesial community, and because he is personally, if not professionally, concerned about the "depth" dimensions of human life, the sociologist of religion performs an important intellectual witness-bearing function for his colleagues. The better sociologists have abandoned simpleminded modernization models which in humankind are in a unidirectional, unidimentional evolutionary hegira from one end of the Parsonian pattern variables to the other. We are not becoming more secular, more universalistic, more achievement-oriented, more specific, or more gesellschaft. The rediscovery of the primary group by such varied sociologists as Lazerfeld, Katz, Shils, and their students has pretty well established that at one end of the alleged modernization continuum we still have human beings who are meshed in a tight network of intimate relationships. Gesellschaft exists, of course, but it builds on a gemeinschaft foundation. The primary group has not evolved out of existence but continues to exist. To the extent that muscle-bound, top-heavy, bureaucratic gesellschaft society operates at all, it operates because of the persistence of the primary group.

More recently, the work of the historical demographers (or the historians of the family, as they are sometimes called) call into serious question assumptions about the other end of the modernization continuum. Private property and the nuclear family, supposedly the results of modernization, can be found in the Western world at least as far back as our solid data go, which is now to the early part of the fourteenth century.

Even though academics in general, and sociologists in particular, may be transient persons living in a temporary society, most human beings are still rooted and value their rootedness, and still belong to belief communities and value their belief. Sociologists may know this in theory, but since they encounter few such people in their daily lives (with the exception of students, and of course students are not really people) they are apt to forget that most people, even in an industrial society like our own, are not rootless alienates like the typical American academic. The Christian sociologist, almost by definition, has roots. His presence in and around campus is evidence that roots are still important for substantial numbers of human beings, even though you would not know it from reading the latest issues of the *AJS* or the *ASR*.

## Excel Professionally and Don't Be a Doormat

7. *The Christian sociologist must be good at what he does; patient with the rigidity of his non-Christian colleagues; and he must be absolutely, totally, and completely unapologetic about his religious position.* Combining the latter two requirements is not easy. For the implicit demand on the Christian sociologist is that he prove that he is capable of objective research, long after others of equal or inferior ability are accepted as approved scholars. It is unfair, biased, and bigoted, but there is no way the Christian sociologist can escape from the never ending responsibility of proving himself other than by leaving the profession (and thus escaping both the pot of boiling water and the lions). If he doesn't like the heat, he simply should not come into the kitchen.°

We bear witness to the Lord Jesus, of course, by our patience, our kindness, our charity, our long-suffering, and all those other traditional Christian virtues which are so easy to articulate—but oh, so difficult to practice. However, the Christian sociologist, while he must practice

---

° He may even find himself accused of bias from those within his own community. Three sociologists from the University of Notre Dame in a book review concluded that since I was a Catholic priest I was incapable of being objective about the present condition of the Catholic Church—thrown to the lions and cast into the boiling pot at the same time!

tolerance and forbearance in the midst of the bigotry of his secular counterparts, ought also to know where to draw the line. I will confess that in my early years as a student at the University of Chicago, and then as a member of the staff of the National Opinion Research Center, I did not draw the line when I should. I let pass the most appalling ignorance, arrogance, and patronizing bigotry (never within the walls of NORC, by the way) on the sincere but mistaken premise that they were nice people and they meant well. In retrospect, they were not nice people, and they did not mean well, and I much prefer the Irish Catholic racists on the southwest side of Chicago to the agnostic nativists in the University of Chicago environment. (Do I need to say that the *majority* of the University of Chicago faculty are not nativists and the *majority* of south side Irish Catholics are not racists?)

We do not engage in witness-bearing, as the late Cardinal Suhard of Paris said, by engaging in propaganda or by militant "convert making," nor by hard-sell evangelism. But neither do we win respect from people by being a doormat. Never pick an argument and never run from one. And when the argument finally does come, do not defend—attack. The bourgeois agnosticism of typical American sociologists is far more incoherent and inconsistent as a meaning system than is Christianity. Do not play the game by their rules because their rules say you defend and they attack. Nowhere is it written that in sociology, or in any other profession, the agnostics are the ones who make the rules. No one wins such arguments, of course. But at least the Christian sociologist will upset his secular colleague and challenge him to think a little about the ambiguities of his own position. (An agnostic, a colleague once remarked to me, is someone who is afraid there might be a God after all.)

I have not run from many fights recently—I may even have picked a few. But then that may be a character flaw found among those Christian sociologists whose ancestors hailed from the Celtic fringe (Wales, Cornwall, Brittany, the Isle of Man, the Highlands of Scotland, the south of Ireland, Queens, and Cook County).

It may be said that the view and the location of the Christian sociologist depicted in the above assertion is dispeptic and melancholy. Possibly. It is also, I fear, an accurate description of the present situation, but the situation may be changing. Though I have no data, I suspect that sociology may be one of the few enterprises of the world where the proportion of practicing Christians is actually increasing (it could not have gone down much more.) One finds more and more young Protestants, Catholics, and Jews who are committed to their religious heritages and will not permit domination of bureaucracies to eject them from their heritage, nor will they permit graduate school village atheists to resocialize them. They are a tough and impressive crowd, utterly immune to the temptations of acculturation which plagued a prior generation. I do not think these young people (such as my colleagues, William McCready and Teresa Sullivan) are going to transform sociology. Nonetheless, the presence of such young people will make the Christian witness within the profession much more difficult to dismiss. One can then face the future of the Christian sociologist with some moderate grounds for hope—the only legitimate stand for a Christian to take no matter how hopeless the situation may be.

### Discussion Questions

1. What do Christians and secular sociologists have in common? How do they differ?

2. Does Andrew Greeley think that sociologists can be value free? Is it the job of the sociologist to advocate social and moral policy? Why? Why not?

3. In what ways are some religious groups and the New Left alike? Why is their position unacceptable to the Christian sociologist?

4. In addition to ethnic minorities, what other minority is discriminated against by some in the sociology profession? What are the fears of the secularist? Is there any basis for it?

5. What problems do Christian sociologists often encounter from within their own denominations? Why are religious bureaucracies often skeptical of sociological research findings?

6. Sociologists often report "bad news," says Andrew Greeley. Can you find any similarity between some sociologists and the great eighth-century prophets of the Old Testament, such as Amos?

7. Do you agree that religious sensitivity is essential to the sociological task? Why?

8. What are Andrew Greeley's criticism of much work done in the field of the sociology of religion? What kind of religious research does he prefer and why?

9. What sort of witness does the Christian sociologist bear to his non-Christian peers? Does society at large support that witness?

10. Why is the stand Andrew Greeley takes, "Never pick an argument and never run from one," consistent with Christian commitment? Does Jesus have anything to say about justice being a manifestation of love? Discuss.

# References

Berger, Peter L.
    1969 *Rumor of Angels*. New York: Irvington.
Durkheim, Emile
    1954 (Trans. by Joseph Swain) *The Elementary Forms of the Religious Life*. Glencoe, Ill.: The Free Press.
Lenski, Gerhard
    1961 *The Religious Factor*. Garden City, N.Y.: Doubleday.
Luckmann, Charles
    1967 *The Invisible Religion*. New York: Macmillan.
McCready, William and Andrew W. Greeley
    1977 *Ultimate Values of the American Population*. Los Angeles: Sage Press.
Weber, Max
    1958 (Trans. by Talcott Parsons) *The Protestant Ethic and the Spirit of Capitalism*. New York: Scribner's.

# 10

# A Christian Perspective
# on Sociology

*George A. Hillery, Jr.*

There is a perspective that pervades most of sociology which may be labeled a "naturalistic" view of man. Though the perspective has not gone uncriticized (e.g. King and Hunt 1974), it nevertheless has some rather outspoken exponents. One of the clearest statements says,

> This naturalistic position ... has gained overwhelming popularity among modern intellectuals. It is the most fundamental premise of a scientific perspective. In its most extreme form it is the argument that any mysterious event ... can ultimately be found to have its origins in natural conditions available to our observation. ... Naturalism does not preclude the existence of mysteries; but ... it attributes them to people's ignorance of how things 'work' in the real world. Mysteries and miracles are not the product of some divine force teasing us with a dramatic display of magical happenings (Cuzzort and King, 1976:6).

The theme of this paper is that there is a viable alternative to this viewpoint that assumes a Christian perspective, as the title to the paper indicates. The perspective is by no means unique. Though its adherents are in a minority, its expression is being heard with increasing frequency. Some, indeed, argue not simply for a Christian perspective on sociology but for a Christian sociology (Jones, 1951; Heddendorf, 1972). Others take a more indirect approach (Ellul, 1964, but see Ellul, 1970; King and Hunt, 1974—the latter also have numerous references).

**George A. Hillery, Jr.**
*Professor of Sociology*
*Virginia Polytechnic Institute and State University*
Mr. Hillery received the PhD from Louisiana and previously has taught at the University of Georgia, the University of Kentucky, and the University of Iowa. He has written extensively in community theory and social organization. He is an active churchman and serves as an officer in the Presbyterian Church. Presently his special interest is the "communal movement." He is coordinator of the *Christian Sociologist.*

The task of this discussion, then, is to attempt to make as explicit as possible the value premises on which an openly Christian perspective on sociology would rest, the direction in which such a sociology would go, and its consequences for sociology in general. In examining such a perspective, it is clear that a select set of values is openly embraced. As even the quote from the naturalistic position should make clear, there is certainly no such thing as a "value-free" sociology. There are only various degrees of success in maintaining objectivity, whether because of, or in spite of, our biases.

As we begin our consideration of sociology from a Christian perspective, we can name a few approaches and subject areas which are now either not treated in depth or are virtually absent in the discipline of sociology generally. However, because sociology has gone as long as it has under the naturalistic approach, no one can hope to outline the full spectrum of a Christian perspective in one attempt. What follows is the thinking of one person concerning the direction that sociology should take from a Christian point of view. In part, it is a reflection of my own interests. More importantly, I hope, it is a position paper outlining certain parameters and constraints encountered in my work both as a sociologist and a Christian. Emphasis will be in substance more than on theory, in part because most attention by others has been given to the theoretical underpinnings (Balswick and Ward, 1976; Heddendorf, 1972, King and Hunt, 1974). Also, I am more of a research sociologist than a theologian, and so my emphasis is placed on the consequences of a Christian perspective more than on its theoretical assumptions.

## Aspects of a Christian Perspective

The question to be asked, then, is: What difference does a Christian perspective make to sociology? I will attempt to answer this question by addressing five topics: methodology, religion, freedom, love, and conflict resolution.

Before proceeding, a basic question must be asked: Is it possible to have a Christian sociology? In the total sense, the answer is negative. When one considers the demographic equation, or the relation between frustration and aggression, the relationships remain as they are regardless of one's religious (or economic or political) persuasion. But when one seeks to ascertain the reasons why a given subject is chosen (or not chosen) for study, then one's perspective becomes quite important. There is, however, a more subtle relationship.

We may begin with the premise that all truth is God's truth. The fact remains, nevertheless, that God allows us freedom to study and discover His truth without acknowledging or recognizing him. It follows, then, that one is free to pursue the act of discovery either "on his own" or as an *act of worship*. It is in this second choice that a Christian sociology develops. And it is in this very act of worship that the sociologists (and indeed any of the behavioral scientists) have an advantage that their colleagues in the natural sciences do not have. It becomes more apparent in the behavioral sciences when one is pursuing subject matter that is more congenial to the Christian perspective. Attempting to understand power, prestige, or wealth can be done from a "value-free" and or a Christian perspective. But attempting to understand love in its more basic meanings (see below) is difficult to achieve from a position of value-neutrality.

Therefore, we may conclude that there may be a Christian sociology insofar as the worshiper would attempt to follow God's will in his research.

### Methodology

Consider first the collection of data. Instead of doing everything for the sake of science, the person or the people studied would be placed first. One could not, for example, obtain data under false pretences—hidden tape recorders, hidden cameras, etc. Nor would one promise subjects a reward for undergoing an experiment, and then tell them that such a promise was only a part of the experiment and was never really meant to be awarded. "Fake" electric shocks, such as were used in certain "teaching experiments," would be avoided. Nor could one release information which could potentially harm an individual or a group.

These are not simply pleasant moral pronouncements. In the first place, each principle has been stated in reaction to some research behavior in which sociologists have been directly involved. But second, and more important, each principle is founded on the teaching of Scripture. The most general principle is that man is created in the image of God and human life is sacred. In the parable of the *Lost Sheep*, Jesus attests to the supremacy of the individual over any "cause" (Matthew 18:12-14). There is also a Christian emphasis on truthfulness. To be sure, such positions do provide impediments to the study of sociology. But the impediments are already largely with us because most sociology is already done within a Judeo-Christian framework of values. The difference between a Christian perspective and the present state of sociology is that the Christian perspective would make explicit the value-premises on which it is based (Heddendorf, 1972).

Since the Christian definitely starts with a number of value-premises, any ill-conceived notions of a value-free sociology would be further discredited. There would still, however, be the obligation to strive toward the *art* of objectivity. It is, in fact, quite possible to have a commitment to a set of values and still be objective. Games such as chess or tennis provide illustrations. Each player is committed to win. And yet, success in winning requires that each player not only be honest, but also able to anticipate the other's moves. Thus, in spite of the commitment *against* one's opponent, one still has the requirement of honestly looking at the world through his opponent's eyes.

A Christian perspective, furthermore, would not limit itself only to that which could be measured or quantified. This position is shared with non-Christian sociologists, but here it is adopted as a matter of principle. There are a number of areas in particular that are essentially not quantifiable, though aspects of it may be. The Christian perspective, further, would not even limit itself to science (though science is not synonymous with quantification.) It would be perfectly free to investigate such topics as the relation between prayer and joy or peace, topics that would be difficult to integrate into the modern schema as sociology is practiced today (Hillery, 1973).

There is also a problem with the choice of a subject. As I look at the work of various sociologists who are Christians, I notice an overconcentration of effort in such fields as the sociology of religion and very little in such areas as complex organization. This problem of concentration in subject areas needs to be more thoroughly researched before it can be stated with certainty. If, however, the charge has substance, let us make plain the admonition that there are few areas, if any, that should be avoided by sociologists because of their faith. While there are certain areas neglected by sociologists in general which a Christian perspective should explore, it is quite another matter to avoid areas of investigation because one feels that the subject matter is incompatible with one's belief. Perhaps there are such areas. But if Jesus could associate with thieves, prostitutes, tax collectors, and even military officers, there is no reason why a Christian sociologist should avoid them.

Before proceeding, it should be made clear that there is nothing in a Christian perspective that would make one avoid or even minimize the importance of science. The truths obtained through the testing of propositional statements—especially quantitative statements—are no less truth because of their objectivity. What is being asked for is more, not less, truth. The position taken here is that there are many kinds of truths, and a few words are required on these.

*Types of Truth*

The problem of exploring the nature of truth is both metaphysical and epistemological (Hillery, 1978). The metaphysical problem involves the nature of the assumptions concerning reality. The scientist limits himself by the assumption that reality is based on physical data, whereas a mystic assumes that there is also a superphysical, i.e., a spiritual reality. (Some assume that *only* spiritual things are real—all else is illusion. For the sake of simplicity, we will ignore this assumption.) Nonetheless, regardless of one's assumptions of reality, there are different ways of experiencing that reality, in the sense of the type of evidence one will accept as truth. The experience may be direct, such as hearing sounds, or being inebriated, or perceiving God. This is the experiential aspect. Such experience can only be communicated to others in part, if at all. On the other hand, some types of experience may be communicated rather precisely, such as the designation of sounds by means of musical notes, or discerning the alcoholic content of blood, or describing the fact that Christians believe in a triune God. This is the objective aspect.

The combination of the metaphysical and epistemological dimensions reveals four types of truth (no claim is made that these are the only types of truth): mystical, theological, sensory, and scientific. They are depicted in Figure 1 on page 164.

Whether scientific or theological, most written discussions are objective, in the sense that "objective" is being used here. Seldom can writing be experiential, though poetry and novels come close. Nonetheless there is frequently a dependence of objective on experiential truth. Just as a scientist tends to be more satisfied when he has done an experiment himself, a theologian's writings take on an added dimension when he has undergone a mystical experience. But the separation between the two types of truth is often quite discrete. An example from sensory truth will help show the distinction. One who has never been

FIGURE 1. Types of Truth

| Metaphysics: Type of reality that is assumed: | Epistemology: Method of knowing: | |
|---|---|---|
| | Experiential | Objective |
| Spiritual | Mystical truth | Theological truth |
| Physical | Sensory truth | Scientific truth |

drunk may do a breath analysis and establish that someone else is drunk. He may understand this analysis sufficiently to cause the drunk to be placed in jail. But he will not experientially understand what it is to be drunk.

The same can be said for mystical truth. The theologian may understand that Christians believe in a triune God. He may have faith in such a God himself, and he may even be able to prescribe certain theological readings to help someone else understand God. But that does not mean that he knows God in that he has had a mystical experience with him.

One of the major purposes in presenting such a discussion is to help to demarcate more precisely the boundary of science. A major assumption of the Christian perspective is that the world cannot be understood purely from the scientific point of view, as here defined. The question arises, then, what is the perspective that exists outside of science? Granted that some of the topics to be treated here are not considered "sociology" as the term is generally used. However, the thesis I am advancing is that in order to understand social behavior and in order to study society properly (i.e., socio*logy*), the customary horizons of sociology must be extended.

Most sociologists concentrate on scientific truth, as here defined. Occasionally, some venture into sensory truth, particularly through participant observation. What I am calling for is research into various kinds of spiritual truth, both mystical and theological. The Christian assumes the reality of a spiritual world. He assumes further that there is a symbiotic relationship, a mutual influencing between the spiritual and the physical worlds. If we logically follow these assumptions, then we must be willing to do research in the spiritual world also.

Such investigations would require one to do such things as interview mystics, charismatics, and pentecostals concerning their experiences. In addition, the investigator should record his own religious experiences, study various types of prayer, and observe what happens to the people and groups who practice them. The problem is not that we do not have such research, but unless the sociologist has had experience, such research is necessarily somewhat limited. It must be admitted from the start, if our assumptions about the spiritual realm are correct, that much of what we study will *not* be translatable into physical sociology. Also we must be willing to face the possibility that some of what was once considered to be in the spiritual realm really belongs in the physical.

I am asking essentially for a return to Weber's *verstehen* (understanding) sociology–and with a vengeance. Prediction is fine, but we need not stop our research if we cannot predict. We must understand, and a basic tenet of Christianity is that understanding is not limited to the physical world.

*Religion*

I must confess, first, that the sociology of religion is not my specialty. Nevertheless, since my research has impinged on this area occasionally, some observations seem pertinent.

In many ways, the study of religion is one of the most difficult for the Christian sociologist. First, the nearly obvious point should be made that a Christian perspective is not synonymous with the study of religion. A Christian perspective signifies a particular point of view rather than subject area. This point of view can be illustrated by examining the way a Christian sociologist would view the field of religion.

Benton Johnson, in an unpublished but extremely challenging article, has leveled the charge that the sociology of religion as it is currently practiced is "to put it bluntly . . . agnostic" (Johnson, 1975:4). Although this charge cannot be made of all sociologists who specialize in the field of religion, agnosticism is plainly evident in certain critical areas. One of the most critical is the very definition of religion itself, as belief in ultimate reality. According to this formulation, practically anything can be religious. The atheist who believes that ultimately all reality is chance and/or chaos is to be considered religious! Such a definition is no definition at all. (See the discussion on this point in Robertson, 1970; also Fallding, 1974).

The Christian perspective would emphasize religion as the belief in the supernatural (see Gould and Kolb, 1964). At the very least, such a definition would alert us to the interesting problem that all cultures (whether or not all people) acknowledge and react to such a belief. As one anthropologist said of anthropology: We should develop a view of religion "that does not presuppose the absence of the supernatural."

## Freedom

A survey of the indexes of the *American Journal of Sociology* (1895-1970) and the *American Sociological Review* (1935-1970) reveals only two and three articles respectively under the heading of freedom. These are, of course, only indexes in themselves of the importance of the topic. Parsons, for example, stressed voluntarism in his early work. But my point is that the study of freedom would be an essential task for those who take a Christian perspective in sociology, since freedom is so central to the Christian view. In spite of abuses, acceptance of Christianity cannot be forced. Further, a Christian view presupposes a free will (within limits, of course), while at the same time it admits to at least some degrees of predestination. The point here is not to argue the validity of either free will or predestination. The point is that a Christian can emphasize neither at the total expense of the other. The naturalistic view of science which maintains that all can be explained by science is simply carrying predestination to its logical conclusion. A Christian sociologist would also investigate the other side of the coin.

The purpose of this discussion is not to develop a sociology of freedom, though that would be in itself an important topic (Hillery, 1978; Hillery, Dudley, and Morrow, 1977). Nevertheless, a few words must be said on the meaning of freedom to clarify my perspective. First, one must distinguish sociological from psychological aspects of freedom (Hillery, 1971). Sociologically, one could define freedom in terms of the norms governing movement over space: (1) the most open type of group would be the most free, one in which anyone could enter or leave as he wished. (2) Most groups require some sort of permission to enter, and thus lose one degree of freedom. (3) Some groups, such as monasteries and certain hospitals, require that at least some of the members (usually, the inmates or clients) have permission to come and go. (4) Prisons and some mental asylums prohibit their members from leaving. (5) Solitary confinement represents the loss of a fourth degree of freedom. (6) Maintaining control over inmates through the use of drugs represents perhaps the ultimate in loss of freedom short of death. Note that these norms have nothing to do with the feelings or attitudes of those involved. We have here a strictly sociological concept of freedom (as opposed to a psychological one).

On the psychological side, one could define freedom in terms of perception. My colleagues and I have identified four types (Hillery et *al.* 1977; Dudley and Hillery, 1977). First, there is the overall feeling of being deprived of freedom. On the other hand, there are (in terms of our research) three different ways of viewing the freedom that one does have. Disciplined freedom refers to the feeling that freedom requires sharing and sacrifice. Egoistic freedom is the type one experiences when he feels that he can "do his thing." Conditional freedom is akin to egoistic freedom, except that other conditions, specifically other people and things, must be taken into consideration.

Trappist monks, more than any other group yet studied, see their condition as one of disciplined freedom. Forty-six groups have now been examined. The "do your own thing" type of urban commune, not surprisingly, exhibits most clearly egoistic freedom, particularly where little more is required of the "members" than they pay the rent. Finally, conditional freedom is more of an institutional phenomenon, particularly well-developed in homes for the aged and boarding schools (Dudley and Hillery, 1977).

It is significant for our purposes that the monks score most highly on disciplined freedom. Further research is needed, of course, but one could suggest that disciplined freedom is the consequence of surrendering egoistic or conditional freedom. Both of these are relatively immature types: egoistic freedom being synonymous with license; conditional freedom being a compromise with reality. Truly, only disciplined freedom comes with commitment. That last statement may be regarded as a prime example of the type of problem which a Christian sociologist would investigate.

*Love*

From the Christian perspective, this topic is clearly the most important. A search similar to that conducted for freedom through the indexes of two of the major American sociological journals shows two references during the 75-year period in the *American Journal of So-*

*ciology* and four during the 34-year history of the *American Sociological Review*. Further, all of these apparently refer to romantic and/or sexual love. Other types of love are not mentioned, in spite of Durkheim's work on altruistic suicide and Sorokin's studies of altruistic love (Sorokin, 1948, 1950, 1954).

Since love is important to the Christian perspective it requires extensive treatment. Accordingly, brief mention should be given to some of the types of love. A central premise, however, is that love cannot be understood unless it has been experienced (Hillery, 1978).

Because of the importance of experiential truth, any verbal description is necessarily limited. Thus, while we can *suggest* a definition and a typology of love, we cannot *give* one (certainly not in an operational sense!). Accordingly, love is that condition wherein one attempts to work for the best interests of the beloved. From this point of view, we may begin with the Greek conceptions of love. One of the words used by Paul and the earliest Christians to discuss love was *agape:* it meant love in its purest sense, i.e., self-giving love. An alternative was *eros,* which has come to denote what Renaissance poets called "profane" love. The original meaning was not limited to sexual love, but we shall emphasize that meaning here (see the entry, "Love," in Gould and Kolb, 1964).

Two other types of love are designated as fraternal and parental, admitting that the terms are not completely descriptive. (The corresponding Greek terms are *philos* and *storgos*—see Lewis 1960.) Fraternal love is that between friends, whether they be brother, sister, or initially a stranger. Parental love refers to both the love of parents for children and vice versa, though emphasis is on parental love. While one could undoubtedly provide additional types, these will suffice here.

These types of love may be seen as related to two variables; physical contact and detachment (see Figure 2). Physical contact is absolutely essential to erotic and parental love, but is not as important to fraternal or agapic love. On the other hand, parental love demands that the parent must be willing to relinquish certain rights to the child; that is, the parent must exhibit some degree of detachment. Normally, one does not consider such a condition necessary to erotic love ("Therefore a man leaves his father and his mother and cleaves to his wife, and they become one flesh." Genesis 2:24). In other words, there is a certain element of possessiveness to both fraternal and erotic love. In the same vein, agape love also carries a sense of detachment; indeed, it reveals the maximum amount of detachment love can have, if we consider Jesus as the prototype.

FIGURE 2. Types of Love

|  |  | Willingness to Be Detached | |
|---|---|---|---|
|  |  | no | yes |
| Physical Contact | yes | erotic | parental |
|  | no | fraternal | agapic |

Love is the central fact of the Christian message. We need only refer to the new commandment (John 13:34) or Paul's superb characterization in 1 Corinthians 13. In fact, love is the entire meaning of the cross and the resurrection. Undeniably we do not live up to this commandment. But the human deficiency does not negate the message. Nor does our deficiency contradict the fact that much of our lives is lived in love. The importance of erotic love in human affairs is obvious. And (again) in spite of our failure, the fact that millions of children grow to adulthood to form new families of their own attests to the significance of parental love.

It is not easy to point to the significance of fraternal love in everyday life, and it is even less easy to speak of the existence of agape. There may indeed be a progressive diminishing in the extent to which these loves are realized: Most encounter erotic love, fewer achieve parental love, less fraternal love, and fewest agapic love. But even so, we cannot excuse the lack of attention given those non-erotic types of love. To give them our research emphasis—whether through scientific and/or other truths—would be the greatest contribution Christian sociologists could make. For then we may come to realize that the ultimate fulcrum in history is neither power nor prestige nor wealth, but love. The human world ultimately turns on love, for all its efforts to turn to other things.

A final caution: Emphasizing the study of love does not mean deemphasizing conflict. Quite the contrary, we need only indicate the lover's quarrel, the parent's punishment of the child, disagreement among friends, and finally, Jesus' conflict not only with the Pharisees but also with his disciples (Peter in particular—see, for example, Matthew 16:23). In fact it can be argued that conflicts of a low level of intensity (generally short of violence) are indispensable to a full development of the love relationship.

### Interpersonal Conflict Resolution

There are numerous other topics that could be addressed within a Christian perspective on sociology, but we shall close with a consideration of interpersonal conflict resolution. This choice is prompted by several considerations. First, if it is true that love requires some degree of conflict, then it is even more critical that conflict resolution be studied. The need to understand conflict resolution is especially heightened since conflict has a way of being escalated beyond desirable limits, such as murder, (to cite the most extreme form). If we are to have love, then we must find some way of resolving conflict. Second, we have emphasized pure research in this discussion, but a Christian sociology must also deal with applied questions. Third, little work has been done on the question of interpersonal conflict resolution, from any perspective.

An important caveat before proceeding: I am a sociologist, not a psychologist, or even a social psychologist. Thus, I am somewhat out of my field, since I study groups rather than individuals. Not that my training makes me completely incapable of working in this area, but the field of interpersonal conflict resolution is not the area in which I feel most comfortable. My concern is that I see few others doing anything about it. Particularly is this true of my colleagues in other fields. We know much about intergroup conflict (such as wars, riots, etc.) and much about intrapersonal conflict (such as psychological problems, psychiatric disorders, etc.), but little about interpersonal conflict (such as quarrels, fights, grudges, etc.). We have such problems whether in monasteries or prisons. I see the problem. And so I feel I must comment (Hillery, 1976).

There is a myth in our culture that conflict is somehow "bad." The fact is, however, that most groups in this world, and practically all groups where members have been together for any length of time, are involved in interpersonal conflict. But before we can say more, we must define conflict. For purposes of this discussion, conflict includes simple disagreements, arguments with tension, antagonisms, arguments with shouting, use of physical force, hurting someone, use or threat of weapons, and ultimately murder. There are, admittedly, other ways of defining conflict; it will be these phenomena which we will include within the concept (Hillery, 1971, Hillery and Morrow, 1976, Hillery, 1978).

To be sure, conflict as here defined covers a wide variety of behaviors. For purposes of simplicity, therefore, we will think of conflict as ranging within two extremes: *disputes* cover disagreements, tensions, and antagonisms; *violence* covers shouting, force, harm, and use of weapons (and/or murder). During the past seven years I have collected data on these concepts from 46 groups having more than a total of 1,600 members. The groups include monasteries, communes, old age homes, boarding schools, prisons, college and university dormitories, military groups, fraternities, sororities, a drug rehabilitation center, and a social work agency. *All* groups have shown a considerable amount of disputes among the members during the year preceding the interview (ranging from 40 to 100 percent). And although only two groups have registered no violence, all others have, ranging to a high of 43 percent of the population being involved in violent acts (in a boarding school for unmanageable children). If a group registers no conflict (even no violence), my first reactions are that (1) the members have not been together very long (as was true in both cases that registered no violence), (2) they do not know each other very well, or (3) they do not interact very much.

Some of my colleagues who are Christian sociologists have expressed the desire to investigate the extent to which they can demonstrate the sociological truths that are contained in the Bible. If there was ever an area in which this could be done, conflict resolution is such an area. For example, Jesus said: "If your brother sins against you, go and tell him his fault, between you and him alone. If he listens ... you have gained your brother. But if he does not listen, take one or two others along with you. ... If he refuses to listen to them, tell it to the church; and if he refuses to listen even to the church, let him be to you as a Gentile and a tax collector" (Matthew 18:15-17).

Again: "Peter came up and said to him, 'Lord, how often shall my brother sin against me, and I forgive him? As many as seven times?' Jesus said to him, 'I do not say to you seven times, but seventy times seven'" (Matthew 18:21, 22). And we should continually recall that Jesus said, "forgive us our trespasses as we forgive those who trespass against us." True forgiveness is not only a means to conflict resolution but can be a true resolution in itself. Once again, for a prescription that we pass over too lightly: "So if you are offering your gift at the altar, and there remember that your brother has something against you, leave your gift there before the altar and go; first be reconciled to your brother, and then come and offer your gift" (Matthew 5:23, 24).

Notice that Jesus does not tell us to become reconciled if *we* have something against our brother—he tells us to become reconciled if our brother has something against *us.*

One should not neglect to mention Jesus' words in Luke 17:3 where he says that repentance should *precede* forgiveness. Approaching the offended individual, asking for forgiveness is one of the easiest ways to resolve conflict and effect reconciliation.

Finally (and these examples are not meant to be exhaustive), Paul says: "Be angry but do not sin; do not let the sun go down on your anger" (Ephesians 4:26). This rule I have found effective in marriages as well as in cloisters, in business as well as in play. In fact, the real problems usually occur when the principle is ignored.

There are more such biblical prescriptions. These are simply a few mentioned to show their relevance and significance. Scripture is, after all, the end product of more than two thousand years of experience. It has something to offer sociology also.

Before closing these remarks on conflict resolution, some distinctions must be made. First, there is the distinction between conflict resolution in the sense of feedback on the one hand, and healing or therapy on the other. This distinction can best be illustrated by an analogy. In the process of driving an automobile, we continually adjust our steering as we get feedback from the road and the conditions around us. The steering may be compared with conflict resolution. But, should the automobile suddenly not respond to our steering, we stop immediately and have the mechanism repaired. The repairs may be likened to healing or therapy. We are all aware of conditions wherein conflict resolution is, if not impossible, certainly not practical. The conflict may have gone on too long for either party, or we may be aware of old scars that are simply not amenable to resolution. What is needed is not resolution but therapy.

Also, we should distinguish between conflict resolution and conflict management. The agreement not to discuss certain matters is an example—as between Democrats and Republicans who are otherwise good friends. No therapy is involved here—simply an agreement to disagree. But neither will there be a resolution, as all are aware. More important, there may be occasion in some instances to "get away"—as on a hike. Tensions build up that may possibly be relieved simply by some form of management. Nothing is resolved. But all may realize that there will be a continuation of things that cannot be changed, and that another hike or picnic or whatever may well be prescribed in the future. Since we know of no other way to correct things, such conflict management is the only apparent way.

## Conclusions

Should a Christian perspective on sociology develop, beginning along the lines suggested here, what difference would it make to sociology as a whole? Initially, very little. Statistical techniques would still have their place. Data would be gathered by participant observation, surveys, secondary analysis, etc., as it has been. Even the topics under which various facets of the discipline are studied would probably remain the same. But I envision some changes gradually making their appearance with increasing frequency. We may eventually expect to find less dependence on quantitative techniques and less insistance that sociology be only a science. (This latter development would probably have to wait until sociology became more certain of its accomplishments.) At any rate, more emphasis would be placed on understanding the human condition instead of *only* predicting it. The specific topic of love in all of its ramifications would be developed—not only its expression through sex. Furthermore, we would explore other topics such as joy, peace, kindness, goodness, faithfulness, gentleness, self-control (Galatians 5:22, 23). I sense there is probably embarrassment even among some Christian sociologists at the mention of such topics, and if so, we should examine carefully the reason for such attitudes. We ignore these areas at our own peril—physical as well as spiritual.

In all probability, we can expect many of the basic issues of sociology to remain. Christian or not, there will always be some who prefer hard to soft data, psychological to organizational approaches, pure to applied emphases, etc. But whatever the issue, there is always a need to understand society, and there is always a need to have our theories agree with our data. These two approaches are at the heart of any sociology, no matter what the issues or the perspective.

Notwithstanding such constancy, the Christian sees things differently. He is concerned with the person of Jesus—not simply his teaching or his example, but with communion with him. And certainly herein lies the ultimate distinction: the Christian no longer writes or does his research for himself. He has relinquished his will and his desire to a higher force, even a personal force, and in the end all the differences will stem from that.

## Discussion Questions

1. In what way is the naturalistic position opposed to a Christian perspective?

2. What areas of sociological research could you propose as being relevant to a Christian perspective, other than those mentioned in the discussion? Explain their relevance.

3. Could you propose other areas of truth than those listed in the discussion? If so, what are they? If not, why not?

4. What is the relation (and the lack of relation) between Christianity and science?

5. What difference does it make to the study of religion in the way in which one defines religion?

6. What does freedom have to do with a Christian perspective on sociology?

7. Draw up a plan of research which would show the relation between the various types of love and social cohesion. (Note there are scales already designed to measure cohesion, and these should be consulted.)

8. Why should a Christian sociologist study conflict?

9. What are some biblical prescriptions for conflict resolution, other than those listed in the discussion?

10. How would one proceed in testing the accuracy of some of the biblical prescriptions for conflict resolution?

## References

Balswick, Jack and Dawn Ward
1976 "The Nature of Man and Scientific Models of Society." *Journal of the American Scientific Affiliation,* 28, pp. 181-185.
Cuzzort, R. P. and E. W. King
1976 *Humanity and Modern Social Thought.* Hinsdale, Ill.: The Dryden Press.
Dudley, Charles J. and George A. Hillery, Jr.
1977 "Freedom and Alienation in Homes for the Aged." *The Gerontologist,* 17, pp. 140-145.
Ellul, Jaques
1964 *The Technological Society.* New York: Random House (Vintage Books).

1970 *The Meaning of the City.* Grand Rapids: Eerdmans.
Fallding, Harold
1974 *The Sociology of Religion.* Toronto: McGraw-Hill Ryerson Ltd.
Gould, Julius and William L. Kolb (eds.)
1964 *A Dictionary of the Social Sciences.* New York: Free Press.
Heddendorf, Russell
1972 "Some Presuppositions of a Christian Sociology." *Journal of the American Scientific Affiliation*, 24, pp. 110-117.
Hillery, George A., Jr.
1971 "Freedom and Social Organization." *American Sociological Review*, 36, pp. 51-65.
1973 "A Sociological Analysis of Contemplative Prayer." Unpublished paper read before the Association for the Sociology of Religion, August 25, New York City.
1976 "Conflict Resolution and Fraternal Correction." *Monastic Exchange*, 8, pp. 50-55.
1978 "Freedom, Love, and Community: An Outline of a Theory." *Transaction/Society*, 15, pp. 24-31.
Hillery, George A. Jr. and Paula C. Morrow
1976 "The Monastery as a Commune." *International Review of Modern Sociology*, 6, pp. 139-154.
Hillery, George A., Jr., Charles J. Dudley, and Paula C. Morrow
1977 "Toward a Sociology of Freedom." *Social Forces*, 55, pp. 685-700.
Johnson, Benton
1975 "Faith, Facts, and Values in the Sociology of Religion." Lecture delivered at King College, Bristol, Tennessee.
Jones, G. V.
1951 "Some Presuppositions of a Christian Sociology." *The Expository Times*, 62, pp. 163-166.
King, Morton B. and Richard A. Hunt
1974 "Moral Man and Immoral Science?" *Sociological Analysis*, 35, pp. 240-250.
Lewis, C. S.
1960 *The Four Loves.* New York: Harcourt Brace and Janovich, Inc.
Robertson, Roland
1970 *The Sociological Interpretation of Religion.* Oxford: Basil Blackwell.
Sorokin, Pitirim A.
1948 *The Reconstruction of Humanity.* Boston: Beacon Press.
1950 *Altruistic Love: A Study of American Good Neighbors and Christian Saints.* Boston: Beacon Press.
1954 *The Ways and Power of Love.* Boston: Beacon Press.

# PART III

# SOCIOLOGICAL THEORY: A CHRISTIAN APPROACH

# SOCIOLOGICAL THEORY: A CHRISTIAN APPROACH

"Don't let the secular society squeeze you into its mold, and don't conform to its patterns of behavior," is an accurate paraphrase of Romans 12:2. Here Paul expresses two basic biblical truths: first, secular society (the "world") is often an evil force that can rob Christians of a fruitful life, and second, you and I have freedom to resist and overcome the constraints of society.

Constructing a model depicting how society is structured and functions is one of the basic tasks of the sociologist. While empirical evidence is usually gathered to support a theoretical model, it is based upon assumptions. One of the difficulties you face is to chose a model that accurately represents the way society functions. Not all sociologists can agree on a single model. You will probably do what most of the Christian sociologists contributing to Part III have done—construct an eclectic model utilizing biblical principles.

The most popular analogies of society are based on evolutionist, functional, or conflict models. The *evolutionist model* envisions society passing through successive stages from "primitive" to "advanced." Herbert Spencer, influenced by Darwin, was one of the early advocates of this model. He was followed by men like Emile Durkheim, Ferdinand Tonnies, and Howard Becker. Generally speaking, they saw society changing from rural, agricultural, and traditional to urban, industrial, and secular. Obviously not all societies change at the same rate.

Even within a given society the rate of change will vary.

The *functional (or structure-functionalist) model* likens society to a living organism in which each part contributes to the well-being of the whole. (Paul used the analogy of the human body for the church in 1 Corinthians 12.) While society is undoubtedly pluralistic (composed of various groups), it is assumed that all share a common consensus about societal goals and values. The skeletal system of the organism, its structure, is composed of the major institutions in society (family, government, economy, religion, education). While these institutions and their various parts all interact with and on one another, a healthy equilibrium is maintained. Threats to the organism are met in such a way as to maintain stability. Talcott Parsons is the leading advocate of this position, but since World War II its popularity has given way to the conflict model.

The *conflict model* accepts conflict as the basic ingredient in society. Conflict develops whenever any group challenges the dominant or majority group in control of resources and power. Marx, the father of conflict theory, saw the rich and powerful (*bourgeoisie*) controlling and exploiting the worker (*proletariat*). It was society, basically the economic institution controlled by the bourgeoisie, that was the oppressor and culprit. For Marx, only a revolution by the proletariat could save man from capitalist oppression. Modern disciples of the Marxian model include scholars such as C. Wright Mills, Ralf Dahrendorf, and Irving L. Horowitz.

In Part III the authors evaluate models by biblical principles. They see the nature of man as one of the keys to model building and understanding society. Some theories view man's behavior as determined or controlled by society. (The old Calvinistic religious notion of *predestination* is replaced by the secular belief in *cultural determinism*.) Persons become pawns in the hands of societal forces. But Christian sociologists do not entirely agree. They view man as a free agent who, though limited by society, can direct and control it.

Stan Gaede critiques both the functional and conflict models, synthesizing them and emerging with a Christian perspective. It is not society or man that is evil—both are. Both, however, can and must be redeemed. Conflict and stability are part of the human condition and essential to a healthy functioning society.

Richard A. Russell argues that philosophical presuppositions lie behind the secular humanism and the positivism that pervades modern sociological thought, and that some kind of religious commitment (ultimate values) is assumed by philosophers. Since scientific objectivity is a myth, he calls for openness to other perspectives in both communities. He also challenges Christian sociologists to build a unique perspective of their own—not an eclectic one composed of "bricks" from non-Christian perspectives and models.

Margaret M. Poloma presents an *interpretative model* of society. She acknowledges that the social structure shapes man, but insists that the individual can also shape the society he lives in "through subjective interpretations of reality." She rejects the extremes of both naturalistic and humanistic definitions of person and society in favor of a biblical/sociological view. Her concept of person is that he/she has fallen, hence a "fallen" society. But in Christ both are capable of renewal.

Coming to terms with Karl Marx is essential. Michael L. Yoder analyzes and compares Marxian and Christian concepts. He suggests that Marx is more in line with the Hebrew prophets' social preachments than Christians wish to admit. Furthermore, mainline Christianity is at odds with the basic teachings of Christ. Richard D. Christy raises the question, Was Marx really a sociologist? Whether a sociologist or not, Marx certainly presents a challenge to Christianity. From the vantage point of a Christian adventist sect he points up some crucial differences between the two systems of thought.

# 11

# Functionalism and Conflict Theory in Christian Perspective: Toward an Alternative View of Order and Conflict

*Stan Gaede*

The functional and conflict models of social reality have been well critiqued in the last two decades.[1] Functionalism in particular, after its post-World War II ascendancy, has become the object of much castigation, verbal abuse, and, at times, ridicule.[2] In part, this critique has been generated by those influenced by the Marxian perspective. The latter's popularity no doubt reflects the growing predisposition among younger social theorists toward the Hegelian-Marxian dialectic. Nevertheless, functionalists have willingly entered the debate, and they have managed to critique themselves as well as the new Marxists.[3]

Every dialogue produces its own mediators, and the functional-conflict debate is not without its synthesizers. While early attempts were aimed either at explaining conflict within a functional model or specifying the functions of conflict[4], numerous contemporary theorists have advocated a third model—a synthesis incorporating the findings of both the functional and conflict models. Outstanding among these are the works of Pierre L. van den Berghe and Gerhard Lenski.[5] Their common assumption is that there is a certain degree of truth in the

**Stan D. Gaede**
*Associate Professor of Sociology*
*Gordon College*
Mr. Gaede received his PhD from Vanderbilt University with a primary focus on the sociology of religion, community, and social stratification. An elder in the North Shore Community Baptist Church, Beverly Farms, Massachusetts, he has also taught at the University of Tennessee and Houghton College, and has published articles in the area of sociology and religion. In addition to his teaching, Mr. Gaede is Dean of Students at Gordon.

polemics of the debaters, and that a synthesis of these truths is both desirable and possible.

In this chapter we will enter the functional-conflict debate in order to examine its philosophical and theoretical roots from the perspective of a Christian world and life view.[6] Our approach will include (1) a brief exposition of the basic assumptions of the functional and conflict models, (2) a review of the critiques and resolutions generated by the synthesizers, (3) the presentation of an alternative model, incorporating Christian presuppositions and addressing the issues raised in the functional-conflict debate, and (4) an assessment of the dominant models and their synthesizers from the perspective of our Christian alternative. Given the global nature of our objectives, the reader may wish to provide us with *a priori* forgiveness for the terse and sometimes superficial manner in which rather weighty issues are handled.

## Functional and Conflict Theory
### *Functional Theory*

The literature on functionalism is immense[7] and we shall not attempt an exhaustive review at this time. Rather, we shall take as a given the credibility of van den Berghe's treatment and allow his summarization of the basic postulates of functionalism to stand as the point of departure for our discussion. Relying on Parsons, Merton, and Davis, van den Berghe reduces the structural-functional position to these seven postulates:

1. Societies must be looked at holistically as systems of interrelated parts.

2. Hence causation is multiple and reciprocal.

3. Although integration is never perfect, social systems are fundamentally in a state of dynamic equilibrium, i.e., adjustive responses to outside changes tend to minimize the final amount of change within the system.

4. As a corollary of #3, dysfunctions, tensions, and "deviance" do exist and can persist for a long time, but they tend to resolve themselves or to be "institutionalized."

5. Change generally occurs in a gradual, adjustive fashion, and not in a sudden, revolutionary way.

6. Change comes from basically three sources: adjustment to exogenous (or extra-systemic) change, growth through structural and functional differentiation, and inventions or innovations by members or groups within society.

7. The most important and basic factor making for social integration is value consensus, i.e. . . . broad aims or principles which most members of a given social system consider desirable and agree on (van den Berghe, 1963:696).

Van den Berghe does an admirable job of enumerating the basic elements of the functionalist position, but he makes no such attempt in his discussion of the "Hegelian-Marxian dialectic." And for good reason. The latter position is embraced by a diversity of individuals, with remarkably dissimilar backgrounds and theoretical inclinations. Moreover, given van den Berghe's discussion of this school of thought, the reader is left with the clear impression that he is much more comfortable with (and competent in presenting) a functionalist rather than Marxian perspective.[8]

*Conflict Theory*

Fools rush in where van den Berghe fears to tread. Despite this, we feel it is important to articulate a conflict position that corresponds to the functionalist statements previously specified. If we do not, we run the risk of critiquing "straw men," not to mention alienating a large segment of our audience. What follows then is a list of seven positional statements attempting to address the issues raised above from the perspective of the conflict theorist. By "conflict theorist," we mean those such as Mills, Dahrendorf, Gouldner, Moore, and Horowitz who have followed Marx in identifying "the underlying reality in all groups" as a "series of more-or-less powerful tensions and conflicts" (Friedrichs, 1970:45). We do not assume that our list of conflict postulates is either exhaustive or explanatorily adequate. We would argue, however, that they are a fair representation of the perspective embraced by those who identify themselves as conflict theorists. With that in mind, let us reduce this perspective to the following elements:

1. Societies are not functional systems, but settings within which societal sub-units (classes, parties, interest groups, etc.) are in constant conflict and struggle.
2. Social conflict arises from the antithetical interests of societal sub-units, each of which is struggling to maintain or achieve advantage.
3. Social equilibrium is brief and temporary, arising from the dominance of one sub-unit and the false consciousness of disadvantaged sub-units.

4. Social change is inevitable and tends to be sudden and cataclysmic.

5. Change is dialectical, the product of conflict between polarized societal sub-units and the continual replacement (or threat thereof) of dominant sub-units by previously disadvantaged ones.

6. The most important factor contributing to social conflict is the domination of power, goods and services, and prestige by one sub-unit and the disadvantaged position of other societal sub-units relative to these items.

7. Material inequality results in value disensus between societal sub-units and social disintegration.

## Synthesis and the Issue of Presuppositions

At first glance, it is difficult to see how any synthesis of these two positions is possible. After all, one posits a society of stability, equilibrium, and consensus while the other assumes instability, disequilibrium, and conflict. Can such a fundamental antithesis be brought to resolution?

Van den Berghe thinks it can and his method is disarmingly simple. His thesis is that societies show *both* stability and instability, consensus and conflict. The major problem with both schools of thought, according to van den Berghe, is that they concentrate wholly upon, and tend to reify, only one aspect of social reality. Their social vision is not incorrect, but only myopically limited. Thus, the main problem with functionalism is not that it assumes a stable, integrated society, but that it fails to account for the fact that many societies "fall far short of complete consensus, and often exhibit considerable dissension about basic values" (van den Berghe, 1963:697). He goes on to point out that functionalism fails to recognize that (1) social change is not always adjustive, but can lead to greater problems, (2) societies can go through long periods of increasing malintegration, (3) change can be revolutionary (not adjustive), and (4) social change can result from internal conflicts and contradictions with society.

Similarly, van den Berghe does not find fault with the Marxist's claim that social conflict is endemic to social structure and that such conflict gives rise to change. It is, rather, the claim that "the dialectical process is the *only* source of change" and that conflicts *always* polarize into pairs of opposites that the author adamantly rejects. Once again, van den Berghe asserts that like the functionalist, the conflict theorist tends to take one element of social reality (conflict) and assume its normativity. Not surprisingly, van den Berghe concludes his paper by calling for a synthesis that assumes the existence of both conflict and consensus and an approach that attempts to explain their dual role in society.

If van den Berghe's analysis is elegantly simple, it is also somewhat simplistic. For while his assertion of the mutual existence of conflict and stability is empirically compelling, it is theoretically and philosophically weak. It ignores completely the fundamental reasons why social theorists in both camps have arrived at their conclusions. In addition, it naively assumes that a simple empirical observation can resolve an issue rooted in long historical debate. Neither Talcott Parsons (a functionalist) nor C. Wright Mills (a conflict theorist) suddenly discovered one morning that there was much order or conflict in the world. They are, more accurately, twentieth-century representatives of two different views of humanity and society, each attempting to explain the very meaning of life itself. If they tend to ignore order or conflict in their sociological analyses, it is not merely due to empirical oversight, but it is also due to a fair amount of logical deduction. And if, as we believe, their empirical conclusions are not wholly satisfactory, it has implications for the whole of their philosophical-theoretical approach. It cannot be corrected by a simple empirical slap on the wrist.

It is his recognition of presuppositional issues that sets off Gerhard Lenski's treatment of the functional-conflict debate from van den Berghe's. In *Power and Privilege* Lenski demonstrates that the perspectives of contemporary conflict and functional theorists are fundamentally rooted in two conceptions of mankind. The first, which he labels the "conservative thesis," has been articulated by such men as Aristotle, Saint Paul, Adam Smith, and Darwin. This view tends:

> (1) to be distrustful of human nature, (2) to emphasize the important role of social institutions in restraining humanity's selfish nature, (3) to emphasize societal needs over individual interests, (4) to be supportive of the status quo, and (5) to find the distribution of goods and services to be justifiable, necessary, and inevitable.

Lenski identifies the second conception as the "radical antithesis." Its advocates, according to Lenski, include Plato, Phales of Chalcedon, Jesus (the Christ), Locke, Rousseau, and Marx. In contrast to the conservative thesis, the radical position assumes:

> (1) a more optimistic posture concerning human nature, (2) a

basic distrust of social institutions, the latter being blamed for most of mankind's negative predisposition, (3) a priority of individual over societal interests, and (4) a critical stance towards the status quo. The radical position finds the distribution of goods and services to be inequitable, exploitive, and in need of change.

Obviously, Lenski has taken some liberties in arriving at these two presuppositional caricatures. Few advocates of either position would embrace all of the postulates in either of the groupings. For example, neither Christ Jesus nor Plato were particularly optimistic about human nature. Nevertheless, the battle between these presuppositions is clear and historically well documented. These are antithetical perspectives on rather basic issues and they are as evident in the thoughts of Aristotle (in response to Plato) as they are in Mills (in response to Parsons). The important point, however, is not that the ideological battle exists, but that it is manifestly obvious in the dispute between functional and conflict theorists.

Functionalism may be viewed as the contemporary version of the conservative thesis. Its emphasis on the needs of the social system, the necessity of stability, and the normativity of integration and consensus neatly parallels the emphases of the conservative model of human nature. Because mankind's instincts are destructive, the system (i.e. order) is stressed. Because social institutions play the "positive" role of restraining selfish behavior, their integrative and stabilizing influence is assumed. Because the status quo is both a barrier against disorder and a justifiable commodity, the functionality and normativity of slow/adjustive change is postulated. In short, the functional position tends to be a defense of the status quo in that it defines order as functional. It acts as a sociological justification of what is.

In contrast, conflict theory constitutes a sociological critique of the present state of affairs. It undermines the legitimacy of the status quo by emphasizing its precarious nature and highly inequitable base. Its dialectical orientation is grounded in the assumption that conflicting sub-units in society give rise to change and social pathology. Thus, social problems can be explained by reference to the nature of society and its structure, rather than to the predispositions of human nature. Indeed, by postulating an endemic quality to societal conflict, this perspective is able to champion the right of the individual and, at the same time, lay the blame for human failure at the doorstep of society in general.

## On Biblical Presuppositions

The significance of Lenski's observations are twofold: first, they force us to acknowledge the close relationship that exists between presupposition and theory. Clearly, sociologists do not simply go about their task, making observations in a philosophical vacuum. Their theoretical conclusions about social phenomena are intricately woven together with their assumptions concerning human nature and society. Second, Lenski's analysis demonstrates that a synthesis of the conflict and functional approaches cannot be achieved at the empirical level only. Any true resolution of the dispute will have to deal with the question of assumptions.

Both of these points should drive every sociologist, and anyone who is interested in the social sciences, back to the issue of presuppositions. We must ask ourselves, honestly and with great deliberation, what assumptions we are employing, and what assumptions we *ought* to be employing in the development of our sociological theories. Moreover, those of us who claim to be Christian sociologists have the further obligation of asking what role our faith should have in the shaping of these foundational presuppositions. And while this is a question worthy of a well-informed discussion, it is not one which we will debate in this chapter. Rather, we shall take as our point of departure the assumption that the Christian is obligated, radically and without reservation, to build his philosophical base upon biblical presuppositions.

This is not a particularly earthshaking statement. Christian sociologists have often called for Christian thinking in sociology,[9] and our argument is far from novel. What is not commonplace, however, are attempts by Christian sociologists to actually develop a presuppositional base that is distinctly biblical, and to use such a foundation to come to grips with the theoretical issues being addressed by contemporary sociologists. What we will try to do in the remaining sections of this chapter, therefore, is to generate a number of propositions about the nature of humanity and society based upon our understanding of biblical revelation. Then, we will apply these propositions to the issues raised in the debate between functional and conflict theorists.

### On Human Nature

Of the many things the Bible communicates about the nature of human beings, we will concentrate upon two of the more obvious fundamental principles. The first is that humans are social beings, obliged by God to live with one another as a member of a community. After the creation of Adam we read in Genesis 2:18 the words of God: "It is not good for the man to be alone" (NAB). In this statement we are not only given the primary reason for the creation of Eve, but also a major statement about the nature of humanity. In a very real sense, Eve was created to complete God's creation. Why? Because human beings were created to need and to relate to one another in a social situation. Loneliness and isolation are abnormal states for individuals. In the words of our God, it is "not good" for his special creation.

The second important event in mankind's history is commonly called the Fall, and it ushers sin into the domain of humanity. For our purposes, there are two important effects of the Fall. First, it meant that relationships, which were once complete, now became strained and difficult to maintain. Sin cut humanity off from intimate contact with God. In Eden there was perfect communication between God and his creation; outside of it, there is a barrier. Mankind has become estranged from God. Sin also disrupted the relationship of man and woman. To the woman God said, "Your desire shall be for your husband, and he shall rule over you." Here we move from partnership to hierarchy, symbolic of the struggle that is now a part of the interpersonal relationships of mankind. This same thought is obviously expressed in the story of Cain and Abel. Cain is also alienated from himself. In short, a major result of the Fall is the alienation of man— from God as well as from himself and other human beings.

A second result of the Fall is a product of sin and the alienated state in which humanity finds itself. For when human beings became estranged from God and one another, they were forced by necessity to look out for themselves in order to survive. Mankind, therefore, becomes a creature of self-interest and the "self" becomes a newfound preoccupation. The Fall, therefore, provides a new motivation for humanity—the protection, maintenance, and survival of the self.

Before concluding this section on the nature of humanity, we ought to point out the basic paradox endemic to the human situation. On the one hand, we are social beings, desperately in need of establishing relationships with one another in order to be fully human (that which God intended us to become). On the other hand, we are unable to maintain full relationships because we find ourselves in an alienated state, motivated by self-interest and preoccupied by our own survival. It should be further noted that Christ came precisely to bridge this gap between God and mankind, and within humanity. To the extent that human beings accept this bridge, they have the *potential* to greatly reduce the effects of alienation and self-interest in their lives and relationships.

## On the Nature of Society

As far as we can tell, the Bible does not provide the kind of explicit information on the nature of society that it does on the nature of humanity. Nevertheless, as we have seen, it is concerned with mankind in a societal context. For that reason, its discussion of the nature of humanity has definite implications for the nature of society.

Since human beings are social beings, it is clear that the Bible assumes the social context as the "normal" one for mankind to be in. Furthermore, it seems to us that it devotes a good deal of energy to the topic of an ideal society. The Old Testament in particular, especially through the eyes of the prophets, presents specific criteria by which societies can and will be judged by God. Amos, for example, says that God is concerned with social justice. He quite boldly condemns unjust class privileges, the abuse of wealth, lack of concern for the needy, and unfair judicial and taxation systems. The Old Testament makes clear, moreover, that the God-given responsibility of government is to provide for the welfare of the people, not the monarch. And furthermore, it is the duty of a God-fearing nation to hold fast the sanctity of marriage and the family. All of this seems to indicate God's concern for the establishment of a just society.

In our opinion, however, one of the most vivid pictures of an ideal community is given in the New Testament, in a portion of Scripture that is not ostensibly dealing with "society" at all. Listen to Paul as he describes the body of Christ in 1 Corinthians 12:12-26:

> For just as the body is one and has many members, and all the members of the body, though many, are one body, so it is with Christ. For by one Spirit we were all baptized into one body—Jews or Greeks, slaves or free—and all were made to drink of one Spirit.
>
> For the body does not consist of one member but of many. If the foot should say, "Because I am not a hand, I do not belong to the body," that would not make it any less a part of the body. And if the ear should say, "Because I am not an eye, I do not belong to the body," that would not make it any less a part of the body. If the whole body were an eye, where would be the hearing? If the whole

body were an ear, where would be the sense of smell? But as it is, God arranged the organs in the body, each one of them, as he chose. If all were a single organ, where would the body be? As it is, there are many parts, yet one body. The eye cannot say to the hand, "I have no need of you," (nor again the head to the feet, "I have no need of you." On the contrary, the parts of the body which seem to be weaker are indispensable, and those parts of the body which we think less honorable we invest with the greater honor, and our unpresentable parts are treated with greater modesty, which our more presentable parts do not require. But God has so composed the body, giving the greater honor to the inferior part, that there may be no discord in the body, but that the members may have the same care for one another. If one member suffers, all suffer together; if one member is honored, all rejoice together.

In this description of the body of Christ, Paul communicates an ideal of community relationships that is remarkably like a functional interpretation of society. Here we have a beautifully cooperative, marvelously efficient, functional community.

There is a fly in the ointment, however. First, it is obvious that Paul is presenting *an ideal* for the church, not society. Second, and this should make us ponder just a bit, it is manifestly obvious that the church, even with the dynamic of the Holy Spirit within it, has rarely achieved the kind of harmony that Paul describes. One can only guess, therefore, how much rarer it will be to find a society that fits this functional ideal. Indeed, we might expect that a society made up of alienated individuals, who are motivated by self-interest, will experience a great deal of conflict.

### Toward Christian Thinking On Order and Conflict

At this point we would like to collect our thoughts and present them in the form of three propositions. While we believe they accurately reflect an aspect of biblical truth, it is important that the reader understand that these are deduced propositions, not biblical propositions. They represent *our* attempts to employ biblical truth for the purpose of sociological insight, and *our* efforts are highly subject to error.

*Proposition A*

If humanity is social by nature, and if mankind's present condition is marked by alienation from God and one another, then we may conclude that humanity is, by nature, in a state of tension between these two forces. Therefore, if tension is a state that is uncomfortable for people to remain in, then one of the basic needs of mankind is to relieve this tension between his social nature and his alienated condition.

The implications of this proposition are numerous, but for the sake of brevity, we will specify only five:

1. We are first of all assuming that every person possesses, simply because he/she is a human being, a need to be in social relationship with others—a social need. This is true whether it is subjectively realized or not.

2. If human beings have a social need, and if it is a driving force in their lives, then much of their behavior can be understood in terms of an attempt to satisfy this need. We would go so far as to assert that a basic reason for the formation of groups is the need for social relationships, although it is by no means the only reason.

3. If society exists in part to provide social relationships and to satisfy the social need of its inhabitants, then one criteria by which a society may be evaluated is its ability to meet this need. This point is particularly relevant for modern industrial societies, since they have difficulty providing adequate sustaining communities.

4. All other things being equal, the society that is able to meet the social needs of its members will reduce their tension (that tension which is attributable to mankind's alienated state), and therefore it is more likely to resemble the functional ideal. Where this need is not being met, society is more likely to be characterized by conflict and disorder.

5. Finally, our biblical assumptions indicate that there is a vertical, as well as horizontal, aspect to social relationships. Human beings have a need to be in a right relationship with God as well as with one another. For this reason man's need for community will not be satisfied solely by human relationships. Therefore, we should not be surprised to discover that people exhibit feelings of alienation even while they are involved in very supportive human communities.

*Proposition B*

If humans are social beings alienated from God and one another, and if they are also creatures of self-interest, and if the objects for which they strive are in short supply, then it is reasonable to expect that a struggle for the objects in short supply will be present in every society.

1. One assumption of this proposition is that people want more than is normally available to them. This assumption is rooted both in

our understanding of human nature as well as in the biblical account of the Fall. Man's orientation towards self-interest produces an insatiable appetite for goods and services, since the desire for self-protection and/ or gratification produces limitless needs and wants. Genesis 3:17 also indicates that, as a result of the Fall, mankind was condemned to toil for basic needs. "Toil" is here associated with the curse God placed on the ground, and it implies that man's needs and desires will not be easily satisfied.

2. Clearly, the fundamental prediction of our proposition is that societies are "likely" to exhibit a great deal of struggle and dissension.

3. However, it also assumes that among societies there will be a great range or variation in the degree and form of disorder and conflict manifested by this struggle. Even if we limit ourselves to the context of the proposition itself, we can say that the degree to which this struggle takes place in any particular society depends upon: (1) the extent to which the self-interest of the members of a given society is controlled (either externally or internally), (2) the extent to which a society is able to provide its members with *what they think* is a just distribution of the goods and services available in that society, and (3) the extent to which a society is able to meet the social needs (Proposition A) of its members.

4. Therefore, all other things being equal, the society that is able to control self-interest, provide a fair distribution of goods and services, and meet the social needs of its members will tend to resemble the functional ideal. To the extent that these criteria are not met, a society is likely to be characterized by conflict and disorder.

*Proposition C*

If mankind was created in the image of God, and if mankind is held accountable for his actions by God, then it is reasonable to conclude that humans are, at least in part, active agents in their own history.

1. While this proposition does not relate directly to the issue of order and conflict, it is important because both functionalism and conflict theory are rooted in deterministic conceptions of humanity (Durkheim and Spencer/Rousseau and Marx). A biblical approach, therefore, must posit at the outset that human beings make real choices which affect their behavior, their lives, and their history.

2. However, we must be careful not to naively conclude that human beings are "totally free." In this regard, we ought to remember

that (1) God is sovereign and ultimately in control; (2) that history has a purpose and, by God's own design, it is going somewhere; and (3) though humans make real choices, they are nevertheless affected by very real forces—forces within them (their nature) and outside of them (their environment). We should never downgrade the coercive power of these forces by concentrating blindly on human freedom.

## Conclusion

The presentation of our model has been brief, skeletal, and needs much more elaboration. Consequently, we have not been able to touch upon many important issues raised by both functionalist and conflict theorists, conservatives, and radicals. More importantly, we have not had the time to defend either our biblical exegesis or our deduced propositions. For all of these reasons, we have run the risk of alienating not only those who label themselves functionalists and conflict theorists, but Christian sociologists as well. To those whom we have slighted or offended, we apologize.

We have managed, however, to present some rather concrete ideas concerning the biblical account of the nature of humanity and society and apply these to the issue of social order and conflict. Before closing, therefore, it might be helpful to compare, in a summary fashion, our conclusions with those made by the functional and conflict theorists.

A major difference between our model (if we may call it a "model") and those of the functional and conflict theorists remains at the level of assumptions. When tied to their philosophical roots, both dominant models differentiate between, and contrast man's nature with, that of society's. Thus, the functionalist is able to distrust human nature while, at the same time, placing great faith in the social system. Conversely, conflict theorists, while distrustful of the operation of society, are rather optimistic about mankind's potential when freed from the chains of society. But to attach different natures to humanity and society is, to us, a tragic mistake. It ignores completely the intimate relationship between individuals and society—the shaping of society by individuals and, in turn, the socializing of individuals by society. If we observe that either humanity or society is corrupt, we cannot magically throw the blame for its condition on the other entity. We must conclude, rather, that corruption is mutual and proceeds from the fundamental nature of both.

There is a second difference between our approach and the ones taken by the functional and conflict theorists. While our model is much more explicit in its assumptions concerning the nature of humanity and society, it assumes much less about the actual behavior of these entities. Functionalists *assume* a cooperative, integrated, stable, and slow-changing society, while conflict theorists *assume* a conflict-ridden, disintegrated, unstable, and revolutionary society. These assumptions are so pervasive that the conflict theorist must talk about "false consciousness' to explain stability, and functionalists must resort to terms like "pathology" and "deviance" to explain radical change. Our model, however, assumes a very wide range of possibilities in various types of societies, depending upon how a society deals with the basic condition of humanity (alienation, social needs, and self-interest). Thus, we would agree with van den Berghe that the empirical assumptions of the functional and conflict schools are myopic and narrow. In contrast to van den Berghe, our approach attempts to provide a presuppositional base for this assertion, as well as an alternative explanation for the empirical variations that exist.

Two more observations are probably in order. First, we would admit that, empirically, our conclusions concerning the expected state of society resemble those of the conflict theorist more than those of the functionalist. It should be noted, however, that this is because our model views conflict, struggle, and tension to be *more likely*, given the nature of humanity and society. We have in no sense assumed a dialectical necessity for conflict. Moreover, we should reassert that theoretically a whole range of societies is possible, from the extreme functional ideal to a society of massive strife and anarchy. Second, from a normative perspective, it is clear that a biblical approach shares certain concerns with both the conservative and radical positions. We share, for example, the functionalist's interest in a society that maintains strong social bonds among its members. In terms of our model, if a society fails to meet the social need of its members, it abrogates one of its basic reasons for existence. On the other hand, all social relationships are not good! A biblical approach is just as concerned about the *kind* of social bonds a society maintains as it is with their simple existence. Moreover, meeting the social needs of its members is only one of a number of normative obligations that a society has. A society that provides cohesive social relationships, but condones wealth for a few and condemns the rest to poverty, is far from the biblical ideal—though it may be the epitome of functionality. In short, a biblical approach will share many of the ethical concerns of both models, but it will not construct its empirical hypotheses simply to augment its ethical bias. It is always concerned, first and foremost, with truth.

## Discussion Questions

1. In your own words, summarize the basic positions of both the functional and conflict schools of thought. Take a major social event (e.g. civil rights movement, Vietnam War and student protest, forced busing, energy crisis) and attempt to explain its development from both a conflict and functionalist perspective.

2. Explain Pierre L. van den Berghe's critique of both functionalism and conflict theory. On what basis does he propose a synthesis? Explain.

3. Gaede has criticized van den Berghe's synthesis on the basis of Gerhard Lenski's analysis of functionalism and conflict theory. What is Lenski's central argument? Compare Lenski's argument with van den Berghe's position.

4. If you were a member of an underground, radical political group, would you tend to view your society in functional or conflict terms? Why? What view of social reality do you think the leaders of your society would embrace? Explain.

5. According to Gaede, sociologists do not make social observations in a philosophical vacuum. What does he mean by this statement? What are presuppositions? Give an example of how antithetical presuppositions on a particular issue can lead to different practical applications.

6. In your opinion, should a Christian sociologist allow his faith to affect the way he does sociology? How do you think the author of this chapter would answer that question? Compare and contrast your position with that of the author's.

7. The Bible has much to say about human nature beyond that discussed in this chapter. Make an attempt to draw out other biblical principles concerning human nature. How might you relate those principles to a Christian approach to sociology?

8. Evaluate propositions A, B, and C in the chapter from a functionalist and/or conflict perspective. Specify points of agreement and disagreement and then attempt to explain their existence by comparing the assumptions of the various approaches.

9. The author claims that while his approach is more explicit in its assumptions concerning human nature and society, it assumes much less about the actual behavior of society and its inhabitants. On what basis does he make this claim? Evaluate his assertions.

10. What is determinism? Try to state the functional and conflict perspectives within a deterministic framework. Can a Christian approach to sociology be deterministic? Explain your answer.

## Notes

1. See Pierre L. van den Berghe, "Dialectic and Functionalism: Toward a Theoretical Synthesis," *American Sociological Review*, 28 (October 1963), pp. 695-705; Ralf Dahrendorf, *Class and Class Conflict in Industrial Society*, Stanford: Stanford Press, 1959; Gerhard Lenski, *Power and Privilege: A Theory of Social Stratification*, New York: McGraw-Hill, 1966; C. Wright Mills, *The Sociological Imagination*, London: Oxford Press, 1959.

2. See particularly Robert W. Friedrichs, *A Sociology of Sociology*, New York: Free Press, 1970; and Alvin W. Gouldner, *The Coming Crisis of Western Sociology*, New York: Avon, 1970.

3. The debate between functionalism and conflict theory is especially interesting in the area of stratification; in this regard, see the exchange between Davis and Moore and Tumin in Melvin Tumin's *Readings on Social Stratification*, Englewood Cliffs: Prentice-Hall, 1970, pp. 367-410.

4. For a discussion of conflict within a functionalist model, please see Robert K. Merton, "Social Structure and Anomie," *American Sociological Review*, 3 (October 1938), pp. 677-682; and Lewis Coser, *The Functions of Social Conflict*, New York: Free Press, 1956.

5. See footnote #1 for references on Lenski and van den Berghe.

6. We would like to argue that our position is that of historical, orthodox Christianity. Since a number of variant groups describe themselves in those terms, however, our theological position may be more cogently described as Evangelical.

7. See van den Berghe *(loc. cit.)*, especially in his second footnote. Lenski *(loc. cit.)* and Friedrichs *(loc. cit.)* also provide excellent biographical information in this area.

8. The reader may note that van den Berghe cites *only* Dahrendorf in his discussion of the "Hegelian-Marxian dialectic."

9. See Russell Heddendorf, "Some Perspectives of a Christian Sociology," *Journal of the American Scientific Affiliation*, 24:3 (September), pp. 110-117; Jack Balswick and Dawn Ward, "The Nature of Man and Scientific Models of Society," *Journal of the American Scientific Affiliation*, 28:4 (December), pp. 181-185; David Lyon, *Christian and Sociology*, Downers Grove: Inter-Varsity, 1977.

# 12

# Theoretical Models of Person in Contemporary Sociology: Toward Christian Sociological Theory

*Margaret M. Poloma*

When I became a Christian after being an agnostic through graduate school and my early professional career, a nonbelieving colleague and friend expressed dismay. This sociologist, whose professional work I greatly admire, quipped: "You can't be a Christian and a sociologist; the two are mutually exclusive categories!" Many of us would like to respond that such an assertion is nonsense. Yet this same point has been raised by Christian students and friends who ask, "Isn't it difficult to be a Christian and a sociologist?"

This question is a hard one to confront, and one to which there is no simple answer. Yet it is not easy to live in the world and not be of it (John 15:18-20; 17:16), nor is it easy to be a practicing sociologist and not experience the strain of numerous sociological assertions that are anti-Christian.

Let me say at the onset that I am concerned about a sect-like Christianity rather than a church-like one. Yinger (1970:257) proposes three criteria by which to categorize a religious group as a church or a sect: (1) the degree to which a group includes all members of a society, (2) the extent to which a group rejects or accepts the secular values of so-

**Margaret M. Poloma**
*Associate Professor of Sociology*
*University of Akron*

Reared in the Roman Catholic Church, Margaret Poloma is active in interdenominational witness on her campus. She is editor of the *Christian Sociological Society's Newsletter*. She holds a BA from Notre Dame College of Ohio and the PhD from Case Western Reserve University. Her special interests include family sociology and Christian covenant communities. She has authored a textbook for undergraduate students in sociological theory, and for five years was coeditor of *Sociological Focus*, the official North Central Sociological Association journal.

ciety, and (3) the extent to which it is bureaucratized. The second point is of particular relevance for our discussion. Biblically, religious groups that are one with the world (church-like) are not following the ideals of Scripture. Jesus promised tension between his followers and the world (Matthew 10:17-23; John 15:18-27; 16:33). "Christians" who have acclimated to the world, who have not accepted Jesus as Savior and Lord, and who accept the Bible simply as a book of "good teachings" may not have as much difficulty reconciling their Christianity and sociology. Those Christians who are more sect-like (regardless of the particular church or denomination to which they belong), who accept the Bible as God's Word, and who acknowledge Jesus as the Son of God and their personal Savior will experience tension. Church-like Christians may question the premise upon which this chapter rests—namely, that there is a tension between Christianity and sociology. To them I can only respond: I am a sect-like Christian and this chapter reflects corresponding assumptions and "biases" (as do all theoretical papers) that I cannot prove.[1]

This chapter will attempt to deal with the dilemma of reconciling sociological theory with Christian tenets. After briefly tracing the history of the tension and the nature of the tension in contemporary sociology, the focus will rest on assumptions about the nature of person upon which different theoretical perspectives are based.

## Tension Between Sociological Theory and Religion

While the appropriateness of Auguste Comte's being the founder of sociology may be questioned, Comte's recognition of the tension between science and theology is readily apparent. His "law of three stages" views scientific explanations as progressive steps beyond either theological or philosophical theories. Moreover, sociology, complete with its priesthood of sociologists and its social sacraments, was to be a new religion that would redeem modern society.

Sociologists would like to believe that as a science we have progressed beyond the social philosophical musings of Comte—and indeed we have. But the fact remains that Comte's positivism and rationalism provide a base upon which modern sociology rests. As we move through other important founders of the discipline, the issue of religion and sociology's incompatibility becomes veiled in discussions of "scientific neutrality." The religion of sociology promoted by Comte and his disciples soon gave way to a sociology of religion as developed by founding fathers Emile Durkheim and Max Weber. Religion became a legitimate topic of sociological analysis, but overt claims of sociology's inheritance of religion's functions in society were muted. As the twentieth century progressed, it seemed possible to separate religion and sociology into different spheres that need not conflict.

Perhaps social scientists were too quick in proclaiming the death of a religion of sociology. The religion-like quality of the discipline for many practitioners has been noted by contemporary scholars (Friedrichs, 1970; Dynes, 1973). Friedrichs, in fact, asserts that the self-image of sociologist as priest or prophet is an overriding paradigm upon which sociological theory rests. In assuming a priest-like position and being at peace with the world, sociologists have failed to reconize their acceptance of the ways of the world. They have ignored the value stance that exists under the cloak of "scientific neutrality." Prophetic sociologists, on the other hand, are critical of the existing social order. They herald theories that speak of doom, and the ways to redeem man from imminent social destruction. This type of sociology, with or without the religious analogy, has forced sociologists of the 1970s to look closely at value-laden assumptions contained in various theories.

Empirical data also suggest tension between serving sociology and Christianity. Sociologists of religion Glock and Stark (1965:289-306), in part based on studies of scientists' values, have challenged the notion that "the war between religion and science that was waged so fiercely during the period since the Enlightenment is now over." Their data suggest that religion and science, due to conflicting images of person, continue to be in tension. While natural science and religion may be establishing greater rapport, it is fallacious to extend this development to the social sciences.

The basic problem for Glock and Stark is one of "natural determinism" (espoused by science) versus "divine intervention" (accepted by religion). Both positions rest to a degree on assumptions, but more of science's assumptions than religion's are empirically demonstrable. Glock and Stark (1965:293) suggest that "the seeming rapprochement between religion and science is illusory" and "without the innovation of a wholly new perspective which would resolve the determinacy issue, there is little prospect for a genuine rapprochement." It is the issue of the determined nature of person that holds the key for analyzing differing theoretical perspectives and their respective compatibility with Christian belief. It would be erroneous to assume, however, that all sociological theory accepts a determined image of person. In fact, two main traditions, naturalistic sociology and humanistic sociology, hold opposing views on the nature of person. As we shall attempt to demonstrate, however, neither ideal type is completely compatible with Christian belief.

## Naturalistic Sociology's Assumptions About Person

Naturalistic sociological theory could be said to rest on two interrelated assumptions that make a scientific study of human behavior possible: (1) human action is empirically observable and is determined by the social surroundings in which we live, and (2) these social surroundings are organized and are also subject to empirical study. Just as physical matter is comprised of atoms and the physicist studies the property of atoms as well as the resultant whole, so too, sociologists are able to study human behavior as it results in social groups. Both atoms and human behavior are subject to the same type of laws which determine action and reaction. Sociological theory is a quest for laws similar to the law of gravity or the law of material density in physics. Although there are varying degrees of adherence to the ideal type of naturalistic theory, naturalistic sociologists are committed to a sociology that fashions itself in the image of the natural sciences.

While naturalistic sociologists would deny they have any value assumptions about the nature of man, careful reading of their works suggests otherwise. Implicit assumptions about man are present which may be correlated with assumptions about the nature of society. Men and women are "fallen" creatures whose redemption is made possible by an ordered social world.

The image of person as a fallen creature is not a new one and, of itself, is compatible with Christian teachings. Where Christians and naturalistic sociologists would part company is in their interpretation of both the freedom men and women have to choose a course of action *and* in the source of redemption from this fallen state. The image of person and society inherent in naturalistic sociology is more compatible with the philosophical treatises of Thomas Hobbes than with Christian teachings. For Hobbes, human action is determined by passions and greed which manifest themselves in violent conflict situations. In addition to such passion, however, men and women are endowed with reason. Reason allows this fallen state of nature to be overcome, and permits violent conflict to be transformed into nonviolent cooperation.

This feat is accomplished through the establishment of a state which provides security for its people from their own greedy, passionate nature. Thus, for Hobbes, man is selfish and warlike, but in need of security. Society evolves to constrain human passions and to socialize men and women into submission.

Within Hobbes' theory we find the assumptions that men and women are naturally egoistic, determined creatures, yet capable of rational action—assumptions that have been built into much naturalistic theory. While most naturalistic sociology would be reluctant to express the view that man is inherently egoistic, it does imply that society is necessary to constrain persons. People are viewed *primarily* as products of the social world, rather than beings who are capable of fashioning and designing their world. Like Hobbes, it observes rationality in men and women—a rationality that will employ necessary means to secure desired goals, and that is inherent within the social order.

### Illustrations of Naturalistic Sociology

Naturalistic theory, built on the model of sociology provided by Auguste Comte, is clearly the dominant thrust in contemporary sociology. This model has dominated structural theory in sociology as well as behaviorism in social psychology. The former is governed by an image of person that Matson (1976) terms the "robot model," while the latter is dominated by the "creature model." Both provide determined concepts of person—the robot model viewing person as a machine, and the creature model emphasizing person as beast. Structuralist theory, including structural functionalism, conflict functionalism, and systems theory is most likely to imply a mechanistic view of person. The less popular behavioral exchange theory or the developing sociobiological theory imply a model of "person as beast." Neither of these models stresses the creative capacity of an individual as a free acting agent that, as we shall see, is basic to the humanistic perspective.

While a determined image of person, whether it be as machine or beast, is implicitly contained in naturalistic theory, the degree to which a theorist accepts such an assumption does vary. Some theorists are quite explicit about their determinism, which they feel is essential for the development of a scientific sociological theory. Social behaviorist and exchange theorist George C. Homans (1967), for example, believes that persons act rationally, but they do so under the "illusion of choice": "I speak of illusion because I myself believe that what each of us does is absolutely determined." Homans acknowledges that we will always have the illusion of free will because it allows us the conviction that we can change our condition. In reality, however, men and women are subject to the same rigid and determined laws that govern the world of natural science.

Unlike Homans' behavioral exchange theory, most structuralist theories imply assumptions about the nature of person without specifically stating them. In structuralism, human beings are treated as determined beings enacting a predesignated script according to the established norms or rules of society. In the Durkheimian tradition of avoiding psychological reductionism, persons are viewed as determined products of norms and institutions that enshrine them—when persons are dealt with at all. This led to criticisms of sociology's "oversocialized conception of man" (Wrong, 1961) and the admonition to "bring men back" into sociological analysis (Homans, 1964). The person presented by structuralism is determined by social constraints or norms with little room for creativity.

The work of Robert K. Merton provides a classic example of structuralism's deterministic model. Merton's main concern is not with individual behavior, but rather with an analysis of social structures. Underlying such an analysis, however, is a complex, yet determined, image of person. As Stinchcombe (1975:12) has observed in commenting on Merton's model, " . . . the core process that Merton conceives as central to social structure is the *choice between socially structured alternatives*." In other words, there are patterns of behavior that are part of the institutional order, thus allowing sociology to develop scientific theory. But there are also alternatives, allowing for a structurally contained voluntarism on the part of persons. Thus people have some choice in their actions; but these alternatives are socially established with corresponding normative demands. While there is room for choice, it is a structured and limited rather than a creative choice.

Such a view of constrained choice may also be found in other leading structuralist theorists. Talcott Parsons' "pattern variables" were developed in order to create a typology exhausting possible rational choices and in order to classify social action. Lewis Coser, in admonishing against the dangers of psychological reductionism, warns that "individual striving is not sufficient to free us from the grip of social constraints." Gerhard Lenski's model of an egocentric and self-seeking person is redeemed by adhering to rules "merely as a form of self interest." The image of person found in these and other structuralist works is one that is determined by social structures which save the individual from his lower nature.

## Humanistic Sociology's Assumption About Person

In many ways humanistic sociology exists as a polar opposite to naturalistic sociology. While naturalist sociology is committed to the assumption that sociology must be a science like the natural sciences, humanistic sociology is critical of any preoccupation with the scientific nature of sociology. While naturalistic sociology adheres to the principle of value neutrality, humanistic sociology recognizes there are values inherent in assumptions on which any theory rests. While naturalistic theory is wed to empiricism and positivism, humanistic sociology is more concerned with the significance of the sociological problem than the method used to collect data. While naturalistic theory devotes much effort to the construction of formal and often abstract theory, humanistic sociology claims to be more interested in depicting reality than building theoretical models. Finally, while naturalistic sociologists may be likened to Friedrich's "priestly model," humanistic sociologists are more likely to lean toward the prophetic self-image. In varying degrees, humanistic sociologists share a concern for the problems of the social world—a concern that leads many of them to speak out for radical social change. These social prophets differ from their priestly counterparts in the image they have of the nature of person and his/her ability to create a better social order.

For the humanistic sociologist, persons are more or less good by nature and capable of pouring out this goodness on their social world. Such a view may be found in the writings of the eighteenth-century philosopher Jean Jacques Rousseau whose philosophy is often contrasted with that of Hobbes. According to Rousseau's model, the natural state of man is one of goodness and his social order should be patterned after this state of nature. In this original state of nature, harmony prevails, and from it can be derived principles to guide the process of social reorganization. Present social evils could be eliminated if the individual were released from the constraints of society. Thus persons are seen as potentially peace loving and good, as individuals who need to be freed from the constraints of a corrupted social order.

While humanistic sociologists may not go as far as Rousseau in acknowledging the positive creative potential of man, their model of person and society is more in accord with Rousseau than Hobbes. Rather than viewing people as creatures who are products of their social order, humanistic sociologists stress the ability of men and women to use their sociological knowledge to fashion and design their world. Rather than being constrained by the goals inherent in the social order, they can formulate new goals based on human nature before the fall from social grace. This goal is a changed and better social world where men and women can live together in peace and harmony.

## Illustrations of Humanistic Sociology

If Hobbes' theory serves as a philosophical base for naturalistic sociology's image of person, it is Rousseau's that inspires the humanistic model. As developed in humanistic social science, Matson observes (1976:209) the model "begins and ends with an act of faith":

> Its starting point is a conception of human nature—an idea of man—not as a fully determinate and predictable "given" but as an open system of shifting parameters, live options, and indefinite possibilities of becoming. The fundamental faith of the humanist is that there is a self worthy of actualizing and a consciousness worthy of the task. . . .

Men and women thus have an inherent goodness and, because of this goodness, an ability to create a better social world.

Many humanistic sociologists look to Karl Marx as their founder. Marx lamented the state of the nineteenth-century European society and desired to see men and women freed from its oppression. A key to the problem facing men and women in industrial society, according to the young philosopher Marx, may be found in alienated labor. The individual's salvation from beastiality lay in his ability to create human products through meaningful and creative labor. Only in humanizing labor could the individual be released from the estrangement he experienced from nature, from other people, and even from himself. Once aware of this condition, human beings could be instruments in the creation of a perfect society—a classless Utopian society that would redeem them from conflicts of the past. Marx would concur with the structuralists who believe that human beings are determined by their social structure, but Marx asserts that people have the ability to create a new society. It is the creator aspect of person rather than the creature model, that is emphasized.

Humanistic sociologists have been much more concerned with practice or application (termed *praxis*) than the development of formal scientific theory, particularly when contrasted with the efforts put into theory construction by their naturalistic counterparts. Birnbaum (1971:129) observes that the Marxist scientific praxis assumes that a totally objective or detached sociology is impossible, and that sociology must be concerned about the direction of society, as well as utopian programatic goals (including abolition of a division of labor). Such a reform orientation has led humanistic sociologists toward discussing social problems and toward constructing theories that may be applied to social action. This deficit in well-formulated theories has been particularly noteworthy in the case of radical sociology. As Mullins (1973:270-71) has noted, radical sociology has had little academic base and has suffered a lack of systematic theoretical development. Although they have had an effect on contemporary theory, the efforts of the radicals have been largely directed toward organization of radical groups and political confrontation, rather than the development of academic theories.

Contemporary nonradical theorists of the humanistic mode are more likely to temper their assumptions regarding the basic goodness of person and his potential to create a more perfect social order. Such muting of Marxist assumptions may be evidenced in the work of C. Wright Mills. Mills' view of person reflects a strain between the person as a social product and a person as creator of his social structure. Cuzzort and King (1976:144) have made the following poignant observation regarding Mills' view of person as interrelated with the social structure:

> Although Mills claimed that power has its locus within supporting institutions, he still was concerned with the fact that it is individuals who make decisions and are responsible for the consequences. Mills was torn on the one hand by an analytic perspective that properly located the individual within the broader system and on the other by a humanistic sensitivity that made him critical of an apparent inability of powerful individuals to assert their autonomy

In commenting on people's freedom, Mills asserts that *all* men and women were free to make history, but indeed that some have much greater freedom than others. Thus the person Mills depicts is partially free and partially determined, depending upon his or her position among the power holders. At the same time, Mills allows for collective action among socially aware citizens to block the power moves of the elite and to participate in the creation of their own destiny. Similar views of person may be found in Alvin W. Gouldner's (1970) call for a reflexive sociology and Amitai Etzioni's prescription (1968) for an active society. Mills, Gouldner, and Etzioni all represent moderated versions of humanistic sociological tenets.

## A Christian Looks at the Dominant Sociological Paradigms

We have tried to demonstrate that the ideal theoretical types presented in contemporary sociology are naturalism at one end of the continuum and humanism at the other. The former is the heir to Comtean theory while the latter may trace its sociological origins to Marx. While specific theories vary in the degree to which they approximate the naturalistic or humanistic ideal type, these two paradigms do represent dominant strains of contemporary theory. Much of what passes for alternate paradigms, such as conflict theory or exchange theory, when examined in light of underlying assumptions, are in fact naturalistic, or less frequently, humanistic.

We would suggest that, in their extreme form, neither naturalistic theory nor humanistic theory reflects a Christian perspective on the image of person. This is due to two interrelated issues discussed throughout this presentation: (1) the essence of man's nature, and (2) the source of, and need for, redemption. Christian assumptions on both issues are partially in accord with naturalism and partly in agreement with humanism, but concur with neither. For example, Christian belief in original sin coincides with the structuralistic assumption (often unexpressed) of a fallen man. Christians would differ with structuralists on the topic of absolute determinism, as well as in structuralism's faith in structural properties as being the source of man's redemption. On the other hand, humanism's view of an unfallen man stands in direct contradiction to the scriptural view of person as a sinner in need of redemption, and of the inability of the individual to save himself. (See Romans 5 for Paul's discussion of salvation and our deliverance from sin and death by Jesus Christ.) It may appear that humanism's dictates are compatible with Christian tenets, but a closer scrutiny of its main assumptions about person reveals only surface similarity between the kingdom of God and the utopia of the humanist. The Christian position on the sinful condition of person and the need for redemption made possible only through Jesus Christ will leave a Christian sociologist at odds with the humanist who is committed to the notion that men and women have the potential to save themselves.

We would suggest that naturalistic sociology may represent a more accurate model of pre-redeemed person than does humanism's utopian visions. While the tenets of naturalistic sociology may be adequate for describing a non-redeemed world, Jesus promised that his kingdom, which was not of this world (Matthew 13:36-43), was close at hand (Matthew 4:17; Matthew 10:7). This kingdom differs from the world in a number of ways, including stratification (where in Christ there is neither Jew nor Greek, male nor female, slave nor freeman—Galatians 3:28-29), leadership (which requires service—Matthew 20:27; John 13:12-15), and authority (which is not to be lorded over anyone—Matthew 20:24-25). Indeed, relationships within the kingdom of God are radically different from relationships in the world. Social exchange has been viewed by many theorists, humanists, and naturalists alike as the base upon which society rests. Jesus' command that we love one another as he has loved us should make reciprocity an unnecessary concept for the person who is born again (John 15:12). We, as Christians, are indeed a new creation (2 Corinthians 5:17) who cannot allow ourselves to be simple products of our social structures. We have been commissioned to actively participate in the building of this new kingdom.

Given these Christian tenets, is there a sociological perspective that can be used to analyze the Christian in the world? We believe there is an existing theoretical tradition in sociology that is fully compatible with the Christian perspective—one which may be used to build Christian sociological theory.

### Interpretative Sociology: Toward a Christian Sociological Model

The sociological model which is most compatible with Christian teaching may be termed interpretative sociology. This sociological tradition represents a synthesis between the creature emphasis of structuralism and the creator model of humanism. By interjecting subjective dimensions of reality into an objectively oriented synthesis, it allows not only for an image of fallen humanity shaped by the social structure, but also for a redeemed person who experiences Jesus as Lord and Savior. It is then redeemed person who acts as creator in the world (through the power of the Holy Spirit) to fashion a more perfect social structure in accord with the plan of God. Interpretative sociology takes seriously W. I. Thomas' famous definition of the situation: "If men define situations as real, they are real in their consequences." Christians have had a transforming experience with Christ and they define their encounter with Jesus as a reality. This encounter has real implications for individual as well as collective lives.

Interpretative sociology rests on three interrelated premises: (1) the importance of studying individuals in interaction in society, (2) emphasis on subjective as well as objective dimensions of the social order, and (3) that any macro-sociology or study of large-scale organizations must include premises 1 and 2. Each of these three premises separates interpretative sociology from both naturalistic and humanistic theories. For the naturalistic sociologist, the individual is treated as an abstract status-role that responds to the needs of the larger social structure of which he/she is a part. In contrast, the humanistic sociologist is more likely to recognize that individuals, not sociological systems, have needs, and that sociology should guide individuals in altering the structures to meet these needs. The emphasis for both remains, however, on the structure. Interpretative sociologists tend not only to acknowledge the importance of the individual but also focus on the individual in interaction as the appropriate level of sociological concern. For them, the concept of social structure or social institution is useful, but it should not be overemphasized nor reified. Instead, sociologists should analyze the manner in which people attach meaning to, or interpret, their social world. The stress is on the subjective or interpretative, rather than the objective dimensions of social reality.

Interpretative sociology also differs from the naturalistic and humanistic positions on the discipline's scientific nature. Interpretative sociologists would agree that sociology is a science, but they would assert that its subject matter is radically different from the natural sciences. This difference is due to the fact that men and women interpret or attach meaning to their social world—something with which humanistic sociologists might concur. On the other hand, interpretative sociology is committed to being value-free and would not share the humanistic sociologist's commitment to particular ideologies. It is, therefore, man's ability to ascribe meaning, or to interpret the social world, that makes the science of society different from the natural sciences. But nonetheless, it must attempt, at the same time, to be value-neutral in studying this subjective dimension of human behavior.

The base for interpretative sociology was well laid by the classic scholar Max Weber. Others have built upon this base, notably American interactionist sociologists, including Charles Horton Cooley, George Herbert Mead, and W. I. Thomas. Theorist Peter Berger, in collaboration with Thomas Luckmann (1966), has developed a sociology of knowledge built on classic scholars that serves as a contemporary example of interpretative sociology. I feel Berger's works provide the best single source upon which to build a theory that is compatible with Christian tenets and which allows for both a religious and scientific perspective to be held simultaneously.

Berger (1977:vii) finds that doing sociology is "often a difficult and painful business." Why? Because as Berger notes:

> To be a sociologist need not mean that one become either a heartless observer or a propagandist. Rather it should mean that each act of understanding stands in an existential tension with one's own values, even those, indeed especially those that one holds most passionately.

Therefore, the committed Christian sociologist, who necessarily holds passionately to Christian truths, must wrestle with the painful process of reconciling his/her beliefs with a sociological perspective. While Berger recognizes the tension, he has not resolved the dilemma.[3]

Berger's theory does attempt to synthesize the objective approach of naturalistic sociology with the subjective approach of humanistic sociolgy. With the naturalists, he does not abandon the model of a value-free sociology, nor does he deny the importance of the social structure to sociological analysis. With most humanists he shares the vision of human input in changing the social order, and he recognizes the importance of including microscopic analysis (the study of individuals and their subjective views) into a macroscopic perspective. Berger's theory reflects both naturalistic and humanistic assumptions on the nature of person and society.

Berger (1977:xv) defines society as "the imposition of order upon the flux of human experience." This order is a restraining force on men and women's potential freedom, but this constraint is paradoxically liberating. As Berger (1977:xvi) notes, "Society protects our sanity by preempting a large number of choices, not only of action but of thought." Yet while for Berger person is structurally constrained by his/her objective social reality, he/she is potentially free. The individual can and does help to fashion the social world, but within limits. Berger (1977:xviii) states that sociology "points up the social limits of freedom—the very limits that, in turn, provide the social space for any empirically viable expression of freedom."

Berger describes his theoretical orientation as "conservative humanism." As a conservative he is skeptical of theories that advance notions of rapid social change because he has "profound suspicions about the benefits of whatever is proposed as an alternative to the status quo" (Berger, 1970-21). As a humanist, he is critical of the shift in the sociological enterprise from theory toward narrowly circumscribed studies (Berger, 1963:8). In calling for sociology as a humanistic discipline, Berger (1963:168) urges an "openness to the immense richness of human life (which) . . . forces the sociologist to permit 'holes' in the closed walls of his theoretical schemes." Only as a humanistic enterprise that cannot be easily molded into a rigid propositional format for rigid empirical testing can sociology reflect the "richness of human life."

At the same time, as we have already noted, Berger is not willing to abandon the model of a value-free sociology. Values continue to be a source of tension and pain for Berger's humanistic sociology, for "the sociologist who (after all) is also a living human being, must *not* become value-free. The moment he does, he betrays his humanity and (in an operation that can be simultaneously called 'false consciousness' and 'bad faith') transforms himself into a ghostly embodiment of abstract science." Berger tackles issues of central significance, including politics and religion, and proceeds with his attempt to engage in this "painful business of doing sociology."[4]

### Discussion and Conclusion

Through an examination of assumptions underlying much sociological theory on the nature of person, we have attempted to demonstrate the source of tension that does exist between Christianity and sociology. Furthermore, we would like to suggest that there is an inherent role strain between the two roles of being a Christian and being a good sociologist. We feel this role strain has been dealt with in three ways: denial, compartmentalization, and compromise. Many of us have been afraid to face up to the potential conflict between sociological tenets and Christian belief. Instead of confronting the problem, it has been easier to deny its existence. Others of us may have avoided or minimized the conflict through compartmentalizing our religious concerns and our sociological ones: "Render to sociology the things that are sociology's and to God the things that are God's." Perhaps without realizing it, we may in fact be denying the things of God by making faulty assumptions that are not compatible with Christian tenets. Ironically, this approach leads to faulty sociological conclusions as evidenced by sociology of religion's failure to predict a religious revival that was well underway, at the time it was sounding a death knell for organized religion. Another solution to the problem of role strain has been to compromise commitments to either Christianity, sociology, or both. Under the guise of being value-free, many sociologists have become technicians rather than scholars. Worse yet, from a Christian perspective, many of us have denied the truth of the Scriptures by rationalizing them to fit into the positivistic mode of sociology.

In this chapter I have suggested that interpretative sociology provides a theoretical model that may be employed by Christians and non-Christians alike. Interpretative sociologists are committed to sociology's scientific method, but not to the manner in which it is expressed by their naturalistic colleagues. They favor a value-free sociology and attempt to prescribe appropriate methods of scientific investigation that would allow researchers and theorists to hold their values in abeyance. Not wishing to distort social reality as they feel naturalistic sociology has done, they are unwilling to openly admit to a value-laden position as humanistic sociology often dictates. While any scientific method for the study of human behavior must include cognizance of the subjective dimensions, this subjectivity must always be approached from the point of view of the subjects being studied, rather than from the biases of the theorist or researcher.

As we have been suggesting, the interpretative sociologist tends to stress a more creative and free person than allowed for by the naturalists. While the interpretative sociologist is aware of the potentially constraining power of our social institutions, he/she focuses on the creative abilities of men and women to shape them. While there may be no attempt to prescribe changes in the social world, there is an awareness that social reality is always in the process of being constructed. Men and women are both free actors in the social world and yet, to some extent, are simultaneously shaped by a world that is already in existence. The emphasis tends to be on the interaction in and interpretation of the world, rather than on the nature of the structure. I have further suggested that the works of Peter Berger provide the best contemporary example of such a theoretical model.

As Christians it is time for us to look closely at our sociological beliefs. While I do not believe Christians can or should develop a unique "Christian sociological theory," I do believe we should examine our theoretical wares carefully before we purchase them. The development of a sociology of sociology within the last decade has made us aware that sociology still can be a religion—complete with a creed demanding our faithful allegiance. It is important for Christians to attempt to sort out the sociological articles of faith from empirical facts.

## Discussion Questions

1. Why does the author identify with sect-like Christianity, rather than church-like Christianity?

2. What are the main differences between naturalistic and humanistic sociology's assumptions about the nature of person?

3. What are the main differences between their assumptions about the nature of society?

4. What are the main differences between their assumptions about the nature of sociological theory?

5. What are the reasons offered as to why naturalistic sociology, in its extreme form, is not compatible with Christianity?

6. What are the reasons offered as to why humanistic sociology, although bearing surface similarities to Christian teachings, does not reflect Christian teachings on the nature of person?

7. What makes interpretative sociology different from naturalistic and humanistic theories?

8. Why is interpretive sociology more compatible with Christian teachings?

9. Is interpretative sociology necessarily Christian; i.e., can there be non-Christian interpretative sociology?

10. How does the author assert that many Christians have combined their roles of being Christian with that of being sociologist?

## Notes

1. For a theologian's discussion of a reconciliation of sociological theory with theology, see Gregory Baum's *Religion and Alienation: A Theological Reading of Sociology*. Baum (1975:262-63) asserts that if sociologists refuse to reduce religion to a purely secular phenomenon (symbolic realism), they will "acknowledge a conception of human life, of which the deepest dimension remains hidden, lies beyond the grasp of science, manifests itself in the world

religions, and finds expression in people's person quest for self-transcendence." Then it is possible for sociology and theology to "move along the same line and theology appears as the critical prolongation of sociological concepts."

2. For a Christian theologian's discussion of Max Weber's "creative religion," (an approach that deals more satisfactorily than that of Comte, Durkheim, or Marx with an analysis of religion), see Baum (1975).

3. Berger's failure to resolve the tension between his Christianity and sociological theory is reflected in his masterpiece, *The Sacred Canopy* (1967). In this sociological treatise, he sounds much like an atheist ringing the death knell of religion. And with other sociologists of religion he failed as a sociologist to predict the occurrence of religious revival underway in the 1970s. Berger did deal with the resiliency of religion in his popularized discussion, *A Rumor of Angels*. In it he allows for a rediscovery of the sacred not discussed in his sociological treatise, *The Sacred Canopy*. In fact, Berger acknowledged that this work, in part, "reads like a treatise on atheism." *A Rumor of Angels* was an attempt to keep *The Sacred Canopy* from being used as a "counsel of despair for religion in the modern world." Clearly the tension between being a Christian and a sociologist is present in Berger's writings, but any resolution or synthesis is lacking.

4. Berger (1977:vii-ix) himself refers the interested reader to his diverse attempts at wrestling with his values and the issue of modernity. "I have explicated my understanding of the impact of modernity on human social existence and consciousness in *The Homeless Mind* (New York: Random House, 1973, with Brigitte Berger and Hansfried Kellner). Finally, the reader who wants to know more about my unapologetically *moraliste* approach to politics may turn to *Pyramids of Sacrifice* (New York: Basic Books, 1974), while *A Rumor of Angels* (New York: Doubleday, 1969) is still the longest statement on how I combine being a sociologist with (I'm afraid) a rather heretical Christianity."

## References

Baum, Gregory
    1975 *Religion and Alienation: A Theological Reading of Sociology*. New York: Paulist Press.
Berger, Peter and Thomas Luckmann
    1966 *The Social Construction of Reality*. Garden City, N.Y.: Doubleday.
Berger, Peter
    1963 *Invitation to Sociology*. Garden City, N.Y.: Doubleday.
    1967 *The Sacred Canopy: Elements of a Sociological Theory of Religion*. Garden City, N.Y.: Doubleday.
    1969 *A Rumor of Angels*. Garden City, N.Y.: Doubleday.
    1970 "Between System and Horde." Peter L. Berger and Richard Neuhause (coauthors). *Movement and Revolution*. Garden City, N.Y.: Doubleday, pp. 11-82.
    1977 *Facing up to Modernity*. New York: Basic Books.

Birnbaum, Norman
   1971 "The Crisis in Marxist Sociology," in J. David Colfax and
        Jack L. Roach's *Radical Sociology.* New York: Basic Books,
        pp. 108-148.
Cuzzort, R. P. and E. W. King
   1976 *Humanity and Modern Social Thought.* Hinsdale, Ill.: The
        Dryden Press.
Dynes, Russell R.
   1973 "On the Institutionalization of Sociology in the United
        States." *Sociological Focus,* 6 (Summer).
Etzioni, Amitai
   1968 *The Active Society: A Theory of Societal and Political
        Processes.* New York: The Free Press.
Friedrichs, Robert W.
   1970 *A Sociology of Sociology.* New York: The Free Press.
Glock, Charles Y. and Rodney Stark
   1965 *Religion and Society in Tension.* Chicago: Rand McNally
        and Co.
Gouldner, Alvin W.
   1970 *The Coming Crisis of Western Sociology.* New York: Basic
        Books
Homans, George C.
   1964 "Bringing Men Back In." *American Sociological Review,* 29
        (December).
   1967 *The Nature of Social Science.* New York: Harcourt, Brace
        and World, Inc.
Matson, Floyd
   1976 *The Idea of Man.* New York: Dalecorte Press.
Mullins, Nicholas
   1973 *Theories and Theory Groups in Contemporary American So-
        ciology.* New York: Harper & Row.
Stinchcombe, Arther
   1975 "Merton's Theory of Social Structure." Lewis Coser (ed.)
        *The Idea of Social Structure.* New York: Harcourt, Brace,
        Jovanovich, pp. 9-20.
Wrong, Dennis
   1961 "The Oversocialized Conception of Man in Modern So-
        ciology." *American Sociological Review,* 26 (April).
Yinger, J. Milton
   1970 *The Scientific Study of Religion.* New York: Macmillan.

# 13
# Coming to Terms with Karl Marx

*Michael L. Yoder*[1]

Karl Marx is hardly a candidate for the list of ten most admired men, at least in the United States. After all, many Americans, particularly Christians, see him and his latter-day followers as the foremost enemies of Christianity and the American system. Suggesting that he who stated that "religion is the opiate of the people" must be taken seriously by students of sociology and by Christians, and that Marx's ideas contain elements of truth which cannot be ignored, may be regarded by some as heresy. Such, however, is precisely the position taken in this chapter.

## Why Marx Should Be Taken Seriously
*Some Basic Contributions of Marx*

Students of sociology, Christian or non-Christian, cannot ignore Karl Marx for the following reasons:

First, Marx, Max Weber, and Emile Durkheim form what sociologists jokingly refer to as the "holy trinity" of sociology. Marx's contributions are especially important in the fields of social stratification, political sociology, social change, sociology of knowledge, sociology of religion, and social theory in general. There is hardly an area of sociology in which Marx has not made an important contribution.

Second, Marx has laid out in compelling fashion the case for the primacy of economic factors in human social events. Simply put, this view says that economic factors ultimately shape all social relations and

**Michael L. Yoder**
*Associate Professor of Sociology*
*Goshen College*
After service as a missions associate in Brazil, Michael Yoder did graduate work in sociology at the University of Wisconsin where he is presently a candidate for the PhD degree in sociology. His specialty has been urbanization, demography, and religion. At Goshen College he teaches a variety of sociology courses. He is a member of the Mennonite Church, Goshen, Indiana.

social institutions (law, religion, politics, education, etc.) in a given society, as well as the way people think and believe. There is much evidence to support his case which cannot be refuted simply by resorting to philosophical or religious assumptions contrary to those of Marx.

Third, Marx is the intellectual father of what might be called the "conflict school" in contemporary sociology. This view, which has recently been gaining ground in American sociology at the expense of the long dominant "functionalist" or "consensus" view, says simply that it is conflict, not consensus, which is most pervasive in human social interaction and which best explains social phenomena. For Marx the conflict is always rooted in economic affairs; all conflict is ultimately class conflict.

Fourth, Marx combined the roles of sociologist, economist, political scientist and activist, historian, and philosopher, if not more. Modern American sociology has become so specialized that we may look to Marx for an example of how to avoid sociological myopia.

*Reasons Why Christians Should Take Marx Seriously*

Christian students of sociology should take Marx seriously and come to terms with him for three additional reasons:

First, although Marx himself was anti-religious and his criticism irreligious, he can quite correctly be seen as a prophet in the best of the Judeo-Christian tradition.[2] Although his theology is certainly not orthodox in a Jewish or Christian sense, his thirst for social justice is rooted in the prophetic tradition of the Old Testament. Marx's message is quite similar to that of Amos who said to the ancient Jews:

> Hear this word, you cows of Bashan, who are in the mountain of Samaria, who oppress the poor, who crush the needy, who say to their husbands, "Bring, that we may drink!" The Lord God has sworn by his holiness that, behold, the days are coming upon you, when they shall take you away with hooks, even the last of you with fishhooks (Amos 4:1, 2,).

The supreme irony here may be that although Marx was avowedly anti-religious, he in fact was quite religious as measured by the Jewish prophetic tradition.

Second, recent developments in theology, particularly the theology of liberation, actually draw considerable inspiration from Marx and his analysis of the human condition. The Christian student of sociology should come to some understanding of the relationship between socioeconomic context and the development of theologies of different content. Marx can help us here.

Third, Marxism has become not only a method of social analysis but a functional religion for many sociologists today. Many of those who no longer believe in the God of Abraham who later revealed himself in Jesus Christ now *believe* the doctrines of Marx with real conviction and attempt to convert nonbelievers to the Marxist belief system. This is particularly true in the graduate schools of the most respected departments of sociology. A Christian sociologist must come to terms with Marx simply to maintain the integrity of his or her faith.

## Marx's Philosophical Assumptions

Marx studied, lived, and wrote in the German philosophical tradition. To be a respected scholar in nineteenth-century Germany required a thorough grounding in philosophy. Marx took the task seriously, so seriously that we today find his emphasis on philosophy overdone, if not a serious stumbling block to understanding him.

### Idealism vs. Materialism

Western philosophy has basically been idealist philosophy. While the Greek philosopher Plato has been the most influential in shaping the idealist tone of Western philosophy, at the time of Marx the most prominent philosopher was a German, Hegel. Marx's rejection of idealism must be understood to grasp the rest of what he said. But that rejection of idealism makes it difficult—particularly for Christians—to understand and accept Marx's propositions.

The following diagram, while an oversimplification, helps us understand the basic differences between idealist and materialist philosophy.

FIGURE 1. Contrast Between Idealist and Materialist Philosophy

| Idealism | Materialism |
|---|---|
| °Ideas | Ideas |
| Material things | °Material things |

Idealist philosophy and thinking says that that which is "really real," which is perfect, changeless, absolute, and eternal exists only in the realm of ideas. Material things are only poor copies, pale reflections, of that reality. For example, the perfect square or the perfect apple exist only in the realm of ideas. Any square that might be drawn, any apple that might be picked and eaten, even the most perfect, will be flawed in some way. There is also the assumption here that ideas precede material things, that material things derive from, and are produced by preexistent ideas. Thus the star in the diagram emphasizes that the level of ideas is most basic, and the arrow indicates the emanation of material things from the world of ideas.

Materialist philosophy takes the opposite view. Here the assumption is that reality exists only in material form, which precedes ideas, and that our ideas of what things are like are really only imperfect derivations from those material things. To use our prior example and turn it around, we can only derive an idea of what a square or an apple is after having seen, felt, and experienced real squares and apples. Thus the material realm is most basic and is preexistent to the derivative ideas which flow from it.

## Idealism and Christianity

It is important to realize that most Christians and orthodox Christian theology have been and continue to be closer to the idealist position than to the materialist:

> In the beginning God created the heavens and the earth. The earth was without form and void, and darkness was upon the face of the deep; and the Spirit of God was moving over the face of the waters (Genesis 1:1).

> In the beginning was the Word, and the Word was with God, and the Word was God. He was in the beginning with God; all things were made through him, and without him was not anything made that was made. In him was life, and the life was the light of men. The light shines in the darkness, and the darkness has not overcome it (John 1:1-5).

In the Christian view an eternal, preexisting, omnipotent God created everything that was made. He created man himself along with the rest of the creation (Genesis 1). Later he incarnated himself in the form of the God-man, Jesus. It is through God and his revelation to us through Christ and the Bible that Christians learn of God's grace, salvation, love, and justice. God's love, righteousness, and justice are perfect. Christians are called to follow after Christ as disciples and to lead lives of righteousness and love, realizing that their own righteousness and love will always be flawed. In fact they will be "as filthy rags." Religion and the church are seen as instituted and ordained by God. They are to follow the biblical pattern, although again, any particular church or religion, albeit Christian, will be somewhat flawed. Such is the lot of sinful man and his sinful institutions, even religious institutions.

## Marx's Materialism

Let us now turn to Marx to illustrate the radical shift he made from idealist to materialist thinking. (Refer back to Figure 1 to see the shift Marx is making). Consider the following statement from Marx and his collaborator, Friedrich Engels:

> In direct contrast to German philosophy, which descends from heaven to earth, here we ascend from earth to heaven. That is to say, we do not set out from what men say, imagine, conceive, nor from men as narrated, thought of, imagined, conceived, in order to arrive at men in the flesh. We set out from real, active men and on the basis of their real life process we demonstrate the development of the ideological reflexes and echoes of this life process. . . . Life is not determined by consciousness, but consciousness by life (Marx and Engels, *The German Ideology*).

Marx is taking "real active men" (and women) and their "real life process" as the starting point. He says that material life and relations are basic, preexistent, and determinative of "ideological reflexes," the ideas which men and women hold about their lives.

> But before there was argumentation there was action. *Im Anfang war die Tat* (In the beginning was the deed.) (Engels, *On Historical Materialism.*)

Contrast this statement of Engels with the biblical "In the beginning was the Word" (John 1:1) and the difference between Marx and Engels' materialism and the idealism of Christianity is again seen. Marx's view of religion, as we might expect, is also quite different from the Christian view:

The basis of irreligious criticism is this: *man makes religion;* religion does not make man (Marx, *Contribution to the Critique of Hegel's Philosophy of Right*).

## Marx's Model of Society

At this point we wish to attempt a fuller diagram of Marx's thinking, one which is really only an elaboration of the idealist model in Figure 1, but which uses some of Marx's own terminology:

FIGURE 2. Simplified Marxian Model of Society

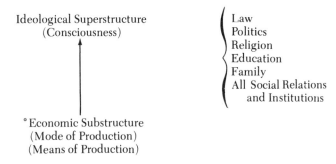

Marx explains:

> In the social production of their subsistence men enter into determined and necessary relations with each other which are independent of their wills—production—relations which correspond to a definite stage of development of their material productive forces. The sum of these production-relations forms the economic structure of society, the real basis upon which a juridical and political superstructure arises, and to which definite social forms of consciousness correspond. The mode of production of the material subsistence conditions the social, political and spiritual life process in general. It is not the consciousness of men which determines their existence, but on the contrary it is their social existence which determines their consciousness (Marx, Introduction to *Critique of Political Economy*).

Marx's economic substructure contains both "the mode of production" and the "means of production." The latter correspond roughly to what a capitalist economist would term the "factors of production," usually given as land, labor, and capital. The mode of production is best understood as the distinctive economic system which combines those means (factors) of production to produce goods and services. Marx was most concerned with the capitalist mode of production under which he was living. But he also spoke of slavery and feudalism as modes of production which had preceded capitalism and looked forward to socialism, and finally communism succeeding capitalism. Regardless of the number and names of the various modes of production, Marx's basic point is that the economic mode of production will condition and ultimately determine all those elements of consciousness (ideology) and derivative social institutions which make up the superstructure. Thus, according to Marx, we should expect to find different systems of law, government, education, family life, religion, etc., under differing economic systems. These not only correspond to a given mode of production; they support and maintain it as well.

For example, under slavery the system of law will exist to maintain and regulate the conditions of slavery. Education will certainly be different for slaves than for their masters. Religion may even be called on to teach slaves that it is God's will that they obey their masters. Under modern capitalism, private property will no longer include slaves, but law will still function to protect property in similar ways.

### Dialectical Materialism

Marx's materialism, however, is not as static as a careless reading of him might suggest. He took pains to disassociate himself from Feuerbach, whose materialism provided for little change. We have already said that Marx saw different modes of production—slavery, feudalism, capitalism, socialism, communism. He often called these "epochs" in human history, or stages in which the mode of production produced a qualitatively different consciousness and pattern of social relations. Human history, then, is one of progression from one epoch to the next. But what is the cause of such change or progression?

Central to Marx's theory of social change is the idea of *contradiction*. Actually Marx simply took this from Hegel's idea of the "antithesis." The idea here is simply that when a phenomenon of sufficient strength, opposed to a prior phenomen (thesis), arises and comes to full flower, the tension between the two will produce a new and qualitatively different phenomenon (synthesis). The dialectical pattern developed by Hegel and used by Marx can be seen in Figure 3 which appears on page 224.

To Hegel this dialectic moved in the realm of ideas. Marx rejected

FIGURE 3. The Marxian Dialectic

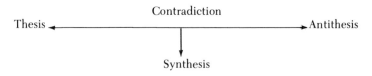

Hegel's idealism, but retained the useful concept of the antithesis or contradiction and applied it to his materialist outlook to produce his unique dialectical or historical materialism. How exactly does this operate? Marx explains:

> At a certain stage of their development the material productive forces of society come into contradiction with the existing production-relations, or what is merely a juridical expression for the same thing, the property relations within which they have operated before. From being forms of development of the productive forces, these relations turn into fetters upon their development. Then comes an epoch of social revolution. With the change in the economic foundation the whole immense superstructure is slowly or rapidly transformed (Marx, from the Introduction to *Critique of Political Economy*).

Thus Marx holds that slavery and feudalism each gave way in turn to a succeeding mode of production when the internal contradictions within them became strong enough. The basic contradiction within capitalism is the class conflict between those who own capital, the chief means of production under capitalism, and those who do not. Marx's term for the class of the owners of capital is *bourgeoisie*. Persons who own no capital are forced to sell their labor to the bourgeoisie in order to live. These persons are designated the *proletariat*. These two classes of persons are the most fundamental groups of people under capitalism.

The capitalist expropriates the value which his workers add to the product they produce in the form of *surplus value*. The capitalist's point of view would be that this profit belongs to him for taking a business risk. Marx feels it is unfairly taken from the worker who has produced it. The capitalist will give the worker a wage barely sufficient to sustain him and to allow him to reproduce, since this is in his economic interest, but no more. The wages paid the worker are less than the productive value of the labor performed. This exploitation of the worker is inherent in capitalism, Marx feels. When the proletariat develops sufficient class consciousness of their oppression, they will revolt, overthrow the bourgeoisie and the capitalist state which supports the bourgeoisie, and abolish private property.[3] The basic contradiction of capitalism will have then resulted in a new stage in human history, socialism, where property will be held for a time by a state in the interests of all. Law, politics, religion, and family life will all be transformed. Religion, in fact, will disappear since it functioned under capitalism only to keep workers falsely content, preventing them from developing true class consciousness. As the vestiges of class antagonism tracing back to capitalism are removed the need for even the state will disappear. Then Marx's utopia, true communism, will be reached—or so he holds:

> When, in the course of development, class distinctions have disappeared and all production has been concentrated in the hands of a vast association of the whole nation, the public power will lose its political character. ... In place of the old bourgeois society, with all its classes and class antagonisms we shall have an association in which the free development of each is the condition for the free development of all (Marx and Engels, *Manifesto of the Communist Party*).

Then, curiously, the dialectic will stop. The class struggle, to which Marx had traced all past historical development, will disappear as private property is abolished and all forms of consciousness tied to private property gradually fade away. Heaven on earth will be a reality. There will be no further stages of human evolution, if we are to believe Marx.

### Marx's Major Contributions
After having looked at Marx's basic philosophical assumptions and a brief diagram of his view of society we now turn to a brief look at what we see as his major contributions. What is there to Marx which rings true, which helps us better understand human social events?

### *The Primacy of Economic Affairs*
We have seen that Marx's materialism holds that *ultimately* everything in the social system, both social institutions and ideology, is rooted in the economic substructure. In the language of contemporary sociology we might say that Marx claims that economic variables

should "explain the variance" in noneconomic variables and not vice-versa.[4] What evidence it there to support this view?

## Slavery in the United States

We have previously referred to slavery as a mode of production. If we look at the pre-Civil War South in the United States, we can clearly see that the social institutions and consciousness which Marx includes in the "superstructure" in fact corresponded very closely to an economy based on slavery. Law, government, religion, education, and the family not only were compatible with slavery, *they resisted any attempt to do away with it*. Laws and government combined to protect most carefully the "right" to own slaves. Slaves were more accurately termed property than people; they were a commodity traded on the auction block. Runaway slaves and those who aided them were severely punished. It was illegal to teach a slave to read or write since such might free slaves' minds and cause them to seek to free their bodies as well, bodies which they themselves did not own.

Religion accommodated itself quite well to slavery. White people were taught that slavery was *not* unchristian, and Bible passages were used to support these claims. Slaves were seen as human enough to receive salvation, but were still taught that it was their Christian duty to obey their masters. It is clearly *not* a historical accident that the abolition movement arose in the churches of the North, where slavery had never taken hold, rather than in the South. It is also no historical accident that the Methodist, Baptist, and Presbyterian churches divided into Northern and Southern branches at the time of the Civil War.

Slavery also helped produce the pattern of social norms regarding sexual contact, which held the slave women were to be accessible to their white masters. But if black males were even suspected of sexual contact with a white woman they were castrated and lynched as an example to others. The exaggerated stereotypes of black sexuality which persist today almost certainly trace to the period of slavery.

## Latin America

Other evidence to support the primacy of economic factors in determining elements of the "superstructure" comes from traditional Latin America. The landed estate, whether producing crops for export or basically for subsistence, has been the central social institution in most of Latin America until quite recently. Its economic domination is reflected in other areas of life, and its influence is still present even where it has been economically superseded by urban industrial capitalism. Latin American politics, particularly on the local and regional level, has been dominated by the most powerful large estate owners. Since the landed aristocracy dominated politics, they were able to write laws in their favor, appoint judges, and raise military and police forces to enforce those laws supporting the system of property relations. In this system the privileged few owned most of the productive land and the poor masses were reduced to offering their labor to the landlords in exchange for what approximated the subsistence existence Marx predicted. Repeated attempts to redistribute land to poor peasants through much-heralded land reform programs have been blocked by the large estate owners and their supporters, except where genuine social revolutions have occurred, as in Mexico, Bolivia, and Cuba.[5] Despite all the publicity given to reform and "revolution," Latin American society, with the notable exception of Cuba, remains a conservative society. There the economic powers that be (including large estate owners, urban industrialists, and increasingly, multinational corporations) block efforts toward meaningful social change which would benefit the poor masses.

*Class Antagonisms in the United States Today*

While evidence from contemporary United States may be somewhat less clear, there is much to support Marx here as well. In the urban riots of the late 1960s which broke out after the assassination of Martin Luther King, police were in some cases ordered to "shoot to kill" looters. The logic of such an order seems to be that the protection of private property is of more fundamental importance than the life of a human being.

In labor relations, we find that the game played is a more or less open power play between labor and management. Labor uses the strike, management the threat of dismissal of "unruly" workers (those "agitating" to form a union), the lockout, or the threat of a complete shutdown. While labor relations in the United States are less violent now than in the early twentieth century, the class struggle which Marx saw as central to human history and social change clearly continues.

A specific case in point here involves the struggle of the United Farmworkers Union, representing largely Mexican-American agricultural laborers, to organize and improve their working conditions and wages paid them by large farmers in the Southwest, particularly California. While the farmworkers gained a good deal of support from college students, intellectuals, church leaders, and urban workers, support was notably lacking among United States farmers. Farmers in the author's own (Mennonite) denomination and other Christian groups showed little support for the farmworkers. Christians must learn from Marx that they are not immune from class interest.

## The Influence of Social Class Position

The salience of social class position in human affairs is so obvious that even non-Marxist social scientists do not dispute its importance. From studies of voting behavior to studies of family size preferences to studies of religious practice, social class position is generally found to be one of the most important explanatory variables. This is true despite the fact that non-Marxist social scientists generally do not measure social class as Marx would prefer.[6]

We conclude that Marx has contributed greatly to social science by stressing the importance of economic factors in influencing the rest of human affairs. While he did not so much prove as assert his case, modern social science has offered solid verification of this important hypothesis.

## The World Economic Order

While Marx dealt largely with individual national societies, his latter-day followers have extended his analysis beyond national boundaries. While various terms are used to describe rich countries and poor countries, the basic idea here is that the rich capitalist countries form a kind of world bourgeoisie and the poor countries a kind of world proletariat. Lenin claimed that imperialism, the oppression of the poor countries by the rich, was inherent in capitalism. More recent thinkers such as Frank and Wallerstein argue basically that poor countries remain poor not because rich countries are not helping them enough (the liberal view), but precisely because the poor countries are part of a world economic order which treats them as economic, if no longer political, colonies. Such a position holds that the United States, while trying to appear magnanimous in offering "foreign aid" to poorer nations, really is serving its own economic interests by using political diplomacy, war, investment in poor countries, extension or withdrawal of credit, and other instruments.

It is difficult, even for social scientists, to calculate the cost vs. benefits that accrue to poor countries because of their relationships, voluntary or involuntary, with the United States. While it is unlikely that all U.S. actions toward poorer nations are undertaken solely out of economic self-interest, it is likely that many are to a considerable degree. To again turn to the cases of Latin America, we find that the United States has intervened repeatedly in Latin America, whether overtly by sending in the Marines or covertly through the CIA or other indirect methods. And while such intervention is usually couched in the language of "preserving freedom" it might be less euphemistically and more honestly recognized as directed toward protecting U.S. economic interests. For example, there was widespread support of Castro's overthrow of Baptista and attempts to begin social reform in Cuba until we in the U.S. learned that by reform he included expropriation of American-owned lands and businesses. United States interventions in Guatemala, the Dominican Republic, Chile, Vietnam, etc., while explained as attempting to prevent the growth of communism, have had as an undeniable objective the long-run protection of U.S. economic freedom to invest in those countries and profit from those investments.

It could well be that the Marxian tradition is again close to the Bible. Note what the Book of James has to say on the origin of strife among men:

> What causes wars, and what causes fightings among you? Is it not your passions that are at war in your members? You desire and do not have; so you kill. And you covet and cannot obtain; so you fight and wage war (James 4:1-2a).

While James is speaking more on the individual level and Marx on the collective level, the similarity is striking. Quarrels and wars result when men and nations covet what belongs to someone else. Marx and his followers have in a way simply offered evidence as to the consequences of violation of the biblical injunction, "Thou shalt not covet" (Exodus 20:17).[7]

*The Role of Religion in Society*

We have stated that Marx's view of religion is that it is a human rather than divine product, that as part of the superstructure it reflects and supports the existing mode of production. While Christians cannot accept all of Marx here (see "A Christian Response to Marx"), the Marxian perspective offers crucial insights on the role of religion and theology which most Christians miss because of their idealist position.

Marx's most quoted statement on religion is that it is the "opiate of the people, the sigh of the oppressed creature" (*Contribution to the Critique of Hegel's Philosophy of Right*). He regarded it as such and therefore favored its eradication, not so much because of any fundamental opposition to religion, but because it was his judgment that on balance religion was strongly counterrevolutionary. Under capitalism it kept the proletariat drugged, it kept them from developing true class consciousness, and it postponed the revolution which he saw as so necessary to achieve communism, the Marxist heaven. Marxism is in a way a secular world religion, one which says that supernatural religion must be done away with if we are ever to reach utopia.

It is not true that Marx and Engels saw religion as always counterrevolutionary. In his *The Peasant War in Germany* Engels notes the revolutionary contribution of the Reformation, particularly among the most radical of the Anabaptists and self-styled prophet leaders such as Muenzer.[8] Yet he notes that Luther, himself of peasant origin, eventually turned vehemently against the peasants, crying that:

> They should be knocked to pieces, strangled and stabbed, secretly, and openly, by everybody who can do it, just as one might kill a mad dog (Engels, p. 61).

Muenzer met a violent death; Luther and Lutheranism prospered and became in Marx's view as counterrevolutionary as the Roman Catholic Church. Since it was their view that on balance religion was quite counterrevolutionary, Marx and Engels opposed it and looked forward to its destruction. It is clear, however, that they did not oppose religion which fed the revolutionary consciousness of the masses. They simply did not see enough of such religion around to put any faith in it.

There is sufficient evidence available to hold as Marx did that religion acts at times as a counterrevolutionary ideological tool of oppression. We have mentioned the role of religion in maintaining slavery in the U.S. Afrikaaner religion in South Africa is clearly a key ideological support to the oppression of black people there. The Catholic Church in Latin America has until recently consistently supported the interests of the rich landowners against the peasants.

Yet there is enough evidence on the other side to show that religion has more often been a liberating force than Marx would admit. In Jewish history we find the zealots, the Maccabees, and modern-day Zionists. Who would deny the religious origins and support for the Abolitionist and Civil Rights movements in the U.S.? Priests are now being tortured in Latin America for their support of the poor.

We conclude then that while Marx is correct that religion often has been used as a counterrevolutionary instrument of class oppression, his conclusion that it almost always plays this role was too hasty. We may learn more from Marx if we look at the specific class situations of different groups and how their religion and theology may have been influenced by their class position.

*Theologies of Liberation/Oppression*

It is no accident that religion is used as a liberating or potentially liberating force more often by oppressed peoples and as a force to maintain the (oppressive) economic system more often by those groups who profit from that system. The Old Testament prophets, Christ, and Marx himself were all Jews, a group of people probably more oppressed throughout Western history than any other. Is it any accident that they should yearn for liberation? Is it an accident that black slaves in the U.S. picked up the theme of liberation from (Jewish) biblical history in their songs and are now building a black theology?[9]

> When Israel was in Egypt land, let my people go
> Oppressed so hard they could not stand, let my people go.
>
> Go down Moses, way down in Egypt land,
> Tell old Pharaoh, let my people go.

Marxist analysis suggests that it is no accident that the theology of liberation has arisen in Latin America, where oppression and the class struggle are perhaps more obvious, rather than in North America or Europe, where theologies are decidedly less radical. The rich and the comfortable do not need a theology of liberation. They find more assuring a theology which stresses order, since this suggests subconsciously, if not consciously, that they will retain their economic position as well as their spiritual salvation.[10] This might help to explain why Christian theology has been so infected with a (pagan) Greek emphasis on order and unchangeableness of God and His creation. ("Change and decay in all around I see. . . . O Thou who changest not, abide with me"). The biblical view which teaches that God *acts* in history to bring "justice for the poor and mercy for the oppressed" is not so often highlighted. It is noteworthy that the name of God given to Moses is "I Am Who I Am" or "I Will Be What I Will Be" explicitly implying that God is one who acts (Ex. 3:13-14).

Central to the author's own religious tradition is pacifism and nonresistant love. This emphasis is more commonly found among religious groups which have arisen as relatively powerless social minorities (Anabaptists, Quakers, Brethren, Jehovah's Witnesses) than among groups which have been part of a state-church tradition of relative wealth and power (Catholic, Lutheran, Anglican, and Calvinist). Marx should teach us that a group's choice of pacifism vs. a "just war" position, for example, is not merely a "theological" matter, but one which has real economic, social, and political implications which may influence that choice.

## Marx's Shortcomings

### A *Christian Response to Marx*[11]

The first and most obvious objection to Marx from the standpoint of Christian belief is that Marx has "thrown the baby out with the bath water." That is, in his view that religion is merely a derivative part of the ideological superstructure dependent on the economic mode of production with no autonomous existence or transcendent origin, Marx has removed the God of both the Old and New Testaments. God and religion become merely human ideological constructions based on and helping to maintain the economic *status quo*.

Along with Marx's denial of a transcendent Creator God in control of the universe is an implicit denial of revelation from God as the source of truth. Truth for Marx becomes little more than true class consciousness, an awareness of one's true class position. Such a position is unacceptable to Christians, who believe that the biblical message speaks to man regardless of his class position. Man is lost without God, no matter how aware he may be of the material conditions of his life. Such, however, are not irrelevant to the perception of the biblical message, as we have seen.

Another serious error of Marx from the Christian point of view is his attribution of *all* evil or sin (Marx wouldn't use these terms) to the holding of private property which is most highly developed in capitalism. That is, Marx attributes evil to the *system* based on private property, and ultimately sees no individual basis for sin, since even the exploitation of the worker by the capitalist is due to their relationship in the capitalist mode of production, rather than to any problem with the nature of man. Marx's naive faith is such that he believes that once the system is changed to abolish private property, all evil will disappear. Christians can easily see through this delusion; they know that since the Fall individual sin is a very present reality, and one responsible for much (not all) of the evil in the world around us. One does not remove individual sin simply by changing the system. It is removed by the redemption offered by Jesus Christ.

Many Christians, however, have fallen into an equally one-sided position of attributing all evil to the individual and none to human institutions. A more realistic Christian view might be that sinful human beings build sinful human institutions and social systems, which are capable of greater evil than individuals alone ever could be. A few of the more obvious examples here are the horrors of slavery, Hitler's Third Reich, Stalinist purges in Russia, and nuclear war, a foretaste of which was given by the U.S. to the world at Hiroshima and Nagasaki. The redemption and regeneration offered by Jesus Christ is desperately needed by individuals and institutions in a groaning, fallen creation.

### A Sociological Response to Marx

The major weakness of Marx from a sociological point of view is that he overstates his case, ultimately reducing all social phenomena to economic causes. In so doing he ends up with a one-factor theory. Marx certainly has good company in this position, but it is no less a failing for him than for others who have done the same with other theories.

The best corrective to Marx's one-sided emphasis on economic factors has been provided by Max Weber. In his classic, *The Protestant Ethic and the Spirit of Capitalism,* Weber provides a compelling accounting of the role of ascetic Protestantism in the development of capitalism. Causality in human social affairs simply does not run *only* from the material to the ideal, or in Marx's terms from the substructure to the superstructure.[12]

Many of Marx's predictions have simply failed to come true. The revolution of the proletariat happened first not in England or Germany, as he expected, but in semi-feudal Russia where urban industrial capitalism had not yet come to full flower. Marx taught that a given mode of production would only supersede another when the latter had reached full development. Such was not the case in Russia.

The proletariat in most Western societies has been quite content to continue working for the fruits that capitalism can provide. For most workers these fruits have certainly been more than the subsistence wage Marx said would be paid them. Many workers have been given the right to strike and to bargain collectively to improve their wages and fringe benefits. Most have been content to do this, and have not worked actively to overthrow the capitalist state. Capitalism has been more flexible in meeting workers' demands than Marx would have thought possible.[13]

Most Western sociologists would disagree with Marx's view of social class, which essentially says that class position is determined by only one variable, namely ownership vs. non-ownership of capital, the chief means of production. Following Weber, most sociologists see class position as determined by a variety of factors, among which are occupation, education, income, and type and location of residence.

Marx felt that the class structure of capitalist societies would ultimately be reduced to the two major classes, the bourgeoisie and the proletariat. Persons occupying middle positions such as *petit bourgeois* (small shopkeepers) would fall into the proletariat, as would a large portion of the bourgeoisie itself, due to intense competition among producers. While there is some evidence to support Marx on this, most sociologists in the U.S. hold to a three-class view of society—upper, middle, and lower or working class. There are clearly many persons in industrial societies who do not fit well in either the bourgeoisie or the proletariat. Self-employed farmers, small businessmen, and professionals are good examples.

## Conclusions

What do we conclude as we come to terms with Marx? First that Marx was correct in stressing the importance of economic (material) factors in human affairs, although he exaggerated that importance. Such is his basic and primary contribution to social science.

Second, that although the Christian can never accept Marx's dismissal of a preexisting, transcendent, creating, and redeeming God, Marx does help us to see that much of religion is a human product, although we may still believe it to be divinely instituted and ordained. Elements of that religion may and often do serve class interests which should be regarded as a form of idolatry. Sincere Christians should continually pray that God might free them to act according to his will, not according to their will and interests.

Third, that while Marx's attribution of all evil to the system rather than to fallen human nature is incorrect and naive, we must admit that there is evil in both individual persons *and* in the institutions they build and maintain collectively, although Christians have tended to ignore the latter. The biblical call to repentance and conversion applies at both levels.

## Discussion Questions

1. Why have Christians often been slow to preach the justice dimensions of the gospel? Why is a theology which emphasizes individual sin and redemption often more comfortable?

2. What meanings have been given to "salvation" by different religious communities? How have these been influenced by socioeconomic positions?

3. How is the way we read and interpret the Bible influenced by class interests? For example, what is the meaning of "thou shalt not steal"? To whom does the command apply? How has it been used by Christians?

4. Is evaluation of capitalism, socialism, or other economic systems possible free of the bias of class position?

5. Why have "priests" been more popular than "prophets"?

6. How do religion, nationalism, and class position in the world economic order combine to defend the interests of Western capitalism against those of Third World nations of different ideology and class position?

7. Why does Marx's dialectic end once communism is reached?

8. What criticism may Christians make of Marx's view of human nature and the nature of evil?

9. To what degree are religious institutions (e.g., denominational organizations, mission boards) and religious practices (e.g., worship patterns) of divine origin? Of human (social) origin?

10. How does Marx's view of social inequality compare with biblical teaching? What did the ancient Jewish prophets and Jesus have to say to the people of God regarding material wealth and the sharing of that wealth? What should Christians today be doing to follow biblical guidelines regarding the acquisition and use of material wealth?

## Notes

1. The author, an associate professor of sociology at Goshen College,

stresses that this article represents only something of his own coming to terms with Marx. Useful suggestions were given by J. Howard Kauffman and Dennis MacDonald.

2. Marx was born to a German Jewish family in 1818. When Karl was six years old, his father had the whole family baptized as Christians. Marx struggled with his Jewishness the rest of his life and is the author of some anti-Semitic statements.

3. Marx's followers have long debated the question of whether a violent revolution is needed to accomplish the transition from capitalism to socialism or whether a peaceful transition, perhaps by democratic processes, is possible. Marx is not entirely clear on the matter. Recent evidence is mostly on the side of the necessity of a violent transition. The democratic election of Salvador Allende as Marxist president of Chile and his attempted transformation of Chile into a socialist state was cut short by a violent counterrevolution supported by what Marx would call "bourgeois reactionaries." Revolutions generally require a monopoly of force if they are to succeed.

4. This is oversimplifying a bit. Marx realizes that the superstructure can act back on the economic substructure to change it. This is partly what happens in the dialectic through revolutionary *praxis* (practice). It is the developing class consciousness of the proletariat, which fits in the ideological superstructure, which eventually results in the overthrow of capitalism. But that developing class consciousness is itself rooted in the capitalist mode of production, and thus is ultimately economically determined as well.

5. For evidence that land ownership in Latin America remains highly concentrated in large estates see Barraclough and Domike (1966).

6. For an example of a Marxist treatment of social class see Wright and Perrone (1977).

7. While Marx and the Book of James seem to agree that covetousness causes social conflict (war), we do not wish to suggest that Marx and the Bible agree on the cause and origin of covetousness itself. While for Marx covetousness arises from a system of unequal property relations and should disappear with the abolition of private property, the biblical view sees covetousness as a part of the fallen human condition, largely irrespective of social class. See "A Christian Response to Marx."

8. Present-day heirs of the Anabaptist movement, the Mennonites, Amish, and Hutterites, have repeatedly tried to disassociate themselves from those such as Muenzer who took up the sword in an effort to bring in the kingdom of God on earth. The actions of Muenzer and the Munsterites are strongly counter to the emphasis on pacifism found among most of the sixteenth-century and twentieth-century Anabaptists. This attempt to renounce Muenzer is partly due to a genuine difference in theology, but also the fact that historians opposed to the Anabaptists used the violent chapters in the Anabaptist movement to discredit it. Nonetheless, the connection to chiliastic violence is here. The present-day attempt to erase it is an illustrating example of the gymnastics that religious groups go through to cleanse their theology and history.

9. James Cone, in *A Black Theology of Liberation*, says, "American white

theology . . . has been basically a theology of the white oppressor" (Segundo, p. 22).

10. Sociologists of religion and church historians have long recognized that different social settings produce differing theological emphases and religious practices. See for example Niebuhr's *The Social Sources of Denominationalism* (1957).

11. The author purposely does not label this section "The Christian Response to Marx" since it is his conviction, and hope, that each Christian can and will make his or her own genuine response to Karl Marx. This is the tentative response of one such person.

12. It is not fair to use Weber to fight against Marx and try to disprove the validity of the materialist position. Weber saw the possibility of ideas influencing material existence and vice versa. See the closing lines of *The Protestant Ethic*.

13. This analysis rests heavily on the case of the United States. It is less true for other Western nations and even less so for others, where the Marxist analysis fits better, as we have seen for Latin America. And in the case of U.S. workers, their prosperity may have been achieved at least partly at the cost of the poor in less developed countries.

## References

Barraclough, Solon and Arthur Domike
1966 "Agrarian Structure in Seven Latin American Countries." *Land Economics*, 42, pp. 391-424.
Cone, James
1970 *A Black Theology of Liberation*. Philadelphia: Lippincott.
Engels, Frederick
1966 *The Peasant War in Germany*. New York: International Publishers.
Frank, Andre Gunder
1969 *Latin America: Underdevelopment or Revolution*. New York: Monthly Review Press.
Lenin, Nikolai
1966 "*Imperialism: The Highest Stage of Capitalism*" in *Essential Works of Lenin*. New York: Bantam Books.
Marx, Karl
1963 *Early Writings*. T. B. Bottomore (ed). New York: McGraw Hill.
Marx, Karl and Frederick Engels
1959 *Basic Writings on Politics and Philosophy*. Lewis S. Feuer (ed). Garden City, N.Y.: Doubleday.
1964 *On Religion*. New York: Shocken Books.
1970 *The German Ideology*. C. J. Arthur (ed). New York: International Publishers.

National Council of Churches of Christ
1952 *The Bible*. Revised Standard Version. New York: American Bible Society.
Niebuhr, H. Richard
1957 *The Social Sources of Denominationalism*. New York: World.
Segundo, Juan Luis
1976 *The Liberation of Theology*. Maryknoll, N.Y.: Orbis Books.
Wallerstein, Immanuel
1974 *The Modern World System*. New York: Academic Press.
Weber, Max
1958 *The Protestant Ethic and the Spirit of Capitalism*. New York: Charles Scribner's Sons.
Wright, Erik Olin and Luca Perrone
1977 "Marxist Class Categories and Income Inequality." *American Sociological Review*, 42, pp. 32-55.

# 14
# The Conceptualization of Karl Marx in Comparative Perspective

*Richard D. Christy*

There are few areas of social life that sociologists ignore in their thirst to analyze human behavior. In sociology extensive literature exists on politics, industry, religion, social class, family, and medicine, to name but a few fields of research. This literature can be divided into two broad categories—theory and empirical investigation. But neither theory nor empirical research can or do stand in isolation from each other. There is an unmistakable interplay between these sociological processes. Each is coloring and energizing the other.

The foundation of sociology was established by the theories of Comte, Durkheim, Weber, Spencer, Pareto, Simmel, and numerous others. Yet these writers were not merely contributing theoretical concepts or assumptions, they have provided the theoretical frameworks and models which continue to guide much of the empirical research in sociology. Equally influential to the discipline has been the conceptual frameworks and theoretical assumptions of Karl Marx. Like each of the above, his work has stimulated a particular research perspective and much theoretical debate.

To consider writing an article on any of the classical or contemporary theorists is to assume an awesome task. But if this is true for other social theorists, it is a particularly onerous task to write on Marx. This

**Richard D. Christy,** *Assistant Professor*
*Wilfrid Laurier University,.*
*Ontario, Canada*
   Richard Christy began his academic career in economics and business administration. This early interest in micro- and macro-economics stimulated his involvement in social theory and the sociology of religion. He earned his MA at the University of Waterloo and his PhD at the University of Toronto. His dissertation dealt with "social change in industrial society." As an active church member, Richard Christy has been a member of the Board of Parish Services of the Diocese of Toronto. He is presently faculty adviser for IVCF at Wilfrid Laurier University.

task is demanding not only because of the extensive writings of Marx, or because of the volumes of books and articles written about him, but primarily because of the intellectual, social, and political controversy that surrounds Marx the man and Marx the theorist.

## Marx and Seminal Thinker

Marx is undoubtedly one of those individuals who, for better or worse, cannot be readily ignored. While he has been a thorn in the flesh of many academics and politicians, he is for others the epitome of Renaissance man. While Marx was writing in the areas of philosophy, history, economics, and political science, he also retained a vital interest and delight in classical literature and Shakespeare. But whatever one's reaction to Marx and his work, all must recognize and appreciate his enormous capacity to come to grips with the basic assumptions of "German philosophy, English economics, and French history" (Aron, 1965:140).

Numerous questions cannot help but flood one's mind as he weighs the possible directions for an article on such a controversial man and career. What version or interpretation of Marx will be presented? What concepts or themes should be introduced or emphasized? Is one required to understand Marx the radical, before he can appreciate Marx the theorist? If one is writing a comparative essay, with whom will one compare Marx? Is it proper to compare the position of Marx to a theoretical position or social-religious movement he never knew?

The comparative perspective is not particularly new in handling the work of Marx. One approach has been used by Nisbet (1966) in *The Sociological Tradition*. Here Nisbet selects what he considers to be the five essential unit-ideas of sociology: community, authority, status, the sacred, and alienation (Nisbet, 1966:6). His objective is not to deal primarily with the conceptualization of Marx, but to consider community, authority, status, and alienation in a comparative perspective. The concept of community is examined in the work of Comte, LePlay, Marx, Tonnies, Weber, and Simmel. Nisbet noted the concept of authority from the perspective of Tocqueville, Marx, Weber, Durkheim, and Simmel. While status or class and alienation have come to be associated immediately with Marx, Nisbet also considers these concepts in the work of LePlay, Taine, Durkheim, Weber, Simmel, and others.

Another comparative approach related to Marx, can be found in the work of Gidden (1971). In his book *Capitalism and Modern Social*

*Theory,* Gidden identifies those central themes and concepts which Marx developed in his earlier writings and also appeared in his later works. What Gidden proposes is an internal contrast between the earlier and later works of Marx. Gidden (1971:19-20) notes that you can find the following ideas in his later writings:

1. The conception of the progressive "self-creation" of man.
2. The notion of alienation. The main implication of his concept is that alienation must be studied as an historical phenomenon, which can only be understood in terms of the development of specific social formations.
3. The theory of the state and the emergence of future form of society began to appear in his writing. The thesis that capitalism would be replaced with the elimination of the separate spheres of the "political."
4. The main rudiments of historical materialism as a perspective for the analysis of social development. Marx stressed that capitalism is rooted in a definite form of society, the main structural characteristic of which is a dichotomous class relation between capital and wage-labor.
5. A summary concept of the theory of revolutionary "praxis." Only by the union of theory and practice, by the conjunction of theoretical understanding and practical political activity, can social change be effected.

As interesting as each of these comparative perspectives might be, I would like to consider two equally controversial issues. First, I will consider those arguments for and against Marx being called a sociologist. Second, I wish to outline some of the issues in the continuing debate between religion and Marx.

Some might ask, why introduce a discussion of whether Marx is a sociologist in an article for introductory sociology? I introduce the issue because I think it is essential in a general sociology course to have an overview of Marx's position in the discipline. True, this issue is being considered in a paper designed to deal with the concepts of Marx in comparative perspective. But, it could be argued that this brief detour, while it is not so much concerned with the conceptualization of Marx, is an effort to see how others categorize or conceive of Marx's position in the history of intellectual thought.

I will then consider the issue of religion and Marx as one way of noting the concepts and theoretical assumptions of Marx in a comparative perspective. I will take a number of his assumptions and compare these with some of the basic characteristics of Christianity. I trust that this approach will be of interest not only to those studying in the sociology of religion, but also those who consider themselves practicing Christians.

## Marx the Sociologist?

For some, Marx's achievements in sociology are quite obvious. Those taking this position argue that while his political action and his intellectual endeavors are numerous, one facet of his work is essential and vital to sociological theory. For example, Coser (1971) admits Marx's position as socialist, theoretician, and organizer. He recognizes Marx as a major figure in economic and philosophical thought, and as a social prophet. But Coser apparently feels he can move all those competing perspectives to one side, for he states, "It is as a sociological theorist that he commands our interest" (Coser, 1971:43).

But for others, the assessment of the role of Marx in sociology and his contribution to social theory is viewed as an exceedingly difficult task. As Boskoff (1966) noted, it is because of his activities as economist, propagandist, and revolutionist that the sociological elements of his writings are blurred and confused. Forced by his activities to meet both scientific and political objectives, Marx was often vague in defining his concepts. And, as Boskoff points out, this lack of conceptual rigor made it difficult for Marx to avoid contradicting himself as he reworked his ideas to match the political-intellectual controversies that marked his career. Taking these factors into account, Boskoff concludes that "Marx's position in sociological thought has been perhaps less dramatic although, nonetheless, quite real and subtly persistent, than the extensive influence of his political and economic doctrines" (Boskoff, 1966:9).

Boskoff is not alone in this cautious evaluation of Marx's contribution to sociology. Nor is he alone in appreciating the encroachment of one aspect of Marx's intellectual interest on others. Aron (1965) is quick to note that Marx's analysis of the economic realities of capitalism were originally philosophical and moral discussions before they became the subject of strictly sociological and economic analysis. In Aron's evaluation Marx the economist and philosopher expresses himself in Marx the sociologist. In his youth Marx made his economic and social comments from a background rooted in philosophical themes. "These philosophical themes—the universalism of the individual, total men, alienation—underlie the sociological analysis of the mature work" (Aron,

1965:147). Aware of this intellectual interplay, Aron concludes that Marx's sociology is essentially a sociology, while it seeks to be philosophy.

Yet not everyone who considers the positions of Marx is willing to come to this conclusion. For example, MacRae (1969) is unable to endorse Marx as one of the "founding fathers" of sociology. He will admit, however, that the influence of Marx on sociology has been great and is perhaps still increasing. But MacRae is equally firm in his judgment that "he was not a sociologist, and his influence has been unfortunate" (MacRae, 1969:59). While MacRae will concede that there may be a latent general sociology in his work, he argues that Marx could not be a sociologist.

> Partly, indeed, he could not be a sociologist, for sociology is a form of inquiry, and he already knew. More profoundly he could not be one for he was concerned not with the social, but with what underlies and explains the social; that is, in his judgement, with the economic order. And lastly, he did not need to be one, for he was concerned, above all, with a philosophic anthropology and his favorite tense was the future. Yet none of this prevents the extraction of something very like a sociology latent in his work, and though I would not entirely agree, it can be argued that this was until recently the most satisfactory and fruitful general sociology available (MacRae, 1969:61).

MacRae reviews Marx's work and finds himself asking what all this has to do with sociology? MacRae does recognize that Marx has not only done social research, but he has also inspired it. MacRae acknowledges Marx to be a culture hero, a great fact of our age. But for sociology as an academic discipline, Marx is primarily a most interesting historical figure. MacRae is by no means isolated in this opinion of Marx as a sociologist or in viewing Marx's work as possibly containing a latent sociology. Henri Lefebvre (1969) also holds this position.

Lefebvre cautions that the title of his book *The Sociology of Marx* should not lead anyone to conclude that he is going to make a sociologist out of Marx. If one assumes that this was his intention, he has either never opened his book or he is acting in bad faith. Lefebvre is quite emphatic about his stance. He states "Marx is not a sociologist, but there is a sociology in Marx" (Lefebvre, 1969:22). To argue this position he points out that it is possible to see in Marx's work a sociology of family, city, subgroups, classes, knowledge, the state, and others.

In summary, one will find varying positions in response to the claim that Marx is a sociologist. Coser is ready to accept Marx's sociological theory without any question. By contrast, Boskoff and Aron both sound a note of caution as to the strictness of Marx's sociology perspective. Their caution is based upon Marx's political action and his demands for social reform. This word of caution grows into a flat denial by MacRae and Lefebvre who both assert emphatically that Marx is not a sociologist. Of course, this discussion is primarily an overview of a much deeper debate. It serves merely to highlight the various positions of the issue. But it also leads us to this question—What is then the contribution of Marx to sociology?

## Marx's Influence in Sociology

Marx's theories remained isolated, for some time, from the social sciences. Their sociological significance was only realized toward the end of the nineteenth century as sociology began to establish itself as a separate discipline. At the first Congress of the Institut International de Sociologie in 1894, Marx's social theory had a prominent place in the discussion (Bottomore and Rubel, 1963:44). Bottomore and Rubel provide a detailed account of the influence of Marx in European social analysis and the eventual movement of his ideas from Europe to the United States.

Many early American sociologists who studied in Europe, and especially those who studied in Germany, were exposed to the ideas of Marx. The early influence of Marx was particularly apparent in discussions on social class. For example, A. W. Small studied Marx and the theory of class conflict. George Herbert Mead and Thorstein Veblen both reflect the influence of Marx in their writings. However, it is far from my intention to review Marx's influence on the sociologists of Germany, France, the United States, or Britain. What must be appreciated· is that Marx's sociological thought has been examined, criticized, or used widely in empirical research by many in sociology.

What appears as the enduring aspect of Marx's thought is not in his theories but in the *problems* and *concepts* he established for the analysis of society. Sociology has acquired from Marx: (1) the institutional analysis of society, (2) the analysis of the economic structure and its relations with other parts of the social structure, (3) the social significance of stratification, (4) the analysis of conflict, tension, and hatred, (5) and the theory of ideology. It is from these perspectives that sociologists have been encouraged to stress the examination of those social factors that are not obvious. Sociologists are to go beyond social appearances in their analysis of society.

## Marx and Christianity

One approach to the conceptualization of Marx in comparative perspective is to contrast the Marxian assumptions on man and society with those found in religion. The historic opposition and rivalry between the two makes such comparison of particular interest. Yet, my interest is not to make a comparison between Marx and all religious perspectives. My desire is to investigate the distinctions between Marx and Christianity, a front on which the controversy and rivalry has been intense. This rivalry has been particularly ardent not only because of the avowed atheism in Marx, but also because of the inhuman and anti-Christian policies of many countries established on Marxian political and social structure.

While, in these opening comments I intentionally used the words religion and Christianity, it is necessary that each concept is understood more clearly. By religion I mean God-confronting religion. Christianity is, of course, committed to belief in God, a personal being who is omnipotent, omniscient, omnipresent, and loving, just, and holy. While this assumption is true in general of Christianity and a dramatic contrast to Marx, I believe that the conflict is especially heated between Marx and the evangelical Protestant Christians.

### The Conversionist and Adventist Sect

Undoubtedly, evangelical Protestants would agree with the above characteristics of God, but because of their religious emphasis and the structure of their religious organization, confrontation with Marx is virtually inevitable. The types of Christianity to which I refer are characterized by Wilson (1959) in his analysis of sect. He suggests that the sect has the following general characteristics.

A sect is a voluntary association with membership dependent upon knowledge of doctrine, a conversion experience, or the recommendation of members in good standing. There is an exclusiveness about the sect, and those who contravene doctrinal, moral, or organizational precepts can be excluded or disciplined. Any misdemeanor against these precepts is considered not merely a sin against the group, but also a sin against God requiring confession and an appeal for forgiveness. The sect also advocates, at least as an ideal, the priesthood of all believers. While this often takes the form of untrained church leadership, it always involves the encouragement of a high level of lay participation. This commitment to doctrine and to the group may express itself as hostility or indifference to the nonreligious values and institutions of society and the state. But this commitment that serves to keep the member separate from "the world," also makes him into a totally committed and well defined member of the religious organization.

It is not solely these general characteristics of sect that distinguish the arch rival of Marxism; the subtypes of sects, conversionist, adventist, introversionist, and gnostic are also useful (Wilson 1959:5-7). Of specific importance to our discussion are the characteristics of the conversionist and adventist sects.

Briefly, the conversionists sect is a Christian group in which teachings and activities center on evangelism. The Bible is taken as the guide of salvation and is accepted as literally true. The criteria for group membership is the acceptance of Jesus Christ as personal Savior and Lord. This is vital because of the sin of the individual and the need for redemption through Christ. The sect seeks to share this message of forgiveness through Christ with everyone who will listen. But at the same time the conversionist sect is distrustful of or indifferent towards churches that do not preach salvation. This distrust, and in some cases hostility, can also be directed to the wider society and its humanism.

The adventist, or revolutionist sect, focuses its attention on the eventual overturning of the present world order. Its emphasis is also on the Bible, but especially on the prophetic books of the Old and New Testament which the sect believes prophesies Christ's second coming. In this approach Christ is regarded more as a divine Commander than a personal Savior. While evangelism is undertaken by way of preaching and teaching, it is to warn of the eventual establishment of Christ's new kingdom. Separation from the "world" is stressed and restrictions are placed upon certain worldly activities. Such doctrinal positions make the adventist sect primarily hostile towards the wider society which they anticipate will be overthrown.

It is conversionist and adventist groups with these specific sectarian characteristics that come to my mind when I think of religious groups at odds with Marx and the Marxian doctrine. Of course, it must be said that this does not mean that other branches of Christianity or other religious systems are not at odds with Marxism. I believe that because of the foundations of the religious perspective, there will be some opposition to Marx. But from the above discussion of this classification of Protestant Christianity, one cannot help but recognize some implicit reasons for disagreements between Christianity and Marx. Let me spell these differences out more clearly.

## Marxist and Christian View of God

Stevenson (1974) examines both Christianity and Marxism as two rival theories of human nature. He notes where each is at odds with the other. For Christianity the existence of a transcendental God is essential. As Eliade (1959:202) notes *homo religiosus* (religious man) always believes there is an absolute reality, the sacred. For Christianity God is transcendent as well as immanent. God is in some sense present everywhere and at all times. Yet, he is also beyond or outside the world in that he is not visible or tangible. "Ever since the creation of the world his invisible nature . . . has been clearly perceived in the things that have been made" (Romans 1:20).

Another vital part of the Christian doctrine of God is that God is the Creator. This is put most precisely in Genesis 1:1a, "In the beginning God created." It implies that if God did not exist, the world would not exist. The world of living things, the world of nature, and the social world exist by his design or at the very least by his permission. The world is very much the design of God the Creator.

By contrast Marx's main theoretical assumptions are rooted in atheism. This is not peculiar to Marx's theory, but it is one of its essential characteristics. God and the religious system that supports the notion of God are a creation of man to compensate for life in a society that rewards and damages. Marx rejects transcendence and refuses all the appeals of the transcendental. Man lives primarily in the history of human societies. For Marx "the whole of history is a preparation for 'man'" (Bottomore and Rubel 1967:85). For Marx, man is the sole subject and agent of history. More precisely, Marx is concerned with a view of man in history which he called materialism. This theory supposes that the laws of history are economic in nature, and that "the mode of production of material life determines the general character of social, political, and spiritual processes of life" (Bottomore and Rubel, 1967:67). Therefore there is no intelligent, powerful God behind the design of the universe. There is only man—more specifically, economic man. The final form to society will be worked out in the class struggles between the bourgeois and proletariat.

Marx was confident that the economic system and structure known as capitalism would become more and more unstable as the class struggle between the bourgeois and proletariat intensified. As the proletariat became poorer and larger in number, they would revolt. In a major social revolution the capitalist phase of economic history would end and the workers would take power and institute the new communist phase of history. Here again one sees Marx's interpretation of society rooted in man and his socioeconomic behavior.

### Marxist and Christian View of Man

The contrast between each perspective does not rest solely on the structure and creation of the society. Examining the origin and needs of man we again observe a great divide between Christianity and Marx.

The Christian doctrine of man sees him essentially related to God. Man is made in the image of God and is to have dominion over the rest of creation (Genesis 1:26). Man is unique in that he has some of the characteristics of God himself. God created man for fellowship with himself, so man fulfills the purpose of his life when he loves and serves his creator. Given this Christian doctrine of man, the conversionist sects would understand the problems of society as sin before God. Man has sinned, he has chosen in his God-given freedom to choose evil rather than good. Therefore, man has disrupted his relationship with God. This interpretation of the plight of man is not merely for believers, for "all have sinned and fall short of the glory of God" (Romans 3:23).

By contrast, Marx's view of man is understood primarily in terms of our *social* nature. He takes the view that "the essence of man is not an abstraction inherent in each particular individual. The real nature of man is the totality of social relations" (Bottomore and Rubel, 1967:83). Marx does not allow for individual human nature. Whatever a person does is essentially a social act. This is true of all human activity, but it is particularly true in the activity of production. Essentially "man makes himself" (Eliade, 1959:203), and he makes himself by the types and quality of his social and economic activities. Unlike the conversionist sectarian who defines the problem of society as the sinful nature of man requiring regeneration, Marx sees the difficulty in society as alienation. For Marx alienation sums up what is wrong with capitalism.

There is some debate as to what Marx means by alienation. In his early works where the idea is most fully developed, he appears to mean a number of things. The means of production and the type of economic exchange are the defining qualities of alienation in capitalism. Factory technology, increased division of labor, and the private ownership of industry have all brought about the estrangement of the industrial worker from his work. There is no hint of a solution to this alienation in the regeneration of man, but in the creation of a new state. This would be a state in which industry is made for man, not man for industry.

*The Christian and Marxist "Solution"*

This brings us to the final issue that I wish to deal with in this comparison of Christianity and Marx. Namely, what are the practical solutions proposed by each perspective? How will each strive to establish its solution? While I have already hinted at the answers to these questions earlier, let me answer them more fully.

For Christianity in the conversionist tradition, the solution is based on God. If God has made man for fellowship with himself, and if man has turned away and broken his relationship to God, then only God can forgive man and restore the relationship. Therefore, salvation, and the regeneration of man are made possible by the mercy, forgiveness, and love of God. Each person must accept the redemption that God has provided in Christ and become a member of the body of believers. Thus, the regeneration of man and the world is possible in and through Christ (2 Corinthians, 5:17). This does not necessarily mean a solitary experience of conversion, nor does regeneration occur all at once; it is a lifelong process that is focused beyond this life to Christ's return (1 Corinthians 13:12). Those of the adventist sect are particularly concerned with the second coming of Christ. While the return of Christ is an important doctrine in the whole of Christendom, for the adventists there is the intense expectancy of seeing "the holy city, new Jerusalem, coming down out of heaven from God (Revelation 21:2).

For Marx there is also the vision of the regeneration of man and the creation of a "new kingdom." But as with all of his theory, Marx thinks these creations must be rooted in society. "If man is, by nature, a social being, he only develops his real nature in society (Bottomore and Rubel, 1967:249). If alienation is part of the social problem, then the solution is the removal of that society. Therefore Marx argues that since alienation is caused by the nature of the capitalist economic system it must be abolished and replaced by a better society. Capitalist society will not be abolished by some wholesale destruction so that socialism can start anew, but the movement of the capitalist system generates the social conditions which provides the new social order. The social change of man and society are linked to this inevitable revolution. This communist revolution will usher in a new social order in which alienation will disappear and man will be regenerated in his true nature. Marx claims that the resolution of the problems of capitalism will occur as the "old regime" gives way to the "new kingdom" on earth. Marx envisages a total regeneration of men, but he expects it entirely within the content of history. He is, of course, not willing to just theorize about the nature of the revolution but proposes that individuals and groups can assist its coming.

It becomes all too obvious that there is a wide gap between Christianity in its conversionist and adventist form and Marxism. The reason for this great divide is that Marxism is firmly established in humanism. For Marx, man and society are the centers of reality. While man is given a unique position in Christianity, his being is rooted in God the source of his creation and the hope of his preservation. Because of "The Fall"—because man has rebelled against God—there is controversy, rivalry, antagonism, and animosity between God and man, and among men. Yet, I believe that as in love so in war, one side benefits from the other. It can be noted that Christianity can benefit from Marxism.

Christianity should be challenged by Marxism to discover afresh the message of Christ to a needy world. Marx isolated some of the tragedy, oppression, and indulgences that are found in capitalism. Marx was unwilling to close his eyes to these problems. Christ was also unwilling to turn from human misery. In his lifetime Christ addressed himself to the needs of mankind. Christ epitomized in his life, death, resurrection, and his promised return, service to others. The disciples of Christ in today's society are to rediscover this "praxis"—that combination of theory and practice. So Marx challenges Christians to "practice the truth." Undoubtedly the failure of Christians to practice the truth in every sphere of social life has given contemporary Marxism the ring of authenticity. Granted, Marxism is grounded in a purely materialistic analysis of man and society, nonetheless its demands radically and comprehensively cut through social appearances. Christ asked no less of his followers: "If you continue in my word, you are truly my disciples, and you will know the truth, and the truth will make you free" (John 8:31).

## Conclusion

Marx has been, and continues to be, a source of much inquiry in sociology. He is one of those academics who wrote numerous books and articles, and about whom numerous books and articles have been written. I defined for myself an exercise which entails discussing Marx in a comparative perspective. This is not entirely new. Nisbet used this approach as he considered the unit-ideas of sociology: community, authority, status, the sacred, and alienation. Gidden follows this as he compares the themes in the earlier and later works of Marx. In this article I took a different approach. First, I considered those arguments for and against calling or identifying Marx as a sociologist. Coser appeared to accept this claim without question. Boskoff and Aron both sound a note of caution in view of Marx's political actions and demands for social reform. These positions were then compared with those of MacRae and Lefebvre who emphatically denied that Marx was a sociologist. Second, I examined the theoretical assumptions of Marx by comparing them with those of Christianity. Using the characteristics of the conversionist and adventist sects, I outlined the divergence and rivalry between Marx and Christianity. Each provides its own definitions and assumptions about man, society, and their regeneration.

## Discussion Questions

1. In sociology there is an interplay between social theory and empirical research. Why is it particularly important to understand this in Marx's writings?

2. What are the unit-ideas of sociology according to Nisbet? Who are the theorists used to contrast Marx's work? Discuss their theoretical position for each concept.

3. What does Gidden consider to be the enduring themes between the early and later writings of Marx?

4. How much truth is there in the statement that Marx is not a sociologist?

5. Is Marx's contribution to sociology related to his social theory? If yes, in what areas? If no, what then are his contributions to sociology?

6. What are some of the general characteristics of a Christian sect? What are the characteristics of conversionist and adventist sects?

7. Contrast and compare the basic assumption of Christianity and Marxism concerning man and society.

8. Can it be argued that Christianity and Marxism are just two differing sets of answers to the needs of man?

9. Is "personal conversion" *the* answer to evils within society, or is there also a need for the conversion and/or modification of our capitalist system?

10. Is there a tendency for adventists to neglect the "kingdom of God" in this present age? Does the New Testament deny the reality of God's kingdom in the world? Discuss.

# References

Aron, Raymond
   1965 *Main Currents in Sociological Thought*, Vol. 1. New York: Basic Books.
Boskoff, Alvin
   1966 "From Social Thought to Sociological Theory." *Modern Sociological Theory* (ed. by Howard Becker and Alvin Boskoff). New York: Holt, Rinehart and Winston.
Bottomore, T. B. and Maximilien Rubel
   1967 *Karl Marx: Selected Writings in Sociology and Social Philosophy*. Middlesex, England: Penguin Books.
Coser, Lewis A.
   1971 *Masters of Sociological Thought: Ideas in Historical and Social Context*. New York: Harcourt Brace Jovanovich.
Eliade, Mircea
   1959 *The Sacred and the Profane: The Nature of Religion*. New York: Harcourt, Brace and World Inc.
Giddens, Anthony
   1971 *Capitalism and Modern Social Theory: An Analysis of the Writings of Marx, Durkheim and Max Weber*. Cambridge: University Press.
Lefebvre, Henri
   1969 *The Sociology of Marx* (trans. by Norbert Guterman). New York: Vintage Books.
MacRae, Donald G.
   1969 "Karl Marx" *The Founding Fathers of Social Science* (ed. by Timothy Raison). Middlesex, England: Penguin Books.
Nisbet, Robert
   1966 *The Sociological Tradition*. New York: Basic Books.
Stevenson, Leslie
   1974 *Seven Theories of Human Nature*. Oxford: Clarendon Press.
Wilson, Bryan R.
   1959 "The Analysis of Sect Development." *American Sociological Review*. Vol. 24.

# 15
# Philosophy and Sociology
*Richard A. Russell*

The conjunction between philosophy and sociology inescapably involves examining the relationship between two areas of fundamental controversy. In both disciplines there are schools of thought whose differences are deep and often longstanding. How one treats this fact appears to vary systematically, depending on the individual's school of thought. Are these differences logically mutually exclusive, merely matters of emphasis, or are they really complementary, capable of a theoretical synthesis? Does the existence of diverse schools of thought indicate that a discipline is still immature and prescientific in that it lacks a paradigm, or are there reasons to believe that it will never rise beyond the level of opinion? Does the existence of these schools of thought indicate a healthy theoretical pluralism which is essential for intellectual progress, or are they a veritable scandal in the academic community? Are these schools of thought a passing development phase which the fuller utilization of scientific method will duly exorcise, or are they something much more endemic?

On this point there has been great controversy about the nature of the scientific method. Recently some philosophers and historians of science have argued that such a method is not apparent in the history of science, and also that such a method is detrimental to scientific progress (Feyerabend, 1975). In short, we find deeply divergent accounts of both the proper methodology and field of investigation in both philosophy and sociology, ramified by deeply divergent accounts of

**Richard A. Russell**
*Trinity College, Stoke Bishop, Bristol, England*

Richard Russell has earned three masters degrees; an MA in philosophy from McMaster University (Canada) (1967), an MA in sociology (1973), and an MEd (1976), both from Bristol University, England. He has taught philosophy at Manchester College, Oxford (1968-9), as well as at Trinity Christian College, Chicago (1968-72). A forthcoming book offers a critique of the control and content of contemporary education. He is director of the Christian studies Unit at Trinity College. He is an ordained minister in the Anglican church.

these, all of which are supported by diverse historiographical accounts of the developments of the two disciplines.

## Christian vs Humanist Perspective

This whole situation seems to provide a *prima facie* case for the view that there is no sociology or philosophy per se, but always sociology *working within one perspective or another*. This paper is an attempt to provide some account of the relationship between philosophical and sociological perspectives within the broader context of a Christian perspective. Such an approach is essential, if it is true that all wisdom and knowledge are found in the revelation of God in Christ (Colossians 2:3). If the great theme of *creation, fall,* and *redemption* in Jesus Christ is the central meaning of created reality, then its significance can hardly be restricted to theology. Nor can it be excluded from philosophy and sociology on the grounds of some established division of academic labor. (Of course, there is a long tradition within Christendom of doing precisely this in terms of a dualism between faith and reason, grace and nature, and sacred science and "natural" science). While there are different explanations of this dualism, they all agree that the integrity of natural or scientific reason necessitates such a dualism. The sciences must be autonomous—free from any notion of revelation. Such integrity assumes that reason is unaffected by "the fall," in no need of redemption or redirection. Such limited autonomy is a huge concession to the central Western philosophical tradition of the unlimited autonomy of theoretical thought (Wolters, 1975). Accordingly, the problems of philosophy and sociology fall within the domain of reason. Therefore a Christian philosophy or sociology is regarded not simply as a complex and difficult project, but as a contradiction in terms. According to this view, such a project cannot be the central responsibility of Christian philosophers and sociologists. The point at issue here is whether, in the last analysis, the Christian religion provides *the sole perspective in terms of which reality is rightly to be understood.*

### Secular Humanism—Reason Autonomous

It hardly needs to be said that the direction of modern philosophy since Descartes, and virtually the whole sociological tradition, is fundamentally opposed to such a recognition of the Christian faith. Rather both are motivated by an antithetical tradition, namely that of secular humanism. Indeed the whole movement of modern thought can be viewed as a massive attempt to eliminate such commitments, prejudices, and presuppositions from human thought and to seek direction from unaided human reason. The Enlightenment philosopher, David Hume (1774), makes clear his exclusive and unqualified commitment to autonomous human thought when he writes:

> Tis certainly a kind of indignity to philosophy, whose *sovereign authority* ought everywhere to be acknowledged to oblige her on every occasion to make apologies for her conclusions, and justify herself to every particular art and science which may be offended at her. *This puts one in mind of a king being arraigned for high treason against his subjects (p. 532).*

Young Karl Marx, in his PhD thesis, rightly interprets and shares the ultimate commitment underlying this quotation. He sees it as a declaration of opposition "against all gods, heavenly and earthly, who do not acknowledge the consciousness of man as the supreme divinity. There must be no god on a level with it" (Marx and Engels, 1955:15). This declaration of autonomy, this confession of the finality of man, is the root of all humanist thought in both philosophy and sociology.

In the academic world today, however, such spirited declarations are rather rare. There are two main reasons for this. In the first place, there is little for the secular humanist professor to protest against, for the mind of the university has been radically secularized, and perhaps is the major agent of secularization. However, if Christian scholars in higher education began to reform scholarship on the basis of the principle we have enunciated (namely, that the Christian religion provides the sole perspective in terms of which reality is rightly to be understood), then the antithetical principle of humanist autonomy would rapidly be articulated. In the second place, those who are committed to the autonomy of reason believe in its neutrality with respect to ultimate beliefs and worldviews. More explicitly, while reason may lead to ultimate beliefs and worldviews as conclusions, it is vehemently denied that its conclusions are more of the nature of the explication of the presuppositions with which it started.

*Positivism as a Secular Humanist Ideology*

A very influential form of this belief in the autonomy and neutrality of reason, or theoretical thought, is *positivism*. Two key figures in the development of positivism are Hume and Comte, the latter of whom gave sociology its name. Positivist epistemology has two major aspects: a view of the *source* of human knowledge, and a view of the *historical stages of the development* of human knowledge. With respect to the former, commitment is to empiricism—the theory that all genuine knowledge derives from and is about sensations. Modern positivism, known as *logical positivism*, has sought to provide a verification principle by which genuine knowledge (genuinely cognitive language) may be distinguished from that which is not. The prime examples of the latter being the claims of metaphysics and religion. With respect to the historical development of knowledge, Comte maintained that it had progressively passed from the level of *theological* explanation (explaining phenomena in terms of gods and spirits), to *metaphysical* explanation (in terms of abstract principles and essences), then to the final and highest stage of *scientific* explanation. For Comte the "world" that science describes is *the* world, and its method *the* method of knowledge itself. He announced his determination not to accept any statement as worthy of belief that could not be verified by the methods of empirical science. "Our real business," he wrote, "is to analyze accurately the circumstances of phenomena and to connect them by the natural relations of succession and resemblance."

This positivist view of the sources and development of human knowledge has become almost common sense to the academic world, at least to those who think of themselves as "scientific." Innumerable textbooks in every "scientific" subject have told how their discipline has freed itself from bondage to religion and philosophy and entered into the freedom of the promised land of the scientific method. The logical positivists propagated the view that any residual problems they experienced would be resolved by the total elimination of metaphysics. This would be achieved by a "rational reconstruction" of the discipline in terms of logical positivist principles. Undoubtedly, some form of positivism or scientism may well remain very influential in the academic world. But there are reasons to believe that positivism in particular, and the dogma of the autonomy of theoretical thought in general, are, at the very least, highly problematic.

### The Case Against Positivism

The structure of my argument against positivism has two steps. First, I will adduce grounds why no science, including sociology, can be philosophically neutral. In other words, it is impossible for any scientific discipline to leave metaphysics behind. Secondly, I will argue that philosophy itself cannot be religiously neutral. Inevitably it is based on religious presuppositions.

My first step concerns the thesis that sociology and all other sciences have philosophical presuppositions. It seems to me that considerable support for this thesis can be derived from two sources: (1) from contemporary developments in the philosophy of science and (2) from a careful consideration of the sciences themselves.

*The Philosophy of Science Argument*

One of the most noticeable features in the philosophy of science over recent decades has been the progressive collapse of the logical positivist view of science (Radnitzky, 1973). The attempts of logical positivism to provide a justified demarcation between the "scientific" (meaningful) and the "metaphysical" (meaningless) have foundered. No satisfactory solution was found to the early recognized self-reference problem of the verification principle itself. The principle maintained that all meaningful propositions are either "empirical" or "analytical," but one must not regard the principle itself as belonging to either category. If it was regarded as some sort of empirical claim, then it was most likely false. But if it was analytical, then there was no reason why it could not be dismissed as a very arbitrary stipulative definition of the terms "meaningful" and "meaningless." If, however, it was neither empirical nor analytical, then the principle was itself meaningless, which brought it precisely into the same category logical positivism used to dismiss metaphysics and theology.

Apart from the status of the principle there were even deeper problems about its content. When strict criteria of meaning were laid down sufficient to exclude metaphysics (this would also exclude the epistemology and metaphysics of logical positivism), upon careful examination it was realized that huge areas of science had been excluded too. When the criteria were liberalized to prevent such exclusion, they signally failed to serve their central purpose, i.e., to exclude (other people's) metaphysics. While the verification principle purported to derive from a universally valid theory of linguistic-and-cognitive meaning, the history of its continuous revisions were clearly controlled by a prior commitment to a scientistic positivism. This itself was made plausible by a yet deeper commitment to a secularized world-view.

## Positivism, Its Epistemology and Metaphysics

For our present purposes, perhaps the most significant breakdown of the logical positivist research program is the formulation of its own position. In spite of verbal denials, it patently could not avoid involvement in epistemological and metaphysical theories and decisions. This was precisely what its program, its revolution in philosophy intended to transcend. In short, in spite of immense industry and ingenuity, this massive attempt to provide a way of "freeing" science from metaphysics has signally failed. Most contemporary philosophers of science will concede, some more willingly than others, that science and philosophy are structurally interconnected. Indeed the positivists' claim that theirs is *a* or *the* "scientific philosophy" is now widely dismissed, because of the huge gulf between the image of science provided by studies of the past and present development of science, and that of the positivist image. The positivist image is now seen by many philosophers of science as little more than a projection of the propositional calculus from the field of formal logic.

In fact, the successive shifts which have occurred in the philosophy of science provide considerable support for the view that the sciences are inconceivable outside of metaphysical frameworks. Henry Skolimowski has formulated the main outline of these shifts:

1. *Facts and observations* of primary importance to logical empiricists and most empiricists.
2. *Problems, conjectures (theories) and refutations* of primary importance to Popper; on this level "facts" and "observations" are determined by our problems and theories.
3. *Paradigms* of primary importance to Kuhn. They determine, at least partially, not only the content of our theories, but also our comprehension of our "facts."
4. *Metaphysical research programs* or *conceptual frameworks:* these not only provide conceptual tools and determine the nature of problems, but usually spell out what counts as genuine science, thereby determining the scope of science; in doing so it implicitly or explicitly defines the meaning of the objectivity of science and not infrequently it suggests the concept of truth (Skolimowski, 1974:490-1).

The pattern that clearly emerges here is that serious attempts to develop a theory of science have required increasingly larger and more comprehensive conceptual units. This suggests a model of science as a hierarchy of frameworks which provide a continuity between facts and

observations at one extreme, and very general metaphysical and epistemological theories at the other.

## The Argument from the Sciences

There are grounds for believing that this model can equally be
supported by a direct examination of the various sciences themselves.
The ubiquitous feature of the sciences, indeed of all fields of scholarship to which I wish to draw attention in this context, is the existence of
*schools of thought.* Schools of thought are by no means restricted to the
humanities and social sciences, but are equally present in mathematics,
physics, and biology. The differences between schools of thought tend
to be systematic. They cannot be resolved by appeal to "facts" and
observations," for what constitutes acceptable "facts" and "observations" for a discipline is disputable. Nor are the disputes merely apparent with the two accounts complementary to each other. For such a
theory would then, if developed, constitute another school of thought
at odds with the others, especially with those it had claimed to absorb
and unify. Nor are appeals to the professional incompetence of one or
more parties likely to withstand examination. In most cases the dispute
will turn out to be at each of Skolimowski's levels 1—4. To put the matter in general terms, the disputes will be about *where one must stand in
order to see the entire field aright, and how one ought to proceed with
theoretical enquiries concerning the field.*

## Sociological Schools of Thought

### Martindale's Position

With respect to schools of thought in sociology there are two works
of particular interest: Don Martindale's *The Nature and Types of Sociological Theory* and Walter Wallace's *Sociological Theory.* Martindale's work is a valuable study of the historical development of the
main schools of sociological theory. He writes:

> Because most schools of sociological theory have, until recently,
> drawn inspiration from Western philosophy, their origins in this
> matrix have been traced, in order to clarify the main propositions
> and problems of the different sociological schools. To ignore these
> philosophical origins is to cut oneself off from insight into some of
> the most fundamental affinities of our discipline with others. . . . In
> the case of every school of sociology to develop except the very
> last—sociological functionalism—discussion has begun with the
> philosophers. As systems of ideas, all the early schools of socio-

logical theory originated as philosophic points of view. ...
Positivistic organicism is made possible by the fusion of older forms
of philosophic idealism and empiricism. Conflict sociology is the
scientific extension of historical empiricism. Formalism was suggested by neo-Kantian empiricism and phenomenology. Pluralistic
behaviorism and social-action theory found their point of departure
in neo-idealism. Symbolic interactionism is the American form of
social science proceeding most directly from pragmatism (Martindale, 1964:viii,x).

While much of the substance of Martindale's book bears out these
contentions, nonetheless his commitment to positivism leads him to
restrict the influence of philosophy on sociology essentially to the past.
In the same context as the quotation above, he writes:

This cannot be taken to suggest that these origins had permanent
importance for sociological theory. Often the philosophical parent
model varies greatly from the sociological theory based on it. This
is inevitable, for the precondition of the scientific development of
an idea is its empirical fertility. The origin of a school quickly
recedes in importance (p.x).

Martindale's positivistic historical perspective comes clearly into view
when somewhat later he maintains:

The separation of sociology from philosophy was long anticipated by the departure of natural science therefrom. In fact, it
was the great success attendant upon the separation of physical
science from philosophy that provided a major motive for the establishment of independent social science. For this reason special
interest attaches to the factors promoting the independence of
physical science (p. 19).

The two crucial factors that Martindale identifies are as follows: First,

...the acquisition of the rational proof permitted philosophy to
acquire an autonomy, a self-determination, which facilitated its
separation from theology. When the truth—establishing function—was located in the thought process itself, no institutional
hierarchy was required to fix the truth. Mythological, theological,
and magical types of thought were thoroughly undermined by the
self-correcting power of the new philosophy (p. 19).

The second factor for Martindale was the extension of this rational autonomy into the area of empirical knowledge by means of experiment.

We are in profound agreement with Martindale's first quotation concerning the vital historical relation between philosophy and sociology. Nevertheless, his positivistic framework which effectively negates the contemporary significance of this insight seems entirely mistaken. While one can agree that there may be very considerable changes between a philosophical school of thought and a sociological perspective to which it gives rise, this in no way eliminates our contention that a philosophical framework continues to structure the discipline. Furthermore, the framework itself develops and may well divide into subschools. Indeed, Martindale himself has not found it possible, in spite of his positivism, to characterize contemporary sociological schools of thought without reference to their philosophical differences.

In our third quotation from Martindale he maintains that natural science has long been independent of philosophy. Of course, this thesis is central to positivistic history and philosophy of science and has become part of the folk wisdom of the academic community. However, both positivistic history and philosophy of science are being increasingly challenged. The best and most recent study of the birth of modern natural science, Eugene M. Klaaren's *Religious Origins of Modern Science*, maintains that

> conflict and reformation in Western theologies of creation made the rise of many natural sciences from the older natural philosophy a distinct and lively possibility; belief in divine creation was presupposed in the rise of modern natural science (1977:v).

While a positivistically inclined philosophy of science (because of its definition of religion, science, and philosophy and their relations) would discount Klaaren's study, more recent philosophy of science is much more open to entertaining the idea of structural relations between science, philosophy, and religion. We will consider Martindale's view of philosophy as autonomous later. For the present it should be noted that his view of science as the combination of "rational proof" and "experiment" remains stuck at Skolimowski's level one, and should be dismissed as obsolete positivist dogma with no real point of contact with the natural sciences—not to mention sociology.

## The One and the Many

The impotence of such a dogma to direct sociology is evident in the last section of Martindale's book which is headed "Toward Integration." After characterizing the diverse sociological perspectives for more than five hundred pages he spends just over one page on the subject of integration. According to classical and modern positivist expectations, once a discipline has become "scientific," schools of thought should be left behind. Surely such divergencies are due to religious and metaphysical prejudices from which devotion to scientific method frees us. Martindale's unspoken dilemma is that he wants to claim that sociology is scientific in a positivist sense, and yet he is not prepared to dismiss all but one school of thought as "unscientific." He maintains that the various schools of thought are "true theoretical alternatives."

Nevertheless, in the interest of theoretical integration he urges us not to look at the "distinctive features in a theory," but to the elements of basic agreement that he claims are "a common stock of terms, concepts and empirical generalizations" that are "increasingly shared by all schools" (1964:54). This latter claim is certainly a central expectation of the positivist theory of science. Such a consensus may only be visible to the eye of positivist faith, for Martindale provides us with no evidence for it. The suggestion that it is a mistake to look at the distinctive features of a theory is hard to distinguish from an avoidance of counter-evidence. Actually there is much in contemporary philosophy of science that would support the view that Martindale *cannot* supply any evidence. The reason for this is that terms and concepts are "theory laden," i.e., their meaning is tied in with the theoretical perspective to which they belong. Furthermore, empirical generalizations must be formulated by means of their theory-laden concepts. In fact, the different sociological perspectives are identified by the distinctive concepts that they employ. Although certain of them use common terms, it is doubtful if they bear the same meanings.

### He Looks for a Positivist Messiah

It is perhaps because the prospects of a positivist resolution of the fragmentation of sociology seems so bleak and hopeless that Martindale's thought takes a millennialist turn in the closing paragraph of his book. He hangs on to his positivist faith against all odds, and awaits the coming of a positivist messiah who will develop the unified theory that will explain and reveal all. He says:

From the perspective developed here, it is possible to offer neither easy solutions for the integration of theory nor utopian hopes for sociology as a boon to mankind. It is not even possible to offer that sop to the Western conscience—all things yield to hard work. In the cooperation of reason and energy, within the tinder is at hand and the sparks are struck from mother wit, sociology or a Maxwell who will take up the materials cast up by chance and worked up with patient labor, clarify them in the crystalline formations of his logic, and fuse them in the fire of his love (1964:541-2).

Therefore, our general conclusion here is that positivism's highly reductionistic conception of scientific knowledge thoroughly incapacitates it from coming to grips with both the historical development and the present shape of science in general, and sociology in particular.

*Wallace's Systematic Approach*

We turn now to Walter Wallace's *Sociological Theory* which has a systematic approach to the diverse sociological schools of thought, rather than a historical one. While his work shares some of the problems of Martindale's, he is able to make much more intellectual contact with the eleven schools of thought he discusses. He is able to do this precisely because he drops, at least in measure, the positivist veto on the recognition of philosophy. This is perhaps inevitable because his attempt to produce a framework for integrating, as well as differentiating, these eleven schools is itself largely an exercise in systematic philosophy. This is not to say that Wallace actively tries to connect sociology with philosophy. In discussing the possible dimensions in terms of which the schools of sociology might be classified, it is the "content," rather than the "relations" of sociology, he has made central. He writes:

> In the present case, I have tried to select dimensions that refer directly to the sociological subject matter as such, and have avoided dimensions that refer, instead, to non-sociological thought systems. That is, I have rejected philosophy of science descriptions like "positivistic," "phenomenological," and "systemic." . . . I have asked in short, What kind of direct observations does each theory imply?—rather than asking, What kind of non-sociological conceptual framework does each theory resemble (1969:2-3)?

Wallace's concern with the content of sociological theories leads him to recognize that in order to locate a sociological perspective two questions are essential:

(1) How is the social *defined?* (2) How is the social *explained* (i.e., by what classes of phenomena)? *Both questions are required, and joint answers to them will be sought here,* because it seems wholly inadequate to differentiate theories in terms of the single, loose, and indefinite question of what they are "interested in," or what their "approach" is, or what they "deal with," although this is often done (1969:5).

## Classifying Sociological Theories

In terms of the definitional and explanatory dimensions embodied in these questions, Wallace proposes the following property space for classifying sociological theories (1969:13):

|  | The Principal Behavioral Relations that *Define* the Social are: | |
|---|---|---|
|  | Objective (Materialist) | Subjective (Idealist) |
| Imposed on the Social (Determined) |  |  |
| Generated by the Social (Free-willed) |  |  |

*The Principal Phenomena that Explain the Social are:*

Wallace's discussion of his taxonomy is highly illuminating. He writes that

> ... some attention should be paid to certain broadly philosophical implications of the property-space itself. Although the dimensions of the space were inductively derived from inspecting the data (i.e., current sociological theories), on reflection it appears that these dimensions are closely related to two central and long-lived philosophical problems (indicative terms for them are given in figure 1). Thus the question of whether the social is to be defined in terms of subjective or objective behavior relations seems to reflect philosophical problems long expressed in the antinomies of idealism and materialism. ... Similarly, the question of whether the fundamental explaining conditions are imposed on, or generated by, the social seems to echo the still more resounding philosophical ques-

tions of whether man is to be considered primarily a determined consequence of prior and/or higher events, or as primarily a free-willed maker of his own constitution and history. . . . Inasmuch as the broadly philosophical differences I have mentioned are at least as tenaciously contested as are the more narrow scientific differences, the connections between the two may help account for an occasional vigor in arguments regarding sociological theory, since what may ultimately be at stake are world-views and not merely society-views (1969:14).

## *Philosophy and Sociology Are Related*

Several comments are in order here. First, is it correct to speak of Wallace's property space as having "philosophical implications" rather than "philosophical presuppositions"? His choice of the former phrase seems to be based on the assumption that science is autonomous with respect to philosophy—scientific theories being " . . . inductively derived from inspecting the data. . . ." Furthermore, the phrase "philosophical implications" suggests that philosophy is not autonomous with respect to science. May not philosophy have "scientific implications"?

Second, in spite of Wallace's tendency to minimize the full significance of philosophy for sociology, his claim that the major contemporary sociological theories can be significantly classified in terms of his property space marks a decisive break with positivism. In short, his claim is that contemporary sociological perspectives make a philosophical choice between materialism and idealism with respect to their *definition* of the social. Furthermore, they make another philosophical choice between freedom and determinism with respect to their mode of *explanation* of the social.

## *Wallace's Impasse and Hope*

In the end, Wallace reaches an impasse—one without the consolation of the hope of a positivist messiah such as sustained Martindale. His final words are analogous to Sartre's thesis that man is a "futile passion" because his desire to be God can never be realized, since the very concept of God within Sartre's philosophical framework is self-contradictory. Wallace writes:

Sociology as a whole . . . may be described as an ultimately vain but irresistible search for a single general theory incorporating at least the dimensions discussed in this essay, and to which all special theories, all empirical generalizations, all hypotheses, and all observations regarding social phenomena can be accurately related and thereby made intelligible (1969:59).

While Wallace does not make it explicit, I would offer two suggestions as to why he is convinced of the ultimate vanity of sociology. First, the ideal of a single general theory is itself thoroughly mistaken. It is part of what Rom Harre[2] has called the "mythology of deductivism," which he has subjected to a devastating critique (1970:1-32). Note, there is no sign of any such theory in physics. This ideal undoubtedly has played a significant role in behaviorist psychology with stimulus-and-response posing as the one general theory. However, far from vindicating this ideal, the history of behaviorism provides something much closer to a *reductio ad absurdum* (Koch, 1964; 1959). Second, Wallace thinks of philosophical positions (e.g., with respect to idealism, materialism, freedom, and determinism) as being tied to world-views and ultimate commitments. The result is, there is no "rational" way to move from the philosophical fragmentation of sociology in terms of these differences to a unified general theory which would clearly need a single agreed philosophical basis.

### Résumé

At this point let us review the rather lengthy course of our argument and introduce the next stage. Our overall task in this paper is to introduce a Christian perspective on the relationship between philosophy and sociology with a view to clarifying the Christian task in sociology. We began with the thesis that "the Christian perspective is the sole perspective in terms of which reality is rightly understood," but this has been radically rejected by the modern philosophical and sociological tradition. We illustrated this by reference to Hume, Marx, and Comte—for whom Christianity was irrational superstition, reactionary bourgeois ideology, and an obsolete form of mythological explanation, respectively. We then focused on positivism as a theory of the source and the historical stages of the development of human knowledge. We chose positivism because it was central to the secularization (de-Christianization) of Western thought in both philosophy and the sciences, including sociology. Consequently what stood in the way of any contemporary Christian reformation of scholarship was the positivist assertion of the autonomy of both philosophy and science with respect to religion, and the autonomy of science with respect to philosophy.

We then argued that positivism should be abandoned both as a philosophy and as a historiography of science. Our main arguments were that positivism suffered from grave internal contradictions and that it had little or no point of contact with the sciences. In particular, we argued that it could throw no light on an important and ubiquitous feature of all forms of theoretical inquiry, the existence of diverse schools of thought. This we sought to illustrate by reference to the works of Martindale and Wallace. By denying that philosophy had any role in contemporary sociology Martindale found himself unable to make any sense of the fragmenting role of various schools of thought. Wallace, although trying to stay close to positivism, concluded that the modern schools of sociological thought could only be accounted for if it was recognized that they rested on conflicting major philosophical assumptions and choices concerning materialism, idealism, freedom, and determinism. Wallace believed that these choices were rooted in different world-views. In part, his conclusion anticipates our next step which is to argue that just as sociology cannot proceed without philosophy, so philosophy cannot proceed without religion or ultimate commitments.

## Philosophy and Ultimate Commitments

While it might seem evident to positivistically minded sociologists that philosophical ideas are "relative" to class, nationality, and values, this has been resisted by philosophers who claim that their theories are universally valid or rationally self-evident. This parallels the way sociologists have resisted any suggestion that their theories are "relative" (especially to philosophical ideas), claiming that their theories are "scientific" and "value-free." The assumption behind these two claims is that sociology cannot be truly scientific until it has freed itself from philosophy, and that philosophy cannot be truly philosophical until it has freed itself from belief, especially religious belief. In the Western tradition this means Christian beliefs.

### Philosophy Needs a Metaphysical Framework

We have already argued that the first of these claims is fundamentally mistaken. We drew support for our argument from contemporary philosophy of science and the existence of numerous schools of thought in sociology. A similar argument can be used to refute the claim that philosophy is autonomous with respect to religion. Indeed, if the contention from the philosophy of science that every science requires a conceptual (or metaphysical) framework can be generalized to theoretical disciplines, and if philosophy is a theoretical discipline, then philosophy also needs a conceptual framework. However, the main stream of twentieth-century philosophy has sought to avoid this suggestion in the interests of neutrality, just as the social sciences have done. Pragmatism, phenomenology, logical positivism, and linguistic analysis have largely presented themselves, not as systematic metaphysics rooted in ultimate commitments, but as *neutral methods.* Concerns with interpretation, evaluation, integration, and synthesis have been disclaimed, while a "scientific" approach involving some form of "logical analysis" or "pure description" has been proclaimed as *the* philosophical method.

## Many Schools, One Method

In this context reference cannot be made to the philosophical literature, but the fact that such claims to neutrality are at least dubious, if not a complete pretense, should be evident from the fact that there are many schools of thought offering *the* neutral method. A closer examination will reveal that each of these schools is divided into subschools, each with their variants on *the* method. It is very hard not to see these various schools of philosophy as guided by various pretheoretical commitments (Gellner, 1963; Pivcevic, 1970). *Perhaps the deepest irony of the situation is that while philosophy has been progressively restricting its field and methods in order to appear "neutral" and "scientific," the sciences themselves (including sociology) have found themselves in an ever deepening philosophical crisis.* Some sense of the chaos of modern thought is provided by Ernst Cassirer (1953). He writes, we

> . . . have amassed an astoundingly rich and constantly increasing body of facts. Our technical instruments for observation and experimentation have become immensely improved, and our analyses have become sharper and more penetrating. We appear nevertheless, not to have found a method for the mastery and organization of this material. When compared with our abundance the past may seem very poor. But wealth of facts is not necessarily wealth of thoughts. Unless we succeed in finding a clue to Ariadne to lead us

out of this labyrinth, we can have no real insight into the real character of human culture; we shall remain lost in a mass of disconnected and disintegrated data which seem to lack all conceptual unity (1953:40-1).

In large measure this disintegration is due to the rapid growth and differentiation of knowledge without *philosophical integration*. This is clearly not a technical problem that can be solved by means of information storage and retrieval, or some more sophisticated form of computerization. The questions and disputes we are concerned with are clearly philosophical disputes that *transcend* the more limited problems with which the sciences deal. Yet, at the same time, they *define* and *structure* the sciences both with respect to their fields of investigation and method of inquiry.

## Philosophical Integration Is Needed

This concern with philosophical integration is, of course, not new. It has been one of the major aims of modern secular humanist philosophy for the past four hundred years. It has produced a whole series of systems—rationalism, materialism, empiricism, idealism, historicism, and evolutionism—all of which have provided integration at the price of reductionism. Each has taken one or two aspects of the creation-order and has attempted to give an account of everything in terms of them. Each one sounded plausible enough at the beginning, but in the end, if consistently developed, resembled a *reductio ad absurdum*. Each school of thought provoked another which advocated that previously omitted aspects were to be regarded as the key to knowledge.

## Again, Humanism or Christianity?

At the end of his book, *The Age of Complexity*, the American philosopher Herbert Kohl concludes his survey of contemporary philosophy with these words:

> There is no single explanation of all phenomena, no single characterization of language, and most of all, no one point of view from which man "must" be considered. Throughout my text there has been no mention of God or religion. . . . Philosophy, insofar as it considers the actual lives men lead these days, must consider life lived without divine guidance or grace. Life has become too com-

plex for simple answers; hence philosophy insofar as it is modern does not consider religion an issue. . . . Life does not have a single great question with a single answer but questions and answers (1965:271).

Let me make three comments on this passage. First, while saying that there is no one point of view from which man must be considered, Kohl immediately proceeds to dismiss any alternatives to his own commitment to modern humanism. Similarly, while saying that life does not have a single answer, he is insistent that the only acceptable answer is what in his terminology he calls a "philosophy of complexity and disillusionment."

Secondly, Kohl seems to be haunted by the memory of an alternative unification—one provided by the Christian religion (instead of secular humanism). Christians view man as the servant of God, finding life through divine guidance and grace. He dismisses Christianity because it is inconsistent with his own disillusioned humanism. The reason he offers is interesting. He thinks that life has become too complex for simple answers. Is Christianity a "simple answer"? It may be that the Christianity Kohl encountered was so reduced and compromised that he concluded that it could not provide the intellectual unification and hope needed to answer the complex problems and disillusionment of the modern world. One further comment on the ambiguity of the phrase "simple answer." It can mean "simplistic," or it can mean "basic" or "foundational"—just as "single great question" can be poking fun at something pompous and pretentious, or it can refer to a question the answer of which determines the direction of all subsequent questioning. Kohl trades on this ambiguity. He is clearly conducting a strategic retreat on behavior of humanism which involves a scorched-earth policy. In short, if humanism cannot find any integration in our complex world, then there is no integration to be found. To think otherwise is to engage in fantasy.

*To summarize*, we have found that no serious case has been made for either the autonomy of the sciences (including sociology), or for philosophy. Furthermore, the anarchy of the various sciences with their diverse schools of thought cannot be helped by humanist philosophy, for it shares, and is part of, the same problem. Indeed, the fragmentation of contemporary scholarship is due to the fragmentation of humanist philosophy underlying it. As modern humanism declines, its highest wisdom seems to be that we should reconcile ourselves with "complexity." This seems little short of intellectual chaos—or expressed existentially, "meaninglessness."

## A Call for Openness

Let us now put together the two stages of our argument. If sociology cannot be philosophically neutral, and if philosophy cannot be religiously neutral, then we may draw two implications.

### What Are the Presuppositions?

First, if sociology is to be *critical* instead of dogmatic, then it must clearly state the philosophical and religious presuppositions that provide its structure and control its development. This reverses the usual formulation inspired by positivism, where a sociological perspective that has an explicit philosophical-religious orientation is dismissed as dogmatic and prejudiced—or as "social philosophy." To this idea, a good number of non-Christian sociologists will show some sympathy and might even suggest that it is slightly passe. For instance, we could mention Alvin Gouldner's paper, "Anti-Minotaur: The Myth of a Value-Free Sociology" (1963). This should not surprise us, for there are many secular humanists who are opposed to the various forms of positivism and scientism (Sorokin, 1965; Andreski, 1972).

### Humanism Revised

Modern humanism since Kant has been torn between two poles— that of *autonomous science* and that of *autonomous personality* (Dooyeweerd, 1958, 1960). This has led to the existence of two antagonistic traditions within modern humanism, and a variety of attempts to arbitrate between the two poles by assigning territory to both the ideal of science and to the ideal of freedom. In that, positivism represents the primacy of the ideal of science. There have been many humanists since Kant who have wished to "limit science to make room for faith." By this they mean to limit the humanist's ideal of science in order to make room for the humanist ideal of personality with its values. All that is being proposed is a revision of humanism. *There is no concern to make room for non-humanist ideals of science and personality.*

### Illiberal Humanist/Positivist Academe

The nature and content of our academic programs and textbooks continue to show the decisive imprint of positivism. They continue to be organized as if disciplines are isolated units, as if all share the same universally valid standpoint and train towards neutral-technical professional competence, and as if controversy were marginal to the academic enterprise and would disappear as disciplines matured. Such an administrative-curricular-textbook pattern is deeply at odds with the academic realities of teaching, learning, and research. In sociology, for example, it does not take long to recognize that departments are solidly functionalist, neo-Marxist, or symbolic interactionist. Many are divided into a number of camps with open or implicit conflict between them. One soon comes to realize that he could not be "at home"—be free to be himself—if he held to a markedly different perspective. In spite of what might be said about "stimulating criticism," if scholarship is something that is centrally communal in character, then one would necessarily be intellectually isolated from his colleagues by virtue of his perspective. Furthermore, one's academic growth would be stunted by this isolation, although it might be overcome, in part, through contact with like-minded scholars in other institutions.

*Teaching:* With respect to teaching, there are also deep dilemmas. Positivism requires neutrality. One can teach that his perspective is the neutral perspective. The only positivist alternative is that one "neutrally" *teach about* all perspectives, concealing his own. If the earlier arguments of this chapter are correct, then there is no philosophical or religiously neutral perspective. The idea of neutral teaching is hardly less problematic. What is to be included or excluded from the syllabus and why? What will be the aim of the curriculum? How will one account for the diversity of perspectives? What will one say or insinuate about those who claim to have the exclusively correct perspective? How will one evaluate the work of students? Would they be expected to give the appearance of suspended judgment in their examinations and papers (Russell, 1979)?

### The Student

In all this, the situation of the students is the most difficult, for they are the most vulnerable—especially if they try to be radically Christian and do not share the philosophical and religious perspective of their teachers. Most of them realize they are not in a position or equipped to dissent, and will play along with what is required, never becoming existentially involved. Their motivation will almost necessarily be reduced to an extrinsic concern, passing exams. This alienation from academic inquiry may well stay with them for life, making them pragmatic and unreflective. Those who do dissent are likely to pay a heavy price. Not only will they have to keep up with the requirements of the program, but they will have to work much harder to present cogent criticism of the ruling departmental perspective and work at the discipline from their own philosophic-religious perspective.

## Lack of Community in Academe

In short, within the present positivist dominated institutional framework there seems to be no way to take seriously the academic freedom of the researcher, teacher, and student, and the communal character of scholarship. This freedom cannot be conceived of in an individualistic manner, but is a matter of working along with those who share a common perspective. The academic reality is that there are two intellectual "communities" in which one participates. The one composed of those with whom one shares an interest in the same discipline, and another of those whose main interest is different but with whom one shares a similar philosophical and religious perspective. Our present departmental organization only recognizes the first community, though there are reasons to think that the second involves a much deeper sense of community. Those who belong to the various communities in this sense could perhaps be served best by a series of research institutes based on campus. In the meantime there is no reason why Christian students and lecturers should not unofficially initiate such an "institute"—a university within a contemporary university. The aim of such an institute would be a Christian academic witness. It would involve the critique of non-Christian perspectives and the construction of Christian alternatives.

## Shared Perspective Is Essential

A final point is that this arrangement would best facilitate the concern that exists for interdisciplinary integration. If the general argument of our paper is sound, then there is no possibility of genuine integration between disciplines that lack a shared philosophical perspective—a necessary prerequisite for academic communication and community. Attempts at integration and communication between disciplines which are themselves philosophically fragmented is a hopeless venture. It is far better to build on shared philosophical foundations with the plurality of integrations it offers. If one does not, attempts at unification will inevitably fail, pushing the academic enterprise into further fragmentation and more academics into that form of intellectual suicide known as dedicated specialism. Those who seriously wish to oppose this gentle pluralization of academic institutions ought to consider carefully the philosophical presuppositions of the "unity" they wish to retain. Should those who do not share such presuppositions have the institutional and academic consequences of them forced upon them? Doubtless the proposed pluralization might give administrators a few headaches, but perhaps this is what they are paid for as servants of the academic community.

### Christians Must Break Clean of Humanism

We now turn to the second implication of our main argument. If sociology cannot escape the control of philosophical and religious presuppositions, then it is mandatory for Christians to break with sociological perspectives with non-Christian presuppositions. If Wallace is correct, this means a break with all the major contemporary perspective, for he maintained that they had all made a choice in their foundations between the freedom and determinism, and between materialism and idealism. This is a choice between the humanist ideal of personality and science in terms of the first alternative, and between two forms of non-Christian ontology (idealism and materialism) in the second. That all these alternatives are between different types of secular humanism is hardly surprising, for the founding fathers of sociology—Comte, Spencer, Durkheim, Marx, and Weber—offer us nothing else. Each was quite explicit about his rejection and interpretation of the Christian religion. Nor has Christianity had any subsequent impact on the sociological tradition. The nature of the contemporary scene is clear enough. Wallace writes in the preface of his book on theory:

> I am not concerned in this book with all sociological theories that anyone might ever have dreamed of (for example, supernatural theories of social life are left out), but only with those that have achieved a relatively high degree of formalization and explicit expression in "the sociological literature"—and indeed, only with the most widely and currently influential of these theories (1969:viii).

Many Christians are not willing to break decisively with the secularist presuppositions of the sociological community—especially those who have been socialized into that community and for whom being a sociologist constitutes a significant part of their identity. Sometimes their interpretation of the Christian religion is adjusted so that no break is required. Sometimes they will maintain that sociology has no such presuppositions, that it is neutral. As we have already argued, this positivist claim is very dubious from both a biblical and epistemological standpoint. Sometimes they feel the claim to be eclectic is a sufficient break, as long as one is not a member of one particular school of thought.

The appeal of eclecticism is that it seems to be the only way to save being boxed in by highly reductionistic schools of thought, while at the same time recognizing aspects of reality that one does not wish to ignore. But there are two crucial points that cannot be avoided. The first is that unless one's selection of concepts, theories, and methods from other positions is purely arbitrary, then one is guided by criteria which are presumably mutually consistent. It is hard to see how this can differ from being a member of a school of thought, except that this school might have only one member and would inevitably be underdeveloped—at least at first. The second point is that the term eclectic suggests purely personal choices, whereas if it is a Christian perspective that guides the choices, then it would be better to say so. However, to put the matter like that is not fully adequate either. In my opinion, a Christian eclecticism mistakenly assumes that all the materials necessary for a Christian sociological perspective already exist in the humanistic sociological literature, and that one can simply select and remove concepts and theories from other perspectives. The assumption is that they are bricks from which one can proceed to build his Christian theoretical edifice. We have already suggested that a theoretical perspective is not like a pile of bricks, but is far more integrated and interconnected. It is like a tree with religious roots, a philosophical trunk, the sciences as branches, and theories as twigs.

*Borrowing Working Hypotheses and Methodologies*

In addition to reinterpreting Christianity, positivism, and eclecticism, there is one final method of making peace with the world of secularized sociological perspectives. This is to claim that one has only taken over assumptions from these perspectives as "working hypotheses" or as "purely methodological" tools, or simply that one finds them "useful."° Sometimes these glib phrases are used to dis claim responsibility for one's intellectual commitments or to evade answering serious criticism. If something better lies behind these phrases, then the individual should be willing to submit to interrogation and justify his commitment to a theory, theories, or research program. One might ask, why work with this hypothesis? Why does it work? Why adopt this methodology? What would lead you to adopt another methodology? What assumptions about the nature of social reality does this methodology presume, and what grounds are there for making that presumption? The word "useful" volunteers even less information, so that one cannot but ask, useful for what purpose? Are those purposes justified?

## The Consequences of Not Breaking with Humanism

Our general conclusion is that these and other strategies used by Christian sociologists to try to avoid making a decisive break with the secular presuppositions of the sociological community will not stand up to serious examination. One reason for not wanting to make this break may be that only the cost of the break has been considered. One should also consider the consequences of *not* making the break. Some of the consequences are as follows:

### It Divides the Body of Christ

It leads to the breaking of the church, the body of Christ, in terms of the divisions that non-Christian sociologists have among themselves. Sadly this is not a new phenomenon. Much of the history of theology itself is a history of synthesis with non-Christian philosophies running from neo-platonism to existentialism, linguistic analysis, process philosophy, and neo-marxism in our own day. It presents the pathetic spectacle of Christian theologians scrambling to get in line with the

---

°These evasive phrases were naturally much utilized by the logical positivists in order to give the appearance of not holding any substantive philosophical positions. They spoke of "methodological materialism," "methodological behaviorism," and even "methodological solipsism" ... but one suspects that they would not have tolerated "methodological idealism" or "methodological mentalism." Some contemporary sociologists have suggested that the sociology of religion should operate on the basis of "methodological atheism." If this atheism is as purely methodological as they insist, then they should have no problems with other sociologists opting for "methodological theism" instead.

"assured results of modern thought." By the time they have gotten in line, "modern thought" has restlessly moved on again, leaving the Christian *avant-garde* not only defending already obsolete ideas, but propagating them in congregations who have not quite absorbed the ideas from the previous era of synthesis. One listens in vain for any complaint that the Christians "have turned the world of philosophical or sociological scholarship upside down." All this serves to confirm the sense of victory that secular humanism has over the Christian faith.

## We Are Under Judgment

To the extent that we synthesize with non-Christian sociological thought, we will share in its crisis. More pointedly, we will share its judgment—judgment in that all thought not submitted to the obedience of Christ eventually suffers. However, having synthesized with the sociological establishment we are more likely to be apologists for that establishment, rather than prophets calling it to repentance and renewal.

## We Neglect Our Evangelical and Prophetic Roles

If we do not see the vanity of secularized scholarship, then we will not understand that the gospel of the kingdom of God is good news for scholarship in all of its many fields and institutional dimensions. If these expressions sound strange and even bizarre, perhaps we should ask if this is because we view the university as the "temple of the un-fallen intellect of man and as the true light of modern culture." Perhaps we have a little too much reverence for the modern university, sym-bolized by the fact that many ministers in Britain wear their university hoods during services—as if that qualifies them to lead the Christian community. Historically, this reverence is not difficult to understand, for until relatively recently most of higher education was church con-trolled. In addition it is difficult to be critical of an institution from which one derives status and distinction and, even more crucially, one's intellectual formation. We are called to evaluate that intellectual formation and to spiritually discern the religious dynamics that have made it what it is. If we have really grasped that academic institutions, traditions, disciplines, theories, and concepts can never be religiously neutral, then the following words of Paul will speak concretely to us. But if we have not, then they will restrict us to "values," "moral out-look," and "pious platitudes."

> Do not conform any longer to the pattern of this world, but be transformed by the renewing of your mind. Then you will be able to test and approve what God's will is—his good, pleasing and perfect will. Romans 12:2, NIV.

As Christian scholars our central task can be none other than discovering and manifesting the genuine liberating power of the gospel for scholarship.

## Ideas Do Have Consequences

We should never underestimate the power of scholarship, or fail to recognize that ideas have consequences. Karl Marx spent years of his life writing and researching in the British Museum library. You can read about the consequences of those ideas in any newspaper, any day, in any country of the world. John Maynard Keynes, perhaps the most influential economist of the twentieth century, ended his *General Theory* (1936) with this statement: "... the ideas of economists and political philosophers, both when they are right and when they are wrong, are more powerful than is commonly understood. Indeed the world is ruled by little else. Practical men, who believe themselves exempt from any intellectual influences, are usually the slaves of some defunct economist."

In our own day the social sciences clearly play a significant role in shaping contemporary society—in legislation, industrial relations, management practices, the administration of law and justice, education, and welfare services. Their power has a twofold source. On the one hand, being "scientific," they are taken to be quite unproblematically reliable and unprejudiced by the decision-makers who claim to base their decisions on them. They in turn claim, that since their decisions are based on "scientific" research, they are the only ones possible. Policy, so we are led to believe, is determined by the facts, so that any dispute about values or ideologies is now obsolete.

On the other hand, there is a second indirect source of influence that, in the long run, is far more powerful—the sociological perspective. The first source has been subjected to considerable criticism. Frequently it is suggested that there is a gap between "facts" and "social policy," and "is" and "ought." According to positivism there is no "logical" way of crossing this gap: no social fact has any policy implications whatever without the introduction of normative principles. Such criticism, however, tends to be superficial and ineffective because it fails to realize that *a perspective* lies behind sociological facts and theories, as much as it does behind social policies and values. The theory *defines* the situation, its necessities, possibilities, probabilities, and impossibilities. Different sociological perspectives do this in often radically different ways.

Once you have accepted a "description" of the situation, certain "prescriptions" seem more or less inevitable (Olthuis, 1969; 1975). In a nutshell it means that if Christians accept "descriptions" of contemporary society that are rooted in a humanist sociological perspective, then any attempt to develop integrally Christian social and political policies by appeal to Christian principles or values will be impossible. One cannot get Christian policies by adding "Christian values" to functionalist or Marxist "descriptions." At present virtually all the "descriptions" we have available are from different humanist perspectives. Consequently this is also true of almost all social and political causes, and it will continue to be true until we have developed an analysis of contemporary society from a Christian perspective (Storkey, 1979).

### Needed, a New Reformation

The task before us is nothing other than the reformation of the sociological tradition as part of the larger task of the Christian reformation of scholarship (Runner, 1979). But where do we start with this? In the first place, if we had not previously recognized the possibility and necessity of such a reformation, then it is highly likely that our worldview has been dualistic. One that has profoundly restricted the meaning of Christian faith and obedience. Consequently we need to recapture the cosmic significance of creation, fall, and redemption in Jesus Christ, and glimpse the possibility of making every sociological theory subject to the obedience of Christ. Second, as we have seen, such a world view needs theoretical articulation to provide a new ontological and epistemological foundation for sociology. In short, we stand in need of a Christian systematic philosophy. It may come as a surprise, but considerable work has been done by Herman Dooyeweerd on the development of such a philosophy, one with a Christocentric worldview and deeply concerned with the reformation of the sciences, including sociology (1958). While the reformation of scholarship that Dooyeweerd proposes is extensive, any serious attempt to develop a comprehensive Christian sociological perspective and theory must include this thought.

## Discussion Questions

1. What is the dichotomy that "science" imposes on human thought? What does Russell see as the critical issue?

2. What is the tradition that lies behind both sociology and philosophy? Consult a philosophy book if need be and identify the basic assumptions and tenets of this tradition. How do they agree/ disagree with those of Christianity?

3. Why does Russell believe there is no opposition to secular humanism in universities today? Is this true at your college or university?

4. What philosophy does sociology identify with and why does Russell object to it? What are his arguments against it?

5. How do Martindale and Wallace seek to explain the various sociological schools of thought? How does each try to integrate them, if at all?

6. What "religious assumptions" lie behind the various philosophical schools? Why does Russell believe that philosophy cannot integrate itself?

7. What problems exist in the modern university that hinder students from developing their full intellectual potential? What alternatives does Russell suggest?

8. Do you agree with Russell's position that a Christian cannot build an eclectic system, drawing "bricks" from non-Christian perspectives and models? Discuss—why, why not?

9. What consequences does a Christian suffer if he does not make a clean break with secular humanism and develop his own unique Christian perspective?

10. Is it realistic to assume that Christians can agree on a single sociological or philosophical perspective? Should this be our goal? Why, why not?

## References

Andreski, S.
  1972 *Social Sciences as Sorcery*. London: Andre Deutsch.
Cassirer, E.
  1953 *An Essay on Man: An Introduction to the Philosophy of Human Culture*. New York: Doubleday.
Dooyeweerd, H.
  1953 *A New Critique of Theoretical Thought*. Nutley, N.J.: Presbyterian and Reformed.
  1960 *In the Twilight of Western Thought*. Nutley, N.J.: Presbyterian and Reformed.
Feyeraband, P. K.
  1975 *Against Method*. London: New Left Books.

Gellner, E.
    1963 *Words and Things.* London: Gollancz (critique of the pretended neutrality of the methods of linguistic analysis).
Gouldner, A.
    1963 "Anti-Minotaur: the Myth of a Value-Free Sociology" in *Sociology on Trial,* edited by Stein, M. and A. Vidich, Englewood Cliffs, N.J.: Prentice-Hall.
Harre, R.
    1970 *The Principle of Scientific Thinking.* London: Macmillan.
Hume, David
    1874 *A Treatise on Human Nature.* Vol. 1, London.
Keynes, J. M.
    1965 *General Theory of Employment, Interest, and Money.* New York: Harcourt Brace Jovanovich.
Kalsbeek, L.
    1975 *Contours of a Christian Philosophy.* Toronto: Wedge Pub. Foundation (an introduction to Dooyeweerd's thought).
Klaaren, M.
    1977 *Religious Origins of Modern Science.* Grand Rapids: Eerdmans.
Koch, S.
    1964 "Psychology and Emerging Conceptions of Knowledge as Unitary" in *Behaviorism and Phenomenology: Contrasting Bases for Modern Psychology,* edited by T. W. Wann, Chicago: University of Chicago Press. *Psychology: A Study of a Science.* New York; McGraw-Hill.
Kohl, R.
    1965 *The Age of Complexity.* New York: Mentor Books.
Martindale, D.
    1964 *The Nature and Types of Sociological Theory.* London: Routledge and Kegan Paul.
Marx, K. and F. Engels
    1955 *On Religion.* Moscow: Foreign Language Publishing House.
Olthuis, J. H.
    1969 *Facts, Values and Ethics.* New York: Humanities Press
    1975 *I Pledge You My Troth: A Biblical View of Marriage, Family and Friendship.* New York: Harper and Row.
Pivcevic, E.
    1970 *Husserl and Phenomenology.* London: Hutchinson.
Radnitzky, G.
    1973 *Contemporary Schools of Metascience.* Chicago: Henry Regnery (an excellent account of the theory and collapse of the logical positivist theory of science).
Runner, H. E.
    1973 *The Relation of the Bible to Learning.* Toronto: Wedge Publishing Foundation.

Russell, R. A.
    1979 *Reason and Commitment in Education*. Exeter: Paternoster Press.
Skolimowsi, H.
    1974 *The Philosophy of Karl Popper*. New York: Library of Living Philosophers.
Storkey, A.
    1979 *Towards a Christian Social Perspective*. Leicester: I.V.P. (a major contribution to Christian social thought using insights from Dooyeweerd to provide a searching analysis of sociology, economics, and political theory. Essential reading for all Christian sociologists).
Tucker, R.
    1967 *Philosophy and Myth in Karl Marx*. New York: Cambridge University Press.
van der Hoeven, J.
    1976 *Karl Marx: the Roots of His Thought*. Toronto: Wedge Publishing Foundation.
Wallace, W.
    1969 *Sociological Theory*. London: Heinemann.
Wolters, A.
    1975 *Our Place in the Philosophical Tradition*. Toronto: Wedge Publishing Foundation.

Note: The Association for the Advancement of Christian Scholarship sponsors the Graduate Institute for Christian Studies (229 College Street, Toronto, Canada, M5T 1R4). It is doing excellent work in a number of culturally strategic areas—philosophy, ethics, theology, history, political theory, aesthetics, education, psychology, and economics.

# PART IV
# CULTURE AND
# SOCIALIZATION

# CULTURE AND SOCIALIZATION

Once a Japanese is employed by a firm in Japan, his position is secure regardless of fluctuations in the economy. When a Muslim is walking on the streets of Baghdad and the call to prayer is sounded, he falls to his knees in prayer. If a male child is born to Jewish parents, he will be circumcized. Aged parents are not sent off to an "old people's home" in China or India. They are treated with dignity and respect within the family home. A young couple in a Goan village (India) refrain from displaying affection in public—it just is not done.

What do all these different customs have in common? They are all regarded as "right" within the respective societies. Not to follow the cultural ways of one's society is to incur varying degrees of negative sanctions.

Culture, sociologically speaking, includes all the ways of feeling, thinking, and acting within a society, including material artifacts. We learn these values and behavior patterns through a process called socialization that begins in infancy and continues throughout life. While we are taught much in the home, school, church, and by peer group, most of our cultural ways and values are *caught*—absorbed in a process analogous to osmosis. As Gabriel Tarde suggested, we learn by imitation.

But not everyone shares the same culture within our society. In your travels you have probably discovered subcultural groups that have "strange ways"—ways different from your's. These may arise from racial, religious, and political, socioeconomic, regional, or age differences. Because self-conscious groups do share a common consensus about societal values, while at the same time subscribing to unique values and behavior patterns, we call them subcultures. Groups that reject the core values of our society and are at odds with it are labeled as counter- or contra-cultural.

Within these cultural and subcultural groups persons occupy various positions or statuses, each having imposed on them by society a set of prescribed norms which define the rights and responsibilities called a role. If the incumbent of a position does not play his role within the prescribed limits, society disapproves. Individuals who exceed these proscribed bounds are labeled as deviants.

Some deviants who "blow the whistle," challenging the various institutions in society to act responsibly, are sorely needed and appreciated—in retrospect and often posthumously. (For example, Moses, Amos, Jesus, Marx, Martin Luther King, anti-Vietnam protesters, *et.al.*). Deviants who "rip off" society—whether "white collar" criminals in executive and corporate offices, or syndicated and "blue collar" criminals are all punished—the latter with greater rigor and severity.

The first essay in Part IV by William Hasker challenges you to think through the problem of cultural relativity and relativism. Are there absolutes, or does it all depend on "how you look at it"? While he acknowledges that cultures are obviously different, and that traits are relative to each culture, he rejects any notion that there are no absolutes or that *truth* is relative. He believes that ultimate truth is found in Jesus Christ and in the Scriptures.

Next, Gary Farley takes you to the funeral parlor, using the experience of bereavement to illustrate the way culture programs us to play specific roles. He points up the limitations of role theory to explain human nature and behavior, and suggests that the image of man presented in the Bible be used as a means of correcting and integrating sociological images.

Jack Balswick discusses the somewhat revolutionary changes in female and male sex roles. In a brief historical sketch he cites the factors contributing to these changes, including the contribution of the Women's Rights Movements. He argues that since sex roles are primarily culturally determined, the church and Christians should reflect the equalitarian views of Scripture and not blindly conform to cultural norms.

Becoming old in America involves a resocialization process that transforms an active, contributing, well-functioning adult into a passive, noncontributing, dysfunctioning person. David O. Moberg challenges both the secular and sacred communities to reevaluate their philosophy or theology, policy, and treatment of old people. *Ageism* (discrimination) and *gerontophobia* (prejudice) must be replaced with a policy that restores dignity and worth to old people.

What do you do with the "improperly socialized" youthful and adult offenders? Do you confine them to prison (a "total institution") and throw away the key? Prisons only further socialize persons into greater depths of criminality, says Richard P. Rettig, an "ex-con" who spent fifteen years in prison himself. He sees the greatest cure coming, not from prison bureaucrats and paid professionals, but from *trained* volunteers who love freely, are nonjudgmental, accepting, and who respect the "con" as a person.

# 16
# Cultural Relativity and Relativism

*William Hasker*

## The Case for Relativism

"It all depends on your point of view." "It's all relative, isn't it?"
Expressions like these reveal an attitude which is rather prevalent, an
attitude we all share from time to time. It is the attitude that, on some
questions at least, there is not any one correct answer but rather several
answers, each of which is "correct" from one point of view, but
"wrong" from other points of views. Or, as we sometimes say, "Different people have different ways of looking at things," and often one
way of looking at a matter is no better or worse than another. Now, if
we take this attitude seriously, and apply it to everything, it becomes
*relativism*, which can be defined as the view that *there is no such thing
as a belief being absolutely true or false; beliefs are true or false only
relative to a given point of view.*

Relativism exists in people's thinking either as an explicit theory,
as I have just stated it, or as a more or less unconsciously assumed attitude—but either way, it is usually supported or encouraged by evidence from the social sciences. Sociology describes for us the process of
socialization, in which we learn and absorb our basic beliefs and attitudes in the course of being brought up within a particular social
group. Psychology describes the formation of the superego, in which we
internalize the rules laid down by our parents, make them a part of

**William Hasker**
*Professor of Philosophy*
*Huntington College (Indiana)*
William Hasker was trained in philosophy and received his PhD
from the University of Edinburgh. Earlier he earned the BD from
Berkeley Baptist Divinity School. Professor Hasker's areas of specialty is in the philosophy of mind, philosophy of psychology, and
the philosophy of religion. He has contributed articles to numerous
journals, and he has served as president of the Indiana Philosophical
Association. A member of the Christian Church, Disciples of Christ,
he is currently an elder in the local congregation.

ourselves until they become our very conscience. History shows us the succession of different societies each with a belief-system which seemed obviously true, right, and natural to the society's own members—and obviously wrong, silly, or fantastic to members of other societies. And finally there is anthropology, which by comparing different cultures shows us the vast range of cultural relativity, with a seemingly endless variety of everything from magic to manners to morals to medicine.

When we encounter these facts and ideas from the social sciences it is hard not to feel that they present an overwhelming case for relativism. If our beliefs have been shaped by our cultural environment, and if beliefs held by others have been shaped by *their* cultural environment, then who is to choose between them? Of course, each of us, *speaking from the standpoint of his own culture*, can say that certain ideas are "true" and that others, which disagree with them, are "false." But none of us can jump outside of his own culture, so as to judge from a "neutral" point of view what is *really* true, any more than you can jump out of your skin in order to look yourself in the face. The idea of some ultimate, "absolute" truth seems meaningless. Truth, of necessity, *can* only be judged from the standpoint of a particular culture.

In many ways this is a comfortable kind of conclusion to reach. When we think of the blood that has been spilled and the persecutions that have been carried out by "true believers" throughout the ages, the more tolerant attitude of the cultural relativist comes as a relief. Relativism undermines at a stroke the superiority complex of "advanced" (read, "white European") cultures towards "primitive" cultures (all the rest). It allows every man to hold and to speak the truth from his point of view, but forbids anyone to claim that his is the *only* truth or to impose it on others by force or intimidation. These are real advantages.

All the same, relativism sometimes makes us uncomfortable. We find ourselves asking, If all truth is relative, what can I believe? Of course, the relativist has an answer for this. He tells us to believe whatever seems right to us, in the light of our own point of view. But this is not completely satisfying, especially when we realize that in doing so we are exactly as right—*and as wrong*—as someone else who holds exactly opposite beliefs as "true" from *his* point of view. It is easy enough to have a tolerant, relativistic attitude toward beliefs held by others, or even toward beliefs of our own that are not very important to us. But when we come to matters that concern us deeply, it is hard to say—and even harder to *mean*—that our own viewpoint is really no more true or correct than its opposite. It would be safe to say that during the sixties and seventies many persons normally inclined towards relativism have found themselves making "absolute" judgments about quite a few things, ranging from civil rights to Watergate and from abortion to marijuana law reform. It is just not that easy to be a consistent, thoroughgoing relativist. The relativist may succeed in cutting the ground from under his opponent's feet, but only at the cost of leaving himself with no place to stand.

But is not relativism unavoidable? Given the facts mentioned above, from the various social sciences, does not relativism follow whether we like it or not? I do not think so. To be sure, it would be foolish to deny the *facts* about socialization, human development, history, and cultural relativity mentioned above. We must try to get the facts straight and challenge those who make exaggerated claims about the differences in moral codes between different societies.[1] But facts are facts, and must not be denied. What we have to show—and I think we *can* show—is that the *conclusion* drawn by the relativist (namely, relativism itself) simply does not follow from those facts.

In this article I am going to suggest two different ways of answering the relativist, which I will call the "short answer" and the "long answer." Each of them by itself is sufficient to show that relativism is unsound and need not be accepted. The "short answer" is concise and rather easy to grasp, but it fails to meet some of the issues raised by the relativist. The "long answer" is more complex and involved (indeed, it cannot be presented in full in a brief article) but in the end it provides a more complete and satisfying answer. We will take the short answer first.

### The Short Answer to Relativism

The short answer consists, really, of just a single question which we put to the relativist in order to see how he responds. What we say is this: "You assert that all truth is relative—that nothing is true or false absolutely—but only in relation to the 'point of view' of the one who believes or disbelieves.

"Now, this assertion of yours—how are we supposed to take it? Do you mean to say that this is *really so*—that there *really is* no such thing as ultimate or absolute truth? Or do you mean only that it seems this way *from your point of view*, so that *for you* relativism is correct but it might very well be false from someone else's point of view?"

How will the relativist answer? Suppose he takes the first alternative, and says that relativism *really is* correct. Is it not clear that in asserting his own position he has undermined it? For he is asserting that at least *one* belief of his *really is true*—namely, the belief that there is no absolute truth! He cannot have it both ways. If there *is* no truth, then *his* assertion cannot be true, and if he thinks that it is true, then he is admitting that truth exists! The assertion that there *really is* no such thing as truth contradicts itself.

Suppose then, that he takes the other alternative. He says, "Oh no, you won't catch me in *that* trap. When I say that there is no absolute truth, I don't mean that *my* assertion is absolutely true! I simply mean that from *my point of view* there is no absolute truth. But if anyone thinks differently, he is entitled to his opinion, which no doubt is correct from *his* point of view."

In saying this, our relativist has avoided the inconsistency pointed out above. But in doing so, he has made it unnecessary for us to answer him. For he has failed to say anything that needs to be answered!

Let me illustrate this point with an example. Suppose you are standing on a hilltop with a companion, watching a storm develop in the valley below. Your companion points to a dark shape in the churning cloud-mass, and says "Look! It's a giant's hand reaching down out of the cloud!" If your companion is a small child and seems genuinely frightened, you will reassure him by telling him that there really is no giant; it is only a shape that the clouds have taken which will soon blow away. If he is old enough to understand, you may support your answer by explaining to him the wind-patterns in storm clouds, and the mechanism by which they produce shapes like the one which has frightened him.

Suppose, on the other hand, your companion is a college graduate with a BA in physics. *He* does not need to be reassured about the giant or told about the wind currents. In fact, there is no need to say anything to him at all, for, unlike the child, he really did not mean to assert anything about a giant in the valley. Rather than talking about a giant who supposedly *really exists*, he is speaking about his own *subjective perception* of the storm cloud. He is saying, in effect, "This is how that storm cloud looks to me." There is no point in your disagreeing with him, or agreeing, for that matter. At most, you might want to look at the cloud yourself and see whether you get an impression similar to the one he is reporting.

Now, back to our relativist. If he claims that his denial of the existence of truth is itself true, he is in the same position as the child in our story: that is, he is making a claim about what is really the case—what is really so. Unfortunately for him, his claim, unlike the child's claim about the giant, is then self-contradictory. If on the other hand he does *not* mean that his statement is itself true, he is more like the physics graduate. He has not said anything about the *actual* existence or nonexistence of truth; it's as if he had said, "I feel as though there isn't any truth at all"—but this simply describes a personal impression of his. And there is no need to quarrel with this impression, for he has not claimed to say anything at all about what is really the case. In particular, he has not said anything which disagrees with the view that there *really is* a definite truth, and that we can know what that truth is.

The relativist, then, finds himself in a dilemma from which he cannot escape. If in saying that "all truth is relative" he claims to be saying something objectively true, then in the act of asserting this he contradicts his own assertion. But if he does not make this claim, he fails to assert anything at all; he merely reports a subjective impression. Perhaps the kindest thing to say to him is, "That's too bad. I hope you feel better soon."

This argument really does show that relativism is untenable—that it is not a position which anyone can consistently hold or advocate. Yet I must admit that it is not in every respect a satisfying answer to relativism. Even if we see that no one can consistently deny the existence of truth, this by itself does not help much towards clarifying what truth is and how we can find it. And it does not give us much help in dealing with those facts and ideas from the social sciences mentioned earlier—the facts and ideas which, when we first encounter them, seem to push us in the direction of relativism. In order to deal with these questions, the "long answer" to relativism is needed, and to it we will now turn.

## The Meaning of "Truth"

A good place to begin is with the concept of truth. Pilate cynically asked, "What is truth?" and a great deal of ink has been spilled trying to answer this question. Still, if we think clearly and are careful to avoid irrelevant side issues, the answer is not too hard to come by.

A first step in answering the question is to stop talking about "truth" as if it were a thing, an object of some kind, and focus instead on the adjective "true," as it is used in statements like, "What you just said is true." (I know that in the previous sections I have been talking pretty freely about "truth" as if it were a thing. I hope this hasn't been confusing, but in this section we need to be more careful.)[2] Now the needed explanation of "true" is really very simple:

> (A) The statement that "Grass is green" is true if and only if grass is green.
> (B) The statement that "Yosemite Falls is higher than Niagara Falls" is true if and only if Yosemite Falls is higher than Niagara Falls.

These examples show a pattern which can be applied to any statement whatever which can be said to be "true" or "false." And strange as it may seem, in the light of the seemingly endless discussions about "truth," this is really all that needs to be said on the subject.

But while this explanation of truth is apparently simple, it has consequences which are extremely important for our present topic, including the following:

1. *Whether a statement is true or false in no way depends on whether or not people believe it.* There are many true statements which nobody has believed until quite recently. For example, statements describing the pattern of craters on the back side of the moon. And there are true statements which, until recent times, almost everyone believed to be false; for example, the statement that there are heavenly bodies which are many times larger than the sun.

2. *Whether a statement is true or false in no way depends on the evidence we have for its truth or falsity.* Of course, evidence has a bearing on what *we believe* to be true or false, and also on what we *know*, since in general knowing something requires that we have evidence in support of our claim to know. But evidence does not *make* a statement true; and there are statements which people have believed on the basis of excellent evidence which nevertheless turned out to be false. For instance, the statement that the earth is flat and motionless is strongly supported by everyday observation, and people in ancient times who believed this were entirely reasonable—yet the statement is false.

When we apply these points to the problem of relativism, an interesting conclusion emerges—the conclusion, namely, that the "evidence" presented by the relativist is irrelevant to the position he is advocating! His evidence consists of pointing out different *beliefs* held by different persons, and suggesting that no one has good *evidence* on which to base a decision as to which belief is correct. But even if he is right about this, this has *no bearing* on the question whether there *is* a truth about the matters in question. In other words, it provides *no support* for his claim that "all truth is relative."

### How Can We Know What Is True?

Perhaps you still are not satisfied. It is all very well, you may say, that there are all these true statements—but what good are they to us if we cannot recognize them? A truth which I can never know is, for all practical purposes, the same as no truth at all.

Your point is well taken. And it is just here that the "long answer" to relativism, in order to be complete, would have to become very long indeed. For the question, "How can we know?" is one that cannot be answered briefly. It is, in fact, the main question of an entire branch of philosophy known as epistemology, the theory of knowledge. Fortunately, it is possible to say some things briefly that may be helpful.

It is a fact of great importance that there are some of our beliefs which do not seem to be subject to the kinds of intercultural conflicts emphasized by the relativist. Take for example the simpler truths of arithmetic—say, "1 + 2 = 3." There is no known culture in which this statement is taken to be false, nor (I think) is there anyone who is seriously in doubt about it.[3] A great deal could be said on the question of *how* we know this, but that we *do* know it is hardly open to question.

Consider, again, our beliefs about the things we perceive with our senses—for instance, my belief that I am now composing this article on a typewriter. Do you really question whether I know that I am doing this? If you have studied philosophy, you probably know that philosophers have suggested ways in which I might, after all, be mistaken. Perhaps I am just dreaming that I am doing this, or hallucinating, and so on. Still, under normal circumstances we do not take such possibilities seriously; rather we confidently assume that we can perceive and correctly identify the familiar objects in our environment.

As we move beyond the things that we see, hear, and touch, disagreement becomes more common, but even so there are many things that cannot reasonably be doubted. Consider, for instance, some of the well-established facts of history. You may personally remember

Presidents Johnson, Nixon, and Ford—is there any doubt at all that these men really were our presidents prior to Carter? Perhaps no one now living remembers President Lincoln, but there is no doubt about his having been president, or that a civil war was fought during his time in office, or that he proclaimed freedom for the slaves. And many other facts about the past are beyond all reasonable doubt. Of course, much about the past *is* doubtful or even entirely unknowable; my only point is that there is also truth about the past which *can* be known by us.

Consider, again, the results of science. The scientist seeks to understand and explain the process of nature, or of society, or of individual behavior. In his explanations he often refers to things which we cannot perceive with our senses—be they atoms, quarks, or Oedipus complexes—and sometimes to things which cannot be observed in any way. Yet there is a fairly well-understood procedure by which hypotheses are invented, elaborated, tested against experiment, revised, and re-tested. Science as a whole is never complete and it is rare even to have a complete explanation of a particular phenomenon. But there is no reason to doubt that the sciences give us the best explanations of the workings of nature that is presently available—incomparably better than anything produced by competing "methods" such as magic or mythology. Indeed, we must assume that the cultural relativist is himself committed to the scientific method as a means to arriving at truth about human cultures—otherwise, the data "from the social sciences" he relies upon is not put forward as being true and need not be taken seriously!

### Christianity and Relativism

Having said all this, the most difficult aspect of the problem lies still before us. For those who stress cultural differences do not normally mean to say that simple arithmetic and everyday sense-perception vary greatly from culture to culture. Nor is the focus on differences in scientific beliefs, even though what we call "modern science" clearly originates within one specific culture. The most striking differences, and those most emphasized by the relativist, concern what are called "world-views." Included among these are not only the different religions and philosophies, but also quasi-religious political systems such as Naziism and Communism. Here, indeed, the differences are real and intractable, and they promise to remain so for the foreseeable future. Differences of world-view carry with them differences over morality, and while these differences have sometimes been exaggerated they are real and extremely difficult to overcome. Here, if anywhere, the claim that "every man has his own version of the truth" (that is, of what *he thinks* is the truth!) seems plausible; and the assertion that there is some one, definite truth which can be known as such seems incredibly pretentious.

Now, I am not going to try to prove to you that the Christian world-view is the true one, even though I firmly believe that it is.[4] Rather, I want to point out to you certain implications concerning relativism which follow if the Christian faith is accepted. Quite simply, a Christian is a person who believes that Christianity is *true*. That is to say, he regards the major Christian beliefs—concerning God, the creation, the sinfulness of man, the God-manhood of Christ, and salvation in him—as genuine affirmations concerning the ultimate nature of things. These are affirmations on which he is willing to stake his life here and hereafter. To be sure, faith in Christ is *more* than merely believing that these affirmations are true. But it does *include* believing these things, and one who does not believe them has no right to call himself a Christian. At this point, Christianity and relativism are simply incompatible.

But perhaps you think I am being too dogmatic. Perhaps you would like to say, "I know that Christianity is true *for me*, but I don't judge anyone else." The trouble with this is that the assertion that Christianity is true "for me" is ambiguous. Perhaps in adding "for me" you wish to emphasize that this is your *own* faith, something which you personally believe and have committed yourself to. If so, well and good. But if you *do* believe the Christian affirmations, then in believing them you believe them to be *true*—not "true" *for* you, or me, or anyone else in particular, but just *true*. Or, if we want to speak of them as being true "for" somebody, then surely we must say that they are true for everyone—for the new convert to Christianity *and* for the resolute atheist, for the child reared in the faith since infancy *and* for the member of an alien culture who has never heard of Christ.

Unfortunately, the claim that Christianity is true "for me" can have a different meaning. The one who says this *may* mean: "I choose to worship and conduct my life according to the teachings of Christianity, but I will leave others to carry on according to their own faith, whatever it is, and no doubt it will come to much the same thing in the end." Thus we represent faith in Christ as something optional, something which may have quite a lot of significance *for me, if* I decide to accept it, but which can equally well be left to one side if something else interests me more. If we really feel this way, then it is questionable whether we do believe in Christ at all. It may be, rather, that we find the Church a convenient focus for certain values, values which we wish to preserve in our lives whether or not Christianity is "really" true— and whether it is or not doesn't much matter. This sort of tolerant, relativistic "culture-Christianity" is all around us, but it has little in common with the faith of the early Christians. A Christ believed on in this relativistic fashion is a Christ whose significance depends on my attitude towards him, but the Christ of the New Testament is Lord of earth and heaven.

### Should We Judge Others?

We still need to come to terms with the widely held notion that a relativistic viewpoint is superior because it promotes tolerance, understanding, and a nonjudgmental attitude towards others. Indeed, relativistic ideas are often deliberately promoted for just these reasons. The belief in single, absolute truth, on the other hand, is thought of as fostering dogmatism and intolerance. We must ask ourselves how much truth there is in this charge. It must be acknowledged, with regret, that the belief in an ultimate truth has sometimes led to these unfortunate consequences. But as a matter of reason and morality, *ought* it to lead to them? In particular, should acceptance of Christ as the ultimate revelation of truth lead us to become dogmatic and intolerant? I think we can see that it should not.

First of all, the fact that there *is* an absolute, objective truth in no way implies that we have grasped that truth at all completely. The true scientist will always echo the attitude of Newton, to whom it seemed that the truth he had discovered was insignificant in comparison to that which remained unknown, as a bucket of water to the great ocean. In theological matters, the Christian claim that Christ is the complete and the final revelation in no way implies that our understanding of that revelation is either complete or final. Nor is it necessary, or wise, to regard our own ethical insights as final. Elizabeth Eliot, after living among the Auca Indians who had killed her husband, came to feel that the morality they practiced among themselves was not inferior to that of her Christian friends and neighbors in America. This is not a judgment based on ethical relativism, but one based on a Christian sensitivity to the ethical values and integrity of an alien culture.

Another way of countering temptations to pride based on cultural heritage is to ask yourself, "Just how much of what I am proud is due to *my own* efforts?" If I had by my own wisdom created the modern scientific understanding of the world, then I might on the basis of this feel superior to the primitive animist who lives without such knowledge. As things are, however, we are about equal in that each of us has learned and accepted what was passed down to him.

This sort of reflection seems especially to the point if we are tempted to compare ourselves with others in the moral dimension. The philosopher Kant points out that as moral beings we all begin on a basis of equality, for a person's moral worth is not measured by the favorable or unfavorable conditions which he faces (including his cultural environment), or by the good or bad disposition with which he is endowed. Rather it is based on his own struggle to do the right, regardless of conditions and the cost to his own inclinations. From a different perspective, the Christian faith destroys our moral pretensions with the observation that "all have sinned and fall short of the glory of God" (Romans 3:23); we are all alike in need of the grace of salvation in Christ. What do we have that we have not received from him (1 Corinthians 4:7)?

I think it would be very difficult to show that belief in an objective, knowable truth has by itself been the cause of judgmental and intolerant attitudes. Such attitudes are rather the product of ignorance (of the achievements and values of another culture), of pride (which both exaggerates our own accomplishments and takes more credit for them than we deserve), and of the desire for domination (which leads us to denigrate others in order to justify taking advantage of them). But ignorance is excusable only if there has not been opportunity to correct it, and pride and desire for domination are directly condemned by Christ. His gentleness and humility are a better cure for arrogance than is the easy tolerance of relativism.

## Conclusion

It is time to summarize. We have seen something of the plausibility of relativism, especially when it is supported by data from the social sciences showing the cultural relativity of beliefs, and the impossibility of reaching an independent point of judgment outside of all cultural influences.

Nevertheless, the relativist is wrong in supposing that what is true depends on what people believe or on the evidence that they have for it: truth itself, as opposed to *our knowledge* of it, is entirely independent of these things. And while the question, "How can we know what is true?" raises important problems, there are many areas in which the truth can readily be determined by a reasonable person.

It is more difficult to prove conclusively that one's own faith, or worldview, is true. But it is the Christian's conviction that the truth about these ultimate matters can be known, since it has been revealed to us in Jesus Christ. Our possession of the truth should not lead us to arrogance. Instead, it should make us humble, grateful to God, and eager to share the truth with others without judging or condemning them. And one final thought: do not forget to ask the relativist, "Do you mean to say that there *really is* no such thing as truth?"

## Discussion Questions

1. Describe briefly an incident in which either you or someone you know made some statement expressing a relativistic viewpoint. Do you feel that this viewpoint was the correct one to take under the circumstances? Why, or why not?

2. Do you feel that relativism is a common viewpoint in our society? Is relativism usually an explicitly formulated belief, or is it more often an implicitly held attitude?

3. What are some of the main reasons which lead people to take a relativistic viewpoint?

4. What is the point of the question (addressed to the relativist): "Do you mean to say that there *really is* no such thing as truth?"

5. Explain why what is true does not depend on what anyone's beliefs are or on the evidence that anyone may have.

6. List a number of statements which (in your opinion) you know to be true—statements of which you think there could be no reasonable doubt. Why do you feel so certain about these statements?

7. Do you view science primarily as a means for manipulating and controlling the world around us, or do you view it primarily as a means of gaining truth and understanding?

8. According to the essay, why can't a Christian be a relativist? Do you agree with this?

9. Is there a sense in which a person *can* be both a relativist and a Christian? If so, what is it?

10. Is it possible to think that one's own world-view is true and that others which differ from it are false, without being judgmental and intolerant?

# Notes

1. A balanced perspective on this is offered by Clyde Kluckhohn, "Ethical Relativity: Sic et Non," in his *Culture and Behavior* (New York: Free Press, 1962). See also Morris Ginsberg, "On the Diversity of Morals" in his *Essays in Sociology and Social Philosophy* (Baltimore: Penguin, 1968), and Richard B. Brandt, "Ethical Relativism," in Vol. 3 of *The Encyclopedia of Philosophy*.

2. Not that the use of "truth" as a noun is inherently objectionable. In many contexts a "truth" is simply a true statement, as in "This truth was discovered only recently." The use of "truth" to name a property is also readily explained: "I wondered about the truth of what he said" means the same as "I wondered whether what he said was true." But for this to be helpful, the adjective "true" must first be clarified.

3. We should not, of course, suppose that the use of different *notations* makes any difference to the mathematical truths which are expressed. Someone who writes, in binary notation, the sentence "10 x 10 = 100" makes *exactly the same statement* as one who writes in our ordinary decimal notation "2 + 2 = 4"—and similarly for Roman numerals and other systems of mathematical notation.

4. The attempt to prove or to persuade others by rational means that Christianity is true is known as *apologetics*. An excellent recent work in this field is *Reason to Believe*, by Richard H. Purtill (Grand Rapids: Eerdmans, 1974). Older but still very much worth reading is C. S. Lewis, *Miracles* (New York: Macmillan, 1947.)

# 17
# Role Theory in Christian Perspective

*Gary Eugene Farley*

The theory of social roles and its related concepts is an important tool used by sociologists in their efforts to understand what happens when people interact with one another. In the first part of this paper I will present the basic elements of this theory. In the second part of the article I will demonstrate the usefulness of this theory by using it to analyze typical "routines" and "rituals" employed by Protestant Middle America in response to death. In the final part I will suggest some issues raised for the Christian by role theory, and indicate how the reader might use role theory for self-analysis.

## Role Theory

*Definition*

One of the most outstanding students of role theory has been Erving Goffman. In this paper I will rely heavily upon his analysis. His fullest discussion of role appears in *Encounters*. There he writes:

> Role consists of the activity the incumbent would engage in were he to act solely in terms of the normative demands upon someone in his position. Role in this normative sense is to be distinguished from role performance or role enactment, which is the actual conduct of a particular individual while on duty in his position.[1]

Interestingly, this definition of role includes elements of two types of definitions and ways of looking at roles current in contemporary so-

**Gary Eugene Farley**
*Professor of Sociology*
*Oklahoma Baptist University*

Gary E. Farley taught at Carson-Newman College for several years before assuming his present position at Oklahoma Baptist University. He received his MA in sociology from the University of Tennessee, and his PhD in social ethics from Southwestern Baptist Theological Seminary. He has also received the MDiv from Midwestern Baptist Theological Seminary. Professor Farley's special interests are ethics, role theory, and authority.

ciology.[2] Some sociologists, particularly those who adopt a structural-functionalist model, focus upon the normative structure of particular roles. Usually these are work and familial roles such as minister, soldier, salesperson, or wife, husband, child—roles are often seen as *positions* within a given social organization or system.

The term *role expectations* is used to indicate that roles come with built-in rights and duties. That is, when a person assumes the role of minister, he either has been or will be socialized into this role. He learns what is expected of him; what norms are used to judge the quality of his performance; what he might rightfully demand from those with whom he interacts; and what sanctions are available to encourage compliance with the role expectations attached to his role. Goffman says:

> In entering the position, the incumbent finds that he must take on the whole array of actions encompassed by the corresponding role, so role implies a social determinism and a doctrine about socialization. ... The function of a role is the part it plays in the maintenance or destruction of the system or pattern as a whole, the terms eufunction and dysfunction sometimes being employed to distinguish the supportive from the destructive effects.[3]

Returning to Goffman's definition of the role, one focuses on performance, and reflects the concern of the second definition and analysis of social role. This approach focuses on the actor's performance of a role, including the internalization of feedback. Here the concern shifts from a position with norms, to a performance in relation to norms.

From the perspective of performance the student may focus on such matters as the style of the actor (expediter, combatant, trickster, rogue, or conciliator), or he may focus on his goals, his commitment to the role, or simply the mechanics of face-to-face encounters. For example, a study from this perspective might focus on the techniques and strategies of incumbents within the ministerial role, variations of performance as one moves between audiences, and the degree to which the self-identity of ministers and their colleagues is tied to the role.

In our reading of sociological material we will find the term role used in both ways, i.e., referring either to position or to performance. The important thing for us to see at this point is that each of us occupies many social roles and that these roles have normative and moral dimensions. Consequently, how we see ourselves and how we conduct our lives is profoundly influenced by our roles. It would be hard to overestimate the impact of social roles upon the way each of us lives.

How do we acquire these roles? Like status, some roles are ascribed, such as sex, race, and class. Others, such as occupation, marriage and/or family, and a vocation, are achieved.

How do we learn to do our roles? We learn to play our roles through socialization—formal and informal. Family, school, church, work, and friends all teach us how to do our roles.

*Situational Properties*

Although roles may be looked at analytically as abstracted from interaction, in reality, roles are "done" or performed through interaction. Interaction does not occur within a vacuum; situational properties always shape the form interaction takes.

Living in a small college town, as I do, there are two places where large numbers of people—often pretty much the same crowd—gather. One is the college field house and the other is the First Baptist Church. By comparing and contrasting the activities in these places, I can demonstrate the function of "situational properties" in the role theory.

*First*, place and occasion tend to define what roles are appropriate and how they are to be played. In a sense it is a stage. Although the Saturday night and the Sunday morning crowds are comprised of many of the same individuals, they conduct themselves quite differently. *Second*, each place will have a number of roles available—roles which are interrelated. In fact it is hard to conceive of a role without an alter or other role. (Perhaps this is why the Apostle John spoke of the eternal Son of God who had fellowship with God the Father.) *Third*, within a large gathering there will be sub-gatherings of couples, friends, and groups with their distinct roles to be played within the larger event. *Fourth*, each place will have places where one can escape from the major function of the gathering—dressing rooms, lobbies, and rest rooms. Here he may experience some "distance" from the role(s) he was playing in the larger occasion.[4] Goffman refers to these as front and back regions. And *fifth*, the actors within these places will have goals for the occasion and perhaps for themselves, and will use their skills to achieve these goals. The formation of one's goals and the means employed to achieve them are subject to being monitored by those with whom one interacts, so in most cases the actor is very sensitive to normative expectations. They observe one's manner of speaking or facial expressions and physical appearance. So much so, that even when he violates a behavioral norm he must be ready to give an accounting.[5]

Not all encounters are so structured. For example, initial and unintended dyadic ones are unstructured. Here it may be to the advantage of an actor to control the interactional sequence by determining the "definition of the situation" in play. In the subsequent discussion of "responses to death" that follows, we will see how sympathetic "others" will accept the definition offered by the bereaved and act accordingly.

In summary, role theory suggests that most human conduct is customary or moral behavior. We conduct our lives in terms of the roles we hold. We are aware of what our fellow actors and audiences expect of us. As we move from situation to situation, we assume the role that seems appropriate for us, and normally we play it to gain the recognition and approval of others—the applause of the crowd. To say this is not to pass moral judgment or to question the sincerity of the participants. It varies. Rather, role theory provides a perspective from which the social organization of human conduct may be perceived and examined.[6]

### Death: Routines and Rituals

While a divinity student, the author worked occasionally as a "professional pallbearer" and "house minister" for a Kansas City mortuary. And I have officiated at almost 50 funerals in the role of pastor. What follows is an attempt to interpret my close observations of bereavement from the role theory perspective. I will, of course, limit my analysis to the nonliturgical, middle-class Protestant bereavement which I have observed. The reader may note some distinctive features associated with death in relation to his own communion.

*Defining the Situation*

Death is seldom received with joy, at least openly, by the family, kin, friends, and acquaintances of the deceased. American culture defines death as tragedy—something bad—that should be avoided as long as possible. As a tragic event bearing sorrow it calls for some adjustment. This adjustment is necessitated because our society believes that happiness is both the ideal, as well as the normal state of mankind.

As in many primitive cultures, Americans have a sense of awe and dread of death which is clearly seen in the well-defined set of norms and roles associated with it. When a member of the family or an acquaintance dies, he knows the role he must play. He also knows how he is expected to respond, although there is some variation as to the age and the nature of the death of the deceased. Death, therefore, sets in motion a series of rituals and routines.

Elements of the performance normally include: (1) demonstration of grief, (2) efforts to comfort the bereft, (3) expressions of thoughtfulness (4) kind words about the deceased and (5) frequently "potlatch"-like demonstrations of affluence and "love" by the family for the deceased through the medium of an expensive funeral. (Interestingly, if the minister is paid at all, it is usually less than 1 percent of this total cost.)

## Roles

When one throws a rock into a placid pool, ringlike ripples emerge from the point where the stone hits the surface and moves in ever-widening circles toward the shore. In a somewhat analogous way there are circles of intensity of bereavement.

1. *The bereft.* Normally the inner circle is composed of the immediate family, e.g., husband, wife, mother, father, and children. In the next circle are somewhat more distant kin, e.g., aunts, uncles, cousins, and grandchildren, and perhaps particularly close friends. A third circle might include more distant relatives and in-laws and other friends and associates. There is a continuum of intensity of expression of the elements of performance listed above. For example, the grief of a widow will likely be more intense than that of a third-cousin-twice-removed. (Note: it is "bad show" for someone, e.g., a secretary to the deceased boss, to demonstrate a greater intensity of involvement than the situation calls for.)

2. *Neighbors and acquaintances.* These are persons who were not close enough to the deceased to be included in the rings of bereavement but who, because of custom and/or feelings of sympathy, become at least a part of the audience. (Others may function alternately as part of the audience and minor performers.)

3. *The professionals.* Any number of professionals, who earn all or part of their livelihood from serving the bereft, will be involved with a family. One of the most important of these is the funeral director. Most families have only infrequent experiences with death, so a professional is called in to aid in preparing for "the performance." Like a stage director he provides and places the artifacts, gives stage directions to the

performers, and often even provides much of the script.

Since many deaths occur at the hospital with a portion of the potentially bereaved present, the doctors and nurses play an important role at the time of the initial encounter with death. Frequently they provide bits of information such as when death occurred, nature of the illness or injury, degree of suffering, and last words. These are repeated many times during the course of the bereavement. (One may notice that a widow repeats these bits of information to each new person who comes to comfort her, quoting the medical personnel as supporting references.) Also medical professionals may be the first ones to enunciate the clichés which cue everyone to assume roles: "It is better this way." "Go ahead and cry; it may help you." "What would he want you to do?" "It must have been God's will."

Frequently the minister plays a key role in the bereavement cycle. He is expected to provide the inner circle of the bereft with consolation based upon the Christian hope of eternal life. Many want the minister to pray with and for them, and some request prayers for the deceased as well. At the funeral the minister is on "center stage."

Other professionals include musicians, funeral home attendants, florists, caterers, and the news media.

4. *The curious.* Whenever someone with a degree of notoriety dies, many who did not personally know the deceased will attend the funeral. Morticians in some communities say that there is a small coterie or group of persons who attend almost all the funerals they direct.

*Social Norms*

When death comes, very powerful psychological forces are at work on the bereft—guilt, a feeling of lostness, and despair about the future. All of these are culturally conditioned. At least the form and expression they take are acquired in the socialization process. The way in which the various roles outlined above are played will depend in part on the personality of the actor, and in part on the situation. Primarily, however, how the actor behaves is determined by the audience before whom one is acting. If he perceives them as significant, he will "perform."

1. *Emotional involvement.* The inner circle of the bereaved are supposed to demonstrate their grief by or through emotional releases. Frequently the bereaved seize center stage and apparently lose self-control. However, it is amazing to see a short time later, the one who

could not be comforted, switch roles and become the comforter of someone else who "refuses to be comforted."

Two typical styles of play emerge: (a) the one in need of comfort; (b) the one offering comfort. The bereaved have a choice of these styles and, as indicated above, they may alternate between them. The one mourning may become the comforter of another mourner.

2. A number of *situational factors* affect one's performance. (a) *Age of the deceased.* As a general rule, the younger the deceased the more intense is the grief. Our norms dictate that we grieve more over the death of a 19-year-old girl than for a 91-year-old woman. (b) *The role of the deceased.* Mothers with small children, fathers, and community leaders held in high esteem are mourned more intensely than bums, criminals, and others perceived as nonproductive members of society. (c) *Cause of death.* (1) Accidents may be divided into two categories: Acts of God and carelessness. Grief is more intense for the former. Death by an accident is more grieved than by an illness because one is less prepared. (2) Illnesses may be divided into two categories: short and long term. Since we shun pain in our society, death from a brief illness is much preferred. (d) *Relationship.* We have already suggested that there is a continuum of grief from the close relative and friend to the more distant ones. (c) *The religious factor.* For committed Christians grief may be less intense if the deceased was a practicing Christian, because of his hope of eternal life.

3. *Pressures for involvement.* It is the height of inconsiderateness for someone who is connected with the deceased or his family not to become involved in the mourning process, either as one of the bereaved or as a comforter. Failure to participate makes one subject to sanctions, unless one can justify his absence. The usual excuse offered to the bereaved is, "I did not hear of it until after the funeral."

4. *Quality of the performance.* (a) Stage settings. Some people, the newly rich or those with guilt problems for instance, feel obliged or pressured to provide elaborate funerals. Others say, "We want to make it simple." This may reflect poverty, lack of feeling, an effort not to succumb to pressure, or common sense and good Christian stewardship.

(b) Manner. We have already mentioned the continuum between the comforter and the one to be comforted. And we have mentioned the concept of the degree of grief being commensurate with the relationship between the mourner and the deceased. In mourning and comforting "given off" expressions are particularly important. Tears, a kiss for the widow, an anguished countenance— these are but a few commonly used idioms of the body. Verbally, certain phrases appear to be standard:

"I lost my . . ." is used by the consoler to establish a relationship between himself and the mourner.

"My, doesn't he look natural . . ." is meant to help console the bereft.

"Did he suffer much . . . ?" is a good opener, for it allows the bereft an opportunity for repeating her story and reaffirming his death. Also the response is a certain "winner" for the questioner. If he suffered, then she may remark that his death was in a way a blessing that he did not suffer as so many do. Perhaps an anecdote or two is added.

"How is she taking it . . . ?" and if the answer is 'Well," then this can be complimented as being courageous. And if the reply is "Not so well," then the comforter feels a particular challenge.

There is always an interest in last words. Widows particularly make a great deal of them. Of course, it would be "bad show" for the bereft to "take it" too well.

(c) Appearance. Mourners and comforters are expected to demonstrate their reverence for the dead by attending the events of the ritual of death in their best attire. They are to project an image of reverence, solemnity, and respect. Perhaps at no other time do the social norms call so strongly for one to be other-directed. For example, one notes how responsive widows are in the weeks following the funeral to those who share a common grief.

In summary, we are to grieve and to be comforted and to comfort. In doing this, we should perform in certain prescribed ways and use certain acceptable lines.

### Procedural Response

A number of stages are involved in what we might call the mourning cycle. Normally six stages can be noted.

1. *Closest kin informed of the death.* Death occurs for a variety of reasons, and it is necessary that the cause and certainty be established. Normally, the coroner or a medical official verifies that a person is dead. The "next of kin" is then notified and the mourning cycle is initiated.

2. *Notification and arrangements.* Often there is a kind of "pecking order" in the notification of kin. Those in the inner circle are no-

tified first, preferably face-to-face, but at least by phone. Next the second circle is notified by phone or by wire. Frequently there is a division of the labor with the second circle, who assist by notifying those in the third circle, lesser friends, and acquaintances.

Normally one member of the inner circle, perhaps the eldest son, is invested with the responsibility of making the arrangements for the funeral. Perhaps in consultation with other family members, he makes contacts with the professionals and arranges for the formal events of the ritual. Arranging for the funeral service carries with it awesome responsibility. In addition it requires diplomacy for often there is a "falling out" among family members over the arrangements. He also provides a model of stability and rationality for those within the circle.

3. *Response of home visits.* Soon the kin begin to arrive. Arranging accommodations for those coming from some distance must be made. The neighbors begin to bring in food, the rationale for doing so is that the bereaved are too distraught to prepare food and, in addition, there are usually added guests to provide for. Frequently the one bringing the food also comes in to console the bereft. As such he is particularly concerned with what Goffman calls impression management.[7] Usually almost everyone involved is uncomfortable in his role becuase he is unfamiliar with it. Perhaps there is no other occasion when so many are so unsure of their roles. At this time it is difficult to distinguish between actors and audience. The comforters particularly seem to vacillate between these positions.

One factor which makes things so uncomfortable for the mourner is that there is no "back stage" really available. He may get off stage, but he can't seem to escape his role. Any thought of role distance would be quickly dismissed as being immoral and unthinkable.

The conversations at these times are of particular interest. Some of the standard lines were mentioned above. Most of the participants, both the mourners and the comforters, are so "other-directed" at the time that they are quite guarded in what they talk about and choose words carefully. Some of the elements seem to be: (a) It is important to keep some kind of chatter going; (b) This should be rather light, nonconsequential, and not very much related to what is really uppermost in the minds of most; (c) Some effort may be made to draw the mourners out, getting them to talk about things which will enhance their own self-image, and deal with any feelings of guilt that they might have. (Both overt and covert expressions of guilt, particularly by the next of kin, are quite frequent. Perhaps one of the primary tasks of the comforters is to allay these guilt feelings.) (d) Reminiscenses about good deeds and good times with the deceased are frequent topics in these conversations. References to evil acts or bad character are inappropriate, at least for the time.

Later, the funeral service as a ritual event becomes a topic of discussion. Elements include: size of the crowd, the many people who came that were not expected, the words of the minister, and the beauty of the floral tributes. The professionals also make appearances. These are regarded as being particularly comforting. (Some morticians have been known to seize upon the opportunity to advertize by distributing favors like calendars and emory boards.)

4. *The reception of friends at the mortuary.* This is still a common practice. It is called "viewing the body," and is perhaps the most tasteless of all the elements of the ritual complex. On the evening prior to the funeral service, the family receives friends before the open casket. At this time people "get a last look" (form a memory picture) of the deceased. Often several hundred people are involved. The bereft are particularly vulnerable at this time. Much of the action is similar to that noted in the previous stage.

5. *The funeral.* This is a rather short service, usually lasting less than half an hour. Frequently it has two parts. The first is a formal memorial service in a church or a mortuary chapel. The second is a graveside service. Normally a minister is in charge. Elements in the first service may include music with a solo or small ensemble, reading of Scripture, reading of the obituary, some brief remarks of an appropriate nature, and prayer. If there is a second service, at the graveside, this is usually limited to Scripture and prayer.

In the funeral service the Goffman dramaturgical model is most evident. Three groups are involved. The professionals are Goffman's actors *par excellance*. An office or a lounge in the church or the chapel provides them with a back region. As professionals they are veterans at these things and frequently engage in byplay. Yet as professionals they can assume the role of mourner or comforter on command. The family functions both as audience and secondary actors. The others serve as the audience.

Frequently, the stage setting is a work of art. Beautiful flowers, organ music, songs, dim lighting, appropriate tints and hues, and reverent ritual—all provide the proper setting. Everyone knows his role well enough to play it rather successfully. Usually it is a good performance, and the audience is cooperative, overlooking miscues.

The graveside service usually involves only the true mourners. Following the service the crowd frequently does a little backstaging itself. Often there is a certain joviality in the byplay of those outside the inner circle. The crowd takes on the character of a reunion. Old friends see one another again. They are introduced to new people.

6. *At home.* After the service the inner circle returns to the family home. Often they are joined by the funeral director and the minister. Both are congratulated for "doing such a wonderful service." More than likely it was, because "they defined it as helpful." The conversation is taken up again in the same "uneasy" way. Everyone is still working hard at his role. After awhile they begin to make their way to their own homes. The family is then left alone with all the problems of making adjustment in role contents to take up the slack left by the death of a family member.

Just here it becomes difficult; and here we must end our analysis. The situation must now be redefined. One of the latent consequences of much of the earlier comforting is that it prepares the mourners to do this. The social gathering is at an end. Later reflection by the actors may help them to give a more creditable performance when called upon again.

*Summary*

This analysis has focused upon the events related to bereavement following the death of a family member. What seem to be the basic elements have been briefly outlined. Also, attention was directed specifically to those elements in the experience that fit role theory concepts. The main point we made was that the mourning ritual provides fruitful resources for applying the role theory concepts and perspective.

To summarize, mourning is a social gathering with rather well-defined bounds. Roles and role expectations are well defined and people have been socialized concerning them. Likewise, the various rules or situational properties are generally well understood. The cycle includes beautiful symbolism.

## Some Insights and Challenges for the Christian

Let me share some insights and responses to the questions which I have posed for you at the end of this chapter.

First, analyzing the roles we play has helped me to realize the customary or "moral" nature of our actions. No one really "does his own thing." Whenever you or I assume a role, we take on and must deal with the moral expectations which come with the role. Provided they do not run counter to the basic teachings of Christ, there is no reason why we should not play the role. (See questions 1-4.)

Second, "social order" demands that there be social roles with attendant moral expectations. Otherwise society would be plunged into chaos. Yet truth demands that expectations be subject to critical analysis. Otherwise, societies would be static and could not adjust to change. Here lies a basic dilemma both for sociology and for Christian theology. How can we have a society which is stable and orderly, yet is malleable and subject to change? In change, how can we keep from "throwing the baby out with the bath water?" Are there Christian "absolutes" or principles which can inform our analysis of social roles, practices, and systems? If so, how do Christians go about seeking to apply these?

Third, I see changes happening with regard to funeral practices in the wake of the recent surge of interest in the sociology of death. I have noted a coming together of the insights of sociology and psychology with theology. The end result has been the planning of funerals, services of worship and praise, donation of human organs for the good of others, and simpler funeral arrangements. In the light of Christian principles, what kind of changes would you like to see with regard to the rituals and practices associated with illness, death, and funerals? (See question 10.)

Fourth, I have found role theory an insightful tool for reflecting on the life, work, and death of Jesus as discussed in the New Testament. This is particularly clear in Matthew's Gospel where he gives an account of how Jesus very carefully fulfilled many of the biblical "role expectations" of the Messiah. However, the public of his day wanted a political savior, not a "suffering servant." Christ lost public support because his concept of the Messiah and his role was in conflict with the role expectations the Pharisees and others held. Hebrews can be read as a hymn of vindication of Jesus' understanding of what the role called for. None of us will be confronted by role conflicts of such monumental proportions, yet all of us will experience such conflicts. Are there any biblical principles available to help us choose between conflicting role expectations? Should we always seek to please the majority, our peer group, the person most important to us, or the crowd immediately present? Or are there some principles which are not subject to compromise? (See question 5.)

Fifth, this discussion points up the most subtle danger of role theory analysis from the Christian perspective. It builds upon a "weak view of the self." By this I mean that discussions of human activity from the role theory perspective tend to posit a self who is responder, a conformer. The image of man portrayed in no way resembles a person free to seek to do God's will as he/she understands it.

It is important for the Christian student of sociology not to take role theory as a total "doctrine of man." Its image of man is generalized and partial. It must be used as a helpful tool, but never be allowed to become dogma. (See questions 6-9.) This point underscores a serious problem confronting the Christian student. Sociology and psychology each has its "doctrine of man." Each tends to push it as dogma, yet each is partial. While both have merit, each must be further informed by the Christian/biblical image of man. Here is one of the great challenges for Christian scholars in the social and behavioral sciences.

### Discussion Questions

1. List all of the social roles you play, e.g., young person, male, Christian, college student, human services major, son, boyfriend, roommate, athletics team member.

2. What roles, held by others interface with each of these roles?

3. What do you see as the major role expectations attached to each of your roles?

4. What conflicts do you experience in trying to handle all of these roles, expectations, and audiences simultaneously?

5. How do you resolve these conflicts?

6. How does memory and the drive for consistency in actions make for the conception of a trans-situational self, rather than of a person who passively conforms to the expectations of whatever situation he is in?

7. Is there room for the freedom of the individual in role theory, or is the person's behavior socially determined?

8. Is there more to you than the roles you play, or is your self only an amalgamation of roles?

9. Is role playing necessary for social order, or is it inauthentic behavior as the existentialists contend?

10. How do you feel about the conduct roles called for in our society by the death of a loved one?

## Notes

1. Erving Goffman, *Encounters* (New York: The Bobbs-Merril Co., Inc., 1961) p. 85.

2. The distinction between two types of role definitions was suggested by W. Richard Scott, ed., *Social Processes and Social Structures*. (New York: Holt, Rinehart, and Winston, 1970), pp. 58-59. "Thus some sociologists use the concept of role to refer to the behavior of an incumbent of a social position, while others, sharing the perspective of Gross and the editor of this volume, define a role as the set of normative expectations applied to the position incumbent. The former definition of the concept focuses attention on how the position holder *does* behave." One is from the perspective of the actor; the other from that of the audience. It is the contention of this chapter that Goffman unites these two perspectives in his definition.

The "normative expectations" kind of definition of role is that which is found most frequently among those sociologists of the Structural-Functionalists persuasion. Talcott Parsons, "*The Social System* (New York: Free Press, 1950), pp. 69-112. A most definitive discussion from this perspective is found in Neal Gross, Ward S. Mason, and Alexander W. McEachern, *Explorations in Role Analysis* (New York: Wiley, Inc., 1958).

The discussion of symbolic interactionists tends to focus on the performance of the incumbent. Building on Mead they focus on how role-taking contributes to the emergence of the social self. See Tamotsu Shibuteni, *Society and Personality* (Englewood Cliffs, N.J.: Prentice-Hall, Inc., 1961) pp. 46-54, and Ralph H. Turner, *Family Interaction* (New York: John Wiley and Sons, 1970), pp. 185-214. In these writings the emphasis falls upon the impact of the role of the individual and interpersonal relations. In the other, the focus is upon the role as a part of a system.

Attention is given to both perspectives in the very important work: Bruce J. Biddle and Edwin J. Thomas, eds., *Role Theory: Concepts and Reseach*(New York: John Wiley and Sons, 1966). In the present study the term "role" will be used in a fashion consistent with Goffman's definition. Role may be used to indicate normative expectations or the performance. The specific intent will normally be apparent in the context. Dennis Brissett and Charles Edgley have gathered a fine collection of writings on this subject in *Life as Theater* (Chicago: Aldine Pub. Co., 1975).

3. *Encounters*, pp. 87-88.

4. Goffman discusses these concepts in great detail in his *Behavior in Public Places* (New York: The Free Press, 1962).

5. An interesting account of "accounting" appears in Goffman, *Relations in Public* (Harper: New York, 1971).

6. Goffman makes this clear in *The Presentation of Self in Everyday Life* (Garden City: Doubleday, 1959).

7. For a clear statement of impression management see *Ibid*.

# 18
# Changing Female/Male Roles in Christian Perspective

*Jack Balswick*

"So God created man in his own image, in the image of God he created him; male and female he created them" (Genesis 1:27). In the majority of societies during most periods of history *changing* sex roles would not qualify as a topic of great interest to sociologists; for it is usually assumed that males will grow up behaving like males, and females will grow up behaving like females. Likewise, most Christians throughout history have assumed that a proper interpretation of Genesis 1:27 means that any differences in *their* society between males and females existed because God created these differences.

It has only been since the emergence of the social and behavioral sciences that we have begun to question the "absolute role" which physiology plays in the formation of sexual temperament and behavior. Through cross-cultural research, social scientists now surmise that culture, rather than "nature," is the major influence in determining the temperamental differences between the sexes.

In Western industrial societies like the United States, where social and cultural changes have been rapid, traditional definitions of sex roles have especially been questioned. Recent changes in the United States and the Western world include an expansion of the number of roles females can play, in addition to the wife and mother role. The Woman's Liberation Movement has been instrumental in redefining

**Jack Balswick**
*Professor of Child and Family Development and Sociology*
*The University of Georgia*

Jack Balswick has published a number of books and articles in the areas of social change, family, and social theory. He is a member of the Evangelical Free Church. He received his PhD from the University of Iowa in 1967.

the female sex role. The movement has "liberated" women from suppressive conditions in our society so that they might have equal opportunity to pursue options previously defined as appropriate only for men. Changes in the women's role—new freedoms and rights—have also had an impact on the male sex role. These changes in the male sex role revolve around security in his own masculinity and position in society. Men have traditionally been defined as independent, task and achievement oriented, objective, competitive, rational, unsentimental, and unexpressive, while women have been defined as dependent, interpersonally oriented, sentimental, emotional, supportive, and expressive. As many of these stereotyped ways of behaving change, they affect changes in other aspects of society—from family life and the nature of religious organization to participation in the educational and economic institutions.

This change in the nature of the sex roles places Christians in a troubled position. For while we must affirm the distinctions between males and females intended by God, we must also be sensitive to the differences between the sexes which are unique or peculiar to a given culture. Even more importantly, we must be aware of culturally defined and produced differences between the sexes which God never intended to exist. There are a number of very important questions which could be addressed, including husband/wife authority in marriage, female participation in the church, and heterosexual and homosexual relationships. Our concern in this chapter, however, will be much broader. We will focus on the nature of female/male sex role differences in society in general. To do this it is necessary to understand something of the background for the changes that are taking place. Thus we will begin by considering physiological and cultural contributions to sexual differences, and the historical roots of the current changes in sex roles. Next we will take a look at the changes taking place in the female role, followed by a look at the changes in the male role. We will conclude by considering the meaning of Christian womanhood and manhood, and the strategy which can be used to bring about a society within which these can develop. (See Donald B. Kraybill's chapter, "Jesus and the Stigmatized" where Jesus' relationship to women is discussed.)

## Sexual Difference: Nature or Nurture?

It may be no accident that it was a woman, the late Margaret

Mead, who did the classic study demonstrating that temperamental differences between the sexes can be explained primarily in terms of culture, not physiological or biological innateness. In her book, *Sex and Temperament*, Mead (1935) reported on the differences in sex roles for three societies in New Guinea. Using ethnocentric Western standards to define sex roles, she found that the ideal sex role for both the male and female was essentially "feminine" among the Arapesh, "masculine" among the Mundugumor, and "feminine" for the male and "masculine" for the female among the Tchambuli. The Tchambuli's definition of sex roles is diametrically opposite to the traditional distinction made between these roles in the United States.

More recently, Hampson and Hampson (1961:1413) in their study of sex orientation and behavior concluded that "an individual's gender role and orientation as boy or girl, man or woman, does not have an innate preformed basis as some have maintained. Instead, the evidence supports the view that psychologic sex is undifferentiated at birth, a sexual neutrality . . . and that the individual becomes differentiated as masculine or feminine, psychologically, in the course of the many experiences of growing up." The environment versus heredity argument has swung far in the direction of the negation of heredity to an emphasis upon environmental factors in the determination of social behavior. However, lest one should too hastily attribute all observable social and psychological differences between the sexes to culture or environment, the contributions made by physiological differences between the sexes should be explored.

There are universal biological differences between the sexes which are important contributors to behavioral differences: (1) although born in greater number, males tend to be less resistant to disease; (2) females generally reach puberty at an earlier age; (3) males are generally taller, larger boned, and heavier, and their physique allows them to lift heavier weights, throw things harder and farther, and run for longer periods of time; (4) females are physically affected by the fact that they menstruate, conceive, carry, give birth to, and nurse children (Ford, 1970: 2728).

Most experts hesitate to argue that biological factors are responsible for more than mere physical differences between the sexes. One of the most qualified to speak to this point, Clellan Ford (1970:28), states that "secondary sex differences in aptitude and temperament are still in good measure a matter of speculation. These are aspects which seem more likely to be related to cultural conditioning, and it is preferable to assume at this point in our understanding that differences between men and women in these respects reflect primarily differential exposure and training." Most experts would not deny the *possibility* that biological factors explain many temperamental differences between the sexes, but would quickly point out that what is explained by biology may just as easily be explained by social conditioning. The strongest evidence that innate temperamental differences may exist between the sexes is the general similarity of males and females in most cultures.

Roy D'Andrade (1966:201-202) in reviewing the cross-cultural literature, summarized the temperamental differences between the sexes as follows: "Males are more sexually active, more dominant, more deferred to, more aggressive, less responsible, less nutrient, and less emotionally expressive than females. The extent of these differences varies by culture. And in some cultures some of these differences do not exist (and occasionally the trend is actually reversed). These differences are related to and presumably influenced by which sex controls economic capital, the extent and kind of division of labor by sex, the degree of political 'authoritarianism,' and family composition."

In regard to temperamental differences between the sexes, it may be safe to conclude that: (1) most societies expect males to differ from females temperamentally; (2) in most societies the male assumes a temperament which corresponds to the "masculine," and the female assumes a temperament corresponding to the "feminine" temperament as defined in Western societies; (3) these model temperamental differences between the sexes are most directly the result of *environmental conditioning* and *physical differences* between the sexes.

It becomes a dangerous trap for Christians to assume that the particular definition of masculinity and femininity learned in their culture is God's ideal. We fall into this trap by reading our cultural expectations into Scripture and also by accepting all biblical accounts of males and females as if they were normative, instead of descriptive. Biblical descriptions of how males and females behaved during biblical times should not necessarily dictate how we should behave. I know of very little evidence in Scripture calling for normative temperamental differences between the sexes. Where the Bible does speak of temperament, it addresses itself to both males and females. Thus in the Sermon on the Mount Jesus calls those blessed who are sorrowful, possess a gentle spirit, show mercy, whose hearts are pure, and who are peacemakers. In listing the fruits of the Spirit Paul makes no gender distinctions when speaking of love, joy, peace, patience, kindness, goodness, faithfulness, gentleness, and self-control. In the life of Jesus we find no "macho" image, no attempt to "prove" his masculinity through toughness, competitiveness, and inexpressiveness. If we really take a close look at the life of Jesus we find a man who had a wide range of emotions, a point which will be developed more fully later in this chapter.

### Historical Roots of Women's Liberation

The history of Western civilization has been one that has glorified woman and, at the same time, viewed her as inferior to man. The church, as the main sanctioning institution during most of the history of Western civilization, set the pattern for society's attitude toward women. The early church father, Tertullian, believed that woman was the gate of hell, the destroyer of God's image, man. Other church fathers took an equally harsh view towards women. St. Bernard described woman as a scorpion, ever ready to sting. St. Chrysostom stated that of all the wild beasts, the most dangerous is woman. The Council of Macon in the sixth century decided by only a one vote majority that women had souls (Vernon 1962:101). While it is true that some church fathers took a stand for equality, most sided with the views expressed. In considering the view taken toward women during the early years of American society, we should keep in mind the view held during earlier years in Europe.

The feminist movement has a long history, and it is only possible to trace its earliest roots to landmark events which precede feminist organizations. The first of these events was the 1792 publication of Mary Wollstonecraft's book, *A Vindication of the Rights of Women*, which came to be the "bible" of early feminists in the United States. The first organized feminist movement was a part of the great rise of reforms affecting American society during the 1830s and 1840s. These reforms concerned rights of Negroes and labor, as well as those of women. Women's rights *per se* has rarely been a single movement; instead it has been tied to numerous other causes. Andrew Sinclair, in his book, *The Emancipation of the American Woman* (1966), has traced the history of reforms in the United States, including the fight for women's suffrage. "The reform wave surged in certain areas of America in the 1830's and 1840's, receded before and during the Civil War, surged again in the hope of the reconstruction of society after the war, receded for twenty years while large industry dominated the government, and surged again in the two decades before the First World War (p. xii)."

It is important to remember that the position of woman in America during the early 1800s was that of a creature regarded as inferior intellectually, legally, socially, and politically. Educationally, while girls could hope for a few years of elementary school, college was out of the question. Legally, a wife could not sign any contract and had no right to her own earnings. Socially, she was "put on a pedestal to be looked down upon," or, as one writer puts it, "women were treated like a cross between an angel and an idiot." Politically, women, of course, could not vote. Sinclair may not be too severe when he states that "early American women were almost treated like Negro slaves, inside and outside the home. Both were expected to behave with deference and obedience towards owner or husband; both did not exist officially under the law; both worked for their masters without pay; both had to breed on command, and to nurse the results."

Although women were expected to assume the subservient role in the early history of our country, the issue over women's rights is nearly as old as our country. In fact, there rarely has been a time when it was not an issue of some sort. Feminists first began to organize in the early 1800s in an attempt to remedy the social problems of the day. In attempting to cope with all kinds of social problems, from poverty, poor housing, and disease, to prostitution, alcoholism, and crime, the social feminists were the forerunners of the social work movement. In addition, and more importantly for our purposes, they redefined and expanded the role of women in American society to include activity *outside* the home. The social feminists were the forerunners of the late nineteenth- and early twentieth-century feminists who were not only concerned about other people's social conditions, but their own. The major victory of the feminist movement came in 1920 when the "suffragist" movement was instrumental in gaining women the right to vote. After 1920, women continued to be discriminated against by law in hundreds of different ways (O'Neill 1969:92), but to the present day the feminist movement is only beginning to regain the prestige and momentum it had during the first decades of the 1900s.

### Women's Liberation Today

Although the roots of the contemporary women's liberation movement can be traced back to the earlier feminists of the 1800s, the present renewal of interest started with the publication in 1963 of Betty Friedan's book, *The Feminine Mystique.* Friedan agreed that the modern woman had been lulled into acceptance of the idea that the only respectable role for a woman was in the home, where she could be a good mother to her children and wife to her husband. She saw the popularization of Freudian psychology and some of Margaret Mead's anthropology, combined with advertising in the mass media, as being the subtle persuaders which encouraged women to maintain their feminine image. As she analyzed the influences which college girls were exposed to between 1945 and 1960, she found one overwhelming message. In order to be happy, normal, and well adjusted, the only role one should contemplate in life is that of wife and mother. Friedan was especially concerned over the intellectual stagnation of the growing number of college educated housewives. Friedan advocated that the educated housewife maintain her intellectual interest by reading professional journals and by venturing outside the home to interact with persons of similar academic interest.

Friedan suggested that any woman who wanted to pursue a career should seriously think of doing so, even though married with children. Not only the husband's, but the wife's career should be taken into account when contemplating a move. Women have much to contribute to society beyond being good homemakers and mothers, and, according to Friedan, society is weaker because women are discouraged from becoming actively involved.

In 1966 Betty Friedan was instrumental in organizing the National Organization of Women (NOW), which is the largest present-day feminist organization. By the standards of some of the more radical women's liberation groups, NOW is quite conservative in its goal—the end of economic and legal discrimination against women.

The more radical women liberationists do not believe that sexual equality can be achieved merely by reforming the present social structure. Instead, they see sexism as built into the very social fabric of American society. Many utilize a conflict or Marxist theoretical model in describing men as the exploiting bourgeoisie, and women as the exploited proletariat. The exploitation of women by men is seen as continuing to exist because of society's means of economic production, reproducing children, rearing children, and a lack of sexual freedom and equality (Firestone, 1970; Mitchell, 1966). The solution to the sexual exploitation of women is seen in establishing a socialist economy in which technical knowledge is utilized to free women from bearing and long hours of rearing children, and in which sexual freedom is secured through the discarding of outdated sexual norms.

It would be a mistake to classify most "women liberationists" in this radical camp, as many people unfortunately do. Most merely want to be treated equally, which they believe can be accomplished by enacting and enforcing laws which will not allow employers, state or private, to discriminate against women in economic hiring, pay, and advancement. The ERA (Equal Rights Amendment) merely stated that "the government shall not discriminate on the basis of sex." One of the curiosities is the extent to which the evangelical church has sided with the anti-ERA forces, supposedly for the sake of maintaining the "God ordained" practices in our society, and to prevent such practices as sexually integrated rest rooms, the drafting of women into the armed forces, and the payment of alimony by women. In actuality, the Bible presents no justification for discriminating against women in employment, and the things which anti-ERA groups predict will happen can take place under existing legislation. The government has the right to draft women, business establishments need not provide separate rest rooms for men and women, and some women are paying alimony to their husbands. The anti-ERA position taken by many Christians is reminiscent of the anti-civil rights position which many Christians took several years ago. It is a tragedy that the church must often learn social justice from secular groups in society, rather than be the initiator of social justice within society.

### Informal Discrimination

While most attention is currently being given to overt discrimination against women, there are more subtle informal types of discrimination which should concern Christians. Perhaps the greatest informal discrimination against women involves the prejudice against them in the norms governing the aging process. It can be argued that it is much more difficult psychologically and sociologically for a woman to grow old in our society than it is for a man. The man who is left widowed may marry down in age and society does not react unfavorably to it. In fact, it is expected that a widower of fifty or sixty will marry a woman in her forties or even her thirties. However, should the widow even think of marrying a man more than a very few years younger than she, the relationship is looked at with suspicion. This form of discrimination, coupled with the fact that women on the average live longer than men, greatly reduces her chances of remarrying following a divorce or the death of her husband. The statistics for remarriage, for those widowed between the ages of 45 and 64, are 70 percent for men and only 2 percent for women (Bell, 1970:77).

The advertising industry plays upon society's discrimination against old women and, in so doing, reinforces and perpetuates its unfair view. There was a very popular magazine advertisement for a famous brand of hat which quite boldly pictured a graying 60-year-old male movie star surrounded by several women in their early twenties. The girls admiringly look up to the man, who is old enough to be their father. It is almost beyond the imagination to picture an advertisement depicting an elderly woman surrounded by adoring young males.

It can also be argued that the advertising media reduce women to a sex object or less. One advertisement pictures a girl emerging from a newly opened crate and the caption reads, "The last word in 1970 office equipment!" A radio station in Boston was quite surprised recently when a young lady walked into the station and proceeded to dump a box of baby chicks on the startled manager's desk. It seems that the day before the station advertised a need for "some chicks to do typing and secretarial work." As the perturbed lady deposited the baby chickens she informed the station manager, "These are chicks, I am a woman."

It is almost too obvious to mention the various ways in which the advertising media reduce women to sexual objects. We have the Brylcreem girl slowly sliding out of the Brylcreem tube, the lightly clad mermaid lying on a floating island asking, "Men, are you ready for a new experience?" and above all, the Noxema Shaving Creme girl breathily exhorting the male shaver to "take it off, take it *all* off."

Hugh Hefner has attempted to create a whole philosophy in which women are reduced to a sex object to be used and discarded by men, like any other disposable commodity. It is ironic that whereas the *Playboy* philosophy purports to emphasize the beauty of women, in reality it substitutes a quite ugly view of women by reducing them to objects. All women, liberationists or not, would argue that it is impossible to conceive of a more perverted view than Hefner's, where women are reduced to a commercial item.

## The Male Sex Role

While most attention has been given to the changing female role in society, it is an error to overlook certain aspects of the male role which is also in the process of change. Masculinity has traditionally been expressed largely through physical courage, toughness, competitiveness, and aggressiveness; whereas femininity has, in contrast, been expressed largely through gentleness, expressiveness, and responsiveness. When a young boy begins to express his emotions through crying, his parents are quick to assert, "You're a big boy and big boys don't cry," or "Don't be such a sissy," or "Try to be a man about it." Parents often use the term "He's all boy" in reference to their son, and by this expression usually refer to behavior which is a demonstration of aggressiveness, getting into mischief, getting dirty, etc. But they never use the term to denote behavior which is an expression of affection, tenderness, or emotion. On the one hand, anger, boisterous humor, competitive or athletic enthusiasm, physical or verbal aggression, and similar emotions which are deemed "manly" are acceptable. On the other hand, however, "feminine" emotions—tenderness, compassion, sentimentality, gentleness, verbal affection, soft-heartedness, and the like—are clearly to be avoided. What society in general, and parents in particular, are really telling the male child is that a real man does not show his emotions, and if he is a real man, he will not express them. Hartley (1959:458) has suggested that families press these demands early in childhood and frequently enforce them harshly. Therefore, by the time male children reach kindergarten, many feel "virtual panic at being caught doing anything traditionally defined as feminine, and are hostile toward anything even hinting at 'femininity,' including females themselves."

As the male child moves out from under the family umbrella and into the sphere of male peer groups, the taboo against expressing feelings characteristic of females is reinforced and continued. According to studies of the male subculture in schools, street corner male groups, and delinquent gangs, to be affectionate, gentle, and compassionate toward others is not to be "one of the boys." The mass media seems to convey a similar message. From comics and cartoons through the more "adult" fare, the male image does not usually include affectionate, gentle, tender, or softhearted behavior, unless expressed by a very small male child (for adults to appreciate, not as a model for other young male children), or an old, gray-haired grandfather.

Family, peer group, and mass media, then, converge to call the tune to which the male must dance. Confronted with the image projected by this powerful triumvirate, most young males quickly learn that whatever masculine behavior *is*, it is *not* an expression of gentleness, tenderness, compassion, verbal affection, sentimentality, softheartedness or similar emotions. Avoidance of such emotions is one of the major badges of manliness. Hartley (1959) argues that masculine behavior is in most cases presented as something males should not do, rather than as something they should do.

The way in which masculinity has been defined within our culture has done much to determine the way in which males play their social roles in society. To be a successful businessman means to be tough, aggressive, and competitive. Thus, success is thought to be possible only by purging one's role of such emotional elements as tenderness, sympathy, and compassion. In the process, men learn to interact with others, both men and women, with a cool detachment. The traditional definition of masculinity may mean that in social relationships many men come close to what Erich Fromm has called the "consumer oriented personality"—one who treats other people as objects to be manipulated towards their own end. These are the aspects of the male role which are currently being challenged in our society—by women, as well as men.

### Christian Womanhood and Manhood

As Christians we must be attuned to the fact that there is currently a women's *and* men's liberation going on in our society. Rather than reacting against such changes we must be actively involved in the process of examining the legitimacy of such change in the light of Scripture. In examining the Bible I see no reason why Christians should not be involved in the process of liberating women from the suppressive societal conditions which have kept them from having equal opportunity with men to pursue options other than, or in addition to, those of wife and mother. Likewise, I see no reason why Christians should not be actively working to liberate males from traditional definitions of masculinity which have hindered them from developing healthy male-female, marriage and father-child relationships, or the development of men's liberation in general. For, in order for there to be a real women's liberation, there must also be liberated men who, being secure in their own masculinity and position in society, can support increased freedom for women.

Secure Christian manhood means that one is so mature that he need not confirm his masculinity at a woman's expense. Such a man will be secure enough not only to work with a woman as an equal, but also to work under a woman supervisor or superior. In addition, within the family, he will be willing to wash a dish or change a diaper at home. True Christian womanhood and manhood will not be a mere reflection of traditional cultural definitions of femininity and masculinity. I believe that there are cultural alternatives, that is, alternative ways in which cultures may define femininity and masculinity and still be consistent with the Bible. From God's point of view it is neither right nor wrong that certain work and activities are done by women in one culture, and by men in another. The real question we should ask, however, is this: at what points are our cultural norms preventing both females and males from becoming fully human as God intended? Although we cannot answer the question in this chapter, it may be helpful to at least begin by considering the personhood of Jesus as he lived his life here on earth.

What was Jesus really like as a person? If we take a look at the total life of Jesus we see a man who experienced a wide range of emotions. The most dominant emotional characteristic we see in Jesus was his compassion or love. The gospels report numerous occasions when Jesus showed both internal feelings (he loved and pitied) and external action (he helped the needy). The compassion and love of Jesus is seen in his relationship to other individuals such as the blind man, lepers, the bereaved widow, the woman at the well, and the mourners of dead Lazarus. His compassion and love for the multitudes are also seen in his acts of feeding the hungry, healing the sick, and in his concern for the lost, whom he described as "sheep without a shepherd."

The compassion and love of Jesus were expressed also in emotions of sorrow and joy. He wept over Jerusalem because of the unbelief of its people. When he saw Mary and Martha, as well as the friends of Lazarus weeping at his death, he, too, wept. In healing the deaf and dumb man, Jesus looked up to heaven with a deep sigh. When the Pharisees sought to test him by asking for a sign from heaven he sighed deeply.

At other times the love of Jesus moved him to express great joy. When the seventy whom he had sent out to witness for him returned rejoicing, we are told that Jesus "rejoiced in the Holy Spirit" (Luke 10:21). He also speaks of joy in heaven when just one sinner repents. Jesus tells his disciples that if they abide in his love then his joy will also be in them (John 15:10-11). The love of Jesus for his disciples can also be seen in his statements to them just prior to his death: "For the moment you are sad at heart; but I shall see you again, and then you will be joyful, and no one shall rob you of your joy" (John 16:22, NEB). In praying to his heavenly Father, Jesus shows his compassion for mankind by saying that he has spoken his truth so that men might be filled with joy (John 17:13).

Although Jesus was meek, mild, and tender, he was also capable of anger and indignation. In a world under the curse of sin, Jesus responded with anger and righteous indignation to man's inhumanity to man, to man's hardness of heart and unbelief, and to man's hypocrisy. The same Jesus who said, "Suffer the little children to come unto me," went into the temple and drove out those who bought and sold animals and upset the tables of the money changers. Jesus' anger at the hypocrisy of the Pharisees can be seen when he called them "whitewashed tombs . . . full of dead men's bones and all kinds of filth," "snakes," and a "viper's brood." His language was equally severe when he called Herod a "fox," those unreceptive of his message "swine," and false prophets "savage wolves."

In his humanity, Jesus possessed a wide range of emotions and was harmoniously complete in his own individuality. He also had the full range of human needs and appetites as he hungered, thirsted, was weary, knew physical pain and pleasure, slept, grew in knowledge, wept, suffered, and died. All that is human manifested itself in perfect proportion and balance in Jesus Christ. Jesus was emotionally mature and able to freely express and show his emotions to himself and to others.

The picture of Jesus that emerges is not one of a man who was masculine or feminine as traditionally defined by our cultural standards, but one who embodied the best of the characteristics that we divide and assign to the two sexes. I would suggest that a fully developed Christian womanhood and manhood are far more similar to one another than our current cultural definitions.

## A Strategy for Change

Scientific social research indicates that it is much easier to effect attitudinal change by changing behavior, than vice versa. Many Christians may be surprised to find that this "discovery" by modern social science is completely consistent with the wisdom of Jesus. In Matthew 6:21 Jesus states, "For where your treasure is, there will your heart be also." Notice that Jesus did *not* say that attitude (heart) will determine right behavior (investing one's treasure in the kingdom of God), but rather that right behavior—the act of investing our treasure in a certain way—will result in the right attitude.

In a similar vein, the most effective way to change sex roles which are currently defined in such a way that they prevent us from attaining full Christian womanhood and manhood, is not by attempting to change sexist attitudes directly, but rather by changing sex role behavior. Sociologically, this means changing behavior by attempting to change *social structures*, rather than directly changing the personalities of people.

An examination of the history of the feminist movements in our society will reveal that significant cultural change came about when attempts were made to change the social structure of society. The early social feminists were successful in passing laws against child labor, slavery, and prostitution. The suffragettes were successful in getting women the right to vote. And the modern feminists have been most successful in bringing about structural changes in our society. Social and cultural change is neither automatic nor predictable. Changes in sex roles have come about most when collective assertive efforts have been made to change the social structure of American society.

Mention might also be made of changes brought about by industrialization, as well as World War I and II which created a demand for women workers. When women were exposed to these new freedoms, it was difficult to get them to relinquish them. Attempts to change the male role are more recent. As an example, in 1974 I wrote an article for *Woman's Day* entitled "Why Husbands Can't Say 'I Love You.' " This article was primarily directed to wives, and suggested ways in which they might attempt to draw an inexpressive husband out of his shell. I believe that there is a place for such an emphasis, for some males are better able to become expressive with the help of an understanding wife. In a well-taken criticism of the *Woman's Day* article, Sattel, a sociologist, points out the danger in burdening the wife with this additional "emotional work" at a time in history when she is probably struggling to define who she is. I might also add that the strategy I suggested consisted of an attempt to change men directly rather than to change the social structure within which men behave. If I were to write another article to wives on this subject (the editor strongly suggested that few husbands would actually read the article), I would emphasize the need for structural change, such as the amounts of time spent in certain roles. I would suggest to wives that they encourage their husbands to assume more of the child-rearing responsibilities in the home. One way this might be induced would be by greater involvement on the part of the wife outside of the home.

Men's consciousness-raising groups have also been utilized as a means of encouraging males to reconsider their masculinity. Such groups, where men feel free to open up to each other and exchange experiences related to their masculine identity, are undoubtedly an effective way for men to develop a more complete concept of manhood. However, a selective factor may be involved in the formation of such groups. The males who are most aware of the stifling effects of our culture's "masculine" emphasis are most likely to be the ones to join such groups.

What is most needed is a change in the amount of time which males are asked to devote to emotion-laden roles. If fathers committed as much of their time to relating to their children as their wives do, it would undoubtedly be reflected in their expressiveness and parenting ability. Part of the needed structural change has already been initiated by women redefining their roles in society; these changes will "force" men to commit greater amounts of time to roles which carry high expressive expectations. A neglected impetus for change is the educating of men to make them aware of the potential gains which changed role relationships can bring. However, even males who are already aware may need to commit themselves to increased proportions of time in roles where expressiveness is encouraged.

In conclusion, when any aspect of our culture is in the process of change, such as sex roles, before either defensively rejecting the change or naively accepting the change, Christians must carefully examine the nature of the change in the light of the Bible. Such a detailed examination was only begun in this paper; I encourage each reader to diligently examine his or her own sexuality and that of our society in light of a careful search of what the Scriptures have to say about sex roles.

## Discussion Questions

1. What are some historical examples of how adherence to cultural tradition has caused the church to misinterpret biblical teachings concerning sex roles?

2. Does the Bible give any indications as to whether found differences between the sexes are culturally or biologically induced?

3. Was Jesus' behavior considered overly masculine or feminine in his day? How would it be characterized today? Would Jesus' relationships with women in traditional patriarchal Jewish society warrant calling him an advocate of women's lib?

4. Discuss examples of where biblical accounts of males and females are descriptive instead of normative.

5. What might Jesus' position be on the current women's rights issue? Can there be a women's liberation movement without a men's liberation movement?

6. How does the church, youth in particular, differ in exploitation of women as sex objects? Consider dress and the behavior of females in musical groups in particular.

7. What is the effect of male inexpressiveness upon marriage? Is the marriage relationship likely to be threatened by males becoming expressive toward all females?

8. Evaluate the following statement: "Even if changes are needed in the way our society defines sex roles, it is not the duty of the church to get involved because the church should not get involved in politics."

9. Do you think that Christians err in "over-feminizing" Christianity or "over-masculinizing" Christianity? Support your answer by giving examples.

10. How different or similar should males and females be? In what ways should the sexes be different and in what ways similar? What is the biblical evidence concerning the nature of "man's work" and "woman's work?"

## References

Balswick, Jack
    1978 *Why I Can't Say I Love You*. Waco, Tex.: Word Books.
Bell, Inge P.
    1970 "The Double Standard." *Transaction*, 8 (November/ December), pp. 75-80.
D'Anrade, Roy G.
    1966 "Sex Differences and Cultural Institutions." Eleanor E. Maccoby (ed), *The Development of Sex Differences*. Stanford, Calif.: Stanford University Press.
Firestone, Shulamith
    1970 *The Dialectic of Sex*. New York: Morrow.
Ford, Clelland S.
    1970 "Some Primitive Societies." Georgene H. Seward and Robert

C. Williamson (eds.), *Sex Roles in Changing Society.* New York: Random House.

Friedan, Betty
1963 *The Feminine Mystique.* New York: Dell Publishing.

Hampson, John L. and Joan G. Hampson
1961 "The Ontogenesis of Sexual Behavior in Man." W. C. Young (ed.), *Sex and Internal Secretions,* Vol. 2 (3rd ed.). Baltimore: Williams and Wilkin.

Hartley, Ruth E.
1959 "Sex-Role Pressures and Socialization of the Male Child." *Psychological Reports,* 5, pp. 457-468.

Mead, Margaret
1935 *Sex and Temperament in Three Primitive Societies.* New York: Morrow.

Mitchell, Juliet
1970 In Betty Roszak and Theodore Roszak (eds.), *Masculine/ Feminine: Readings in Sexual Mythology and the Liberation of Women.* New York: Harper and Row.

O'Neill, William L.
1969 *Everyone Was Brave: The Rise and Fall of Feminism in America.* Chicago: Quadrangle Press.

Sinclair, Andrew
1966 *The Emancipation of the American Woman.* New York: Harper and Row.

Vernon, Glenn M.
1962 *Sociology of Religion.* New York: McGraw-Hill.

# 19
# Sociology of the Aging and Christian Responsibility

*David O. Moberg*

A truism we often forget is that everyone is aging. Aging begins at the moment of conception. It is the subject of social gerontology, the social and behavioral science which studies the aging process and people, as well as of geriatrics, the professional care of adults in their later years.

However young a person may be, he or she already is preparing for retirement (even before choosing a career!), old age, and death. This is obvious whenever wages are reduced by payroll deductions for FICA, the Social Security tax which covers retirement benefits as well as disability and survivor's insurance. It is less obvious in relationship to eating habits; physical and mental exercise; use or abstention from tobacco, alcohol, and other drugs; social relationships; self-conceptions; education, and other investments of time, energy, and money. Our behavior patterns and our relationships to ourselves, others, God, and the distant and near environment are preparing us either for an improved or a deteriorated set of circumstances in our later years. Preparation for the future is a lifelong process. It begins in childhood and continues through youth, adulthood, and even retirement itself. All the biblical principles of Christian stewardship pertain directly to it.

In spite of the lifelong nature of the aging process, most references to the aging pertain to persons in their "later years" or "old age." Be-

**David O. Moberg**
*Professor of Sociology*
*University of Marquette*

As an active Baptist layman, David Moberg has held various positions of leadership in interdenominational organizations. He has also served as moderator, and held various other offices in local Baptist churches. Since earning his PhD in sociology at the University of Minnesota in 1952, he has had two Fulbright appointments and has participated in many professional organizations and research projects. Currently he is a member of the National Advisory Committee for Project GIST (Gerontology in Seminary Training) of the National Interfaith Coalition on Aging.

cause the sixty-fifth birthday was used as the time at which people could begin to collect retirement benefits when the Social Security program was established in 1935, most data on aging use 65 as a cutting point between middle age and old age. This is just as arbitrary as using the eighteenth birthday to inaugurate adulthood. On the basis of physiological criteria, some people are still "young" at 70, but others are "old" at 45. Because so many of the disabilities and limitations of health and mobility associated with the end of the life cycle are concentrated in the older category, there is a growing tendency to distinguish between the "old-old" who are past age 75 and the "young-old" aged 65 to 74.

Sociologically a person is old when she or he has relinquished the roles, relationships, and statuses typical of middle-aged adults and been given those which are more characteristic of persons in "late life." In preliterate societies it often is relatively easy to classify people functionally by age, for distinct roles involving ceremonial leadership, midwifery, child care, preparation of food, repair of clothing, or other active responsibilities are assigned to older people (Simmons, 1945). In industrialized urban societies, however, no definite place is established for the aged, so it is not possible to define old age on the basis of clearcut sociological criteria.

Indeed, one of the problems of aging in our society is the lack of a recognized and respected place in the social system. The "roleless role" of the elderly combines with the great veneration and admiration for youthfulness in our culture. This not only makes them feel "on the shelf," unwanted, not needed, and ignored, but also disappointed and disillusioned. The "golden years" of old age and retirement tarnish quickly; they are a period of frustration and maladjustment for many. At the same time, however, we must recognize that never before in human history has such a high proportion of the population reached their sixties and seventies, and never before has such a large percentage of those past 60 remained in good physical health.

Because of the difficulties of using psychological, sociological, or other functional criteria to define old age, the chronological measure of age in years is used for nearly all data on the subject. In July 1974 the 21,800,000 persons aged 65 and over comprised 10.3 percent of the total population of the United States. Both the total number and the percentage are increasing; by 1985 it is predicted that there will be about 26,700,000 people in that age category, 11.4 percent of the nation's people (Metropolitan Life Insurance Co., 1975). In 1900 only one person in every twenty-five was aged 65 and over; by 1950 the ratio had reached one in twelve, and by 1985 it will exceed one in nine. Similar trends are evident in other nations; they are the most pronounced in the "developed nations."

Life expectancy at birth has been rising steadily as well. In 1900 it was 49 years in the United States, but by 1970 it had risen to 71 (67 for men and almost 75 for women). The majority of this trend is accounted for by improvements in childhood through the child-bearing age. If ever there should be a major breakthrough in regard to the control of cancer and diseases of the heart and circulatory system, we can expect a significant jump in longevity. Currently, however,

The years of our life are threescore and ten,
or even by reason of strength fourscore (Psalm 90:10).

Compared to the eternal nature of God, our 70 or 80 years are like a flickering moment. At their longest, they are like dust or grass which briefly flourishes, then is shriveled by dry summer winds (Psalm 90:3-6; 103:13-18; 1 Peter 1:24-25; 2 Peter 3:8-9). Those who are wise will not try to disguise and repress the temporary nature of their sojourn on earth! Yet such attempts are a major source of the emphasis upon youth in contemporary society. They contribute to frustrating efforts by many members of the older generation to remain youthful in appearance and actions. The denial of death and efforts to avoid reminders of it are also related to the fears and anxieties of people who are not prepared to face their Creator.

### The Elderly as a Minority

A sociological minority may be defined as an identifiable group that is kept subordinate by the dominant majority, that has fewer life chances because of ascribed characteristics, or that suffers disadvantage due to prejudice or discrimination. Regardless of the definition chosen, the elderly can be interpreted as a minority in American society.

Compulsory retirement forces older adults out of the job market in most occupations, regardless of their capabilities. Then even if they would like to work and are capable of it, they are not counted among the unemployed because of their age. Employment discrimination against them begins much earlier in the life cycle; when people past the age of 45 lose employment, it often is very difficult to find another job because of discrimination against "the older worker."

.

An "invisible poverty" characterizes a substantial number of senior citizens. About one third of them live below or near the poverty level, yet they tend to identify politically and socially with the socioeconomic status of their working years. Pension plans into which payments were made on their behalf often are uncollectable. Savings accumulated to help meet the needs of their later years are eaten away by inflation. Problems of housing, nutrition, health care, transportation, and participation in clubs and other social groups emerge from their inability to meet the financial costs that are involved. At the very time of life when they have more time for leisure pursuits and participation in social activities, their means to satisfy these interests are inadequate.

Other discrimination is evident. Humor is often directed against "the old codgers" who are alleged to be "out of step with the times." The suggestion has even been made that all persons should lose the vote at retirement, at age 70, or when they migrate to another state after age 55. (Stewart, 1970). Removed from most positions of leadership and power on the basis of their chronological age, the majority of the elderly are the victims of both ageism and gerontophobia.

*Ageism* is a term used to denote acts of discrimination directed against the elderly sheerly on the basis of their age. It is a form of bigotry that is analogous to racism and sexism, and the institutionalized consequences of this inequality is similarly evident in income, occupation, and other variables (Palmore and Manton, 1973). Although the phenomenon of age discrimination was present much earlier, the term was coined only in 1969 by Butler (1969). In 1972 the Gray Panthers were organized under the leadership of Margaret E. (Maggie) Kuhn to combat it. Their goal is to liberate older persons from the "paternalism and oppression with which society keeps us powerless." They desire to make old age a victory rather than a defeat, a privilege rather than a punishment (Hessel, 1977).

*Gerontophobia* is an underlying attitude of prejudice against aging and the aged. Some scholars view it as a relatively rare "unreasonable fear and/or constant hatred of older people" and include prejudicial attitudes and stereotypes among the characteristics of ageism (Palmore, 1972). However, I prefer to define gerontophobia more broadly, as the prejudice which provides the attitudinal basis for ageism. Just as prejudice and discrimination are differentiated in the analysis of racism, the analogous concept of gerontophobia can be distinguished from ageism. As defined by Bunzel (1972), gerontophobia consists of the unconscious and irrational psychological tendency to fear one's own aging, hence to shun anything that reminds one of it, including contacts with aging people. Cultural attitudes prejudicial to the aged in our youth-oriented society may not be interpreted as symptoms of "unreasonable fear," nor as an "irrational psychological tendency," but their consequences for both the hate-bearers and their victims may be all the more harmful because they are so widespread and "normal" that they acquire the significance of "truth."

Like prejudice against women, racial groups, or ethnic minorities, gerontophobia cannot be reconciled with the Christian virtue of calling no human being "common or unclean" (Acts 10:28). The importance of extending and sustaining justice toward all people, including the poor and needy, aliens and strangers, employees and servants, and youth and elders, is a persistent theme in the personal and social ethics of the Bible.

Ageism differs from racism and sexism in the sense that everybody who survives to the later years—with the possible exception of a few persons at the highest levels of wealth or prestige—becomes its victim. We ourselves are tomorrow's minority, yet we all tend to be trapped into sinful conformity to cultural norms and patterns when we fail to give explicit thought to our attitudes and conduct. Gerontophobia and ageism are perpetuated by a vicious cycle of continual reinforcement in which stereotypes of the elderly, myths about aging, discrimination against the aged, and denigrating expectations of the aging process become part of a cultural self-fulfilling prophecy. Older persons themselves internalize the predictions and, as a result, experience many of their negative features as if they were natural and inevitable.

The "myths of aging" which are believed by a substantial majority of people need to be eliminated in order to eradicate the social diseases of ageism and gerontophobia. Among them are these falsehoods:

| Myth | Fact |
|---|---|
| 1. That the elderly are all the same. | 1. There are greater differences among them than among people at any other segment of the life cycle. |
| 2. That they no longer can learn. | 2. They frequently are compelled to adjust to new circumstances and learn the requirements associated with them. |

3. That they are devoid of sexual interests and capabilities.

3. Healthy married couples share the intimacies of sex even in their 80s and 90s.

4. That they wish to be relieved of all responsibility.

4. They may wish to carry a lighter load, but they desire the self-respect and sense of worth that comes from serving others.

5. That old age is a disease or a problem in and of itself.

5. It is the natural and inevitable terminal period of the life cycle but not in itself a handicap, except as social and cultural attitudes and practices have made it so.

6. That most of the elderly are physically incapacitated or mentally senile.

6. Only about 5 percent of all who are past 65 are in institutional care facilities at any given time.

7. That it is unwholesome for older people to reminisce about their past.

7. The life review process of reflecting upon the past is wholesome and therapeutic; it enables many to make sense of the tangled web of their experiences and the puzzles of their life story for the first time.

8. That it is no use working with older people because they are too old to change, to be converted, or to be rejuvenated.

8. The facts are contrary. Like younger people, some elderly are resistant to change while others welcome it; some become very fruitful as in Psalm 92:14, while others are so self-centered that they seem impossible to rehabilitate.

Since Christians are the followers of him who is known as "the Truth" (John 14:6), they ought not to perpetuate and disseminate the lies that constitute the core of the myths of aging! In contrast to gerontophobia, their attitude ought to be one of *gerontophilia*—love of the aging.

The middle-class values which dominate American society aggravate the problems of the aging. They were reared in an era in which a man's work was a sign of success and lack of work a mark of failure. For women, the opposite perspective prevailed; it was a declaration of failure for a married woman to take a job outside the home. Today in their own later years compulsory retirement rules take away the employment of the typical man, and many older women are compelled to find work outside the home under circumstances which they internally, if unconsciously, interpret as indicative of "failure."

The measurement of success by material possessions and wealth also accentuates their problems, since retirement income is seldom as large as anticipated. Savings, social security, and pension funds are all diminished by inflation, and what may have seemed large when initiated years earlier by a labor union, employer, or insurance company, is seldom enough. The end result is that the level of living must be adjusted sharply downward.

> This in turn may lead to impaired dietary habits, diminished participation in social organizations (including the church), and other harmful consequences. If emergency medical expenses or other costs emerge, society is reluctant to provide help until the person has, in effect, declared himself or herself to be a pauper. The problems of ageism—discrimination against the elderly—and its underlying unconscious discrimination of gerontophobia have made the goal of long life to become an evil to be feared, not just a blessing to be claimed. Retirement for all too many is a curse, so the aging have ambivalent emotions about it (Moberg, 1978:4).

## Theories of Aging

Theories of aging, like other sociological theories, frequently incorporate or reflect a normative value position even when they claim to be based purely upon empirical evidence. Presumably, all the major sociological schools of theory can be applied to the study of aging people and processes, but the theoretical development of social gerontology is still in its infancy. Two theoretical perspectives predominate and vie with each other for acceptance.

*Disengagement theory* (Cumming and Henry, 1961) states that aging persons gradually withdraw (disengage themselves) normally from the roles and relationships which they maintained earlier in the life cycle. They are prodded by the interests of society to do so, and they are rewarded for complying with its pressures and punished for resisting them. The process is functional for both society and its individual members. Typically it begins in middle age by the departure of children, followed later by retirement from work by men and widowhood by women. Friends die, children move to distant locations, and voluntary association offices are relinquished. Eventually the elderly person is no longer capable of the minimum adaptive behavior necessary to maintain health, cleanliness, or propriety, so someone else enters to do so, reducing the person to the social condition of infants. Thus a progressive process of reduction and simplification occurs; the individual gains increased freedom from obligations which earlier had bound him or her into an interlocking system of divided tasks.

It is rewarding to the individual to disengage during the later years, but the process is mutual, for society also desires to discard older members in favor of younger ones, who allegedly can achieve more. Disengagement affects various temperamental types differently. For each person involved it constitutes an inner experience, a social imperative, a response to changing roles, and changes in solidarity bonds (Cumming, 1963). The final stage in the disengagement process is death. Life satisfaction results from conforming to social expectations that the aging person will withdraw from others in the social system and develop a new equilibrium based more upon socioemotional than upon instrumental roles.

In contrast, *activity theory* holds that there is a positive relationship between activity and life satisfaction, so the greater one's loss of roles, the lower the level of satisfaction, morale, adjustment, and/or happiness. Roles which are lost can be replaced by new roles and relationships. The path to wholesome aging therefore involves replacing departed or deceased friends with new ones, work positions from which one is forced to retire with part- or full-time employment or with voluntary service positions in social organizations, and finding other functional equivalents to substitute for roles which are lost.

Activity theory has emerged out of role theory and symbolic interactionism. Those who accept it believe that the emergence of a subculture of older people is a wholesome trend (Rose, 1965), for it provides a new status system and opportunities for social activity that will contribute to the well-being of aging people.

Obviously the perspectives on successful aging in disengagement theory are directly opposed to those of activity theory. Empirical evidences marshaled to test disengagement theory generally have failed to support its implications for morale and life satisfaction, while data generally tend to support the hypotheses that various types of activity are associated with mental health and a sense of well-being. Lemon,

Bengtson, and Peterson (1972), however, carefully specified concepts and types of activity (informal, formal, solitary) from activity theory and found that only informal activity with friends (not even with relatives and neighbors) was significantly associated with life satisfaction. Their research, which reviewed the results of many other studies, concluded that

> neither activity theory nor disengagement theory by themselves can adequately account for optimal aging. Perhaps it is good to be reminded again of the *variability* of aged individuals in terms of their value systems, personalities, physical and social situations, and the danger of stereotyping or of building theory that is overgeneralized (p. 521).

The defects of the two leading theories have led Atchley (1977:26-27) to suggest a *continuity theory* which assumes that individuals develop habits, commitments, preferences, and other dispositions that become a part of their personalities. As they grow older, they are predisposed toward maintaining these, regardless of explicit circumstances, in a constantly evolving process of interaction among all elements of preferences, capabilities, opportunities, and experience. Continuity of personal identity and of participation in voluntary associations characterizes successful aging according to this perspective.

The overlap of these three theories with structural-functional theory, symbolic interactionism, labeling role theory, age stratification, the elderly as a minority, and other sociological and social-psychological perspectives needs to be developed systematically in the sociology of aging.

### Values and Aging

The perspectives toward aging of many social and behavioral scientists reflect an implicit exchange theory. Since we will be old someday, we ought to improve the status of the elderly so that our own condition will be more satisfying when we ourselves are old. Demeaning the elderly actually contributes ultimately to demeaning ourselves.

Explicitly Christian values also reflect some aspects of exchange theory, but much more is clearly expressed in numerous teachings of the Bible.

Although it does not specifically mention the elderly, the fifth of the Ten Commandments (Exodus 20:12) can be interpreted to do so because the Decalogue is addressed to adults even more than to youth. This commandment to honor our fathers and mothers is described as the first commandment with a promise, for obeying it would result in long life (Ephesians 6:2-3). By implication, it was reaffirmed by the apostle Paul in his insistence that the material needs of widows and other family members among Christians should be met by their immediate relatives whenever possible (1 Timothy 5:3-8, 16). If, however, the relatives failed, they would not be allowed to suffer, since the Christian community was expected to extend loving care toward them. The example of providing food, clothing, and other material needs for widows in the early Christian church is reflected in Acts 6:1-6 and I Timothy 5:3-16. "Social ministries" received just as much attention then as what many today call "spiritual ministries." They did not draw a line of separation between evangelism and social concern, though a division of labor was established to be sure that all was done well. In part this may be attributed to the biblical concept of the soul. In contrast to Greek thought, the Hebrews believed the soul was the very essence of the person—the totality of one's being—not a separate part. (The nearest equivalents today are the concepts of the self, ego, or person.) Ministering to the needs of people, therefore, covered all of the domains which we today tend to label analytically as body, mind, and spirit or what might be called the physical, economic, social, psychological, political, and spiritual dimensions of individuals' lives (see Moberg, 1977, for current applications).

Christian love should not be limited to Christians. It extends to all people (Galatians 6:10), even though members of the household of faith have first claim to energies and resources. Jesus summarized the Ten Commandments by lumping all of them into two—to love God and to love your neighbor as you love yourself (Matthew 22:36-40). He also answered and clarified the question, who is my neighbor? He made it clear that it is any person who, like the Good Samaritan, shows compassionate love to people in need (Luke 10:25-37). Applying this means discovering those who are in need, and being a good neighbor to them.

In part, the theological basis for such concern resides in several basic biblical truths: (1) that all human beings are made in the image of God, (2) that helping people in need who are even "the least of Christ's brethren" is a form of serving him (Matthew 25:34-40), (3) that we should be imitators of God who loves the unworthy and showers his blessings upon the evil and unjust as well as upon the just and good

(Matthew 5:43-48), (4) that every Christian has a spiritual gift to use in his or her ministry of service (1 Corinthians 12; Romans 12:3-8; Ephesians 4:11-16; 1 Peter 4:10-11), and (5) that stewardship responsibilities demand an active social concern. (See Moberg 1965:13-58 for further elaboration of biblical principles.) While none of these is limited to the aging, they all obviously include an implied responsibility for the elderly.

The ethical teachings of the Bible also exhibit a strong emphasis upon justice and mercy. When explicit groups are mentioned in connection with those virtues, they typically are the poor and widows, both of whom are overrepresented among the elderly. Add to this the many references to "elders," their important roles, and the need to respect their judgments, and it will be all the more evident that biblical values require that we honor the aged members of the church and community.

Aging individuals whose lives are oriented toward spiritual values receive many rewards in this life; it is not merely "pie in the sky by and by." Research which gets beyond mere labels of church membership or religious identity reveals that committed Christians who engage in personal devotions (prayer, meditation, and Bible reading) enjoy higher levels of life satisfaction, personal adjustment, or morale than do others who lack such faith and piety (Gray and Moberg, 1977: Chapter 4).

### Implementing Christian Values

It is much easier to verbalize general normative statements than it is to put them into practice. In a complex, urbanized society it is usually easy to get Christians to agree upon general principles for social action, but specific application of those principles may arouse considerable disagreement. Sometimes this is a consequence of erecting certain generalized value orientations above others, such as adopting an unyielding overall conservatism or liberalism in political affairs. Or it may be analogous to making commitments to a political party, occupational group, or socioeconomic class primarily and only later and secondarily seeking a biblical basis for supporting them. More often, however, failure to manifest social concern for the aged arises from several sources: (1) ignorance of the facts, (2) blindness to the suffering of people, (3) acceptance of cultural myths about the elderly, (4) belief in fictions about welfare clients or other stereotyped groups, (5) slowness to recognize the intergenerational changes in the situation and needs of the aged, or (6) accent upon one set of biblical teachings while another

Christian group stresses a different set which seems to imply different actions.

Whenever people state, "The *Bible teaches* that . . . " with reference to any specific doctrine or action program, we need to remember that they really are saying, "*My interpretation* of what the Bible teaches is that. . . . " It is very important, therefore, for Christians to share their understandings with one another in the process of developing action programs and their supporting rationale.

When others disagree with us, it is not necessarily they who are wrong in thought and action. Nor should we label "them" by saying that "they are not acting as Christians." It is quite possible that we are in error, or both camps may need to find a third position which is more consistent with revealed truth and the realities of the situation.

The specific actions which can be taken to help the aging and elderly on the basis of Christian values are so numerous that an extensive literature of denominational and other studies has developed (for a beginning, see Clingan, 1975; Gray and Moberg, 1977; McClellan, 1977; Moberg, 1971, and the references included in each). The actions desirable in one community or church setting may be inappropriate for another. Therefore, planning should involve research to identify needs and available resources, clarification of goals and objectives, prediction of the likely outcomes of alternative courses of action, program development and implementation, gaining legitimation and financial support, and evaluation and feedback, which leads to a new modified cycle of similar action (see Moberg, 1965: Chapter 10).

Basic to Christian ministries in the area of aging is the cultivation of proper attitudes and values. For example, since every individual, however young or old, is created in God's image as a unique person, and was loved so much that Christ died for him or her, it is sinful to react to the aged as if all are the same. Rather, their autonomous, self-directing nature should be respected, and their creative powers should be drawn out and developed, not squelched.

People are of greater value than possessions. If property rights clash with the human rights of the aging, the latter should be given priority. Similarly, institutions are made to serve humanity, not vice versa—this is the implicit meaning of Jesus' words, "The sabbath was made for man, not man for the sabbath" (Mark 2:27). Churches, as well as governments, therefore exist to serve people, not people to serve them.

Many ethical teachings of the Bible are personalized. They therefore are easily used to support antisocial individualism. It is important to remember that the only way to help the elderly or other individuals, in many instances, is by sweeping actions to serve an entire class of people. To help only selected victims of social problems may be equivalent to pulling straws out of a burning haystack that destroys ever more victims than we can personally rescue; putting out the fire by getting at its source will save far more individuals. Thus the need for a balance between aiding persons and engaging in remedial and preventive programs to change the social, economic, and political circumstances which cause their misery must be recognized. Ageism cannot be eliminated merely through scattered efforts to help those few aging individuals whose paths cross ours. Like Jesus, our concern should extend to both persons and the masses (Matthew 9:36).

Numerous programs of activity to serve the aging and elderly are possible in Christian churches. Educational ministries at all levels can correct the myths of aging and help to prevent the gerontophobia that supports ageism. The churches can also contribute to wholesome personality development at all ages and assist in the solution of personal and family problems. In addition they can help with material, physical, social, and recreational needs, support congregate nursing care facilities and retirement homes, work to influence civic affairs and politics, cooperate with other associations promoting the well-being of the aging through service or research, and create opportunities for the elderly to serve others (Gray and Moberg, 1977: Chapter 8).

Good intentions alone are not an adequate basis for Christian action. For example, compelling retired people to be inactive except for swaying the proverbial rocking chair may be highly detrimental to their physical, psychological, social, and even spiritual health. Being overly solicitous and helpful to the point of reducing the exercise and mobility of elderly people has caused a great deal of unhappiness, has cut off many years of useful living for thousands of them, and thus has contributed to the social impoverishment of our nation.

While home care of the old-old may require supportive services for housekeeping and health needs, it is far less expensive than institutionalization and generally much more satisfying to them. Even during terminal illness many people would rather endure extra pain in order to die at home in the midst of the normal round of life than to be in the costly "sterile atmosphere" of a hospital receiving professional care.

We must become more aware of the subtle ways we demean people, ignore their desires, and bring about latent dysfunctional consequences by our acts. We also should evaluate more realistically and carefully those that are manifest and functional.

At the core of whatever the Christian church does are the spiritual nature and needs of humanity. In the midst of the joys and satisfactions, the burdens of economic deprivation, chronic illness, rejection from social life, bereavement, and the other problems faced by most of the elderly in our society, are spiritual values. These values can bring rejuvenation to the elderly, as well as correction to those whose violations of human rights and Christian virtues have helped to cause and perpetuate the problems. Whatever else may be done by a church, it must always keep its spiritual concerns in the forefront. Without them, all its other ministries eventually will fade as well. With them, it will lead its members into ministries that serve the whole person in every dimension of life as it teaches them to observe everything that Christ commanded (Matthew 28:20).

## Summary

Everyone is aging, and all are preparing in many ways for their own old age. Nevertheless, the elderly in modern society do not have a recognized social role and face so many circumstances of discrimination (ageism) that they can be viewed as a minority group. Beneath this discrimination are the prejudicial cultural attitudes of gerontophobia. These are sustained by many "myths of aging" and perpetuated in a vicious self-reinforcing cycle of prejudice that illustrates the self-fulfilling prophecy.

Although all major sociological schools of theory can be applied to the study of aging, gerontological theory is an underdeveloped subject. Disengagement theory, which holds that older adults gradually withdraw voluntarily or compulsorily from their social roles, has been opposed by activity theory, which teaches that successful aging involves taking on new roles and relationships as old ones are relinquished. While more sociologists are inclined toward activity theory, it also has weaknesses. Among other theoretical perspectives is continuity theory, which assumes continuation of the individual's personality traits, identity, and social participation with only gradual evolutionary changes throughout the life cycle.

Numerous values from Christian social ethics pertain to our attitudes, relationships, and actions with reference to the aging. The Fifth Commandment (to honor our fathers and mothers), the examples of Christ and the early Christian church, the instructions to love others, the emphasis upon mercy and justice, and numerous other theological and practical instructions of the Bible provide the value basis for Christian action.

In attempting to implement these values, Christians sometimes disagree with each other. Nevertheless, Christian social responsibility demands the cultivation of wholesome attitudes and values and the implementation of explicit activities to serve the aging. The latter will vary by community and congregation or parish, but in all instances the cultivation of spiritual life must take priority in the work of Christian churches.

## Discussion Questions

1. Make an analysis of the age, sex, and income distribution of the population of your home city, village, or county. How does it compare with your state and the nation as a whole, especially for the age categories past 60? What do these findings imply with reference to the elderly people of your community?

2. Is your church congregation aware of the number of elderly persons in its membership and the surrounding community? What is it doing to identify and serve their unique needs?

3. Make a list of relatives and acquaintances who are past the age of 65. What specific needs and problems do they face? What are their assets and advantages? Do you note any difference between the "young-old" and the "old-old?" How can you benefit from them? What can you do to alleviate their burdens?

4. Identify one older person who seems to have a happy, satisfying life and one who does not. What variations in their social situations, philosophies of life, religious values, personalities, and other characteristics can be hypothesized to account for the differences? If time allows, test your hypotheses by observing and interviewing other elderly people.

5. Ask a grandparent or other elderly person to review selected experiences from his or her life with you. Notice contrasts between your own situation and that which prevailed for the aged when they were at the equivalent stage of life. In what ways are general social trends to which sociologists refer reflected by and illustrated in the life of that person? What has been the impact of spiritual experiences in the "living history" recounted by your interviewee?

6. Collect the attitudes of at least five adolescents about old

people and those of at least five elderly people about adolescents. Does either group tend to stereotype the other? Can representatives of each group come into a group of the other in your church to discuss your findings?

7. Do any of your family members show symptoms of gerontophobia? How about yourself? What can a Christian do to be freed from this sinful conformity with the spirit of our age (Romans 12:2)?

8. Which influences in your personal experience have contributed to gerontophobic attitudes, and which have contributed to gerontophilia? What can you do to improve the situation so that persons coming after you will have better experiences than you?

9. Compare Psalm 71:9-12 with Psalm 103:5. How can you account for the contrasting reflections of personal experiences? Are both types of attitude evident among older people today? May both be present in the mind of a single person?

10. Read Ecclesiastes 12, preferably in two or more translations. Does the graphic picture of emptiness in old age in verses 1 through 8 describe the situation of elderly people in modern society? How do the recommendations of the conclusion (verses 13-14) relate to current facts and theories of aging?

# References

Atchley, Robert C.
> 1977 *The Social Forces in Later Life: An Introduction to Social Gerontology,* Second Edition. Belmont, Calif.: Wadsworth Publishing Co.

Bunzel, Joseph H.
> 1972 "Gerontophobia Pervades U.S. Life, Sociologist Says." *Geriatrics,* 27 (March), pp. 41-49.

Butler, Robert N.
> 1969 "Age-ism: Another Form of Bigotry." *The Gerontologist,* 9, pp. 243-246.

Clingan, Donald F.
> 1975 *Aging Persons in the Community of Faith.* Indianapolis, Ind.: Institute on Religion and Aging.

Cumming, Elaine
> 1963 "Further Thoughts on the Theory of Disengagement." *International Social Science Journal,* 15, pp. 377-393.

Cumming, Elaine, and William E. Henry
> 1961 *Growing Old: The Process of Disengagement.* New York: Basic Books.

Gray, Robert M., and David O. Moberg
> 1977 *The Church and the Older Person* (rev. ed.). Grand Rapids, Mich.: Eerdmans.

Hessel, Dieter (ed.)
1977 *Maggie Kuhn on Aging*. Philadelphia: Westminster Press.
Lemon, Bruce W., Vern L. Bengtson, and James A. Peterson
1972 "An Exploration of the Activity Theory of Aging: Activity Types and Life Satisfaction Among In-Movers to a Retirement Community." *Journal of Gerontology*, 27, pp. 511-523.
McClellan, Robert W.
1977 *Claiming a Frontier: Ministry and Older People*. Los Angeles: University of Southern California Press.
Metropolitan Life Insurance Co.
1975 "Profile of Elders in the United States." *Statistical Bulletin* 56, (April) pp. 8-10.
Moberg, David O.
1965 *Inasmuch: Christian Social Responsibility in the Twentieth Century*. Grand Rapids, Mich.: Eerdmans.
1971 *Spiritual Well-Being: Background and Issues*. Washington, D.C.: White House Conference on Aging, Government Printing Office.
1977 *The Great Reversal: Evangelism and Social Concern* (rev. ed.). Philadelphia: Lippincott.
1978 "Numbering Our Days: Aging and Christian Stewardship." *Radix*, 9 (January-February), pp. 4-7.
Palmore, Erdman B.
1972 "Gerontophobia Versus Ageism." *The Gerontologist*, 12, p. 213.
Palmore, Erdman B. and Kenneth Manton
1973 "Ageism Compared to Racism and Sexism." *Journal of Gerontology* 28, pp. 363-369.
Rose, Arnold M.
1965 "The Subculture of the Aging: A Framework for Research in Social Gerontology." Arnold M. Rose and Warren A. Peterson (eds.). *Older People and Their Social Worlds*. Philadelphia: F. A. Davis Co., pp. 3-16.
Simmons, Leo W.
1945 *The Role of the Aged in Primitive Society*. New Haven, Conn.: Yale University Press.
Stewart, Douglas J.
1970 "Disfranchise the Old." *The New Republic*, 163 (August 22-29), pp. 20-22.

# 20
# The "Whole Man" Approach Through Nonprofessionals in a Prison Setting

*Richard P. Rettig*

We use a lot of terms to describe the work we do with troubled persons. We can talk about *rehabilitation,* which means to restore someone to his former capacity, office, or position. Or, we can use the concept of *regeneration,* which implies a complete moral reform on the part of the offender. The notion of *reformation* means the improvement or amendment of what is wrong, corrupt, or unsatisfactory. These are all worthy motives for action and can serve to inform a meaningful treatment policy. But I like to talk and work through the notion of *redemption* as a process that can include those with "troubled identities" who have tended to be marginal men and women in the system. When a person is redeemed, he is rescued from whatever attitudes, behaviors, and circumstances of yesterday that contributed to his criminality. He is redeemed into a new lifestyle, released from captivity to financial mismanagement and debilitating moral practices. He is set apart from old values and ideas—he is totally changed.

One meaning of *redemption* given by Webster is: conversion of paper money into specie (coin, gold, or silver). In a redemptive process, then, we work toward the potential of changing the "paper man"—full of frailties, subject to being blown about by the winds of circumstance, burned in the fires of life, wasted in fruitless living—into a man of value to himself, for himself, and for society.

**Richard P. Rettig**
*Associate Professor of Behavioral Sciences*
*Oral Roberts University*
Richard Rettig is the author of several books and numerous articles in the area of deviancy, criminology, and penal institutions. His interests include the sociology of education, group dynamics, and social theory. He earned a PhD in sociology at the University of Oregon and has taught at Humbolt State University and Nipissing University College in Ontario. He participates in many community activities related to penal reform. He was ordained at the Faith Bible Church, Albany, Oregon, in 1977.

## The Need for Radical Prison Reform

If we are to provide the solution to crime problems and prison problems, we must be willing to face the facts about what causes these problems. It is essential for us to recognize the mistakes of the past and the problems of the present, if we are to provide remedies that will address issues and solve systemic, as well as individual, problems. Any kind of meaningful reform must be innovative and radical (the true Christian posture), and must address itself to the needs of the whole man—body, soul, and spirit. If lasting change is to come, we must attempt to change some of the structures within society—in political, economic, and social sectors of society.

### Negative and Positive Deviance

It is not deviance, per se, that needs to be eliminated from society, it is *destructive* deviance that must be addressed. We need to minimize that deviance that hurts society, maims individuals, and subverts young people. But we should remember that there is *positive* deviance as well as *negative* deviance. Those in contemporary society who are standing up for moral rectitude, integrity, and cleanliness of mind are a minority group—today's deviants. We need to enlist more in this minority who reject the new permissiveness on behalf of spiritual-ethical values rooted in Christ. We need to feel free to deviate from what seems to be "the drinking ethic," the "drug ethic," the "free sex ethic," the "prono ethic." The greatest service that we can render inmates, residents, clients, and friends is to present ourselves as a living example of the Christian individual—clean in mind, body, and spirit. Furthermore, we must go on to cultivate a political astuteness and capability that will enable us to undertake a meaningful advocacy role (cf. Knapp and Polk, 1971: Chapter 1).

### Prison Bureaucracy Neglects "the Spiritual"

I would suggest that the prison bureaucracy has over-conformed to the standards of the world in de-emphasizing the spiritual needs of its clients. This general de-emphasis of belief is precisely why we have so many people returning to prisons and jails in these times. God has been defined as distant or "dead" and nothing has been invented to take his place as a regulatory agent. There is nobody to "stand in the gap," as it were. I would challenge you as students in the social sciences to *deviate* from the mainstream of a correctional ideology that is rooted in the dead-end street of the "natural man," emphasizing only sterile humanism and merely a-spiritual social work methods. Tomorrow's radical prison reformers will be among those who recognize the need to identify, confront, and support "the inner man." They will need to take the time, interest, and money to devise and maintain programs which bring men out of disenfranchisement and social abuse through an exposure to the gospel. God is working in today's world everywhere—even on the prison yard. It's about time Christian sociologists and social workers bit the bullet. I get letters every day from prisoners telling me how God is working in their lives. Religious life and spiritual values form a powerful agency for change in the lives of individual convicts. And the prison administrator, politician, lawyer, or interested student who fails to recognize what salvation and discipleship will do for the offender is missing a change agency with particular promise.

## Prisons Are Largely Dysfunctional

We should recognize that when we initiate a locking-in process, we automatically cultivate a locking-out process. That is to say, we do not just lock the offender away behind concrete walls and steel bars. Our maximum security measures, by definition, lock him out of a legitimate world in which he will have to live someday (95 percent of all incarcerated people will someday return to society). And our present penal system does little or nothing to assist its inmates in adjusting their lives so that they might avoid criminal behavior next time (Burger, 1970:13-16).

Therefore this article is written to you—future administrators, office-holders, voting citizens, and volunteers in corrections—who through an informed Christian educational experience desire to effect changes in our depersonalized and hostile prison institutions.

### The Predicament of the Prison Inmate

Numerous changes have been made in our correctional institutions in recent years. We have added professional and social services, built new maximum security facilities, and expended large sums of money and energy to rehabilitate the offender. What has it accomplished? If we accept the opinion of most penologists, our system of corrections is bankrupt (Murton, 1976: xi-xii; Rettig, et al., 1977:66-108, 215-221).

We might well ask, *why?* And I am sure we have. But have we looked for the answers among those who might have them? First, what is the nature of the man in prison? Is he radically different from any other man? If so, how? And if we can determine differences, what can we do to bring *him* into line with *us*? Second, what is prison like to the incarcerated offender? What happens to him? Why does the system fail to leave its rehabilitative mark on him? It's time we asked *him*! As one who has been "up the river"—in the joint—for more than 15 years, and has studied the problem theoretically for several years, let me advance a partial answer.°

*Imprisonment a "Culture Shock"*

Incarceration sometimes places the new inmate in a terrifying predicament—especially if he is young. He is usually, in one way or another, stripped of his personal property, all credentials, licenses, his rights as a citizen, and all legitimate supportive relationships in the community. He is deprived of most social, and many physical, helps without which the normal person cannot live successfully (Irwin, 1970:38-41). He brings with him into prison whatever emotional conflicts, psychological problems, and troubles in personal relationships that he had failed to work through on the outside. He internalizes an immediate awareness that he has become an object of fear, hatred, and scorn in most areas of the community from which he has been banished. He carries the stigma of excommunication, of being swept beneath the rug of life. As a consequence of his incarceration, the new inmate experiences a deep sense of alienation, loss, failure, and rejection; and he is often gripped by a feeling of terror because of the inmate subculture to which he must adapt (Ogburn, 1972).

He is given a number, a set of blue denims, a lecture on custody and security; then he is processed as a unit of merchandise, an object, a thing. He enters and becomes part of the life of an institution where there is often the threat of harassment, violence, rape, and even death. He is deprived of liberty, of goods and services, of normal heterosexual relationships, of autonomy, and of personal security. He becomes subject to a vast body of impersonal rules and arbitrary commands designed to reduce his personality to a cipher and to control his behavior in minute detail. All opportunity to be self-determining is severed. He is not only deprived of privacy, but he also loses his "ci-

---

°This article will reflect my personal experience and that of men I knew in several prisons, where I spent 15 years off and on between 1944 and 1966.

vilian" identity as he is resocialized into a "con-culture" from which he picks up his new identity and values (cf. Rettig et al., 1977; Irwin, 1970; Minton, 1971).

*Prisons as "Total Institutions"*

Despite the professional rhetoric, a prison is a *total institution*—an experience that affects every aspect of your life (Goffman, 1971: Chapter 1). We can discuss concepts of deterrence, rehabilitation, and education, but retribution often seems to be the articulated goal in the present process. We in the public sector would like to think that the time an individual spends in confinement initiates a utilitarian process where he ponders the uselessness of his ways, regrets past actions, and forms resolutions toward a new lifestyle. The public often believes this but it is a myth and a lie. We inmates used to say: "If a man is rehabilitated in the prison process it is in spite of the system, not because of it."

Prison is an unreal experience. The prisoner lives life in a dream with little feeling of the passage of time. The mist of unreality, or fantasy, evaporates only when the inmate has a visit, or a parole hearing, or some other contact with the outside world. This trancelike condition may explain why the effect of prison is slight, and why the recidivism rate is so high. The work program, educational tokenism, drug therapy, and other aspects of the correctional program may serve as "cooling out" processes, but they have little permanent effect on the personality.

In fact, prison may well encourage its members to function on lower physcial and psychological levels. In depriving the inmate of numerous experiences of adulthood, society reduces him to a childlike state of being. Then, when he is released into today's demanding world, we expect him to immediately function as a mature, middle-class adult (Irwin, 1970:109-112).

*The Inmates' Psychological State*

More often than not, inmates compensate for the emptiness of prison days and the loneliness of prison nights by fantasizing an impossible future and a distorted past. When this dreamlike state disintegrates, or is punctured like a balloon, the prisoner often "blows his top," becoming physically or mentally unstable. Or he develops into a psychopath who repeatedly strikes back at his environment.

Life, for the prisoner, means helplessness and unbelongingness.

He experiences what it is to be blocked at every turn, cut off from every normal desire, and often agitated into madness—much like a caged circus animal. One constant danger the prisoner faces is the certain feeling that he can do little about his predicament. Often he is overwhelmed by feelings of emptiness, helplessness, and uselessness.

As any psychologist knows, man cannot exist for long in a condition of emptiness. Man must be growing toward something; he will not stagnate for long (cf. Maslow, 1968:4-8). He will realize his potential sooner or later—either for good or for evil. When a man experiences emptiness over a period of time, he may break under the conviction that it is impossible for him to act as a voluntary agent directing his own life, or to change other people's attitudes toward him. The convict soon learns that he cannot influence any legitimate world to which he is exposed and in which he must function. Therefore, he either acquires an attitude of futility and despair, or he directs his attention toward illegitimate ends.

### The Public and the Inmate

Public images of the offender are often stereotypical. We view him as a "raving criminal beast," "a subhuman," or "a depraved being" for whom there is no hope. We "lock up" people who are already in bondage to their poor economic circumstances and emotional conflicts. We lock them into a structure and process where hundreds of other fearful, frustrated, hostile, despairing human beings are collected and restrained. In the process, we subject him to numerous ceremonies of degradation, many disquieting, humiliating, restrictive, punitive experiences which inevitably evolve out of any maximum security prison setting. We banish our offender to a treadmill existence for life on the installment plan. We often place him in the custody of keepers who do not understand his internal struggles. For the most part, custodial personnel fear and hate him and his "kind," and, in the line of duty, they work out their own psychological frustrations on him, safe from reprisal and reprimand. They are also untroubled by their own conscience since they rationalize that they are correcting or punishing a convict whom they identify as an animal (cf. Rettig, et al., 1977).

Just as the ancient Jewish custom called for the "sinner" to write his offenses on parchment, tie them to a goat's back, and send the goat off into the desert to die for his sins, so the criminal often serves the public as a scapegoat. We, the people, send our "goats" into the desert-prison hoping to free ourselves and society of our sins.

Therefore, what most of us do as members of the dominant group in society is refuse or neglect the ordinary one-to-one identification with members of the "out" group—sometimes because the institution will not allow us to communicate, but usually because we do not care. So, we leave the offender outside the circle of normal relationships, neatly disposing of him—"flushing" him and his kind.

Society's refusal to identify with and accept convicts as human beings has created ignorance and fear both inside and outside of prison. The man in prison, who is locked out of the system, alienated, and oppressed, feels terribly threatened by external circumstances and by the emotional conflicts generated out of our neglect, apathy, and fear. He feels intense shame and humiliation; most of all, he experiences a sense of powerlessness that leaves him helpless against his situation. What can be more shameful for a man than to be confronted and threatened by degrading and humiliating circumstances before which he feels totally powerless? The offender, in these circumstances, usually feels intense frustration and rage—often mixed with a deep sense of guilt. Quite possibly, he will act, if he gets a chance, to destroy others or himself. Sooner or later he will strike back, and when he does, this often leads to the crushing punishment that he is unconsciously seeking.

### The Sociological Imagination and the Problems of the Offender

If we are going to be of any use to the offender, and to society, we need to understand and deal openly with the factors that contribute to his predicament. We will have to examine, understand, and demolish the faulty assumptions and approaches that have led to failure in the past. We must be willing to open our imagination to bold new possibilities, and apply our energy toward instituting new methods of care and concern.

*First* of all, we must realize that in most instances the primary purpose of the correctional institution or the prison is that of most organizations in our society—to maintain and extend itself (Murton, 1976:106). It solicits, programs, handles, and treats clients. Ask yourself this question, "What if they had a prison and nobody came?" Prisons are in the business of relating to social deviance. You might say that it is in the best interests of any state penal system that social deviance continue in society. Therefore, one might make a case against *a redemptive process that works*, one that would effectively "resocialize," since it would undermine the ongoing penal institution because the prison population would be systematically reduced. It may be a matter of no small importance that on "dress out day" the man at the front gate always waved good-bye to me saying, "I'll give you six months out there, and you'll be back." Perhaps he hoped I would be back so he could continue to draw his check!

*Second,* we need to recognize that our penal institutions tend to be boxed in by their primary purpose for being, by their own discrete policy and procedures, and by the thinking of their officials. Consequently, any dynamic revolutionary change in penal policy is seldom engendered from within the system (Murton, 1976:97-107). New and highly imaginative ventures are seldom welcomed or implemented by the established prison bureaucrat, or by a particular prison within the system.

*Third,* we need to understand that there is little indication today that in the foreseeable future any radically innovative large scale changes will be effected in the correctional structure or process. Let us place the blame for the lack of penal change directly where it belongs— on you and me as members of society. After the President's Commission on Law Enforcement and the Administration of Justice called for massive and sweeping changes in 1967, a Lewis Harris poll found *that professionals in the corrections field were looking for change and were willing to accept change.* Therefore, it is the average citizen, the uninformed man or woman in the public sector who stands diametrically opposed to innovative and imaginative penal procedures.°

Therefore, today in our correctional system—mainly in our maximum security prisons—the primary concerns are with *security* and *custodial care,* not rehabilitation or redemption. Incarceration itself is normally punitive and is usually a factor in undermining rehabilitation. Deprivation, overcrowding, and idleness, combined with the coercive and abrasive life in the "convict subculture" breeds and perpetuates a pervasive climate of criminality. The lifestyle generated by this process usually insures that rehabilitation will not take place, and tends to reinforce the criminal lifestyle by contributing to recidivism, decay, and death (Irwin, 1970:83-85).

---

°To be clear, some administrators are against innovation, e.g., Warden Crisp, Oklahoma State Prison, recently came out against prerelease community centers (*Tulsa World,* January 11, 1978).

*Fourth,* we need to realize that our professional and social approaches to the offended are institutionally centered, not person-to-person centered. Even in the most benign and well-intentioned institutionally centered approach, the individual is not seen as a person, but as an offender, a convict, a unit, a number, or, at best, a client.

Each institution has its hierarchy of authority or chain of command, staff and line operation, rules and regulations, and its own rational purposes to which the incarceree is subordinate. He is always cast in the inferior position within a superordinate—subordinate arrangement, a position which creates resentment and confusion in him, making it difficult for him to be open to help, if it is forthcoming. Is it not strange, and somewhat ironic that, although most offenders have an authority problem, *they are perpetually sentenced to precisely those situations which intensify and develop authority* problems?

Penal institutions are by nature and design impersonal and isolating. And the larger the facility, the more impersonal and isolating, the more complex and alienating its structure, the more intricate and suprarational its procedures and relationships, and the more barriers there are to inhibit meaningful personal encounters.

If we assume that major changes in our penal organization are not forthcoming, is there any process whereby we can act to free the prisoner from his predicament? Not free him *from* his responsibilities, but free him *to carry out* his responsibilities. If we cannot change his physical environment, and the basic arrangements of his confinement, how can we be of service to him? Can we intervene so as to offer our prison inmates the kind of help they require to "make it" in our complex society?

### The Promise of a Forthright Helping Relationship

In my fifteen years in prison I learned that most inmates feel dependent, inadequate, unworthy, confused, fearful, hostile, and frustrated. Sometimes they hid these feelings behind a facade of intellectualism or bravado, but they are there nonetheless. Nothing that I have heard or seen since that time has caused me to believe that they experience anything different. I see again and again men who have been institutionally programmed (i.e., earned high school certificates, learned a trade, gone through Alcoholics Anonymous, group therapy, Dale Carnegie, Toastmasters, Great Books, Gavel Club) getting released on parole into what promised to be a supportive situation. But in a few weeks, or months, they were right back "in the joint." Why? Because the rehabilitative processes to which they were subjected were institutionally oriented, not people-to-people oriented. There is something about the professionally focused effort at rehabilitation that fails to communicate a ministry of help. It is an abstract process which fails to tell the "client" that people care, that someone is concerned. It is always *duty-bound* and never *love-free*.

The first thing that must be done to institute meaningful helping relationships in the prison setting is to eliminate the traditional we-they syndrome common to existing institutions. Relationships must be we-they in a framework of "us"—"you and me, friend!" This would mean structuring maximum involvement of inmates with people in the community, and the community with the inmates. This would necessitate changing the cardinal rule of the penologist which states that the system must not be exposed to outsiders.

The helping relationship is truly genuine and progressive when the helping person comes not from the superordinate position (from which the prison teacher, counselor, correctional officer, and administrator come), but from the position of person-to-person or eyeball-to-eyeball from which the *trained* volunteer comes. In this equalitarian relationship, the "client" is treated always as a person of value—his judgment respected, his voice heard, and his contribution acknowledged for what it is worth. In this relationship, two people get together and consider alternative solutions to problems. Each is able to see viable solutions, and feelings of mutual interest, concern, and trust are generated. I have seen few correctional officers, and fewer chaplains and prison psychologists, who could engage in this kind of helping relationship with the inmate. The institutional imperative for formalized relationships between the "con" and his "keeper" inevitably intervenes. One of the best possible answers to the prison problem in America is the *trained volunteer*. The trained volunteer serves as a "bridge" wherever walls have been erected to keep convicts *in* and people *out*.

Allowing for this kind of person-to-person concern, invites opportunity for the offender to experience feelings of independence, worth, competency, belongingness, adequacy, confidence, usefulness, and trust. He can begin to assimilate a better self-image and a less fragmented and disturbing view of his world. There is opportunity for him to be exposed to authority based on a personal and social competence that he can trust, respect, and appreciate because it is presented to him head-on, not from the superordinate position of the "professional heavy." The net result of the helping relationship being suggested is essentially this: authoritative and guiding relationships can exist— volunteer to inmate—in which both will be strengthened, enlightened, and built up. The inmate will not feel diminished, or fearful, or hostile interacting with this kind of authority. And the volunteer sponsor will gain as much from the relationship as his "match-up."

The most viable opportunity for the rescue of today's criminal offender from his predicament lies in a helping relationship. "No man is an island" (Burger, 1970:1). All of us live in relationship to others. Human warmth, understanding, and acceptance enable the offender to feel that he is a person of value, that people care about him, and that others have respect and confidence in him. It is by interacting in these relationships that the "con" will come to understand that others are not just objects for controlling, using, and manipulating. He will learn to serve and to be served, to give and to take, to love and to receive love. The citizen will learn that the inmate is a person to respect, value, and love—someone who can be "helped" and returned to society.

### Helping the Whole Person

Let us assume that there are three interdependent aspects to our personhood, whoever we are, or in whatever circumstances we are. *First* of all, man has a body and physical needs. He has a need for safety, comfort, and physiological well-being. He must be reasonably warmed, fed, and housed. If these needs are not met, the chances are slight that the other "higher" needs *can* be met (Maslow, 1968: Chapter 3).

*Second*, man has a soul, like his body, derived from God. It is classically defined in three parts—intellect, emotion, and will. His intellectual and emotional needs must be nurtured if his will to live and grow is to survive.

*Third*, man has a spirit as part of his created being. There is an unmeasurable, only partially definable part of man which vitally determines how he will cope with reality. It is particularly in this realm of the spirit of man that we see him as the image of his Maker and can understand his potential to become a "whole man" (Lyon, 1975:58-60).

Man, in his tripartite nature, resembles God in his trinitarian nature—the Father, Son, and Holy Spirit. The Father, Creator, correlates most closely with the physical nature of man. God the Father is the creator, the sustainer, and the supplier. The love of God begins on the physical level in warmth, fullness, safety, and well-being. The Son most closely exemplifies the soulful nature of man. He shows us the way to a perfect balance of intellect, will, and emotion. He identifies with man at all points, understands the yearnings and seekings, and knows the feelings of acceptance and rejection. And the Spirit of God informs the spirit of man, providing that man is aware of God and open to a relationship with him.

In the very depths of the convict, powerful, forbidden feelings thrust against walls raised up to contain him. The prison barriers wall off the offender not only from others in society, but also from the truly profound part of himself—the higher regions of his soul and spirit. Because these regions are strange and terrifying to him, he never seeks to map them for fear of getting lost in areas where he cannot cope. The mind and the spirit of the convict are unmapped territories within which he is prisoner, until he discovers the "promised land" of opportunity, to be and to do legitimately, and to enter into redemptive regions.

The convict is generally unable to discover the promise of a redemptive life alone. He does not desire to, or dare to, because there are socio-emotional and spiritual forces within him—and perhaps within his friends and family—that are as terrifying to him as they were when he initially failed to cope with them in the past. Left alone in his prison cell, the inmate will continue to work around erroneous assumptions and draw inaccurate conclusions about everything in life. Because he intensifies and perpetuates his failure by repeating the untrue assumptions and conclusions over and over again, he often spins the web of his next felony conviction—even before his release from the present one.

He needs someone who will sit down and rap with him. Someone who will go with him into the valley of decision. Someone who will enter the untracked and unknown country of the searching soul and the troubled spirit with him, in love. He needs someone who will be with him both in the valley and on the mountaintop. He needs interactions where he can experience true encounter, not phoniness and facade. He needs to have relationship in which he knows the other person really cares about him, wants the best for him, appreciates him for what he brings to the relationship, and treats him as a person with value.

A friend who can care for the prisoner, meet him at the point of his need, is a *living key* that can undo the damaging effects of past experience. Genuine friendship is the key that will free him from his fear and hostility, his view of the world as a battlefield full of enemies, his compulsion to defend his pitifully inadequate territory, and his continual effort to shore up a shaky self-concept with a phony facade. Caring for him as a friend cares is a key which can release him from his "I-centered universe" and make it possible for him to feel that other persons exist and have meaning. With sincere, earnest help from one who cares, the hardest, meanest, most socially depressed convict may be able to travel out of his broken, dead-end world of "living death" into the sunlight of a creative existence for good.

But caring involves considerable risk. Until he feels safe and accepted, until you have proved yourself to him, perhaps several times, the fear and hostility he has carried may cause him to reject you. Any hint of rejection, domination, duplicity, dishonesty, or neglect on your part is enough to cast you in the image of "all the rest of those dirty, lying, low-life freaks out there." What you will be experiencing, if this happens, will be his attempt to identify you with one of the hated, threatening persons he has encountered in the past. Even if something like this happens, you must continue to create a climate of safety for him by being a solid friend who is consistently concerned about him, even when he expresses his hostility and fear.

### Harnessing Religious Motivation

You will do well to leave the prisoner alone in his cell if your motivation is to "claim another scalp for the Lord." This kind of "love 'em and leave 'em" relationshiop always does more damage than good. Address yourself to the needs of the whole man by meeting him where he hurts. For example, nobody ever listens to a con in prison, so *listen to him*. Listen and communicate your interest in him, your appreciation for him, and your concern for his well-being. Understnd and accept how he feels, and what he says, because this will help him understand and accept those thoughts and feelings that tend to frighten and confuse him.

You must always make clear with a look, a phrase, or a gesture, that your esteem for him is in no way diminished by what he says, or how he says it. You must always *listen* and respond to him as a person of value instead of reacting negatively to hostility or frank language. This doesn't mean that you should never respond with expressed irritation. You would be phony if you didn't, and he would be the first to know it.

You must never respond with ridicule, contempt, or condemnation. You must never play games with him. Answer his questions directly and honestly. When he sees that you have "soul," that you have spiritual depth, he will often allow you to lead him out of whatever is troubling him—his inferiority conflicts, his sexual hang-ups, his authority problems, his existential or search-for-meaning conflicts. You may well get the chance, sooner than you think, to help him find a way out of his predicaments, motivate him to take some positive steps, and help him gain the confidence that he can be a *winner*.

To accomplish this, you yourself must know "the *truth* that sets men free." You must see the *truth* about *him*—that he is a person of value because he is endowed with creative potential for good. You must have the faith to know that no matter how far into crime he has gone, no matter what has happened in his life, he has the God-given capacity to live, love, and create.

You must be willing to try and sever what he did from what he is. What he did was kill, rob, rape, steal, dope. What he is, is a person of value—for whom Christ died. He has feelings, aspirations, and energy set in motion by God. He is a man that has the potential to walk in pathways of the highest and most magnificent purpose.

You must "remember his sins no more." This does not mean that you condone what he has done. Nor does it mean that you condemn. The prisoner is aware of the crimes he has committed and he is looking for forgiveness, acceptance and a new identity. Therefore, you must not approach him as a murderer, rapist, thief, or doper. Only in forgiveness can there be identity; only in identity can there be true meeting.

You must help him to see that real freedom means assuming full responsibility for his existence; that he must learn to make wise choices, rejecting unwise alternatives. If you are a real person who is learning to transcend your bonds, you will be able to help him see that he can transcend his bondage, give meaning and value to his life, and become his true self—a child of the living God!

You will, of course, in attending to the "whole man," help him to operationalize those educational, vocational, recreational, therapeutic, and spiritual opportunities available to him. Beginning with him where he is, walking by his side, providing opportunities for him to seek and find higher values, you can escort him into the land of discovery where he will experience a good job, faithful friends, and growing intellectual and spiritual relationships.

## Conclusion

It may seem that this kind of a para-professional helping relationship is impractical or impossible in many penal situations. True, many traditional programs allow little time to volunteerism and even less to Christian service workers. But the door is opening in many places. This writer has worked to establish Christian volunteer programs in two states. Today in Oklahoma, Volunteers in Corrections (VIC), a Christian nondenominational service organization, has over a thousand members. Over five hundred match-ups are presently in place and functional. Trained volunteers are matched with prisoners who are coming up for parole in a few months. They visit, become friends, help find employment, post-release housing, and serve in other ways.

However, the main purpose of a VIC match is to foster constructive Christ-centered relationships—one concerned, open, sensitive, praying individual outside, with one inside who needs to know that someone cares, that someone stands ready to help.

If Oklahoma, not in the forefront of penal reform, can provide an institutionalized process whereby redemptive relationships are often formed, so can other jurisdictions. Matthew 25:31-46 stands as a challenge to comfortable Christians, especially verse 36c, "I was in prison and you came to me." Meaningful involvement can be one effective process, and a Christian ministry of helping relationships is much needed in the prison yard today.

### Discussion Questions

1. Compare and contrast the concepts of rehabilitation and redemption. Can the notion of redemption be secularized?

2. Discuss the socialization process which most young "first-time offenders" go through in prison.

3. Follow up on the Goffman citation so as to be familiar with his perspective on "total institution." How would the acceptance of volunteer workers be a breakdown of the total institutionalization process?

4. Compare and contrast the notions of "custodial care" with rehabilitation in terms of their respective goals and means.

5. Outline the four or five most important variables one needs to consider in becoming a "helping person," according to Rettig.

6. Describe the "whole person" according to this article. What does this concept of man indicate with respect to meeting his needs?

7. Discuss this chapter from the labeling or stereotyping viewpoint.

What specific steps does Rettig advance for reducing the label?

8. Compare and contrast the need to ensure prisoner rights with the need to promote and build individual responsibility in the offender.

9. Does this chapter point to the need of maintaining a proper balance between the prisoner's rights and responsibilities? Discuss.

10. Formulate a code of ethical conduct for volunteer prison workers and justify it both in terms of the prisoner's needs and the needs of the system.

## References

Burger, Warren
   1970 "No Man Is an Island." Speech presented to American Bar Foundation, February 21.
Goffman, Erving
   1961a "The Inmate World" in Donald R. Cressey (ed.) *The prison: Studies in Institutional Organization and Change*. New York: Holt, Rinehart and Winston (Chapter 1 on the characteristics of total institutions).
   1961b *Asylums*. Garden city, N.Y.: Doubleday.
   1963 *Stigma: Notes on the Management of Spoiled Identity*. Englewood Cliffs, N.J.: Prentice Hall.
Irwin, John
   1970 *The Felon*. Englwood Cliffs, N.J.: Prentice-Hall.
Knapp, Daniel and Kenneth Polk
   1970 *Scouting the War on Poverty*. Lexington, Mass.: Heath Lexington Books.
Lyon, David
   1975 *Christians and Sociology*. Downers Grove, Ill.: Intervarsity Press.
Maslow, Abraham H.
   1968 *Toward a Psychology of Being*. New York: Van Nostrand Reinhold (2nd Edition).
Minton, Robert T., Jr.
   1971 *Inside: Prison American Style*. New York: Random House.
Murton, Thomas O.
   1976 *The Dilemma of Prison Reform*. New York: Holt, Rinehart and Winston.
Ogburn, Larry, #43324
   1972a "A Letter to the People." New York: Fortune News (June).
   1972b "Would You Be Normal?" New York: Fortune News, 1972 (August).
Rettig, Richard P., Manual T. Torres, and Gerald R. Garrett
   1977 *Manny: A Criminal-Addict's Story*. Boston: Houghton Mifflin

# PART V

# SOCIAL ORGANIZATION

# SOCIAL ORGANIZATION

Modern society is composed of a multiplicity of groups and organizations. These vary in structure from the informal peer group to the formal, highly organized bureaucracy within society. While many people enjoy picnicking, hiking, and vacationing in rural areas, three fourths of our population live in urban areas—cities, suburbs, exurbs. Even the lifestyle of most non-urban people is urbanized, due to the purvasive influence of the complex institutions (economic, political, educational, and religious) that are located in metropolitan areas. Our mass society is extensively shaped and influenced by the mass media as well, which also is situated in major metropolitan centers.

The city is as old as civilization. It was in the city that "culture" first flourished, as well as trade, commerce, learning, and religion. It was there that the division of labor and specialization developed to their fullest. There man not only competed, but also cooperated and compromised to develop the major institutions that help regulate society. Louis Wirth identified size, density, and heterogeneity as three basic characteristics of the city. While he tended to think of cities as unwholesome places to live, not all agree. Harvey Cox, in *The Secular City* celebrated the advantages of its institutions. Nonetheless, we must face up to it; most major cities in the United States wrestle with serious social problems, not the least of which is minority/majority relations. The racial and ethnic groups not only encounter the problems the majority face, but also individual and institutionalized prejudice and discrimination.

While the Constitution of the United States says that "all men are created equal," you and I know that this is only true in the eyes of God. Social stratification and inequality are facts of life. Inevitably some statuses or positions are ranked higher than others. For instance, in income, power, and prestige, the medical doctor ranks higher than the minister/priest, teacher, engineer, plumber, or mechanic.

While stratification is inevitable, most Christians question whether the spread or gap between the highest and lowest rungs need be so great. Can we harmonize Christ's teachings with the present state of inequality? Or is business business, and religion merely a matter of the "spirit"? But if stratification poses a problem for those living in a developed country, it is an even greater one for those in less developed countries where mere survival is the main problem.

Today most countries are sensitive to birth and death rates, as well as immigration and emigration. Aside from the developed countries in both the East and the West who have achieved a near zero rate of population growth, most less developed countries are being threatened with a population explosion. In the less developed countries people are flocking to the cities. But, unlike the developed nations, which are highly industrialized and can provide employment for most of their residents, the cities in developing nations suffer from severe unemployment and slow industrial growth. While the developed nations have a large middle and working class that is relatively affluent, the others suffer from extremes—a small rich elite and a large number of poor and destitute.

In Part V many of these problems are addressed. Larry M. Hynson Jr. discusses the pros and cons of the city as a viable place to live. Is it a blessing or a curse? Does it civilize or dehumanize its citizens? Your answer depends to a large extent upon what you think God is trying to do in the world. Hynson sees it in a positive light, a place where one can not only find self-fulfillment, but also serve others through the church's outreach.

Racial and ethnic minorities are a part of most major cities. Edgar R. Chasteen discusses the problems of prejudice and discrimination which the American Indian still faces, and the Japanese Americans faced earlier. In addition, he speaks about "rednecks, longhairs, and hardhats." The underlying assumption of his article is that the egoistic nature of man must be crucified with Christ and raised to a new attitude of genuine brotherhood.

Donald B. Kraybill analyzes the place minority groups occupied in the thought and ministry of Jesus Christ. Surprisingly, his ministry was primarily directed towards the poor, powerless, and despised groups—the stigmatized. Kraybill sees Jesus as a deviant in the Palestine of his day, an advocate of equal rights for women in a male chauvinist world. He challenges you to follow Christ's teachings and work for "downward mobility"—servanthood.

Calvin W. Redekop analyzes the problem of inequality—social stratification. Domination and power are inextricably related concepts. He reviews the structure functionalist, the conflict, and the hierarchy of ascending orders perspectives and critiques them. The Christian approach to stratification is to do away with it—at least within the Christian community—and to work for equality of status. He concurs with Kraybill by emphasizing the "servant model."

With millions perpetually hungry and thousands dying daily of starvation, what should be the Christian response? Two demographers tackle the problem from different perspectives, but each arrives at the same conclusion. Bee-Lan Wang discusses five theoretical perspectives to the problem, critically analyzing each and concluding that "both on the basis of Christian morality and scientific analysis" the hungry should be fed. Peter R. Uhlenberg discusses the possible responses we (in the developed countries) could make to the problems of the less developed countries regarding hunger and overpopulation. He rejects both the noninterventionist and the triage positions for aid programs that feed the hungry, as well as help them develop technologically and educationally. Both authors challenge you to make a personal response to the problem.

# 21
# The Meaning of the City

*Larry M. Hynson Jr.*

The study of the city provides the keys for unlocking the doors of greater understanding and opportunity. What we learn about ourselves and others could ultimately become the basis for significant action. Too often, however, "the most important thing . . . that we can know about a man is what he takes for granted, and the most elemental and important facts about a society are those that are seldom debated and generally regarded as settled" (Wirth, 1936). We take for granted that in the world today most people live in cities and participate in group life. Even more, we fail to analyze what this all means. In order to gain a historical and contemporary perspective on the city, let us examine the relationship between man, the city, and the meaning of the city.

### Man Creates the City

Approximately 6,000 years ago in lower Mesopotamia the first cities emerged. Lewis Mumford states that two of the three reasons for the city's creation were religious. Nomadic people formed cities for the purpose of worship and for burial sites, as well as for commercial reasons. In today's cities however, the domination of religious purposes has given way to manufacturing, distribution, commerce, and other activities—some not so noble. Nevertheless, noble purposes may yet be realized. One of these, according to Mumford (1961), is "to unite the scattered fragments of human personality into complete human beings. Like a magnet people are drawn to the city, the living organism of man."

**Larry M. Hynson, Jr.**
*Associate Professor of Sociology*
*Oklahoma State University*
Mr. Hynson has taught at several universities and is currently teaching and serving as the Director of University Cooperative Education at Oklahoma State University. He received an MA in behavioral sciences from Texas Christian University and the PhD in community development from the University of Tennessee. Broad interests and research in psychology, sociology, and resource development has resulted in numerous articles and several books. Larry Hynson is an active member of the Southern Baptist Church, where he serves as a deacon.

Leonard Riessman (1964), another optimist, sees the city as the highest achievement of man. It is in the city, or because of it, that modern man has accumulated so much knowledge, the highest developed mentality, a high standard of living, materialism, and the power to create. Others see freedom enhanced because of urbanization. "The contemporary urban region represents an ingenious device for vastly enlarging the range of human communication and widening the scope of individual choice. Urbanization thus contributes to the freedom of man" (Cox, 1965:3).

While some may espouse noble visions of the city as a heaven on earth, others condemn and ridicule this idea. "What absurdity can be imagined greater than the institutions of cities? Cities originated not in love but in war. It was war that drove men together in multitudes and compelled them to stand so close and build walls around them" (Peabody, 1971)

The first city was built by Cain after he killed his brother and it is in the city that this killing has continued (Ellul, 1970). Thus others perceive the city to be more like hell, for here is found war, disease, exploitation, hunger, misery, frustration, inconvenience, congestion, slums, alcoholism, drug addiction, psychosis, and suicide. In fact the city has transformed life from a "struggle for livelihood into an inhuman struggle for gain" (Simmel, 1969). Louis Wirth predicted the superficial, anonymous, and transitory character of urban social relations (1938).

More recently the psychologist Stanley Milgram explains stress in cities as a function of psychic overload. Because of so many diverse and varied relations, people in urban Jife filter out some relations, allocate time carefully, establish clear social boundaries, protect and block unwanted associations, maintain superficial relationships, and follow highly specialized occupational goals (1970).

Both sides in this debate present cogent arguments and can cite impressive statistics. This dual aspect of man's creation, namely the city, may reflect his own limitations and potentials. According to the Bible man was created just a little lower than the angels and, like the angels who rebelled, man has fallen from his original state of innocence and obedience. The city thus reflects the very nature of man himself. This fact, in turn, affects another feature of urban life, particularly the socialization of the young.

Because man was created in the image of God, he, like God, also creates. This creative potential of homosapiens places the species in an altogether different category from other animals. For as God spoke and created the world and all therein, so man speaks his social world into existence. But unlike God, man has the capacity to destroy that which has been made as well as to create. Thus destructive elements are also part of the city, man's creation. This is true because these elements originate within man.

Just as God desired communion and union with man, so does man. The triune God created both male and female as partners for each other and himself. This idea, along with the family, formed the basis for community life. Even today community life is enhanced where males, females, and different age-groups all interact as a close social group. Consequently, what man creates in community life reflects part of God's original creation and design. Two are better than one because they can help in times of trouble. So, too, a community can accomplish more than individuals acting alone.

### The City Creates Man

The social institutions of the city are the factories that produce people by predisposing them toward certain values and behavior. Sociologists have shown the importance of society in shaping the mind and self. Meaningful human interaction in family and community life is critical in producing mature responsible adults. Today in our plastic urban environment there is often a disintegrated world for children. Twenty-five years ago one in fourteen parents was a single parent; today that figure is one in seven. Divorce rates are seven hundred times what they were fifty years ago. Several developments in our urban setting have accelerated family and community disorganization.

> In our modern way of life, it is not only parents of whom children are deprived, it is people in general. A host of factors conspire to isolate children from the rest of society. The fragmentation of the extended family, the separation of residential and business areas, the disappearance of neighborhoods, zoning ordinances, occupational mobility, child labor laws, the abolishment of the apprentice system, consolidated schools, television, separate patterns of social life for different age groups, the working mother, the delegation of child care to specialists—all these manifestations of progress operate to decrease opportunity and incentive for meaningful contact between children and persons older, or younger, than themselves (U.S. Senate, 1974:152).

More significant is the fact that both individuals and families are isolated as the social fabric of the community, neighborhood, and extended family breaks down. The responsibility for child rearing falls to parents, a parent, or to no one at all since many times neither parent wants the children. The end result can be documented with these trends:

The killing of infants under 1 year of age—infanticide—has been increasing since 1957. Although the number of infant homicides accounted for only 2.2 percent of the total homicides in 1964, the rate of 5.4 deaths per 100,000 population was higher than that for all persons aged 55 years and over. The 74 percent increase from 3.1 in 1957 placed infanticide in 1964 at the highest level recorded since 1945 (U.S. Senate, 1974:153).

More recently Richard J. Gelles reported what he called conservative and low estimates of violent acts toward children in the United States. In 1975 there were 46 million children between 3 and 17 living with both parents. "Of these children between 3.2 and 3.9 million have never been kicked, bit, or punched; while between 1.2 and 1.7 million were kicked, bit, or punched in 1975" (U.S. Senate, 1977:23). The research by Gelles also revealed that violence of this type is not a one-time occurrence, rather it is repeated many times and becomes a pattern of family interaction.

These findings are consistent with those of Marvin E. Wolfgang and F. Ferracuti (1967). The lack of social bonding and emotional support · in the formative years produces people without feelings. Moreover, a pattern of violence stemming from the home environment becomes a lifestyle and part of a youth subculture. Thus an urban society characterized by love-withdrawal and violence creates children adapted to violent behavior. In fact in certain deprived and lower socioeconomic urban areas, violence and physical exertion are status symbols.

In our urbanized society we do not have time for one another or for family life. What we fail to realize is that these relationships "are the juice of life, the longings and frustrations and intense loyalties. We get our strength from those relationships, we enjoy them, even the painful ones. ... If we'd pay as much attention to families as we pay to firearms and football, this country would be a lot healthier and happier" (Bronfenbrenner, 1977:47).

The city and its social institutions exhibit a certain entropy over time. Institutions tend to decay, move toward rigidity, de-emphasize individuals, and polarize people. The issue of renewal and revitalization become all important. Often most of the institutional effort is toward maintainance of a status quo. Howard A. Snyder examines the church structure in a secularized and urbanized world and concludes that the same faults that plague other institutions prevent the church from dealing with the more relevant issues of today. Using the analogy of new wine in old wine skins, he suggests radical changes in the church structure. "For the ever-new wine we must continually have new wine skins" (Snyder, 1975:23). While Snyder advocates renewal for the church, renewal in the city and its other social institutions is also needed as well.

The direction that revitalization of the city and its institutions takes ultimately depends upon one's basic philosophy and assessment of the root problems. Augustus Certillo (1976) has grouped the major lines of evangelical Christian social thought as conservative, liberal, and radical. The conservatives viewed society as largely atomistic with preference for limited government, free enterprise, and management over labor. The individual Christian applies biblical truth to his situation and specific issues.

In contrast, the liberal stresses application of social research to our urban society, and rejects an exclusively individual approach to problem solving. Various facets of social life including family, labor, commerce, science, and the church need to be considered in this revitalization process.

Finally, the radical view underscores a simple, community life devoted to God and separated from the techno-materialistic urban society.

With these and other prevalent philosophies, several reactions and/or solutions to the inhumanness of city life are possible. Many just accept the status quo, reasoning that the problems are just too complex for any solution. It is a resignation to powerlessness and helplessness and the inability to bring about any significant change. Others advocate revolution. This can be in the form of the overthrow of the government by means of military control, disintegrated elites, and a basic climate of relative deprivation. Still others strive after the ingredients which make for healthy institutions. These include pluralism, decisive leadership, techniques of conflict resolution and problem solving, individual development, and proper moral values, among others.

Finally there are those who see the "regeneration" of individuals within the city as the most appropriate step to revitalization. Someone has said that an optimist is one who seeks to change individuals, a lunatic is one who tries to change society without changing individuals.

John Gardner, former secretary of HEW, once noted that flaws in human nature inhibit true social transformation. Somehow these flaws as seen in prejudice, greed, hate, and the quest for power in order to tyrannize and control others must be contained. People today like Charles Colson, Jeff McGruder, Graham Kerr, Malcom Muggeride, President Jimmy Carter, Eldridge Cleaver, Larry Flint, Senator Mark Hatfield, and former Senator Harold Hughes all testify to "second birth" experience. Regeneration then becomes one approach in dealing with the flaws of human nature.

### The City Is an Objective Reality

The city today literally dominates the whole world. Here are found most of the world's population, the cultural centers, the political seats of government, the industrial manufacturing centers, the mass media (TV) centers, and transportation centers. The city or geographical locations can give individuals and groups identities. Common place of residence in cities is often the basis upon which people establish friendship and maintain continued interaction. Even professional and amateur sports are supported on a geographical and urban basis.

Somehow the objective artifacts of skyscrapers and freeways give some sense of identity to modern man. Perhaps it is because these cities are self perpetuating and lasting. Emile Durkheim thought that this reality suggests the notion of God and immortality. After all a city exists before one's birth and continues after one's death. It is an external reality that stands outside the existence of man's individual or social world.

Because the city is an external reality which was both produced by man and, in turn, produces man, it can be evaluated objectively as well as subjectively. Historically, the opinion of most Americans about urban life has been more negative than positive. The city is seen as a corrupting influence on man's spirit, for here is found secularism, sin, violence, alienation, noise, pollution, and dirt. Data from public opinion surveys of city life reflect this negativism. Even the majority of city dwellers prefer not to live in the city. On the other hand, there is also a more positive evaluation of the city. For it is in the cities that real opportunity exists, and it is there excitement is found—the pulsebeat of any society.

American attitudes toward the city have always reflected this ambivalence. We are dependent upon the city and like visiting there, but at the same time we do not like it. While there may be excitement and majesty about cities, the life there is also prosaic. Something is lacking in modern urban life. In spite of all our technologies and innovations, city life is meaningless by itself. To build cities for profit alone, as we have done, is not good enough. The commercial activity of cities does not necessarily preserve liberty and freedom. In the past, however, there have been grand old cities built for other reasons. "They reflect an official concern with the question of what is the purpose of human life" (Berns, 1973:77). The cultural monuments of the Parthenon in Athens, St. Peter's in Rome, Notre Dame in Paris, and the religious shrines in Jerusalem all point backward and forward toward that missing ingredient in our modern urban life. Cotton Mather put it this way, "Come hither, and I will show you, an admirable Spectacle! Tis an Heavenly CITY . . . A CITY to be inhabited by an Innumerable Company of Angels, and by the Spirits of Just Men" (1710:1-2, 45).

### Strategies for Action

Most of us have lived or may live in a metropolitan area at sometime. In the development of professional pursuits people move in and out of the major urban centers of our society. Any information or insight which comes from readings or studies on community life can help the Christian and the church as they seek to fulfill the "Great Commission."

The cities today are the gateway to evangelizing the world. Paul gave priority to urban outreach because the cities were centers of influence, and a means of reaching out from the cities to the surrounding towns and countryside. In fact all of the cities in which he started churches were centers of Roman administration, Greek civilization, Jewish influence, or commercial significance.

Too often the church's response has been to flee the cities and move to the suburbs. Whenever a group has resisted this strategy some interesting and unusual things have happened. David Mains, former pastor of such an inner-city church, gives testimony to this fact in his book *Full Circle*. The struggle was not easy and the victories came hard. Nevertheless, the vision of Mumford to unite the fragments of humanity became a reality. The large concentration of people with diverse backgrounds, experience, and lifestyles became a united community.

The crisis in the city has been described as a spiritual and moral one. The true resources of cities are not the artifacts, but rather the people. The city is people. It is for these that Christ died—the rich, poor, powerful, weak, old, young, all races, and all classes. What action we take on behalf of these people depends upon our own meaning and interpretations of the city.

## Discussion Questions

1. Why do you think the everyday experiences of community life are taken for granted and often not debated or discussed?

2. Mumford states three reasons why the city emerged. What are the major functions of the city in our society?

3. Compare and contrast the optimistic and pessimistic views of the city.

4. How do the doctrines of the creation and fall help us interpret the meaning of the city? How does the gospel apply to the redemption of both the individual and the city?

5. What are the essentials of community life and what enhances social cohesiveness?

6. What sort of job are the social institutions in our society doing in terms of producing people? How can they do better?

7. How does the issue of new wine in old wine skins relate to the social institutions of our urban life?

8. What are the reactions and solutions given to the inhumanness of city life? Which do you recommend?

9. Why are Americans ambivalent toward the city?

10. How significant are cities to world evangelism? How important were they during the New Testament era?

## References

Berns, Walter
    1973 "Thinking About the City." *Commentary*, 56 (October), pp. 74-77.
Bronfenbrenner, Urie
    1977 "Nobody Home: The Erosion of the American Family." *Psychology Today*, 10 (May), pp. 41-47.

Certillo, Augustus
1976 "A Survey of Recent Evangelical Social Thought." *Christian Scholar's Review*, 5, pp. 272-280.

Cox, Harvey
1965 *The Secular City*. New York: Macmillan.

Ellul, Jacques
1970 *Meaning of the City*. Grand Rapids, Mich.: Eerdmans.

Gelles, Richard J.
1972 *The Violent Home*. Beverly Hills, Calif.: Sage.

Mather, Cotton
1710 *Theopolis Americana: An Essay on the Golden Street of the Holy City*. Boston, Mass.: B. Green.

Milgram, Stanley
1970 "The Experience of Living in the City." *Science*, 167 (March), pp. 1461-1468.

Mumford, Lewis
1961 *The City in History*. New York: Harcourt Brace Jovanovich.

Peabody, Elizabeth Palmer
1971 *Cited in The Urban Reader*. Susan Cahill and Michele F. Cooper (eds). Englewood Cliffs, N.J.: Prentice-Hall, p. 3.

Riessman, Leonard
1964 *The Urban Process*. New York: Free Press.

Simmel, Georg
1969 "The Metropolis and Mental Life." *Classic Essays on the Culture of Cities*. R. Stennet (ed.) New York: Appleton-Century-Crofts, pp. 47-60.

Snyder, Howard A.
1975 *The Problem of Wine Skins*. Downers Grove, Ill.: Inter-Varsity Press.

United States Senate
1974 *American Families: Trends and Pressures*. Washington, D.C. U.S. Government Printing Office.
1977 *Extension of the Child Abuse Prevention and Treatment Act*. Washington, D.C., U.S. Government Printing Office.

Wirth, Louis
1936 Preface to *Ideology and Utopia*, by Karl Mannehim. New York: Harcourt, Brace.
1938 "Urbanism as a Way of Life." *American Journal of Sociology*, 44 (July), pp. 3-24.

Wolfgang, Marvin E. and F. Ferracuti
1967 *The Subculture of Violence*. London: Tavistock.

Wong, James Y. K.
1974 "A Strategy of Evangelism in High-Rise Housing Apartments." *Reaching All*. Minneapolis, Minn.: World Wide Publications, pp. 87-92.

# 22
# Racial and Other Minority Groups: A Challenge to Christians

*Edgar R. Chasteen*

Over 218 million people in the United States make it the world's fourth largest country. The diversity of its people, its historical commitment to individualism, its creed of justice and equality, the practice of prejudice and discrimination by many—all these make American society one of unending ferment and intrigue.

America is a nation of minorities. That is a big part of our problem. American society is said to be governed by majority rule, but it has no majority. What we have is an ever-changing alliance of minorities, cooperating on certain issues and at certain times, holding together only so long as each member group is having its vested interests served.

The United States is one of the most color conscious societies in the world. Our national literature is filled with references to white, black, red, and yellow races, as if such things were real. The majority of Americans think that color is a reliable index of racial heritage despite the fact that science employs half-a-dozen other criteria in its definition of race. But as in other societies, Americans have created a social definition of race bearing only a slight resemblance to the scientific.

The scientific definition of race is based solely on genetic characteristics passed sexually from one generation to another. The social definition includes both genetic and cultural characteristics in a Pandora's box of sloppy thinking, religious perversion, political self-

**Edgar R. Chasteen**
*Professor of Sociology*
*William Jewell College*

A member of the Southern Baptist Church, Professor Chasteen has taught at several colleges including Southwestern State College (Oklahoma), before coming to William Jewell. With a PhD in sociology from the University of Missouri, Ed Chasteen has published extensively, including several books. His specialities include population, social movements, and racial and minority relations. He is also director of the Ethnic Activities Center of Mid-America.

interest, and psychological sickness. While science says only that the races are different, society says that some are better than others. And because the social definition of race includes cultural traits, the number of social races is infinitely greater than the number of scientific races.

Americans talk about the Jewish race as if Jews were born and not made, as if Jewishness issued from the blood rather than the synagogue. European Americans think of Indian Americans as being a distinct race and all of a kind. "If you've seen one Indian, you've seen them all." "Indians are all drunks and bums"—with such statements do descendants of Poles, Irish, Italians, Germans, Slavs, Czechs, Russians, Croatians, English, French, and other varieties of European Americans delude themselves and destroy Indians. To dismiss as "Indian" the hundreds of different tribes, with their multiplicity of lifestyles, religions, housing patterns, family forms, ways of making a living, and their other cultural differences, is to reduce a vital and varied people to a sterile and unjust stereotype.

### The Indians: A Case Study

Today the descendants of once powerful Indian societies live on those few million acres of desert, mountain, and swamp which "white" Americans did not want. Every now and then the "white" man, sometimes the White House, has a change of mind and decides that the Indian land is desirable after all. Treaty and law not withstanding, the reservation shrinks in size when oil or uranium is discovered, a new lake is built, lumber is needed, or more pasture is wanted. Can you imagine the Indians taking back Manhattan Island? Yet in 1834 most of what is now Oklahoma was designated Indian Territory by Congress, and many tribes were forced (the "Trail of Tears" it was called) to move to this land. In 1907, Oklahoma, however, was made a state, and the Indian land was reduced to a few parcels in north central and western Oklahoma. We think of an Indian giver as one who takes back a promise, but it was the "white" man who took back the land. Nonetheless it is the Indian who is called unreliable. But that's what power does. You can take what you want, yet see to it that it is the other fellow's reputation that suffers.

Many a European American longs for the "good old days" when his or her particular group flourished. Certainly native Americans (such as the Blackfeet, the Sioux, the Chippewa, the Crow, the Cheyenne, the Arapaho, the Shoshone, the Pueblo, the Navajo, the Zuni, the

Apache, the Choctaw, the Potawatomi, the Winnebago, the Oneida, the Onondaga, the Penobscot, the Cherokee, the Eskimo, the Creek, the Seminole, the Ute, the Caddo, the Delaware, the Wichita, the Kiowa, the Modoc, the Hopi, the Seneca, the Sac, the Fox, the Shawnee, the Kickapoo, the Wyandotte, the Gros Ventre, the Cree, and the scores of other Indian tribes) long for the good old days before America was "discovered," when their societies flowered, making war and peace, worshiping and working as they chose. Those were the good old days when an Apache was not a camping trailer, a Pontiac was not a car, a Winnebago was not a motor home, Kickapoo was not a drink, the Seminoles were not a football team, and Indians lived in India.

### The Changing Character of Indian Policy

The relationship of whites to Indians in the colonies, and later the United States, has run the range of human interaction—conflict and competition, assimilation and amalgamation, segregation and stratification, removal and mass expulsion, pograms and genocide, tolerance and sympathy, sentimental romanticism and cultural pluralism. Many of these attitudes and actions occurred simultaneously throughout the four centuries of Indian and white encounters. It is possible, however, to identify the dominant themes of specific times.

1. *Indian tribes as separate nations.* From about 1700 to 1850, white settlers followed a policy of dealing with the various tribes as independent sovereign powers, recognizing their title to land, paying them for it, and negotiating by treaty. This policy led to conflict for at least two different reasons. First was the fact that the Indian concept of land and property was different from that of the European settlers. The Indians believed that air, water, and land belonged to the Great Spirit and were free to all men. They owned no real estate, and they felt that whites who claimed land were sacrilegious; hence came religious resistance to the settlers by the Indians. Thus occurred another of the ironies of history and society: Europeans came to America to establish religious freedom, but their coming destroyed that freedom for the people who were already here.

This policy of dealing with Indians by treaty led to conflict for a second reason. To draw up and sign a treaty implies a degree of social organization and authority which neither Indian nor white society possessed. No one Indian tribe could sign a document binding another to a particular course of action. The governing processes in the colonies were so poorly developed that any document was practically meaningless. Since the colonies and the early states had no means of insuring that whites would honor their treaties, such documents often produced the very conflict they were designed to avoid.

2. *The segregation of Indians.* Beginning about 1850 the policy of dealing with Indian tribes as sovereign nations ended, and in its place came a policy of segregation and isolation. Between 1850 and 1880, most of the Indian reservations, now numbering about 200, were set up. Prior to the Civil War many Indian claims to land were declared illegal by white courts and legislation. After the war, lands belonging to Indians who had fought for the Confederacy were taken from them, even though white Southerners were allowed to keep their property. In 1871 an act was passed making it illegal to enter into treaties with Indians. From that time on they were declared wards of the federal government and were to be segregated from white society by confining them to reservations.

This policy of segregation was no more successful than the prior policy of negotiation. Many Indian tribes were nomads and hunters and could not adjust to the more stationary and settled life of the reservation. The white man's law confined the Indian to reservations but it did not change the migratory habits of the buffalo, deer, and other animals on which the Indians depended for food and shelter. Since Indians could no longer move about in search of game, they quickly became dependent on food rations supplied by the government through Indian agents. Many of these agents used their position to abuse the Indians and to increase their profits by withholding a portion of the Indian food allotment and selling it to white settlers. Because Indian society had been structured around food getting and preparation, the denial of their right to hunt disrupted every aspect of their lives and reduced them to a state of despised dependency.

3. *Compulsory assimilation.* By 1880 this policy of segregation was such an obvious failure that a new policy was begun designed to assimilate Indians into white culture. This policy set out to destroy tribal organization and to suppress Indian religion and language. Indian hair was cut in length and styled in a manner acceptable to white standards. Native Indian dress was outlawed, and other features of Indian culture were annihilated. Indian reservations were broken up by the General Allotment Act of 1887 which gave each Indian a share of reservation land. This end to communal ownership of land was intended to create a

spirit of free enterprise—selfishness—in the Indian and make him more like whites (Berry, 1951: 235).

During this period of time, Indian children were put in boarding schools in an effort to weaken family ties and to indoctrinate Indian children with white values. Though these schools did not succeed in transforming the Indian young into "apples"—red on the outside, white on the inside—they did teach a consuming self-hatred reflected clearly in rising rates of Indian alcoholism, suicide, and a pervasive apathy.

This policy of compulsory assimilation dominated Indian-white relations for some forty years, from the 1880s to the 1920s. It seems odd that such great efforts to assimilate Indians during this period did not include making them citizens. But such was the case. Not until 1924 were Indians granted American citizenship, and it was years after that before they were given the right to vote. It seemed as though white society wanted to transform the Indian, yet at the same time keep him "in his place."

White society was not successful in its efforts to assimilate Indians, but the policy was not without effect:

> The boarding school nearly destroyed the Indian's family institution, and the concerted attack upon his culture had a devastating effect. Economically it ruined him. When the Dawes Act was passed in 1887, Indians owned some 140 million acres of land, an area larger than the state of California. Within 45 years they had lost all but 48 million acres, and a large part of what remained had never been good land and much of it had become worthless through overgrazing. An investigation made in the 1920s revealed that only 2 percent of the Indians had incomes of over $500 a year. Death rates and infant mortality were extremely high, tuberculosis and trachoma were widespread, housing conditions were appalling, sanitary provisions were lacking, diet was poor, and the reservation, far from disappearing, was the only friendly refuge for children leaving the boarding schools and the center of existence for those who never went to school (Berry, 1951:237).

4. *A policy of pluralism.* Under President Herbert Hoover in the early 1930s, a new Indian policy of cultural pluralism began. On June 18, 1934, the Indian Reorganization Act was passed. The philosophy of this act was stated by John Collier, Commissioner of Indian Affairs, as the "simple principle of treating the Indians as normal human beings capable of working out a normal adjustment to and a satisfying life

within the framework of American civilization, yet maintaining the best of their own culture and racial idiosyncrasies" (Berry, 1951:238). This policy encouraged the redevelopment of Indian tribes, religion, family, arts and crafts, as well as other features of Indian culture.

It's difficult, if not impossible, however, for a people who have been subjugated and dependent for generations to regain their identity and integrity. What makes it especially difficult is that the majority of the population loses patience with the experiment when the inevitable tensions and conflict arise. And because the majority always possesses the power to institute still another policy, another effort to accomplish another objective always follows.

5. *Back to assimilation.* And so it was in the early 1950s that the official U.S. Government policy shifted back to assimilation. In 1953 Congress passed Joint Resolution 108 which terminated the status of Indians as Federal charges and gave to individual states the right to govern Indian affairs within their borders. This meant that states were free to take Indian land and destroy Indian organization. This policy was strongly supported by the timber, ranching, and mining industries who stood to reap great profits from the forced sale of Indian land.

In 1961, a conference was held in Chicago which called for an end to this policy and for greater involvement of Indians in shaping future policies.

With the Civil Rights Movement among black Americans during the 1960s, Indians began to see that they could have a bigger role in deciding what happened to them. With the coming of age of the post World War II Indian generation, the emergence of "black power" in 1965 and "red power" shortly thereafter, the American Indian has demanded that policies be made by and for Indians. Tribal councils have been strengthened, jobs and industries have been attracted to the reservation, Indians have begun to discover that "red is beautiful," and a long-lost determination to manage their own destinies is now returning to the Indian population.

As we have seen, however, Indian-white relations have a yo-yo quality, and no one knows what the next policy will be. Indian, black, Oriental, and all other American racial and ethnic minorities never know how they will fare from the next political deals which usually place their interests second to those of winning an election or maintaining power in some other form.

To be an Indian in modern American society is in a very real sense to be unreal and *a*historical. It is this unreal feeling that has been welling up inside the Indian people and threatens to make the 1980s the most decisive in history for Indians. Indians are reexamining themselves in an effort to redefine a new social structure for their people. Tribes are reordering their priorities to account for the obvious discrepancies between their goals and the goals whites have defined for them. Indians are searching for a middle way, a way to remain Indian and yet deal with a white society.

### The Political Definition of Minority Rights

Rutherford B. Hayes compromised the newly won rights of black Americans in 1876 in order to win the presidency. His Southern strategy was essentially the same as that of Richard Nixon in 1968 and 1972: appease the whites because that is where the votes are. If blacks are relegated to second-class citizenship in the process, that is unfortunate. But politicians enter elections with winning in mind. If they must rewrite the rules of the game to accomplish that objective, so be it.

*The Case of the Japanese American*

Japanese Americans also learned that political expediency often speaks louder than humanitarian principles or constitutional rights. When Japan bombed Pearl Harbor in 1941, Japanese Americans found themselves suspected of political treason and denied the protection of law. White Californians began to urge the federal government to do something about the Japanese Americans. So it was that President Franklin D. Roosevelt authorized the removal of all West Coast Japanese Americans to relocation centers in other parts of the country. These centers were little more than concentration camps where the government herded thousands of Americans, there to be locked up for years without indictment or trial.

White America permitted and justified this gross denial of legal rights by claiming that it was a necessity of war. Since the United States was at war with Japan, Japanese Americans had to be considered potential saboteurs and fifth columnists. National security demanded that they be confined and isolated. So at least the official reasoning went. But America was also at war with Germany and Italy, yet German and Italian Americans were not rounded up and locked away. Why the difference?

No one can say for sure, but two things are obvious. First is the fact that Japanese Americans owned much valuable farm land in California, as well as many prosperous businesses. They were forced to sell these on a few hours notice, and many simply had to abandon their property. It was the whites in the California area who agitated for Japanese American removal, and it was whites in the California area who realized huge profits from the property the Japanese had to leave. It was, at the very least, a most fortunate coincidence that the exercise of patriotism by native Californians (as the whites called themselves) went hand in hand with a profitable business deal. One cannot help but wonder whether patriotism or profit was uppermost in their minds at the time.

The second thing that must be mentioned in accounting for Japanese removal, and not German or Italian, is racism. It does seem uncommonly strange that the one group which differed in physical appearance from white America just happened to be the group that was jailed. Of course it did not just happen. When put together with the history of black Americans, Indian Americans, Mexican Americans, Chinese Americans, and other physically distinct Americans, this treatment of Japanese Americans makes sense when explained in terms of white racism—a psychological and political tendency to react to color in a hostile and stereotyped fashion.

### Rednecks, Longhairs, and Hardhats: Notes on the New American Tribalism

Color is the usual basis of discrimination in most societies. The reason is fairly obvious. Color differences are highly visible and are not subject to change. Individuals or groups discriminated against because of their religion, their politics, their lack of education, their dress, or any number of other acquired characteristics can change, or they can pretend to if they so desire and if they wish to escape discrimination. A person's color, on the other hand, cannot respond to social pressures. An undesirable status based on one's color can be protested in a variety of ways, but it cannot be prevented by a change in color. If people were chameleons and able to adopt the protective coloration of their social environment, the character of social interaction would be profoundly changed. Individuals could decide what color would be of the greatest social benefit to them and color themselves accordingly.

Though color is the usual basis of discrimination, it is not the only one. Other factors behind discrimination are the amount of education, length of hair, and the type of work one does. Rednecks, longhairs, and hardhats are prominent victims and mutual antagonists in present-day America. These groups confront each other with an intensity that might strike the uninvolved observer as comic farce, if it were not so potentially destructive. These groups are deadly serious and socially dangerous.

Of the three groups, longhairs are the easiest to recognize. Their shoulder-length tresses are a throwback to the days of Wild Bill Hickock and Jesus Christ, decidedly different from the crew cuts and mohawks of the 1950s. Just as longhairs are the easiest to recognize, so are they the easiest to join or to quit. Skipping a few haircuts will get you in, and a visit to the barber will get you out.

It might seem that a status so easily acquired and surrendered would evoke little social reaction. Not so! The hostility directed toward longhairs by rednecks and hardhats is reminiscent of the race riots and lynchings of the 1920s and 1930s. Longhair to these two tribes is an enemy uniform, signifying an alien and unworthy creature incapable of ordinary human emotions and actions. In an almost ritual reenactment of such childhood games as cowboys and Indians, dress-up, hide-and-seek, and charades, rednecks, longhairs, and hardhats play a game of social interaction which no call to supper can end. How did such relationships develop? To answer that question we must first describe these three tribes.

## Rednecks

Rednecks are those Americans, usually of rural residence, always of rural origin, who have done little traveling and have little education. They can, in most cases, write, read, and figure, but their value systems and thought patterns have been fashioned by the provincial prejudices of their isolated, insulated, uninformed little communities. They are hostile towards strangers and foreign ideas, which they define as anybody or anything coming from further away than the county seat. A "fur piece" in their dictionary is not something to wear, but the distance between themselves and the outside world. Physically, they reside in the present; psychologically they live in a dream world where only those identical to themselves have a right to exist. In trying to make the physical world conform to their psychological image, their dream becomes a nightmare to which the whole society is unwillingly subjected.

Rednecks are not easily recognized on sight, particularly today. Overalls and denim shirts are no longer peculiar to this tribe, having been adopted by the longhairs as a symbol of their rejection of materialism. Of course, the presence of shoes and the absence of abundant hair still make it possible to distinguish the redneck from the longhair by visual inspection.

Rednecks have short hair, but not all shorthairs are rednecks. A redneck is a shorthair who associates long hair with communism, the devil, sexual excess, laziness, radical students, "soft politicians," and crime in the streets. Like a prize fighter who goes into a crouch at the sound of the bell, the redneck moves to the attack at the sight of long hair. It is a conditioned reflex, just as it is with the bull who charges the matador.

Why are rednecks called rednecks? I do not really know, anymore than I know why Caucasians are called white. I suppose rednecks got their name because their face and neck, when they are about their business of "doing somebody in," becomes flushed. Anger, anxiety, and great expenditures of energy draw blood to the extremities of the body and it is particularly visible in the hands, face, and neck.

*Hardhats*

Hardhats are those Americans who make their living in the construction, mining, and manufacturing industries. They may or may not actually wear hard hats on the job, but regardless of what they wear on their heads, they carry in their hearts an abiding love for "working people" and a contempt for eggheads, welfare recipients, campus demonstrators, and hippies.

Hardhats generally work at monotonous jobs for good pay. They strike when their union tells them and they work where their company puts them. Many of them get even with their employers for "treating us like animals" by stealing from them or sabotaging their products.

Hardhats may be of rural origin, but they usually live in urban areas adjacent to their work. They do not like the city though. It has too many "niggers," "spics," "greasers," "dagos," "wops," "pollocks," "slant-eyes" and others whom they consider undesirable and un-American. They cannot keep them out of the city, but they make it difficult for them to join their unions. And if these minority Americans go to the welfare office because the union hall is closed to them, the hardhats call them lazy loafers.

## Longhairs

Hardhats think of universities as places that make arrogant snobs out of young "kids," and make excuses for the behavior of bums and chislers. To hardhats, longhairs are rich kids who have been ruined by stupid ideas planted in their heads by radical professors and weak-kneed administrators. When longhairs side with minorities, protesting racism in unions and society at large, it only aggravates the problem.

When longhairs condemn the military-industrial complex and criticize the injustices within "the establishment," hardhats think they, too, are under attack. When longhairs take up communal living and shun material comforts, hardhats feel that their way of life is being ridiculed. They have worked hard to buy a house and fill it with labor-saving and pleasure-creating devices. They resent longhaired kids who "never had to work a day in their lives" telling them it was a stupid thing to do.

Long hair, although not as popular today, is everywhere today: the college campus, the high schools and grade schools, big business, the church, government, even the military has let its hair down. From coast to coast and border to border, small town and big city, FHA to SDS— long hair is an "in" thing. In most cases, however, it is only fashionably long, meaning that it is a little fuller and a little longer than was acceptable several years ago. Fashionably long hair, however, does not make a longhair. To be a true longhair requires hair of a greater length than that styled by barbers or worn by style-conscious status seekers.

Longhairs, of course, are status seekers, just as rednecks, hardhats, and all the rest of us are. It is only that longhairs seek another status. Theirs is a self-conscious and often self-righteous attempt to announce to their society that they are different—and perhaps even better. They have recognized the system for its true corruptness. They have courageously indicted it by both confrontation and escape. They have the strength born of conviction and a zeal born of conversion. Their conversion is to a kind of physical and psychological nomadism, and their conviction is that traditional American dedication to hard work and the straight life is a cop-out. It does not permit the individual to "do his own thing" or "tell it like it is." It compromises individual freedom and creates gigantic, impersonal bureaucracies which strangle human initiative and erodes integrity.

Longhairs put down hardhats because they see them as willing slaves to an outmoded work ethic, selling their bodies to an industrial system which pollutes and destroys in the name of profit. Longhairs make little effort to understand the frustrations and fears of the rednecks, preferring to ignore them as irrelevant and to intimidate them with their large vocabulary.

## Why Call Them Tribes?

You may have wondered why I referred to rednecks, longhairs, and hardhats as tribes. Americans are accustomed to thinking of tribes in Africa, South America, or Southeast Asian jungles. With the exception of those red Americans now stared at by tourists who visit reservations, no American thinks of tribes in the good ole U.S.A.

The *World Book Dictionary* gives ten different definitions for "tribe." The first one says that a tribe is "a group of people united by race and customs under the same leaders." Each of the three groups under consideration is racially homogeneous and distinguishable from one another by their peculiar customs. To this extent each would qualify as a tribe under this definition. These groups, however, are scattered all over the United States and would not conform to the second definition of "tribe": "a group of persons forming a community and claiming descent from a common ancestor." Rednecks, and to a lesser extent, longhairs and hardhats are sometimes antagonistic to those of their own emotional make up if they come from another place or hold slightly different prejudices.

But the third definition of tribe fits these three groups: "a class of persons; fraternity; set; lot (now often contemptuous): *the whole tribe of gossips.*" "*Society is . . . formed of two mighty tribes, the Bores and the Bored*" (Byron). Rednecks, longhairs, and hardhats certainly are three distinct classes of persons and each in its own way is a worthy candidate for social contempt. Contempt, however, implies that the group holding such an opinion of another is superior to it. As this chapter has pointed out the intergroup behavior of the entire American society qualifies all its members for their share of contempt. Such an attitude is likely, however, only to worsen an already intolerable situation by producing still more factions and frictions.

## A Christian Perspective

In 1919 the late distinguished criminologist Edwin Sutherland was a member of the faculty at William Jewell College, where I have taught since 1965. He was in the same department as I currently am; then, however, it was called the Department of Christian Socialism. The department is now called Sociology.

What's in a name? More than you might think. Christian Socialism is a bluntly eloquent statement of philosophy and program. There is no doubt that such a department is committed to a program of social and personal change. Such a department would never house "value-free" observers whose commitments were to the latest research project.

Sociology as currently practiced is impotent because it is impartial: a search for facts does not provide sufficient thrust. People, sociologists not excepted, must have a power source, a sense of purpose and direction, a consuming conviction of the indispensability of what they do.

Because the value free sociology of the past thirty years has become increasingly deficient in this respect, new schools—each committed to different, sometimes contradictory, perspectives and programs—have emerged. Marxist sociology is one such school and has exerted widespread influence, particularly in the Third World.

Christian sociology has also been reborn. As yet it is not taken seriously. Perhaps because some think it was tried before, maybe because those who advance it are too cautious or too little known; it might even be that its solutions are inadequate when tested against the unyielding realities of the everyday world. We simply do not, cannot, know. We can only believe—and work.

Christianity is dedicated to the brotherhood of man, the reign of peace, the kingdom or rule of God coming on earth, and the meeting of human need through the medium of human compassion. Christianity is anti-materialistic, the champion of the poor, the defender of the weak, the voice of the mute, and the eyes of the blind. Christianity has no truck with pomp. It addresses no man by title, and knows all men by name.

Christian sociology would rid the world of bigotry and prejudice. Difference of color would become a design for celebration; human diversity would be welcomed as a deliverance from boredom and a provider of alternatives. The Christian loves God and serves him more fully when he works to help other people—all kinds of people—than by any other method.

Christian sociology is not warmed-over Sunday school verbalizing. Its goal is a disciplined and energetic commitment to a world order free of hate and indifference, a world bound forever to the breaking down of barriers and the coming together of people in Christ.

## Discussion Questions

1. How do we join Christianity and sociology? Do we change either in the process?

2. How can we come to see that we are all racists, whatever our color? What do we do about it?

3. If we rewrote history and eliminated mention of racial injustices, would this make it easier for the races to get along? Why? Why not?

4. Can a Christian condone inequality and injustice? How does a Christian oppose these conditions?

5. Why is discussion of racial and ethnic prejudice, as well as many other kinds, an essential for the church and Christians?

6. What can you do as a college student to improve race relations where you are? What is the "next step" you should take?

7. How does one come to endorse group differences, rather than simply enduring them? Is it necessary to do so? Is it desirable?

8. Does the Christian have a different or greater obligation in the field of race relations? Why?

9. What group differences, other than race, evoke hostile behavior? Why? How can this be combatted?

10. Why should the Christian sociologist be a more diligent student of intergroup behavior?

## Reference

Berry, Brewton
  1951 *Race Relations.* Boston, Mass.: Houghton Mifflin.
Berry, B. and Henry L. Tischler
  1978 *Race and Ethnic Relations,* Boston: Houghton Mifflin.
Brown, Dee
  1971 *Bury My Heart at Wounded Knee,* N.Y.: Bantam Books
Deloria, Vine, Jr.
  1969 *Custer Died for Your Sins,* N.Y.: Avon Books.
Haselden, Kyle
  1959 *The Racial Problem in Christian Perspective,* N.Y.: Harper Torchbooks.
Rose, Peter I. and Stanley Rothman and William J. Wilson
  1973 *Through Different Eyes: Black and White Perspectives on American Race Relations,* N.Y.: Oxford University Press.
Simpson, G. E. and J. Milton Yinger
  1965 *Racial and Cultural Minorities: An Analysis of Prejudice and Discrimination,* 3rd Ed., N. Y.: Harper and Row.

# 23
# Jesus and the Stigmatized: A Sociological Analysis of the Four Gospels

*Donald B. Kraybill*

### The Thesis and the Gospels

This chapter utilizes a sociological perspective to describe certain aspects of the life and teachings of Jesus in the four Gospels. Before a Christian sociologist can engage in sociological analysis of present issues it is imperative to develop an understanding of some of the sociological dimensions of the message of the Christian faith in its original social context. This chapter will analyze the ministry of Jesus in the four Gospels, focusing primarily on his relationship with stigmatized groups and individuals. The thesis which we propose to verify in the documents of the four Gospels is that Jesus focused his ministry primarily on individuals who were members of stigmatized groups in Palestinian society in the first century AD. We will also note that Jesus rejected upward social mobility and urged his disciples to serve the powerless and poor.

There are a number of assumptions made in this survey of the Gospels which should be identified:

1. The actual social behavior and teachings of Jesus are fundamental to understanding the essence of the incarnation itself.

2. The Gospel documents as we have them today consist of a composite of the teachings of Jesus, teachings from the early church, and

**Donald B. Kraybill**
*Associate Professor of Sociology*
*Elizabethtown College*

After having served in the pastorate and on the staff of the Mennonite Mission Board, Don Kraybill studied at Temple University and earned his PhD in sociology. He now teaches at Elizabethtown College. His areas of special interest include the sociology of religion, sociology of Mennonites, and social rehabilitation. Mr. Kraybill has written several books and columns for Mennonite periodicals. He is a member of the Mt. Joy Mennonite Church.

material contributed by the writer himself. Although distinguishing among these three strands of content is helpful, I will view them as a single entity representing a holistic statement of the nature of the Gospel.

3. The Gospels provide us with reliable historical evidence of the general outline of Jesus' ministry.

4. Although I will accent the social dimensions of the life and teachings of Jesus, I assume that they have significant theological implications for our understanding of the Christian faith. In other words, the distinct social shape of Jesus' ministry informs us about the intent of God for humanity, since we assume that the life of Jesus was a concrete manifestation of the will of God.

5. Finally, I also assume that the behavior and teaching of Jesus are normative for his followers today. I do not mean that we are to duplicate every aspect of his life (e.g., wearing sandals), but that general principles of his life and thought provide relevant behavioral guidelines for his disciples today.

## Racial Purity and Stigmatized Groups

The stratification of social roles, groups, and positions is a pervasive phenomenon in all societies, and Palestine in the first century AD was no exception to this widespread reality.

The German scholar Joachim Jeremias (1975:274) points out that racial purity was the critical social factor which formed the basis of a rigid system of social stratification. At the top of the Jewish social ladder were Israelite families with pure ancestral ties. Five other major groups of people were under the pure families in descending order: those with a slight racial blemish, those with grave blemishes, Gentile slaves, Samaritans, and Gentiles. Within these major strata there were numerous subdivisions.

### Gentiles

It is clear from historical and biblical sources that Gentiles were at the bottom of the social hierarchy in Palestine. A Gentile was considered to have the same impurity as a corpse (Jeremias, 1975:321). Gentiles were synonymous with heathen. They were considered to be fatherless because, in the extreme judgment of the rabbis, all heathen women were thought to be immoral and suspect of prostitution. The problem of how to relate to Gentiles is one of the central issues in the

Acts of the Apostles. Although the early church engaged in a Gentile mission in Acts, it began during the ministry of Jesus where we see him healing and associating with Gentiles, which was contrary to current Jewish social norms. One of the problems in characterizing Jesus' attitude toward Gentiles is the variation found between Matthew and the other Gospel writers. Because he was writing to a Jewish audience it appears that Matthew may have portrayed Jesus with typical Jewish attitudes (Matthew 15:24 and 10:6). Mark and Luke in contrast seem to underscore Jesus' acceptance of Gentiles.

Luke (4:14-30) places the Gentile issue in the center of the crowd's reaction to Jesus' inaugural sermon in his hometown of Nazareth. After hearing the sermon, Luke (4:22) reports that "all spoke well of him, and wondered at the gracious words which proceeded out of his mouth." Then Jesus went on to describe two occasions in Old Testament history when Gentiles were used by God in a special way. This reference to Gentiles and the inference that the kingdom which he was announcing also included Gentiles insulted Jewish pride. Luke then tells us that "all in the synagogue were filled with wrath. And they rose up and put him out of the city, and led him to the brow of the hill on which their city was built, that they might throw him down headlong" (4:28b-29). Clearly Jesus had offended their ethnic pride by suggesting that despised Gentiles would be accepted in the kingdom of God.

In Mark's Gospel the feeding of the five thousand (6:35-44) and the feeding of the four thousand (8:1-10) demonstrate Jesus' welcome of Gentiles (Swartley, 1973). The first feeding of five thousand was in traditional Jewish territory on the western side of the Sea of Galilee and included five loaves and resulted in twelve baskets of leftovers. The symbolic meaning in the first feeding is clearly Jewish with five representing the five books of Moses and twelve symbolizing the twelve tribes. In the second feeding there are four thousand people with seven loaves and seven baskets of leftovers. Four signifies the four corners of the earth, while seven was the Jewish symbol for perfection and unity. This feeding was on the eastern side of the lake on Gentile turf. All the symbolism in these passages points to the acceptance of Gentiles in the new kingdom. Sandwiched between the two feedings is an episode with a Syrophoenician woman who was a Gentile. As Jesus moves into Gentile territory the woman begs him to heal her daughter of a demon, and after an initial hesitation the daughter is healed.

In another instance Jesus heals the servant of a Roman centurion.

Jesus commends this Gentile by saying, "Truly, I say to you, not even in Israel have I found such faith" (Matthew 8:10). In another occasion Jesus heals a Gentile demoniac in Gentile territory and then instructs him to go and tell his friends about the healing, which contrasts sharply with what Jesus told Jews who were healed (Mark 5:19). In these encounters Jesus is deliberately relating to three Gentiles who were not only stigmatized by ethnicity, but also by sex, politics, and mental illness.

### Samaritans

Apart from Gentiles, Samaritans were at the lowest echelon of social stratification in Palestinian society. The first century AD was a period of embittered relationships between Jews and Samaritans (Jeremias, 1975:354). Jews viewed Samaritans with utter contempt because they operated a rival temple on Mount Gerizim. The Samaritans traced their roots into the Old Testament and claimed that their temple was the true place of worship, and insisted that their priests had pure blood ties to the royal priestly lines in the Old Testament. The Scripture attests to the belligerent racism between the two groups. John (4:9) says the "Jews have no dealings with Samaritans." The disciples James and John were so infuriated when some Samaritans refused to give Jesus lodging that they begged Jesus to destroy the Samaritan village with fire. Jewish leaders called Jesus a "Samaritan" as a derogatory nickname, equating it with someone controlled by a demon (John 8:48). When Jesus was about twelve years of age a group of Samaritans scattered human bones over the temple porch and sanctuary in Jerusalem, an act which exacerbated Jewish/Samaritan antagonism Jews could not eat unleavened bread made by a Samaritan nor could they eat any animal killed by a Samaritan. Samaritan women were considered to be perpetually menstruating from the cradle and their husbands were perpetually unclean. Any place where a Samaritan woman lay was considered unclean, as was any food or drink which touched the place. A whole village was declared unclean if a Samaritan woman stayed there. Galilean Jews on pilgrimages to Jerusalem were frequently attacked by Samaritans. In short, Jewish/Samaritan relations were abrasive and hostile during the ministry of Jesus.

In light of this social background it is astonishing to find Jesus selecting a Samaritan as a model of Christian love in the story of the Good Samaritan (Luke 10:25-37). This was in response to the lawyer's question, "How does one inherit eternal life?" and "Who is my neighbor?" For Jesus to use a Samaritan as an example of perfect love and to simultaneously place the Jewish leaders, priests, and Levites in a derogatory role was an unthinkable act which shattered his audience's ethnic prejudice. This unbelievable story was an outrageous affirmation of Samaritans.

A second extraordinary act by Jesus was his conversation with a Samaritan woman. This encounter was compounded by the fact that this person was not only a Samaritan, but also a promiscuous woman. This act was clearly out of line with normative Jewish behavior, which prohibited public contact with both Samaritans and women. In fact, Jesus violated five explicit social norms in his request for a drink of water. In the first place he violated territorial norms. Second, this was a Samaritan who should be avoided. According to Jewish custom a man should not converse with a woman in public—not even his own wife. This woman had a bad sexual reputation. And finally, by touching anything that she touched, Jesus was making himself ceremonially unclean. By asking for water which she had touched, he was contaminating himself and would need to go through a long series of ritual purification. In addition this is one of the few persons in all the Gospels to whom Jesus disclosed his messianic identity. When she speaks about the Messiah Jesus tersely responds: "I who speak to you am he." In this dramatic moment Jesus accepted a person branded with numerous stigmatized labels.

We discover that the only one of ten healed lepers who returned to give thanks was a Samaritan. We find that Jesus refuses to honor the request of James and John to consume a Samaritan village with fire. These incidents dramatize the care and concern which Jesus demonstrated toward what the Jews considered to be half-breed Samaritans.

## Women

A third stigmatized category of persons which Jesus related with was women. Unlike today, women were excluded from public affairs (Jeremias, 1975:359-376). Outside of the house, women wore two head veils to conceal their identity. Women could even be divorced for talking to someone on the street; in short, public life was the exclusive domain of men. In the house a woman was considered the same as a Gentile slave and was expected to serve her husband, who had the sole right to divorce her. The woman's basic function was the production of male babies; consequently, great sorrow was expressed at the birth of a baby girl, but great joy when a male child was born. A daily prayer offered by the male thanked God that he had not made him a woman. Women were not permitted to study the Holy Law—the Torah. They were not allowed to go beyond the court of the Gentiles and the court of the women in the temple area. During their monthly period of purification from menstruation they were not allowed into the temple area at all. They were forbidden to teach or take instruction in religious matters, and they could not even pronounce a benediction at a meal. In legal affairs women could not give testimony in a court of law because they were generally considered to be liars. The extremely low opinion of women excluded them from public life, valued them chiefly as producers of male children, viewed them as religiously inferior, and reduced them to servants of fathers and husbands. The Hebrew adjectives for "pious," "just," and "holy" interestingly do not have a feminine form in the Old Testament.

In light of this background Jesus' attitude and behavior toward women is surprising. We have already noted his encounter with the Samaritan woman. In another unusual encounter we find Jesus forgiving the sins of a prostitute (Luke 7:37-50). In fact, during a special meal hosted by a Pharisee Jesus spends most of the time talking with this woman, to the dismay and consternation of the Pharisees. In a joyful response to her forgiveness, the prostitute takes the tainted perfume of her trade and anoints Jesus. She is the one and only person who has the honor of anointing the Messiah (which means "the anointed one").

On another occasion Jesus was touched by a woman with a 12-year hemorrhage (Mark 5:25-34). Such a person was considered ceremonially filthy and unclean because she was viewed as perpetually menstruating. Anyone who touched the things which she touched would also be ceremonially unclean. Apparently she perceived an attitude of acceptance from Jesus and was willing to take the risk and touch him, even though the typical rabbi would have cursed such a woman if she touched him. Jesus accepts her and heals her regardless of her sexual stigma.

Luke (7:11-17) reports that Jesus had compassion on a widow and healed her only son who would have been her only source of financial support. Luke (10:38-42) also records the visit of Jesus to the house of Mary and Martha. By affirming Mary's interest in theological issues,

Jesus was overturning the conventional Jewish definition of the role of women as household domestics who could not participate in religious discussions.

Apparently many women were incorporated into the disciple group as Jesus moved from Galilee toward Jerusalem. Luke (8:1-3) names three women and "many others" who followed him and used their financial resources to help support the disciples. By permitting women to travel in public with his group and to participate in their religious discussions, Jesus was disregarding the stigmatized label attached to the female role in Jewish culture. Interestingly the female disciples are loyal in the moment of crisis at the cross when the male disciples scatter in fright. All four Gospels report that the same women who followed from Galilee also watched the crucifixion. In a dramatic moment at the resurrection these women, who were not permitted to give testimony in Jewish courts because they were considered liars, are the first witnesses to the resurrection. Mary Magdalene is honored as the first person to see Jesus after the crucifixion, and as usual, the male disciples do not believe the words of the women who reported Jesus' resurrection. "These words seemed to them [the males] an idle tale, and they did not believe them" (Luke 24:11).

Beyond specific encounters, Jesus also highlighted women in his teaching. He commended a widow as a model giver. He used female imagery to describe his compassion for Jerusalem, "How often would I have gathered your children together as a hen gathers her brood under her wings" (Matthew 23:27). On another occasion Jesus compares God to a woman searching for a lost coin (Luke 15:8-10). In his ministry and teaching Jesus and the Gospel writers removed any stigma that might be associated with the woman's role. Although his behavior appears very routine today, it was radical enough within the context of the Jewish culture of his day for him to be labeled as deviant.

### The Poor

Another group of people who received special attention from Jesus were the poor. The term "poor" in the biblical context has three different meanings. First of all, it referred to material poverty. Second, it was used to include those who were oppressed and despised—captives, slaves, sick, destitute, prisoners—as well as the powerless in the social system. The third connotation of the term "poor" comes out of an Old Testament tradition which regarded those who were humble in spirit as poor. With this meaning the poor were those devout ones who stood before God as beggars with outstretched hands pleading for his mercy. It was this poorness of spirit which Matthew had in mind when he records Jesus' words, "Blessed are the poor in spirit." In contrast, Luke clearly had the materially poor in mind.

In the sermon on the plain (Luke 6:20-26) Jesus warns the wealthy, "Woe to you that are rich," but affirms the poor, "Blessed are you poor." In his inaugural sermon at Nazareth, Jesus (Luke 4:18) proclaims that his mission is to "preach good news to the poor." When John's disciples ask Jesus if, in fact, he is the Messiah, he responds by pointing out that "the poor have good news preached to them" and, probably because of that statement, he concludes by saying, "And blessed is he who takes no offense at me" (Luke 7:22, 23). The disciples are instructed to sell their possessions in order to give alms for the poor (Luke 12:33). Instead of inviting the rich, the disciples are urged to invite the poor when they give a banquet (Luke 14:13). The rich young ruler is admonished to distribute his property to the poor (Luke 18:22). After conversing with Jesus, Zacchaeus decides to give half of his goods to the poor (Luke 19:8).

In a stinging parable (the rich man and Lazarus), Lazarus, the poor man, ends up in heaven, while his rich neighbor who ignored the plight of the poor is condemned (Luke 16:19-31). These passages suggest that the poor, contrary to current Jewish thought, were not the recipients of divine wrath, but were the focus of God's special concern and interest. In contrast to the rich and powerful who trample the poor, Jesus demonstrated particular compassion and concern for them.

*The Powerless*

We also find Jesus initiating contacts with other persons from various social groupings, all of whom were stigmatized. He invites Simon, a Zealot, to join his band of disciples. The Zealots were a left-wing revolutionary group which did not hesitate to use violence to overthrow Roman domination. The radical Zealots were despised by the moderate Sadducees who operated the temple in Jerusalem, and who benefited from their Roman political connections.

Tax collectors were hated and sometimes killed by Zealots who viewed them as political traitors, since they were Jews who cooperated with the Roman oppression. In addition tax collectors were considered dishonest and disreputable because their tax-collecting operations were usually fraudulent. We find a tax collector, Matthew, welcomed by Jesus as a member of the disciple cohort. The Gospel records indicate that Jesus frequently associated with tax collectors and sinners. He invited them to meals (Luke 15:2) and joined in their parties (Mark 2:15 and Matthew 19:10). The Pharisees were infuriated by this unorthodox behavior and mocked him by calling him "a glutton and a drunkard, a friend of tax collectors and sinners!" (Matthew 11:19). Perhaps the most familiar story of Jesus' warm acceptance of despised tax collectors is his luncheon with Zaccheus, the chief tax collector of the Jericho district.

He also touches lepers who are quarantined outside the city walls. We find him healing all sorts of sick people—the unproductive social cast-offs—who typically are avoided and trampled on by the powerful. In addition, he welcomes a criminal into the new kingdom as he hangs on the cross.

In all of these encounters we find Jesus initiating interaction with social undesirables. Although he also related to the powerful and esteemed, they usually took the initiative in their encounters with him. For example, Nicodemus, Jarius, the synagogue ruler, the rich young ruler, the chief priests, and the lawyer all took the first step in relating to Jesus. In contrast, Jesus himself deliberately aimed his work and ministry in the direction of the poor and helpless. The biblical texts do not provide the social detail which allow us to document this proposal precisely, but the basic narratives do seem to confirm the fact that Jesus took the initiative aggressively in ministering to the disinherited, while the privileged had to take the initiative themselves. While it is true that some of the sick and impoverished reached out and cried out to Him, the major thrust of his effort was deliberately directed toward such persons. We find Jesus continually touching the untouchables, loving the unlovables, and accepting the unacceptable—the stigmatized.

In addition to his actions he frequently mentions a similar catalog of people in his sermons and parables; the poor, blind, lame, and the oppressed. This list of persons is at the center of his inaugural sermon at Nazareth where he indicates that in his ministry he will:

Preach good news to the poor,
proclaim release to the captives,
recover the sight of the blind, and
set at liberty those who are oppressed  (Luke 4:18).

When asked by John's disciples if he indeed is the Messiah, Jesus responds not with a definitive yes or no, but by pointing to the destitute persons who are being transformed by his ministry:

> The blind see,
> The lame walk,
> The lepers are clean,
> The deaf hear,
> The dead come to life,
> The poor hear good news (Luke 7:22).

Jesus explicitly tells his disciples not to follow the conventional norm of reciprocity by inviting friends, relatives, or *rich neighbors* to a dinner or banquet—they do not need it, they can return the favor. Instead invite the stigmatized to meals—those who really need it:

> The poor,
> The maimed,
> The lame,
> The blind (Luke 14:13).

In one of Jesus' parables, it is this same catalog of powerless classes who are invited to come to a great banquet, in place of the prominent guests who rejected the invitation. In a vision of the final judgment a similar listing of social outcasts appears. In this case all the nations of the world are punished or rewarded on the basis of whether they have ministered to six categories of people: the hungry, thirsty, naked, strangers, prisoners, and the sick (Matthew 25:31-46).

The categories and images which we find here are not exhaustive. Jeremias (1971:104) reminds us that in the East these are images of the dead. These are people with no hope; ones who find living too miserable to call it life. Jesus brings life to those who are as good as dead—healing, walking, talking, sanity, social acceptance, dignity, and self-respect. These individuals who were denied privilege, power, and prestige in the Palestinian social structure now are members of a new community where they have hope and dignity.

### Downward Mobility

In addition to Jesus' own focus on the socially deprived he also rebuked the Pharisees' status-seeking and encouraged his own disciples toward downward mobility. Jesus pinpointed three tools which the religious leaders used to flaunt their eminent position on the Jewish ladder of social stratification. Their first instrument of prestige was ostentatious clothing. Jesus describes them as wearing long robes with special fringes at the bottom and broad phylacteries to impress the people of their superior status (Matthew 23:5).

The physical structure of social events also reinforces patterns of social stratification. Here the Pharisees utilized another opportunity to display their prominence by selecting prestigious seats in the synagogue and at feasts. In the synagogue they sat on the seat of Moses located at the front of the room facing the people, and at feasts they rushed to the distinguished chairs on the right side of the host. Jesus derides their status-seeking and makes it clear that such behavior is inconsistent with his new kingdom (Matthew 23:6).

Finally the rituals that the scribes used reminded the common people of their lofty position. Since a greeting represented a communication of peace, there were strict ceremonial rules governing to whom, and how, a greeting was to be given. The scribes insisted that men call them "rabbi" or teacher (Matthew 28:8). Jesus debunks such status reinforcement when he tells them, "But you are not to be called rabbi, for you have one teacher, and you are all brethren" (Matthew 23:8).

## Models for Christians

### The Child

The interest in status-seeking is not only a Pharisaic problem; it emerges three different times among the disciples. On the way to Capernaum Mark reports that the disciples were discussing "with one another who was the greatest" (Mark 9:34). On another occasion James and John asked if they could sit on the right and left hand of Jesus in his new kingdom (Mark 10:37). And of all times, at the last supper Luke (22:24) writes that a dispute arose among them as to "which of them was to be regarded as the greatest." After all of Jesus' teaching about servanthood and suffering, and even after seeing his selfless ministry to the poor, the disciples in the final analysis are still concerned about upward mobility and the achievement of status and prestige. To counterbalance their status-striving, Jesus holds up two examples of powerlessness as role models in the kingdom of God—the child and the slave.

When the disciples first aspired for recognition as "the greatest," Jesus holds a child in his arms and says, "If any one would be first, he must be last of all and servant of all" (Mark 9:35). On another occasion when the disciples were pushing the children away so that Jesus could deal with "important" people, Jesus was indignant and said that "whoever does not receive the kingdom of God like a child shall not enter it" (Mark 10:15). In both of these situations Jesus points to the powerless child as an important symbol in his kingdom.

A child certainly does not signify prestige and status. In virtually all societies children are at the bottom of stratification hierarchies, since age generally correlates positively with social status and prestige. The small child has no economic or organizational resources. The child is utterly dependent on other members of the society for care and security. Because of limited socialization, the child is unable to make the fine social discriminations related to prestige which are at the center of adult social life. In the child's mind there is no sense of greatest and least, important or unimportant, esteemed or stigmatized.

Obviously ethnicity, occupational prestige, nationality, title, and social position are meaningless to the young child. The social neophyte is not able to maneuver and manipulate other people to his own advantage through subtle interpersonal tactics. The child also has psychological attributes of trust, emotional authenticity, and forgiveness. Rather than encouraging his disciples to be upwardly mobile, and instead of telling them to "grow up," Jesus advises them to "grow down." He wants them to develop a childlike mentality which disregards distinctions in social status, prestige, and privilege.

## The Slave

The other social role which Jesus holds up as an ideal to stifle his disciples' ambitions for social greatness is that of slave/servant. Although there were few slaves working in industries at the time of Jesus, there were a considerable number of Gentile slaves working in Jewish households. Jeremias (1975:345-351) points out that slaves were the absolute property of their master. They could own no goods and their master received all the products of their efforts, including anything which they were given or which they found. Like other possessions they could be sold or given away and were considered part of the master's inheritance.

In the context of the last supper, as the disciples dispute over greatness, Jesus tells them that among the heathen, kings exercise lordship over their subjects "but not so with you; rather let the greatest among you become as the youngest, and the leader as one who serves. For which is the greater, one who sits at table, or one who serves? Is it not the one who sits at table? But I am among you as one who serves" (Luke 22:26-27). The answer to Jesus' question according to conventional logic is that the chairman of the board is much more important socially than the waitress who serves. Anyone can be a domestic slave or servant—that takes little special training or ability—but few are competent to function as the master of a large estate. So surely the master should be the recipient of considerable privilege and prestige. Rather than identifying the master as a Christian example, Jesus points to the servant and says that his own life was one of service, and that it should serve as a model for his disciples.

In an even more dramatic move John (13:4-5) tells us that in the course of the last supper, Jesus himself took the towel and basin and washed his disciples' feet. In Palestinian culture it was customary for the household slave to wash the feet of the guests as they reclined on couches eating their meal. As the master of these disciples, Jesus had the traditional right to demand and expect that they wash his feet. However, he categorically rejects the customary privilege which is his and turns things upside-down in a dramatic role reversal. The towel and basin are the tools of the slave. Washing dirty feet is certainly not prestigious and fulfilling work. Jesus voluntarily picks up the towel and basin as symbols of what his entire life was all about and places himself in the subordinate position. In that dramatic moment the others are elevated to the position of master—but not for long; because as the disciples join him in washing each other's feet, the whole distinction between master and servant explodes. In this sense the basin becomes the most fundamental symbol of Christian faith, since it represents the spirit and intent of Jesus' entire ministry.

What Jesus has done by his teaching, behavior, and now by his example is to invert our conventional social equations which assume that:

greatness (prestige) = master, ruler, powerful,
    adult, first, top

He inverts the traditional formula to read:

greatness = servant, slave, last, child, youngest, bottom

He is not simply turning the old social hierarchy upside-down. Rather, he is suggesting that service instead of social position is the criteria of greatness in the kingdom of God. In addition, when he says that the last become the first and the least become the greatest, he is mocking our conventional hierarchies of prestige. He is suggesting that in his new kingdom everyone is a great person, regardless of social position. Rather than encouraging aspirations of upward mobility Jesus rewards his followers who serve the "least of these"—the hungry, thirsty, and imprisoned—those who are at the very bottom of the social ladder (Matthew 25:40). In place of ingratiating superiors, Jesus directs the attention of his followers toward the social throwaways, those who have little access to power in the social system.

## Conclusion

In conclusion, it's important to note that from beginning to end, the Gospels are filled with the symbols of the powerless and disinherited, rather than with the symbols of prestige and status. Instead of the symbols of success and power—mansions, thrones, white stallions, swords, chariots, and armies—we find stables, mangers, deserts, donkeys, basins, a crown of thorns, and a cross. These are not the symbols of achievement and social success; they signify stigma, service, punishment, and failure.

## Discussion Questions

1. What new insights emerge when Jesus' ministry is described from a sociological perspective?

2. In what ways is the life and ministry of Jesus normative for his followers today?

3. How do the values and symbols which characterize the ministry of Jesus compare with fundamental values and symbols in our modern society?

4. Identify some of the stigmatized groups in contemporary society which might be equivalent to stigmatized groups mentioned in the text.

5. What are some implications of this description of Jesus' ministry for the mission of the church today?

6. Do you agree with the author that the basin represents the fundamental symbol of Christian faith?

7. Can you identify any situations in the Gospels where Jesus' ministry is not congruent with the position taken in this article?

8. What might be some theological implications of this kind of sociological analysis of Jesus' life and teachings?

9. Does this description of the ministry of Jesus have any implications for a Christian's vocational decisions?

10. Is it possible to serve the powerless and stigmatized today by changing the structure of social systems as well as by face-to-face contact?

## References

Jeremias, Joachim
1971 *New Testament Theology.* New York: Scribners.
1975 *Jerusalem in the Time of Jesus.* Philadelphia: Fortress Press.
Kraybill, Donald B.
1978 *The Upside-Down Kingdom.* Scottdale, Pa.: Herald Press.
Swartley, Willard
1973 *A Study of Markan Structure: The Influence of Israel's Holy History upon the Structure of the Gospel of Mark.* Unpublished PhD dissertation. Princeton Theological Seminary.

# 24
# Social Stratification, Power, and Domination: A Christian Perspective

*Calvin W. Redekop*

> Classes struggle; some classes triumph, others are eliminated. Such is history; such is the history of civilization for thousands of years. To interpret history from this viewpoint is historical materialism; standing opposite to this viewpoint is historical idealism.

With these words Chairman Mao Tse-tung (1972:8) begins the second chapter of the little red book which most party faithfuls in China carried and read. It is not unfamiliar philosophy, for Marxism, on which it is based, has been influential for a turbulent century. But Marxism/Maoism is not the only perspective that assumes the presence of classes, of struggle, and of some classes being dominated by others. Among many other evidences that stratification, power, and domination are real life forces, one need only read the literature of liberation of many Third World countries. Feminism in its many forms expresses recent aspects of the same phenomena.

Although we will define the terms and concepts below, it is in order here to say that social stratification, power, and domination are almost universal historically and geographically. Joseph Kahl, for example says, "Every complex society known to scholarship has been stratified" (1960:14). Kingsley Davis, a foremost authority on power, status, and stratification, states, "Looking at the cultures of the world

**Calvin W. Redekop**
*Professor of Sociology*
*Conrad Grebel College and the University of Waterloo*
Prior to going to Conrad Grebel College where he holds a joint appointment with the University of Waterloo, Calvin Redekop taught at Goshen and Earlham colleges. He earned his PhD in sociology at the University of Chicago with special emphasis on minority sociology and the sociology of religion. He has done considerable writing and research in sectarian and minority sociology. Other interests include sociological theory and stratification. He is a member of the Mennonite Church.

one finds that no society is 'Classless,' that is, unstratified" (1949:366). Robert Bierstedt has stated, "Power, in short, is a universal phenomenon in human societies. It is seldom absent except from those social relations in the narrower sense that the sociologist Georg Simmel called relations of 'polite acquaintance' the kind of interaction that appears at cocktail parties and at wedding receptions" (1974:222).

The exertion of power by one class over another (the actual application of power) is termed domination, or in Georg Simmel's terms, superordination. He states that "relationships of superordination and subordination play an immense role in social life" (1950:183). Dominance is defined, according to Simmel, as the pressure to "break the internal resistance of the subjugated . . ." (1950:181).

We are proposing, therefore, that stratification, power, and domination are universal and important aspects in the social fabric. Before we arrive at the point where we can present a Christian perspective on these phenomena, it is necessary to define the concepts carefully, provide a resume of the theoretical aspects of the concepts and their utility, and the problems inherent in them. But to define these three concepts will not be easy, since other related elements determine their relevance and significance.

## Survey of Theory

### Stratification

According to Davis, stratification means the unequal distribution of rights and duties to various positions in society. Thus, social positions, such as father, or factory owner, have different rank. Rank itself is determined by societal processes which are explained in varied ways, depending upon the theoretical orientation of the scientists. Classes in the stratification system thus emerge because "there is an underlying similarity in the kind of positions put at the top, the kind put at the middle, and the kind put at the bottom of the scale" (1949:371). Those persons occupying a certain position or positions, therefore, are members of a class because they possess similar social status (rank, esteem, and prestige).

Class refers, therefore, to those people who occupy generally the same status in social rank. They may be aware of their status, or they may not. This again depends upon who is defining class. Some people say that class, by definition, implies conscious behavior (lifestyle), while others say that it is merely a category. Caste refers to a system where mobility in or out of class is almost impossible or determined by heredity. The characteristics of classes are disputed, and attempts to delineate the boundaries of specific classes meet with little success.

### Power

Max Weber, who is generally considered the first to have systematically studied power, defined it as "the chance of a man or of a number of men to realize their own will in a communal action even against the resistance of others who are participating in the action" (1972:180). Power, as defined above in terms of results, however, needs further explanation. Bierstedt suggests that "power is not force and power is not authority, but it is ultimately related to both." He proposes three aspects of power: "(1) power as latent force, (2) force as manifest power, and (3) authority as institutionalized power" (1974:229).

We are dealing with institutionalized power in this discussion, since force as manifest power is coercion, and is clearly normally rejected by most societies as undesirable, except in situations such as war and police action. Institutionalized power, or authority, thus is the phenomenon which was defined above as being universal and needing analysis. It remains to be said that all persons who fill any social positions possess some modicum of power. Thus a parent, teacher, student, child, grandparent, the wealthy, and even the poor possess certain types of social power (authority).

### Domination

According to Bierstedt, domination is a psychological factor and not a sociological one. But that depends upon one's definition of the meaning of domination. Bierstedt himself provides us with one of the better definitions of domination when he shows how the majority (not necessarily a statistical plurality—it can be a small group) imposes its will and desires on other groups:

> It is the majority, in short, which sets the cultural pattern and sustains it .... It is the majority which requires conformity to custom and which penalizes deviation—except in ways which the majority sanctions and approves (1974:217).

Domination, in short, may be stated as the exercise of one's will against the will of a subordinate.

Domination is a sociological fact which operates universally. Simmel, who has written some of the most provocative and creative materials on the concept of superordination and subordination, describes this relationship in the form of domination by individuals—individual states, churches, schools, families, military organizations, and many others. Simmel discusses the limits and contexts of superordination-subordination and states that only in the case of "direct physical violation" is domination coercion. In all other cases there is some participation of the person or group that is being dominated.

These three concepts, very briefly defined, are clearly interrelated and interdependent. Dominance is clearly not possible without the possession of power, and in fact, domination may be defined as power in action. Stratification is closely integrated in the dynamic relationship in that dominance implies an imposition of desires and wishes of one group or "class" on another. Superordinate declares that one entity is "above" the other—the subordinate person. In one section, Simmel states that the stratification system is descriptive of subordination. He says:

> The particularly unfavorable situation of the lowest element in a complex scale of super-subordination derives from the fact that the scale permits a certain continuous downward-gliding of the pressure. . . . This is the tragedy of whoever is lowest in any social order. He not only has to suffer from the deprivations, efforts, and discriminations which, taken together, characterize his position: in addition every new pressure on any point whatever in the superordinate layers is . . . transmitted downward, and stops only at him (1950:237).

Power, the last of the triad, is predominantly a matter of social position. For aside from coercion which finally is a matter of physical might, power is usually based on the esteem of people in societal positions which carry a certain amount of rank and prestige.

The following diagram may be helpful to conceptualize the interrelationships of the three variables, with the arrows indicating in which direction the influence or relationship flows:

Domination is a consequence of class, and is the effective expression of power, while power creates domination and class but is enhanced by class.

## Theoretical Aspects of Stratification/ Power/ Domination

Before we review briefly the major theories which have been advanced to explain these phenomena, a few observations need to be made. (1) In most discussions of one of the three elements the other two are usually ignored, and this is not helpful because it allows the analyst to avoid certain value judgments. (2) It is precisely the value judgments which need to be made in order to put the elements into their proper perspective. Thus, for example, studying power without referring to domination and stratification allows the researcher to remain untouched by the implications of the process. (3) A host of other related sociological concepts should be included in the analysis because they are related, but space considerations make this impossible.

### The Structural/Functional Theory of Stratification

In this analysis, we will focus on stratification and assume that stratification normally involves domination, and that both are an expression of power. Kingsley Davis is one of the foremost expositors of the functional theory of stratification:

> Any society must distribute its individuals in the positions of its social structure and induce them to perform the duties of these positions. It must therefore solve the problem of motivation at two levels: to instill in the proper individuals the desire to occupy certain positions, and, once in these positions, the desire to perform the duties attached to them (1949:366).

The problem is motivation to do societal tasks, and Davis suggests that social rewards are the answer. "Social inequality is thus an unconsciously evolved device by which societies insure that the most important positions are conscientiously filled by the most qualified persons" (1949:367).

According to this theory, society has developed (evolved?) a series of requirements which must be satisfied if it is to survive and act. These requisites are the various and multitudinous elements which allow a society to exist, such as teaching young people, regulating commerce and transportation, and providing resources for institutional functioning. In order for individuals to be motivated to perform these functions, society supports various techniques by which individuals are selected to do the jobs, and are motivated to faithfully carry out the responsibility. The motivation is achieved by offering socially acceptable and desired rewards such as status or money. The selectivity in preparing for the roles is determined by power and wealth possessed by the individual involved.

By definition, therefore, social inequality (differential rewards for fulfilling functions which vary in importance) "is thus an unconsciously evolved device by which societies insure that the most important positions are conscientiously filled by the most qualifed persons" (Davis,1949:367).

## The Conflict Theory

This approach rejects the idea that inequality is necessary in order to have societal needs performed, but believes it is the result of power differences. This view assumes that there are always groupings in a society whose power is unevenly distributed due to historical or adventitious circumstances, and that these groups will not relinquish their power without a struggle. This is also known as the "conflict theory" of society. This view "invariably questions the legitimacy of existing practices and values ..." (Horton, 1975:57). This view maintains that social problems and social change arise "from the exploitive and alienating practices of dominant groups" (Horton, 1975:57).

Marxist theory, which is in many ways the leading proponent of conflict theory, has developed a theory of history as well as a theory of social organization. In it, the exploited will eventually emerge from their exploited position and become in turn the "ruling" class, although there will theoretically not be any exploited class."The proletariat goes through various stages of development. With its birth begins its struggle with the bourgeoisie" (Marx, Bottomore, 1963:184). The modern class system of the West is based on the idea that three classes—"wage-labourers, capitalists and landowners, form the three great classes of modern society ..." (Marx, Bottomore, 1963:178).

There are other variants of conflict theory, some deriving from the so-called "formal" school of sociology, especially formulated by Georg Simmel. In this approach, conflict and domination is a natural outgrowth of various sociological dynamics beginning with the idea that man is an "egoist"; it is argued that conflicting goals and objectives between individuals cause conflicts and antagonists. There are conflicts over objective causes and ideals as well as the conflicts among groups over scarce resources. Conflict, however, is also an integral force for the creation of cohesion and integration, which is normally not recognized.

However, at the center of conflict theory is the idea that one group or layer of society is in a more privileged position than another, and that the resultant inequity makes for a tendency to exploit, or even extort. This theory assumes that from the beginning of social history there have been differing contexts which have produced groups with differing perspectives on their environment and other groups, as well as, access to power and resulting domination. Harmony is either a future state or not achievable at all. The main dynamic of the social order is conflict: continuing the struggle to remain in power or gain power.

*Hierarchy of Ascending Orders*

In its historical ascendancy during the Middle Ages, this concept of stratification was described as operating as follows:

> Society is a great hierarchy of ascending orders, in which every man has his God-appointed function and recognized obligations, and at the same time his rights and privileges. . . . All men exist in and for each other, and are bound to each other by an intricate network of mutual obligations (Barnes, 1948:19).

This view has also been termed the "chain of being" or the "organismic" view of society. Society, like an organism, is "nothing but a continuation of Nature, a higher manifestation of the same forces which lie at the basis of all natural phenomena" (Sorokin 1928:202).

This view of society is not new, and Christians will remember that the apostle Paul talks about the body, and that we are "fitly joined together" having functions and responsibilities requisite with our "abilities" or callings. This organic view of society has been prevalent through many centuries, and in the Middle Ages became a dominant philosophy, with the state and the church being God-ordained institutions to direct society and thus considered analagous to the head in the body.

This organismic orientation continued its development in the evolutionary philosophy which stressed the development of higher forms of life, and the significance of the gifted and intelligent. Auguste Comte, the initiator of the science of sociology, followed the organismic analogy and said that the "grades of society correspond to, and have their function in, the three fundamental functions of man's cerebral system—feeling, action, and intellect" (Barnes, 1948:92). From this starting point Comte developed the "Philosophe Positive" or what has later come to be known as positivism (upon which modern sociology is based). In positivism the division of labor within society is ranked according to these three functions, and the "hierarchy" of "being" is adjusted accordingly. From this orientation he developed his famous idea that the intellect of society should come from a "church" which was to be a "religion of Humanity and should be administered by the priests of that cult" (Barnes, 1948:91).

The organismic view of society, out of which comes the idea of the objective division of function, or labor, to use Durkheim's conceptualization, is still pervasive in human society. In fact, it may be more powerful than the other two outlined above, for it tends to have a religious and/or "scientific" basis—that is to say, a natural basis. The former is clearly a matter of accepting the idea that some people are destined to have "authority over us" (Romans13), while the second is based on an extrapolation of what nature teaches us—that there are ascending orders of being. Aldous Huxley's *Brave New World* is one picture of what this view will produce.

There are some other ways of looking at the stratification/domination/power system, but they are basically derivative or variants of the three above. Thus, for example, the seemingly fatalistic, deterministic stratification system exemplified in India would be defined by the functionalist as a variant of the functionalist view. If one is taking the position of a person in the system, if one believes that one's position in life is determined by God, or a religious system as in India, this immediately transposes the analysis from an objective position to that of a participant. And in this case, it would clearly represent the third view, namely the "hierarchy of ascending orders."

## Analysis

As was indicated in the last paragraph, the view of stratification one takes is to a large degree dependent upon the position of the observer. If he is looking at the phenomenon from the outside as a "dispassionate" scholar, he will see something different than if he is a member of an "oppressed" group, or at least emotionally identified with the oppressed. Hence the functionalist view of stratification is different from the conflict view, as exemplified by Marx. Marx, a great humanist, identified with the oppressed and wanted to unite a scientific view of human existence with a program for man's salvation.

### The Moral Perspective

There are several perspectives from which the problem can be seen. The first is the *moral*. The fact of stratification, domination, and power, is one type of phenomenon when approached from a moral plane. Thus if the platform is that of equality of opportunity, such as is widely proclaimed in America, then rigid stratification might be bad because it blocks upward mobility. But a mobile system is good, for it allows the aggressive and ambitious to move ahead. If the perspective is Christian, which espouses brotherhood and a Christian love, then there is, as I shall develop later on, a different view to be taken toward stratification.

### The Objective Perspective

The second perspective is the *"objective"* view which assumes that inequalities, domination, and power are everywhere present, and they must be seen as an inherent aspect of social organization. This position is taken by the functionalist view, where the very nature of society is dependent upon a system of rewards and motivational factors. The division of labor theory, popularized by Emile Durkheim, is premised on the assumption that there is an inherent increase in the division of labor as the society increases in dynamic concentration (interaction) (Durkheim 1933:260).

Durkheim's law states:

> The division of labor varies in direct ratio with the volume and density of societies and, if it progresses in a continuous manner in the course of social development, it is because societies become regularly denser and generally more voluminous (1933:262).

The division of labor brings with it, or is in fact dependent upon a development of dependencies and hierarchies of importance, where some services and activities are more important than others.

Durkheim acknowledges the possibility that the division of labor could create conflict between the various groupings. He states, "If the division of labor does not produce solidarity in all these cases, it is because the relations of the organs are not regulated, because they are in a state of anomie" (1933:368). Durkheim's solution to achieving solidarity is for the "opposite sciences" to create that unity by providing the collective conscience of unity. Durkheim, an organismic sociologist, reasons by analogy from the body and decides that the various parts of the body need the brain to tell them what to do and assure each that it is as important as the next.

Differences in social function exist, Durkheim states, but these differences should not be considered on a moral plane. Instead, they should be seen as interdependencies, with each having its own intrinsic rewards and purposes, and in which each person adapts. The individual's concept of happiness is not something he creates, but it reflects the norms and the collective conscience of the society around him. In fact, Durkheim believes that "individual personality develops with the division of labor" (1933:403). The subjective aspects of differences in position and its meaning are thus totally ignored in this "objective" view of stratification

## The Ideological Perspective

A third way of analyzing the reality of stratification is to approach it from an *ideological* perspective which assumes that everyone has a concept of the nature of reality, a Weltanschauung (a world-view) that he imposes upon the world of experience. Although this includes most of the various Marxian perspectives, it is not limited to it. Thus this analysis of stratification is very clearly a subjective perspective, although the Marxist view has maintained it is of all perspectives the most objective, therefore the most correct. From this view, stratification can be viewed as the result of individual egotism to get the most for oneself, or one's group which is organized to maximize success. There have been numerous attempts to explain the workings of stratification using this analytical perspective. The Judeo-Christian belief in the "fall of man" assumes that it is natural for men to compete and struggle with one another, as has been immortalized in the conflict between Cain and Abel.

Many subscribe to the pragmatic idea that man is motivated by a desire to subvert social goals and resources to his own end, and that the only evil is to fail. Thus Machiavelli in *The Prince* portrays the most bold-faced approach to this view. But other more "respectable" philosophers such as Nietzsche have promoted the idea of the "super man" whose will to power is the ultimate goal. Nietzsche had something to say to modern feminism as well, for he believed that equality between men and women is impossible. Peace "comes only when one or the other is acknowledged master" (Durant, 1954:432). Nature "abhors equality, it loves differentiation of individuals and classes and species" (1954:433, *ibid.*). Masters and slaves, therefore, is the ultimate achievement of strength and nobility.

## The Normative Perspective

A fourth approach to understanding stratification is to suggest that it is a *cultural* or *normative phenomenon,* an expression of an internalized norm which states that "it is a good thing to dominate others." Thus the view of Nietzsche could be one expression of this cultural value which has somehow developed and been given cultural sanctions. This view states it is not functionally necessary to have stratification, it is merely the expression of the cultural value of "lording it over people." There is evidence to suggest that some societies have very little stratification and little, if any, awareness of status differences which would argue for the cultural source of stratification. However, Durkheim argues that an undifferentiated society which has no division of labor has an individualized differentiation, i.e., a stratification of individuals among themselves. The status differences of parents and children, older and younger, and a few other social categories suggests that there is an inherent differentiation which is not due to cultural value system.

Regardless of which orientation or explanation one takes, there is an objective reality to the existence of some type of class structure in most societies. Joseph Kahl's comprehensive survey and evaluation of the various studies of class in the United States not only indicates that an astounding amount of research on class has been done, but also that everyone agrees that a class structure exists. W. Lloyd Warner *(Yankee City)*, August B. Hollingshead *(Jonesville)*, Robert Lynd *(Middletown)*, and others have established that fact in impressive studies.

While there is unanimous agreement on the existence of a class structure, there is less than total agreement about the exact nature of the class system, how it operates, or what its consequences are. For example, W. Lloyd Warner believes he can best describe the stratification system with six classes, while Hollingshead documented five. What is more problematical is that there has been even less agreement on the criteria for determining class factors—should it be subjective—how people feel about their rank, or should it be objective sociological factors? There has developed, however, a general consensus that occupations are closely related to class membership. For example, a medical doctor enjoys a higher class membership than a day laborer.

Income, education, and occupation and the resultant lifestyles are also considered important aspects of class membership, and one factor is seen to exert a significant influence on the others. Thus the amount of income a person commands determines what style of life he can promote, and where he will live. But education is considered as important or more important than some of the others because of its ability to provide upward mobility. Education thus has become an important vehicle of rapid upward mobility and has tended to undermine the exclusiveness of the "blue bloods" who reckon their class standing in terms of inherited wealth and position.

This latter idea infers a self-conscious awareness of class, or an ideology which promotes a class consciousness based on political philosophy or social ideas. This has been defined by Richard Centers as follows:

> ...a person's status and role with respect to the economic processes of society imposes upon him certain attitudes, values and interests relating to his role and status in the political and economic sphere ...(Kahl, 1960:159).

The consciousness of belonging in a class involves several steps: "objective interests in common, recognition of that common bond, and evolving group or class consciousness, and finally, organization to promote the common advantage" (Kahl, 1960: 159).

The description of the class system, and the resultant access to differential power, and the domination which follows, cannot be documented here. In addition to the wealth of sociological research, there is a plethora of popular literature of which John Marquand's *Point of No Return*, or Sinclair Lewis' *Main Street*, are two excellent examples. For those with experience or interest in a cross-cultural perspective, the description of the *hacienda system* in many Latin American countries will adequately describe the objective aspects of the domination of the lower class (peons) by the upper.

### Some Problems with Social Stratification

There are many theoretical, logical, and empirical problems with the material on stratification. A full analysis would require a major treatise. A few points, however, deserve attention here.

1. Most of the theories of stratification can be interpreted as defending or promoting the interests of certain groups or individuals. Thus the structural functional view of stratification has rightly been accused of being conservative and supportive of the status quo. A functional view of stratification does not inherently offer hope that an individual can or should change his lot. Admittedly upward mobility can be seen as the mechanism which allows people to improve their lot, but the "relative deprivation" idea undercuts that argument, since if all were millionaires, those with billions would, under this theory, still be higher on the ladder. The conflict theory is more concerned about the abolition of classes, but in actuality, most conflict theorists believe everyone would be equal when "their" group is in control!

2. The fallacy of composition states that what is good for the group is not necessarily good for the individual, and vice versa. It may well be that a stratification system is a requirement for the functioning of a society, but seen from the perspective of the individual, or a group, it may not be right after all. A parallel may be made with unemployment and the free enterprise system, a not unrelated idea here. If free enterprise economics is built on a certain hard core of unemployed in order to keep labor prices competitive, it may well be seen as a desirable factor from the perspective of the stockholders and managers of the business enterprise. But if seen from the perspective of the unfortunate "hard core" unemployed, it is the cruelist form of victimization.

The counter argument that the people at the bottom enjoy their status or that they do not want to change their position is a spurious argument which reflects either cynicism or ignorance, or both. It is only the most uninformed or the most unsympathetic cynic who could subscribe to the above. The black "Uncle Tom" mythology has been exploded so completely that many of the traditionally bigoted feel that there must be some conspiracy to explain why the blacks should suddenly want to be like "us white folk."

3. The theoretical problem of arguing from the actual or real to the ideal is as sinister as any that can be imagined, since it is so happy for those in power. That is to say, there are great philosophical problems in arguing that *what is,* is what *should be.* In some areas, like physical health, we have not argued that man by definition gets sick

easily, and dies early. We have, and still are moving from the real to the ideal in the realm of physical life. (A recent news report tells of a breakthrough in the search for eternal youth—the freezing of cells for later injection into the same body for rejuvenation purposes). Why should this be different in the body politic?

That there were different views of the ideal is proven by the tremendous flurry of utopian literature in the nineteenth and early twentieth centuries, although utopian literature goes back into the thirteenth century (Seibt, 1972). The utopian movement of the nineteenth century emerged because of a strong reaction to the pragmatic and utilitarian views of the positivist and utilitarian philosophies of the eighteenth and nineteenth centuries. And of course the rampant growth of communalism in the twentieth century is a direct response to traditional cultural values. Veysey suggests that this "cultural radicalism" is a process of reacting to "going through life maintaining the values imbibed during a gradual, more or less routine process of socialization" (1973:61).

The upshot of this theoretical problem is that it is very difficult to tell whether a scientific problem is couched in the framework of traditional cultural values (not wrong in and of itself), or whether it is informed by a higher vision or dream (not necessarily good in and of itself either).

4. The empirical problems with stratification, both in terms of its theory and in terms of its measurement and testing, are legion. The difficulty of defining in an operational way what stratification, class, and lifestyle are have already been alluded to and there are many descriptions of the "real" stratification system. Are there three, five, six, or a dozen classes? Is a class composed of persons aware of their class membership, or do they participate in a common culture? These are theoretical questions, but they are also empirical, because the canons of social science suggest that a theory should have empirical referents.

Another problem is the gathering of data on the stratification system. Society is a dynamic changing system, never standing still or at the same place. Therefore, what was probably a relatively accurate description at one point, soon becomes inaccurate or obsolete. Stratification in "Yankee City" may have existed as described by W. Lloyd Warner thirty years ago, but is it the same today? Further problems relate to the generality of the stratification system—is America stratified according to Hollingshead's five class system or is it a local phenomenon? Is a person who is on the top rung of the class system in a local community also on the same rung in the region or nation? Local wisdom says no, for the "big fish/little fish versus big pond/little pond" confuses the issues and makes a coherent system of stratification theoretically very complex and possibly even contradictory at points.

These points are not to question the reality of stratification as discussed earlier, but rather to suggest that it is a difficult field to study, and even more problematical to establish "laws" of social structure and process which includes these phenomena.

## A Christian View of Stratification/ Domination/ Power

This section will be more of a confessional statement than a careful survey/analysis of the subject because of the limitations of space. It needs to be said at the outset, however, that this topic is one of the most difficult, problematic, and significant of all sociological concepts for the Christian faith. The relationship between the Christian and the world is nowhere more intertwined and mixed than in the area of power and hierarchy. It is a well-known fact that churches are stratified like the society around them, and that the organizational structure of a congregation reflects the stratification/power profiles of the larger community. These facts illustrate the point well.

The biblical story, beginning in the earliest pages of the Old Testament, recount the fact of levels of human kind, of one lording it over another. The Cain/Abel story is one of the most signally important archetypes of human existence, and has haunted us through aeons of human history. And the presence of outsiders—"pagans," "Samaritans," "infidel Muslims," etc.—have come to plague us as well. H. Richard Niebuhr points up the apparent contradiction between the church' message and practice:

> But a skeptic world notes with amusement where it is irreverent and with despair where it longs for a saving word, that the organization which is loudest in its praise of brotherhood and most critical of race and class distinctions in other spheres is the most disunited group of all, nurturing in its own structure that same spirit of division which it condemns in other relations (1957:9).

It requires but little investigation to convince us that the Christian tradition has itself been enmeshed in the web of the stratification/domination/power motif discussed above.

## The Kingdom of God

Among the many approaches to a biblical analysis of the stratification complex, the one that makes most theological sense is to focus on God's purpose for his creation, namely, to establish the kingdom of God among men. The concept of the kingdom of God is foreshadowed in the Old Testament, but in the New Testament it becomes the central theme of God's revelation. As Jesus said; "Repent for the kingdom of God is at hand." Over the centuries Christians have been preoccupied with this theme, as illustrated by H. Richard Niebuhr's *The Kingdom of God in America*. But nowhere has the kingdom of God as a perspective on God's doing in the world been more strongly stressed than by the Anabaptists.

> Early Anabaptist theology did not stop with a backward look at the pristine primitive church. Rather, our fathers and mothers in the faith believed and experienced the biblical call for the death of the old and the birth of a new creation, which was seen not only as salvation for the individual but as the restoration of right relationships in all of life. Menno Simons wrote of two opposing princes and kingdoms. We live in a period of two overlapping aeons, one pointing backward to life lived apart from Christ, the other pointing forward to the fullness of the kingdom of God (Brown in Burkholder and Redekop, 1976:270).

The "kingdom of God," even though defined differently in the Reformed, Lutheran, Catholic,and Anabaptist traditions, nevertheless embodies the kernel of the way in which Christ preached and taught. He promised that at the end of time, the kingdom of God would come in its completeness and fullness. In the interim, we were to live as though the kingdom had already come. Hence Christ could proclaim that the kingdom of God is at hand, while at the same time he pointed to the future time when the kingdoms of this world would become the kingdom of our Lord.

The parameters of the kingdom of God, even if only dimly envisioned or realized in this life, are central to our ability to understand how we can analyze the stratification problem and relate it to the Christian faith. It is most direct if we go to Christ's teachings regarding the nature of the kingdom of God, which is being created already. Christ's life and teaching, for they can only be considered together as a unified expression of God's will, is unequivocally simple. He taught and lived the absolute value of the individual person, and he regarded as sinful all attempts to place oneself in any manner above one's neighbor.

### Christians as Christ's Servants

We can only allude to a few of his *many teachings* on the subject. One statement, the theme of which is repeated in all the Gospels, is: "For even the Son of Man did not come to be served; he came to serve and to give his life to redeem many people" (Mark 10:45 TEV). On another occasion, when there was discussion about who was the greatest, he said, "Whoever welcomes this child in my name, welcomes me; and whoever welcomes me, also welcomes the one who sent me. For he who is least among you all is the greatest" (Luke 9:48, TEV). On still another occasion, Jesus seems to cut at the heart of the functionalist view of the stratification process (status and reward seeking) when He said, "For everyone who makes himself great will be humbled, and everyone who humbles himself will be made great" (Luke 14:11, TEV).

But his life also indicated the ethics of the kingdom of God. He was concerned about the poor and needy, and did most, if not all, of his healing among the poor. He restored sight to the blind and fed the poor. For Jesus, class distinctions did not constitute a barrier, since he was accused of "eating with sinners," and associated with "declassed" people such as Zacchaeus, the tax collector. He was not a respecter of the prestigous and upper class, for he was particularly disdainful of the Pharisees. He was not intimidated by power, for he refused to be cowed by Pilate. The moneychangers and their obvious exploitation of the poor did not impress him, for he was angered *to the point* of using force against them, the only time when it could be *inferred* that he became violent!

### Equality in the Kingdom

Jesus, his teaching and his life, need to be seen in the context of the entire sweep of the Old and New Testament. There are many themes that can be derived from the Old Testament, but none is more powerful than the one which focuses on the fact that God expects the children of Israel to treat each other as equals. If they fail to obey God, the prophets make it clear that God's wrath/anger will be displayed against all who exploit or dominate. Amos said:

The Lord says, The people of Israel have sinned again and again,

and for this I will certainly punish them. They sell into slavery
. . . men who cannot pay their debts, poor men who cannot repay
even the price of a pair of sandals. They trample down the weak
and helpless and push the poor our of the way. . . . In the temple of
their God they drink wine which they have taken from those who
owe them money (Amos 2:6-8, TEV).

This oppression was not a matter of the children of God being oppressed by the pagans; rather it was brother exploiting brother. This
theme is found throughout the prophetic books.

In the New Testament, the theme is continued, and among Jesus'
many statements on domination, none is more universally appealing
than his reading in the temple, "The Spirit of the Lord is upon me, because he has chosen me to bring good news to the poor. . . . To set free
the oppressed and announce that the time has come when the Lord will
save his people" (Luke 4:18-19). And thus he quoted verbatim a prophetic statement from Isaiah (61:1-3).

The stringent rejection of domination and oppression provides us
with some of the elements of the kingdom of God, and among the foremost is the fact that in the kingdom of God, the citizens are to "prefer
one another," to take the lower seats, and "to love one's neighbor as
oneself." There are to be no distinctions between male and female,
black or white, nationality or ethnic background, but all are to be
members of the society in which all men are equal. In addition, each
should be concerned about the other's welfare, even to the point of
sharing coat and scarf. It will mean that we lend without expecting
interest or return if the neighbor cannot pay (Luke 6:34).

But we recoil with apprehension. This cannot be meant for the real
world! It would not be possible to survive even a month if there were
not the creation of capital and that means lending, taking risks, etc.! It
would be impossible to get anything done, inside the church walls and
without, if we could not organize and create a "chain of authority or
responsibility." And of course, though the kingdom of God may be the
ideal, we know that it simply cannot be achieved. Niebuhr concludes a
chapter on "The Churches of the Middle Class" by saying, "Yet it (the
Christian church) remains the religion of the middle class which excludes from its worship, by the character of its appeal, the religious
poor as well as those who live within the lower ranges of economic and
cultural respectability" (1957:105).

The sociologists have the last laugh! It seems to be a fact that the

Christian church has behaved no differently from the rest of human society. Not quite. There were "eruptions" of the "kingdom of God" before Christ, now known as the Essenes. The early church exhibited flashes of brotherly love—caring and sharing. The protest and sect groups in the early Middle Ages, radical reformation and nineteenth century groups, and the communal groups of our day are in various ways responding to the call to "love thy neighbor as thyself." None of these has achieved it fully, or even partially. The Rappites and Shakers, among many others, are only memories. But they pointed to a possibility whose blueprint is roughly seen in the New Testament—the kingdom of God.

### Tension Between Two Kingdoms/Worlds

A Christian answer to the problem of stratification, domination, and power would suggest that the Christian lives in two worlds at the same time—the kingdom of God, and in the secular world. As a citizen of the former, which claims highest loyalty, he strives to live by the ethics contained in the two Testaments, but because he is not free from the claims and realities of the present order, he needs to live in an eternal tension. As a parent, for example, he will de facto possess more power, status, and necessity of domination than his children. As a Christian parent, however, he will obey the heavenly vision of living with his children as though Christ already reigns in the present order.

In regard to the fact of stratification, he will realize that to obtain an advanced degree, a PhD in theology, for example, means an increase in status, and he will be inadvertently a part of the functional system of stratification. But he will not use his position to oppress or dominate others. He will use his power or his wealth to help others. Nowhere in the New Testament is wealth or power condemned as such—it is only how it is used in relationship to others that one reveals whether or not he is practicing the ethics of the kingdom of God.

It is necessary to recognize, therefore, that we face a paradox. There is on one hand a general realization on the part of Christians that the sociological fact of stratification and domination is present in almost all societies, and that the more developed and dense societies become, the greater the stratification and domination will become (Durkheim). Sociologists provide strong evidence that a nonhierarchical system is impossible. On the other hand, the sociologist who is also a Christian will admit that domination and stratification is present even in the

Christian community, *but that it does not need to be present.* Sociological primary groups tend to be less stratification and domination oriented, and occasionally avoid them altogether, showing that brotherhood is possible. Primary group relationships are very prevalent in Christian experience—Christian social relations have duration through time, are face to face, and are often very unstructured, even for instrumental purposes.

The Christian can live in both kingdoms, since he has been called to do so, but he will be motivated to increasingly follow Christ in all his actions and relationships. This will mean that he will obey Jesus in every area of life which will do several things: it will downgrade status differences, result in helping a neighbor in trouble, help him when he is sick, inform him of the reconciliation available in Christ, and in general draw him into membership in the kingdom of God. The basic Christian response to the question of stratification and domination is not to seek mastery over other people, but to serve them. The heart of the structural/functional theory of stratification and domination is the assumption that each person is motivated to enhance his own position relative to his neighbors, otherwise the motivation for the reward system breaks down.

*Goodness and Servanthood*

If the Christian is motivated by the value system of Jesus, he will not "buy in" to the system of competition and struggle. He will rather compete in doing good, which does not carry much danger of exploiting and dominating other people. The key variable is the degree to which Christians reject the values of the secular environment, and separate themselves to become a peculiar people, a royal priesthood, and members of the kingdom of God. Jesus told his disciples, "Nor should you be called 'Leader,' because your one and only leader is the Messiah. The greatest one among you must be your servant. Whoever makes himself great will be humbled, and whoever humbles himself will be made great" (Matthew 23:10-12, TEV).

Christians will therefore express the servant role on the most primary level, in relationships between husband-wife, parent-child, and friends. In the Christian community, individuals will prefer one another in honor, and be concerned about each other's welfare. In this way the congregation will not discriminate on the basis of "class," nor will members dominate one another, but it will be an expression of *koinonia*—fellowship in the spirit where no distinctions make any difference (Kraus, 1974). In the world of secular pursuits, such as business and industry, the Christian will not employ worldly standards but, instead, he will use his influence to help level status, rewards, and authority differences. Profit sharing, employee stock ownership plans (ESOP), and similar practices will be developed to the fullest.

### *"Balkans" or "Colonies of Heaven"*

Christians will not aggressively attempt to destroy status and domination in secular society. The Marxist/socialist system has tried just that, and as a result the means have made the ends meaningless. In other words, it makes little sense to be concerned about the plight of the individual, as Marx clearly was, and then foment a program that destroys persons in the attempt to achieve the ideal.

Adam Schaff, an erudite interpreter of Marx, says:

> Socialism is a doctrine of neighborly love both in its point of departure and in its goals. But since it approaches the problems of love not abstractly but in a concrete way—that is, on the hard ground of struggle for its related basis and goals—Marxist humanism must struggle against what contradicts this love, and so against all that makes man debased, oppressed, exploited—in a word unhappy (1970:173).

Marxism saw full well that the individual man could not be helped without changing the society which forms man. But the tragedy was that society could not be changed without employing violence which hurt individuals that it intended to help.

The Christian way of abolishing the class struggle is to break down the monolithic affiliation of individuals into little "balkan" states, where the love of Christ can operate at all levels of the social, economic, and political spheres. These little "colonies of heaven" will, of course, still bear some resemblance to the secular society, but they will also exhibit characteristics of the kingdom which is to come, but which has already broken into history in Christ.

> The kingdom has come. It is here now. Those who have been reconciled unto God are its citizens. They constitute the colony of heaven in the midst of a world which has not yet acknowledged the sovereignty of the King. ... The kingdom which now is, is the earnest, the guarantee of that which is to come (Hershberger, 1958).

## Discussion Questions

1. How is the increasing division of labor (especially bureaucratization) going to affect the reality of classes and their influence?

2. How does the social system control the tendency for the powerful to become more powerful?

3. What social theory propounded either in this chapter or in the reader best explains the presence of classes, and why?

4. Does the Marxian theory have a theoretically reasonable answer to the use and misuse of power?

5. Each society rationalizes its use of power, domination, and stratification. Discuss this statement and indicate whether it is possible to make an objective analysis of the subject.

6. Most societies have experienced attempts at revising or destroying systems of power and domination. But no society has been successful. What conclusions can be drawn from this?

7. The chapter states that Christians cannot avoid the facts of domination and stratification. What does this mean for the way Christians and the Christian faith affects social structure?

8. What would a society look like that was totally Christian, especially in reference to domination and classes?

9. What would a Christian congregation look like if it were organized like Jesus taught and lived?

10. What problems does a scientific approach to power, domination, and classes face? What additional contribution does a Christian perspective make?

## References

Barnes, Harry Elmer
> 1948 *An Introduction to the History of Sociology*. Chicago: University of Chicago Press.

Bierstedt, Robert
> 1974 *Power and Progress. Essays on Sociological Theory*. New York: McGraw-Hill.

Brown, Dale
> 1976 "The Free Church of the Future" in J.R. Burkholder and Calvin Redekop. *Kingdom, Cross, and Community*. Scottdale, Pa.: Herald Press.

Davis, Kingsley
> 1949 *Human Society*. New York: Macmillan.

Durant, Will
> 1954 *The Story of Philosophy*. New York: Pocket Books.

Durkheim, Emile
> 1933 *The Division of Labor*. Glencoe: The Free Press.

Hershberger, Guy Franklin
    1958 *The Way of the Cross in Human Relations*. Scottdale, Pa:
        Herald Press.
Horton, John
    1966 "Order and Conflict Theories of Social Problems as Compet-
        ing Ideologies." *American Journal of Sociology*, 71 (May
        1966), pp. 701-713. Quoted in Norman R. Yetmand and C.
        Hoy Steele, *Majority and Minority*. Boston: Allyn and Bacon,
        1975, pp. 54-63.
Kahl, Joseph A.
    1960 *The American Class Structure*. New York: Rinehart.
Kraus, C. Norman
    1974 *The Community of the Spirit*. Grand Rapids: Eerdmans.
Marx, Karl
    1963 *Early Writings* (trans. by T.B. Bottomore). New York:
        McGraw-Hill.
Niebuhr, H. Richard
    1957 *The Social Sources of Denominationalism*. New York: Living
        Age Books.
    1959 *The Kingdom of God in America*. New York: Harper
        Torchbooks.
Schaff, Adam
    1970 *Marxism and the Human Individual*. New York: McGraw-
        Hill.
Seibt, Ferdinand
    1972 *Utopia*. Dusseldorf: Verlag L. Schwann.
Simmel, George
    1950 *The Sociology of George Simmel*. Glencoe: Free Press.
Sorokin, Pitirim
    1928 *Contemporary Sociological Theories*. New York: Harper and
        Brothers.
Tse-tung, Mao
    1972 *Quotations from Chairman Mao Tsetung*. Peking: Foreign
        Language Press.
Veysey, Laurence
    1973 *The Communal Experience*. New York: Harper and Row.
Weber, Max
    1972 *From Max Weber: Essays in Sociology*. New York: Oxford
        University Press.

# 25
# The Population and Food Dilemma: Christian Perspectives[*]

*Bee-Lan Chan Wang*

In the last few years, the United States government has faced conflicting pressures in determining its role in the face of mass hunger around the world. Since 1954, this country has had a policy of sending surplus food to poor countries, most of it on easy credit terms. In emergency situations, food has also been given away free of charge. However, since the early 1970s, the United States has not had much surplus food, and these shipments to poor countries fell to a small fraction of their former amounts. At the same time, mass famines have occurred in large parts of Africa, India, Bangladesh, and elsewhere, leading Third World leaders to call for greatly increased aid from rich countries. The United Nations conservatively estimated the number of seriously and chronically malnourished people in the world to be 460 million, or about one out of every eight persons then living. How should the U.S. respond?

In this chapter, attention is focused on what appears to be a vexing ethical dilemma faced by the United States and other industrial nations that are in a position to send aid to poor countries. On the one hand we

---

[*]This chapter appeared in *Christian Scholar's Review*, Volume IX, No. 3, December 1979 under the title, "Demographic Theories and Policy Positions on Population and Food."

**Bee-Lan Chan Wang**
*Assistant Professor of Sociology*
*Wheaton College (Illinois)*
Mrs. Wang obtained a BA in Biochemical Sciences *cum laude* from Harvard University, and a PhD in Education from the University of Chicago. She has done scholarly work in comparative education and women in the Third World. Mrs. Wang and her husband have two children, and the family is affiliated with the Christian and Missionary Alliance. Malaysian born, she grew up as a Chinese under British colonial rule and Western missionary influence.

find individuals and groups, such as the Environmental Fund (EF), an organization of scientists and other prominent persons, who sound the warning of impending worldwide disaster as a result of uncontrolled population growth. EF believes that sending food to hungry people is a prescription for disaster because:

> Each piece of land has a specific carrying capacity ... [and] there are definite limits to how many people a given unit of land can support. Food aid violates the carrying capacity principle by *artifically* allowing more people to live *on* the land than can live from it...the inescapable result of saving lives today will be an even greater number of lives lost tomorrow.°

Therefore, EF recommends a suspension of all U.S. food and technical assistance to any country which has a population growth rate above the world average unless that country adopts population control measures that are stringent enough to satisfy the U.S.

On the other hand, the U.S. Congress passed the Right to Food Resolution in 1976 and established that U.S. foreign policy shall be guided by the principle that every human being has a right to adequate nutrition. The Right to Food Resolution implies that those in a position to extend food aid to starving peoples are morally obliged to do so, in direct opposition to the EF position.

The Environmental Fund bases its position on the contention that increased food available to starving people reduces the death rate without influencing the birth rate, thus accelerating population growth. This in turn will mean increased human misery (there will be *more* hungry people in the future), since agricultural production cannot keep pace with population growth. It appears, therefore, that we are faced with two choices: either we allow people to die today through lack of help or we feed hungry people today and allow them to multiply. The latter choice will result in starvation on a greater scale tomorrow, since we will not be able to alleviate human hunger on such a grand scale.

Whether these are indeed the alternatives we face is the issue of this chapter. If the EF's analysis of the world population-food situation is correct, then the obvious conclusion is that biblical teachings in this

---

°"Depend on US for More Hunger," position paper of the Environmental Fund, published in *Science,* 196 (428), April 1, 1977.

area are ultimately foolish and, indeed, immoral from the utilitarian point of view. The Bible clearly commands us to feed the hungry (for example, Deuteronomy 15:11; Matthew 25:31-46; James 2:15-17). Are we to obey if doing so will mean causing greater total human misery tomorrow, misery that cannot be met by the resources available? Before answering this question, let us examine more closely the premises of EF's analysis. Is population growth really the basic cause of mass starvation and malnutrition today? Will feeding hungry people indeed cause greater population growth? What is needed to bring population growth under control? The following section will summarize five perspectives on interrelationships between population growth and food. Then these perspectives will be evaluated in the light of social science research findings and their philosophical assumptions examined from the perspective of biblical teaching.

## Theoretical Perspectives on Population
*Classical Malthusianism*

Thomas Robert Malthus was an English economist whose controversial *Essay on the Principle of Population*, first published in 1798, underwent several editions throughout the nineteenth century. The basic principles of Malthus' theory are very simple: (1) food is essential for the existence of man; (2) "passion between the sexes" will continue to exist and to result in population growth; (3) population grows "geometrically" whereas at best food increases only arithmetically. The rising curve of population growth together will the straight line increase of food supply means that periodically population overshoots the capacity of given resources to support it, at which time "positive checks" operate to keep population down by increasing the death rate. These checks are such things as famines, disease, and wars, the likelihood of which is increased at times of inadequate resources for human needs and wants. Thus, the population growth curve fluctuates around the limits set by the available food supply, and, given human propensities to procreate faster than food can be produced, most of mankind is poor most of the time.

In second and subsequent editions of his *Essay*, Malthus allowed that "preventive checks" might also operate to keep population growth down by reducing birth rates. These are essentially what he termed "moral restraint" through later marriage, reduced frequency of sex relations within marriage, and no premarital or extramarital sex relations. However, Malthus did not think the effect of "moral restraint" would be significant. Further, he did not approve of the practice of contraception.

The classical Malthusian theory of population implies that an increase in the food supply or income would result in either fewer people dying, or in more marrying earlier and having more children. In either case both would result in increased population growth, thereby nullifying the effects of the additional food or income. Thus, Malthus looked with disfavor on welfare programs in England during his day and, if he were living today, he would probably think it equally unwise to send food to starving people overseas.

## Technological Optimism

Malthus wrote his *Essay* at the time of a debate among English intellectuals regarding the perfectibility of man. Enlightenment philosophy, together with the impressive amount of economic and technological progress made by modern science at the time, led many thinkers to believe that man's ability to produce to meet his needs were limitless. Indeed, some believed that one day it might even be possible to grow "food for all in a flower pot." Therefore, many rejected the idea that the unavailability of food would serve as a check on population growth.

The long history of human population growth, as far as archaeological methods can determine, does contain evidence to support the optimists' position. Human population grows along an S-shaped curve, as do most biological populations in a constant environment. Each species placed in a particular environment multiplies slowly at first and then at an accelerating rate in exponential fashion, until "environmental resistance" exerts significant negative pressure on the "biotic potential" for growth. The rate of growth slows to zero and the population growth curve flattens out at the top of the "S." There is a basic difference between man and other creatures, however, in that man possesses culture, which includes a store of knowledge that is constantly being increased. Through improved technology, man can change the environmental resistance to his growth or, to put it another way, to alter the carrying capacity of the land.

Thus, during the hunting and gathering era, before agriculture was known, it is estimated that the human population grew only very slowly if at all. Man was limited in his ability to feed himself, since he had to expend a considerable amount of energy finding his daily food. The introduction of agriculture at about 8,000 BC brought a revolutionary improvement in the energy output-input ratio of man's food producing activities. Man was able, for the first time, to control his food supply by harnessing the natural ability of plants to convert solar energy into food energy. Civilizations sprang up around the world as a result of the agricultural revolution. At the same time, the size of the human population expanded from about 5 million around 8,000 BC to 200-300 million at the time of Christ, and then to about 500 million by 1650, in typical S-shaped fashion.

Then the eighteenth century brought the industrial revolution to Western Europe. Through the application of modern scientific knowledge man was able to harness inanimate sources of energy, fossil fuels, to supply his needs. In addition, agricultural techniques and medical knowledge greatly improved. Together, these developments increased birth rates somewhat and decreased death rates significantly, resulting in a population explosion in Europe that did not slow down until well into the twentieth century. As the effects of modern science, particularly medical science and new measures of public health and preventive medicine, spread to other parts of the world, other continents also began to trace a similar population growth curve. After World War I, and especially after World War II, death rates in the Third World declined dramatically, resulting in a population explosion in these countries. For the whole world, then, the new knowledge discovered during and since the Enlightenment has enabled man to grow in numbers beyond previous limits.

It is evident, given present technological practices, that we are once again pushing against the limits of the environment. The mass famines occurring simultaneously in different parts of the Third World during 1973-1974, together with the energy crisis, point to the limits of the carrying capacity of the earth. The world's rate of population growth appears to have slowed; it is now 1.7 percent per year (1978) compared to a 1.9 percent last year. However, the present growth rate is still far too high and it will mean increased mass starvation, if indeed we have approached the carrying capacity. Furthermore, the highest rates of growth, 3 percent or more, are occurring among the poorest countries, and, if present growth rates continue, this will mean a doubling of their combined population in less than a generation.

Present-day technological optimists, however, argue that we will be able to support additional billions of people if we can shift our main source of energy from exhaustible fossil fuels to inexhaustible supplies such as nuclear or solar energy. Also, in addition to improved seeds and more intensive agricultural techniques, new sources of food such as single cell protein and cultivated aquatic plants and animals are also very promising in terms of food possibilities. In short, it is believed that man's ingenuity will once again bring about a technological breakthrough and raise the carrying capacity of our environment. Countries that are presently poor should be helped by teaching them to use new scientific methods of agriculture.

### The Environmental Crisis Perspective

In contrast to the above perspective, many observers, especially ecologists such as Garret Hardin and Paul Ehrlich, believe that in many parts of the world, if not the world as a whole, population growth has already overshot its carrying capacity. These scholars believe that no present or foreseeable technology can reverse the damage already caused to the environment. The carrying capacity of the earth has been reduced by such activities as overgrazing (example, the Sahel), deforestation (examples, Ethiopia and India), ill-conceived "development" projects (example, the Aswan dam), and chemical pollution of the environment (especially in industrialized nations). Any attempts to grow more food by altering the environment, such as forest clearing or irrigation, is viewed with caution for two reasons. First, in the long run it may reduce the carrying capacity of the region by interfering with the ecological balance. And second, it exacerbates, rather than eliminates, the basic cause of hunger—too many people.

When a population exceeds the carrying capacity of its environment, the inevitable result is massive disaster. Malthus' "positive checks" of misery and vice, famines and disease, come into full play and death rates rise dramatically. The population growth dynamics of some biological species such as annual plants and insects exhibit what will happen. Their populations increase at an accelerating pace until environmental conditions change (for example seasonal climatic cycles), at which point a massive die-off occurs because the total population exceeds the carrying capacity. A graph of the population plotted against time in such a case yields a J-shaped curve. The extent and precipitousness of the die-off is proportional to the degree to which the population had exceeded the carrying capacity.

The classic statement of this position is probably Garrett Hardin's "The Tragedy of the Commons" (1968), which has been reprinted many times in different books. He begins with the premise that the problem of overpopulation has no technical solution. Rather, it is a question of values or morals. In a situation where pasture land is open to all (the "commons") and ownership of cattle is private, individuals acting in their own interests would tend to increase their herds as much as possible. They would do this because the cost of an additional cow (the grass eaten) is spread among everyone, while the gain goes in its entirety to the individual owner of the cow. However, when all the herdsmen do the same thing, the result is overgrazing and destruction of the pastures, bringing tragedy to all. Thus, "freedom in a commons brings ruin to all."

Our society, observes Hardin, is like a commons, given the philosophy of the welfare state which takes care of the basic needs of the poor. However, since freedom in a commons results in disaster for all involved, the welfare state means that freedom to breed must be curtailed. By this reasoning, therefore, the United Nations' *Universal Declaration of Human Rights* contradicts itself. If every man, woman, and child is entitled to food, health care, education, and so on, this implies that the state or the world has the responsibility of meeting these needs. It logically follows, therefore, that people cannot be entitled to have as many children as they want. Yet the *Declaration* states that the family is to be given the right to decide on the number of children they wish to have (implying that contraceptive information and devices should be made available only so families will not have *more* children than they want). Hardin believes this is a recipe for disaster.

Essentially the same moral issue is posed by another metaphor, that of the lifeboat. If there is a lifeboat capable of carrying only fifty people, and there are already fifty on board, what should be done about the people outside the lifeboat? If they are brought aboard, *all* will die. This would be a greater tragedy than refusing to permit those outside of the lifeboat on board. In brief, on the assumption that overpopulation is the basic cause of world hunger, this perspective calls for the application of strict population control measures, rather than freely dispensing food and/or technical assistance to enable poor countries to increase their agricultural productivity. This is similar to the position of the Environmental Fund summarized earlier.

## Demographic Transition Theory

The demographic transition is one of the most widely documented generalizations in social science. It has taken place in all of the industrialized countries, and apparently it is being repeated in some of the more advanced Third World countries such as South Korea, Taiwan, Singapore, and Costa Rica. It is a transition from high birth and death rates, to low birth and death rates. This takes place in three stages. The first stage is one in which high birth rates are matched by high death rates. This is characteristic of preindustrial societies. In the second stage, improved nutrition and health causes death rates to fall while birth rates remain high, resulting in high rates of natural growth in population size. In the third stage, birth rates fall, eventually reaching the low level of the death rates, resulting in zero population growth.

Europe experienced its population explosion during the eighteenth and nineteenth centuries, and entered the third stage of the transition around the turn of this century. By today most European countries have completed the transition. Most Third World countries entered the second phase of the transition in the last fifty years, especially since the Second World War. As a result, they have been experiencing a population explosion. While a few of these countries have recently experienced a significant reduction in their birth rate, none has completed the transition. Birth rates are still above the now low death rates, and population growth continues. Demographic transition theorists expect the Third World countries to complete the downtrend in birth rates as they become more developed. As a theory, however, demographic transition suffers from lack of an adequately detailed explanatory model. Just why and how did birth rates decline in Europe? Are the same forces operating in less developed countries today?

Historical evidence indicates that the existence of effective birth control techniques and the extent of knowledge about them are not as important in explaining the decline of birth rates as the *decision* by humans to use whatever techniques exist in their society. Even without the pill and sterilization, which became widely available only in the last fifteen or twenty years, preindustrial and ancient societies were able to control their population size by a variety of means—abortion, infanticide, celibacy, delayed marriage, abstention from sex relations, *coitus interruptus,* and other birth control practices. Fertility control is governed both directly and indirectly by cultural norms and social factors, and it is in the area of human motivations in relation to social and economic factors that we must find explanations of changes in the fertility rate.

During the same period when birth rates were declining, European society underwent some basic structural transformations that are functionally related to an industrialized economy. *First*, the population became increasingly urban, beginning with the eighteenth century and accelerating in the nineteenth, so that today most of the people in Europe are urban residents. Fertility declines were first experienced by the urban dwellers in Europe. This was not true of the rural people until after 1900. Likewise today, in most of the less developed countries, urban residence is correlated with low fertility. However, there are exceptions to this pattern, such as India and Northern Africa. These exceptions lend support to the idea that it is not urban residence *per se* that causes families to bear fewer children, but rather the kind of lifestyle and economic circumstances that characterize most urban communities.

The *second* transformation of European society that was correlated with the decline of birth rates was the growth of the middle class, and the spreading of middle-class lifestyles and values to the other sectors of the population. The proportion of the people living and working as peasant farmers today is negligible, as farming is now almost entirely commercial. The wage earner has become the most common type of person in modern industrialized societies. Under these circumstances, and especially since the abolition of child labor, children are no longer the economic assets they once were. The availability of pensions and government sponsored old age security plans is also a feature of modern societies that has reduced the need for children to provide for the aged. While in less developed countries the middle-class lifestyle is true of only a very small proportion of the people, the same forces are at work among them. The middle classes have smaller families than the majority of the people who are poor.

The *third* major social change of importance is the rise of public education, especially compulsory education laws. As children stay longer and longer in school, their economic role within their families of origin disappears. Instead, to a great extent, they become economic liabilities, and that for a longer period of time. In addition, the necessity of secondary and post-secondary education for those who aspire to modern occupations serves to increase the average age at marriage, thus postponing childbearing. This negative effect of education on family size has been observed among women in India, Taiwan, and Costa Rica, as well as in many other countries.

The above social changes influenced parental decision-making greatly, in that a large number of children no longer made economic sense. Thus birth rates tell. Proponents of the demographic transition position therefore argue that the way to reduce the birth rate in poor countries is not simply to promote family planning, and certainly not by withholding aid. Rather, what is needed is greater socioeconomic development within these countries. This can best be done by increased aid from industrialized countries, especially in the areas of education and employment in modern occupations.

*Distributive Justice*

The fifth perspective on the population-food issue emphasizes distributive justice. Adherents of this position agree with transition theorists that the socioeconomic development of poor countries is the only ultimate solution. However, its focus is more on food than on population dynamics, and it places heavy emphasis on maldistribution of resources and the fact that "the rich get richer and the poor get children."

The world's resources are undoubtedly distributed extremely unevenly in terms of where they are consumed. For example, the United States comprises about 5 percent of the world's population but consumes more than one third of its total nonrenewable resources, such as oil and other minerals. In the case of food, similar inequities exist. The annual grain consumption is about four hundred pounds per person in India, but close to two thousand pounds in the United States. In the latter case, most of the grain is consumed indirectly, by feeding it first to livestock, particularly cattle, which are then consumed by human beings. The feeding of grain to cattle, in effect, reduces the amount of food calories and protein available for human consumption by a factor of about ten or more.

George Borgstrom, in *The Food/People Dilemma* (1974) and other books, presents statistical evidence showing that the rich nations (North America, Europe, and Japan) import more protein from the poor nations than vice versa, programs such as Public Law 480 ("Food for Peace") and common American beliefs notwithstanding. Much of the world tuna catch, for example, is consumed by American people and pets, and one third of the African peanut crop goes to Europe for livestock feed (Lappe', 1975).

Such facts as these underscore the statement that *demand*, not need, determines where the world's food and other resources go. Demand as an economic concept means the amount of a given commodity that the market will buy at a given price. Demand is therefore generated by people with cash to spend. Need, on the other hand, is equally true of all human beings. Whether rich or poor, we each need protein in the amount of about .08 pecent of our body weight. Most Americans could cut meat from their diet and still eat enough protein. Besides, too many Americans are overweight from eating too many calories. Clearly, world consumption patterns are guided by purchasing power, not basic human need. The demand versus need concept is expressed in another way by Lester R. Brown, who considers growing affluence an equal, if not bigger, challenge to the earth's ecological limits compared with population growth (1974a,b).

Proponents of the distributive justice position further argue that millions are hungry today, not because population has outrun the earth's capacity to produce food, but rather because of wasteful and excess consumption by people in rich countries. In addition, they argue that much of the world's best cropland is being used to grow non-essentials for the rich. Many tropical countries have given over their most fertile soils to the production of such commodities as rubber, coffee, bananas, and sugar cane for export to the affluent countries. In return, the elites of the Third World countries import manufactured goods, automobiles, and luxury items for their own use, as well as oil and machines needed to run their fledgling industries.

Social scientists, such as dependency theorists, argue that trade in itself is not bad, but the patterns of trade between rich and poor countries have benefited the rich and exploited the powerless poor majority. For one thing, over the last few decades, the prices of manufactured goods sold to the Third World have risen much more than the prices of raw materials produced for export to the industrialized West. Furthermore, much of the commmercial agriculture in poor countries is controlled by multinational corporations whose chief interest is to reap as much profit as possible from the poor countries, rather than to make sure poor people earn enough to eat.

In brief, this position puts the blame for world hunger on an inequitable world economic system, not on population growth. While it cannot be denied that rapid population growth in poor countries aggravates the problem, supporters of distributive justice point out that birth rates will be brought down only when the poor are assured a decent level of nutrition, health, education, and security. This will make children unnecessary as economic insurance for their parents. Therefore, a new world economic order of fair trade and increased aid—and in many cases land reform in Third World countries themselves—is called for.

## Evaluations and Conclusions

If we wish to do good, should we send aid to starving peoples overseas? Will we be causing even *more* hunger and suffering if we try to feed the hungry now? The answers to these questions rest on three basic issues:

(1) Is the world in a lifeboat situation? That is, has world consumption of food and other resources exceeded, or will it soon exceed, the carrying capacity?

(2) Is population growth the greatest threat to worldwide ecological balance?

(3) Will feeding hungry people cause population growth to increase?

In regard to the first issue, it must be noted that carrying capacity is a changeable quantity, depending on the technology man employs to gain a living from his environment. The technological optimists' position is that current and future scientific breakthroughs will enable man to increase his numbers beyond the apparent Malthusian limits of today. However, many nonrenewable resources, such as oil, are being so rapidly depleted that many scientists have warned that unless man changes not only his technology but also his values and economic systems, and unless he engages in population control, he will face worldwide ecological disaster. This would result in a kind of final doomsday when our life support systems break down. They predict that this will happen within a couple of generations.

The reference to values and economic systems leads us to the second issue. If we exceed the carrying capacity of the earth, or come close to it, who is to blame—the poor who multiply more rapidly, or the rich who consume resources at a rate several times that of the poor? Edwin Schumacher, a noted economist and a Christian, had a very simple calculation is his book *Small Is Beautiful*. He reveals that despite the slower population growth rate of the rich countries, their higher rate of consumption of oil means that most of the future increase in world oil consumption will be due to the rich. The clear conclusion is that if carrying capacity is in danger of being exceeded, the biggest culprit is the growing consumption on the part of the rich. The economic systems of the world, be they capitalist or socialist, are based on increasing material production and consumption. "More is better" is the value assumption. Is it? The Bible warns us about the dangers of materialism, and tells us not to live "by bread alone." Industrialized economies have made an idol of material production and consumption, and will ultimately have to pay for this sin. Worldwide ecological disaster, if and when it comes, will come more because of the consumption of the rich than because of the reproduction of the poor.

Nevertheless, it cannot be denied that population growth is a contributing factor, and the poor are the ones with the highest population growth rates. There are countries such as Bangladesh and Niger, where the growth of population has apparently outstripped the ability of the land to support it. These countries are thus faced with a situation of chronic famine. Are we to assist them by either shipping food to them, or by allowing their excess population to migrate here? Environmental crisis thinkers such as Garrett Hardin say, "No," on the premise that "injustice is preferable to total ruin" (1972). Feeding people who are already reproducing too fast will only keep them alive longer to produce even more offspring. To return to the lifeboat metaphor, it will only sink the boat if we allow more people on it. According to this view, it is better that some die rather than that all die (Paddock and Paddock, 1967; Ehrlich, 1971; Fletcher, 1976).

Biblical injunctions to share with the poor would indeed be folly in a situation where population has exceeded the carrying capacity, if it is true that well-fed people produce more babies than those who are poorly fed. Is it? The answer is "No, " in the long run. A thorough review of studies bearing on the effects of reduced mortality on fertility found that when fewer children die, mothers eventually bear fewer children in total, so that their completed family sizes either remained constant (as when more children had died) or even diminished. This was true in about half of the cases studied. In the other half of the studies, which had time horizons of two to five years, mothers experiencing fewer child deaths ended up with more living children; that is, any reduced fertility only compensated partially for the reduced mortality (Schultz, 1976).

Mothers have reduced fertility when fewer children die for two reasons, biological and behavioral. The biological factor involves the fact that lactation frequently prevents ovulation. When a baby that is being nursed by the mother dies, the mother ceases to produce milk and her ovaries begin to produce ova again, so that she is again capable of becoming pregnant.

The behavioral factor involves subconscious decision-making on the part of parents. In many poor countries it is extremely important that at least one son lives to adulthood, so that he can suppport his parents in their old age. Under conditions of high child mortality, village families need to start with at least five children to ensure the survival of one son (Taylor, 1973). For example, under current infant and adult death rates in India, computer simulation showed that a couple must bear 6.3 children in order to have a 95 percent probability that one son will survive to the father's sixty-fifth birthday (Berg, 1973). The average number of births per family in India is 6.5, confirming the finding in another study that "families continued to have children until they were reasonably certain that at least one boy would survive. Once they had this number, they attempted to stop having more." [°] Yet another study, this one in an urban area in Peru, showed that the poorest mothers have a greater number of live births than their less poor counterparts and that mothers with more deaths among their children had more live births (Frisancho, et. al., 1976).

Adults seem to base their expectations of how many children will survive on what they observed to be true among their siblings and friends when they were children. Thus reduced infant and child mortality through improved nutrition and health measures will have the effect of reducing fertility twenty years hence—a long-run effect. However, it is probably possible to shorten the time lag "by using child health services deliberately to make awareness of child survival a direct and conscious reason for accepting family planning" (Taylor, 1973).

The above review of the evidence shows that while feeding hungry people will in the short run cause population growth to increase by reducing deaths, in the long run births will also be reduced so that population can be brought under control. One of the qualities that we

---

[°] Carl E. Taylor and Marie Francoise Hall, "Health, Population and Economic Development," *Science*, August 11, 1967, p. 4, as quoted in Alan Berg, *The Nutritional Factor: Its Role in National Development* (Washington, D.C.: The Brookings Institution, 1973:33).

possess as human beings made in the image of God is the ability to anticipate future events and to make decisions based on such planning. Poor peasants are behaving rationally, not stupidly, when they have large families under conditions of high child mortality. Study after study has shown that when conditions of life improve so that children are no longer as likely to die, when people feel secure about being provided for in old age, and when modern education and jobs are available, the birth rate falls.

In the book of Genesis, we read that God gave man authority and responsibility over the rest of his creation. Rationality and free will, aspects of the image of God in man, are to be exercised in the carrying out of this charge. In direct disobedience to God, however, man has tried to be his own master and has sought after other gods. The god of materialism and man's disrespect for God's created world have led to a situation today where we face ecological disaster if we continue carelessly exploiting the world's nonrenewable resources and polluting the earth.

Throughout the Bible, God reveals his character as one of justice and love. Human economic systems have fallen short of justice. Inequity and inherited poverty are evident throughout the world, in contrast to the kind of society God favors, where people are assured of a productive livelihood and just wages (Deuteronomy 15, Amos 2:6-8; 4:1; 5:11-12; James 5:1-8). God knew that human injustice would result in a situation where "the poor you will have with you always," and therefore instructed his people to reflect his character by being generous to the poor and needy (Deuteronomy 15:11 *et. al.*).

Feeding the hungry and meeting other basic needs, including livelihood, security, and education, are not foolish things to do. This author disagrees with Malthusians and the environmental crisis thinkers in this, both on the basis of Christian morality and scientific analysis. The demographic transition and distributive justice positions come closest to reflecting both biblical and secular truths. While the position of the technological optimist gives credit to man's God-given rationality and power over nature, it runs the risk of putting ultimate faith in technology alone. Man's technology can be used either as a tool to carry out God's will in the world to help eradicate hunger, or it can be used to pursue the false god of irresponsible and uncaring economic growth in production and consumption. How do you think it should be used?

## Discussion Questions

1. In what ways might or might not human fertility patterns be similar to those in the animal world? How does this relate to the central issue in this chapter?

2. Which of the world's countries had the first government-sponsored family planning program (1951), as well as is the first and only country to have legislated a mandatory sterilization program for its people? What is the status of fertility rates in that country today? What does this show about the effectiveness of governmental "encouragement" of family planning in the absence of changes in socioeconomic conditions?

3. Do you regard America as a "lifeboat" in the face of the world hunger situation? Why or why not?

4. If consumption and depletion are what we are concerned about, would it be fairer to compare rich and poor countries in terms of growth in population-consumption-equivalents, rather than merely in numbers of people?

5. Name a few examples of commodities or services which are distributed on the basis of economic demand, rather than human need.

6. Discuss: "Freedom in a commons brings tragedy to all."

7. Is there a "right" to have children? Does one have the right to have as many children as one wants?

8. Is there a "right to food"?

9. Is it possible to answer "yes" to *both* questions 7 and 8? Why or why not?

10. What would be the most effective way for Christians to respond to chronic famine in, say, Ethiopia, in the light of what you have learned about the relationship between food and development and population growth?

## References

Berg, Allan
    1973 *The Nutritional Factor: Its Role in National Development.* Washington, D.C.: The Brookings Institution.
Borgstrom, Georg
    1972 *The Hungry Plant.* New York: Collier-Macmillan.
    1974 *The Food/People Dilemma.* Belmont, Calif.: Duxbury Press.
Brown, Lester R.
    1974 *By Bread Alone.* New York: Praeger.
    1974 *In the Human Interest.* New York: Norton.
Ehrlich, Paul
    1971 *The Population Bomb.* New York: Ballantine.
Fletcher, Joseph
    1976 "Feeding the Hungry: An Ethical Appraisal," in George R.

Lucas, Jr. (ed.), *Lifeboat Ethics: the Moral Dilemmas of World Hunger*. New York: Harper and Row.

Frisancho, A. Roberto, Jane E. Klayman, and Jorge Matos
1976 "Symbiotic Relationship of High Fertility, High Childhood Mortality, and Socio-Economic Status in an Urban Peruvian Population." *Human Biology*, 48, pp. 101-111.

Hardin, Garrett
1968 "The Tragedy of the Commons." *Science*, 162, pp. 1243-48.

1972 *Exploring New Ethics for Survival: The Voyage of the Spaceship Beagle*. Baltimore: Penguin.

Lappé, Frances Moore
1975 "The Banality of Hunger." *Harper's*. February.

Malthus, Thomas Robert
1958 *An Essay on Population*. London: Dent (reprinted).

Paddock, William and Paul Paddock
1967 *Famine—1975!* Boston; Little Brown and Co.

Schultz, T. Paul
1976 "Interrelationships Between Mortality and Fertility," in Ronald G. Ridker (ed.), *Population and Development*. Baltimore: Johns Hopkins University Press.

Schumacher, E.F.
1973 *Small Is Beautiful*. New York: Harper and Row.

Taylor, Carl E.
1973 "Nutrition and Population," in Alan Berg (ed.), *Nutrition, National Development and Planning*. Cambridge: MIT Press.

# 26
# Population Problems and Christian Responsibility

*Peter R. Uhlenberg*

> Man, for instance, is related to all he knows. He needs a place wherein to abide, time through which to live, motion in order to live, elements to compose him, warmth and food to nourish him, air to breathe. He sees light; he feels bodies; in short, he is in a dependent alliance with everything. —Pascal (Pensees).

We live in a finite world, on a planet so small that astronauts can circle it a dozen times in one day. Surrounding this planet is a thin envelope of air, water, and soil, an envelope we call the biosphere since it contains the necessary elements for life. Within this biosphere exists an intricate network of interdependent relationships between all living things—microbes, plants, and animals. One of these hundreds of thousands of living species inhabiting the surface of the earth is man, and, like all other species, he is part of a complex and intricate ecological system. Man is bound to this system through a series of links that form a web relating all living things to one another. For the system to survive through time a balance, or ecological equilibrium, must be achieved and maintained between the constituent parts. If certain limits are exceeded by one species, not only that species, but the entire system, is threatened with painful repercussions or even extinction.

So we locate man as one species within an immensely complex ecological system which is contained within the biosphere of a small

**Peter Ralston Uhlenberg**
*Associate Professor of Sociology*
*University of North Carolina*
A specialist in demography, Peter Uhlenberg earned his MA and PhD in this area of sociology. He has been active in demographic associations and served on publication boards. He has served as a member of the Advisory Panel for the Center for Population Research, NIH. Associate Professor Uhlenberg has served as adviser to the Inter Varsity Christian Fellowship, and is an elder in the Chapel Hill Bible Church. He has done considerable writing and speaking on family demography and minority demographic issues.

planet. Man is part of this system, but he is also unique. He stands out from the other components of the system because he occupies the dominant position. More than any other creature, man has the power to manipulate the environment to suit his preferences, and he does manipulate it. In recent years humans have leveled mountains, changed the courses of rivers, altered climates, eliminated diseases, exterminated species of animals, and produced unprecedented quantities of material goods. Some demonstrations of man's ability to influence the environment have been intentional; others have not been. In either case, new problems are created for the human population as a result of it being freed from earlier constraints. Indeed, man at the end of the twentieth century is facing many serious problems. These are the result of having radically altered parts of the ecological system without adequate regard for the consequences that these changes have for the continued functioning of the intricately interrelated system of life on this planet.

In this chapter we are examining one of the most fundamental of these problems—the problem of the unprecedented rapid growth of the human population. Through application of science and technology, death rates around the world have fallen precipitously over the past century, so there now exists a serious imbalance between births and deaths. The magnitude of this imbalance is difficult to fathom. Each day there are 200,000 more births than deaths; each year the excess of births over deaths exceeds 70 million. This means that a number equivalent to the total population of the U.S. is added to the world population every three years. Whereas it took from the creation of man to the year AD 1830 for world population to grow to one billion, it took only 100 years from this date for an additional one billion to be added to world population. Since 1930 we have added 2 billion more! It is no misnomer to label this growth a "population explosion."

The growth of population is not distributed evenly over different regions of the earth. Rather, the most rapid growth is occurring in the poorest countries. If the world is divided into two parts, the developed countries (DCS) and the less developed countries (LDCS), we find the rate of growth in the LDCS is nearly three times that of the DCS, and 88 percent of the total annual increase in world population is occurring in the LDCS. Many population experts are deeply concerned about the consequences of this concentration of population growth in the poorest regions of the world, and they are proposing various governmental policies to reduce growth rates. The challenge that I hope you will accept is to gain an understanding of what is happening in the world today, and then strive to integrate this information into a comprehensive Christian world-view.

## Bringing God into the Picture

From first to last this has been the work of God. He has reconciled us men to himself through Christ, and he has enlisted us in this service of reconciliation (2 Corinthians 5:18, NEB).

Few sociologists concerned with population problems approach their research and writing from a perspective which includes the existence of a supernatural God who created and sustains the universe. Nevertheless, it is a serious error for the Christian student to set up the social sciences as an enemy of Christianity, or to reject or dismiss as unimportant the findings of sociology. To the extent that sociologists do good research, the results of their scholarship provide insights into human society which can greatly enrich our understanding of the world we live in. The exciting challenge confronting the Christian student is to take the material that is offered, and to test it against what is revealed in the Bible. Through this process some findings must be rejected as contrary to a Christian understanding of reality, but much can be incorporated into a larger Christian world and life view. By accepting this challenge, our understanding of life can be enriched, and with greater understanding we can more faithfully work out how we are to live as responsible Christians in the contemporary world. As Christians we do not have the option of stopping with a disinterested analysis of social problems, but we must go on to ask the question, What should our response be? We need to function as whole persons in all areas of life—not separating the intellectual from the emotional and behavioral.

As we explore the division of the world into rich and poor countries, and examine the implications of population growth for poor countries, and survey the policies being suggested to alleviate the problems, we need to keep in mind a Christian perspective on history. And the Bible reveals a good deal about the meaning of history. The Bible begins by boldly stating that in the beginning God created everything. Behind all of the physical, material world that surrounds us is an invisible, supernatural God. As we read through the Bible we see the unfolding drama of man and God's continuous dealing with him. We read of man's rebellion against God, and the subsequent frustration of God's intended purpose for his creation. But we also learn that God has not turned his back on the world. Rather, God is at work to restore the world to its intended purpose. When Jesus came, he announced the establishment of the kingdom of God within the world now, although it remains partial and incomplete. It is with the return of Christ at the end of time that God's kingdom will be perfectly restored (see Romans 1-8).

Now we can locate our place in history. God has called us to be reconciled with himself, and thereby to experience authentic life. And he has given us a task of tremendous significance—to be his agents of reconciliation in this broken and twisted world (2 Corinthians, chs. 4-6). We are to proclaim the good news that man can be rightly related to God, and we are to work toward the real healing of nature. (For a more complete discussion of this idea of "substantial healing" of nature, see Schaeffer, 1970). With this Christian perspective in mind, let us proceed to look at the current division of the world into two sectors.

## Developed and Less Developed Countries

Our world today is in reality two worlds, one rich, one poor; one literate, one largely illiterate; one industrial and urban, one agrarian and rural; one overfed and overweight, one hungry and malnourished; one affluent and consumption-oriented; one poverty-stricken and survival-oriented.           —Lester R. Brown.

There is increasing recognition that the countries of the world are interrelated, and that in a very basic sense the world forms a unity. But it is in this context of increasing awareness of world unity that the vast differences in economic levels between nations comes into sharpest relief. On the basis of economic conditions, the nations of the world can conceptually be divided into two categories—the economically developed and the economically less developed, or, more simply, the rich and the poor. Obviously such a distinction is a simplification of reality, since there are countries at all stages of development, and within each country there exists a wide range of economic levels. Nevertheless, the dichotomy of countries by economic criteria is very useful for the study of population problems, since there are fundamental differences in the kinds of problems facing countries in each category. Therefore, let us specify more clearly the differences between DCS and LDCS.

*The Developed Countries*

The emergence of countries in which large portions of the population enjoy considerable affluence is something very recent in world history. Prior to the modern era, poverty was the universal lot of almost all men in all countries. A few individuals amassed fortunes in earlier eras, but never did whole nations experience affluence. The LDCS, where the battle against hunger and illness continue and where most people live at or near a subsistence level, experience a continuity with the past; it is the DCS that are unprecedented in history. As John Kenneth Galbraith aptly puts it, "Few people at the beginning of the nineteenth century needed an adman to tell them what they wanted." The people wanted the basic necessities of life—food, clothing, and shelter. In contrast, advertising and salesmanship now provide a key function of creating "needs" in wealthy societies, where the basic physical needs are easily satisfied.

There is general agreement that the DCS consist of the countries of Europe, North America, and Oceania, plus the U.S.S.R., South Africa, Japan, and Israel. (Sometimes a few additional countries are included, such as Argentina, Chile, Venezuela, and Brazil in Latin America, and Taiwan, Hong Kong, and Singapore in Asia; and several Eastern European countries are excluded, such as Albania and Romania). While the overriding characteristics of DCS are their high per capita incomes and advanced industrial, technological economies, there are a cluster of other characteristics that accompany them.´ Some of these common characteristics are: low mortality rates, low to moderate birth rates, large proportion living in cities, high rates of literacy, advanced educational systems, adequate nutrition levels, and widespread medical care.

*Less Developed Countries*

Having identified the DCS, it follows that the LDCS are the remaining countries of the world—most of Asia, Africa, and Latin America. These nations, marked by poverty, have not begun to, or are only in the early stages of, transforming their economies into the modern systems characteristic of the DCS. Peasant agriculture remains the occupation of most people in this sector of the world, and hunger and malnutrition are pervasive. Birth rates remain high, and educational levels low. But statistics of poverty are completely inadequate to convey an appreciation for conditions in LDCS to a person who has never visited or lived in a poor country. To understand, one must see thousands of people crowded in a shantytown where whole families live in a single room that has no electricity, no running water, and where an open sewer runs beside a dirt road a few feet from the doorway. One must see the protruding bellies and discolored skin of children suffering from protein malnutrition, the flies on open sores of prematurely old men and women. And one must see the begging of people with no hope for the future, before the desperate poverty in LDCS is really comprehended. Of course not everyone in LDCS experiences this extreme deprivation, but a staggering number do. And only a handful of individuals in LDCS experience a life of comfort and affluence that is taken for granted by the majority of people living in the United States, Canada, and the rest of the Western World.

Many more people are currently living in poor countries than in rich ones. Of the approximately 4 billion persons living in the world today, 70 percent are living in LDCS and only 30 percent DCS. Furthermore, the percent of world population living in LDCS is increasing, since their population growth rates are about three times as high as those in DCS. By the year 2000, it is projected that for every person living in a developed country, there will be three living in LDCS. It is disturbing to discover that on a world scale, the number of people living in poverty is rapidly increasing, and that the gap between the rich and poor countries is widening. The role of population growth in aggrevating the already serious problem of economic inequality between nations is stated clearly by Donald Bogue: "A disproportionate share of the current population growth in the world is concentrated in the poorer regions and is inundating them just as they are making a major effort to improve their economic condition. Thus not only is the world growing at an explosive pace, but its growth is concentrated in exactly those spots where it can be afforded least (from the point of view of reducing world poverty and raising levels of living)" (Bogue, 1969:47).

## Problems Related to Rapid Population Growth

The population explosion and its concomitants have transformed man's attitudes, values, institutions and, in general, his way of life. Moreover, they have generated unprecedented problems, chronic and acute; local, national and international; personal, social, economic and political.

—Philip M. Hauser.

Much has been written regarding the implications of rapid population growth in poor countries. In this literature there is considerable disagreement regarding the precise role of population growth in causing various social and economic problems. Nevertheless, there is widespread agreement among demographers that rapid growth is detrimental to societal welfare. Several of the basic arguments that lead to this view are summarized in this section.

*Land and Resources*

The most popular, although not the strongest, argument for the negative effects of rapid population growth is the imbalance it will cause between the population and the supply of land and natural resources. From Thomas Malthus on, dire prophecies that population growth will lead to shortages of food and nonrenewable minerals have been common. Much of this discussion has been simplistic and has failed to include any serious consideration of the role of technology and innovation. Nevertheless, while alarmist positions may be flawed from a lack of objective analysis, very real problems are created by continued population growth in a world with finite supplies of land and natural resources.

Consider the implications of current growth rates. The average rate of population growth in Latin American and African countries is about 2.7 percent annually, a rate which leads to the doubling of a population every 26 years. By the time a person living in such a country reaches age 66, the total population would be 6 times larger than it was when he or she was born. Thus in the lifetime of an individual, the production of food, and every other commodity, must be increased sixfold to simply maintain the already critically low level of living. In densely settled countries this creates tremendous environmental strain.

Responses to rapid growth in rural areas where the supply of arable land is limited have been a fragmentation of farms and a massive migration from the countryside into cities. Both of these responses are creating serious social and economic problems. The fragmentation of farms tends to reduce agricultural efficiency, and farms rapidly become too small to support a family. Migration from rural areas has produced enormous growth in the major cities of every LDC. In these cities most persons are living in urban poverty. Expansion of opportunities for useful employment cannot keep pace with the growth of individuals seeking jobs. It is clear that they cannot keep expanding indefinitely in a

world with finite space, and there are obvious advantages to a population which reaches a stationary state before its environment is seriously
overstrained.

## Age Distribution

A high birth rate in conjunction with a low death rate (the situation in LDCS today) not only produces rapid population growth, but
also produces a population with a very young age structure. A comparison of LDCS and DCS demonstrates the profound effects of high
birth rates. In the low growth countries of Western Europe, about 23
percent of the total population is under age 15. In contrast, in Latin
America 42 percent of the population is children under age 15; in Africa
the figure is 44 percent, and in Asia 38 percent. More than half of the
population in almost every LDC is below age 20. What are the implications of such a large proportion of youth in the population?

1. The future economic growth of a society is critically dependent
upon the level of skills possessed by the population. When there is a
very large proportion of children, the problems of educating and equipping the young with useful skills is greatly exacerbated. Provision of
classrooms, trained teachers, and educational material are all strained
in poor countries because of the large and constantly growing number
of children. But it is these children who will be the new workers entering the labor force in coming years. The future not only of the children
themselves, but of the whole society, would be brighter if more
resources could be invested per child.

2. The large number of children relative to persons in the labor
force restricts the level of investment in new capital. Basic consumption
needs—food, clothing, shelter—are greater in a population with a large
proportion of children. Hence, less is left over for savings and investment which could lead to future increases in per capita production.

3. In a rapidly growing population, the number of children born
each year greatly exceeds the number born in the previous year. Over
time, therefore, the number of children arriving at any particular age
(e.g. 15) is constantly expanding. This becomes especially critical at the
age for entrance into the labor force, because it means that each year a
growing number of new jobs need to be created. Poor countries cannot
meet this challenge to create enough new, productive jobs to accommodate the supply of persons seeking to enter the labor force. Consequently, in most LDCS there exist serious problems of unemploy-

ment and underemployment, and there is much wastage of human potential. If there was slower growth, it would not only be possible to reduce this waste, but it would be possible to accommodate individuals into the work force more easily.

*Family Size*

Problems of rapid growth can be discussed at the societal level (as above), but the basic cause of rapid growth is that individuals are having large families. Hardships occurring within families as a result of excessive numbers of children are not difficult to understand. A number of studies have pointed out the following problems that are experienced more often by children in large than in small families.

1. Children born into large families have fewer life chances. Given limited resources (food, medical care, etc.), children in large families have less available than they would if they had fewer siblings, and this is reflected in their higher rates of illness and greater probabilities of dying during infancy or childhood. Children born with very short birth intervals are particularly disadvantaged.

2. A child with a large number of siblings is found to suffer more often from malnutrition and, at any given age, is physically smaller. The impact of poor nutrition upon physical and mental development during childhood may permanently impair an individual's ability to function normally throughout later life.

3. Related to the above consequences, as well as to the reduced amount of possible time for parent-child interaction, children from large families tend to perform more poorly on standardized educational tests. Further, the possibilities for schooling are more limited for children in large families because of the lower per capita resources available to them.

The evidence summarized above indicates some negative consequences that rapid population growth may have, and the human suffering associated with them. This discussion is not "Christian," and it is not "non-Christian," but rather it is an effort to discover the actual situation. Obviously a Christian should not remain unmoved by the suffering and degradation caused by poverty. The individuals suffering are human beings created in the image of God, and they are suffering as a result of sin which has affected every aspect of creation. But, beyond feeling compassion, how should we respond? The next section discusses responses that various social scientists have suggested. An evaluation of these proposed responses should give us a good basis for working towards a Christian response.

## Responses to Population Growth

There is nothing more frightful than ignorance in action.
—Goethe.

While keeping in mind the importance of viewing our lives holistically, we may find it useful to distinguish two levels of response to the problems of population growth. First, on an intellectual level we need to grapple with the question of what is the ethically correct action for governments to take. Obviously this is such a complex issue that it would be arrogant to assume that we have complete answers, but this should not keep us from attempting to find some answers. There are moral issues involved, and Christianity is relevant to these issues. Second, on a personal level, what should our response be to the understanding we have? Along with a deeper understanding of the world around us comes a larger responsibility to live lives that are faithful to our calling to be "agents of reconciliation."

### Should the Government Respond?

In attempting to answer the question of what the American government should do, we may start by asking, "Where should it direct its efforts?" Following this we deal with "How should the government respond?"

Where should we direct our efforts? Three distinct positions have been forwarded in response to this question. Let us consider each.

1. *No intervention.* This approach argues that there is either no need for government intervention, or that we do not know enough to intervene effectively and thus are better off doing nothing. This *laissez-faire* perspective often refers to the DCS where birth rates fell as a result of economic development, and suggests that a similar balance between mortality and fertility will occur "naturally" in LDCS. Each country is left to work out its own population problem.

But is it so simple to remove responsibility to offer aid from the U.S.? First, the U.S. is largely responsible for producing the current rapid population growth in LDCS. By introducing public health measures around the world, U.S. technology has drastically reduced mortality rates. Thus the U.S. has not played a neutral role in creating the present situation. Second, to use the historical example of a balance being achieved in the DCS is misleading when applied to currently LDCS. LDCS today are experiencing rates of natural increase that far exceed those which occurred earlier in the history of DCS. Also, high fertility in LDCS is a major impediment to the economic growth which is suggested as the solution to the population problem. Third, the U.S. cannot become isolationist without severe consequences for all of mankind. If we are to consume resources from other parts of the world, we must concern ourself with its problems of poverty. And Christians especially should resist emphasizing national boundaries which unnecessarily hinder cooperation and sharing in God's creation.

2. *Triage.* Since it was suggested in 1967 by Paddock and Paddock, the triage principle of determining which countries should receive U.S. aid has gained considerable support. This principle begins by dividing the LDCS into three categories: those with such serious population and poverty problems that they "can't be saved"; those that will succeed without aid; and those that can be saved if considerable aid is given. The suggestion, taken by analogy from battlefield medicine, is that aid be given only to countries in the last category. Countries such as India (population = 645 million) and Bangladesh (population = 84 million) would be classified "hopeless," and would receive no aid. The justification for this approach is that aid given to "hopeless countries" is wasted, and a better strategy is to concentrate upon fewer countries where progress may be expected.

Is this a good strategy? And is it good ethics? The analogy of battlefield casualties and human populations is not really so helpful. Individual soldiers either die or survive, but countries are going to continue. India and Bangladesh are not going to disappear by being ignored. Christians do not need to be sentimental in making hard decisions, but they are not free to disregard the call for help from suffering people. Our inability to see any solution to a problem such as India's poverty does not relieve us of responsibility to work for a solution and to strive for at least partial healing.

3. *Aid where possible.* A third perspective suggests that it is our responsibility to offer assistance in reducing population growth in countries wherever it is possible. This view considers the U.S. to be part of a global community and, as the economically richest country in the world, to have an obligation to assist poorer countries. The level and

type of aid considered appropriate varies among proponents of this position, but there is a common concern that we not ignore the problems of population growth. Arguments against this position are primarily the other sides of the arguments given in support of the other two positions. (It may be obvious from the way the material is presented here that I consider the third position to be more compatible with a Christian view of the world than either of the others. You should grapple with this issue for yourself.)

## How Should We Respond?

Assuming that the U.S. should respond in some way, there remains the very controversial issue of what kind of response this should be. Many possible responses have been suggested, but to permit a consideration of different options some simplifying scheme is required. Here four analytically distinct positions are presented.

1. *Economic assistance only.* Rather than attempt any direct action to reduce birth rates, some believe the best approach is to only aid LDCS to increase per capita income. The underlying assumption is that a population will automatically reduce its fertility as a consequence of economic growth, and that in the absence of economic growth measures to limit fertility will be ineffective. Without minimizing the importance of economic aid, however, it can be questioned whether this is the best approach.

First, prospects for significant economic development within the foreseeable future for many poor countries (with hundreds of millions of inhabitants) are dim. Thus it is an extremely pessimistic view to say that nothing can be done to curb population growth in these countries in the coming decades. This is a particularly dismal picture because the rapid population growth is a major factor in perpetuating poverty. Second, it is not clear that fertility does respond very quickly to improved economic conditions. In a recent study of Mexico over the past 20 years, Ansley Coale (1977:423) a leading demographer, found that,

> The Mexican population in 1975 was more than 72 percent literate and more than 60 percent urban, the per capita income had nearly doubled in 20 years, the expectation of life at birth had risen to about 65 years and was still increasing; nevertheless, fertility until about 1975 was, if anything, somewhat higher than it was 20 years before.

The problems with this first position appear to be not primarily ethical, but whether it is correct.

2. *Family planning.* The most popular view of what should be done to reduce growth is to support family planning programs. The U.S. government in recent years has strongly supported this approach. This strategy is clearly described by Bernard Berelson (1970:1):

> By "Family Planning Programs" we mean deliberate efforts, typically governmental in funding and administration, to provide birth control information and services on a voluntary basis to the target population: to the end of lowered fertility among other objectives, e.g., maternal health, child health, reduced resort to nonmedically induced abortion.

Recently the family planning approach has tended to support availability of legally induced abortion, in addition to contraception, as a means of helping women avoid unwanted pregnancies.

While this approach may be supported as a public health program and as a way to increase freedom of choice by individuals, it has been severely criticized by sociologists as a solution to the problem of population growth. The basic criticism is that it does not deal with the motivation of individuals to have children, and hence cannot really solve the problem of population growth. Surveys in LDCS reveal that women, on the average, still want a large number of children. If this is so, then a family planning program could be completely effective by eliminating unwanted pregnancies, but the population would continue to grow at a rapid pace.

On ethical grounds, the major question that Christians must deal with is the morality of encouraging abortions. Christians are divided on this issue, and it is one that merits careful and prayerful consideration by all of us. Rather than dogmatically starting with a position, we should openly examine both sides of the issue, and retain Christian charity toward those who come to an opposite conclusion from our own.

3. *Social change.* Those who criticize the family planning approach as being ineffective argue that much deeper changes in the social system are required to motivate persons to have fewer children. If people are strongly motivated to avoid pregnancy, it is argued, they will find the means. The social institution that needs to be altered in order to effectively change orientations toward childbearing is the family.

Sanctions against nonmarriage and childlessness, sex roles for men and women, and a wide range of other pronatalist aspects of society must be changed. At the same time, policies can be introduced which raise the cost of childbearing and child rearing for individual couples. Singapore is an example of a country which has taken some of these steps: education of women is stressed; contraception, abortion, and sterilization are readily available; tax relief is only granted for the first three children; only two maternity leaves are permitted for public employees; housing allocations favor small families, etc. Whether or not in response to these measures, the birth rate in Singapore has rapidly declined in recent years.

This approach must be carefully considered, because it is grounded in a sociological understanding of how reproduction is related to other components of a social system. A pragmatic question may be raised concerning whether or not measures that radically alter the social system can in fact be introduced into traditional societies. But there is evidence (China most dramatically) that a strong government can quickly alter the nature of a society. On the other hand, it is unlikely that these measures could be implemented without a powerful, repressive government (whether it be communist or right-wing military).

There is much for a Christian to consider with respect to this approach. One issue is, What means should we accept to achieve a desirable end? Assuming that a slower rate of population growth would be beneficial to the whole society and to future generations, is it acceptable to achieve this by severe restrictions on individual rights? (This question is central to the next position, also). What is the role of the family in God's intended purpose for the world, and when does manipulation of family structure violate this purpose? For example, legitimization of sexual activity outside of marital unions may significantly weaken the institution of the family and, hence, reduce motivation for having children. But I believe the Bible clearly teaches that this is contrary to God's will for men and women.

Another question raised by this position is, How ethical is it to introduce negative sanctions for childbearing when the effect is to penalize children? If society withdraws support for children born into large families (educational support, housing support, medical care, etc.), the children as well as the "irresponsible" parents suffer. Likewise, liberalization of divorce laws to increase the independence of women may have the consequence of increasing the number of children being reared in broken homes. In general, policies intended for one purpose often have significant unintended consequences in other areas. The approach of introducing social change via public policy may be a risky way to reduce fertility because the total ramifications cannot be anticipated.

4. *Coercion.* The final approach included here is the most severe: limit the number of children individuals may produce through coercive techniques. Strategies such as enforced sterilization of women after giving birth to a second child, or the licensing of parents to procreate, both have articulate spokespersons. The argument is that voluntary reduction of fertility to replacement levels will not succeed, and that continued growth is so harmful to societal welfare that countries will be forced to adopt coercive measures.

The issue raised by this position which confronts a Christian is fairly obvious. Does the goal of controlling population growth justify this kind of totalitarian control by a government? If a government has the right to forcibly sterilize individuals, is there any limit to the control of the state over individuals? The possibility of this solution is not so unlikely that we can afford to ignore it.

### A Personal Response

Throughout this chapter a number of issues have been raised and questions posed. In most cases I have not developed my personal answers to these questions because I think it is desirable for each of us to struggle with them personally. But I have given thought to these questions. And while I do not have answers to many of them, I have made certain decisions regarding some. I close by summarizing my response below. The purpose of this is not to indicate how others should respond, nor to claim that this is *the* Christian response. Rather, it illustrates the response of one Christian.

Given our understanding of population problems, my wife and I decided that we should not produce more than two children. However, we also felt that God had given us the ability to provide a good Christian home for more than two children, so after our two biological children reached school age we adopted four children who were in need of a home. In our home we try to remember that God cares about the whole world. We keep a map of the world available, and in our family prayer time we frequently choose a country and pray for it. We support two children living in a Christian orphanage in South Korea, and part of our support is prayer for their development.

Further, I received a visiting faculty position for one year at a university in a LDC, and our family lived in that country last year. An important reason for this decision was our desire to be exposed to the life and culture of a poor country. Hopefully we will gain from this new insight into our own lives, as well as into the problems confronting people in poor countries. It is my goal to develop a fairly simple lifestyle, and not to become so encumbered with the concerns of material possessions that I am unable to respond to the needs of others.

On the political level I am not an "activist," but generally I support a generous foreign aid policy by the U.S. And I pray for further insight into how I should live as a responsible Christian at the end of the twentieth century, and for strength to do it.

## Discussion Questions

1. Liberal abortion laws have greatly accelerated the decline of birth rates in several countries, and medically induced abortion early in pregnancy is no more dangerous than having a live baby. Nevertheless, many Christians are opposed to making induced abortion legal. What are the issues involved, and what do you consider the correct position?

2. Policies to slow population growth range from completely voluntaristic approaches to complete coercion. Is there some point on this continuum that the disadvantages of restricting personal freedom outweigh the advantages of population control? (All but anarchists accept the legitimacy of governments imposing some laws which limit personal freedom.)

3. Frequent appeals asking for contributions for famine relief are made. Some argue that while famine relief may offer short-term help, in the long run it intensifies problems of overcrowding and poverty because it delays the time at which populations must control their growth. How should we respond?

4. Christian missionaries in LDCS have been attacked from two sides. Some say they should concentrate more upon meeting the spiritual needs of the population because this is of eternal significance. Others say they should concentrate more on meeting the pressing physical needs of people. What do you think is the proper balance?

5. Is the Christian view of the future optimistic or pessimistic? Develop a biblical response to this.

6. What do you consider to be "responsible parenthood" for Christians?

7. Some argue that the only way to really improve the welfare of a significant number of people is through structural change in society via government action, and that we should direct our efforts at this level (change U.S. government policy). Others argue that our primary responsibility as Christians is to deal directly with individuals who have needs rather than working through bureaucratic structures. Using Christian principles, develop your view of an appropriate response.

8. In response to problems of poverty and population growth in the world, what do you feel is the lifestyle God is calling you to develop? Are you willing to accept this?

9. As indicated on the first page of this chapter, the human population is one important element in a complex ecological system. In Genesis we learn something about God's design in the creation of this system. Discuss the implications of the biblical account of creation for our position on environmental issues.

10. What does Paul mean in 2 Corinthians 5 when he writes that Christians are "agents of reconciliation"? Does this include a responsibility to work for the restoration of the environment?

# References

Berelson, Bernard
    1970 "The Present State of Family Planning Programs." *Studies in Family Planning*, 57, pp. 1-11.
Bogue, Donald J.
    1969 *Principles of Demography*. New York: Wiley.
Coale, Ansley J.
    1977, "Population Growth and Economic Development: The Case of Mexico." *Foreign Affairs Quarterly*, 56, pp. 415-429.
Schaeffer, Francis A.
    1970 *Pollution and the Death of Man: The Christian View of Ecology*. Wheaton, Ill.: Tyndale House.

# PART VI

# SOCIAL INSTITUTIONS

# SOCIAL INSTITUTIONS

Society is a social system, similar to an organism in which all groups, associations, and institutions interact on one another. The major institutions in society are designed to meet man's basic needs: physical, emotional, spiritual, intellectual, and social. At different periods throughout history, one institution predominates, exerting influence over the other institutions. For example, religion (the church) was the dominant institution during the Middle Ages. Without a doubt, the economic institution within Western society exerts the greatest influence today. Since it is inevitable that one predominates, the questions that need to be asked are: Which should predominate? How, and how much should it dominate? What kind of balance and relationship will best meet the needs of the whole man, as well as society?

There is a tendency for many American Christians to rail against "Godless, atheistic communism," yet no society is more materialistic than the United States. We have the highest standard of living in the world—material standard! Does man live by bread alone? Can we serve God *and* mammon?

The pervasiveness of the economic institution is seen in its influence on the others. Although the nuclear family has existed for centuries, it is fragile and fragmented because of the demands of business and industry. Our cultural emphasis on individualism, freedom, and happiness dovetails nicely with the needs of modern industry and business for "movable" personnel. Even divorce, once regarded as an "evil" is now seen to be functional—but for whom?—the individual, the children, or the corporation?

Education, likewise, is responsive to the needs of the economic sector. Business and industry dictate changes in curriculum, as well as initiate changes in administrative and teaching methods. The "business model" is now the model for education at all levels. The electronic revolution, the computer technology, has revolutionized education in virtually every discipline.

The political sphere is inextricably linked to economic factors—regardless of the form of government prevalent in the country. In the United States, for example, the controllers of big business (including big unions) exercise a firm guiding hand in government—overtly or covertly. This is true of both domestic and foreign policy.

Even religion has not escaped the pervasive influence of the economic institution, as denominations draw on the expertise of men and women who also happen to have financial clout. Their influence is reflected in the nature of the message of popular clergy. One could hardly compare them to a "Nathan" or an "Amos" who called rulers (kings), businessmen, and judiciaries to task for immorality, oppression, exploitation, and injustice. But not all have bowed the knee to Baal, as Paul Hanly Furfey and Anthony Campolo point out.

Obviously, each major institution could be treated so that its effect upon the others could be seen. But there is little doubt that the economic institution has wrought the greatest influence. We are not being pessimistic. It is realism—"that's the way it is." Have Christians allowed the secular world to squeeze them into its mold? Marxists challenge us to prove them wrong!

Edward A. Bagdoyan, a corporate executive and engineer who has engaged in worldwide business transactions in both the free and communist world, presents an overview of our modified capitalist system. Ideally, he sees the free enterprise system as completely compatible with Christian principles. When the system goes wrong, he sees the root cause to be the nature of man, not the free enterprise system.

"Politics and Principalities and Powers" presents an examination of the relationships between government, economics, and the church. Biblically, government is ordained by God and we should obey "the powers that be." But the Christian ought not to be involved in corrupt practices of either politics or business. Anthony Campolo discusses the apparent symbiotic relationship between the church and the state in America which has given rise to a "civil religion." He points out the close ties between government and multinational corporations, and he challenges the church to speak out prophetically as the National and World Council of Churches has done.

Four areas in family sociology are presented. J. Howard Kauffman treats comprehensively the alternatives to traditional monogamous marriage. His coverage includes swinging, communes, single-parent families, trial marriage, living together, homosexuality, and polygamy. He does not see the family vanishing. Robert W. Herron asks, "What Makes a Family Christian?" He rejects the notion that it is the traditional patriarchal family structure, insisting that mutual love, respect, and submission is the key. He supports his thesis with both solid biblical and sociological evidence. Charles P. De Santo discusses the issue of premarital sex. He relates sexuality to the whole person and the total social context. He discusses the pros and cons in the light of biblical principles.

J.H. Phillips' article presents the case for monogamous, egalitarian marriage, supported by fresh biblical insights from the teachings of Jesus, as well as from the Apostle Paul. He also draws support from "secular prophets" in the fields of sociology, psychoanalysis, and marriage and family counseling. He suggests that partners within marriage find fulfillment through a "permanent," "exclusive" relationship.

Religion gets extensive coverage. E. Steve Cassells opens with a discussion of the sociological and psychological functions of religion for both the individual and society. He sees no necessary conflict between sociology and Christianity. Christianity, he believes, best meets man's needs. Paul Hanly Furfey demonstrates that New Testament principles shed light on ways of dealing with social problems. He emphasizes the New Testament doctrine of *works* as evidence of faith—a neglected doctrine in Protestantism. The problems of the sick and the poor, as well as slavery, sexism, and war can all be ameliorated and/or resolved when biblical principles serve as guides.

Margaret M. Poloma presents her research of the Mana Community—an intentional urban one. She analyzes the contributions it makes to the personal lives of its members and to the community through their service. She calls attention to the dangers of institutionalization that inevitably quench the free working of the Holy Spirit.

Richard J. Stellway's research into the exercise of the clergy's prophetic role illustrates how mitigating factors often restrain him. He cites intervening variables such as congregational opposition, theological perspective, denominational polity, and personal ambition as all playing a part in a minister's preaching and leadership relative to social problems. He challenges the laity—you and me—to support clergy in the exercise of the prophetic role.

# 27
# Capitalism and Christian Principles

*Edward A. Bagdoyan*

> Has religious opinion in the past regarded questions of social organization and economic conduct as irrelevant to the life of the spirit, or has it endeavored not only to Christianize the individual but to make a Christian civilization? Can religion admit the existence of a sharp antithesis between personal morality and the practices which are permissible in business? Does the idea of a church involve the acceptance of any particular standard of social ethics?
> —R.H. Tawney, *Religion and the Rise of Capitalism.*

> The superlative value of individualism through its impulse to production, its stimulation to invention, has, so far as I know, never been denied.
> —Herbert Hoover, *American Individualism—Economic Phases.*

As an undergraduate student at New York University, I once prepared a paper for a humanities class in which I tried to explain my philosophy of life as centered on areas like economics, family, ethics, etc. At that time (1949) I based my personal philosophy of life on the premise and belief that there is a God, and that the Judeo-Christian teaching of Scripture that pervades my cultural and religious background influenced not only my thinking, but also my actions.

Now, after nearly thirty years, I can still say that my philosophy of life (circa 1979) is still influenced by the same tenets of the Christian faith. This does not mean that there has not been any intellectual

**Edward A. Bagdoyan**
*Staff Assistant to the Vice-President of Sales and Engineering*
*Kennedy Van Saun Corp., Danville, Pennsylvania*
Mr. Bagdoyan, a chemical engineer, has traveled extensively as a sales representative to countries in the free world, as well as to communist block countries. He is famliar with the complexities of the business community, and he has authored articles for trade and chemical journals. An ordained elder, he is active in the United Presbyterian Church. He earned a BS in chemical engineering from New York University in 1950.

development over the past three decades; but, if anything, it means that there has developed a deeper regard and a greater realization that perhaps an honest effort to base our social thinking on Judeo-Christian principles may be the thrust of the future.

## Sociology and Economics

The sociology of industry will be considered against the background of the American capitalist or free enterprise system. Under this system, American culture and civilization has developed and produced the highest standard of living in the world, concomitant with the development of stable democratic social and political order. Neither sociology nor economics is an exact science; each deals with a sphere of human activity which does not easily lend itself to precise definition or to neat categorization. It is because of this factor that any article dealing with the sociology of industry must, of necessity, be subjective to a large degree. The general goal of this chapter is not to present an overview of either economics or of sociology. Instead, my goal is to point out some thoughts that should be helpful to one as an individual and as a group member so that he can exercise considered judgment against the background of Judeo-Christian concepts. Hopefully, his actions, whether individual or in concert with his fellowmen, will be based on sound reason and fair play.

We live in a world and in a society in which people interact with each other on many levels and in different contexts. One such area of interaction or relationship is economics—not the esoteric world of Galbraith, Friedman, and Marx—but the everyday world of business and industry, of buying and selling, and of producing and consuming. Economics and economic judgements are involved in many commonplace activities in which all of us are involved to varying degrees. For example:

(1) The housewife who buys the family's groceries, deciding which of the many competing brands of bread, soap, or dog food she will purchase;

(2) the farmer who plants his wheat in the expectation of a favorable growing season and a good crop;

(3) the chemical plant or automobile factory worker who produces the goods and materials for the marketplace; and

(4) the plant manager who establishes production schedules to meet the needs of his customers.

The economic relationships of people have undergone significant changes, modifications, and alterations during the past several centuries; however, the underlying consideration has been to provide members of society with the basic necessities for survival, commonly referred to as food, clothing, and shelter. Regardless of the times or situations, questions such as, "Who will produce?" "What will be produced?" "Who will share?" and "In what proportion will the goods and services be distributed?" have always required answers.

## Capitalism—An Overview

The history of the United States and of Western civilization, which has come to influence world thought, customs, and actions has its moral and ethical roots in Judeo-Christian teachings. Within the context of this teaching, the individual is not only held in high regard, but oftentimes there is a one-to-one relationship such as exists between God and man. This emphasis on individuality with personal rights, responsibilities, actions, and decisions spills over into, and plays a significant role in, the area of economics and industry.

In today's world there are two basic economic philosophies, which may simply be categorized as capitalism and socialism, with their many and varied forms; however, we will limit ourselves to the capitalistic or free enterprise system.

Capitalism, as a distinct phase of economic life, can be traced back to the thirteenth century with the emergence of merchants and bankers from the binding restrictions of feudal society. This led to the period of mercantilism when, under the protection of the state, markets were opened up, sources of raw material procured, and the standard whereby one measured success was wealth. The mercantilist state, through which the merchants worked, had as a primary object the enhancement of political power through wealth.

The subsequent doctrine of individualism was developed in part by the philosophy of John Locke. He argued that men as individuals possessed natural rights, such as the right to own property, and these rights could best be exercised when government regulation or activity in the economic field was reduced to a minimum. These ideas reached their culmination in Adam Smith's *Wealth of Nations* (1776/1969) and, with the advent of the Industrial Revolution, capitalism came of age.

Basically, capitalism or the free enterprise system may be characterized by the following features:

(1) *Private Property*—defined as the right to own capital goods or the means of production, and the right to use them in any legal way.

(2) *Freedom of Enterprise*—defined as the freedom to utilize property in whatever field one choses and, in so doing, to assume the risks of loss as well as the prospect of gain.

(3) *Profit*—defined as the expectation of gain or profit from a venture. The enterpriser will, with the expectation of gain, exert his ingenuity and skill to operate in the most efficient and productive way.

(4) *Competition*—defined as the interaction of forces in the marketplace to stabilize prices, profits, wages, and costs. In a competitive system no one producer controls the market for a particular commodity. It may be viewed as the automatic or built-in regulator of capitalism.

The emphasis is on individual action, initiative, and responsibility. As Herbert Hoover said, "The superlative value of individualism through its impulse to production, its stimulation to invention, has, so far as I know, never been denied."

An economic system does not exist in a vacuum. It is an integral part of a political system. Capitalism, as we have experienced it, has developed in democratic countries that guarantee individual rights and freedoms and allow a plurality of political thought. Theoretically, capitalism could develop under any form of government as long as the concepts of private property, freedom of enterprise, profit motive, and competition are allowed to interact. It is interesting to note that modern capitalism has developed almost hand-in-hand with political democracy. In each case, the emphasis on individualism and individual rights and responsibilities has been, and is, an important catalyst.

### Religion—Influence and Relationship

Judeo-Christian teaching has been used as a guide to the development of economic rules of behavior for several millennia. While we will not give an overview of this historical development, we will offer specific thoughts and ideas for consideration which will allow the reader to decide how, and in what way, they may be applicable to today.

There are sociologists and historians who believe that the development of the modern capitalistic economic system is a direct outgrowth of Christian principles enunciated during the Protestant Reformation—more specifically Calvinistic principles (Weber, 1905/1958). Just as the Reformation emphasized personal and individual responsibility and response, so did the development of capitalism require individual initiative and development. Other scholars disagree with this cause-and-effect relationship and maintain that the capitalistic spirit is as old as history, and that it would have developed regardless of the fact of the Reformation.

In this time period of greater awareness of the roles of the various segments of society and of their influence on the quality of life we enjoy, there has been renewed interest in the part capitalist principles should or ought to play. There have been attacks on the industrial community for its lack of sensitivity. Some of the more prominent areas of attack have been:

(1) *Environment*—that the industrial community alone is responsible for the problems of air pollution, water pollution, and the irresponsible use of land resources.

(2) *Unethical behavior*—the proffering of bribes and other inducements to clients, both domestic and foreign.

(3) *Obscenity of profits*—that the profit motive which is one of the basic elements of capitalism is somehow obscene and ought to be eliminated.

(4) *Social callousness*—that industry has regard only for its own well-being and has no regard for the effects of its actions on society.

All too often, these attacks have been made in simplistic terms, with no attempt made to present a balanced picture or argument.We will neither defend nor pass judgment upon the industrial community or its attackers. But what we will do is point out a few Christian or biblical guides which, if followed to their logical conclusions, would allow the various elements of society to interact to their mutual benefit.

At an early date in the development of capitalist thought, its exponents succeeded in formulating a religious and an ethical philosophy. Many recognized that it was not possible to separate man's actions in the economic world from his actions in the religious and ethical worlds. They believed that economic relations are merely a facet of human behavior for which each is morally responsible. This responsibility is not the result of an impersonal mechanism, but the application of religious and ethical principles.

Basically, the idea of a dual standard of behavior was attacked as not being consistent with Christian principles. This attitude is still with us today, and it is reflected in the saying that one ought to practice what he preaches (believes). In effect, it is incumbent upon us to put into everyday practice, in all facets of our lives, those Christian principles which we profess on Sunday. Many Christian businessmen insisted that the Christian demonstrates his commitment to Christ by adherence to his ethical standards. Furthermore, they believed that observance of these standards was obligatory in the economic world, as well as in all other areas of the private and the public sector.

One of the leading thinkers of the seventeenth century in this area was the Puritan clergyman and scholar, Richard Baxter, who strongly argued against the notion that religion has nothing to do with business. He preached that the Christian is bound to consider the golden rule in business, as well as in religion. Furthermore, he said that business must be carried out in the spirit of one who is conducting a Christian service.

### Biblical Guidelines for Businessmen and Christians
*Biblical Guide (1)*

Let us go beyond Baxter to the teachings of the Bible for a few injunctions which ought to serve as guides in the area of business ethics, as well as religion. The prophet Amos addressed himself to the socioeconomic conditions of his day. He cried out against the practices of unethical businessmen of his day and, in effect, told them to bring into the marketplace their ethical teachings and not to separate their religious life from their business life. Amos did not mince any words when he said, "Listen, you merchants who rob the poor, trampling on the needy; you who long for the Sabbath to end . . . so you can get out and start cheating again" (8:4-5, *Living Bible*).

Amos catalogs injustices such as the use of short weights, inflated prices, poor quality of workmanship, and shoddy merchandise. He also criticized employers who were overly severe with their poorly paid employees who owed them money. Amos, as well as Baxter, recognized that business must be guided by principles of biblical ethics. Amos, in particular, was saying that there was a need for the buyer-seller relationship or consumer-business relationship to be based on the precepts of justice and honesty (5:24).

*Biblical Guide (2)*

Another aspect of Christian teaching which we may consider is that of fairness, of not taking advantage of another's weakness, and of living up to one's promises. Admittedly, the previous statement could have been divided into several propositions, and each one treated separately. However, perhaps at the risk of oversimplification, we will speak of fairness. The gospel writer Matthew speaks of the vineyard owner who hires men to work in his vineyard. He hires them throughout the day and agrees to pay to each one a set amount of money. At the end of the workday, the accounts are settled and each worker is paid the agreed upon sum. As it turned out, those who started to work in the morning were paid the same amount of money as those who worked only a half day. Naturally, there were grumblings that the system was not fair, and that the owner was discriminating—not treating them fairly. Note, however, the answer of the owner, "I did you no wrong! Didn't you agree to work for me all day for a set sum? I want to pay all of my workers the same amount. Is it against the law to give away my money if I want to? Why are you angry with me because I try to be considerate?" (Matthew 20:13-15).

Here simply expressed is the sentiment that an employer, an owner, a businessman should treat his workers with fairness. He should not only agree to pay each the worth of his labor, but he should also keep his word. The implication here is that the workers and the owner have entered into an agreement or a contract to do a specific job for a specific amount of money. In our complex society, labor-management relations (as were those between the biblical vineyard owner and the workers) are agreed upon by the process of collective bargaining. Representatives of both sides meet to settle differences and agree upon items such as fringe benefits, working hours and conditions, types of work, and pay rates.

Underlying all of these agreements or contracts should be the principle of fairness; that is, that the agreed upon contract should be fair to the worker as well as to the owner. There is, in addition, the added dimension of responsibility to fulfill the terms of the agreement or contract.

### Biblical Guide (3)

The golden rule, "So whatever you wish that men would do to you, do so to them (Matthew 7:12), introduces the idea of accountability or of stewardship. The Christian teaching of stewardship states that all that we have, we have as free gift from the Almighty (1 Corinthians 4:7), and that we are only stewards or caretakers (Deuteronomy 8:17-18; 1 Corinthians 4:1-2). This includes entrepreneurs and corporate executives.

Matthew (25:14-30) also tells us about a ruler or an owner who, upon going away for a while, calls his workers and gives them certain sums of money for investment purposes. He gives to each according to his station and to his apparent ability. During the absence of the ruler, several manage to invest the entrusted funds and soon begin to show a profit. One who was afraid and timid buries the money and, upon the return of the ruler, returns it. The ruler reviews the actions of his workers and rewards them according to their degrees of success.

One of the implications of this story is that those who are entrusted with business matters are to act and to work in the best interests of those who have invested their money and of the enterprises in which they work. This may be expanded to say that the worker should perform his duties in the best possible way, trying not only to improve his situation, but that of the organization for which he works.

Still another corollary concept which may be derived is that of social responsibility. Along with the concepts of making a profit, of engaging in free trade, of hiring workers, etc., there is for capitalism the added implied responsibility of social stewardship. There are intangible areas in which the businessman should be active. For example, he should cope realistically with the problems of environmental pollution, not only because it is the proper technological action to take, but also because it is the moral action to take as the steward of goods and services.

It was this same steadfast concept of stewardship which prompted Andrew Carnegie and John D. Rockefeller to donate vast sums of money to hospitals, libraries, colleges, and other social institutions.

## Conclusion

It appears as if by a fortunate coincidence that some of the very virtues enjoined on Christians, e.g., diligence, moderation, sobriety, thrift, and prudence, are also the qualities deemed conducive to success in the business world. The seventeenth- and eighteenth-century writers carried this analogy to logical conclusions while pointing out the similarities between the religious and business attitudes. Virtue is good; vice is bad. Bad company, speculation, gambling, fanaticism are traits which the Christian is admonished to avoid, as is the businessman. It was noted that the needs of society and the needs of the individual coincided.

There is, however, a gulf between theory and practice. The theory that Christian precepts of morality can and should be synonymous with business ethics is an ideal towards which we should strive. If followed, they would surely allow mankind to develop a social structure which is fair to all, free of injustice, and always conscious of the commonweal. We are, however, dealing with and speaking of finite and fallible human beings who often speak of achieving perfection, but then seem to work in an opposite direction.

Today, in our century, our political, social, and economic philosophies are being questioned and challenged by those who would destroy, as well as by those who would improve. It is hoped that honest probings will allow us to improve our social and economic fabric. While it would be a miracle indeed if, after all these years, Christian principles were invoked and used as guidelines, it is a goal towards which we should strive.

## Discussion Questions

1. Does the idea of being a Christian and a church member involve the acceptance of any particular standard of social and business ethics? Why? Why not?

2. In the United States where we try to "separate church and state," should a businessman put his religious and ethical beliefs into actual practice or should he adopt a dual standard of morality?

3. If in making a purchase you find that an error has been made in your favor, should you take positive corrective action or should you accept it as a rightful windfall?

4. Should an American businessman working in a foreign country follow the proverb of, "when in Rome do as the Romans do"?

5. Can industry and business be considered as social activities and can (or should) they be rightfully studied as sociological phenomena?

6. Why are sociological studies of business and industry a must? Who benefits?

7. When working in a foreign country, an American businessman is faced with the dilemma that, in line with local practices, substantial bribes must be offered in order to be considered for, or to obtain, an order. In such a situation, should ethical principles of "no bribery" be followed and a potential order lost, or should one follow local customs? What biblical principles can you cite to support your answer?

8. Based on your knowledge of Christian and biblical teachings, what other guides would you suggest which might supplement or complement the text?

9. Do we expect individuals or nonbusiness people to be responsive to one set of ethical standards and business people to another? In

effect support a dual standard which says, "If I do it, it's okay because I'm a little guy; but if General Motors does it, it is wrong because General Motors is a corporation"?

10. Is the Bible supportive of the free enterprise system? Of any other system? Discuss.

## References

Butterfield, Herbert
    1965 *The Whig Interpretation of History.* New York: The Norton Library.
Grunewald, D. and H.L. Bass
    1966 *Public Policy and the Modern Corporation.* New York: Appleton-Century-Crofts.
Smith, Adam
    1969 *The Wealth of Nations.* New York; Penguin (1776).
Tawney, R.H.
    1937 *Religion and the Rise of Capitalism.* New York: Harcourt, Brace.
Wasserman, L.
    1944 *Modern Political Philosophies and What They Mean.* Halycon House.
Weber, Max
    1958 Trans. by Talcott Parsons) *The Protestant Ethic and the Spirit of Capitalism.* New York: Scribner's (1905).

# 28
# Politics and Principalities and Powers

*Anthony Campolo*

### The Universality of Political Institutions

Every society develops a political system through which social control is exercised over its members. There must be some way to maintain order, to prevent deviants from disrupting the life of society, and to make those decisions which determine the destiny of society. The structures which serve these functions may be as simple as a kinship system ruled by the elders of the tribe, or they may be as complex as the bureaucratic monstrosities which have come to characterize highly industrialized societies. Regardless of their nature, these political systems exercise power over the members of society. They constrain behavior and orient the populace to reach the requisite goals which insure society's survival.

Emile Durkheim leads us to understand that political institutions, like all social facts, emerge *sui generis* from the meaningful interactions of members of society. They are created by society, but, once they develop, political institutions take on an autonomous character. They seem to have an existence of their own, independent of the people who gave them birth. Political institutions become reified entities. The people from whom they emerge forget that they are the creators and

**Anthony Campolo**
*Professor of Sociology and Department Chairman*
*Eastern College*

Anthony Campolo is the author of a book and numerous journal articles. He is a popular speaker and lecturer, and has appeared much on the mass media. Before entering the teaching profession, he served as a Baptist minister to several congregations in New Jersey and Pennsylvania. His field of special interest is the family. In addition to his teaching at Eastern, he has also taught at the University of Pennsylvania and Regent College of the University of British Columbia. He has served in a humanitarian corporation that has programs in the Dominican Republic, Haiti, and Niger. His academic training was received at Eastern Baptist Theological Seminary, and he earned his PhD in sociology from Temple University.

treat political structures as entities which have lives of their own.

## Scripture and Government

When the Bible speaks of political institutions, it refers to them as "principalities and powers." Berkhof (1962), a Dutch theologian, has brought the biblical idea of "principalities and powers" into sociological discussion. He claims that this phrase, used so often by the Apostle Paul, refers to those elements of reality which Durkheim calls "social facts." This means that when Paul speaks of "principalities and powers," he is referring to all elements of the culture which constrain the behavior and thinking of people within society. Into this category fall the political institutions.

Whatever the process by which they come into existence, the Apostle Paul makes it clear that political systems are "principalities and powers" which originate with God. In Colossians 1:16 we read:

> In him everything in heaven and on earth was created, not only things visible but also the invisible orders of thrones, sovereignties, authorities, and powers: the whole universe has been created through him and for him (NEB).

Furthermore, Christians are reminded by the Apostle Paul to obediently submit to the power exercised by political systems.

> Let every soul be subject unto the higher powers. For there is no power but of God: the powers that be are ordained of God. Whosoever therefore resisteth the power, resisteth the ordinance of God: and they that resist shall receive to themselves damnation (Romans 13:1-2).

This passage from Romans seems to provide theological legitimation for the existing political structures. Furthermore, any rebellion against the political system of a society apparently is rebellion against God.

### Religion Can Bolster Corrupt Government

Voltaire clearly saw how useful this religious legitimation could be for the political system. He recognized that if political leaders could convince the populace of society that its political system was ordained of God, then opposition to the political leaders would be interpreted as a sin against God. That French philosopher would have had a cynical analysis of the close association which former President Nixon sought with evangelist Billy Graham. Voltaire probably would have argued that Nixon was trying to convey the impression that his policies were approved by God, because Christianity's most famous preacher seemed to be lending tacit support to the Nixon administration.

## Natural Law Can Anthenticate Government

Religion is not the only way of legitimating a political system. As the world becomes increasingly secular (or "rationalized," as Max Weber would say) other means of legitimation have been sought and found. Max Weber (1964:124-133) points out that a political system also can be legitimated by "natural law" or by "legality."

Legitimation by "natural law" means that the people of a society discern a particular order to the universe, and the political system is structured to be in harmony with that order. The founding fathers of the United States legitimated their new society on "natural law." In their Declaration of Independence they stated that this new political system was one to which "the laws of nature and nature's God entitled them." The universe was conceived to be a gigantic machine governed by fixed laws and the political system was viewed as an expression of those laws. These political leaders were sure of the legitimacy of their system because it appeared to be in accord with the laws which governed the rest of nature. Auguste Comte, the founder of modern sociology, would have labeled a social system which legitimated its normative order in this fashion as one in the metaphysical stage of evolutionary development. Nevertheless, a political system legitimated by "natural law" was more "rational," given Weber's understanding, than one which was legitimated by divine right.

## The Consent of the Governed—Legality

The most usual basis of legitimacy in today's world is through legality. Such a system is authenticated by the consent of the governed. They recognize that their rulers are in positions of authority because the majority in the society willingly accept them as rulers. Since authority for a legal system is derived from the people of the society, they are aware that they can take this authority away and give it to others.

## To Obey or Not to Obey

Christians, in many circumstances, have had a hard time dealing with political systems because they have tended to legitimate them religiously. Indeed, the thirteenth chapter of Romans does seem to give to political systems legitimation from God. Regardless of how the secular society views its rulers, it seems as though the Apostle Paul admonishes Christians to view their rulers as ministers of God.

> For he is the minister of God to thee for good. But if thou do that which is evil, be afraid; for he beareth not the sword in vain: for he is the minister of God, a revenger to execute wrath upon him that doeth evil (Romans 13:4).

During the days of the Hitler regime some Christians believed that it was wrong to oppose the government in spite of its obvious immorality. They reasoned that it was their religious responsibility to "obey the higher powers," and that God would not hold them responsible for what the government did or ordered them to do. There were others who reasoned that "the powers," or government, though created by God, had become rebellious against their Creator and was now under the control of Satan. To obey the dictates of such a political system, or to lend it support, would be to cooperate with demonic powers. Hence, they believed that it was their moral responsibility to resist the government.

As the Civil Rights movement developed in the United States, the question of how Christians should relate to the immoral dictates of government was once again a live issue. At first, Martin Luther King contended that the local laws maintaining "Jim Crow" were unconstitutional and therefore not legitimate. Disobeying unconstitutional laws, consequently, seems permissible. Eventually, King was faced with the necessity of standing against a federal injunction. Then the issue of civil disobedience had to be faced squarely. King did disobey the laws of the government, but when he did, he offered himself to the authorities to be jailed. He contended that submitting to "the powers" was to choose from the options that that state offered. The state had the right to expect conformity to its ordinances, and the right to jail those who refused to obey. King chose to disobey, but in so doing he recognized the authority of state by submitting to its punishment.

More recently, the same sort of question arose in relation to the draft resisters during the Vietnam War. Some would argue that the draft resisters did the moral thing by fleeing the country—usually to Canada. Others contended that if they believed that what the government required was against the will of God, then they should have submitted to the government by going to jail. Thus they would have recognized the God-ordained power of the state over them but, at the same time, refused to do what they believed to be contrary to God's will.

## Governmental Support of Religion

Structural functionalists, who dominate sociological theory on the contemporary scene, are not only concerned with the legitimating role which religion has in relation to the government, they are also very interested in the ways that government functions to serve the interests of religion. Certainly there is reciprocity between the political and the religious institutions. Even in the United States, a nation that prides itself in maintaining a separation between church and state, there is tacit support of ecclesiastical institutions by the government.

### Federal Funding of Religion

First of all, the government does not tax church property. Many claim that this is a covert means of the state providing financial support for religious institutions. The state cooperates to enable the churches to grow wealthy as the property increases in value. Furthermore, the state provides police protection, fire protection, roads, and other services which the churches use, but for which they do not pay.

Second, the state supports the church by providing chaplains for the armed forces. Here we have tax payers paying the salaries of religious leaders. Some argue that chaplains should be supported by churches and denominations in the same way that ministers and missionaries are supported, rather than out of the government's treasury.

There are a great number of people who still think that the government sponsored public school system should have Bible reading and prayer, if not outright religious education as part of the academic program. This was one way the government endorsed religion in former times and many believe that such practices were proper.

The government supports the church in other ways which are even more subtle. Peter Berger (1961), in his book *The Noise of Solemn Assemblies*, makes an excellent case that, in spite of claims to the contrary, the government supports the church handsomely for the legitimation which it receives in return.

## "*Civil Religion,*" *Government and Christianity*

Perhaps the ultimate legitimation for the government comes from what Robert Bellah (1967:1-21) has called "civil religion." It is his claim that in our pluralistic society, there has developed a religion which underlies the denominational and sectarian variants of the American people and encompasses religious values which we all hold in common. These values express themselves not only in "civil religion," but in the legal structure of the political system. Consequently, the more loyal we are to those values, the more loyal we are to the state.

Many argue that this "civil religion" which legitimates the social order has become an unconscious alternative to Christianity. They claim that churches unwittingly propagate this religion, thinking that they are advocating a biblical faith. Instead, they fool people into thinking they are Christian when these believers have become adherents of a religion which enhances ethnocentricism and keeps people from a God who transcends the cultural system.

## *True Christianity in Conflict with* "*Principalities and Powers*"

There are some who go beyond criticizing "civil religion." They suggest that "true New Testament Christianity," rather than legitimating the existing political-economic system, judges it and provides an ideology for challenging that system. Some Christian leaders, particularly in the Third World and in the American black community, utilize the biblical message as a means of legitimating opposition to the government. They see the gospel as "the new wine," which tears apart the old wine skins (i.e., the government). They see Jesus as a revolutionary figure who challenged the "principalities and powers" of his day and was eventually crucified by them. In crucifying Christ these powers had their true diabolical character revealed.

> On that cross he discarded the cosmic powers and authorities like a garment; he made a public spectacle of them and led them as captives in his triumphal procession (Colossians 2:15, NEB).

These "Christian revolutionaries" accept the admonition of the Apostle Paul when he writes in Ephesians (6:12) that we are to fight against principalities and powers. They may believe that this fight is to be carried out in a nonviolent manner or they may believe that violence is justified. Still others, like Howard Yoder (1972) in the Anabaptist tradition, suggest that the Scripture dictates that Christians be an alternative community standing with Jesus, while the established political system collapses in its sinful violent lifestyle. What is significant is the fact that religion does not always legitimate the political system as some overly simplistic Marxians might claim. It can be used, as Karl Mannheim (1936) saw, as a legitimation for those who would challenge the established political system with visions of the kingdom of God.

### Economics, Governmental Control, and Politicians

Marxians claim that political systems are simply extensions of the society's dominant economic system. Those who control the means of production and the capital of the society, control the society and express that control through the political system. To the Marxist, it is impossible to separate the political and economic systems. They claim the two are one and the same. Through the political system the ruling economic class exercises power over those whom they would exploit.

Without going as far as the Marxians, a case can be made that the government of the United States has become subservient to special interest groups. This has become the case primarily through campaign financing. To successfully run for the United States House of Representatives costs a candidate about $100,000. The high cost of campaigning is the result of the employment of television as a medium for political advertising. Without employing television a candidate cannot gain the kind of recognition that wins in national elections. Unless the candidate is personally wealthy, he must turn to donors to finance the campaign. Generally, the corporations and business firms underwrite the campaigns of Republican candidates and the labor unions underwrite Democratic candidates. However, if a candidate accepts large donations for a campaign from some special interest group, can that candidate still claim Jesus as Lord? Are the decisions made by that candidate, once elected, dictated by the Holy Spirit or by the concerns of the special interest group which financed the candidate? This is an issue with which every Christian candidate for national office must grapple.

### The Problem of Multinational Corporations

Most observers of the American political scene are aware of the role that corporations, unions, and other special interest groups play in financing campaigns and, consequently, in influencing political decisions made by those whom they help to elect. However, there is much less awareness of the political ramifications of corporations expanding to the point where they have greater wealth and power than many of the nations of the earth (Barnet and Muller, 1974:15).

If we compare the annual sales of corporations with the gross national product of countries for 1973, we discover that GM is bigger than Switzerland, Pakistan and South Africa; that Royal Dutch Shell is bigger than Iran, Venezuela and Turkey; and that Goodyear Tire is bigger than Saudi Arabia.

These companies often function as monopolies or oligarchies, and can control the supply of resources which are crucial to the survival of nations even as large as the United States.

Seven large energy corporations, often referred to as the Seven Sisters, control most of the oil supply of the world. The policies of these corporations can determine the destiny of wealthy industrial nations, as was demonstrated by their policies following the Yom Kippur War in the Middle East.

*Loyalty to Stockholders*

Such corporations openly acknowledge that they have an allegiance which transcends any nation. These multinational corporations exist for the express purpose of making a profit for their stockholders and that interest takes precedence over the interest of any particular nation. Because their primary financial transactions are not limited to boundaries of any nation, the trade regulations and antitrust regulations which might control their activities and influence their decision-making prove meaningless. Our laws are designed to regulate what goes on within a nation and do not regulate what they do extraterritorially. Hence, the emergence of the multinational corporations become huge units of power which national governments find increasingly difficult to keep from determining what goes on in the world.

*The Church "Takes on" the Corporations*

The National Council of Churches has lobbied for legislation to foster social justice. For instance, the Council played a significant role in pressing for civil rights legislation during the 1960s. But as power began shifting from the national government to the multinational corporations, the Council has seen the need to exercise influence over the decision-making processes of corporations. One means of doing this has been to have the representatives of the National Council of Churches attend the annual stockholders meetings of these corporations and question policies that seem to foster injustice and oppression. The Council can easily do this, because member Christian denominations usually have stockholdings in such corporations, thus providing the right to be heard when the stockholders' meetings take place.

*Do Multinationals Assure Peace?*

That the multinational corporations are coming to dominate political structures is a reality which is readily admitted to by the leaders of these companies. The president of IBM claims that the concept of the national state is outmoded and calls for a new world order which validates the roles and functions of multinational corporations. He and many other such corporate executives point to the fact that they are the creators of world peace. They claim that by interlinking the economies of the various nations, they have created an interdependence between nations which makes war increasingly impossible. That claim might be easy to maintain except for the fact that these companies foster consumption styles which deplete the world's limited unrenewable resources (i.e., oil, bauxite, copper). As the rich countries find these resources more and more scarce they will become increasingly belligerent in their relations with each other as each endeavors to get a disproportionate share.

Thorsten Veblen, taking the ideas of Edward Bellamy, as set forth in his delightful book, *Looking Backwards,* suggests that the national state eventually may be discarded as a dominant form of political organization. Even as consanguine tribal units were transcended by the national state, so the national state will be transcended by another kind of social order efficiently run by corporations. Already there are executives whose loyalty to their companies exceeds their loyalty to their nations, thus establishing a new collective consciousness fit for such a new world. If efficiency is what is supposed to make an increasingly complex world function effectively, then a society coordinated and run by corporations has great possibilities. Who can doubt the efficiency of corporations?

From a Christian perspective, these corporations may appear to have assumed an idolatrous nature. Having been willed into existence by God, as have all "principalities and powers," they no longer function in accord with the will of God in the service of humanity. But instead, they make humanity subservient to their vested interests.

## Vesting Power and World War III

Another development which is greatly affecting the political structures is the increasing sophistication of warfare technology. In a world in which one nation almost instantaneously can destroy another, it becomes necessary for each national government to develop the capacity to immediately respond to threats from enemy powers. When a nation faces an attack, retaliation must be immediate to be successful. The delay of even a few minutes could swing the outcome decisively in favor of the enemy.

This need for instantaneous retaliation requires a setting aside of democratic decision-making processes. If the alarm for an attack is sounded, the conditions created by modern technological warfare do not leave time to poll public opinion or to call Congress into session in order to determine what to do. Debates, discussion, and other characteristics of democratic-decison making must be ignored simply because they take too long. If the response to the threat is to be instantaneous, then the decision to react must be concentrated, in all probability, in one person. When Pearl Harbor was bombed in 1941, the United States was able to have its Congress called into session to discuss what response would be appropriate and to vote for a declaration of war. There would not be time for such a process if World War III were to suddenly break out. Our military response would have to be immediate or not at all. Thus, in the face of a national emergency we have given the Commander-in-Chief of the Armed Forces, the President of the United States, the right to make the decision to set loose our entire arsenal of atomic weapons without consulting Congress.

Christians have to consider the ramifications of concentrating that much power in the hands of one person. They believe that power distorts the one who holds it and that the egotistic nature of humans is not to be trusted. They have, consequently, always maintained a system of checks and balances on political leaders. Now they find that they must yield unchecked power to one person, knowing that such power could corrupt that person, and that his egotistic nature could lead him to abuse such awesome power.

## The Role of the Christian In Politics

*The Anabaptist Tradition*

Lastly, we must discuss the role of Christians *in* politics. Some, like many in the Anabaptist tradition, argue that the Christian must not become involved in a system that uses power to force others to do what is "right." Jesus did not use power, but rather emptied himself and took on the form of a servant (see Philippians 2). To deal with people from a position of power is contrary to the style of Jesus and, therefore, unbefitting a follower of Christ. They contend that any government which uses violence in dealing with its adversaries, and legitimates killing to provide national defense, cannot be a social system in which followers of Christ can participate. Hence, most Anabaptists (Mennonites, Amish, Brethren) will not hold elected offices, will not bear arms in national defense, and often will not even vote.

*The Reformed Tradition*

Other Christians, particularly those in the tradition of John Calvin, argue that the task of the Christian is to be one of God's agents in the world and to be used as an instrument for transforming the world into what it should be. They claim that God did not separate himself from the world, as the Anabaptists would have us do, but incarnated himself in it. He loved the world and gave himself for it (John 3:16). He calls upon us to go into all the world with his message of liberation (Mark 16:15), and that must include that sector of the world which maintains political power. This attitude assumes that Christians are called to invade society and to act as the leaven which can transform society from within. They claim that noninvolvement in government by Christians leaves this awesome power system in the hands of those who lack a commitment to the Christian value system. This in turn will result in government that could be oppressive and immoral. These Christians of the Reformed tradition argue that Paul calls them to participate in the deliverance of a fallen creation from its corrupted condition (Romans 8:21-23). There is no question but that those who become involved in politics run the risk of being corrupted by the system, but it is a risk they are willing to take in order to fulfill the call to responsible discipleship.

In all probability, the dialectic tension which exists between these two positions is good for the church and for the world. Society needs a glimpse of the kingdom of God which can somewhat be revealed by a community of believers living apart from worldly involvements. It also needs the participation of those who are willing to work out their own salvation with "fear and trembling" as they take their places in the power structures of our age. The church needs both groups to remind her that, on the one hand, Christians are called to demonstrate the kingdom of God through a communal lifestyle of love, humility, and servanthood; and, on the other hand, that they are called to be in the world as instruments to effect God's changes on the social order.

## Discussion Questions

1. The author equates the biblical expression "Principalities and Powers" with social institutions, so the fair and correct interpretation of what the Apostle Paul meant by this expression is. . . .

2. Does the church have a responsibility to try to influence the political system for good? If so, in what ways should the church exercise influence on the political system?

3. Do you believe that civil disobedience can be reconciled with the biblical teachings of Romans 12?

4. Do you believe the church property should be tax exempt even though many claim this represents a form of government support for religion?

5. Do you think that it would be a good idea for military chaplains to be supported by churches rather than by the government?

6. Do you think that following the teachings of Scripture would make you politically dangerous to society?

7. How do you feel about campaign financing and its relationship to the commitments of elected officials?

8. Can Christians assume power and support the violence that is associated with governmental rule?

9. Some say that the concept of separation of church and state is no longer viable. Do you agree or disagree?

## References

Barnet, Richard J. and Ronald E. Muller
    1974 *Global Reach*. New York: Simon and Schuster, p. 15.
Bellah, Robert N.
    1967 "Civil Religion in America," *Daedalus*, 96 (Winter), pp. 1-21.
Berger, Peter L.
    1961 *The Noise of Solemn Assemblies*. New York: Doubleday

Berkhof, Hendrik
  1962 *Christ and the Powers*. Scottdale, Pa.: Herald Press.
Mannheim, Karl
  1936 *Ideology and Utopia* (trans. by Louis Wirth and Edward
        Steels). New York: Harcourt Brace and World.
Weber, Max
  1964 *The Theory of Social and Economic Organization* (trans. by
        A.M. Henderson and Talcott Parsons). New York: The Free
        Press, pp. 124-133.
Yoder, John Howard
  1972 *The Politics of Jesus*. Grand Rapids, Mich.: Eerdmans.

# 29

# Marriage and Family Alternatives

*J. Howard Kauffman*

It can be reasonably argued that marriage and the family are mankind's oldest social institutions. In one form or another, the family has existed in all societies (Murdock, 1949). This is true of societies dominated by non-Christian religions, as well as those primarily infuenced by Christianity.

Likewise every society has norms or rules regarding marriage and the family. There seems to be a basic and persistent need for people to know who is married to whom. This is because marriage involves certain rights, privileges, duties, and obligations. Society expects individuals to recognize and assume specific roles as they establish homes and rear children.

In modern societies many of these standards become codified into civil laws designed to protect individuals from injury and injustice when duties and obligations are not properly performed. In nonliterate societies there are many unwritten "customary laws" which are equally binding on family members and kinsmen. Whether they are modern statute laws or primitive unwritten codes, these regulations provide definitions of social expectations that give marriage and family patterns stability and continuity over long periods of time.

Marriage and family codes and regulations are deeply rooted in the basic cultural values of a society. These cultural values, in turn, often spring from the prevailing religious beliefs of a people. For

**J. Howard Kauffman**
*Professor of Sociology*
*Chairman Social Science Division, Goshen College*

With extensive training and research in family relations, Professor Kauffman has been involved in family life conferences and commissions, and has written extensively on that subject. His other interests include sociology of religion and social research. Mr. Kauffman received his PhD in sociology from the University of Chicago. An active churchman, he is an elder at the College Mennonite Church, Goshen, Indiana.

example, the traditional Chinese family system emphasized patriarchy, obedience of children to their parents, and reverence for ancestors. These values were rooted in the religion of Taoism and the ethical teachings of Confucius (Noss, 1949). Hinduism stresses the necessity of marriage and childbearing to insure the soul's reincarnation into a higher social status in the next life. In Western society many of the social regulations pertaining to marriage and family patterns can be directly traced to the Judeo-Christian teachings of the Old and New Testaments. Thus to understand the continuity and changes in Western family patterns, a knowledge of Judeo-Christian values is very important. It is the purpose of this chapter to examine contemporary alternative family patterns from the perspective of Judeo-Christian values.

## Family Patterns

Before we discuss family patterns, we need to clarify the meaning of the "family." Usually we refer to the "nuclear family," consisting of a husband, wife, and one or more children. Generally we stretch the word to include a married couple without children or a single parent with one or more children. An "extended family" includes one or more additional persons related to the nuclear family, such as a grandparent, grandchildren, son- or daughter-in-law, or an additional spouse in the case of polygamy. For purposes of this chapter we will be dealing primarily with alternative forms of the nuclear family.

In general, a family has these basic elements: (1) a mating (sexual) relationship legally or socially recognized as a marriage, (2) a common habitation, (3) a shared family name, and (4) shared economic resources. However, some units called families may not meet all of these criteria.

Family members are related by ties of marriage, blood, or adoption. Although the marriage normally is legalized by a license and a ceremony, it is not always so. Some states and countries recognize "common law marriages." Although these "marriages" have never been ceremonialized, they have all the other earmarks of a normal marriage and family, including children.

What makes a marriage a marriage? Except for the recognition of common law marriage in some states, in the eyes of American law a marriage exists if and when a legal ceremony (religious or civil) is performed. But there are other views as to what constitutes a marriage.

The Roman Catholic Church holds a sacramental view of marriage, that is, a marriage is not merely a human act. It is a *permanent* union established by the gift of divine grace. Since the ministry of the church is necessary to invoke the blessing of divine grace (the sacrament), a proper marriage is performed by a priest. Protestants, rejecting the sacramental view, regard a civil ceremony as equally efficacious, although most prefer a religious ceremony.

Others have argued that the essence of marriage is the sexual union. They cite the words of Jesus (Matthew 19:5, quoting Genesis 2:24), "the two shall become one flesh" (Miller, 1973). In this view, marriage begins when the couple give themselves to each other in the act of sexual intercourse, whether or not there has been a ceremony. Needless to say, many people who have had intercourse do not regard themselves as married.

Still others view marriage as a rational, voluntary commitment to continuous companionship and mutual support, whether or not a ceremony follows to give public witness to the commitment.

It is the view of the writer that a couple is not married until there has been a commitment, a ceremony (religious or civil), and a consummation through the sexual union. From a Christian viewpoint, the events should occur in *that* order.

In this chapter the following forms of the nuclear family or alternative arrangments which approximate a family will be considered:

(1) Single-parent families where one spouse is absent due to death, separation, or divorce.

(2) Single-parent families where there never was a spouse.

(3) Two or more nuclear units sharing a common habitation, including communes and group marriage.

(4) A couple living together but not legally married, whether it is a "trial marriage" or merely an arrangement of temporary convenience or expedience.

(5) Common law marriages.

(6) A homosexual couple occupying a common habitation and sharing their resources.

(7) Polygamy.

It should be noted that none of these forms is new. However, interest in these alternatives has mounted, as more have chosen unconventional patterns. Some writers argue that the nuclear family is taking a beating—that the onslaught of industrialization, urbanization, and technological advances is tearing the family from its traditional roots (Cooper, 1971; Young, 1973). Writing in the 1930s and viewing the effects of urbanism on the family, P.A. Sorokin (1937:776) made the dire prediction that

> The main socio-cultural functions of the family will further decrease until the family becomes a mere incidental cohabitation of male and female while the home will become a mere overnight parking place mainly for sex relationships.

Residential and occupational mobility have removed many families and individuals from the communities where their kinsmen live. The striking increase in the rate of marriage dissolutions has further fractured the family and precipitated much greater numbers of single-parent households. Currently in the United States there are over 1,000,000 divorces per year, or one divorce for every two marriages (U.S. Department of HEW, 1978). The increasingly strong impact of individualism—emphasis on personal freedoms and individual rights— has weakened the traditional sense of duty and obligations to family members. The recent Yankelovich study of the American family (General Mills, 1977) highlighted the tendency of the "new breed" parent who stresses self-interest. "New breed" parents have

> rejected many of the traditional values by which they were raised: marriage as an institution, the importance of religion, saving and thrift, patriotism and hard work for its own sake . . . New Breed parents are less child-oriented and more self-oriented.

Can the nuclear family survive in Western society, or will a variety of family alternatives take over? *Should* the family survive? Are these family alternatives to be seen as improvements over the traditional forms? Are they merely last ditch attempts to achieve or retain human values which are lost when the nuclear family disintegrates? Is there some vital link between the Christian faith and the survival of the nuclear family? Should we assume that the needs of a variety of persons are met by a variety of family forms?

## Biblical Perspectives on Marriage
Christian views on marriage and family alternatives have been derived from the holy Scriptures and from church tradition, the latter, of course, resting on the former. Biblical teachings set high standards,

and Christians through the ages have struggled with the question of what to do when people fail to achieve these standards. Should the standards be lowered or altered to accommodate those who fail to maintain them? Or, should the churches exercise a discipline that excludes those who depart from the standards? Current trends include widespread increases in sexual relations outside of marriage, increases in marital dissolutions, and the "coming out" of homosexuals. In an attempt to accommodate the churches to the social realities of contemporary society, many churches are modifying and/or abandoning the more orthodox views of the past. Is this the way to solve the disjuncture between time-honored standards and current shifting practices?

Both the Old and the New Testament take the view that marriage is ordained of God and that it is a lifetime commitment (Genesis 2:24; Matthew 19:4-6; Romans 7:2). The Mosaic law grudgingly allowed divorce (Deuteronomy 24:1-4; Matthew 19:8), while both Jesus and Paul took a strong position against divorce and the remarriage of divorcees (Matthew 19:9; Romans 7:2-3, I Corinthians 7:10-11). The Old Testament allowed polygamy (Deuteronomy 21:15-17; Exodus 21:10-11). Although the New Testament has no specific statement against polygamy, the apostles and early church fathers opted for monogamy as the only acceptable form (I Timothy 3:2; I Corinthians 7:2-3).

Influenced by Greek philosophies of body-spirit dualism, the early church fathers developed the doctrine of celibacy as a higher moral attainment than the practice of sexual relations in marriage. Only in recent decades has Christian scholarship freed sexuality and sexual intercourse from the stigmas attached to them by traditions developed in the early Christian centuries (Wynn, 1966). Despite certain passages (Matthew 19:12; I Corinthians 7:8-9) that have been used to argue for the superiority of singleness, the New Testament definitely teaches an honorable view of marriage (Matthew 19:5; Hebrews 13:4). At the same time, remaining single under certain circumstances was viewed by Jesus and Paul as a desirable option.

Both Old and New Testaments clearly teach that sexual intercourse outside of the marriage bond is wrong. The proscription of adultery (sexual intercourse of a married person with someone other than his or her spouse) was a part of the Ten Commandments (Exodus 20;14), and it was included among sins listed by both Jesus and Paul (Matthew 15:19; I Corinthians 6:9-10). The Jerusalem Conference agreed that essentials of the Judaic law should be carried over into

Christianity, including the decree that Christians should abstain from "unchastity" (Acts 15:29). Likewise, fornication (sexual intercourse between unmarried people, but sometimes used as a synonym for adultery) is included in the same lists of sins. Many passages in both Testaments speak against the evil of "harlotry," that is, prostitution (e.g., Leviticus 19:29; 1 Corinthians 6:13-16).

The Bible takes a hard line against the practice of homosexual acts. The Mosaic Law prescribed death for a man who has intercourse with another man (Leviticus 20:13). Practicing homosexuals, or sodomites, are included in Paul's lists of those who cannot "enter the kingdom of God" (1 Corinthians 6:9-10). Although the Old Testament does not refer to female homosexuals, Paul does mention them in his letter to the Romans. (Romans 1:26).

Beyond these basic ethical issues, the Bible has little to say about marriage and family life. It makes no prescription about the nature of courtship, procedures for betrothal or engagement, payment of bride price, forms of a wedding ceremony, whether marriage should be under the control of the family or the church, the use of family names, or relationships between kinsmen. It appears to forbid marriages between close kin or blood relations. It seems to support the partriarchal family structure, with decreed roles for husbands and wives. It tolerates double standards between men and women on certain points. Despite his statements which seem to support male dominance, Paul apparently tries to move Christians away from the strong patriarchy of both Jewish and Greek cultures of that time toward a more equalitarian relationship between men and women (Galations 3:28; 1 Corinthians 7:2-4; Ephesians 6:21).

We must conclude that the prophets, Jesus, and the apostles felt it was necessary that marriage and the family be hedged about with certain minimum restrictions or limitations. The question is, should these restrictions be viewed as normative and binding for Christians today? Or should they be viewed as outmoded standards that hinder the achievement of the sexual freedoms so loudly proclaimed today?

Pragmatically, are marriage restrictions needed for the long-range happiness of mankind? Are there psychic and social benefits that would be lost if every individual were free to follow his impulses in establishing sexual liaisons wherever he wished? Would a person gain more satisfaction than he would lose?

Suppose we had no record of the Word of God to prophets and

apostles. Would human experience lead to the formation of social norms that would be as controlling as those stemming from Holy Writ? Indeed, when it comes to personal morality and social ethics, humanism and Christianity have much in common. The values of love, kindness, patience, honesty, helpfulness, and unselfishness are not the province of Judeo-Christian ethics alone. In the absence of religious doctrines or laws, man still experiences the need to establish pragmatic, humanistic norms that generate attitudes and behavior patterns that promote the maximum common good. We need positive and negative sanctions to encourage behavior favorable to man's well-being and to restrain detrimental behavior.

Those who wish to engage in sexual relations outside of marriage will view biblical standards as a roadblock to human pleasure, as violating principles of personal freedom. Ideally, intercourse expresses values of love, intimacy, and tenderness. Is intercourse before and outside of marriage acceptable now that the undesirable consequences of sex (detection, infection, and conception) can be avoided by modern technology and medicine? In reviewing marriage and family alternatives we need to keep before us the tension that exists between traditional biblical norms to which Christians should conform and the natural human desire to be free of any limitations in the pursuit of personal pleasures.

## Alternatives to Traditional Marriage
### *Communal Arrangements*

One alternative to the isolated nuclear family is for two or more nuclear units to take up residence in a common household and to share some or all of their economic resources. The usual functions of a communal arrangement are to economize on living costs, to provide mutual aid, and to enlarge the circle of close companions. The latter two functions are particularly important to couples and young families living a long distance from kinfolk who would normally be a source of mutual aid and companionship. Indeed, the upsurge of interest in urban communes in recent years can be seen as an attempt to recover some of the values that formerly were realized in the extended family.

There are, of course, various types of communal arrangements. At one end of the continuum there are groups of unmarried students sharing a common household near a university campus, while at the other end there are large communes composed of ten or more monogamous nuclear family units—such as the Hutterite colonies in the United States and Canada.

Communes have existed for centuries. Some have been "creedal," that is, organized around a set of religious or philosophical doctrines, while others have been non-creedal. Some were celibate, such as the Shakers (organized in 1787 in New York State) who strictly prohibited pairing and marriage. Others, notably the Oneida Community of New York (organized in 1848) went so far as to institute a type of mate sharing which they called "complex marriage." This, however, proved to be problematic and was later abandoned.

There is much to be said in favor of communal arrangements, since they provide a variety of personal and social need-satisfactions. In order to function effectively, individuals need a lot of affection, acceptance, support, and security. In societies that have strong kinship ties and close interaction with neighbors, these emotional needs are met through close relationships with many persons. But if a married couple is isolated from kin and they have few close friends, emotional and affectional needs must be met entirely by the marriage partner. This places a burden on the marriage relationship that is often greater than it may be able to bear. A communal arrangement, therefore, not only widens the base of emotional support, but it also takes some of the load off the marriage partner. The communal setting can also provide a ready framework for social interaction in work settings, leisure time activities, and worship.

Communal groups vary greatly in the scope and intensity of their sharing, and thus in the degree to which they perform the functions of a family. It was indicated earlier that a family normally is identified by the elements of a mating (sexual) relationship, a common habitation, a family name, and shared resources. When individuals and/or nuclear units form some type of commune, they usually share a common household and financial resources. Usually they do not all take the same family name. If pairs (mates) are formed, they are usually faithful to their spouses, particularly if marriages have been legalized. Communal arrangements would seem to offer excellent possibilities for the realization of Christian values and virtues. Sharing is an obvious virtue, and there would seem to be no moral limit on the degree of sharing, except for sharing mates. Maintaining this exception is not only justified on biblical principles, but also on pragmatic grounds. Although shifting from one sexual partner to another might seem to some people to enhance sensual pleasures, deep-seated psychic problems of jealousy and insecurity often emerge. In a study of 35 urban middle-class communal households, Kanter, *et al.* (1975), observed that multiple sexual relationships are hard to maintain. They also found that such relationships were found in only a few of the communes studied. They concluded that "the family-like intimacy that is the goal of communes does not include shared sexual relationships."

In a commune where nearly all aspects of life are shared, does a nuclear unit really exist? Is the nuclear unit *displaced* by the commune? Spiro (1954) raised this question in his study of the Israeli kibbutz. In the kibbutz, a couple's life is no different after marriage than before, except that they now share a room together. The kibbutz takes care of all social and economic arrangments, including child rearing. Thus the nuclear unit performs few functions, even though it is still identifiable.

It should not be assumed that a communal arrangement is an *easy* alternative to the problems that confront the isolated nuclear family. Sharing imposes significant limitations on personal freedoms. Commitment to group values seems to run counter to the goals of individualism that stress the right of each person to "do his own thing." Group life can function successfully only when members are willing to yield much of their time and resources to group controls. Many who attempt communal living find it difficult or impossible to do this. Thus many communes die an early death. In many that do survive, there is a frequent turnover of members whose commitment to the group lasts only so long as their personal benefits exceed the sacrifices required by the group. Nonetheless, for those persons who have the psychic and spiritual resources to merge their own identities with a larger group, the commune offers many satisfactions that the isolated nuclear unit has difficulty supplying.

*Remaining Single*

In recent years, a growing proportion of young Americans are opting for singleness instead of marriage. For some this merely represents postponement of marriage; for others it means avoiding marriage altogether.

In a study of the population aged 14 to 34, the percentage of males never married rose from 51 in 1960 to 56 in 1977; for females the increase was from 38 to 46 percent (U.S. Bureau of the Census, 1978b). The trend is most noticeable in the 20 to 24 age bracket where from

1960 to 1977 the proportion of single males rose from 53 to 64 percent and for females, from 28 to 45 percent. By contrast, the proportion never married among those *over* 35, actually declined slightly.

Not only are more young people remaining single, but they are also marrying later. The average age at first marriage for males went from 23.1 in 1967 to 24.0 in 1977; for females the increase was from 20.6 to 21.6.

Part of the increase in singleness may be due to the growing number of younger persons who choose not to marry at all. When the current young generation gets old, will larger proportions choose not to marry? Only time will tell. One apparent reason for the growth in singleness is the fact that more couples are choosing to cohabit without benefit of legal marriage. This option will be discussed in a later section.

The term "singles" sometimes includes those who were *formerly* married but are currently widowed, separated, or divorced. Although widowhood has gradually declined through the years, the census (U.S. Bureau of the Census, 1978a) reports that from 1970 to 1978 "the proportion of households maintained by a divorced or separated person increased from eight percent to twelve percent." While many of the formerly married have one or more children and choose to live alone for a time, most will remarry. Statistics show that four out of every five divorced persons eventually remarry. But some disillusioned individuals never remarry. Some may be members of a church that disapproves of divorce and remarriage. Those who remain unmarried, for whatever reasons, often find that they face the same kinds of problems that confront singles. They will need to cope with occasional moods of isolation and loneliness, and uncertainties concerning their social acceptance. Some will experiment with new forms of sexual outlets or will need to find ways to sublimate sexual impulses.

Singleness, however, does have advantages. It offers more independence, and freedom from obligations to family members, and it permits greater mobility. Particularly for women, singleness is compatible with career development. The Apostle Paul felt that his Christian ministry was enhanced by being unmarried, and in his first letter to the church at Corinth he advised Christians to remain single, if they could do so with integrity (1 Corinthians 7). His sentiments were reiterated by the early church fathers who promoted celibacy as the norm for church leaders. The age-old controversy over the requirements of celibacy for the priesthood and the holy orders is much in debate again today.

The prevailing sentiment today among both Christians and non-Christians is that singleness and marriage should be regarded as options of equal merit. This has been a particular emphasis of the women's rights movement. Since colonial days, Americans have often discriminated against singles, especially women, not only through popular attitudes and jokes, but also through the legal system (Scanzoni and Scanzoni, 1976: 150-53). It is unreasonable that discrimination should continue in an era that elevates the values of social equality, social justice, and maximum personal development. Churches are often as guilty as other institutions in their differential treatment of singles. This is seen for example, in the organization of separate classes for single persons and married couples who are of similar age.

In the Middle Ages celibacy was elevated above marriage. In Prostestant colonial America, marriage was viewed as superior to singleness. Will the twentieth century culminate in a true sense of equality between married and single individuals?

*Single Parenthood*

Among those who may choose to be unmarried rather than married are an increasing number of parents. The large majority of single parents is such because of the death or divorce of a spouse. Census data indicate that single parent families, either men or women, represent a growing proportion of all families. There were one third again as many of these families in 1977 as in 1970. In these seven years the number of divorced persons maintaining families has doubled. Five sixths of these are women (U.S. Bureau of the Census, 1978b).

The number of *never-married* single parents has also greatly increased. Although the number of widows with families remained constant over the period 1970-77, the number of never-married women maintaining families increased by 71 percent during the period. There were just over a million such women in 1977, and 1.3 million children under the age of 18 were living with them. However, this constituted only 2 percent of all children under 18.

It can be assumed that many single parents have not succeeded in reaching their goal of marriage, their children having been conceived and born unintentionally outside of marriage. There also appears to be another group, small but increasing in size, who want children but do not want marriage. Most of these obtain children through intercourse but some through adoption (in states that now permit unmarried persons to adopt children), and a few, recently, by artificial insemination.

It has been generally assumed in the past that a child's psychosocial development is enhanced by having two parents, thus a role model for each sex. Adoption agencies (with recent exceptions) have reflected this view in placing children only in two-parent homes. Nevertheless, proof that children from two-parent homes have better developmental outcomes is weak. To date, little empirical research has been done in this area. Much more important than the *number* of parents is the *quality* of the parenting and the quality of the relationships between the two parents. Nye (1957) established that it is better for children to have one happy divorced parent than two unhappy undivorced parents. However, all things being equal, such as the quality of parenting, the two-parent child would seem to have definite advantages, e.g., financial advantages, emotional and social security, as well as two role models.

The increase in single parenthood, therefore, needs to be questioned from the child's standpoint. The unmarried parent who elects to obtain a child for his or her own satisfaction, and refuses to provide the other-sex parent, can be charged with putting his or her own interests ahead of the child's. But for the person who is prevented from finding a spouse, and who has the personal qualities to provide good parenting, the role of single parent poses a viable option. From a Christian perspective, however, the child should be obtained by adoption, rather than by intercourse. This also avoids the problem of illegitimacy in those states where laws and/or public attitudes still stigmatize the child (and its mother) when the child is born out of wedlock.

### Living Together Unmarried

Perhaps the alternative to marriage that has been most controversial and most widely discussed is that of cohabitation without benefit of legal marriage. This situation exists in a variety of forms: (1) singles sharing a room or apartment for the sake of convenience and with no intent to marry, sometimes referred to as "shacking up", (2) trial marriage; (3) common law marriage, often extending for decades and involving children, distinguished from other families only by the absence of a ceremony; (4) elderly persons living as unmarried couples, with or without sexual relationships; (5) "swinging" or "wife swapping", and (6) group marriage.

Of these forms, only common law marriage has ever achieved the status of legality. Rooted in English common law, state laws have provided (in the past, if no longer) for the legitimization of the union if it survives a minimum number of years, and thus also the legitimization of the offspring.

1. *Swinging:* is defined by Ramey (1972) as involving two or more couples who mutually decide to switch sexual partners or engage in group sex. Singles may be included in the arrangement either as forming a three-person group or by two singles forming a pair for facilitating swinging with a married pair or pairs. Swinging is not really an *alternative* to marriage, but it deviates from monogamous marriage. Sharing the sexual relationship with an additional person or couple does not normally mean sharing living arrangements as well, unless a commune is formed.

There is no reliable information on the extent of swinging. Ramey (1972) reviews several investigations indicating that it is found most frequently in large urban centers among the more educated, professional classes. It often involves persons who are otherwise strangers to each other. Apparently some persons who get involved soon discover that it is not for them. Other couples develop relationships in greater depth and for longer periods of time. Ramey notes that "having sex with people with whom one does not relate gets stale pretty quickly, for most people." The woman "may begin to feel like a prostitute," and the man "may become impotent."

Thus the pragmatics of swinging, wholly aside from the moral issues, appear to precipitate emotional complications and identity problems that very few persons are capable of handling. It would appear that swingers tend to experience very unstable, short-lived, risk-laden relationships in their effort to find sexual satisfaction in the absence of a stable, faithful, monogamous marriage. Although Ramey's own conclusions are less negative, his evidence strongly suggests this.

The values obtained through swinging are questionable, to say the least. The desire to obtain sexual variety is probably uppermost in the participant's mind. But this not only reflects a failure of the individual's marriage to provide satisfactory sexual relations, but also to meet the more basic emotional and social needs. Some claim that swinging improves the marriage, but case material reported by Masters and

Johnson (1970) suggests that outcomes are often devastating to marriages, self esteem, and sexual abilities. Some argue that sexual variety enhances personality growth or provides an avenue for "finding oneself." Those are ill-defined values and often suggest a floundering and increasing instability of the personality structure. An urge to escape societal norms often seems to be an underlying factor. The behavior obviously violates Christian norms. From a Christian viewpoint it is really consensual adultery.

2. *Group Marriage:* Group marriage has been studied and reported most extensively by Larry and Joan Constantine (1972), who estimated that there were as many as 1,000 such groups in the United States. They include group marriage in their concept of "multilateral marriage" which they define as "any marriage of three or more persons where each partner considers himself/herself married to at least two other partners." The word "marriage" is a problem in that it infers a legal marriage. Of course, no person in the United States or Canada can be legally married to two persons at the same time. Thus the phenomenon might be called group mating, although that is also inaccurate in that a person with two or more mating partners can be legally married to one of them but not to the others.

As compared to swinging, group marriage is longer lasting and involves a greater depth of personal relationships. The Constantines conclude from their studies of 60 respondents that group marriage "is an incredibly complex and difficult form of marriage, but one holding significant potentials for satisfaction and growth."

Individuals in the groups observed by the Constantines ranged from 23 to 60 years of age, and were formed of from three to six partners per unit. Some groups were still in existence after five years, although most had terminated. The average existence of dissolved groups was 16 months. The multilateral experience often led to the dissolution of the previously existing marriages. The Constantines concluded that multilateral marriages dissolve because the partners are incompatible in rather basic personality traits. Multilateral marriage involves an intensity of interpersonal relationships much greater than that of the average marriage. The experience may reveal otherwise unseen individual and marital pathology. Couples who enter such a complex relationship hoping to solve their marital difficulties usually fail to find solutions. These and other findings indicate that group marriage is likely to provide satisfactions for only a very few persons.

3. *Unmarried couples living together.* Although only a very small minority of the American adult population participates in swinging and group marriage, cohabitation (unmarried couples living together) is a much more extensive phenomenon. Apparently the number of single college-aged couples who are sharing the same household has greatly increased in the past decade, particularly in the vicinity of university campuses.

Census data indicate that in the United States in 1977, 1.9 million adults were unmarried and living with an unrelated adult of the opposite sex. Although this was slightly less than one percent of the total population it represents nearly 4 percent of all unmarried adults, and 2 percent of all couple households. The number of such couples increased by 19 percent from 1960 to 1970, but by 83 percent from 1970 to 1977 (Glick and Norton, 1977).

Unmarried couple households exist for a variety of reasons. For some (40 percent in one survey) it is a prelude to marriage (Population Reference Bureau, 1978). For others it follows a broken marriage, and may be a prelude to a remarriage. Some are elderly men needing a housekeeper. Some are middle-aged or elderly women who take in a young male as a tenant. In all these cases the desire to obtain companionship and to economize on living expenses are likely reasons for the arrangement. Sexual partnership is likely desired in most cases. For some young couples, this may give them status among their peers. Ordinarily sharing a household with a mate is one of the earmarks of full adulthood.

The trend is probably more than a passing fad. Martin Marty is quoted as seeing it as "not a momentary phenomenon, but a symbolic shift in attitudes that has great social significance" (Population Reference Bureau, 1978:2). The trend is more evident among persons living in large cities, more among blacks than whites, more among those with less than a high school education, and four times as evident among those who never went to church as compared with those who attend church weekly.

Cohabitation prior to marriage is probably a factor in the recent increase in age at first marrige. Apparently some want to avoid or postpone the responsibilities of legal marriage, if they can have all the privileges without it. The availability of contraception has doubtless encouraged cohabitation. Abortion, as a procedure of last resort to prevent having children, has been facilitated since 1973. Nevertheless, the proportion of all babies born to unwed mothers continues to rise and is now about 13 percent. In 1950 it was 4 percent. The "sexual revolution" is obviously not a change in attitudes only, but also in behavior.

How should these trends be evaluated from the standpoint of Christian ethics? Is the norm of limiting sexual intercourse to married couples still relevant? If norms are substantially liberalized, will this threaten the institution of marriage and will it tend to reduce the likelihood of achieving maximum human well-being in the long run?

In an age that emphasizes individualism and maximizes personal freedom, moral standards are often criticized as outdated and unduly restrictive. The more liberal elements in society, and radical elements in the churches, have bent the rules within the context of "situation ethics." They have not suggested that the rules should be abandoned, but that they should be administered with flexibility, allowing for exceptions where a humanistic or pragmatic value (such as love) seems to be served. For example, sexual relations should be acceptable prior to marriage, if the couple has developed a deep-seated love relationship and has made a firm commitment to marry.

4. *Trial Marriage:* A more radical alternative to conventional monogamy is the idea of "trial marriage." Advocated by Bernard Baruch in the 1920s and Margaret Mead in the 1960s, the idea is that an adequate premarital test of compatibility cannot be made unless the couple lives together for a time. The need for compatibility testing is real, but is trial marriage a valid test? On the surface it might seem to be a more valid test than courtship without living together. But it is often carried on secretively and there may be guilt feelings associated with religious, family, or community attitudes. Furthermore, the couple has little basis (unless they have had previous trial marriages) for judging whether a given amount of friction between them is, or is not, compatible with "compatibility."

Marital success is much more dependent on a couple's attitudes *after* marriage—their commitment to make marriage work—than on experimentation before marriage. And sexual compatibility is not fixed by one's biology. It depends on attitudes and personality traits that cannot be changed by premarital sexual experience. In other words, there is little to be gained and much to be lost (one's moral integrity particularly) from living together before marriage. For those whose trial marriages fail, a pattern of drifting from one sexual partner to another may develop, with possible negative conditioning for faithful marriage. Statistics show a substantial correlation between the incidence of extramarital sex and premarital sexual experience. Thus the increases in sexual activity before marriage can only be expected to result in more adultery in the future.

There is no evidence to date that those who lived together prior to marriage are more successful in marriage than others. Indeed the evidence is generally to the contrary. Those not having intercourse prior to marriage, in the studies reported, have consistently outscored others on marriage success scales (Burgess and Wallin, 1953; Landis and Landis, 1977; Christensen, 1966). The ability to defer sexual intercourse until marriage is an evidence of personality strength, since in many respects life's long-range goals can be obtained only by sacrificing short-run pleasures.

The writings of George and Nena O'Neill have received considerable attention recently. They advocated "open marriage" as contrasted to traditional "closed marriage" which they see as restricted by age-old norms of marital-role and sex-role differentiation, along with inadequacies in communication between the spouses. They emphasize the need for self-growth and flexibility in marriage roles. They define open marriage as "a relationship in which the partners are committed to their own and to each other's growth" (O'Neil and O'Neill, 1972). They emphasize that no person can himself or herself fully satisfy the spouse's needs (emotional, social, sexual, economic, intellectual, and otherwise). Thus relationships with persons of the opposite sex need to be cultivated *outside* of marriage as well.

What the O'Neills are saying is generally acceptable within an orthodox Christian perspective, except their unwillingness to limit sex to marriage. They report that many couples who came to them for counsel admitted they could not cope with the feelings of sexual jealousy related to extramarital sex. Although these couples claimed some benefits from extramarital sex, the O'Neills observed that such experiences were not really enhancing the couples' marital relationships. On the contrary, they observed that "frequently it obscured relationship problems, became an avenue of escape, and intensified conflicts." The O'Neills admit that "only a limited few" could achieve the guidelines of a truly open marriage.

So then, for whom would extramarital sex be a growth experience? From what the O'Neills are saying, only a theoretically limited few who possess a high degree of interpersonal relationship skills. But such skilled persons should be having some of the world's best marriages and should not need to find sexual satisfaction outside of marriage. Thus the reports of the O'Neills have not provided any grounds for assuming that extramarital sex can enrich an ongoing marriage. Their case material points rather toward the opposite conclusion—that it damages marriages. Their argument, developed on principle, does not seem to be supported by their empirical findings.

It is instructive to look at societies where sexual gratification outside of marriage is widespread. Caribbean society is one such example. In her study of Jamaica, Judith Blake (1961) found that 72 percent of births were illegitimate. Similarly high rates are found also in Trinidad, Belize, and other areas formerly parts of the British West Indies. Marriage usually occurs after some years of living together, often after a sequence of "common law marriages." Blake found a pattern of males drifting from one woman to the next, with these common law marriages lasting an average of three years. The pattern is one of extreme male irresponsibility. In return for her sexual favors, meals, a place to sleep, and for bearing him a child or two, the man will provide whatever financial support he can muster. If the woman badgers him for more support he will simply leave her and find another mate with whom to share bed and board until the next fall-out. The woman bears the pain since, not being married, she has no legal recourse. Because of her poverty, she is forced to take in the next man who comes along and promises to be responsible for her and the children she is gradually accumulating. The children, of course, lack adequate role models for fatherhood, responsible living, and marriage, and simply repeat the pattern of male irresponsibility and exploitation of females in the next generation. If we continue the present American trend of separating sex from marriage, how long will it be until the United States catches up with the Caribbean?

## Polygamy

As an alternative form of the family, polygamy has had little relevance to the American scene since being outlawed in Utah in 1890. Some cases can still be found in the villages of the Great Basin, and there are, of course, covert bigamy cases elsewhere in the United States. Polygamy is illegal in all 50 states.

From a Christian perspective the issue of polygamy is relevant where Christianization has taken place in the Third World, particularly in Africa where polygamy has been valued almost universally in the past. The Muslim faith prevails in Northern Africa, and males are permitted up to four wives. In Sub-Sahara Africa there has been a rapid shift from traditional religions supporting polygamy to Christianity which has opposed it. Catholic, Anglican, Methodist, Presbyterian, and other denominations that have been established in Africa in the past century have insisted on monogamy for church members. In recent decades hundreds of "independent churches" have sprung up under African leaders. Many of these openly permit and even promote polygamy.

Polygamy in Africa takes the form of polygyny, that is, one man married to two or more women. A man must have considerable land and cattle resources before he can acquire additional wives. Consequently at any point of time, not more than a third of the males will have two or more wives, even though a majority (in some areas) may acquire more than one wife in their lifetimes. With urbanization and industrialization taking place, there are movements afoot in some countries to make polygamy illegal. Indeed, in one country, the Ivory Coast, it has already been rejected by legislation. Support of this movement comes as much from the women's rights groups in those countries as from the churches.

Should churches insist that monogamy is the only permissible form for Christians? In the past decade leadership of African churches has been shifted to Africans, and the issue has been widely debated among them. As a leader of several seminars on Christian family life some years ago in Africa, the writer participated with several dozen African church leaders in reviewing this and other issues. From the African viewpoint, the Bible is not clear on the subject. The Old Testament is cited, of course, as supporting polygamy. And although the Apostle Paul prescribed monogamy for the bishops and deacons, it can be argued that he was not asking it of all Christians. New Testament grounds for monogamy are implicit rather than explicit. It was the influence of the early church fathers that led ultimately to the church's adoption of monogamy as the only acceptable form. Jesus left no specific word on the subject.

Arguments in support of monogamy may be more practical than biblical. Polygamy is a pattern of male dominance and thus incompatible with notions of sex equality. As a form of extended family, polygamy is much less practical in the cities than in agricultural and pastoral societies. Social and political forces may be more potent than the church in ultimately moving Africa toward monogamy as the norm. Meanwhile, a position of tolerance might be best. The testimony and positive witness of Christian converts who are also polygamists should not be ignored. Up to this point many Africans have viewed the missionary's insistence on monogamy as an imposition of Western norms, a corollary of colonialism. Under African leadership, African Christians will be able to find fitting African solutions to an age-old issue on which God's Word is less certain than we Westerners have generally claimed it to be.

### Homosexuality

If heterosexual sex outside of marriage is a big issue, homosexuality is even bigger. It is not necessary to remind the reader of the force with which the issue has hit the mass media. Is there any issue, secular or religious, that can generate as much heat as this?

There is still much to be learned about the nature and causes of homosexuality. Without reviewing the detailed arguments, suffice it to say the prevailing opinion holds that the sources of homosexuality are environmental rather than hereditary. This means that homosexuality is learned, and results from conditioning factors that operate on the individual from infancy to adulthood. The prognosis for changing homosexuals into heterosexuals is poor although some psychiatrists have claimed success in some cases (Jones, 1966). The strategy of counselors working with homosexuals has been primarily to help them understand and accept their own preferences and to work out a *modus vivendi*, or a way of living in a society generally hostile to "gays." From an ethical standpoint, the issue is not just the question of the rightness or wrongness of homosexual practices, but even more important, what does Christian love require in accepting and working with homosexuals.

It is necessary to distinguish between homosexuality and homosexual acts. Homosexuality is the *tendency to prefer* relationships with a person of the same sex, whereas homosexual acts are behaviors involving sexual arousal and/or intercourse with a person of the same sex. Thus it is possible to be homosexual and not perform homosexual acts. Also it is possible for homosexual acts to be performed by heterosexuals.

It is also important to note that homosexuality-heterosexuality is not an either/or matter. It is a continuum, and every person is somewhere on the continuum between extreme homosexuality and extreme heterosexuality. Homosexuality is a matter of degree, varying from minimal to maximal involvement. Those with minimal development often marry heterosexually and have children, perhaps not discovering their homosexual inclination until later. Also some heterosexuals may have homosexual dreams of fanatasies and even engage in homosexual acts. The extent to which a teenage or adult homosexual can move along the continuum, toward or away from homosexual preferences is not well understood, but it is possible that homosexual experiences may increase the homosexual preferences, depending of course, on whether the experiences are satisfying or not. It is very doubtful whether a Christian conversion experience could change a homosexual into a heterosexual even if the individual strongly desired it. His Christian experience, however, might affect his readiness to engage in homosexual acts.

Homosexuality is believed to be much more frequent among males than among females. It is an alternative to heterosexual marriage and family life only if the homosexual remains single or "marries" another homosexual (of the same sex, of course). So far homosexual weddings have been rare, but homosexuals frequently live together.

Public attitudes have generally made it very difficult for known homosexuals to exist. Consequently homosexuals have had to live in fear and anxiety lest, if discovered, they might lose their jobs and be socially ostracized. It has taken great courage for gay leaders to "come out" and lobby for individual rights. It is likely that in the future homosexual rights will be legally guaranteed along with those of other minorities. How can homosexuals be denied their civil rights, if they really cannot change their sexuality any more than a person can change his race or his national origin?

Christian attitudes toward homosexualtiy are rooted in strong biblical statements against it, and these in turn were reinforced by church tradition. Because it had not been an open issue in the past, many churches are only recently being forced to face the question, and are placing the matter on their study agendas. The United Presbyterian Church established something of a landmark when its 1978 Assembly adopted a policy of allowing *nonpracticing* homosexuals to serve as clergy, while at the same time holding that "the practice of homosexuality is a sin." In effect, the church is asking that homosexuals remain celibates. The Presbyterian action may serve as a precedent for other denominations. Some churches, however, have declared against any tolerance of homosexuality. Most have, as yet, said nothing at all.

Is homosexuality something to be feared? Will it spread farther? Is it a long-run threat to mankind? Is it a product of modern urbanized society? Certainly it has existed since Sodom and Gomorrah and probably as long as man has been on the earth. Why is it more prevalent in some societies than others? It seems to be virtually unknown in Africa.

Only time can provide the answers to these perplexing questions. In the meantime, it behooves Christians to accept homosexuals as human beings with human rights. Perhaps the analogy to alcoholism is useful. It is said that "once an alcoholic, always an alcoholic." That is, even if the alcoholic is a total abstainer, he is always vulnerable to that next drink. We do not ostracize or penalize the abstaining alcoholic. Should we do less for the nonpracticing homosexual?

## Summary and Conclusion

This paper has attempted to establish the following summary points:

1. Throughout mankind's history, and throughout the world today, marriage and family life have been regulated by legal or customary codes. Monogamy has been the prevailing form of marriage, even in societies which permit polygamy.

2. Variations or deviations from the monogamous norm have existed from ancient times. Current interest and attention to alternative forms reflect the recent "sexual revolution" characterized by increased liberalization of attitudes and behaviors in respect to sexual norms.

3. Biblical, particularly New Testament, norms favor faithful monogamous marriage and proscribe sexual intercourse outside of marriage.

4. Communes can provide an effective alternative to the isolated and vulnerable nuclear family unit and to individuals who lack a supporting kinship group. Christian ethics are compromised if communal sharing includes sexual partnership with a person to whom one is not married.

5. Remaining unmarried is an alternative of equal merit to marriage. Society should not discriminate against single persons.

6. Obtaining a child by adoption is valid for a single person wishing to be a parent, provided the person has good qualifications

otherwise for parenting. Obtaining a child by intercourse with a person to whom one is not married is immoral, from a Christian standpoint.

7. Living together unmarried, though occurring with increasing frequency, still occurs only among a very small minority of the population. Though some benefits are claimed by those who practice it, there are many risks and undesirable consequences. Among these are unwanted pregnancies, broken relationships with family members and kin, exploitation of one partner by the other, abandonment of one by the other, and subsequent guilt feelings that are not easily resolved. This adds empirical support for the Christian stance against sexual relations outside of marriage.

8. Though the biblical position favoring monogamy is preferential rather than obligatory, the early church fathers opted for monogamy as the only legitimate form. Westerners have probably been too zealous in the demands that Christian converts in non-Western societies give up polygamy as a condition of church membership.

9. Apparently homosexuality results from conditioning processes over which the homosexual has had little control. The homosexual does have a choice regarding the practice of homosexual acts, and biblical and church traditions, as well as most current church pronouncements, strongly oppose the practice of homosexuality. More understanding and concern for the homosexual is mandatory for Christians.

The central issue still remains. Can we continue to advocate faithful monogamous marriage as the Christian idea.? It is this writer's opinion that we not only can, but we must. Under the many pressures to legitimize a variety of alternatives to marriage and family life that deviate from orthodox norms, we must by all means avoid throwing out the baby with the bath water.

At the beginning we noted that the increased interest in marriage and family alternatives has followed an increasing disillusionment with traditional monogamous marriage as it has been known in the past. Some are saying that this means faithful monogamy is inadequate and will need to be replaced with one or more alternatives. But will the alternatives be any better? If persons fail to find happiness in faithful monogamy, is *marriage* the culprit, or are the individuals at fault? After all, there are a great many successful monogamous marriages and many of us will testify that marriage has brought much joy and satisfaction.

There is a subtle human tendency to blame the institution instead of the person when things go wrong. If the child fails in school it is the school's fault! If the worker is unemployed, the "system" is inadequate! Institutions certainly have their inadequacies, but so do persons. Perhaps much more emphasis needs to be placed on careful mate selection and on marriage enrichment. In addition, greater effort must be made to help persons find satisfaction within the marriages they have, rather than tantalizing them with risky alternatives that may simply add to the load of insecurities, anxieties, uncertainties, and guilt they are already carrying.

After all, monogamous marriage may be man's *best* alternative. The mere fact that it still prevails after thousands of years of human trial and error may be the best testimony to its utility. Surely if there were a better alternative, it would have been found long ago.

Some people are critical of traditional faithful marriage. They think that it is too restrictive and that it limits personal freedom too much. Marriage is seen as as trap from which people cannot extricate themselves easily. This view is unfortunate not only for the persons involved in the marriage, but also for their children who are subjected to negative views of marriage. This negativism does not prepare them to expect and find happiness in marriage.

Again we must remind ourselves that marriage, imperfect because persons are imperfect, nevertheless provides for most people the best possible matrix for the personal growth and fulfillment of both husband and wife. Happy are those children whose parents provide them models of joyful living that will serve them as they choose spouses and marry.

What shall we say, in conclusion, regarding the moral codes that undergird faithful monogamous marriage? Were they established merely to restrict human sexual freedom, or to prevent people from enjoying sex? It may appear so to some. But would removing the moral codes really bring greater happiness and well-being to mankind in the long run? Definitely not. We would not make driving on the highways more pleasant by abandoning traffic laws. Freedom from traffic rules would bring bondage to fear, anxiety, and insecurities in traveling. Only by giving up some of our personal freedom so as to secure the rights and safety of all can we all be free from the dangers and insecurities of traffic chaos.

So it is with marriage and family life. The moral codes which undergird these institutions are the ultimate source of our freedom—the freedom to grow up in a family environment where love, security, and well-being proceed from a pair of stable parents who are secure in their own lifetime commitment to each other. and who can provide a healthy environment where children can gain the emotional fortitude and the social standards that will make them competent to face the challenges of life.

## Discussion Questions

1. Monogamous marriage has been more prevalent in human history than polygamy, group marriage, or other alternatives. Why?

2. Why has there been a notable increase of persons involved in marriage and family alternatives in recent years in America?

3. Is the recent increase in marriage and family alternatives merely a shortrun fad or is it likely to continue? What explains the substantial increase in single parenthood in recent years?

4. In taking a clear moral position against sexual intercourse outside of marriage, were biblical writers simply evidencing a human or divine arbitrariness, or does human experience also justify such a limit?

5. Should the ancient biblical norms be viewed as binding on Christians today? What are the arguments for and against "situational ethics" in respect to marriage and sexual standards?

6. What are the arguments favoring a liberalization of attitudes toward sex outside of marriage? Would a liberalization of attitudes make a positive or a negative contribution of the long-range well-being of the institutions of marriage and family life?

7. Is the legal control of marriage necessary and good, or is it merely a denial of personal freedoms and therefore undesirable?

8. Why do the fathers of children born out of wedlock so often refuse to accept responsibility for the child and its mother? When males can get "free sex" outside of marriage, does it lead to increased male irresponsibility for their own offspring?

9. What do you think should be the twentieth-century Christian attitude toward homosexuality? Toward homosexual practices? Toward homosexuals?

10. If nuclear families lack the traditional support of kinsmen, are communes a reasonable alternative? Or can other support systems be found, such as churches or friendship groups?

## References

Blake, Judith
1961 *Family Structure in Jamaica*. Glencoe: Free Press.
Burgess, E.W. and Paul Wallin
1953 *Engagement and Marriage*. Philadelphia: J.B. Lippincott.

Christensen, Harold T.
  1966 "Scandinavian and American Sex Norms: Some Comparisons with Sociological Implications." *Journal of Social Issues,* 22, pp. 60-75.
Constantine, Larry L. and Joan M. Constantine
  1972 "Dissolution of Marriage in a Nonconventional Context." *The Family Coordinator,*21, pp. 475-462.
Cooper, David
  1971 *TheDeath of the Family.* New York: Pantheon Books.
General Mills
  1977 *Raising Children in a Changing Society: The General Mills American Family Report, 1976-77.* Minneapolis: General Mills, Inc.
Glick, Paul C. and Arthur J. Norton
  1977 *Marrying, Divorcing and Living Together in the U S. Today.* Washington, D.C..Population Reference Bureau.
Jones, H. Kimball
  1966 *Toward a Christian Understanding of the Homosexual.* New York: Association Press.
Kantner,  Rosabeth Moss, Dennis Jaffe and D. Kelley Weisberg
  1975 "Coupling, Parenting, and the Presence of Others: Intimate Relationships in Communal Households." *Journal of Marriage and Family* 24, pp. 433-452.
Landis, Judson and Mary G. Landis
  1977 *Building a Successful Marriage.* Seventh Edition. Englewood Cliffs: Prentice-Hall.
Masters, William H. and Virginia E. Johnson
  1970 *The Pleasure Bond.* New York: Bantam Books.
Miller, John W.
  1973 *A Christian Approach to Sexuality.* Scottdale, Pa.: Mennonite Publishing House.
Murdock, George P.
  1949 *Social Structure.* New York: Macmillan.
Noss, John B.
  1949 *Man's Religions.* New York: Macmillan.
Nye, F. Ivan
  1957 "Child Adjustment in Broken and Unhappy Unbroken Homes." *Marriage and Family Living* 19, pp. 356
O'Neill, Nena and George O'Neill
  1972 "Open Marriage: A Synergic Model." *The Family Coodinator,* 21, pp. 403-10
Population Reference Bureau
  1978 "Marriage, Divorce, and Living Together." *Interchange.* Washington, D.C.: Population Reference Bureau.
Ramey, James W.
  1972 "Emerging Patterns of Innovative Behavior in Marriage." *The Family Coordinator,* 21, pp. 435-46.

Scanzoni, Letha and John Scanzoni
    1976 *Men, Women, and Change*. New York: McGraw-Hill.
Sorokin, Pitirim
    1937 *Social and Cultural Dynamics,* Vol. 4. New York: Harper &
        Row.
Spiro, Melford E.
    1954 "Is the Family Universal?" *American Anthropologist*, 56, pp.
        839-846.
U.S. Bureau of the Census
    1978a "Households and Families by Types." *Current Population
        Reports*. Series P-20, No. 327.
    1978b "Marital Status and Living Arrangements: March 1977."
        *Current Population Reports*. Series P-20, No. 323.
U.S. Department of Health, Education, and Welfare
    1978 "Births, Marriages, Divorces, and Deaths for 1977." *Monthly
        Vital Statistics Reports*, 26, p.12.
Wynn, John C.
    1966 Sex, Family, and Society in Theological Focus. New York:
        Association Press.
Young, Leontine
    1973 *The Fractured Family*. New York: McGraw-Hill.

# 30
# What Makes a Family Christian?

*Robert W. Herron*

The word "family" stimulates a multitude of meanings. The "Christian family" also sparks many images. For some the picture might be the well-dressed family sitting reverently in a church pew. For others it might recall a stern father exhorting his children. Our family of origin often colors our model of the family as we think it should be.

Because it is difficult to browse through history and compare notes with families throughout the world, we tend to assume that our version of the American family is ideal. However, if we listen to foreign missionaries or read a book such as *The Family in Cross-Cultural Perspective*, by Willliam N. Stephens, we must be impressed by the immense variety of family structure.

### Historical Changes in the Family

Two historical examples that are more familiar to us can highlight the ever shifting variety of the family.

*Family in the Bible*

Within the Bible we note a marked development. The patriarchs. Abraham, Isaac, and Jacob, enjoyed the status of wealthy nomads, and therefore could afford to have more than one wife. If a wife could not bear a son, another wife or concubine was added so the male lineage could be preserved. Polygyny (having more than one wife) was taken to the extreme with Solomon. The father had absolute power, at least le-

**Robert W. Herron**
*Executive Director, Presbyterian Personal and Family Life Center*
*Greensboro, North Carolina*

An ordained minister of the Presbyterian Church, Robert Herron combines pastoral experience with academic training in his counseling. He has graduate degrees in Familial Social Science, a PhD from the University of Minnesota, and a BD from Union Theological Seminary in Virginia. Specializing in marriage and family relations, Mr. Herron has been active in professional and community activities.

gally, over his entire household—to the point of putting them to death. This included his sons and their children.

Contrast this with New Testament norms for family life. Monogamy is prescribed by Jesus (Matthew 19:5-6) and by the apostle Paul (1 Timothy 3:2). Dictatorial powers are stripped from the father and replaced with what would be termed children's rights today: "Fathers, do not provoke your children to anger. . ." (Ephesians 6:4).

Over a period of two millennia the biblical portrait of the family shifts dramatically. The reason for this is that the family can never be isolated from the winds of culture. The family can only exist and be understood in its historical milieu. This should caution us against referring to "the biblical view of the family" without specifying the particular historical era. This is not to imply that the Bible is merely a reflection of its culture. I am contending that we cannot accurately understand the eternal principles of Scripture without considering the changing cultural context in which it was written.

## Family in Early America

The second readily available example of historical development is the family in North America. We recall with fond nostalgia the Puritan family. The Puritans were intent upon creating an entire society that was harmonious with God's will. Nevertheless, the structure of the New England Puritan family was influenced a great deal by its environment. Out of necessity most functions were centralized in the family. Food was produced and processed by the family. The contribution of children to these tasks was essential. Children primarily learned the skills they needed to contribute to the nuclear family's welfare. Most education occurred in the home. Some provision was made for formal education in schools but this was generally limited to males. Since Sunday schools did not come into being until the nineteenth century in the United States, all religious instruction took place in the home.

The Puritan father assumed a role much like the Hebrew patriarch. In some colonies laws stipulated that disobedient children could be put to death. While parents influenced mate selection, their control amounted to veto power. Because of the distance between homes and scarcity of fuel the practice of bundling evolved. Courting couples were allowed to sleep in the same bed if they were fully clothed and separated by a bundling board. The success of bundling has been questioned!

What does seem incontestable is that current modern families are quite different from the colonial family. Due to the mechanization of agriculture and the urbanization of our society, most families consume food which was produced and processed by others. Secular and religious education have been transferred from the home to other institutions. Because most fathers are employed some distance from their homes, it is an impossibility for weekend fathers to assert the kind of power exercised by their Puritan predecessors.

As with the biblical notion of the family, we must guard against speaking of "the American family." Because of varied geography and rich ethnic heritage, families in North America have an inexhaustible diversity. The social and economic status of families must be taken into consideration.

Attempts to create a Christian family in Canada and the United States have been just as varied. The Amish and the Oneida communities stand as distinctive ventures. In almost all cases this involves creating a community separate from the rest of society. Would most middle-class North American Christians want to adopt such a separatist lifestyle?

In presenting the two historical examples above I have attempted to show that Christian families, like families in general, have taken many shapes and expressions. It is therefore an impossiblility to define the Christian family in terms of unchanging structure, roles, or functions. We must look more to the spirit than the letter, to processes rather than structure.

## Christian Qualities of a Family

The main point of this article is that family structure, roles, authority, and functions constantly adapt to changing cultural environments. To speak of the Christian family or the family in biblical perspective means that we must focus on how people relate to each other rather than on the static shape of their relationship. For instance, a husband who loves and cherishes his wife can occur in a male-dominated or equalitarian marriage. Self-giving is not confined to one particular model of marriage.

What makes a marriage distinctively Christian is the degree of self-giving (vs. self-centeredness). Its model is Jesus Christ rather than the structure of any human institution. This is best summarized by the apostle Paul:

> Do nothing from selfishness or conceit, but in humility count
> others better than yourselves. Let each of you look not only to his
> own interests, but also to the interests of others (Philippians 2:3-4).

Describing the lifestyle of the Spirit as opposed to the destructive ways
of the flesh Paul uses the following trademarks:

> But the fruit of the Spirit is love, joy, peace, patience, kindness,
> goodness, faithfulness, gentleness, self-control; against such there
> is no law (Galatians 5:22-23).

It seems to this writer that the fundamental credentials of Christians living in a family have to do with whether or not the fruit of the Spirit is in evidence. These spiritual and personal qualities supersede the shape of authority and roles in a family.

Ironically, the concern of the church through the centuries has been with the form instead of the dynamic content of what makes a family Christian.

### Was Paul a Chauvinist?

It can be anticipated that readers will question how this squares with the apostle Paul's crucial passage on family relations in Ephesians 5:21—6:4. It is curious how a phrase of one sentence in this passage has been lifted almost exclusively to define the meaning of Christian family living: "Wives, be subject to your husbands. . . ." Most of the time the sentence is not completed. Paul said ". . . as to the Lord." This seriously violates one of the rudimentary rules of biblical interpretation—to read a verse or part of a verse with reference to the paragraph or chapter in which it is found.

In spite of running against the current of historical interpretation and contemporary beliefs, I contend that Paul in this passage formulates a model of mutuality for the Christian family.

The tone of the entire passage is set in the first sentence: "Be subject to one another out of reverence for Christ" (Ephesians 5:21). In other words, subjection is not the sole responsibility of wives. This harmonizes with Paul's admonition elsewhere that we regard each other more highly than ourselves (Philippians 2:3).

After setting forth his thesis the apostle balances responsibilities for husbands and wives, parents and children. Neither can claim the absolute authority once granted the ancient partriarchs. In the following table, I have outlined how Paul offers a model of mutual submission rather than the hierarchical model of submissiveness that is generally ascribed to the maligned apostle.

TABLE I

Ephesians 5:21—6:4

Thesis: Be subject to one another out of reverence for Christ (v. 21).

| Wives | Husbands |
|---|---|
| Wives, be subject to your husbands, as to the lord. For the husband is the head of the wife as Christ is the head of the church, his body, and is himself its Savior. As the church is subject to Christ, so let wives also be subject in everything to their husbands. (vv. 22-24). | Husbands, love your wives, as Christ loved the church and gave himself up for her, having cleansed her by the washing of water with the word, that he might present the church to himself in splendor, without spot or wrinkle or any such thing, that she might be holy and without blemish. Even so husbands should love their wives as their own bodies. He who loves his wife loves himself. For no man ever hates his own flesh, but nourishes and cherishes it, as Christ does the church, because we are members of his body (vv. 25-30). |

Restatement of thesis: "For this reason a man shall leave his father and mother and be joined to his wife, and the two shall become one." This is a great mystery, and I take it to mean Christ and the church (vv. 31-32).

| | |
|---|---|
| and let the wife see that she respects her husband (v. 33b). | however, let each one of you love his wife as himself (vv. 33a). |

| Parents | Children |
|---|---|
| Fathers, do not provoke your children to anger, but bring them up in the discipline and instruction of the Lord (v. 4). | Children, obey your parents in the Lord, for this is right. "Honor your father and mother" (this is the first commandment with a promise), "that it may be well with you and that you may live long on the earth" (vv. 1-3). |

After the opening injunction for mutual submission Paul balances the responsibilities of both spouses. If either spouse is called upon to sacrifice or adapt, it is the husband. Generally the reverse is true for most American marriages. Research indicates that wives adapt most to the husbands' needs.

The key to the passage hinges on the meaning that one gives to the phrase, " . . . as Christ loved the church and gave himself up for her" (Ephesians 5:25). Again it seems to me the meaning of that love is portrayed best in Philippians 2:1-11. There we see that it means taking on the role of a servant and humbling oneself to the point of death. This is hardly male chauvinism.

Some might contend that this is simply a biased reading. But consider Paul's advice regarding marital sex:

> The husband should give to his wife her conjugal rights, and likewise the wife to her husband. For the wife does not rule over her own body, but the husband does; likewise the husband does not rule over his own body, but the wife does (1 Corinthians 7:3-4).

Neither partner has the upper hand. Both husband and wife are responsible to and for each other's satisfaction. This is certainly consistent with Paul's declaration of equal status in the Christian community (and family?): "There is neither Jew nor Greek, there is neither slave nor free, there is neither male nor female; for you are all one in Christ Jesus" (Galatians 3:28).

### Jesus and Women

A great deal has been written recently concerning the attitude of Jesus toward women. Scanzoni and Hardesty's book is a good example (1975). (See also Kraybill's and Furfey's articles—both elucidate on Jesus' attitude toward women). Being removed from the Middle East culture, we often fail to realize how radical Jesus' departure was from the customs of his times. A man conversing with a woman at a public well does not strike us as unusual. But the incident with the infamous Samaritan woman (John 4: 1-42) was as scandalous in Jesus' day as it would be today in the Middle East.

The status of women stands at the heart of discussions concerning what makes a family Christian. For the Christian, the life and teachings of Jesus Christ must serve as the guide and standard for all we do. It seems clear to me that Jesus made a revolutionary break with his culture. The Gospel of John tells us that they marveled that he was talking with a woman . . . (4:27). They were shocked because rabbis did not talk to women in public, not to mention questionable women. By his actions Jesus demonstrated that women, as well as men, are created in the image of God. Women are equal in worth and dignity. There is no distinction in the personhood of males and females before God.

## A Model of Mutual Submission

The implications of this, of course, are far reaching for Christian family living. Instead of the hierarchical, authoritarian model of the world, the Christian is called upon to adopt a stance of mutual submission (to use Paul's terminology) or servanthood:

> But Jesus called them to him and said, "You know that the rulers of the Gentiles lord it over them, and their great men exercise authority over them. It shall not be so among you; but whoever would be first among you must be your slave; even as the Son of man came not to be served but to serve, and to give his life as a ransom for many (Matthew 20: 25-28).

As I interact with Christians today I do not encounter many who utilize this model for family relations. Instead, models are drawn from other sources: the military (someone has to be the general), sports (someone has to call the signals), business (the buck must stop on someone's desk). The human tendency is to control for one's own sake and status. The way of Jesus, however, is service to each other out of love. Jesus turns the tables on any notion of a chain of command, calling his followers to model giving and serving rather than commanding.

## Research on Family Power in Biblical Perspective

The question of power and authority in the family leads us to research conducted by sociologists. Power within marriage and family is one of the liveliest topics in current research. Of particular interest to this paper is whether male dominated marriages result in higher marital satisfaction.

A comprehensive study by Blood and Wolfe (1960) has shaped subsequent research and provided many insights. The authors defined power in terms of which spouse usually makes the decision in eight central areas:

1. What job the husband should take.
2. What car to get.
3. Whether or not to buy life insurance.
4. Where to go on vacation.
5. What house or apartment to take.
6. Whether or not the wife should go to work or quit work.
7. What doctor to have when someone is sick.
8. How much money the family can afford to spend on food.

From this they defined four basic patterns of decision-making: (1) husband dominant, (2) syncratic—decisions made jointly, (3) autonomic—decisions divided and made separately, and (4) wife dominant.

Blood and Wolfe's analysis of 909 Michigan families reveals that the highest level of marital satisfaction was found in families reporting a syncratic decision-making pattern.. The next highest was the autonomic in which the couple divide areas of responsibility. The male dominant pattern came next.

The lowest marital satisfaction occurred with couples indicating the wife dominant pattern. Running counter to societal norms appears to have a negative influence on marital happiness.

Centers, Ravens, and Rodrigues (1971) essentially confirmed Blood and Wolfe's results. In a sample of 776 couples in the Los Angeles area 73 percent of those in the husband dominant reported being "very satisfied" with their marriage. The other percentages were: syncratic, 70; autonomic, 79; and wife dominant, 20.

Both studies seem to corroborate the proposition that mutual decision-making enhances rather than threatens marital well-being. If one spouse assumes a disproportionate amount of power, it is better if this is the husband. For centuries the predominant pattern has been that of male dominance. Couples who deviate too radically from this norm are likely to experience less marital satisfaction.

The question needs to be raised concerning Blood and Wolfe's definition of power. Are their eight areas of decision-making representative of marital interaction? It can be safely asserted that the eight areas are not of equal importance for all couples. What they do highlight is the fact that we cannot refer to authority or power abstractly. The question is often posed: "Who is the head of the family?" or "Who has the most power?" To answer adequately we must know what area of family decision-making we are talking about. It makes a difference if we are deciding on which brand of beans to buy, how to invest three thousand dollars, or whether to have sex. Who has the most power depends not only on the area of the decision-making but also on the circumstances.

*Marriage and Talents*

The biblical concept of talents is extremely relevant at this juncture. Jesus teaches that persons are to use their unique abilities (Matthew 25:14-30) rather than suppress them. Applying this to marriage and family relationships means that each spouse and each family member has a gift to offer. A family is being obedient to Christ when it brings forth and utilizes these unique qualities in individuals.

*Clinical Examples*

My experience as a counselor has revealed that we face two dangers when talents are denied. The first can be deceptive game playing. Frequently, for instance, it is the husband who is the most vehement in asserting his rights as head of the house, yet he does not remain at home long enough to exercise his "right." On the other hand, I am equally skeptical of the woman who cannot tell you enough about how submissive she is to her husband. Invariably I find this to be a front for wholesale manipulation: "I need to make my husband feel like he is in control." Although possibly overstated, "the real aggressors are the female killer sharks in the guise of submissive females" (Farrell, 1974).

I am acquainted with a Christian couple who have financial difficulties. The wife is adept at math and finances; the husband is not. Yet they play the game "since the husband is the head, he should be in charge of finances." This is a perfect example of denying and misusing the Lord's gifts. This couple and many others have tried to impose a model that does not fit them. Consequently they are forced to play games that will eventually jeopardize their marriage. In my opinion, it would be both biblical and more beneficial to their relationship if each would ascertain and utilize his or her talents.

Clinically I often encounter another pattern that causes marriages to run awry. I am thinking of a couple who are both committed to Christ. The wife believes she should be submissive and that her needs are not important. This pattern seems to run smoothly. There is only one problem. Every two or three months, the wife explodes with defiance and hostility. The dumbfounded husband does not know what is wrong with his compliant wife. The wife is equally puzzled. After all, isn't she doing all the right things?

## What Is Submission?

If one-way submissiveness means annihilation of one's self and needs, then it is doomed for disaster. If a model for marriage teaches or implies denial of self-worth, then it is fundamentally opposed to the Christian way. The implication of traditional teaching about women in the church has often amounted to this. Sadly this has resulted in gradual atrophy or in emotional eruptions, as in the above case.

For a marriage or family to be Christian, I believe there must be an acceptance of the importance of each person's needs. This does not mean that every family member's needs can be met all of the time. But recognition must be given their importance. Emotionally, if some needs are not met on a fairly regular basis, personal growth is inhibited and resentment inevitably festers.

If one adopts the model of mutual submission for a Christian marriage, it means that each partner will be concerned with the other's need fulfillment. It means that Christian couples who seek to apply this will shape their relationship according to their unique strengths. In certain areas one may take the leadership because he or she has the most skill, competence, or motivation. The other partner will assume responsibility in other areas.

If problems arise they usually stem from one of the partners not assuming his or her fair share of responsibility. This is a snag for any marriage model.

Occasionally I meet a wife who wants her husband to take charge, but he is unable or unwilling to assume any responsibility. Or he will assume responsibility only if his wife's decisions or plans are identical to his own. Adopting the male dominant model does not necessarily guarantee success. Failure to cooperate will wreak havoc with any marriage regardless of its power structure.

## Practical Implications

I am also asked frequently, "Who is going to make the final decision if you have an equalitarian marriage?" My experience has been that when a couple maintains trust and respect for each other very few decisions (less than one percent) come down to: "It has to be my way." However, if one person does have to make the final decision, it is my opinion that the person with the greatest expertise should make the decision. If an impasse is reached, it is better for the matter to be discussed openly rather than covertly. The more an adversary relationship develops between spouses, the more the couple will find themselves enmeshed in a win/lose situation.

When my wife and I were asked, "Who makes the final decision if you cannot agree?" we were unable to answer. We had never thought in terms of one or the other's way prevailing. Not that we always agree. Much depends on the framework with which one approaches decision-making and differences. If I expect decisions to go my way most of the time, then there must be a winner and a loser. But if I trust my partner and we cooperate (mutual submission), both of us can win and find a higher degree of fulfillment.

### Summary

To answer the question, what makes a family Christian, I have looked to history, research, and foremost to the model of Jesus Christ.

The family is a fluid institution. It influences and adapts to the cultures of humankind. Consequently we cannot accurately speak of "the family" or "the Christian family." Both have assumed wide variety of expression. What makes a Christian family distinctive is the quality of love demonstrated, rather than a particular power or role structure. Christlike caring is not confined to a particular family model.

From the teaching of Jesus and Paul one may conclude that the New Testament supports a position of mutual submission instead of hierarchical dominance. This principle is best illustrated in the upper room when Jesus took a towel and washed his disciples' feet, work traditionally performed by slaves (John 13;1-17). His model is characterized by love and mutual service rather than by one lording it over another, or by a chain of command.

Research on family power indicated that an equalitarian relationship is not contrary to marital happiness. Sharing of decision-making seems to be supportive of marital satisfaction.

From a Christian perspective couples should ascertain and utilize their unique talents. If we do not make use of these God-given gifts, our relationships may degenerate to destructive game playing.

No pattern of authority within the family is perfect because the family consists of persons who are selfish and tainted by sin. For a family to be Christian, there must be a pervading sense of need for

God's forgiveness, as well as each other's. Fortunately God accepts us as we are, and his grace is sufficient for whatever model of marriage and the family we choose.

## Discussion Questions

1. What images immediately arise when you hear "Christian family"?

2. What are some of the different types of family structure with which you are acquainted?

3. Why was polygyny accepted in the Old Testament?

4. Do you think it is beneficial that many family functions have been transferred to other institutions?

5. Can weekend fathers in contemporary America exert a great deal of power?

6. Do you think the author makes a valid case for mutual submission based on the apostle Paul?

7. In your experience do wives, or husbands, have to make more adaptations in marriage?

8. What areas of family decision-making would you add or subtract to the eight outlined by Blood and Wolfe? Which areas do you think are most appropriate for males? For females?

9. Do you know couples who must play games to maintain a male dominant marriage pattern? How do you feel about it?

10. Do you think it is realistic to adopt a cooperative, mutually submissive model of marriage?

## References

Blood, Robert O., Jr., and Donald M. Wolfe
    1960 *Husbands and Wives: The Dynamics of Married Living.* New York: The Free Press.
Centers, Richard, Bertram H. Raven, and Aroldo Rodrigues
    1971 "Conjugal Power Structure: A Re-Examination." *American Sociological Review*, 36, pp. 264-278.
Farrel, Warren
    1975 *The Liberated Man.* New York: Bantam Books.
Scanzoni, Letha and Nancy Hardesty
    1975 *All We Were Meant to Be: A Biblical Approach to Women's Liberation.* Waco: Word Books.
Stephens, Williams N.
    1963 *The Family in Cross Cultural Perspective.* New York: Holt, Rinehart and Winston

# 31
# The Future of Monogamous Marriage from a Christian Perspective

*James H. Phillips*

## Monogamous Marriage in Trouble

It is quite apparent that monogamous marriage in this country is in a perilous state. Indeed, as the renowned Joseph Fletcher warned, "In the opinion of some, it is actually getting close to terminal illness" (Hart, 1972:189). Another interpreter, a psychiatrist who has spent a lifetime in the field of marriage and family therapy, states, "From where I sit, the picture of marriage and family in present-day society is a gloomy one" (Ackerman in Hart:13). Dr. Urie Bronfenbrenner of Cornell University, recognized as one of the foremost educators of our time, was referred to in a *New York Times* article as seeing monogamous marriage and the family in a "desperate decline" (Nov. 27, 1977).

*Divorce, Symptom of the Problem*

Perhaps the most obvious evidence of the troubled condition of marriage is the divorce factor. For every three marriages performed in this country in 1972 there was one marriage terminated by divorce. Professor Max Lerner of Brandeis University predicted in that year that "the national rate in the decades ahead will probably become one out of two" (Hart, 1972:98). Actually the rate was more accelerated than he could know because only seven years later that proportion had been

**James H. Phillips**
*Professor Emeritus of Religion*
*Duke University*
After receiving his BD and PhD from Yale University, James Phillips served as an associate minister in historic Foundry Methodist Church, Washington, D.C. He was a chaplain in the Air Force in World War II, and later taught at American University. In 1946 he began teaching at Duke University in the undergraduate department of religion. He served as chaplain of the university for five years. His long career has included much counseling, reasearch and writing about human sexuality, marriage, and the family from a Christian perspective. Mr. Phillips is married, the father of two daughters.

realized (Bureau of Census, 1978:79). Vance Packard's startling prediction ten years ago may prove to be more realistic. On the basis of his very extensive survey of college students and young adults, reported in *The Sexual Wilderness* (1968:284), he concluded that the marriages made in the United States of America in the late 1960s have about a 50-50 chance of remaining nominally intact. I should add hopefully, however, that some authorities believe that the current rate is leveling off.

But even the current divorce rate does not tell the whole story. William J. Lederer° reports in *Marriage: For and Against* on a research project which used as test cases 601 couples, who on the average had been married 8.7 years. Husbands and wives were interviewed separately and confidentially. Here are several key questions they were asked with the author's corresponding conclusions:

The first question was; "Do you love your spouse?"

Only 11 percent of the sampling answered unhesitating, "Yes, I love my spouse."

The next group, consisting of 12 percent of the total, delayed for considerable time, hemmed and hawed, and then said approximately, "Well, let's say we get along better than most."

The largest segment, 43 percent, gave what Dr. Jackson called "defensive replies." For example, "I don't like Mary because she's mean and vindictive. But I appreciate the fact that she works hard at looking after the kids."

The wife, Mary, said, "Harry and I have lots of arguments. He drives me and the kids crazy. But I can't deny he's a good provider and is generous with what he makes."

Members of this group (the 43 percent), when required to list what they liked and what they disliked about their spouses, listed more bad characteristics than good.

The remaining 34 percent frankly said that their marriages were unsatisfactory.

All the couples—from the "happy" ones down to the outspokenly discontented— were asked the following as the last question; *If you could wave a magic wand which would divorce you and your spouse immediately, without inconvenience, without suffer-*

---

°Dr. Lederer is coauthor, with Don D. Jackson, of *The Mirages of Marriage* (New York: W.W. Norton Co., 1969), which is considered by many psychiatrists and psychologists to be the most realistic and helpful work on marriage published in recent years. The research project referred to above was one of the results of a 4½ year study for the publication of this book.

ing to anyone in the family, without social censure or expense, would you wave the magic wand and get a divorce?

Almost three quarters of them answered in the affirmative in some degree.

The survey concluded that over half of all married couples stay together, not because they love each other, but because divorce is too painful, difficult, or expensive; and that three quarters of all married couples frequently and seriously think about divorce (Hart, 1972:135-136).

Little wonder perhaps that Mervyn Cadwallader explodes:

Contemporary marriage is a wretched institution. It spells the end of voluntary affection, of love freely given and joyously received. Beautiful romances are transmuted into dull marriages; eventually the relationship becomes constricting, corrosive, grinding and destructive. The beautiful love affair becomes a bitter contract (quoted from *Current*, 1967, by Otto, 1970:3).

And one commentator, Kathrin Perutz, gives a less than subtle hint to her treatment as she entitles her book *Marriage Is Hell!*

*Alternatives to Monogamy Called For*

Are these commentaries accurate? Is marriage hell? Is it anachronistic? Is monogamous marriage on the way out? What are the marriage and family authorities saying? I can only summarize at this point, although I shall be documenting opinions later when I deal with specific subjects. The views of most of these authorities can be generalized as follows: They do not believe that marriage and the family are headed for extinction, but they are convinced that they are experiencing changes in terms of new forms. Furthermore, many of them have gone beyond the role of social scientists and have become apologists, sometimes even zealots, in endorsing and prescribing those changes. For example, Herbert A. Otto, chairman of the National Center for the Exploration of Human Potential, affirms with confidence:

After five thousand years of human history, man is now at the point where he can create marriage and family possibilities uniquely suited to his time, place, and situation. It is my suggestion that the "option to pluralism" offers a compelling challenge;

namely, that we develop new forms of marriage and family which might conceivably add more warmth and intensity to human existence than we ever dreamed possible (Otto: 1970:9).

Or as Sidney Jourard, professor of psychiatry at the University of Florida, puts it:

Polygyny, polyandry, homosexual marriages, permanent and temporary associations, anything that has been tried in any time and place represents a possible mode for existential exploration by men and women who dare to try some new design when the conventional pattern has died for them. Not to legitimize such experimentation and exploration is to make life in our (plural) society unlivable for an increasing proportion of the population (Otto, 1970:46).

Alvin Toffler in *Future Shock* puts it more shockingly. Referring to the debate between extreme pessimists who predict the monogamous family's demise and optimists who argue that the family is at the beginning of a golden age he concludes that neither is likely but rather that the family "may break up, shatter, only to come together again in weird and novel ways" (1971:239).

### Rediscovering the Christian Perspective

In order to bring this contemporary picture into focus on my topic, let me raise this question: What is the relation of the *Christian* tradition to this *cultural* phenomenon? As would be generally acknowledged, the Christian tradition has been largely responsible for, and supportive of, Western culture's monogamous family pattern. Indeed, to this tradition are attributed many of the faults in that pattern, and critics from all directions attack this tradition, especially its support of a patriarchal structure, its demands for permanence, and its claims for sexual exclusivity.

Now, how shall those of us who are in the Christian tradition respond? Shall we concede the traditional monogamous family pattern to be anachronistic, and thereby accommodate the winds of change? Or shall we probe further the traditional Christian claims for the validity of monogamy, and firmly resist the advocates of change who assault its integrity? These questions are the main inquiry of this paper. It is hoped that a juxtaposition of opinions and convictions on these matters may help us come to grips with the vital issues and lay a basis for further reflection and response by readers beyond the scope of the treatment in this chapter.

## The Old Testament Patriarchal Tradition

*First,* let us consider the *patriarchal* structure of traditional monogamy. Here the Western family tradition, up until the modern age, had a taproot in the biblical tradition. "Since marriage was patriarchal among the people of the Bible, the family was a community of persons, related by ties of marriage and kinship, and ruled by the authority of the father" (*Interpreter's Dictionary of the Bible,* Vol. II, 1962:240). Marriage, by divine ordinance, was a covenant between two families and was maintained by its high sense of corporate responsibility, which in turn was sanctioned and supported directly by four of the Ten Commandments. A premium was placed upon female virginity before marriage; and adultery by the wife was a crime so serious that it warranted the death penalty. The central issue involving both virginity and adultery was the assurance to the husband that any male child born to him was his own, for the continuity of the bloodline.

The woman's destiny was in truth—as Freud was later to reaffirm—tied to her anatomy, and a barren womb was regarded as a curse. One recalls the poignant cry of Rachel, "Give me children, or I shall die!" Yet, while subordinate to her husband, the fruitful wife commanded respect and esteem in the family system. And in certain instances, she even commanded equal status with her husband: The Fifth Commandment required honor from her children—"Honor thy father and thy mother." And the proverbial wife who was "far more precious than jewels" and whose "children rise up and call her blessed" has come resounding down through the centuries as the female image most desired, *i.e.,* until mid-20th century! In this society children were cherished, female as well as male. It is a significant fact that there is not one shred of evidence that female infanticide was ever practiced, as it was in some other ancient societies—notably among the Canaanites and Romans.

These were the central features of the Israelite family system, a way of life which, with significant qualifications, has gained the plaudits of distinguished authorites, such as D. Sherwin Bailey. He comments that "in spite of manifest imperfections, the Jewish sexual ethic and conception of marriage and family life were never surpassed in antiquity, and were maintained with remarkable consistency

(1962:18).° And most of these features passed into Christian practice.

## Jesus on Relationships in Marriage

It can be argued plausibly that the relative scarcity of Jesus' teachings on the family, in contrast to the proliferation of family references in the Old Testament, can be viewed as evidence of his *general* affirmation of this *tradition*. Later, however, we shall refer to several notable exceptions regarding adultery and divorce. Though remaining unmarried himself, Jesus in one of his most significant teachings endorsed the sanction of complementary coequality in marriage as the will of the Creator; "'God *made* them male *and* female.' 'For this reason a man shall leave his father and mother and be joined to his wife, and the two shall *become one* flesh.' So they are no longer two but *one* flesh"(Mark. 10:6-8). This teaching was taken by the church to preclude polygamy. But contemporary theological reflection has also seen in this teaching the key to the "one-flesh doctrine" of human sexuality. Bailey comments: "On the finite plane Man, the image or reflection of God, is found to be essentially a 'being-in-relation'—just as true human existence is essentially 'existence-in-community.' The 'adam' is not a single human individual, but a mysterious sexual duality of which man and woman are the relational poles." And he concludes significantly: "Here is the clue to the meaning of human sexuality" (1962:80).

## Pauline Thought on the Married Relationship

We should add to this salient teaching the illuminating and radical insight of the apostle Paul, "There is neither male nor female; for you are all one in Christ Jesus" (Galations 3:28). When this teaching is set within the broader context of his treatment of freedom and equality in Christ, we have a significant biblical frame of reference that can provide a positive basis for ethics on human sexuality and man-woman relationship. Unfortunately, neither teaching became a part of the legacy that formed the Western sexual tradition.

To the contrary, the church, under the impact—note you well—of

---

° Dr. Bailey's two initial books, *The Mystery of Love and Marriage* (New York: Harper & Row, 1962) and *Sexual Relations in Christian Thought* (New York; Harper & Row, 1959), are widely regarded as creating a breakthrough toward a more sensitive and constructive Christian theological understanding of sexuality. Bailey's interpretation moves toward complementarity and coequality in a Christian view of the marriage relation.

non-biblical influences for the most part, became pro-celibate and anti-sexual in its teachings of a "higher" way. And the church, even in its Protestant forms, perpetuated a patriarchal family system involving subordination of female under male—a system that has had lasting effects, many of them admittedly, ill effects.°

Paul has been pointed to by many writers as the chief culprit. A writer in a *Newsweek* issue (November 9, 1970:8) quoted this passage from 1 Timothy 2:11-14: "Let a woman learn in silence with all submissiveness. I permit no woman to teach or to have authority over men; she is to keep silent. For Adam was formed first, then Eve; and Adam was not deceived, but the woman was deceived and became a transgressor. Yet, woman will be saved through bearing children." Then, the writer added: "Among today's liberated women, of course, St. Paul rates a high place on the list of all-time male chauvinists—and for good reason."

Admittedly, an honest and appropriate "defense" of Paul will be partly ambiguous. And unfortunately a full consideration of Pauline teachings relevant to our concerns here obviously cannot be undertaken in this essay, but a few observations may at least help us toward getting a realistic and fair perspective on Paul that is much needed.

In the first place, there has been a wide consensus among scholars that Paul is *not the author* of 1 Timothy. It is scarcely fair to Paul to hold him responsible for what later interpreters, such as the unknown author of 1 Timothy, have made of Paul's teaching. Second, while there is still legitimate room for debate concerning the authorship of Ephesians, we may in any case note the ironical fact that interpreters— mostly males—have over the centuries been more prone to emphasize "wives, be subject to your husbands" (5:22), and have tended to neglect "Husbands, love your wives, as Christ loved the church" (5;25) and "Let each one of you love his wife as himself" (5:33)!

---

°This statement does not intend to minimize the gains to marriage from the Reformers' attack on the celibate ethic. For an illuminating treatment of these gains see "Theological Reflections on the Reformation and the Status of Women" by David C. Steinmetz, *The Duke Divinity School Review*, Vol. 41, No. 3 (fall 1976), pp. 197-207. But in a footnote Professor Steinmetz admits that Protestant theology taught "the subordination of women to men within the context of family and the home" while claiming that this theology moderated traditional practice—*i.e.*, for Protestants— and formed inherently the rationale for women's eventual liberation.

Third, we need to note that in the passages in 1 Corinthians in which Paul himself is indeed setting forth a *subordinate* role for women, Paul is not appealing to the authority of a revelation from Jesus Christ. Rather he appeals to his own personal right to prescribe standards for church life in churches he has established (not unlike Wesley's prescriptions of rules for his societies!) and to other kinds of "authority" which are *not as such Christian:* "nature," "the (Old Testament) law" and "the traditions." Consider respectively:

> Judge for yourselves; is it proper for a woman to pray to God with her head uncovered? Does not *nature* itself teach you that for a man to wear long hair is degrading to him, but if a woman has long hair, it is her pride? For her hair is given to her for a covering (11:13-15).
> As in all the churches of the saints, the women should keep silence in the churches. For they are not permitted to speak, but should be subordinate, *as even the law says* (14:33b-34).
> I commend you because you remember me in everything and maintain the *traditions* even as I have delivered them to you. But I want you to understand that the head of every man is Christ, the head of a woman is her husband, and the head of Christ is God (11:2-3).

If these passages are viewed on their own terms and in their own context, it should be clear that in assigning a subordinate role to women Paul was neither claiming to express a directly Christian revelation nor prescribing binding legislation for all future time.

Finally, and most importantly, any overarching perspective on Paul should focus on the point that at the center of Pauline theology is the *vision of a liberating community* of faith and love in which each person—male, female, husband, wife—has equal status before Christ and neighbor. Paul accordingly depicts a completely *coequal* and *complementary* pattern of sexual relationship *as given by God* (1 Corinthians 7:3-4) "The husband should give to his wife her conjugal rights, and *likewise* the wife to her husband. For the wife does not rule over her own body, but the husband does; *likewise* the husband does not rule over his own body, but the wife does."° It is indeed striking to see

---

°The theme of mutual rights in sexual relationships is a prominent one in current secular literature on sexuality, although it is likely that most authorities would be amazed to learn that, of all writers, Paul antidated them by nearly twenty centuries! The famed team Masters and Johnson in *The Pleasure Bond;*

that in the very midst of arguing from "the traditions" and the teachings of "nature," Paul feels constrained to remind his readers that "nevertheless" in the Christian understanding of man-woman relationships there is coequality and *fully reciprocal interdependence* between male and female (1 Corinthians 11:11-12): "Nevertheless, *in the Lord* woman is not independent of man nor man of woman, for as woman was made from man, so man is now born of woman. And all things are *from God*."

Jesus expressed the view (Mark 10:5) that the hardness of male hearts—contrary to the revelation of the will of God—lay behind the Jewish law (Deuteronomy 24:1) for divorce as a uniquely male privilege. Perhaps similarly the hardness of male hearts may have had something to do with the fact that over the centuries Paul has predominantly been seen as the vehicle of divine revelation establishing once-and-for-all the rightful dominance of men over women. A more just view of Paul will recognize him as a man of his time who, in part, accommodated his teaching on man-woman relationship to his own inherited Jewish traditions and the existing conditions of society in the Roman world. But it will also more strongly contend that, through his understanding of and faith in Jesus Christ, Paul became a man beyond his time: one who has offered, for those with eyes to see, *an egalitarian vision of male-female complementarity as the gift of God in Christ*—a vision that may still lure us toward fulfillment.

### Contemporary "Secular" Prophets
With this biblical background, let me become contemporary and make a few observations about the relevance of this egalitarian vision to the diagnoses and prescriptions of several modern secular "prophets."

*Jessie Bernard's "Shared Role Ideology"*
One of the sanest treatments of marriage, in terms of "the way it

---

*A New Look At Sexuality and Commitment* (Boston: Little, Brown & Co., 1974), describe this generation's progression in a knowledgeable husband's sexual responsibility from "doing something to his wife" to "doing something *for* her sexually." But in their sexual therapy they insist upon one further step toward sexual fulfillment, namely, the *mutual* attitude of achieving fulfillment "with each other, not to or for each other" (pp. 5-10). This book is highly recommended also for its emphasis upon the essential need of commitment and the benefits of fidelity in facilitating "the pleasure *bond*" in marriage.

really is, was, and will be," is *The Future of Marriage* by Jessie Bernard, widely recognized as one of America's leading sociologists. "The what it is" is aptly summarized as his and her marriages, "His, not bad, and getting better: hers, not good, and badly in need of change." And she cites the evidence:

> Because we are so accustomed to the way in which marriage is structured in our society, it is hard for us to see how different the wife's marriage really is from the husband's, and how much worse. But, in fact, it is. There is a very considerable research literature reaching back over a generation which shows that: more wives than husbands report marital frustration and dissatisfactions; more report negative feelings; more wives than husbands report marital problems; more wives than husbands consider their marriages unhappy, have considered separation or divorce, have regretted their marriages; and fewer report positive companionship. . . . Understandably, therefore, more wives than husbands seek marriage counseling; and more wives than husbands initiate divorce proceedings (1972:26-27).

This evidence propels her to her task; "So now to the first order of business [the reader hears it as a shout!]: To upgrade the wife's marriage." And that is what this book is all about.

And I am moved to say that I see nothing but full support from the biblical egalitarian vision for that! Equality, personhood, self-fulfillment. . . . These are all legitimate claims and concerns. And especially consistent with this egalitarian vision is Bernard's "shared-role pattern," which she prefers to "role-reversal," especially where children are involved. But she warns that it takes a considerable amount of sophistication to understand, let alone to accept, the logic and the justice of the shared-role ideology, and a considerable amount of goodwill to implement it. To the fear that this ideology would depolarize the sexes she provides this very interesting rejoinder:

> If we are thinking in terms of maleness and femaleness rather than masculinity and femininity, we have no cause for alarm. I am convinced that women and men are intrinsically so different that nothing we do will obliterate or even reduce the differences. I do not think men have to worry that women will become unsexed or women, that men will. In fact, the freer we become in allowing both sexes to be themselves, the more the fundamental and ineradicable differences will show up. I think that women will find maleness better than masculinity and men will find femaleness better than femininity (1972:255-56).

Though Jessie Bernard probably would be astounded at the comparison, I think this is a profound modern, secular, exegetical treatment of the biblical text, "God made them male and female." Furthermore, her "shared-role ideology" is a practical implementation of becoming "one-flesh."

### O'Neills' "Open Marriage"

In many important respects, I think this can also be said about the O'Neills' best seller *Open Marriage*. (There are some exceptions to this overall assessment. Several qualifications will be introduced later in this essay, and the most notable exception will be dealt with in the final section on the exclusivity of traditional monogamous marriage.) Contrary to a spate of current books that denigrate monogamous marriage, the O'Neills, after coming to grips with the question, "Why Save Marriage at All?" (the title of Chapter 1), reaffirm monogamy and proceed to build a model they call "open marriage:" this "is expanded monogamy, retaining the fulfilling and rewarding aspects of an intimate in-depth relationship with another, yet eliminating the restrictions we were formerly led to believe were an integral part of monogamy" (1972:43). Especially intriguing is their concept and development of "synergy," which is defined as "one plus one equals more than two, that the sum of the parts working together is greater than the sum of the parts working separately" (1972:41). The following paragraph demonstrates the working of synergy. Open marriage is

> a relationship in which the partners are committed to their own and to each other's growth. It is an honest and open relationship of intimacy and self-disclosure based on the equal freedom and identity of both partners. Supportive caring and increasing security in individual identities makes possible the sharing of self-growth with a meaningful other who encourages and anticipates his own and his mate's growth. It is a relationship that is flexible enough to allow for the change and that is constantly being renegotiated in the light of changing needs, consensus in decision-making . . . and openness to new possibilities for growth. Obviously, following this model often involves a departure, sometimes radical, from rigid conformity to the established husband-wife roles and is not easy to effect (Smiths, 1974:62).

Again, this is what I would call the biblical egalitarian vision in a new idiom! The intrinsic virtues of that vision reappear here: equal freedom within the context of interdependence; equal worth that assures individual identity and the satisfaction of essential personal needs (but a worth that is placed under a higher goal, larger than either one's desires would command alone); and growth, both self and mutual, toward that goal that is supported by deep and persistent caring.

A major criticism, for me, of *Open Marriage* is that its focus is on the married couple *alone.* How to picture *children* within their model appears, by omission, to be of no concern. Neither does the role of the family within the larger context of *society* emerge as a matter of concern. Apparently the authors themselves were sensitive to these omissions, for in a later publication they had this to say:

> Children cannot be taught the value of supportive love and caring, responsibility, problem-solving, or decision-making skills unless the parents have first developed these qualities in their own relationship. The inadequacy of our organized institutions to instill these values and skills is only too apparent. Therefore, intimate, long-term relationships such as those of marriage and the family must provide them. . . . Building from within strengthens the individual, the couple, and then the family unit, and thus the entire social structure, since the fundamental unit of society is the family. Whatever forms the family unit may take, its strength will still depend on the rewards gained from interpersonal relationships. It is in this sense that the individual and the married couple can become not only a fulcrum for change but also a key factor leading to the strengthening of the social structure. . . . It is hoped that open families can evolve to an open society and eventually to an open world (Smiths, 1974:66).

However, when I contemplated their definition of synergy as the definitive base for their "model marriage" I exclaimed: "So help us God!" I only wish the O'Neills had said *that*, because what they envision calls for rare wisdom, personal character, and mutual growth that, in my estimate, *transcend mere human effort*. But still, I thank God for these modern, albeit secular, prophets who, in a confused time, see egalitarian visions for monogamous marriage and point the way. I, for one, have learned much from them. But what has especially excited me is that these writers are (unknowingly perhaps) reaffirming, in a new idiom, basic biblical values supportive of monogamous marriage in a time when the rejection of any and all biblical "norms" is taken for granted by many critics.

## Permanence: Till Death Us Do Part?

Let us turn to the *second* feature of traditional monogamous marriage now under attack: the claim to *permanence*. I can—and must—treat this more briefly because a case for commitment to permanence has been partly made in our preceding reflections.

### Youth, Freedom, and Change

For many young people today the case for impermanence appears far more compelling. Many have experienced the trauma of the wrecked marriages of their own parents. To be sure, I have heard students from such homes declare their determination to make their own marriages succeed, in spite of their parents' failure, but they are the exception. The majority, either from experience or observation, find the current rate of marriage failure just one more strike against monogamous marriage.

But divorce is not the only compelling factor. There is a change in mood, in expectations. Whereas in the past the ideal was characterized largely by fixity, stability, security, these are the last things many young people seek today. According to Jessie Bernard, the motif of those who are "with it" is freedom. Consequently, many are turning to other directions. Increasing numbers do not see marriage as fitting into their lifestyle at all and are opting for the single life. Most students who cohabit, I'm told by students, are not marriage-oriented in their cohabitation. Others turn toward "group marriage," which characterizes at least some of the current communes. Still others (usually males!) theorize about sequential or serial marriages, with a new mate to fulfill changing needs as life develops.

### Mead's "Two-Step" Marriage

Some students who are more seriously oriented toward enduring commitment are intrigued by Margaret Mead's "Marriage in Two Steps," first published in a popular magazine in 1967. Let her explain:

> Such a marriage would be a licensed union in which two individuals would be committed to each other as individuals for as long as they wished to remain together, but not as future parents. As the first step, it would not include having children. In contrast, the second type of marriage, which I think of as parental marriage, would be explicitly directed toward the founding of a family (Otto, 1970:80).

As she goes on to elaborate, the first step is designed to be exploratory and maturing. While commitment is called for, this step could be terminated easily. But every parental marriage would have as background a good individual marriage. "And as a parental marriage would take much longer to contract and would be based on a larger set of responsibilities, so also its disruption would be carried out much more slowly" (Otto, 1970:83).

She notes that her proposal has some similarities to Judge Lindsey's "companionate marriage" as it was proclaimed in the 1920s. I remember well as a boy the storm that was stirred in public and church circles by Lindsey, and I see by vivid contrast not even a ripple provoked by Mead's proposal! Such has been the change in the public mood.

## Changing Attitudes in the Church

Even the churches, traditionally the main source for public and legal resistance to divorce, are changing their position—and I think generally for the better. Most Protestant churches no longer interpret Jesus' stringent teachings on divorce (in the Jewish context of an exclusively male prerogative!) as legal proscriptions binding on church members. And I have been personally predicting for some time now that the Roman Catholic Church, for which divorce has been anathema—barring divorced members from communion—will increasingly be forced to place this subject on its agenda for debate and revision. Recent official actions have begun to confirm this expectation. One such action, approved by the Vatican, extends the traditional limited basis for annulments—i.e., finding so-called marriages invalid—to include psychic irregularities, lack of due discretion, and plain immaturity. In fact, Monsignor Stephen J. Kelleher, who served as chairman of the Committee of the Canon Law Society of America (which authored "The American Procedural Norms"—on annulments—approved by the U.S. bishops and the pope), reported: "As things now stand, in some tribunals, a good canon lawyer can obtain an annulment for any person whose marriage has broken down" (*Commonweal*, 1977; 366). But Monsignor Kelleher is critical of the tribunal process for "annulment" as "a dehumanizing process" and counters the continuing proscription of "divorce" by affirming its necessity:

> The only alternative to annulment is divorce. As a lawyer, I think a couple whose marriage ceases to be existentially alive should get a

divorce and, if they desire, marry again.—The Church is out of order in forcing persons to submit to psychiatric examination or psychological tests under the threat of denying them the right to re-marry and to continue to receive Holy Communion (1977:365).

What, in essence, all this points to is that the churches are finding that legal proscriptions are not the solution to the human problems involved in marital breakdown, and that the mission of the churches in this area is to be expressed principally in preparation for marriage that leads to informed commitment, in educational and counseling services that strengthen good marriages and aid to those that are faltering, and finally, when marriages fail, to minister redemptively, making possible what one family scholar calls "realized forgiveness." Restoration of a sense of personal integrity is a deep need of the separated and divorced, whether or not they later enter into a new marriage—as most do.

What the churches institutionally and Christians individually should do in the public sector toward influencing needed legal reforms is a matter for serious study and dialogue. Various proposals are now under public discussion: the establishment of specialized courts for divorce; no-fault divorce; "do it yourself" divorce; compulsory marriage counseling—these constitute a few. Should marriage be made easier, indeed easy, to terminate? This is an important question. A more permissive answer is certainly gaining ground. Some serious students say, "Yes, easier to terminate but made more difficult to enter upon." With discernment, they deplore the fact that it is easier in most states to secure a license for marriage than for driving. Their call is for family-life education in public schools from kindergarten through high school, in churches and even in college, though that is a bit *late*.

I have no blueprint to offer. But I am urging that churches and their members need to get involved in these issues much more than we have. While Christians may differ on precise interpretations of Jesus' stern teachings about divorce—some saying they constitute irrevocable law; others saying, not law but an ideal—it seems to me that there is a minimal Christian stand: that we take those teachings with deep concern, as Jesus certainly taught them; that we regard divorce as human failure; and that we reform and work beyond the current legal entanglements, that so often deepen emotional scars, toward humane procedures that foster renewal and new beginnings.

After much serious study, I am persuaded that we need to give far more attention to *prevention* than we have to the "cure," if we can call it that. I agree strongly with those who have pointed out that the fundamental defect in our legal system is that our present matrimonial statutes are concerned primarily with the rules of terminating, rather than preparing for and preserving a marriage. Far more appropriate is the cardinal principle underlying most of the standard college texts designed to prepare students for marriage: the principle of mutual commitment for making marriage succeed. That is the lesson to be understood, appreciated,and applied.

In concluding our consideration of permanence in marriage, I remain convinced, while some may scoff, that there is a world of "common sense" (and also, implicitly, a trusting invocation of the grace of God beyond any merely "autonomous" human capabilities) in the old traditional vow: "to have and to hold, from this day forward, for better, for worse, for richer, for poorer, in sickness and in health, to love and to cherish, till death us do part, according to God's holy ordinance; and thereto I plight thee my troth."

## Sexual Exclusivity

Now, let us turn to the *third* and final problem in this presentation. Perhaps no claim of traditional monogamous marriage has come under more acid attack than its claim to sexual *exclusivity*. From all directions we are engulfed by evidence that increasingly appears to make that claim a pious pretension: the evidence of sex researchers from Kinsey in 1948 to Morton Hunt (1974:Cf. Ch. 5) in the mid-seventies; daily "triangle" themes in movies, TV, magazines, and paperbacks; the sensational accounts of mate-swapping ("wife-swapping" is "out" because of its chauvinistic ring!) and swinging (no longer hinted at in news releases but treated at length in scholarly books) with an estimated one half to eight million couples involved.

It appears self-evident that extramarital sex is on the increase with new and, to some, fascinating forms of expression. To raise the question of "why?" would demand attention to a complex of causes far beyond the scope of this essay. But I want to call attention to one source that is having increasingly persuasive influence among college students. That source is what many "authorities" are now saying in contrast to what most "authorities" used to say.

### The Permissive Bias of Texts

A review of the outstanding college texts on marriage and the family of only a decade ago will reveal, almost invariably, a "pro-bias" supporting fidelity in husband-wife relations. Today, there is a strong trend toward the opposite: a "pro-bias" justifying extramarital sex (rarely called "infidelity"—that's a loaded and "outdated" term)—referred to by Albert Ellis, a longtime crusader for sexual freedom, as "civilized adultery." Jessie Bernard admits this trend as a significant fact: "One of the most interesting indications of change now taking place is the apologia which is becoming fashionable among researchers in discussing extramarital relationships. It has now become the positive, functional aspects which are increasingly emphasized rather than, as in the past, the negative and dysfunctional aspects. . . . The current trend seems sometimes to be, in fact, not only in the direction of tolerance but even, in some cases, of advocacy" (Smiths, 1974:149-150).

A plethora of statements can be found from a number of writers. But for our purposes here the recent collection of essays, *Beyond Monogamy* (from which a few quotations have already been given), may, with a few exceptions, be taken as representative. The editors, James and Lynn Smith, who are co-directors of a Self-Actualization Laboratory, wrote the introduction and a chapter entitled "The Incorporation of Extramarital Sex into the Marriage Relationship." I have selected the following quotations from the Introduction:

> The consequences [of "transmarital"—note the term!—permissiveness] for marriage are significant and dramatic. By eliminating or at least reducing the deceit associated with conventional adulterer's behavior and by transcending the intramarital demands of sexual exclusivity, and at the same time achieving new levels of candor and freedom about sexuality, the conjugal relationship can be transformed into something very different which may be more trying and challenging but also more rewarding and fulfilling (p. 19).
>
> We remain more impressed with the way in which monogamous heterosexuality denies the multiplicity and latitude of sexual and interpersonal experience that are available to healthy and mature persons than with the dire warnings that sexual freedom will always and everywhere be twisted into sexual license and unchecked promiscuity. From an interpersonal point of view, living in a monogamous relationship is not unlike having sex with one's clothing on: it diminishes sensitivity and restricts movement (p. 33).
>
> Monogamic marriage is, in its own macabre way, a legitimized and normalized form of emotional and erotic bondage, as evidenced by its obligatory character intended as a matter of course to

insure social and familial stability against the wild winds of sexual passion. Historical and social conditions, especially the current rate of divorce and the increasing frequency of extramarital sexual contacts, now suggest that this grand strategy may have backfired.... There is the aching feeling abroad that something is wrong, not with marriage per se, but with the monogamic system of institutionalized customs and habits that has its prime expression in contemporary western culture. There is a recognition that monogamy pushes as many persons apart as it brings together and that this 'forsaking-all-others' and 'til-death-do-us-part' business is neither realistic nor humane (p.35).

The increasing frequency and incidence of swinging and swapping (as forms of consensual adultery) could ... be viewed not as evidence of the decline of western civilization or Christian morality through promiscuity and debauchery but as restless ... attempts which presage a new era in sexual and interpersonal relationship (p.38).

This permissive stance has already received expression in other widely read sources. Let me refer to two examples. In *Open Marriage* the O'Neills redefined fidelity in broad terms (1972: 256-257) as "loyalty and faithfulness to growth, to integrity of self and respect for the other, not to a sexual and psychological bondage to each other," and they then proceeded to say that in a marriage

in which each partner is secure in his own identity and trusts in the other, new possibilities for additional relationships exist, and open [as opposed to limited] love can expand to include others. ... These outside relationships may, of course, include sex. That is completely up to the partners involved. If partners in an open marriage do have outside sexual relationships, it is on the basis of their own internal relationship—that is, because they have experienced mature love, have real trust, and are able to expand themselves, to love and enjoy others, and to bring that love and pleasure back into their marriage, without jealousy. We are not recommending outside sex, but we are not saying it should be avoided, either.

It is significant to note (and not merely parenthetically) that in a more recent publication (1978) Nena O'Neill has presented a strong reaffirmation of the values of sexual fidelity to the marriage relationship. And she deplores the fact that "open marriage" has popularly "become a term, not for the new relationship of equality we had described, but for everything from a *sexually* open marriage to almost anything else" (p. 203). Several critical questions might be raised: Is this popular usage due to an over-accent in *Open Marriage* on the freedom of each partner in the total marriage relationship which caused the undiscerning reader to overlook or ignore the prerequisite of their cardinal principle of synergy? Indeed, in the very allowance of extramarital sex which assumed the realization of synergy, did they not open the floodgate to all-too-human justification? The readers of *Open Marriage* should read *The Marriage Premise*.

In the second example, Della and Rustum Roy's *Honest Sex* (which the authors claim to have written from a Christian perspective, and which for the most part, in my judgment, has considerable merit), the authors see as an extension of agape love the inclusion of a lonely person. They especially mean to include a single woman or widow (one might wonder: why not also especially a single man or widower!) into a co-marital relationship which would afford that person's fulfillment, including, if desired, sexual involvement. Indeed, they confidently declare, "Such relationships can serve as the vehicle of faithfulness to God" (1968:121). For relevant critique of this ostensibly "Christian" position, one is not limited to the pronouncements of traditionally oriented Christian theologians. Masters and Johnson have employed penetrating psychological insight in analysis and scathing judgment on this, and similar, "Christian justifications" of sexual "inclusiveness" (1974:187-191).

*How Should the Christian/Church Respond?*

Again, we raise the question, what should be the response of the church, and of individual Christians, to this increasing contravention, both in theory and practice, of sexual exclusivity in marriage? The position of the church has certainly been clear and strong. "Thou shalt not commit adultery" is probably the best known of the Commandments. Are there strong reasons for "holding the line"? My answers will be brief but pointed.

Many Christians would say that the teachings of Jesus make mandatory calling adultery what he called it: a sin against God's purposes for human sexuality. That Jesus was emphatic about this is clear. In fact, he was more emphatic than the traditional Jewish view of adultery. Jesus went beyond identifying adultery with the behavioral act and equated it with lustful intention. He placed his chief emphasis (perhaps as a reaction against the male-dominated ethos of his culture) on male, rather than female, sin. And he extended adultery to sexual relations (in act or intent) with any woman, not just "another man's" wife, as the traditional view interpreted the Commandment—a view that sanctioned the double standard of some sexual freedom for the husband and none for the wife. And finally, he taught within the context of his teachings on divorce that a man could commit adultery against his own wife and not simply against another husband's rights— another radical extension of the meaning.

I cannot see how the church or any Christian could disavow or fail to take seriously these teachings without compromising Christian moral integrity. At the same time, these teachings should certainly be kept in proper perspective, as Jesus himself did. To make the Seventh Commandment the central one and to preach it negatively with stern "thou shalt nots"—and the church has been guilty of this—is to misread him. It is noteworthy that Jesus was far more lenient with adultery than with spiritual pride, and that adulterers were among his followers, while religiously proud men were his enemies. And he proclaimed his primary mission as not to condemn but to save, to make life whole.

### Fidelity—Pro and Con

And this leads me to my second answer. The majority of authorities are commonly agreed that the function remaining distinctively and, in some ways, uniquely with marriage and the family is the affectional and volitional function; and that as life becomes more automated and impersonal, this function increases the continuing need, indeed, the imperative need, of marriage and the family. Furthermore, it is commonly agreed that this function makes central the factor of interpersonal relationship. The O'Neills declare that "the central problem in contemporary marriage is relationship" (Smiths, 1974:58). If this is so—and I think unquestionably it is—then in marriage the paramount need is to utilize those means that enrich and deepen the one-to-one relationship and resist those attitudes and acts that erode and destroy it.

Let me quote to you two authorities who place the question of extramarital sex in striking contrast. From the O'Neills:

> If outside companionships are to be more than causal ones, and might involve sex, then those relationships too should be approached with the same fidelity to mutual growth, and with the same measure of respect that you would show your partner in open marriage (O'Neills, 1972:258).

A quotation in contrast is from Rollo May in reaction to "generalized love" as characterized by the free-sex movement. Such love

> ends in something which is not fully personal because it does not fully discriminate. Distinctions involve willing and choosing, and to choose someone means not to choose someone else. . . . But what of fidelity and the lasting quality of love? Erotic passion not only requires capacity to give one's self over to . . . the power of immediate experience. But it also requires that one take this event into one's own center, to mold and form one's self and the relationship [with another] on a new plane of consciousness which emerges out of the experience. This requires the element of will (1969:279).

These statements suggest the popular question so often raised by students: "Can you love—in a full, intimate sense, including sexual love—more than one person at a time?" The O'Neills say "Yes"; Rollo May says "No." It is at least suggestive, I think, to recall that Rollo May is a practicing psychoanalyst.

Support for May's position comes, perhaps unexpectedly, from another significant secular source. Masters and Johnson conclude their treatment on "Extramarital Sex" as follows:

> It is true that when one partner finds satisfaction in extramarital relationship, this may turn a potentially destructive marital relationship into a cautious friendship, or a supportive "acquaintance-ship" and in that sense it is better than open marital warfare with all its attendant bitterness and destructiveness. But this *is not marriage in the sense of two human beings with full regard for each other*, sharing the wish to negotiate differences between them and developing mutual pleasures to the fullest extent possible. Making do in marriages is not fulfillment through marriage. Even if infidelity represents the first step in a positive direction—toward making do instead of making war—it is still a long distance away from the goal of becoming committed: true to oneself and loyal and vulnerable to one's partner (1974:139).

I believe the Christian answer to the question would be much closer to May and to Masters and Johnson rather than to the O'Neills, not only because the affirmation of sexual exclusivity has a hard-nosed practicality about it (that is astonishingly overlooked by the O'Neills), but also because of the implied affirmation of a mysterious sexual duality, polarity, and complementarity between husband and wife that finds its deepest needs fulfilled in the "one flesh" union of a one-to-one marriage relationship. This is the positive approach to the Christian claim of exclusive sexual fidelity.

## Conclusion

What is the future of monogamous marriage from a Christian perspective? As we have seen, the current rate of marriage failures and other negative data constitute for some authorities compelling evidence for a pessimistic outlook or motivate others to advocate blueprints of extreme alternatives. My own reflections, on a more comprehensive basis that includes Christian insights as treated above, have led me increasingly to a primarily optimistic—or at least hopeful—position. Realistically there remain, of course, not only deep concerns, not only blatant causes for temporary pessimism, but also complex problems, for which there are no easy answers. But I am persuaded that there is a significant trend in attitudes toward a meaningful understanding and mutually fulfilling realization of the (God-given) possibilities of monogamous marriage, which presents Christians and the church with a unique opportunity. This trend consists of an increasing *correlation* of a great deal of *secular* research findings with authentic *Christian* teaching. If the distinctive cohesive factor that enables marital life not only to survive but to build toward fulfillment is *the quality of interpersonal relationships*, as many secular marriage authorities are urgently affirming (e.g., McCary, 1975:Cf. Ch. 5), then equality, commitment, fidelity, and a dedication to marital success are not only imperative components of that quality, they are inherent components of our Christian faith. Hence, the way for cooperative endeavors between concerned secular and Christian marriage authorities toward strengthening our marriage system is widening. But more importantly, the church has a distinctive function for its opportunity and responsibility in that it now has a reconstructed *positive biblical base* to provide a faith dynamic to this endeavor. This is the salient factor for hope, even for optimism.

## Discussion Questions

1. Some authorities in the area of sexual decision-making contend that religion plays no major or even minor role in students' thinking. Is this your experience? In your observation of your peers, do you think this is generally true? If the answer is "yes," what are the reasons for religion's irrelevance?

2. We have observed in this chapter that modern biblical scholars have reconstructed a very significant biblical base for a primarily positive attitude toward human sexuality. But for centuries the church has conveyed an anti-sexual stance. How do you account for this contradiction? Does your denomination in its official statements, its preaching and teaching still convey this negative tradition? If so, what can be done to change it?

3. How do you reconcile the Bible's patriarchal view of marriage and the family with its teachings about equality before Christ? Did Paul's teachings resolve the problem for you? Is the contemporary clamor for women's liberation resolving it? What should be the Christian view?

4. Is "living together" before marriage good preparation for marriage? What are its contributions? What are its liabilities?

5. In my counseling situations with students living together, the vast majority contend that their sense of commitment is as strong and valid as that of married couples. What is your reaction to this contention?

6. What are your reactions to Margaret Mead's proposal of "two steps" in the marriage process? Compare her proposal with the traditional Christian process.

7. Should the church in its own policy and its influence in public policy support the trend toward easier divorce? What, in your Christian opinion, should be the church's primary functions regarding divorce?

8. What was your reaction to the Roys' position that the Christian husband should regard his relation, even if it involved sexual encounters, with lonely single women, especially widows, as a religious duty?

9. What was your reaction to the O'Neills' and Smiths' positions on extramarital sex? Do you believe that the increasing incidence of premarital sex and living together will increasingly popularize their respective view? What should a Christian, the church do about the problem of increasing infidelity?

10. We are obviously in a transitional, experimental era regarding attitudes and conduct concerning marriage. What basic trends do you see? Do you think that the traditional Christian concept which has been dominant in Western culture will remain dominant? Or does the traditional Christian concept and practice need some changes that would still conform to basic biblical principles?

# References

Bailey, D. Sherwin
    1962 *Common Sense About Sexual Ethics: A Christian View*. New York: Macmillan.

Bernard, Jessie
    1972 *The Future of Marriage*. New York: World.
Bronfenbrenner, Urie
    1977 Nov. 27 "The Family in Transition: Challenge from
        Within."*New York Times*.
Bureau of the Census
    1978 *Statistical Abstracts of the U.S.*
*The Durham Sun*
    1977 Nov. 29.
Hart, Harold H. (ed.)
    1972 *Marriage: For and Against*. New York: Hart Publishing Co.
Hunt, Morton
    1974 *Sexual Behavior in the 1970's*. Chicago: Playboy Press.
*Interpreter's Dictionary of the Bible*, Vol. II
    1962 Nashville: Abingdon.
Kelleher, Monsignor Stephen J.
    1977 June 10 "Catholic Annulments: A Dehumanization Process."
        *Commonweal*, Vol. CIV, no. 12. Harden City, NY: Double-
        day.
Masters, William H. and Johnson, Virginia E.
    1974 *The Pleasure Bond: A New Look at Sexuality and Commit-
        ment*. Boston: Little, Brown.
May, Rollo
    1969 *Love and Will*. New York: W. W. Norton
McCary, James Leslie
    1975 *Freedom and Growth in Marriage*. Santa Barbara: Hamilton.
*Newsweek*
    1970 Nov.2.
O'Neill, George and Nena
    1972 *Open Marriage*. New York: M. Evans. Cf. Nena O'Neill's
        *The Marriage Premise: A Celebration of the Values That
        Make Marriage Work*, 1978, New York: Bantam Books.
Otto, Herbert A. (ed.)
    1970 *The Family in Search of a Future*. New York: Appleton-
        Century-Crofts.
Packard, Vance
    1968 *The Sexual Wilderness*. New York: David McKay Co.
Roy, Della and Rustum
    1968 *Honest Sex: A Revolutionary New Sex Guide for the Now
        Generation of Christians*. New York: Signet Books.
Smith, James and Lynn (eds.)
    1974 *Beyond Monogamy: Recent Studies of Several Alternatives
        in Marriage*. Baltimore: John Hopkins.
Toffler, Alvin
    1971 *Future Shock*. New York: Random House, Bantam Books.

# 32
# Premarital Sex: A Christian Perspective

*Charles P. De Santo*

## Changing Sexual Attitudes and Practices

*A Biblical View of Sexuality*

Whenever we discuss premarital sex it is best to place it in biblical perspective, as well as sociological perspective. Unfortunately sex is too often discussed in isolation, as if it were unrelated to the rest of life. It ought not to be treated this way. Sex must be related to the totality of life's experiences—family, church, and community, as well as to one's male or female friend. Sex is not something we do—we are sexual beings. Our sexual expression is a manifestation of the kind of persons we are. Our behavior toward others really reveals not only who we think they are, but also who we think we are.

As Christians we affirm the goodness of God's creation, and this includes his creation of us as sexual beings. Man and woman were created by him to complement each other, to interact with each other for the enrichment of life in community. When we think of the physical demonstration of affection—necking, petting, and sexual intercourse—we believe that this, too, is good within the bonds of marriage. The physical demonstration of affection, including sexual intercourse, becomes evil only when we use it to exploit another person for our own satisfaction. But when a couple are wholly committed to each other in marriage and mutually submissive, the sexual expression of affection

**Charles P. De Santo**
*Professor of Sociology and Department Chairman*
*Lock Haven State College*

Charles De Santo earned an MDiv from Louisville Presbyterian Theological Seminary, an MA from Ball State Univeristy, and the PhD from Duke University. His special interests include family sociology, deviance, and the sociology of religion. He has written two books and several articles. He is an ordained minister in the United Presbyterian Church. Before coming to Lock Haven he taught sociology at Huntington College, and previously taught religion and philosophy at Maryville, Wheaton, and Sterling colleges.

becomes a means of ministering to one another, as well as means of strengthening the relationship.

*Culture Influences Sexual Ways*

Let us think of the concept of culture as it relates to the expression of affection prior to marriage. It is too easy for us to be culture and time bound—to think that necking and petting as expressed in our society is the way it has always been, and that this is the way it is in all societies. Actually this is not the case. From antiquity to the turn of the present century, for the most part, necking, petting, and sexual intercourse prior to marriage was not only frowned upon, but carried severe penalties. If it was practiced, as indeed it was among a minority, it was usually among the very affluent or among those who were at the other end of the social ladder. Furthermore, young people did not "date" as we know it today. Dating is really a post World War I invention. Prior to the war "dating" was goal oriented; one courted with a purpose— marriage. Dating just for "fun," with no particular goal in mind, is a relatively recent phenomenon. It has spread to the rest of the world along with Western industrialism, ideas of democracy, individualism, and modern films.

We should note, also, that each country has different norms or standards for male-female interaction. Anthropologists tell us that many societies permit premarital sex. Margaret Mead's (1949:1930) writings have informed two generations about the sexual practices of those in New Guinea and Samoa. While we as Christians recognize the right of each society to establish its own norms for sexual behavior, we believe that for the Christian—regardless of his society or culture— there is only one standard for premarital sexual behavior, namely, ab- stinence. It is interesting to note in passing, however, that every society regulates sexual behavior. The family is too basic an institution to go unregulated.

*Changes in the United States*

But even in the West, in the United States in particular, we have passed through phenomenal changes in attitudes and behavior patterns with regard to premarital sex and the demonstration of affection. Dur- ing the colonial period those who were found guilty of engaging in pre- marital sex were flogged and compelled to make public confession before the church congregation. Adulterers were compelled to wear a letter "A" or they were branded with an "A" on their forehead. While bundling was practiced by some, the individuals were fully clothed, wrapped in separate blankets, often with a board between them. Furthermore, they usually slept in the same room with the rest of the family. Courtship was brief, with betrothal and marriage following shortly thereafter. Virginity was highly prized, and woe to the young lady who brought discredit to herself and her family by becoming pregnant before marriage (Kephart, 1972:146-151; Queen and Habenstein, 1974:331).

Gradually, however, courtship and sexual attitudes changed from the strict puritanical standards of the colonial period to the more permissive ones of the nineteenth century. The real changes, however, did not come until the twentieth century. Courtship customs became much more liberalized, as did sex mores. As Kephart (1972:275) said: "The emancipation of women, accelerated urbanization, decline in secular and religious controls, a more permissive attitude on the part of the public—all tended to reduce the backlash of the Puritan tradition." He cites three things that further contributed to change: (1) the automobile, (2) the availability and the mass production of contraceptives, and (3) the relatively quick and easy cure for venereal disease. Most of these changes took place after the Second World War.

The twenties brought another shift toward greater permissiveness. Women had achieved great gains legally, politically, economically, educationally, and socially. The double standard of sexual morality was being challenged as women demanded the same sexual freedoms men enjoyed. Dating without chaperons was not in vogue, a custom which we take for granted today. With the continued emancipation of women over the past several years, permissiveness, by contrast, seems to have gone to seed. Whereas seventy-five years ago courtship took place under the watchful eye of parents, today within ten minutes a young couple can drive away unchaperoned to some quiet, secluded spot.

*Critique Cultural Ways by Biblical Principles*

The point that I am making here is that dating and courtship customs do and *have* changed. Therefore, it is the Christian's responsibility to critically evaluate these changes in the light of Christian principles. It is Christ over culture, not culture over Christ. When we turn to the Scriptures we find a definite theology of human sexuality. First of all our Lord states that "love for God and love for neighbor" are to be our guiding principles. He said in the Sermon on the Mount that adultery is a sin. He did not dwell upon premarital sex because this was not a serious problem among the youth of his day within the Jewish community. Marriages were arranged by parents. The Apostle Paul (1 Corinthians 6:13 ff.) admonishes Christians to avoid fornication. He tells us that our bodies are the dwelling place of God's Spirit and belong to Christ. We are not to engage them in immorality.

When the Christian, therefore, thinks of physically demonstrating affection before marriage, he ought to think of his obligation to God, as well as to his near neighbor—the member of the opposite sex he or she is with. Since someone he "loves" is a "neighbor," he ought to strive to love that person as he loves himself. Just as he would not want to be exploited sexually, so he should not exploit his neighbor.

## Environmental and Cultural Factors
*Attitudes Toward Sex Are Learned Early*

Let us now turn to the subject of the acquisition of our sexual attitudes and morals. We are largely the products of our family socialization. Our parents' behavior toward each other says to us, "We love each other," or "our love has grown cold." If concern and consideration for members of the family are shown by the many little things we can do for one another, then the children absorb the loving attitude and become loving persons too. If our parents are demonstrative in their affection, embracing and kissing in our presence, this says to us, "Affection is normal and good." Our attitude toward sex, therefore, develops early—either positively or negatively.

Later on, as we move out into our peer groups, we begin to learn the "facts of life" from a different perspective. Hopefully, if our parents have talked with us, and we have been given suitable sex education literature, we are not disturbed by the often incorrect and coarse instruction our peers give us.

### What About Masturbation?

During this early adolescent period we begin to become aware of the secondary sexual changes that take place during puberty. How we handle these changes depends to a large extent on our education prior to these changes. I will not go into the physiological aspects of sexual development. This has been done elsewhere and the student is referred to the bibliography for suggested readings. However, I would like to

say a word about masturbation. Masturbation is something that virtually all boys, and a growing number of girls, experience during
adolescence. As a physician said on one occasion: "Ninety-five percent
of the boys admit to masturbation and the other five percent lie about
it!"

I remember reading some religious tracts, as a teenager, which
said that people who masturbate go insane. Thank God we have largely
passed from that benighted period. Masturbation will not drive one
insane, nor will it cause warts to grow on the palm of one's hand, nor
will it cause one's penis or clitoris to grow larger or waste away. I do not
mean to treat the subject lightly, however, as it is not a practice to be
encouraged. R. A. Sarno, in his excellent book, *Achieving Sexual
Maturity* (1969), differentiates between "habitual masturbation" and
"accidental masturbation." While habitual masturbation will not injure
the body, it is probably a sign of some psychological problem for which
the individual should seek counseling. Accidental masturbation occurs
through the process of self-discovery and is eventually abandoned.
Sarno rightly points out that "solitary sex" may make it difficult for an
individual to share the act of love in the mutuality of marriage, since he
or she is apt to bring this self-centered approach into marriage. I personally believe that one of the reasons we feel guilty about the practice
is not only because we believe it is wrong and society frowns upon it,
but also because we ourselves realize that sexual satisfaction was never
intended to be a solitary experience. It ought to be a mutual sharing
within the bonds of marriage.

*Biological and Cultural Conditioning*

Before we consider philosophies of premarital sex, and the pros
and cons of it, let me make two important points: (1) Christians are not
biologically different from non-Christians and (2) men and women differ in their expression of physical affection and in their attitudes toward
sex.

My first point ought to be obvious to all—that just because one is
Christian it does not change our biological make-up. Our response to
sexual stimuli is the same as that of non-Christians.

Let us consider some aspects of male and female sexuality of which
we should all be aware. A woman's sex organs, for example, are not localized as they are in the male. They are distributed throughout the female body, e.g., her breasts are exposed, while her vagina and ovaries

are inside her body. The male's genitals, however, while localized in the groin, are outside of the body cavity. Also, while men experience a build-up of seminal fluid, women do not—a fact which many believe is significant. As one gynecologist punned: "That makes a vas deferens!" Not only is man designed biologically to be the aggressor, but our culture encourages him to be aggressive, whereas women are designed biologically to be receptive and they are nurtured to be passive. Therefore, both for biological and cultural reasons men are generally recognized as being erotic, whereas women are seen as romantic.

Christian young men become sexually aroused just as easily by visual stimuli (pictures, literature, persons), and by physical contact with members of the opposite sex, as non-Christians do. Christian young women also respond to physical contact and to expressions of affection just as non-Christian girls do. The point that I am making is simply that Christians are biologically no different from others when it comes to sexuality.

Therefore, it is important to realize that beyond a certain point of physical intimacy, biology overtakes reason! Christians can get "carried away" and lose control just as easily as anyone else. Witness the number of "hurry up marriages" in your church, community, or on your campus. Therefore, it is important for Christian young people to think through their philosophy of sexual expression realistically and to make sure reason prevails.

Second, we should be aware of the fundamental differences in attitude and temperament between men and women—differences due both to our biological make-up and to the impact of our culture upon us. It might be helpful to list some of the important differences.

| Men | Women |
| --- | --- |
| Biologically built to be aggressive | Anatomically built to be receptive |
| Erotic | Romantic |
| Tendency to separate sex and love | Tendency to correlate sex with love |
| Culturally conditioned to be exploitive | Culturally conditioned to be trusting and sharing |

| | |
|---|---|
| Subconsciously think, "If she's a good girl she'll not have sex." | Tendency to think, "Since we're in love and he wants to have sex, I'll yield." |

While there are exceptions to the generalizations made above, for the most part Christians have been socialized by their peers and the mass media to respond in somewhat the same manner as non-Christians. On the one hand, if a woman loves a man, she tends to be trusting and often yields to his affectionate advances. The male, on the other hand, if he is serious about a girl, hopes that she will not be too easy to engage—even as he makes advances. Because of these differences, young people would find it helpful to write out their philosophy of sex or affectional expression. Discussing these views with one's male or female friend may help both come to some consensus about their sexual relationships and help both maintain their Christian principles.

### Four Premarital Sex Standards

At this point let me share four premarital sexual standards which Ira L. Reiss (1960) has identified. The first is the *single standard* which we identify as conservative and Christian. This standard insists that both men and women should abstain from sexual intercourse before marriage. While the contemporary sexual revolution has taken its toll on this, it still remains the ideal for Christians.

The *double standard* is a second one. This standard is popular in both the Eastern and Western world. It has always been challenged by Christians, and more recently by the women's liberation movement. The biblical commandment to abstain from fornication applies equally to both men and women. With regard to the liberation movement, women are saying that if men can engage in premarital sex, then so can they. Recent statistics indicate an increase in the number of women engaging in premarital sex. This has caused some men to reconsider the validity of the double standard.

The third standard is *permissiveness with affection*, the idea that it's all right to engage in premarital sex if you're "in love." This notion is quite popular in our society, especially among college students. Class surveys I have taken over the past few years indicate that most of my students prefer this standard. One of the difficulties with this standard is that one does not know how long the affection will last. Since over 50 percent of the engagements made are believed to be broken, it should cause young people to think carefully about the time and place of sexual intercourse. If it is the expression of love one hopes to share with a wife or husband, wouldn't it be best to wait until one is actually married?

*Permissiveness without affection* is the fourth standard of premarital sex. This philosophy says that sexual intercourse is no different from eating—it is a bodily function that gives pleasure and, therefore, premarital sex is a normal experience and should cause no guilt. While individuals who subscribe to this view are often brash and vocal, it is quite possible that their bravado and braggadocio are attempts to cover up a deep-seated sense of insecurity and feeling of personal inadequacy. R. F. Hettlinger (1968) reports that "bed-hopping" is often a sign of neurosis. It is, after all, difficult to satisfy an inner psychological or spiritual need for genuine love, acceptance, and security by a physical act devoid of genuine caring. Robert Blood's (1969:156-7) observations, after discussing these standards, are worth noting. "Before I became a sociologist, I was against sexual conservatism," he says. "However, the longer I have studied the evidence from scientific research, the more I have been forced to recognize the positive consequences of restraint. . . . Waiting [until marriage to have sexual intercourse] has two long-range advantages: (1) it provides a secure setting for children conceived from sexual intercourse; (2) drawing a sexual distinction between not married and marriage accentuates the importance of marriage and contributes to its stability."

## Rationalizations for Premarital Sex

With all the talk about sex in schools and colleges today, as well as in the mass media, it is inevitable that Christian young people will be challenged to defend their standard of sexual morality. Therefore, it might be well to state the pros and cons of premarital sex. I am drawing upon the rationalizations for premarital sex that Kephart (1972:377-80) mentions in his marriage text, with modifications.

The first is the *physiological release* argument. This is used by men who argue that there is a biological build-up of seminal fluid which needs to be released. Therefore, if the girl really loves him, so the argument goes, she will consent to sexual intercourse. The obvious response to this argument is that there is no medical evidence that sexual restraint results in psychological or physiological harm. (Our Lord abstained, as have millions of men and women over the centuries.) In fact, nature provides for release through nocturnal emissions or "wet dreams." Also, masturbation is a common practice which provides release.

The second argument is the *"other society"* one. This is one used by students who have read about other cultures with mores that differ from our own. Many nonliterate societies permit premarital sex. Therefore, the argument goes, since it is done in "New Guinea," why not here in the United States? The response notes that cultural traits usually form a consistent pattern—they support one another. We cannot lift practices and integrate them into our culture unless we "buy" the whole set of values or provide the necessary changes the "borrowed trait" will bring about. Besides, from a Christian perspective we would argue that these are non-Christian cultures and not relevant to our situation. What others do is never accepted as justification for what *we* do.

The *bandwagon* argument is the third. In this we are told that everyone is doing it. Therefore, we should get on the bandwagon. Actually everyone is *not* doing it! While the incidence of premarital sex has increased, it is by no means the universal practice. Sexual statistics are difficult to acquire, and the trustworthiness of the information is suspect. Furthermore, many of those who have engaged in premarital sex report that they did so with their fiancés, or on one or two occasions (Kephart, 1972:146-151; Queen and Habenstein, 1974:311). In any case, as Christians we do not base our ethical standards on statistics, but on Christian principles. No one would argue that since most Americans drink, and many drive while under the influence of alcohol, that everyone should be permitted to drive while intoxicated.

The fourth argument is the *hedonistic* or pleasure argument which states that sexual intercourse is a pleasurable experience. Why, therefore, shouldn't we enjoy it? After all, if two consenting adults agree, and no one is hurt by it, why should society object? First of all, we would not deny that sexual intercourse is a pleasurable experience. But the thing that makes it an act of communion, and enjoyable, is the fact that there is a spiritual commitment there and a willingness to assume complete responsibility for the other person. This is only the case within the bonds of marriage. But the question is: "What are the criteria of measurement?" Are we talking about the short-run or the long-run? While there may not *appear* to be any immediate negative consequences, there may well be long-range ones. For one thing, it is worth noticing that many parents who were once permissive now have switched in their thinking to the conservative single standard (Kephart, 1972:275). Apparently the short-range pleasure did not outweigh the long-range pain they experienced. While a couple may reap some pleasure from premarital sex, unintended consequences such as (1) pregnancy, (2) venereal disease, (3) guilt, (4) dissolution of the relationship, (5) loss of self-respect, and (6) early marriage due to pregnancy, may turn the joy to mourning. For the Christian, the hedonistic argument is invalid because one cannot derive pleasure by willfully violating a clear-cut Christian prohibition.

A fifth argument is that *"If you really love me you'll have intercourse with me and prove it."* This argument is one of the most frequently used. Of course, the perfect squelch is, "If you really love me, why do you ask me to violate my ethical standards?" It is wise to keep in mind that love can be a fragile emotion. The Old Testament tells of Amnon's affair with Tamar (2 Samuel 13:1-15). It is interesting to note the comment of the writer regarding Amnon's feelings after intercourse with Tamar. "Then Amnon hated her [Tamar] with very great hatred; so that the hatred with which he hated her was greater than the love with which he had loved her." Jeremiah (17:9) tells us that "the heart is deceitful above all things, and desperately corrupt; who can understand it?" It is difficult to second-guess the response after an experience of sexual intimacy outside of marriage—even with someone we "love."

Finally, there is the *compatibility* argument. This one raises the question, "How can we be sure we are compatible sexually unless we try it?" This argument is not valid for several reasons. Kephart (1972) presents two hypothetical cases. Couple "A" is compatible in every way, except sexually. They find that when they test for sexual compatibility, they experience some difficulty. Should they break off their engagement? And what if couple "B" are compatible sexually, but ill suited in most other areas? Should they marry on the basis of their physical compatibility? David Ruben, in an article in *Redbook*, observed that premarital sexual compatibility in no way guarantees sexual compatibility in marriage, since we cannot simulate the actual married experience. When one is married he assumes an entirely new set of roles and responsibilities which make married sex different.

Furthermore, as Kephart implies, there is a great deal more to compatibility within marriage than the sexual aspect, as important as I believe that is. God has made us so that virtually any two people can relate physically. The female vagina is elastic and flexible; it can accommodate the male penis, whether small or large, without any difficulty. "Plumbing," or the physical fit, is not the determining factor in sexual compatibility, and neither is technique. Sexual intercourse is basically a spiritual experience. If two people are communicating and are attuned to one another, then, and only then, can true sexual compatibility be achieved.

From a Christian perspective there is no logical reason why the two states, courtship and marriage, should be confused. It is difficult for me to separate the notion of exploitation from premarital sex—it is difficult to get away from the notion that one person is using another, or both are using each other. As Christians, we see sexual intercourse as a vital part of marriage. It is something beautiful that needs to be shared on a regular basis within marriage, as Paul said (1 Corinthians 7:2ff.). From a Christian perspective, sexual intercourse is the one expression of love that should be restricted until the couple is willing and ready to assume complete responsibility for the total well-being of each other.

### Forgiveness and Renewal

Since I have been emphasizing the *ideal* Christian standard, the single standard, I do not mean to imply that if one has had premarital sex, he has committed the "unpardonable sin." The grace of God that forgives us for other sins, also provides for forgiveness of sexual sins. Nonetheless, it is true that premarital sexual intercourse is a different kind of sin. Paul (1 Corinthians 6:18) says that "any other sin a man commits does not affect his body; but the man who is guilty of sexual immorality sins against his own body" (TEV). Since the sex act involves more than the physical union of two persons, it is one of the most intimate of all human experiences, and it is virtually impossible to forget. However, the Bible does assure us that God's forgiveness awaits all who freely repent and turn to him.

From a Christian perspective then, premarital sex is something that Christian young people should strive to avoid. It is an experience which God has established to be enjoyed within the bonds of marriage. But while sex is certainly an integral part of the married relationship, it is far from being the sum total of it. (See the author's book, *Love and Sex Are Not Enough*, for a fuller treatment of Christian courtship.)

## Discussion Questions

1. In what ways do our attitudes and behavior with members of the opposite sex reveal (1) our Christian faith in God and Christ, and (2) our love for our neighbor (see Genesis 39:7-9; Mark 12:31)?

2. When does sex become something "evil" or "sinful"? Who is responsible for our behavior—societal forces, others, or ourselves? Compare Genesis 1:26-31a with James 1:13-15; 4:1-7; and Hebrews 13:4.

3. What industrial, social, and political factors have contributed to the permissive attitudes towards premarital and extramarital sex?

4. What criteria and principles should a Christian use when he is evaluating cultural values and norms? Are there any absolutes?

5. Values are "caught" as well as taught. Which primary groups are most influential? At what ages? Why? What does Paul urge in Ephesians 6:1 and Romans 12:1-2?

6. What do you think of the distinction the author makes between "accidental" and "habitual" masturbation? Discuss societal practices and attitudes and evaluate them in the light of God's Word.

7. What differences do you observe between male and female attitudes toward the physical demonstration of affection? Do you agree with the author's analysis? Why? Why not?

8. Of the four premarital sexual standards, which can you publicly acknowledge and justify in the light of biblical teaching and in view of the long- and short-run consequences?

9. The author does not believe that there is really any justification for premarital sex. Do you agree or disagree? Why? Why not?

10. Write your own personal philosophy of human sexuality and sex relations. Show how this relates to the "good" of self, others, the church, and society. Compare Colossians 3:17, 1 Corinthians 10:31, and Matthew 7:12.

## References

Blood, Robert O., Jr.
1969 *Marriage*. New York: The Free Press.
Hettlinger, R. F.
1968 "Portrait of the Freshman as a Sexual Being" in Charles W. Havie (ed.), *Campus Values*. New York: Scribner.
Kephart, William M.
1972 *The Family, Society, and the Individual*. New York: Houghton Mifflin.
Mead, Margaret
1949 *Coming of Age in Samoa*. New York: Mentor.
1930 *Growing Up in New Guinea*. New York: Mentor.
Queen, Stuart A. and Robert W. Habenstein
1974 *The Family in Various Cultures*. Philadelphia: Lippincott.

Reiss, Ira L.
> 1960 *Premarital Sexual Standards in America*. New York: The Free
>> Press.

Sarno, Ronald A.
> 1969 *Achieving Sexual Maturity*. Paramus, N.J.: Paulist Press.

## Suggested Books on Sex

Amstutz, H. Clair
> 1978 *Marriage in Today's World*. (Chapter 2, Human Sexuality),
>> Scottdale, Pa.: Herald Press.

Dalrymple, W.
> 1969 *Sex Is for Real*. New York: McGraw-Hill.

Jones, K. L., et. al.
> 1969 *Sex*. New York: Harper & Row.

Miles, H. J.
> 1972 *Sexual Understanding Before Marriage*. Grand Rapids: Zon-
>> dervan.

Pierson, E. C. & W. V. D'Antonio
> 1974 *Female and Male*. New York: Lippincott.

# 33
# The Functions of Religion in Christian Perspective

*E. Steve Cassells*

### Religion and Magic

The sociology of religion can be a disturbing field for young (and not so young) social scientists who are also Christians, because many of the reasons held by them for having a commitment to Christ and worshiping regularly seem to be belittled by the secular scientific world. A Christian who is accustomed to a negative stance from local nonbelievers may feel somewhat more threatened when the negativism is espoused in print from the pen of a "neutral" social scientist.

This perceived threat need not be seen as a threat at all. The main premise of this paper is that standard anthropological and sociological positions on religion do not have to be interpreted as diametrically opposed to Christian perspectives.

Emile Durkheim, one of the founding fathers of sociology, defined religion as a "unified system of beliefs and practices relative to sacred things, uniting into a single moral community all those who adhere to those beliefs and practices" (1947:47).

In defining religion as such, Durkheim not only brings out some of the ideological aspects of religion (beliefs and sacred things), but he also touches on one of its functions (binding people together). Other definitions of religion may differ from Durkheim's, depending on the perspective of the writer, but they generally involve a social group that acknowledges belief in some form of spiritual reality. The actual issue of the existence of God is not a provable item in these definitions, but

**E. Steve Cassells**
*Assistant State Archaeologist*
*Colorado Heritage Center, Denver, Colorado*
Steve Cassells received a BS in biology, and an MA in anthropology from the University of Arizona in 1976. A member of the Evangelical Free Church and active in youth activities and the Fellowship of Christian Athletes, Mr. Cassells has done research in archaeology in the Midwest and published numerous articles. He is also a part-time instructor in anthropology at Metro State College, Denver, Colorado. He taught four years at Judson College, Elgin, Illinois.

rather these definitions point to the human reactions based on their beliefs.

Religion is known as a cultural universal. In other words, all cultures, to some degree, adhere to some beliefs in the supernatural, though the form it takes may differ considerably from society to society. Additionally, not all members of a given society need to subscribe to the beliefs in order for religion to be considered universal. In some societies, religion may be practiced by only a small segment of the population.

A variant known as *magic* is generally considered separate from religion. Bronislaw Malinowski (1958) and J. G. Frazer (1911-1915) deal extensively with the differences. Frazer felt that in many cases magic appears to mimic science, though Malinowski did not agree. Malinowski saw magic going beyond science. The fact that primitive groups have a form of science, as well as magic, was Malinowski's rationale for the distinction. Malinowski felt man used magic to "control chance, to eliminate accidents, to foresee the unexpected turn of natural events, or to make human handiwork reliable and adequate to all practical requirements" (1958:88). In general, magic tends to be more manipulative. Instead of a supplicative attitude from the participant, as in the case of religious worship, a devotee of magic is more haughty, having a greater self-centered control. He presumes that given the proper incantation or other behavioral requisite, the end will be accomplished to the satisfaction of the practitioner. The magical approach is more cookbook-like than the religious, but this is not to say that some cultures might not have incorporated both perspectives. In some instances, cultures that have been evangelized by modern missionaries reflect both the old ways (often magic) along with the new Christianity—in effect "covering all the bases."

### The Functional Perspective

One sociocultural perspective that has been used to study and analyze religion for some time is the "functional approach." The title of this paper refers to it. It is basically a simple idea, though it can cause confusion when heard for the first time in sociology and anthropology. Briefly, it is a *way* of looking at parts of a culture and/or society. Anthropologists Malinowski and A. R. Radcliffe-Brown are well known for their use of the functional approach. This perspective examines a particular cultural trait in order to determine its *contributions* to the society as a whole. If it contributes, it is "functioning." In the case of Durkheim's definition, religion serves the function of "uniting into a single moral community all those who adhere to those beliefs and practices."

In the opinion of many anthropologists and sociologists, all cultural features have at least one purpose. In other words, they perform a function. Therefore we (as outsiders) should not "judge" the rightness or wrongness of cultural features based on their differences from our own background. This, in essence, is the basis for the concept of "cultural relativism," dealt with by William Hasker in this same anthology.

There are many functions that have been attributed to religion. What follows is a partial, but representative list derived from sociology and anthropology.

## Social Functions of Religion

*Social Control*

Religion defines "normal" behavior for the society, perhaps from the perspective of a belief that the Deity has ordained only certain behavior as acceptable. Marx saw this as a way of perpetuating and justifying the people in positions of power because he saw the belief as *only* coming from society. Christians would differ by saying that though any belief would come under some societal form, the society is not necessarily the sole source of that belief. This perpetuating aspect can be viewed as carrying over into other areas of society as a conservative influence that "retards the wheels of progress." On a more positive note, religion provides a set of ideals for the members of a society. Religion illustrates role prototypes for family members that can help in maintaining harmony. Societal relationships outside of the immediate family may also be modeled with similar results.

*Social Welfare*

Biblical injunctions to "love one another" have led many groups to social outreach, assisting families that have experienced hardships. During national disasters (floods, earthquakes, famines) it has traditionally been organizations and individuals with religious connections that have entered in, bringing food, medicine, and construction skills, to aid in returning the victims to their predisaster condition. Humanitarian concern has led Christians to help abolish slavery, improve factory work conditions, and many other things. Missions to foreign countries often have a "Peace Corps appearance," i.e., humanitarian and philanthropic character about them, with medical and technological assistance in conjunction with the religious thrust. The parable of the "Good Samaritan" is only one of many examples of scriptural exhortation about ideal social behavior.

## Social Psychological Functions of Religion

*Explanation*

Features of the universe that are "mysterious" to the observer (death, life, meaning of life, relationship to extraterrestrial features) often are dealt with by the religious institutions. Scientific research often cannot empirically demonstrate these sorts of things, and religion becomes the only source of knowledge. Some have suggested that religion "fills the gap between the time when people first become aware of a natural phenomenon and the time when they find a scientific explanation for it" (Dressler and Willis 1976:322). Of course, if this last statement were really true, it would mean that religion would be ultimately useless. This progressive dwindling of religion's utility does not do justice to the nature of religion. One must recognize theologically the implications of what is termed "Providence" (Col. 1:16, 17) and the possibility of the miraculous, even though the scientific method cannot deal with these categories. Christians do not believe in a God only of the "gaps." God will not vanish as we learn more about our world, but because he is our Creator, Redeemer and Sustainer, he grows larger as we learn more about his creation.

*Identity Formation*

Group membership can be a most satisfying condition for social beings, such as humans. A religious group can be a point of reference, an anchor of dependable friends in what may otherwise be interpreted as a hostile world. Taking on the identity and norms of an "in-group" may restrict the person from things he was previously involved in, but this need not be regarded as entirely negative. By introducing a bit of hardship—responsibility, sharing, and service—this could add value to the new social group *because* of the cost.

*Comfort*

Traditions adhered to over extended periods of time, and rituals that are repeated regularly, can serve to comfort individuals in times of stress. If one feels "isolated" socially, a believer can be in communication with a "higher power" and receive a sense of comfort as well. Often individuals who occupy a marginal status in society—because of economic, social, and health deprivations—take comfort in their knowledge of "eternal life." Some might term this hope "the pie in the sky by and by." Even a statement such as Marx's, that religion is the "opium of the people" (1968:33), bears some measure of behavioral credibility. Unfortunately, there are people who do use religion solely as a means of escape (comfort?), laying aside all effort of critically evaluating their environment and social networks.

## Manifest and Latent Functions

Robert Merton (1947:49-61) deals with some interesting features of functionalism, dividing functions into those that are intended by the participants and those functions that are unknown to the participants or at best are considered secondary in importance. Intended or recognized functions are termed "manifest" functions, while functions that are not intended or not recognized by the participants are known as "latent" functions.

These distinctions are germane to the discussion of religious functions. They allow for a separation of some of the secular functions from the spiritual ones. Latent functions often operate independently of the manifest functions, and can even work at cross-purposes. For example, it may well be that religion is an opiate in the lives of some adherents, but this does not negate other more positive effects.

All of the functions that are mentioned in sociology texts are observable behavioral functions, and they would apply to religion whether God really exists or not. This becomes a point of contention with some Christians, but realistically one must recognize the limitations of outside observers. God's existence is not a sociologically demonstratable possibility. This is not to be taken as an excuse, however. We should press all observers for completeness of evidence.

There often can be a significant difference between an observer interpreting the intentionality of a subject and what may be the subject's own intention. It is understandable that many sociologists would treat the topic of religion as exclusive of God's reality because they cannot observe him. They do recognize religion as an institution and feel some need to explain its survival over thousands of years. This "neutral" treatment of religion is disconcerting to many Christians because it appears to say that religion is a psychological invention of humanity, a fabrication of man's imagination. This neutrality should rather be seen as the limitation of scientific methodology. To say that religion is a psychological invention is to exceed scientific evidence.

Just because religion can perform certain functions of a psychological and/or social nature doesn't negate its spiritual reality: This is just some researchers' way of explaining religion's presence without necessarily stating their belief or lack of belief in a transcendent being and spiritual values and reality.

Marx was notably outspoken about the lack of spiritual reality in the world, but we must not overlook his materialistic assumptions. There have been others who have reiterated his position—that the religious institution is based upon fraud. To be fair, it must be admitted that some fraud exists and often people have been shamefully exploited. Furthermore, some religion has little depth beyond a quasi-materialism.

How can a Christian look at religion, and specifically Christianity, and evaluate its contributions to society as a whole? Immediately, a larger dimension is entered than science can handle. Certainly one must take into consideration the functions previously mentioned, but there is no need to stop there.

To the person who is committed to Jesus Christ and is sensitive and obedient to the leadings of the Holy Spirit, far deeper functions are performed. There is a richness of experience with this person that is partially concealed from any spectator, scientist, or layman. From a state of relating strictly to a functioning institution (the church, irrespective of God's reality), a Christian can now involve the vertical relationship attendent to true worship. Even though the God-man relationship cannot be completely validated by empiricism, it exists none-the-less.

What follows is a representative list of functions derived from biblical and other Christian sources.

## Spiritual Functions of Religion

### Salvation

The assurance of life after death and a continuing relationship with God is a spiritual experience, based on faith. Faith is a source that contributes meaning to life. The relationship of meaning and understanding needs to be closely examined. The human mind cannot be limited to the scientific method. Of course, this faith-truth in God's existence does have an impact psychologically on its recipients. However, by only looking at the psychological impact, the greater interpretive function is bypassed. Religion also functions as a bridge to the living God.

## Communication

Religion opens the pathway through which God can be reached daily. Communication with Him through prayer enables the believer to better understand God's will. Likewise, God discerns the seriousness of the petitioner, and he does answer prayer. This two-way interchange is a fulfilling of the Christian's life, and the satisfaction he obtains from this is certainly one of God's intended functions for religion. The sociologist can only see the relationships (man to man), but we should not be limited to conclude that what the sociologist sees is either the *total* function, or the whole of reality.

## Prophecy

Religion has provided the base from which the prophets, as well as Jesus, could act as critics of society. From this springboard they appealed to a higher state of morality (now in the Bible) and called men to repentance.

## Filling the Spiritual Void

This is perhaps the harder of the four to explain. Personal philosophizing has led this writer to believe that God created in us a *need* for a spiritual life. This, in a way, is closely akin to early social theorizing about the "psychic unity of man" as an explanation for cultural universals. In Ecclesiastes 3:11 it says, "He has also set eternity in the hearts of men" (NIV). An analogy might be like an automobile that was manufactured with a gas tank. The internal combustion engine is designed to run on refined petroleum. The car has need for that void (the tank) to be filled. Ideally, gas is the fluid that fills it, and the gas is subsequently conducted into the engine to be used. Other fluid products put into the tank make the car run less efficiently. By the same token, God has given us the capability to have a full spiritual dimension—a relationship with him. Each individual tries to fill that void in some way (behaviorists would consider it part of the "comfort quest"), whether the intended way—with God, or some other way—drugs, sex, money, or fame. Whatever fills that void—becoming central in a person's life—will determine the operating efficiency the individual can obtain. Thus, another function of religion is to satisfy a *God-implanted* need. The finite cannot satisfy the need for the infinite. One may speak of it as a search for "the ground of being."

The secular functions mentioned (plus many more) exist in varying degrees, but they do not reveal the whole spectrum encompassed by religion, nor do they invalidate the existence of God. Peter Berger has stated that "secularized consciousness is not the absolute it presents itself as" (1969:120). Man has a need to transcend his own age. The functional approach to sociocultural analysis is a valid one, but it is not (nor was it intended to be) a source of total explanation.

To a Christian, at least, the social and psychological functions are latent functions, while spiritual ones are manifest functions.

## Discussion Questions

1. What would be your reply to a person who told you that religion had outlived its utility now that science had achieved its current state of sophistication?

2. What characteristics led Marx to conclude that religion was an opiate?

3. Are Marx's conclusions beyond the realm of scientific verification?

4. List the functions that religion performs in your life. Put them in order from the most important to the least important.

5. Does it appear your faith life is an inward-directed or outward-directed one? Which dimension is subject to scientific scrutiny?

6. What are the ways that genuine Christian religion and symbol have deteriorated into magic?

7. What is the danger of overritualization?

8. In what ways are rituals the true expression of religious commitment?

9. When does the prayer ending "in Jesus' name" seem a valid religious expression and when a type of magical formula? Consider communion in the same terms.

10. What are some of the religious surrogates within our society and, more specifically, on your campus? Does Christianity meet human needs more completely and satisfactorily?

# References

Berger, Peter L.
    1969 *A Rumor of Angels.* Garden City, N.Y.: Doubleday.
Dressler, David, with William M. Willis, Jr.
    1976 *Sociology, the Study of Human Interaction.* New York: Alfred A. Knopf.
Durkheim, Emile
    1947 *The Elementary Forms of the Religious Life.* New York: Free Press (orig. 1912).
Frazer, J. G.
    1911-1915 *The Golden Bough: A Study of Magic and Religion* (12 vols.). London: Macmillan.
Malinowski, Bronislaw
    1958 "The Role of Magic and Religion" (orig. 1931) in *Reader in Comparative Religion: An Anthropological Approach.* W. A. Lessa and E. Z. Vogt, eds. Evanston, Ill.: Row, Peterson.
Marx, Karl
    1968 "Contribution to the Critique of Hegel's Philosophy of Right" (orig. 1844) *Marxism and Christianity,* Herbert Aptheker, ed. New York: Humanities Press.
Merton, Robert K.
    1947 *Social Theory and Social Structure.* Glencoe, Ill.: The Free Press.

# 34
# New Testament Principles Applied to Social Problems

*Paul Hanly Furfey*

Charity looms so large in the New Testament that the Christian's duty of attacking social problems must surely be very important. For social problems translate into suffering for one's neighbor. To reduce that suffering, then, one must surely try to conquer these problems.

### Social Action as Our Only Duty
One attacks social problems by performing works of mercy. This duty is so emphasized in the New Testament that sometimes it appears to be our only duty. Consider the description of the last judgment in the twenty-fifth chapter of Matthew's Gospel.

#### The Last Judgment
Matthew describes the call of the just in these words: "Come, O blessed of my Father, inherit the kingdom prepared for you from the foundation of the world; for I was hungry and you gave me food, I was thirsty and you gave me drink, I was a stranger and you welcomed me, I was naked and you clothed me, I was sick and you visited me, I was in prison and you came to me" (Matthew 25:34-36). These words will surprise the just. They will ask when they did such things for the Lord. The answer will be: "Truly, I say to you, as you did it to one of the least of these my brethren, you did it to me" (25:40).

On first reading these words strike one as a bit strange. No one is

**Paul Hanly Furfey**
*Professor of Sociology, Emeritus*
*The Catholic University of America*
Ordained a priest in 1922, Father Furfey has had a long career as a social activist, including the Catholic Peace Fellowship. He earned his PhD at the Catholic University of America. His areas of research interest focus on the problems of youth, the deaf, delinquency, and poverty. He has published extensively in these areas, including a number of books and many articles. He has held various teaching positions at the university where he continues his productive work as emeritus professor.

rewarded for fasting and prayer. Not even martyrdom is mentioned. The sole route to heaven seems to be a willingness to help one's neighbor in need.

This impression is reinforced by the parallel passage in which the evil are condemned. "Depart from me, you cursed, into the eternal fire prepared for the devil and his angels; for I was hungry and you gave me no food, I was thirsty and you gave me no drink, I was a stranger and you did not welcome me, naked and you did not clothe me, sick and in prison and you did not visit me" (Matthew 25:41-43). Like the just, the damned are surprised at the judgment. When they too ask an explanation, they receive the same sort of answer. "Truly, I say to you, as you did it not to one of the least of these, you did it not to me" (25:45). So the general principle is clear. As one treats one's neighbor, so one treats the Lord.

Yet a problem remains. It is easy to understand why those who perform the works of mercy are rewarded, and why those who neglect them are punished. Here, however, these works are treated as the *only* duties of the Christian. To neglect a hungry neighbor is indeed wrong; but is it not still worse to rob or murder him? Stranger still, there is no mention at all of duties toward God. Does no one get condemned for blasphemy?

*The Explanation*

Briefly, the explanation is that those who *do* perform the works of mercy will also fulfill their other duties toward their neighbors, while those who *do not* perform these duties will be delinquent in other ways. In order to understand this, it may be helpful to examine the specific duties mentioned.

Six works of mercy are specified. Three of these may be classified as forms of almsgiving, feeding the hungry, giving drink to the thirsty, and clothing the naked. The recipients of such alms are presumably needy people. On the other hand, visiting the sick or prisoners and acts of hospitality may be good works to people above the poverty level. After all, even the wealthy get sick. There is a good deal written about hospitality in the New Testament. The apostle Peter wrote: "Practice hospitality ungrudgingly to one another" (1 Peter 4:9). So an ordinary Christian on a trip could expect food and lodging from other Christians. Charity means loving someone else, no matter who.

An essential point in all this is that the works of mercy all imply going out of one's way to help another. Some persons live quietly and at peace with their neighbors and are careful not to injure anyone in any way. This, however, is not enough (see Luke 16:19-31). To feed a hungry person is something more than simply not injuring him. It means going out of one's way. It means doing something positive. And to do something positive is a clear manifestation of love, in this case, the specific Christian love of charity. So the saved mentioned in Matthew's description of the last judgment proved by their acts of mercy that they possessed charity. Of course this virtue makes other sins against one's neighbor impossible. A man who goes out of his way to feed the hungry will surely not want to cheat or rob or kill. Thus there was no need to mention these other sins. Feed the poor and you merit heaven.

But another difficulty remains. There is no mention of sins directly against God. Idolatry and blasphemy are not mentioned. The reason for this should be clear. Charity is a single, indivisible virtue. The saved performed the works of mercy out of charity, and this fact was enough to prove that they loved God as well as neighbor. Helping one of these least brethren is a clear proof of one's love of God.

## Social Action in the Early Church

The New Testament chronicles many instances of mutual charity in the early church. Of course all of these were, in a sense, instances of social action. However, two sorts of charity were particularly common, and they soon became more or less organized, namely, aid to the sick and the poor. These deserve separate discussion.

### The Sick

In the New Testament help extended to the sick is most commonly miraculous. The most conspicuous exception is the act of the Good Samaritan who helped the wounded man found by the wayside who was already "half dead" (Luke 10:29-37). He did this by binding "up his wounds, pouring in oil and wine." Then he "brought him to an inn, and took care of him." Finally, on leaving, he paid the innkeeper for further care.

Christ performed a remarkable number of miraculous cures. The gospels record 17 specifically, but they make it clear that many others were performed, though not described (Matthew 4:23; 9:35; Mark 6:56; Luke 4:40). The cures covered a very wide range: from temporary minor illnesses, through leprosy, paralysis, blindness, to the raising of the dead. It is worth noting that some cures were performed when Christ was distant from the sick person, for example, the cure of the centurion's servant (Matthew 8:5-13; Luke 7:1-10). Therefore they cannot be explained by the power of suggestion.

In some cases the cure of the illness is described as the expulsion of a demon. Occasionally this seems to be a mere matter of terminology. Satan brought evil into the world, including physical illness; so the cure of a sick person is a rebuff to Satan and his minions. Thus the boy described in Mark who "fell on the ground and rolled about, foaming at the mouth" (9:14-27) would appear to be a case of epilepsy. However, it does not follow that no case of literal diabolical possession is to be found among the cures wrought by Christ.

After the ascension, miraculous cures of the sick became a regular feature in the life of the nascent church. It seems clear, therefore, that mercy toward the sick was a regular feature of the Christian ethic. One point must be made in this connection. Miraculous cures were works of mercy, but they were also proofs of Christian doctrine. This double purpose is often quite clear. For example there was the paralytic at Capernaum (Mark 2:2-12). Christ said to him, "My son, your sins are forgiven." This scandalized some unbelievers who were present. "Who can forgive sins but God alone?" So Christ worked a miracle, saying: "Why do you question thus in your hearts? Which is easier, to say to the paralytic, 'Your sins are forgiven,' or to say, 'Rise, take up your pallet and walk'? But that you may know that the Son of man has authority on earth to forgive sins—he said to the paralytic—'I say to you, rise, take up your pallet and go home.' And he rose, and immediately took up the pallet and went out before them all"

Although it is clear that miracles, in general, had a double purpose in the New Testament, the fact remains that one purpose throughout was to show mercy. Christ and the apostles healed the sick because they loved them. So the lesson is clear. Concern for the sick must be a constant attitude among all Christians.

## The Poor

The most systematic and elaborate plan for helping the poor was that organized by the Christians in Jerusalem. "Now the company of those who believed were of one heart and soul, and no one said that any of the things which he possessed was his own, but they had everything in common. . . . There was not a needy person among them, for as many as were possessors of lands or houses sold them, and brought the proceeds of what was sold and laid it at the apostles' feet; and distribution was made to each as any had need" (Acts 4:32; 34-35). This systematized charity involved a good deal of work. The apostles found that they could not handle this mass of detail and at the same time do justice to their spiritual duties. So seven men, the deacons, were appointed for this duty (Acts 6:1-6).

Later the apostle Paul organized a systematic collection among the various churches he had founded to aid the Christians in Jerusalem. Thus for example he advised his followers at Corinth "to put something aside" every week "and store it up." He promised that when he came back to Corinth he would send their gift to Jerusalem by "those whom you accredit" (1 Corinthians 16:1-4). The total from all the various churches probably added up to quite a considerable amount. Evidently the Jerusalem church was in rather great financial difficulty. One may infer that the highly idealistic system of Christian communism mentioned in the preceding paragraph did not work out very well. By selling their "lands or houses" the believers were impoverished and they lacked sources of income. So Paul had to come to their rescue.

## The New Testament and Ourselves

Now comes a very important question. What can we moderns learn from the New Testament about the treatment of our social problems? While facing this question, two highly important principles must be kept in mind. *One* is that we, as Christians, must accept all the dogmatic statements in the New Testament. They are infallibly true. Thus what Christ tells us about the criterion for distinguishing between the saved and the damned at the last judgment is a fact which we must not question. The *second* principle is that, although the example of the early Christians usually deserves our imitation, this is not always the case. The Christian communism at Jerusalem reflected very generous intentions, but it proved impractical. There is no reason for us to imitate it.

These two principles are exceedingly important when we consider the handling of intergroup relations, the next topic in this chapter. The dogmatic principle is clear beyond the slightest doubt. Paul stated it bluntly and very clearly. "There is neither Jew nor Greek, there is neither slave nor free, there is neither male nor female; for you are all one in Christ Jesus" (Galatians 3:28). To argue that certain classes deserve preferential treatment is thus a direct denial of Christian doctrine. However, following the principle of equality in everyday life does raise problems. How successfully the early Christians solved these problems is a matter for discussion. It will be discussed in the following sections which deal with special groups.

### Slavery

The early Christians did not try to abolish slavery. On the contrary, they urged acceptance of the system. "Slaves obey in everything those who are your earthly masters, not with the purpose of attracting attention and pleasing men . . . but in singleness of heart, fearing the Lord. Whatever your task, work heartily, as serving the Lord not men, knowing that from the Lord you will receive the inheritance as your reward; you are serving the Lord Christ" (Colossians 3:22-24). Since the system was accepted, the slave was doing something more than merely bearing wrongs patiently; he was performing the duties of his status in life. Of course slaveholders had their reciprocal duties. "Masters, treat your slaves justly and fairly, knowing that you also have a Master in heaven" (Colossians 4:1).

The Christians did not insist on the abolition of slavery, but their personal attitude toward the slaves themselves was very different from that of the pagans. This fact is brought out beautifully and dramatically in the short epistle of Paul to Philemon. Onesimus, a slave of Philemon, had escaped his master and made his way to Rome, where he met Paul and was converted. Now the slave is sent back to his master, Philemon, with this letter asking his forgiveness, and also asking that Onesimus may return "no longer as a slave but more than a slave, as a beloved brother, especially to me but how much more to you, both in the flesh and in the Lord" (Philemon v. 16).

The refusal of the Christians to demand the immediate abolition of slavery was one of those practical decisions which, according to the principles enumerated above, does not imply divine approval of the institution. It would seem, however, to have been a prudent decision. Christianity had to work gradually. Slavery was eventually abolished, and the doctrines of the Christians seem to have had a major part in bringing this about. However, to have insisted that slavery be abolished at once would have been very disruptive, and it would have made the spread of Christianity very difficult indeed.

In considering this matter, one should carefully keep in mind the nature of slavery in the first-century empire. It was different in one essential respect from American Negro slavery. Many Americans believed that their black slaves were an inferior subspecies of the human family. They were incapable of anything more than routine manual work. On the other hand, the Romans looked on their slaves as simply ordinary human beings who had lost their liberty. In antiquity, many were enslaved during war. So a slave might simply be one who had the misfortune to be on the losing side.

Romans often had Greek slaves to teach their children Greek language and literature. They might be better educated than their pupils' parents. Some freed slaves became very prominent in Roman politics. Furthermore, some freed slaves probably amassed huge fortunes. The first-century Latin writer, Gaius Petronius, in his *Satyricon* has an uproarious account of a feast given by the ex-slave, Trimalchio, for a group of his friends, ex-slaves themselves. He talks of Trimalchio's fabulous wealth and his utterly ridiculous extravagance.

Roman slavery was often cruel. However, the difference just explained made the toleration of slavery by the early Christians more understandable in one respect. Paul insisted on the essential equality of the slave and the free. Roman slavery destroyed this equality, but it did so by creating an artificial legal inequality. American Negro slavery, on the other hand, rested on the belief that Negro inequality was an inborn characteristic. When the early church tolerated slavery, therefore, this toleration was less clearly contradictory to their doctrine than was the later toleration of American slavery.

*Male and Female*

The example of Christ was highly favorable to the status of women. Roman Catholics believe his Virgin Mother was the greatest of the saints. Holy women ministered to him during his public life (Luke 8:1-3). He had a close personal friendship with Martha and Mary (Luke 10:38-42). After Christ had been condemned to death, association with him became dangerous. Peter did not dare to be identified as a follower. But many women openly expressed their loyalty. On the way to Calvary, the "Daughters of Jerusalem" followed him, wailing and lamenting (Luke 23:27-28). And we read: "Standing by the cross of Jesus were his mother, and his mother's sister, Mary the wife of Clopas, and Mary Magdalene" (John 19:25). Finally, the first news of the resurrection was communicated to women, and only through them to the apostles (Matthew 28:1-10; Mark 16:6-8; Luke 24:1-12; John 20:1-2, 11-18).

Christ forbade polygamy, divorce, and the breakup of the home. This meant much for the status of women. Previously the wife and mother might be summarily dismissed from the home on almost any pretext. Of course this placed women in a degraded position.

No women were ordained priests in the early church, but on the other hand there is no prohibition against the practice. However, women were ordained deaconesses. Phoebe, a deaconess of the church at Cenchreae, was "a helper" to many, including Paul himself (Romans 16:1-2). Apollos, a fervent and eloquent convert, had been poorly instructed in the faith; so Priscilla, as well as her husband, Aquila, took him aside "and expounded to him the way of God more accurately" (Acts 18:24-26). So women played their part in the ministry in spite of Paul's opinion that it was "shameful for a woman to speak in church" (1 Corinthians 14:35).

For those of us who defend the equality of the sexes in New Testament doctrine, probably the greatest difficulty is presented by the passages in which Paul preaches the subjugation of wives to their husbands. The following is probably the most extreme of these passages: "Wives, be subject to your husbands, as to the Lord. For the husband is the head of the wife as Christ is the head of the church, his body, and is himself its Savior. As the church is subject to Christ, so let wives also be subject in everything to their husbands" (Ephesians 5:22-24). The apostle goes on to admonish husbands to love their wives "as Christ loved the church" or as they love "their own bodies" (5:25, 28). So the duties of spouses are mutual. There is no suggestion that the wife should be a mere servant of her husband. The difficulty is that the decision-making process seems reserved entirely to the man.

The socioeconomic conditions of the first century may explain the dominance of husbands, although of course they do not justify it. Wives were enormously more house-bound than they are now for two reasons. For one thing both the high mortality rates of the time, and particularly the high infant mortality rates, made it necessary for women to go through many pregnancies to keep the population from declining. Second, housework was then enormously more laborious than now. Modern wives take all sorts of conveniences for granted, from hot and cold running water to a multitude of electrical gadgets. In addition they can buy prepared foods—frozen, canned, and pre-cooked! But the first-century wife had to stay at home. Only her husband could go out and earn money. And money means power. No wonder husbands were dominant.

Of course Paul could not suddenly alter social conditions. The wife was more or less constrained by the social conditions of the times to stay at home and busy herself with children and housework. But it is hard to understand why Paul did not feel that family decisions should be mutual. Why should not wife and husband have an equal say in decisions about child rearing, about the family diet, about where to live, about relations with neighbors—in short, about the whole range of family life? It seems almost incredible that Paul should endow husbands with a sort of divine authority. Wives should be subject to them "as to the Lord."

To the present writer, it seems that Paul was not stating any divinely revealed truth in this passage. He was simply trying to decide on a practical problem. Just as he did not urge the abolition of slavery, so he did not favor women's liberation, even to the modest extent of mutual family decision-making. These were just practical problems. However, to the present writer, it would seem infinitely easier to tolerate slavery for the time being, than to tolerate such extreme male dominance within the Christian family.

### First-Century Society and the New Testament

The social, political, and economic conditions of the first-century Roman Empire were of course very, very different from those prevailing among us today. As a result of this, even rather simple concepts have changed their meaning. It is often very hard to find an English word that accurately translates a Greek word in the New Testament; for the meaning of a word often depends on contemporary conditions. The importance of this fact will be illustrated in the following sections.

*Christ, the "Carpenter"*

The occupation of Christ, and of Joseph, is described in the gospels by the word *tektōn*. The standard translation for this is "carpenter." This is passable, but it is an illustration of the difficulty just mentioned. The job of the *tektōn* was much broader than that of the modern carpenter. He spent much time making furniture, beds, tables, chairs, stools, and benches, also, for purposes of storage (since there were no closets), boxes, chests, and cupboards. Houses were commonly made of stone or mud brick, but the *tektōn* had to make doors, doorframes, and lattices for windows. At the time locks for doors were also commonly of wood. If we are to believe Justin Martyr, Christ also made "plows and yokes." In short, the first-century *tektōn* was not just a carpenter, but a wide-ranging, unspecialized worker in wood.

The first-century woodworker had most of the hand tools used by his modern counterpart. However, there are some interesting differences. For example, the drill was a bowdrill, not a bit and brace; and saws cut on the pull stroke instead of the push stroke. It is important to realize that highly sophisticated techniques appeared very early in history. The evidence for this fact comes largely from Egypt where the dry climate well preserved wooden objects. However, it is certain that the same techniques had spread to Palestine. The ancient woodworker did not have the sophisticated power tools now available. It took him longer to do a job. But finished woodwork from the ancient world compares well with modern work. Some people imagine that Christ's work at Nazareth was rough and unskilled. It was anything but that. It was highly skilled. And one must remember that well-made furniture has also an element of the artistic.

The social status of craftsmen was very low among the Greeks and Romans. However, this was not the case among the Jews. For example, few of the famous rabbinical writers of the time had independent incomes; and many were not ashamed to support themselves by manual work. If Christ at Nazareth had poor social status, it was because he refused to follow the complicated observances of the Pharisees and not because he was a manual worker. In any case, the lesson for us Christians is a lesson in the dignity of labor.

Was the "holy family" of Nazareth poor? The answer depends on how we understand the word. It seems clear that they were not poor in the sense that they lacked any of the basic necessities of everyday life. During much of the time at Nazareth the holy family had two full-time workers. Moreover, it appears that Joseph owned his own shop, and thus he probably earned more than hired hands did. The poverty of the holy family was the poverty of their class. It meant having all the necessities, but none of the luxuries. It was "evangelical poverty" in the perfect sense. In contrast, to lack any of the real necessities was poverty in an evil sense. It is this latter sort of poverty that we are commanded to try to eliminate by feeding the hungry, clothing the naked, and so forth.

*The Rich*

Again and again the New Testament makes it clear that riches are a grave hindrance to salvation. Perhaps Christ's most famous statement on the subject is: "Again I say to you, with difficulty will a rich man enter the kingdom of heaven. And further I say to you, it is easier for a camel to pass through the eye of a needle, than for a rich man to enter the kingdom of heaven" (Matthew 19:23-24). When the disciples expressed their astonishment, Christ added, "With God all things are possible" (Matthew 19:26). This seems to mean that the rich can, in some cases, be saved; but this requires a miracle of grace. Not a very consoling thought for the wealthy! There are many parallel passages. Paul goes so far as to tell Timothy that "covetousness is the root of all evils" (1 Timothy 6:10).

To interpret these passages correctly, it is necessary to understand exactly what the word "rich" (*plousios*) means in the New Testament. That is to say, we must ask just who were these evil, worldly men who were condemned so emphatically. To answer this question, I once systematically examined the use of *plousios* and its cognates in the New Testament (Furfey, 1943). Such words occur 68 times, but only 34 times in a literal sense. Of course these literal instances are the only ones relevant here. One can think of different kinds of rich men. Some inherit their wealth. Some have money by virtue of their position, as in the case of a king, a general, a statesman. Finally, some become rich by actively seeking wealth, the "self-made" rich. Surprisingly, in all the cases where the source of wealth can be traced, all the rich in the New Testament belong to this third class. The inference is that not the mere possession of wealth, but the active pursuit of wealth is that which is condemned.

The rich men in the New Testament fall into three classes according to the way they attained their wealth. First, there were the rich farmers. Some of these had large farms, hired laborers to run them, and then sold their product. In his epistle, James says to some of these that they fraudulently held back "the wages of the laborers who mowed your fields" (James 5:4). Other rich farmers were *rentiers*. They did not till the soil themselves, but rented it out to others. For example, there was the absentee landlord who owned a vineyard and "let it out to tenants and went abroad for a long time" (Luke 20:9).

A second category of rich men consists of merchants engaged in interregional trade. They are described—prophetically—as mourning the fall of "Babylon" which symbolizes the Roman Empire. "The merchants of the earth weep and mourn for her, since no one buys their cargo any more" (Revelation 18:11). The merchants are not moved by human sympathy. It is only that the "great city" is no more, "the great city where all who had ships at sea grew rich by her wealth!" (Revelation 18:19).

Another category of the rich may be described roughly as financiers. These were men who became rich by dealing directly with money. These would include bankers. Then as now bankers engaged in foreign exchange. So the moneychangers whose tables Christ overturned in the temple were certainly men in the banking business. The publicans belong here also. These men paid the Roman Empire a fixed sum for the right to collect certain taxes such as customs, tolls, and the like. Having paid this fixed sum, they kept whatever taxes they could collect. Not surprisingly, they tried to collect as much as possible, even by unjustly overcharging.

All the rich in the New Testament are acquisitive. They not only possess money; they love it and seek it passionately. Therein lies the evil. Merely to have money is not a fault. Many of the saints were rich in this sense. But to devote oneself to the attainment of riches is to be enslaved by a passion. "No man can serve two masters. . . . You cannot serve God and mammon" (Matthew 6:24). The competition for wealth is a fierce competition. To succeed, one must consider all else to be secondary. One cannot become holy if the love of God is only a secondary consideration.

*War*

The New Testament has little or nothing to say about war in a literal sense, although military terminology is often used to describe figuratively the struggle between good and evil. To cite one instance, Paul admonishes his followers: "Put on the whole armor of God, that you may be able to stand against the wiles of the devil." He goes on to speak of "the breastplate of righteousness," "the shield of faith," "the helmet of salvation," and "the sword of the Spirit" (Ephesians 6:11-17).

However, military personnel do appear in the literature of the New Testament. Can we learn something from the texts about the Christian attitude toward the military? The attempt has been made (O'Rourke, 1970). In a scholarly article, O'Rourke examines all the instances in which military personnel are described. He concludes: "Certainly there is no trace of any polemic against the military as such. . . . There is no evidence of conscious bias against the military as such." The inference might seem to be that the early church did not regard war as particularly evil.

O'Rourke, however, seems to have overlooked one extremely important point. Soldiers in ancient times (and, indeed, until rather recently) performed the duties of modern law-enforcement officers, as well as their military duties. They were patrolmen, jailers, and executioners. In the New Testament the activities of soldiers or centurions described belong entirely in these categories. Soldiers crucified Christ. Then we read of Peter in prison guarded by "four squads of soldiers" (Acts 12:4). Paul was sent to Rome with "some other prisoners" in care of a centurion named Julius (Acts 27:1). In Rome he was kept under house arrest "with the soldier that guarded him" (Acts 28:16). And so on. In those days most soldiers probably spent their entire military career in police functions without ever having faced an enemy in war. O'Rourke is literally correct. Yet it seems dangerous to conclude much from his study about the early Christian attitude toward war.

Even if there were direct statements in the New Testament about the morality of war, another point would have to be considered. War was different, very different in those days. It meant that comparatively small bands of professional soldiers would attack each other with swords and spears, or shoot at each other with bows and arrows. Or a city might be besieged for months and months until its inhabitants starved. Compare all this with modern war in which a whole city may be wiped out in an instant by an atom bomb, a bomb perhaps launched a continent away.

The best we can do in this matter is to draw abstract moral principles from the New Testament and apply them to modern conditions. This does not fall within the scope of this chapter.

*Politics*

One extremely important fact must be kept in mind while considering the attitude of early Christians toward social problems. They lived under the Roman Empire which was totalitarian. Citizens could not vote. It was dangerous for one to criticize, however mildly, the imperial policies.

Today, it is the duty of good citizens to speak out against social injustice because by speaking out they can often end the injustice. Think, for example, of the civil-rights movement of the 1960s. The rights of black citizens at the polls, in education, and in employment had been seriously abused in many parts of the country. The civil-rights movement remedied this to a very large extent. Public opinion on the matter was so clearly and forcefully expressed that officeholders had to follow suit. Citizens were politically effective by virtue of their voting powers.

The important point to remember is that we must not expect to find anything parallel to this among the early Christians. It would have been utterly ineffective—in fact, impossible.

### What Can We Learn from All This?

To be a Christian means not only to believe *in* Christ, but also to *follow* Christ. Therefore we must imitate his life as described in the New Testament and as exemplified in the lives and teachings of his early followers. We must imitate the way Christ treated others. But we also must do more than this. We must imitate his social attitudes, his actions as a member, and as a critic, of his contemporary society.

The imitation of Christ involves difficulties. First of all, it demands heroism. Then there are other difficulties. Christ attacked health problems by miraculously healing a great many of the sick. We cannot do this, although well-authenticated miracles of healing do occur now and then in modern times. Then there is the fact that the whole social, economic, and political environment in which Christ lived was radically different from our own. So we can seldom imitate him literally. What we must do is to seek out the fundamental moral principles that underlay his work and try to apply these principles to our own society.

In this task, the example of the modern Roman Catholic saints should be helpful. In one study (Walsh, 1937) the lives of the most recent 25 canonized or beatified nonmartyrs were studied. Walsh excluded martyrs because many of them lived in remote lands and few details about their daily lives and habits were available. What did these holy people do about the social problems of the modern world? How does saintly perfection relate to the alleviation of social evils? The answer should be interesting.

One fact stood out clearly. Every one of the 25 was deeply concerned about social problems. Some organized works of charity on a grand scale, like St. John Bosco who founded the Salesians, famous for their work with boys. Very different was the Blessed Anna Maria Taigi, a married woman of very humble status, who nevertheless showed remarkable skill in helping persons involved in all sorts of social problems. Perhaps the most surprising result of Walsh's study was that even the contemplative life does not hinder active charity. St. Teresa of Lisieux spent her whole adult life in a cloistered convent; but she very consciously offered this hidden life of prayer for the good of her neighbor, predicting that its effect would be a "shower of roses," that is, a multitude of benefits for those in need.

Our clear duty, then, is to love our neighbor and show our love by helping him. It is also clear that this help must involve not only helping individuals in need, but also trying to abolish oppressive social conditions that make whole classes of people suffer.

Trying to change society is often dangerous. Often it means trying to eliminate the privileges of a dominant class which oppresses and exploits the poor for its own selfish advantage. To oppose the powerful forcefully often means taking one's life in one's hands. Christ's accusers before Pilate brought the indictment: "He stirs up the people, teaching throughout all Judea, from Galilee even to this place" (Luke 23:5). Christ did indeed stir up the people. In their presence, he predicted hell for the rich. He called the powerful scribes and Pharisees "hypocrites" and compared them to "whitewashed tombs, which outwardly appear beautiful, but within they are full of dead men's bones and all uncleanness" (Matthew 23:27). Surely that was stirring up the people. A social agitator must be willing to pay the price which, in Christ's case, was Calvary.

The application of New Testament principles to the social problems of our own day is far from obvious. Indeed one of the first duties that Christian charity imposes on us is to study the sources of these problems and possible solutions. If the problems are built deeply into our society, then society itself may have to be changed. In Latin America the "liberation theologians," as they are called, espouse this view (Gutierrez, 1973). The present author has argued that something similar may need to happen here (Furfey, 1978).

In any case, one principle is clear from the New Testament. There is no limit to the love we must show for our neighbor in need. Our eternal salvation depends on our generosity. Of course we must help the needy individual. But we must be willing to go beyond that. We must, like Christ, be willing to stir up the people. And we must be willing, like Christ, to suffer the consequences.

## Discussion Questions

1. Paul says, "He who loves his neighbor has fulfilled the law" (Romans 13:8). Does this statement imply that the Ten Commandments have lost their force? Explain.

2. Perhaps the sick cured by Christ and the apostles suffered merely psychosomatic illnesses, that is, illnesses caused by abnormal mental attitudes. It is known that such illnesses can be cured by suggestion. Perhaps the so-called miracles of the New Testament can be explained by the power of suggestion. Discuss.

3. Christ is said at various times to have expelled demons. What is meant by this?

4. The early followers of Christ at Jerusalem practiced a sort of Christian communism. Why was this not imitated by other churches?

5. The early church tolerated slavery. Why? Does this mean that American Negro slavery can be justified?

6. Many women had close ties of friendship and loyalty to Christ. Give examples.

7. Paul said: "Wives, be subject to your husbands, as to the Lord" (Ephesians 5:22). Can you explain this? Can you justify it?

8. Explain the nature of Christ's work at Nazareth. How poor was the holy family?

9. Why were the rich condemned in the New Testament? After all, the church has canonized some wealthy saints.

10. What did "soldiers" do in New Testament times? Were any of those mentioned in the New Testament actually engaged in war?

## References

Furfey, Paul H.

    1943 "PLOUSIOS and Cognates in the New Testament." *Catholic Biblical Quarterly*, 5, pp. 243-63.

    1955 "Christ as TEKTON." *Catholic Biblical Quarterly*, 17, pp. 204-15.

    1978 *Love and the Urban Ghetto*. Maryknoll: Orbis.

Gutierrez, Gustavo

    1973 *A Theology of Liberation*. Maryknoll: Orbis.

O'Rourke, John J.

    1970 "The Military in the New Testament." *Catholic Biblical Quarterly*, 32, pp. 227-36.

Walsh, Mary Elizabeth

    1937 *The Saints and Social Work*. Silver Spring, Md.: Preservation of the Faith.

# 35
# Christian Covenant Communities: An Adaptation of the Intentional Community for Urban Life

*Margaret M. Poloma*

Within the last decade or so attempts to create intentional communities have multiplied. In addition to the much-publicized, short-lived, do-your-own thing anarchistic communes of the hippie crash pads of the 1960s, other communities have flourished based on either political or social scientific theories, or much more commonly, on religious commitments. The essence of intentional communities is (1) a mutual commitment of members that (2) focuses on the organic conception of society in which the whole is greater than its member parts (Bouvard, 1975:9-10).

Intentional communities appear to be a response to three human desires frustrated by American culture that are vividly described in Philip Slater's (1970) account, *The Pursuit of Loneliness*. These human desires are:

1. The desire for *community*—the wish to live in trust and fraternal cooperation with one's fellows in a total and visible collective entity.

**Margaret M. Poloma**
*Associate Professor of Sociology*
*University of Akron*
Reared in the Roman Catholic Church, Margaret Poloma is active in interdenominational witness on her campus. She is editor of the *Christian Sociological Society's Newsletter*. She holds a BA from Notre Dame College of Ohio and the PhD from Case Western Reserve University. Her special interests include family sociology and Christian covenant communities. She has authored a textbook for undergraduate students in sociological theory, and for five years was coeditor of *Sociological Focus*, the official North Central Sociological Association journal.

2. The desire for *engagement*—the wish to come directly to grips with social and interpersonal problems and to confront on equal terms an environment which is not composed of ego-extensions.

3. The desire for *dependence*—the wish to share responsibility for the control of one's impulses and the direction of one's life (Slater, 1970:5).

Most institutions in our advanced industrial society frustrate such desires. Our cultural values, including those of individualism, utilitarianism, and pragmatism (all commonly accepted guiding ideologies), war against such desires. The family seems to stand alone as an institution where the desire for community, engagement, and dependence may be partially satisfied; but even in this already overburdened institution, such values have come under attack. While modern man may be questing for community, our guiding cultural values are largely anticommunity. As Benjamin D. Zablocki has observed:

> Under ideal circumstances a sense of community can be found on three different levels. A man has pride in the achievements of his city. He is involved in the affairs of his neighborhood. He is nourished by the love of his family. At all of these levels, he encounters restrictions on his freedom. Postindustrial man has gained an unprecedented degree of freedom, but he has lost his sense of community on all three of these levels.

Not only have the values and structure of the larger post-industrial society undermined community features of the larger social order, but they have also destroyed much of the potential community in the family.[1] In looking at the American family from a cross-cultural perspective, Zablocki (1971:295) states:

> A closer look at the American family indicates that it is not merely barren, but positively destructive of community, and destructive of community-building potential in the children it rears.

It is out of this frustrated quest for community that the contemporary intentional community movement has developed. Literally hundreds of communities have been created within the past fifteen years, many of which were doomed to failure. Yet despite the obstacles some intentional communities are thriving. In this chapter we will look at one such venture, the convenant community, with particular focus on the nuclear family as a foundation for its developement.

## Intentional Communities and the Family

Intentional communities have traditionally treated the nuclear family in one of two ways: (1) as a source of strife and disharmony which must be eliminated if the intentional community is to succeed in achieving its vision of a more perfect social order or (2) as the building block from which the larger intentional community draws its sustenance. If the latter model is employed, balance must be sought to alleviate tensions between nuclear family and community loyalties. We will briefly consider both of these models along with some historical and contemporary illustrations.

### *The Intentional Community as a Replacement for the Nuclear Family*

The view that the monogamous family is a less than perfect institution that should be eliminated for the ruling class of people was advanced by the ancient greek philosopher Plato. Plato (1945:155-64) prescribed "group marriage" for the guardian class that would abolish private homes and families in order that the ruling class might form a single family. This would enable the guardians as rulers to put community interests over family and personal ones, and ensure the greatest possible unity to the state.

This model of group marriage was implemented in the famous nineteenth-century utopian community founded by John Humphrey Noyes. Believing that Christ had already returned to earth in AD 70 and that liberation from sin was an accomplished fact, Noyes asserted that, given the proper environment, men and women could lead perfect lives here and now. In an attempt to provide this environment for the practice of his gospel of Perfectionism, Noyes and his followers established Oneida in the state of New York (Kephard, 1976:52-104). William M. Kephard (1976:79) has provided the following description for the Oneidans' practice of complex or group marriage—a practice central to the achievement of perfection.

According to Noyes, it was natural for all men to love all women, and for all women to love all men. He felt that any social institution which flouted this truism was harmful to the human spirit. Romantic love—or "special love," as the Oneidans called it—was harmful because it was a selfish act. Monogamous marriage was harmful because it excluded others from sharing in connubial affection. The answer, obviously, was group marriage, and throughout the whole of their existence, this was what the Oneidans practiced.[2]

Plato and Noyes were not alone in their convictions that monogamous marriage and the nuclear family were not in the best interests of the perfect society. One of the sharpest criticisms of the traditional family came from Karl Marx. Seeing the exploitation of the workers under the early industrial system, Marx was highly critical of capitalism and the family system he believed it spawned. In exploiting the labors of women and children, as well as men, capitalism was destroying the traditional family. As Marx expressed it:

> However terrible and disgusting, under the capitalistic system, the dissolution of the old family ties may appear, nevertheless, large-scale industry, by assigning as it does an important part in the process of production, outside the domestic sphere, to women, to young persons, and to children of both sexes, creates a new economic basis for a higher form of the family and the relations between sexes (Marx, 1956:254).

For Marx the new economic system of communism would witness the end of the nuclear family unit as modern man has known it.

The Marxist belief that monogamy was a source of strife and a threat to true communal sharing was incorporated into the modern kibbutz of Israel. In it we find attempts at drastic modification of the family and socialization in an attempt to live a truly collective, communal life. In its earliest days, it appears attempts were made to follow strict Marxist ideology in eliminating the family. Unlike Oneida, which succeeded in replacing monogamy with complex marriage, the kibbutz has moved back toward monogamous marital unions, creating a modified family that fits well with the communal life of the kibbutz. George A. Hillery (1968:180) comments: "The family, as reduced to its minimum in the kibbutz, seems to be the type of group which can always be expected in human communal organizations."

Although in theory there is support for the notion that a strong intentional community must abolish distinctions between families and merge them into the larger collective, successful intentional communities have generally modified, rather than eliminated, the nuclear family. Rosabeth Moss Kanter (1973), for example, notes that most communes are a large blanket social order that contain smaller family units. Unlike Oneida, which perhaps did not last long enough to revert to monogamy, the contemporary kibbutz reflects a successful intentional community which sought to eliminate nuclear family ties, only to find them strengthened in the modified family system of the adults who were born and raised in the kibbutz.

*The Intentional Community as an Extension for the Nuclear Family*

The attempt to eliminate the nuclear family has been less frequent than the attempt to use the family as a base and model for the larger intentional community. This is particularly true for religious intentional communities which sought to incorporate families into the community. A notable exception being Catholic celibate religious orders. The Bruderhof, a successful Christian commune founded in Germany in 1920, which moved to the United States (via Paraguay) in the 1950s, provides an illustrative case:

> Life in the Bruderhof is not an alternative to family life. ...[T]he Bruderhof does everything to strengthen the family. Each family has private living quarters, and there are special times set aside during the daily routine so that families can be together. Moreover, because the community is total and includes work, play, education and worship, Bruderhof families have more opportunities for spending time together than families in the outside world whose members work and learn often at great distances from home. Married parents are the dominant social class in the Bruderhof, and most families have several children, for a large family is considered wholesome (Bouvard, 1975:50).

Other examples of successful Christian intentional communities where the family is viewed as the base for the community may be found in the Hutterites (see Kephart, 1975:243-280), Koinonia (see Bouvard, 1975:56-67), and Reba Place Fellowship (see Bouvard, 1975:76-76).

The attempt to live out a Christian commitment within a larger community dates back to the Acts of the Apostles. In Acts 2:44-46, Luke reports:

> All the believers continued together in close fellowship and shared their belongings with one another. They would sell their property and possessions, and distribute the money among all, according to what each one needed (TEV).

The Anabaptists of the sixteenth century emphasized this principle for a full Christian life—a principle kept alive for some 450 years by the Hutterian Brethren. As farmers, deliberately isolated from the larger social world, the Hutterites appear quaint in both dress and lifestyle—relics of a bygone era.

Two other groups, one rural and one urban, developed during this century as successful attempts for contemporary but radical Christian living. Koinonia community was established in 1942 in Americus, Georgia, by Clarence Jordon. He established the community "to practice the brotherhood of all men, the sharing of goods, and conscientious objection in a society characterized by racism, competition, and militarism" (Bouvard, 1975:56-57). While Koinonia is found in a rural southern setting, Reba Place was founded by John and Louise Miller in 1957 in the large, cosmopolitan city of Chicago. Reba Place shares with Koinonia, however, similar motivation and commitment:

> Reba Place communalists believe that injustices such as hunger, racism, and war must be confronted. They also believe, however, that individuals who confront the larger society must have group support. The nuclear family cannot in many cases bear the brunt of the emotional demands of its members. While Reba Place individuals are monogamous and traditional in their viewpoint toward sex, they feel their communal group provides much more emotional security than the isolated family (Roberts, 1971:68).

It is this conviction that the isolated family needs support in living out a total Christian commitment that gave rise to the development of covenant communities. Although they share Christian commitment with other Christian intentional communities, the development and growth of covenant communities within the past decade is unprecedented in the history of the other groups mentioned here. The topic of covenant communities, in general, and the Mana Community, in particular, will provide the subject matter for the remainder of this article.[3]

## What Is a Covenant Community?

The covenant community represents one stream within the Catholic charismatic renewal (the other stream being prayer groups). Both streams "tend not to be parish groups but are rather transparochial, embracing members from a number of parishes" and "tend to be ecumenical in character, even when membership is predominantly Catholic" (McDonnell, 1978:23). The covenant communities, which frequently developed out of prayer groups, share lives with co-members along a wide spectrum, including "prayer, teaching, sometimes living quarters, and, to different degrees, finances" (McDonnell, 1978:24). The community bonds are reinforced by an intensified commitment of the community members to each other.

The covenant community clearly does *not* represent an attempt to establish a new church. On the contrary, members are encouraged to aid in the healing of the divisions within the Christian churches—not to further divide. Their emphasis rather appears to be on creating a type of religious supra-family in which Christians can be nourished and supported in order to better live out their lives as believers.

McDonnell (1978:24) also points to the discipline and formation that members of covenant communities received that are absent in many modern lives:

> Because the covenant communities have tighter bonds than the prayer groups, arising out of mutual submission of the central teams, they form groups of unusual strength. In discipline, formation, pastoral care, personnel, and financing, they have resources far beyond what the ordinary prayer group can hope to attain. This strength comes partly from size. By breaking the community into smaller units they have been able to maintain the intimacy which is so characteristic of the smaller prayer group. But by retaining the large unit they have increased their strength and bear witness to the Lord and have been able to safeguard their personnel resources for pastoral care and formation.

Covenant communities are highly structured for the most effective use of resources. Not only is each well structured internally, but presently covenant communities are being tied together by a network of national and international leadership. McDonnell (1978:24) observes:

> There are differences from community to community, but there is a conscious attempt to build one style of life so that a member of one community could be transferred to another community, live there, and be quite at home with the pattern of life.

Covenant communities have developed largely during the late 1960s and through the 1970s. They range in size from less than 100 members to over 2,000 members. In total they number around two dozen communities in the United States, with others in existence in both Europe and Latin America. Although all of them may be said to still be in varying degrees of formation, the covenant community appears to be on firm institutional grounds.[4] To further illustrate the principles found in covenant communities and to assess them sociologically, the remainder of this article will focus on one small but growing community found in Midwest, U.S.A.

## Mana Community

### Origin

Unlike most covenant communities which have developed out of already existing prayer groups, Mana Community is a result of the vision of its founder and leader, Paul Ducet.[5] Ducet regards 1968 as the turning point in his life—a time spent recovering from tuberculosis contracted while serving in the Peace Corps. While having no specific model in mind, Ducet was convinced of two points: (1) any kind of renewal had to be based on prayer, and (2) it would have to be committed to the poor in some way. After visiting a number of different existing communities that potentially met these two criteria, Ducet felt the Lord was calling him to establish a community in Midwest, U.S.A. Mana Community was established in 1970, even though its founder readily admitted that at the time he knew little about starting one. Although this admission may be true, the Holy Spirit has given Ducet the wisdom to carry out his vision of establishing a Christian community.

During its eight years of existence, Mana has moved from a relatively unstructured small group to a covenant community of about 100 persons, and it appears to be a process of continued growth. Sociologically, its development can be attributed to the successful way it handles areas of critical concern for a community: a sense of purpose, commitment to members of the community, leadership and decision-making, socialization of new members, and in handling other dilemma situations. We will deal briefly with each of these points with special emphasis on the Mana Community.

### Sense of Purpose

Ron E. Roberts (1971:81) has cited a community's sense of purpose as one of the single most important ingredients for a successful intentional community. This sense of purpose that goes beyond the community's immediate needs, Roberts argues, gives religious structures (such as Mana Community) an edge over nonreligious ones because they share a common ideology and fulfill a need for transcendence.

As has already been noted, Ducet was convinced, even before founding the community, of its need to be based in prayer and to serve the poor. These two goals have become stronger and the vision clearer, as Mana continues its pattern of growth and development. The community emphasizes the need for every member to participate in both personal and group prayer. In addition, one of its main outreaches into the community is to host a weekly prayer meeting. Much emphasis is placed on personal holiness and on growing in union with the Lord. Members desiring a deeper commitment to the community than attending the weekly prayer meeting, seek out additional involvement and undergo the socialization process discussed later in this article. There is no question that prayer and a personal relation with Jesus remains central to the Mana Community.

The second of Ducet's convictions, namely that of serving the poor, remains, but this has temporarily been de-emphasized in order to build relations within the community. Although members of the community care for several retarded and handicapped persons and are personally committed to a simple lifestyle, social action outreach is limited. This is not due to Ducet's abandoning a central reason for Mana's existence. But rather as he notes, "I began to realize, if we really wanted to serve the poor, we would have to learn to relate to each other." He feels that only as they grow in community will members of Mana be equipped emotionally and spiritually for any kind of social outreach. We have seen that Reba Place and Koinonia, two Christian communities briefly discussed earlier, are both committed to reaching out to bring Christian love and justice to a larger environment. Mana shares this concern, but appears to still be in a formative stage where solid community ties must be developed before effective outreach programs can be realistically begun.

The prayer emphasis takes priority over social action. As Ducet commented: "An early problem that we had to face was a recognition that we could not serve the poor on our own power. We learned that we have to rely on the power of the Holy Spirit." The community believes that through prayer the Holy Spirit will guide them to develop a more effective social outreach to the poor than they could have divised personally, and that the Spirit will provide the power necessary for that outreach.

## Leadership and Authority

Mana Community has a highly structured authority system, one resembling other religious international communities. Ducet noted that, "One of the first things we had to face is authority—what is authority and what does Scripture say about authority?" In an interview on the topic of "Authority in Christian Communities," the leader of another covenant community Steve Clark (1975) emphasizes that it is "impossible to have community unless people submit their lives to some kind of authority." In the covenant community, the heads or leaders are responsible for the community as a whole and, therefore, "also have responsibility for people's personal lives to the degree those lives are put in common." Clark (1975:24) further states:

> I think there are a number of reasons why people would want to have relationships involving headship and submission. One is that headship enables the body to function in unity. The more a particular group or community wants to act in a disciplined, unified way, the more likely the members are to want some kind of authority.
>
> A headship relationship also provides a context in which formation can take place. A disciple enters into a master-disciple relationship in order to be formed. By agreeing to submit to the person who is doing the formation, the disciple's growth in the Christian life can take place more quickly and effectively.

Mana Community stresses the importance of headship and submission. Although he sees himself under the authority of the local Catholic bishop and is in dialogue with heads of other covenant communities, Ducet is unquestionably the leader of Mana Community. Under him is a recently constructed "brotherhood of pastors" consisting of seven men (suggested by community members but appointed by Ducet), who attempt to guide the community. Within families, women and children must submit to husbands as the head of the family, with the husbands in submission to other men in the community. Single men and women are assigned heads to whom they pledge submission. There is, in short, a highly structured system of submission and inter-submission arranged in a clearly hierarchical way.

While such a structured system may be upsetting to libertarians, in actuality there is a blend of personal freedom along with the authority deemed necessary for the smooth running of an intentional community. Through a commitment to personal and group prayer, it is believed that the Holy Spirit will guide both leaders and followers. The prayer for unity is frequent and fervent. In questioning members, it is apparent that they do not feel that they are deprived of freedom—and they know that they have found community. This observation of Mana is reminiscent of Zablocki's (1971:287) comment on the Bruderhof, another successful religious community: "Alienated Western man does not feel that he really possesses community, but members of the Bruderhof feel they really possess freedom." Zablocki then suggests that modern man may often be confusing individualism with freedom. Freedom is valued by communitarians, but individualism is viewed as problematic for the desired goal of community.

### Commitment to Community Goals

Not only must the community have a goal or purpose, as well as effective leadership and decision-making, but it must also have mechanisms for building commitment. Kanter (1973:99-100) describes committed members as "loyal and involved," as deriving their rewards from participation in the community, as having a "sense of belonging," and as feeling that "the values of the group are an expression of their innermost selves." They are also described working hard, participating actively, and deriving love and affection from the communal group. In order to build such commitment, reports Kanter (1973:100), "members must both shake off vestiges of the old way (of life) and gain a sense of the joys of the new way (of life)."

Mana prayer meetings and gatherings frequently revolve around the theme of Christians being a new creation. This biblical theme of the old person having died and having been born anew in Christ is central. Also emphasized at meetings open to nonmembers is the need to commit one's life to a community, not necessarily the Mana Community, in order to fully live out the gospel. The socialization mechanisms are directed toward forming model Christians living in community with other Christians.

### Socialization Mechanisms

Committed community members become a reality only if there are effective socialization mechanisms. Failure to socialize members into a community's ways inevitably leads to its dissolution. Community, as we have seen, implies to total sharing and giving of oneself. Ideally, it is hoped that the community and the person will be mirror images. This only begins to approach reality if prospective members ·and new members are provided the mechanisms and incentives to take on the community's values and way of life.

Socialization into the Mana Community is highly structured. Attempts are made to discipline prospective members so that they assume the demands of a fully committed Christian life, hopefully within Mana Community. The uninitiated are first encouraged to seek a fuller life in the Holy Spirit, and then a fuller life in Christian community.

Mana is part of the growing charismatic (neo-Pentecostal) movement which teaches Christians to be open to the full range of the gifts of the Holy Spirit. These include praying in tongues (glossolalia), the gift of prophecy, healing (both physical and spiritual), and other gifts described in Scripture as being part of the mature Christian's life. (See 1 Corinthians 12, 13, and 14 for Paul's discussion of some of the spiritual gifts.) For those who have not yet experienced a release of the power of the Holy Spirit in their lives (frequently referred to as "baptism of the Holy Spirit"), the first course is an eight-week seminar entitled "Life in the Spirit." The person is encouraged at this point to continue attending Wednesday evening prayer meetings (open to members and nonmembers), and to make a commitment to complete the course.

Towards the end of the Life in the Spirit seminar (which has marked the spiritual turning point of many lives), those interested are invited to attend a "community weekend" designed to provide more information on the Mana Community. They are then encouraged to make a commitment to continue the learning program through a twelve-week course called "Foundations in Christian Living." If the person's interest continues, additional commitments are made to the Mana Community. One is an invitation to attend a Saturday prayer gathering intended only for Mana members. Another is to join a "sharing group," a structured small-group session with other community members. The "sharing group" is not only a further means of socialization, but also a means for avoiding serious deviance problems. Prayer, service to others, religious study, and community relations are all regular topics for the small-group sharings. Also sometime during this Foundations seminar, the prospective member will be asked to pray about making a regular financial contribution to the Mana Community.

Following Foundations there is a twelve-week "Service Workshop," aimed primarily at further developing relations within the community. During this time, for example, women attend a regular Bible study for fellowship with other women, while men may work together one evening a week on community projects. The emphasis appears to be on men building brotherly relations with other men and women building sisterly relations with other women. In addition, six other instructional courses are offered, although not in any particular sequence, dealing with such topics as fruits of the Spirit, emotions, personal relationships, and being disciples of the Lord.

During this period deeper commitments may be made to the community and to its way of life. A period of at least three years is recommended before a person, in mutual decision with the community, commits himself/herself to a covenant with the Mana Community.

This covenant entails entering into a family-like relationship with all other members of the community. It implies a full personal commitment of lives, responsibilities, and resources to other covenant members. Although persons still retain personal title to homes, bank accounts, etc., the commitment implies a willingness and readiness to share with the community as described in Acts 2:44-46. The socialization is gradual and attempts to be non-threatening, with full realization of lack of trust that most Americans have. The attempt is to build trust first, and then ask for commitments. From the Life in the Spirit seminar on, members are encouraged to build trusting relations with each other. Buoyed with a trust of community leaders and other members, prospective members eventually are able to make a more complete pledge of lives and resources to the community by agreeing to the conditions of the covenant.

### Dilemmas as Facilitators of Social Process

What we have discussed thus far is the nature of structural features common to intentional communities with specific description of the Mana community's practices. Emphasis on structure, however, overlooks the process through which the structure is created and the process through which it changes. A viable community is more analogous to a living organism than a well-oiled machine. There is not only structure and day-to-day operation, but also change and growth. Concentration on structural traits and practices has the weakness of failing to present the dynamic aspects of this living organism called community.

In order to supplement our structural description and to portray aspects of growth and areas of potential development, we will describe some of the dilemmas faced by this particular covenant community. Dilemma involves some paradox, in that an attempt to achieve a desirable end will also produce undesirable results. For example, traits that allow a person to develop as leader of a group (those characteristics which afford him/her popularity as the leader) are often at odds with his/her exercise of that leadership. It is not surprising, therefore, that a popularly elected president may experience a decline in his popularity as he makes decisions in office. His decisions are bound to be unpopular at different times with different groups. As Peter M. Blau (1964:57) observes, "Many social phenomena rest on incompatible conditions that pose a paradox and create dilemmas. . . ." A few such social conditions already mentioned in this article that we would like to explore further are: (1) the dilemma of personal freedom versus the community structure, (2) the dilemma of maintaining nuclear family ties while creating a larger community family, (3) the dilemma of being in the world yet not being of it, and (4) the dilemma of encouraging personal religious experience as a builder of community, versus the institutionalization of religious experience.

## Personal Freedom Versus Community Structure

As we have already noted, lack of structure and leadership is fatal to a community. Yet at the same time, Christ's followers have a freedom in him. As Paul exclaims:

> Freedom is what we have—Christ has set us free! Stand, then, as free people, and do not allow yourselves to become slaves again. Galatians 5:1 (TEV).

In spite of this biblical admonition and others like it, historically Christians have become enslaved by new Pharisaic laws to replace the ones Jesus freed us from! Similarly in covenant communities there is the ever-present danger of members being enslaved by the leadership and rules of the community.

This is a dilemma that will always be present as long as the community is a viable one. Its resolution once and for all would result in either the end of the community or the loss of this freedom. The history of communal failures testifies to the dangers of allowing individualism to run rampant, yet the freedom we have in Christ should not be sacrificed, even in the name of community. Overstructuring and over-regulation is a danger that may be evidenced from the rigidity of many Roman Catholic religious orders (priests, nuns, and brothers) before the liberating Second Vatican Council in the 1960s.

Mana Community deals with this dilemma by stressing the need for personal prayer and by encouraging members to be open to the power of the Holy Spirit in their personal lives. While allowing and encouraging personal freedom, decisions are always discussed with others and ultimately require the approval of the community.

At present it appears as if rigidity could set in unless the community leaders recognize the seriousness of this dilemma and continually strive for a balance between freedom and authority. In an attempt to socialize persons into the community, there remains the real threat of oversocialization. Should this occur, Mana would not long continue to be the viable community it is today.

*Nuclear Family Ties and the Larger Community*

We have already seen how some utopian writers, including Plato and Marx, have called for an end to the nuclear, monogamous family in order to achieve true community. The feasibility of putting this into practice is unclear, as evidenced by Oneida and the kibbutz. Moreover, any attempt to eliminate the monogamous couple as the unit of reproduction and replace it with complex or group marriage is not in accord with the teachings of Scripture. There is a dilemma, however, in balancing the nuclear family needs with communal interests that remain part of any community attempting to do so.

The Mana Community does attempt to incorporate the nuclear family into its structure, making every effort to strengthen rather than to weaken it. As Ducet noted in his interview with this author:

> The core of the community has to be the nuclear or extended family. The community should support the family. I don't think today that it is possible to have a strong family life without community. The vision is that each person will learn to take responsibilities for others to the extent that they are able to, and that they would be taken responsibility for, to the extent that they need that.

Yet this vision of intercooperation and a supra-family community, as with most worthwhile things in life, is not easy to attain. Dilemma or problem situations will continue to arise, forcing changes in one area of community relations that may create imbalances in other areas or on other levels. For example, at present attempts to integrate new couples into the community may at the same time be creating divisions between single adults and families. Will Mana go the way of the Bruderhof where married parents are accorded higher status than single members? This is always a possibility. If it happened, it surely would create problematic status distinctions in the community.

Another family-related dilemma concerns the issue of changing gender roles in our present society. The role of married women in the Mana Community is clearly in accord with traditional values. The husband is head and breadwinner-provider; the wife is submissive to her husband and serves as homemaker. It is encouraged that married women with children do not work outside the home. This practice undoubtedly affects the supra-family of the community where women expect men to be the leaders and men expect to lead. In this respect, Mana reflects the traditionalism of the conservative Christian churches and the subsequent loss of a less-than-full development of female potential. Although admitting to the equality all Christians have in Christ, the hierarchical patterns which leave women out of positions of leadership in covenant communities mirrors Paul's own ambivalence about the role of women in the church.

Still another dilemma exists with regard to male-female relations. After observing that men were not relating well with men and women with women, great emphasis has been placed on women associating with "sisters" and men with "brothers." In an attempt to create a balance in same-sex relations, an imbalance now exists in brother-sister relations. Yet emotional closeness between young people of the opposite sex who have only recently come together (not actually being raised in this "family") can create even more serious problems for the community. Trying to create a family out of socialized adults proves to be more difficult in practice than in theory.

Yet the Mana Community, as we have already seen, has a well-developed program of socialization to initiate prospective members into its way of life. When problem areas arise, teachings are given in an area to help correct the problem. Sharing groups also are used to reinforce the teaching on a small-group level. Respect for authority and authoritative teachings is one of the first areas of socialization and appears to run deep. At the same time, however, there remains a flexibility and openness to change on the part of leaders.

*In the World But Not of It*

In praying for his disciples at the Last Supper, Jesus said, "I do not ask you to take them out of the world, but I do ask you to keep them safe from the Evil One" (John: 17:15 TEV). Many Christian communities have isolated themselves from the world and its problems in rural settings where a more complete community life is feasible. Mana Community, however, is an urban community with members holding diverse jobs outside the community. Although some attempt is made to encourage a clustering of people living in several different neighborhoods within the urban area, members live in regular houses rather than some large community structure. In no sense are members physically isolated from the larger urban society. Instead, they rely on Christ and his prayer for the Father's protection, and they pray that their lives will be a light to the people of the Midwest.

Their dilemma in this regard is one that all committed Christians face. How can a follower of Jesus be in the world but not of it? For Mana members it is actually less of a dilemma than for those without community support. They are constantly reminded by others that they are committed to Christ to love and serve, and that they are a people set apart for God's use. Another key for balancing this dilemma (and others) is the scheduling of time and activities, a program again guided by leadership. A list of priorities is clearly established. The schedule allows for the balancing of time between two top priorities: the community and the nuclear family (or single people with whom one is living). The job is not permitted to interfere with these two priorities. Only after family, community, and work responsibilities are met do they turn to other relationships or non-community activities. Mana Community, through a disciplined schedule and leadership appears to have this dilemma by the horns—better than many other Christians.

*Personal Versus Institutionalized Religion*

Another dilemma that the Mana Community shares with the larger Christian church is the problem of attempted institutionalization of religious experience. The late humanist psychologist Abraham Maslow (1964) suggested that the attempt to institutionalize experiences of God result in the subsequent loss of that experience for the individual. This he saw as an age-old problem of established churches. For Maslow, the founding of the great religions of the world and their sacred writings were the work of those who have experienced a sense of the Ultimate. The problem they face is trying to put their experience into communicable language. Maslow (1964:24) states:

> Much theology, much verbal religion through history and throughout the world, can be considered to be the more or less vain efforts to put into communicable words and formulae, and into symbolic rituals and ceremonies, the original mystical experience of the original prophets. In a word, organized religion can be thought of as an effort to communicate peak-experiences to non-peakers, to teach them, to apply them, etc. Often, to make it more difficult, this job falls into the hands of non-peakers.

The danger is that the symbols and practices become concretized, and a form of idolatry comes into being where sacred things and sacred practices are worshiped rather than the living God. Maslow concludes that this idolatry "has been the curse of every large religion."

The charismatic renewal within the churches, and covenant communities as its offshoot, have represented a fresh outpouring of the Holy Spirit on the church. Establishing a personal relationship with God through Jesus by the power of the Holy Spirit is central to this renewal. It allows Christians to see the Scriptures not as a dry historical document, but as a personal word of God's love which all of Jesus' followers may experience. The dilemma is that as social beings we cannot live by feelings alone. Coming together in groups, men and women attempt to develop theology and social structures based on the experience. In the case of covenant communities, instructional programs have been instituted to socialize interested persons into the structure and presumably into the experience. The danger, as Maslow points out, is a routinization of the practices, in this case, losing sight of the power of the Holy Spirit who began the entire process. When the programs, rather than the voice of the Lord, become the invitation to "graduate" to a new spiritual level; when the community, rather than Jesus, becomes the center of life; when religious practices become ends in themselves rather than means to achieve a closer walk with God; covenant communities will have experienced Maslow's curse of idolatry.

These and other dilemmas exist, the balancing of which will permit growth and development for the community. A problem with rigidly organized groups is that they attempt to eliminate as many dilemmas or conflict situations as possible, rather than allowing them to be a source of life and growth. The direction the Mana Community will take—that of rigid organization versus the continued development of an organization through interaction—depends upon the wisdom of its leadership. If it is able to live with dilemma situations (rather than attempting to eliminate them), Mana will come closer to its own goal of being truly a living organism.

### Postscript: Role of Christian Sociologist as Observer

One of the tests of whether an analysis is scientific or not is whether another researcher could observe the same phenomena. The present description of the Mana Community is one that I believe any sociologist could and would verify in terms of its structural features and its dilemma situations. To this extent the author is playing the role of a sociologist. I have attempted to describe this community through the eyes of a trained observer.

Such observation has its limitations. It can describe, but fails to explain. (See Homans, 1967 for a further discussion of sociology's inability to explain.) As someone committed to the Lord and confident of his desire to guide us, I believe Mana Community's very existence can be explained only by the power of the Holy Spirit, who uses sound sociological principles to keep the community in existence. As a Christian sociologist I felt it was mandatory, even within the context of sociological analysis, to give the Holy Spirit his due. I believe it is he who leads and guides the Mana Community and will continue to do so as long as leaders and followers are open to his guidance. Although I do not contend all the Community does is of the Lord (any more than any individual Christian always hears and responds to the Lord's gentle voice), I do contend that God brought the community into being. This is a matter of faith, going far beyond the realm of what is demonstrable by my training as a sociologist.

Not all sociologists would be in agreement with the appropriateness of this merging of faith and science. As Hillery (1978) reported from a roundtable discussion on the "Interface Between Sociological Theory and Christian Sociology" at a regional sociological meeting:

> At least two alternative Christian views of society may be discerned, "Christian Sociologists" and "Christians in Sociology." The difference is, we believe, more than trivial. Persons who prefer to be identified as Christian sociologists are probably more comfortable identifying with a "value advocation position." Others who identify themselves as "Christians in Sociology" believe that

regardless of sociologists' *personal* commitments, all sociologists have a common starting point in utilizing the values of science to study human social life. Most sociologists who are Christians represent varying degrees of adherence to these positions (Hillery, 1978:10).

Never having been a believer in the feasibility of a truly neutral, value-free sociology, I readily admit that I am a Christian sociologist.

## Discussion Questions

1. What is an "intentional community"?

2. Describe the dilemma posed in absorbing nuclear families into an intentional community. How is this dilemma handled in the Mana Community?

3. What is the purpose of a covenant community? How widespread are they?

4. How are each of the following critical areas handled by the Mana Community: A sense of purpose? Commitment to members of the community? Leadership and decision-making? Socializing of new members?

5. What is Abraham Maslow's theory regarding the idolatry that "has been the curse of every large religion"?

6. Sociologically speaking or thinking, what type of people are drawn into intentional communities? Why are persons closely integrated into the extended family and ethnic communities less apt to join?

7. What advantages do Mana members have to witness and serve that are not open to those in monasteries and convents or to the ordinary nuclear family member?

8. Was the decision to devote time to prayer and learning to relate to each other in the Mana Community a wise one? Should they have integrated prayer with service to the poor? How did Jesus minister?

9. Do you see the development of "intentional communities" as an indictment of the church? Or are these merely another form of "family" organization that supports the institutional church?

10. What is the role of a Christian sociologist?

## Notes

1. The best-selling book *Open Marriage* (O'Neill and O'Neill, 1972) serves to illustrate the value of individualism over the collectivity in marriage. What it actually describes is "married singlehood," where both partners retain individual preferences and lifestyles, rather than the creation of a new institution in marriage.

2. Kephart further discusses the biblical basis for the Oneidans' practice of complex marriage:

Noyes's views on matrimony were also based on biblical interpretation. In the *Bible Argument,* published by the Oneida Community, the following statement appears:

> In the kingdom of heaven, the institution of marriage—which assigns the exclusive possession of one woman to one man—does not exist (Matthew 22:23-30).
>
> In the kingdom of heaven, the intimate union, which in the world is limited to pairs, extends through the whole body of believers ... (John 17:21). The new commandment is that we love one another, not by pairs, as in the World, but en masse.

3. Mana Community is a pseudonym given by the author to a covenant community is the Midwestern section of the United States. Although the head of the community has read this article, he personally prefers that the community not be publicized through this research. I have protected the anonymity of the community at his request.

4. For descriptive accounts of a few early covenant communities and their practices see Horning (1974), Cavnar (1974), Jahr (1975 a, b, c), Pickens (1975), Conniff (1975), and Jahr (1976). While there are certain to be differences among the covenanted communities, there appears to be (as noted earlier) an attempt to converge practices.

5. "Paul Ducat" is also a pseudonym.

## References

Blau, Peter M.
  1964 *Exchange and Power in Social Life.* New York: John Wiley & Sons, Inc.
Bouvard, Marguerite
  1975 *The Intentional Community Movement.* Port Washington, N.Y.: Kennikat Press.
Cavnar, Jim
  1974 "Nonresidential Households." *New Covenant* 4 (November):18-19.
Clark, Steve
  1975 "Authority in Christian Communities." *New Covenant,* 5 (December), pp. 24-27.
Conniff, Cindy
  1975 "Living the Gospel in a University Dorm." *New Covenant,* 5 (September), pp. 12-13.
Hillery, George A., Jr.
  1968 *Communal Organizations.* Chicago: The University of Chicago Press.

Hillery, George A., Jr.
  1978 "Meeting in New Orleans." *Newsletter: Christian Sociologists*, 5 (June), p. 10.
Homans, George
  1967 *The Nature of Social Science*. New York: Harcourt, Brace & World.
Horning, Bob
  1974 "Faith Village: the Lord's Landlords." *New Covenant, 4 (November), pp. 9-11*.
Jahr, Mary Ann
  1975a "*An Ecumenical Christian Community: The Word of God, Ann Arbor, Michigan.*" *New Covenant*, 4 (February), pp. 4-8.
  1975b "Living Together in the Word of God." *New Covenant*, 4 (February), pp. 13-14.
  1975c "Coming Together in Christian Community." *New Covenant*, 5 (September), pp. 8-10.
  1976 "We Are One." *New Covenant*, 5 (January), pp. 25-27.
Kanter, Rosabeth Moss
  1973 *Communes: Creating and Managing the Collective Life*. New York: Harper and Row.
Kephart, William M.
  1976 *Extraordinary Groups*. New York: St. Martin's Press.
Marx, Karl
  1956 *Selected Writings in Sociology and Social Philosophy* (trans. by T. B. Bottomore). New York: McGraw-Hill Book Company.
Maslow, Abraham H.
  1964 *Religions, Values, and Peak-Experiences*. New York: The Viking Press.
McDonnell, Kilian
  1978 "Prayer Groups and Communities." *New Covenant*, 8 (July), pp. 23-27.
O'Neill, Nena and George O'Neill
  1972 *Open Marriage*. New York: Avon Books.
Pickens, Dick
  1975 "The Well." *New Covenant*, 5 (September), pp. 24-26.
Plato
  1945 *The Republic of Plato* (trans. by Frances MacDonald Cornford). New York: Oxford University Press.
Roberts, Ron E.
  1971 *The New Communes*. Englewood Cliffs, N.J.: Prentice-Hall.
Slater, Philip
  1970 *The Pursuit of Loneliness*. Boston: Beacon Press.
Zablocki, Benjamin D.
  1971 *The Joyful Community*. Baltimore: Penguin Books.

# 36
# Factors Mitigating the Clergy's Prophetic Role

*Richard J. Stellway*

> Come now, you rich, weep and howl for the miseries that are coming upon you. Your riches have rotted and your garments are moth-eaten. Your gold and silver have rusted, and their rust will be evidence against you and will eat your flesh like fire. You have laid up treasure for the last days.

Karl Marx did not make this statement, not was it spoken by some contemporary political agitator. Actually, it comes from the Bible (James 5:1-3). Hardly an isolated passage, it represents a theme which resounds through Scripture. From Jeremiah to James and from Amos to Jesus, those who perpetrate injustice—even tolerate it—are denounced and threatened with God's judgment.

## The Prophetic and Priestly Traditions

The call for justice and the demand that socioeconomic and religious evils be rectified in order to avoid God's judgment is a theme which has become known as *the prophetic tradition*. As such it contrasts markedly with *the priestly tradition*. While the latter is concerned with reconciling itself with existing social arrangements and with emphasizing personal faith and piety, the prophetic tradition challenges the legitimacy of institutional arrangements which victimize people by causing undue misery and hardship. Furthermore, the prophetic tradition

Richard J. Stellway
*Assistant Professor of Sociology*
*Chairman, Department of Sociology and Anthropology*
*Wheaton College (Illinois)*

Modernization and development, the sociology of religion, aging, and marriage and the family constitute the major sociological interests of Richard Stellway. Before coming to Wheaton College he taught at Millikin College and at the U.S. International University in San Diego. Although currently attending an interdenominational church, he holds membership in the Nazarene Church. His research interests center on behavioral correlates of religious beliefs, child welfare, and the problems of the aging.

challenges believers to put their faith to work by rooting out evil and by taking action against injustice. The very existence of evil is a mockery to a righteous God, and his judgment most assuredly rests on those who actively perpetuate or even passively tolerate injustice.

It is the contention of this paper that contemporary Christian lay leaders, and most particularly parish clergy, have become so preoccupied with the message of the priestly tradition that they have neglected the prophetic tradition. Indeed, on issues of social morality and corporate responsibility, the contemporary clergy have time and again been strangely silent.

## *Little Rock Ministers and Integration*

Before proceeding to analyze the source of this silence, it is appropriate to first examine some of the evidence bearing on the alleged state of affairs. One of the classic studies bearing on this issue is Ernest Q. Campbell and Thomas F. Pettigrew's study (1959) of Little Rock ministers. This study is particularly noteworthy because it examines ministers' behavior in a situation which provided a real test of their commitment to justice and fair play. It was a situation in which they had something to lose by taking an unpopular stand. The setting of the study involved the impending 1957 desegregation of formerly all-white public schools in Little Rock, Arkansas. Upon compiling a list of twenty-four ministers commonly judged to be the most influential in the community, Campbell and Pettigrew added the names of five ministers who were known to have integrationist sentiments. All twenty-nine ministers were interviewed. Of the twenty-nine, twenty-four favored school integration, despite the fact that virtually all of their respective congregations held a predominately segregationist sentiment.

Partially because of this fact, many of these twenty-four proved to be inactive integrationists. In the weeks preceding the forced integration, only eight ministers continued to defend integration as a Christian imperative. Moreover, only two of the twenty-nine dared to devote a sermon to the subject of integration the Sunday before the event took place.

The reason the inactive integrationist ministers gave for not making their "unpopular" integrationist views public was their fear of being penalized by their congregations. We shall examine the content of these reasons more thoroughly later on. For the moment it can be safely said that Campbell and Pettigrew's findings add support to the contention that parish clergy are quite reluctant to speak out in a prophetic vein.

The critical reader may observe at this point that the above study involved an atypical situation. For this reason it is fair to ask whether parish clergy behave differently under more normal circumstances. The astute reader might also have noted that the ministers were not randomly sampled. The bulk of the ministers interviewed were popularly perceived as being "the most influential." But what about ministers in general? Is their behavior any different? A study by Rodney Stark, et. al., (1971) may assist in answering these questions.

### The Study of California Clergy

Seeking to determine the inclination of ministers to speak out on controversial issues, Stark, *et. al.* (1971), in a random sample of ministers from nine major denominations in California, secured responses from 1, 580 ministers. The study was conducted in the spring of 1968. The timing is particularly noteworthy since, as the investigators observed, the twelve months preceding their study were quite traumatic. Race Riots broke out in several American cities, large portions of them were burned the preceding summer, the Kerner Commission issued its monumental report on the racial crisis, and Martin Luther King was assassinated. Also, the Tet Offensive brought a new wave of concern over the Vietnam War, and the Middle East was recovering from the shock of Israel's 1967 war. With this backdrop of events, and with the air literally seething with social unrest, the investigators sought to determine the inclination of ministers to speak out.

Upon compiling their data, Stark found that a majority of the ministers surveyed had at sometime during the past year delivered sermons which touched upon controversial social or political topics. However only 25 percent reported that they had given more than four sermons which dealt mainly with such issues during the past year. Moreover, 25 percent reported that they had never done so. When one recalls that a minister delivers from forty-five to one hundred sermons in the course of a year, it is clear that dealing with such issues was not their usual pattern. But what makes these findings particularly interesting is that a full 73 percent of the ministers surveyed thought it very important for sermons to "apply Christian standards to judge human institutions and behavior."

## Church, Clergy, and Social Problems

For centuries Christians have been divided over how involved the church should become in dealing with issues of social evil and moral injustice. The issue of slavery is a notable example. Before the Emancipation Proclamation of 1865, ministers and laity of many Northern congregations—whose members had little or no vested interest in the institution of slavery—saw the issue as a moral one and publicly opposed the practice. In contrast many members of Southern congregations interpreted Scripture and doctrine in such a way as to support the practice, thereby eliminating it as a moral issue worthy of comment. Still other Christians chose to define the issue as a strictly civil matter to be decided by the government (see Johnstone, 1965:218-221).

### The Role of Theology

The debate over whether slavery was a moral issue on which the church should take a stand tended to occur along geographic lines. Since the modernist-fundamentalist controversy of the early part of this century, however, the debate over the church's legitimate involvement in issues of social evil and moral injustice has tended to proceed along theological lines. Therefore in seeking to determine why some ministers speak out in a prophetic vein while others do not, it seems appropriate to consider the particular theology espoused by these ministers. Stark, et. al., sent out a questionnaire to clergy to learn what their theological views were. With this data in hand, they constructed an orthodoxy index.° Upon comparing ministers' positions on this index with their inclination to comment on social issues, some rather dramatic differences appeared. During the previous year 66 percent of the least orthodox ministers reported devoting five or more sermons to controversial political or social topics. In contrast, a mere 10 percent of the most orthodox ministers reported doing so. When asked whether they had ever taken a stand on some political issue from the pulpit, an overwhelming 93 percent of the least orthodox (mostly liberal) ministers had done so, but only 42 percent of the most orthodox ministers.

One possible means of accounting for this difference involves the perceived purpose of a sermon. Earlier we mentioned that a majority of

---

°A high score on the orthodoxy index indicated unwavering belief in the existence of a personal God, the divinity of Jesus, life beyond death, the literal existence of the devil, and the necessity to believe in Jesus in order to be saved.

ministers felt it very important to "apply Christian standards to judge human institutions and behavior." In response to this one item both highly orthodox (73%) and highly unorthodox (72%) ministers expressed overwhelming endorsement. However in responding to other statements of purpose, the two groups differed widely. Thus while 77 percent of the most orthodox ministers agreed that it is very important for a sermon to "point out the existence of human sin," only 32 percent of the least orthodox ministers agreed with this statement. And while 87 percent of the most orthodox ministers felt it very important to provide "spiritual uplift and moral comfort," only 39 percent of the least orthodox ministers saw this as very important. From the responses to these latter two items, it is apparent that, in contrast to liberal ministers, theologically conservative ministers are more inclined to stress the comfort theme and the personal sin theme. They neglect preachment about social injustices and corporate evil.

Does the relatively greater emphasis on these themes offer any explanation for the greater reluctance of theologically conservative ministers to deal with issues involving social injustice? One hypothetical explanation might involve the time dimension. Theologically orthodox ministers would quite likely spend more time dealing with the topics of sin (salvation) and comfort from the pulpit, thereby having less time to spend on other topics. However, considering the volume of sermons a pastor normally delivers in a year, time alone should not prevent him from dealing with social issues.

A second possible explanation involves the prospect that the themes of sin (salvation) and comfort somehow preclude comment on social and political issues in the mind of the orthodox minister. The ministers' responses to one additional item adds credence to this explanation. When asked whether they agreed with the statement: "If enough men were brought to Christ, social ills would take care of themselves," a full 77 percent of the most orthodox ministers responded affirmatively, while a mere 7 percent of the least orthodox ministers did so. Perhaps it is in this response that the fuller explanation lies. The logic of a majority of highly orthodox ministers appears to be that if enough people were converted to Christ, social ills would subside.

To this writer there are some gaping holes in such logic. First of all, the prospect of the majority of people becoming Christian seems unlikely. In Matthew 7:14 Jesus said: ". . . strait is the gate, and narrow is the way, which leadeth unto life, and few there be that find it."

Second, even if all people should become converted to Christ, it would be naive to suppose that all men would instantly obtain sainthood upon conversion. All one need do is look at the frequent reluctance of Christians to overturn unjust social arrangements from which they derive personal profit, or consider the difficulty Christians sometimes have in living at peace with one another. Third, it fails to acknowledge the complex nature of social problems, many of which persist as a consequence of structural imperfections. To suppose that such problems would be eradicated once all were converted to Christ is to assume the acquisition of all wisdom and knowledge upon conversion. But social problems do not vanish just because individuals are converted.

Despite the shortcomings of logic that assumes social problems will be eradicated if man is converted, it appears that this logic partially explains the reluctance of conservative ministers to deal directly with issues of social injustice from the pulpit.

## Reference Systems

In the foregoing section we examined the significant role theology plays in determining the amount of emphasis religious leaders give to the prophetic tradition. Theology is not the only variable, however. There is an increasing amount of evidence that other factors also play a significant role. In accounting for the differential behavior of Little Rock ministers, Campbell and Pettigrew relied heavily on reference group theory. They did so by distinguishing between three reference systems: the membership reference system, the professional reference system, and the self-reference system. The *membership reference system* involves members of the local congregation. Insofar as the demands and desires of this group influence the thinking and behavior of their minister, it constitutes an active reference group. The *professional reference system* consists of officials in the denominational hierarchy, as well as other ministers whose opinions and conduct serve as a source of influence. Finally the *self-reference system* constitutes a minister's personal beliefs and convictions. When these three systems are in agreement, a state of consonance or harmony exists. However, whenever a minister's self-reference system is out of line with either the membership reference system or the professional reference system, a state of dissonance occurs. Unless his beliefs and convictions are strong, a minister might resolve the dissonance by modifying his behavior and possibly his beliefs to correspond to the most influencial reference group.

In studying the attitudes and behavior of Little Rock ministers during the school desegregation crisis, Campbell and Pettigrew found that the majority of ministers they interviewed (24 of 29) held integrationist sentiments. However all of them served congregations with predominantly segregationist sentiments, thereby creating a state of dissonance (the self-reference system and membership reference system were inconsistent). Faced with this situation, only eight of the twenty-four integrationist ministers persisted in openly defending integration as a Christian imperative. The majority of them (sixteen of the twenty-four) chose to keep their views to themselves thereby behaviorally accommodating themselves to the interests and sentiments of the membership reference system. Campbell and Pettigrew noted that this was particularly likely to occur when no prominent ministers in the respective denomination (professional reference system) took a strong integrationist stand.

Campbell and Pettigrew's study illustrates the division which may occur between ministers who are committed to social reform, and members of the lay community who are committed to preserving the sociopolitical status quo. While this situation might seem unusual, there is an abundance of evidence to suggest its frequent occurrance. One source of continual devisiveness has been the civil rights issue. Unrest over this issue hardly ended with the North-South denominational splits which occurred prior to the civil war. In a survey of metropolitan Detroit, Lenski (1961:315) found that while 74 percent of the white protestant clergymen felt that ministers should take a stand on the civil rights issue, only 42 percent of the laity were of this persuasion. Hadden's 1967 nationwide survey revealed a similar disparity in that while a scant 8 percent of the clergy disapproved of the civil rights movement, 44 percent of the general sample of white respondents registered such disapproval. In light of such evidence it is hardly surprising to find that in a survey of California ministers, a full 83 percent of those who openly opposed an anti fair-housing amendment to the California Constitution experienced opposition from their congregations (See Quinley, 1974)

As Harold E. Quinley has observed, a congregation may tolerate a minister's stand against civil and social injustice only so long as the issue does not affect them personally. However, as a study by Dean Hoge (1976) reveals, when a minister expresses concern over, for example, justice for the oppressed and legal representation for the poor, he is likely to incur the ire of laypersons who have a vested interest in maintaining the existing state of affairs.

### Authority Structure and Sanctions

Simply stated, Campbell and Pettigrew's thesis asserts that a minister may modify his outward behavior to conform more closely to the interest of his membership and professional reference groups. However, if his personal convictions remain unchanged, as they did for the majority of the inactive integrationists surveyed, this strategy may prove problematic. In essence, by revising his outward behavior to conform to the interests of his church membership, the minister is merely substituting an external source of dissonance (between the membership and self-reference systems) for an internal one. This external source of dissonance results from the inconsistancy between his personal conviction and his outward behavior. But why should he opt to replace one inharmonious state for another? All other things being equal, a minister who is personally convinced by his self-reference system that he should take a stand against social injustice might well choose to disregard the views of his local congregation and the church hierarchy and wage an all-out fight for justice and social reform. But in actual practice all else is not equal and this is why we must consider the authority structure of the organized church.

### Authority Structure and Negative Sanctions

The authority structure of a religious organization is of singular significance in that it determines what group the minister is responsible to, and the way negative sanctions are meted out. With some oversimplification, three types of authority structures may be distinguished. In one structural arrangement, generally referred to as the congregational form of government polity, the minister derives his formal authority from the congregation. The hiring and firing of the minister is under the congregation's control and he remains directly responsible to that body. Under this arrangement, a minister's tenure of office closely depends on his continuing to function in a way which meets with the approval of the lay congregation. Just as Old Testament prophets incurred the wrath of many for making unpopular pronouncements, so ministers operating under this form of polity encounter opposition. Disapproval ranges from verbal warnings to outright dismissal.

The authority structure is somewhat different in the Presbyterian and Episcopalian polities. In the Episcopal Church authority flows from the highest offices down to the local congregation, while in the Presbyterian Church authority flows from middle-level "presbyteries" composed of both lay persons and clergy. In both of these forms of polity—in contrast to the congregational form—the minister's authority is derived from the church hierarchy rather than from the local congregation. In actual practice, this hierarchical structure serves as a buffer between the minister and his congregation. Consequently, if he chose to take a stand on some unpopular issue that would alienate his congregation, the risk of being dismissed is lessened since the congregation cannot act unilaterally. It must go through several channels and follow specified procedures before he can be removed.

With these safeguards in operation, it seems reasonable to expect ministers serving congregations that lack the power to hire and fire them, to display more boldness in pursuing a prophetic ministry. Indeed there is some evidence to support this line of reasoning. In his study of twenty-eight religious bodies, James Wood (1970) sought to determine the impact of church structure on the inclination of church leaders to push for strong integrationist policies. Wood found the integrationist policies of hierarchical organizations to be significantly stronger than those of nonhierarchical ones. While local ministers did not necessarily have a hand in formulating the organization's integrationist policies, Wood observed that they enjoyed the support of church leaders within the hierarchy when publicly affirming these policies.

In addition to looking at church polity, Wood also traced the relationship between a church's theology and its position on civil rights. Not surprisingly, conservative theology was negatively related to strong support for civil rights. It is noteworthy, however, that a positive relationship between church hierarchy and support for civil rights *persisted* within theologically conservative religious bodies.

While ministers may be more inclined to speak out on controversial issues when their authority flows from the church hierarchy, it would be naive to suppose that the statements and policies of church officials are not influenced by lay discontent. In the final analysis, the stability of the church organization rests on continued loyalty and financial support from church members. As Quinley (1974) observed in his study of California ministers who spoke out in opposition to an anti-open-housing amendment, members are quick to wage a pocketbook rebellion—even withdraw their membership—when they take offense at a position their minister has taken. For this reason, it is not surprising that organizational officials frequently advise their ministers to proceed slowly and cautiously when dealing with controversial issues (see Campbell and Pettigrew, 1959).

## Authority Structure and Positive Sanctions

Thus far we have seen how ministers who jeopardize organizational harmony and stability incur negative sanctions. However, it is also important to observe how positive sanctions serve to reward ministers who effectively accomplish organizational ends.

One overriding concern of many church organizations is numerical growth. In fact it is common to evaluate a minister's performance in terms of such growth. Since this is an important evaluative criterion, a minister quickly finds that there are numerous rewards which flow from working diligently at increasing church membership. These rewards are reflected in increased status and recognition, a larger parsonage, a higher salary and greater fringe benefits, additional staff, a more attractive church assignment, and upward mobility in the organization.

It is not hard to see how the close affiliation between church growth and reward may serve to inhibit the exercising of the minister's prophetic role. Out of a desire to "bring them in," they may be quick to point out the benefits and advantages of becoming a Christian and joining the fellowship. Key people may be selected to give testimonials of how Christ blessed their business or helped them attain wealth and recognition. The message, of course, may be quite genuine. But unless it also contains reference to suffering and sacrifice for the kingdom, it distorts the Gospel. The zeal to add to the fellowship may cause them to minimize the theme of Christian responsibility. Having brought new members into the church with the promise of personal comfort and gain, attendance-conscious leaders may be loath to promote the prophetic challenge of social responsibility and structural reform.

## Conclusion

To summarize these last three sections, theology, reference groups, and the authority structure all play a role in determining the extent of emphasis religious leaders place on the priestly and prophetic traditions. Their combined effect is to reduce the attention given to the prophetic role, while increasing the attention given to the priestly role. What should be the Christian response to social, political, and economic injustice? Let me suggest some important considerations as one seeks to decide his response.

Each of us will have to decide the extent to which the church must take a stand on issues involving unfair arrangements, immoral practices, and social injustice. We will have to decide when the church has a God-given mandate to "meddle" in the affairs of the world.

Christians who are aware of social injustice and convinced of their personal and corporate responsibility for reform should find this sociological research helpful. For it reveals the complexity of a social issue and the many variables that influence the decision-making process. But lest we judge inactive religious leaders too harshly, we must acknowledge our role. Prophetic leaders cannot lead unless they have willing and supportive followers. The ability of church leaders to responsibly relate God's love and justice to a needy world depends on the sincere and informed dedication of the laity. Are laypersons willing to follow their "prophetic" ministerial leadership? More specifically, are laypersons willing to urge them to take the lead in tackling knotty social problems, offering Christian solutions?

## Discussion Questions

1. In their study of Little Rock ministers, Campbell and Pettigrew distinguished between segregationist, inactive integrationist, and active integrationist ministers. Which camp do you suppose you would fall into under similar circumstances and why?

2. What kinds of social issues are Christians likely to find themselves divided over?

3. Under what circumstances might a minister (rightly or wrongly) be accused of meddling? Could such meddling ever be considered a God-given mandate? (In reflecting on this it may be helpful to recall the issue of Nazi harassment of Jews that confronted the German church in the years preceeding and during World War II or the issue of slavery that confronted the U.S. church prior to the Civil War.)

4. In what ways does your theology encompass a prophetic ministry? How does it influence your present behavior with respect to responsible action?

5. Is the author's contention that the contemporary church often emphasizes the priestly tradition at the expense of the prophetic tradition true of your experience? Explain.

6. What reference groups have had a part in shaping your Christian life? What dimensions of Christianity have they tended to emphasize?

7. Do you personally favor a hierarchical or a congregational form of church polity? What do you see as the particular strengths and weaknesses of each form?

8. To what extent is numerical growth taken as a measure of success in your local church or denomination? What are the consequences (manifest and latent) of using church growth as a criterion of success? Can you think of other indicators of success?

9. What are the implications of structuring the church as a voluntary organization? What are the implications of structuring it as an involuntary organization in which people have little choice but to belong?

10. It has been said that if the church is a club of selected members, it is the only club which has as its focus the welfare of nonmembers. To what extent is this true of your own experience?

## References

Campbell, Ernest Q. and Thomas F. Pettigrew
    1959 "Racial and Moral Crisis: The Role of Little Rock Ministers."
        *American Journal of Sociology*, 64 (March), pp. 509-516.
Hadden, Jeffrey K.
    1969 *The Gathering Storm in the Churches*. New York: Doubleday.
Hoge, Dean R.
    1976 *Division in the Protestant House*. Philadelphia: Westminster Press.
Johnstone, Ronald L.
    1975 *Religion and Society in Interaction: The Sociology of Religion*. Englewood Cliffs, N.J.: Prentice-Hall.
Lenski, Gerhard
    1961 *The Religious Factor: A Sociological Study of Religion's Impact on Politics, Economics, and Family Life*. New York: Doubleday.
Quinley, Harold E.
    1974 "The Dilemma of an Activist Church." *Journal for the Scientific Study of Religion*, 13 (March) pp. 1-21.
Stark, Rodney, Bruce D. Foster, Charles Y. Glock, and Harold E. Quinley
    1971 *Wayward Shepherds: Prejudice and the Protestant Clergy*. New York: Harper and Row.
Wood, James R.
    1970 "Authority and Controversial Policy: The Churches and Civil Rights." *American Sociological Review*, 35 (December), pp. 1057-1069.

# 37
# Jesus Our Healing Savior and the Sociology of Health

*Frederick C. Depp*

> And [Jesus] . . . went about all Galilee, teaching in their synagogues, and preaching the gospel of the kingdom, and healing all manner of sickness and all manner of disease among the people. (Matthew 4:23).

Each specific healing by our Lord was always meant to lead to a complete healing of the person. Thus teaching and preaching the gospel of the kingdom necessarily accompanied his healing all manner of sickness and disease.

The comprehensive approach of Jesus to healing is found expressed in his temple proclamation.

> The Spirit of the Lord is upon me, because he hath anointed me to preach the gospel to the poor; he hath sent me to heal the brokenhearted, to preach deliverance to the captives, and recovering of sight to the blind, to set at liberty them that are bruised (Luke 4:18).

## Reconciliation Underlies Healing

Healing in God's sight refers primarily to reconciliation between himself and the individual. Healing is necessary because man's sinfulness has resulted in his spiritual separation and isolation from God. Healing comes through Jesus, the Father's only provision for our reconciliation, the Lamb of God who made the one, perfect, and sufficient sacrifice of himself for the sins of the whole world. When man sur-

**Frederick C. Depp**
*Research Sociologist*
*St Elizabeths Hospital, Washington, D.C.*
Mr. Depp's research is in the area of social pyschiatry. He has also lectured and taught courses in the sociology of hospital/patient relationships and psychosocial environment of hospitals. Mr. Depp received his PhD in sociology from the University of Pennsylvania. He and his wife counsel together at the Shalom Biblical Counseling Center, Rockville, Md.

renders his life to God through the Messiah, Jesus Christ, and asks him to come into his heart and take over the direction of his life, profound healing begins. As John testifies, "He that hath the Son hath life; and he that hath not the Son of God hath not life" (1 John 5:12). The healing that begins through new life in Christ may occur simultaneously in body, soul, and spirit. All believers witness to the fact that they have experienced "new life" after being reconciled to God in Christ.

## God Desires Healing

God's loving intention to heal mankind is evident everywhere in the Scriptures. Morton T. Kelsey (1973:54) observes that nearly one fifth of the entire Gospel is devoted to Jesus' healing ministry and discussions related to it. The healing, reconciling, and restorative emphasis of Jesus' ministry is expressed well in Kelsey's statement (1973:53) that

> sometimes it is forgotten that medicine owes its greatest debt not to Hippocrates, but to Jesus. It was the humble Galilean who more than any other figure in history bequeathed to the healing arts their essential meaning and spirit. . . . Physicians would do well to remind themselves that without this spirit, medicine degenerates into depersonalized methodology and its ethical codes become a mere legal system. Jesus brings to methods and codes the corrective of love without which true healing is rarely actually possible. The spiritual "Father of Medicine" was not Hippocrates of the island of Cos, but Jesus of the town of Nazareth.

Therefore, Jesus is not only the necessary foundational presence within which all who practice the healing arts must work, but he brings into lives surrendered to his ways the assurance that " . . . with his stripes we are healed" (Isaiah 53:5). The sacrifice of Jesus the Christ has purchased for us eternal life—free from fear, sickness, and disease. We are healed because we have been forgiven for our sins and reconciled to the Father. We are healed because we are sealed by his Spirit. We are healed because Jesus gives us hope by bringing into our lives increasing evidence which confirms the new life we have inherited in him by faith—new life with more hope, faith, and love, and less fear, guilt, and doubt. These are the ingredients within which personal health in body, soul, and spirit flourish.

## The Sociology of Health

Given the light of the Gospel, what meaning do we find in a specialized area of human concern such as the sociology of health? What does the knowledge and wisdom of the Holy Spirit grounded in the Word of God show us about such an area of professional concern?

David Mechanic indicates that medical sociology, which usefully represents the issues and problems of the sociology of health " . . . is not a single fabric to be woven together, but rather a series of threads going in many directions at once" (1968:1). Thus, we note that natural understanding obtained by data from our sensory faculties suffers from theoretical and empirical incoherence. The Lord says " . . . my thoughts are not your thoughts, neither are your ways my ways . . . " (Isaiah 55:8). God's ways create a single fabric woven together, a seamless garment, while man's ways produce a series of threads going simultaneously in many directions. While we experience new-life and wholeness in Christ, complete freedom and deliverance will not be experienced until God makes all things new. "God shall wipe away all tears from their eyes; and there shall be no more death, neither sorrow, nor crying, neither shall there be any more pain: for the former things are passed away" (Revelation 21:4).

> Mechanic suggests that the basic perspective in medical sociology views much of human activity and the activity surrounding illness within an adaptive framework, and such behaviors are seen as aspects and reactions to situations where persons are actively struggling to control their environment and life situation (1968:2).

Using a Christian perspective one must note that God has called us first to love him and to love our brother—to cooperate and help one another. The Christian rejects the idea that we should struggle and compete with one another in life-situations. For as Paul says, " . . . though we walk in the flesh, we do not war after the flesh" (2 Corinthians 10:3). Nonetheless, we do acknowledge with the apostle Paul that we do struggle with demonic forces. Paul says, "We wrestle not against flesh and blood [the natural realm], but against principalities, against powers, against the rulers of the darkness of this world, against spiritual wickedness in high places" (Ephesians 6:12).

## Illness as Opportunity

The Christian is encouraged to stand on the truth of God's Word. His principles encourage the Christian to rest in God's love confident that nothing shall separate him from the love of Christ, neither " . . .

tribulation, or distress, or persecution, or famine, or nakedness, or peril, or sword" (Romans 8:35). Clearly, sickness, disease, plague, and chronic lifelong disability must be understood within the promise of Romans 8:35. When we live in this promise by faith we experience its reality. We know the Spirit's presence and find the hindrances of ill health transformed mysteriously into benefits. Illness often develops new strengths of character with new opportunity to experience the grace of God, and testify to the sustaining grace of God (2 Corinthians 12:9). Often illness, sickness, and disability are an opportunity for God to work within us the precious fruits of his Spirit— "love, joy, peace, longsuffering, gentleness, goodness, faith, meekness, and temperance" (Galatians 5:22, 23), further replacing our Adamic natures with his nature.

Often illness and disability are opportunities for God to show us areas within our lives in serious need of inner healing. Unforgiveness and resentment, life-dominating problems of addiction to drugs, alcohol, or other deeply rooted sin patterns usually lead to psychological or physical ill health, or both. Prayerfully considered, God will open our understanding and permit us to discern our own needs and the needs of others. On the other hand, the sociology of health focuses on limited aspects of man's condition and is unable to consider the unlimited need of man for God. While the sociology of health captures certain specific consequences and symptoms of man's problems (e.g., heart disease, stroke, hypertension, cancer, mental illness), it fails to grasp the essential ground from which such life problems spring, e.g., covetousness, adultery, self-centeredness, hatred, and the lusts of the flesh (Galatians 5:19-21).

### Contrasting Views of Health and Illness

The sociology of health relies to a significant extent on the conceptual framework used in theories of deviance. From these perspectives the ill and the disabled may be understood in part as "deviant" persons, different from the normal or "healthy" according to whatever defining criteria one applies. For example, one may consider a person deviant because we see him using aids, such as a wheelchair or Seeing Eye dog, or we may observe symptoms such as a body temperature of 103 degrees, or by noting assigned labels such as "schizophrenic." All of these evoke particular patterns of expectations, attitudes, and behavioral responses from others.

However, from a Christian perspective it is important to recognize the relativism implicit in such theorizing about those labeled as disabled or in ill health. For example, the evangelical Christian views homosexuality as a sin, not as an "alternate life-style" as many have come to view it in our rapidly changing society. In Jay Adam's words (1973:191-216), it is a "life-dominating problem." It will never change its character before God. God has condemned it in the Scriptures and he is unchanging, in him there " . . . is no variableness, neither shadow of turning" (James 1:17).

While sociology documents the fact that in contemporary American society what is regarded as deviant behavior may change by societal consensus and gain widespread acceptance and legitimation, the Christian does not alter his standards in response to the latest Gallup or Harris poll. He must " . . . hold fast that which is good" (1 Thessalonians 5:21) and, if necessary, he himself accept the label of deviant because of his resistance to such "progress." Only by holding fast to biblical standards can we properly identify such human needs for healing when these are being redefined by society. Paul Tournier (1965:131) confirms this principle when describing a successful treatment of a woman with lesbian tendencies. He indicates "if medicine is inspired by the desire to know and obey God's will, it will aim at making women real women and men really men."

There are other major aspects of the tension between Christian sociologists who hold to a faithful biblical perspective on social life and the majority of sociologists who subscribe to a secular humanistic view. These aspects can be illustrated in the sociology of health. By examining these tensions, we can see at least two reasons why the secular sociologists' study of social life does not fit neatly together with God's Word. First, man's scientific methods do not easily embrace important scriptural truths for operational study. Second, and more important, modes of explanation and interpretation often are applied which are contrary to the Word of God. McKay calls such explanations and interpretations "philosophical parasites" (1974:52), since these often cling to, distort, and obscure valid natural observations of the creation.

*Flesh and Spirit*

With reference to the problem of method, consider the depth of biblical meaning given to pivotal constructs such as faith, man's heart, man's soul, God's mercy, and God's glory. Can the methods of science begin to plumb the significance, power, and mystery in these central dimensions of the God-man relation operative moment by moment in our lives? I think not. These irreducible terms are converted frequently with some minimal usefulness to uninspired and dimly equivalent notions, thus giving us belief *for* faith, caring *for* heart, and psychological mechanisms or feelings *for* soul. However, the latter terms are unique, divinely inspired. They do not issue from the mind of man and, therefore, cannot be consensually assigned true operational referents.

Because of this tension between the natural and the spiritual, Peter Berger (1967:3-28) believes one must opt for "methodological atheism." That is, one ought to exclude deliberately from scientific study any transcendent conceptions with nonempirical referents. The alternative would be to relax one's scientific frame to allow inclusion of nonempirical categories. Unfortunately, by doing so one loses the scientific object of address, thus vitiating this apparent solution. The problem of method is certainly a vexing one that has troubled sociology since its inception, with many opting against the positivist position. Pitirim Sorokin, for example, comes close to an acceptance of spiritual realities in social life when suggesting " . . . only through direct empathy can one grasp the essential nature and difference between a criminal gang and a fighting battalion; between a harmonious and a broken family" (1956:160).

The ideological content of interpretation in explanation is also fraught with problems. Consider Freud's attack upon the God-man relation in *The Future of an Illusion* (1975). In this work he argues that the primary indicator of progress and health for modern man is to be found in his reduced adherence and personal commitment to systems of religious belief. Contemporary variants of Freud's philosophy and other "Enlightenment" theories operating in lives estranged from the living God must be clearly identified so that the hope of Christ can be presented in their place. Without this hope, there will only be secular-humanistic principles of living founded on satisfying the self-centered desires of man.

One frightening possible outcome of a monolithic secular-humanistic system of explanation and interpretation for man's social relations is that it may further stimulate immoral behavior. The end result of this would be explanations that are increasingly congruent and plausible, that take the form of a self-fulfilling prophecy. Using a simple example, if man chooses to believe his behavior is not subject to the life-giving influence of God's Spirit, then he will believe that he is influenced either by his own human desires or by demonic influences—and he will be. Such "modern-day" rejections of God were expressed in New Testament times by Jude, who referred to those who " . . . know naturally, as brute beasts" (Jude 1:10) and by Paul in Romans, where he said " . . . professing themselves to be wise, they became fools . . . [changing] . . . the truth of God into a lie [they] . . . worshipped and served the creature more than the Creator . . . without understanding" (Romans 1:22, 25, 31).

Sensitive to these modern tendencies of thought, Rene Dubos writes pessimistically:

> Western man may rediscover wisdom in Plato's social philosophy when the world becomes crowded with aged, invalid and defective people (1961:214).

Jacques Ellul (1973:124) believes man has taken upon himself so much of this kind of false "wisdom" in the modern age that

> God who has let himself be put to death in Christ, withdraws himself into his discreetness before the absence of love, the absence of filial relations, the absence of trust, the absence of self-discipline, the absence of freedom, the absence of authenticity. God makes himself absent in this world of absences, which modern man has put together with enthusiasm. Man certainly has not killed God, but in creating this world of absence for himself he has brought about the discreetness of God, which is expressed in his turning away.

## Applying Biblical Truths

One can examine Ellul's notion of man absenting himself from God within the sociology of health. R. K. and P. A. Jones, following Rodney Coe (1975:163) divide this subject into a number of areas of interest and investigation. One area refers to the patterned distribution of diseases and illnesses by social groupings. For example Jackson and Holmes found a relationship between alcoholism and tuberculosis (1960:175). They observed that certain relationships were present in the lives of tubercular alcoholics preceding onset which are not present in nontubercular alcoholics. These life factors can be profitably subjected to scriptural examination to check Ellul's notion.

For example, prior to the onset of tuberculosis, the Joneses found tubercular alcoholics were more anxious, felt that their condition was more hopeless, and they were more withdrawn from others. Compared to their alcoholic cohort, the authors suggest that these persons put themselves in a position of reduced resistance to the disease. From a spiritual perspective, we might say that they placed themselves further from the reach and embrace of God. But we know that "God hath not given us the spirit of fear; but of power, and of love, and of a sound mind" (2 Timothy 1:7). As Christians, we know that the prescription for fear—now called by the euphemism anxiety—is God's power and love. Hopelessness needs to be cast out and hope engendered with the kind of assurance found through faith in God's power to sustain one (1 Corinthians 10:13). Those who are withdrawn need to be surrounded with the love and concern found in the community of God's people.

The authors further describe these alcoholics as fiercely independent. In scriptural terms this is clearly understood as a problem of pride and rebellion, a common sin which has been allowed to grow to very serious proportions. The important point in this examination of Jackson and Holmes' work is that one can bring to bear scriptural truths on the study of human behavior in order to allow assessment of methods of study and theoretical assumptions. In addition, if called to intervene personally, one would then have the effective scriptural approach for ministry—whether to an alcoholic, a tubercular patient, or a tubercular alcoholic. Observing man's health problems, both individual and corporate and using the power and wisdom of God's Spirit to illuminate God's Word, one can increasingly discern the spiritual meanings in these human needs.

### Healing Only Slightly

One major aspect of the sociology of health focuses on the institutions man has erected to treat ill health and disease. Many of these institutions bear testimony to the consequences of secularized perceptions and collective responses to human needs apart from scriptural understanding. How often we see an illness or disease process which is principally rooted in the need for salvation, a need for surrender to God in his Christ! And how often is that need incorrectly identified in our day as one that requires institutional intervention. This barely ameliorates the real human need. "They have healed also the hurt of the daughter of my people slightly, saying, Peace, peace; when there is no peace" (Jeremiah 6:14). As C.S. Lewis says, "God whispers to us in our pleasures, speaks in our conscience, but shouts in our pains: it is his megaphone to rouse a deaf world" (1945:81).

## What Then Shall We Do?

For us, every theory and conceptual understanding of disease and ill health must seek to define problem elements and the most effective responses related to the God-man relationship. When we take this assumption seriously we become profoundly sociological because the God-man relationship underlies and informs all human relationships, no matter what their character or nature. As Lewis (1945:17) puts it:

> . . . being Christians, we learn from the doctrine of the Blessed Trinity that something analogous to "society" exists within the Divine being from all eternity . . . within Him, the concrete reciprocities of love exist before all worlds and are thence derived to the creatures.

### Sacralizing, Not Secularizing

For this reason, a believer in Christ is in the best position to pursue a sociological understanding of health. This is not arrogance, but simply the product of deductive reasoning. We begin with who God is, who we are, and what Scripture tells us about the sources of health, illness, and disease. In Tournier's words, "One cannot tend the body without tending the mind and the spirit. There is no physical reform possible without moral reform. And there is no moral reform without spiritual renewal" (1965:63). In other words, we are being called or drawn by the Spirit to sacralize our professional lives, not secularize them. As sacralists we affirm that there are absolutes which govern man's existence, that accident and random occurrence do not regulate our lives, and that our choices are embedded in God's plan and purpose for this world he has created. We affirm the personhood of God and his separateness from the creation. We also affirm the propositional truth of the Scriptures and the great gift of salvation he has given us in Christ Jesus our Lord. As sacralists, we seek to live against "the fate of our times" which Max Weber says (Gerth and Mills, 1958:155) is

> . . . characterized by rationalization and intellectualization and above all, by the "disenchantment" of the world. Precisely the ultimate and most sublime values have retreated from public life either into the transcendental realm of mystic life or into the brotherliness of direct and personal human relations.

*Jesus at the Center*

As sociologists in the health field we do this in a number of ways, some of which we have already discussed. Most importantly, we do this by testifying in our lives and in our work to the full truth about health and illness: that the God-man relationship is foundational. Illness and disease have spiritual meaning. All point to the Creator and our high priest, Jesus. He must be the one at the center of our thoughts, words, and actions in the health field if the whole person is to have profound and valid health. There is a difference between ministering Christ's love and merely "providing health care". As Mother Teresa of Calcutta has said, "If our actions are just useful actions that give no joy to the people, our poor people would never be able to rise up to the call which we want them to hear, the call to come to God" (Muggeridge, 1971:78).

Tournier (1965:127) also emphasizes the need to assess the spiritual when considering the limitations of science evident in the anatomical method used to evaluate medical problems. He says:

> It is true (the method) in what it affirms but false in what it denies. When, for example, it shows that the symptoms of locomotor ataxia are always accompanied by anatomical lesions of the posterior columns of the spinal cord, it is revealing a true causal relationship. But if it illegitimately goes on from there to deny that a spiritual fact, such as rebellion against God, can have any material, anatomical or physiological consequences on the body, it is denying another causal relationship which is no less true.

Similarly, the anatomical method does not capture many positive spiritual dimensions of man's existence. For example, it does not address Mother Teresa's joy nor the other fruits of the Spirit which support life in its fullness, a fullness which can be experienced whether in affluent America or the slums of Calcutta.

*In the World, But Not of It*

Howard E. Freeman, *et. al.* (1963:479-484), in summarizing the status of medical sociology some years ago addressed the difference in perspective between a medically trained practitioner and a sociologist in the same setting. Similarly, Christian sociologists must also expect to experience tensions in explanation and understanding because our perspective is different from the secular medical sociologists for whom Jesus is not the source of life, hope, and sustenance. Because Christ is at the center for us, our witness should joyfully and clearly affirm that all healing comes from God. Francis MacNutt, a Roman Catholic priest, who has been especially called to the ministry of healing, says:

> The ideal it seems to me, would be when we reach a time when doctors, counselors and psychiatrists would—as some already do—pray for the patients that God might do what they cannot do, or even that God might perform that same kind of cure that medical science can provide, but in a more perfect, more speedy, and less expensive way (1974:274).

As sacralists we must pray for such prayerful interventions and affirm, in contrast to secular-humanists, that the God-man relationship is always present. There is no actual line separating the sacred from the profane. For as the psalmist declares:

> Whither shall I go from thy spirit? or whither shall I flee from thy presence? If I ascend up into heaven, thou art there: if I make my bed in hell, behold, thou art there (Psalm 139:7, 8).

Malcolm Muggeridge expressed it in his account of Mother Teresa's lifework, "either life is always and in all circumstances sacred, or intrinsically of no account; it is inconceivable that it should be in some cases the one, and in some the other" (1971:16).

## The Christian Response

As believers we must apply this orientation when interpreting the variety of differences in the way social factors affect health, illness, and disease. For example, some are indifferent and calloused to certain social groups that have unusually high rates of infant mortality. Too few medical personnel and medical care facilities are accessible to the urban and rural poor. This may mean that those in professional roles are deaf or unresponsive to God's call to service in such areas, areas that call for real sacrifices.

On the other hand, the high infant mortality rate may be explained in other ways. Pregnant women who face a high risk of losing their child may neglect their prenatal care, even with available resources and knowledge. Furthermore, they may be hesitant to seek out appropriate assistance for cultural or other reasons. Regardless of what the reasons may be, we can be sure that if expectant mothers lived by scriptural principles, the infant mortality rate would be drastically reduced.

While the state or federal government can advocate salary bonuses to attract medical personnel to areas of high infant mortality, as Christians we can do more. We can accept the challenge and call to work in deprived areas. In addition, those who work with clients in need can intercede for them in prayer. Furthermore, we can, if so led by the Spirit of God, move personally and corporately to seek redress and constructive change.

It is important that Christian sociologists who are involved in efforts to improve health care realize that, in every instance, our attempts to measure and explain change will always be only partially successful. This is the reason why social scientists speak of "unexplained variance" in their data. However, if they attribute it solely to our corporate ignorance of the phenomenon or to our primitive methodologies, they are neglecting to account for the workings of God's Spirit, who mercifully intervenes for us in our daily affairs.

He is sovereign. He cannot be totally understood nor "explained." He is at work among us and in us as our creative and life-sustaining God. As Jeremiah said, "Behold, as the clay is in the potter's hand, so are ye in mine hand, O house of Israel" (Jeremiah 18:6).

When we recognize that we are in his compassionate hands, then our joy is full and our hope strengthened and renewed. Those without such hope suffer a distressing kind of pervasive demoralization. Jerome Frank, a prominent psychiatrist, believes "the chief problem of all patients who come to psychotherapy is demoralization" (1974:217). He defines demoralization as "a state of mind which ... results from persistent failure to cope with internally or externally induced stresses." Frank suggests its primary characteristics are feelings of impotence, isolation, and despair.

In our broken world, the Gospel message we bring is called Good News. How many of the patients who have lost hope, or more correctly, have come to recognize the sinfulness and hopelessness of our earthly condition, hear the Good News in psychotherapy? Not many. A false hope is often given, a hope that does not sustain life or radically infuse it with God's love. Only his love is capable of neutralizing the despair, isolation, and impotence Frank emphasizes. Francis Schaeffer, in *The God Who is There*, describes modern man without faith as "under the line of despair" (1968:15). That is, he now lives without the previous optimism found in twentieth century rationalism, a belief system intent on building a world-view outward from man apart from God.

### "Take Off the Roof"

Schaeffer views the Christian witness to modern man as one that requires us to "take the roof off," exposing his purposelessness and sense of despair because of the emptiness or sterility of his basic assumptions for living. Then the Gospel can be presented, as always, as a message of salvation and new life.

We must fashion a variant of Schaeffer's message for modern man in the field of health. Patients, clients, social workers, general practitioners, and fellow sociologists must be more effectively reached with the Gospel. We must begin with the present inadequacies of our interventions—be they medical, psychological, or social. We must "take the roof off" in the sociology of health, laying bare empty assumptions that do not lead to healing, and methods of understanding that neither accord with God's truths about the human condition nor lead men to Christ the Savior.

In the depths of every human heart there is an unarticulated yearning for God, to know him, to serve him, and to follow him. There is also a knowledge of sin and a consequent guilt before him. As Christians working in the health field, we must get on with the work of the kingdom, proclaiming that our Redeemer lives to forgive sin and relieve guilt!

Max Weber feared for man's spirit in the twentieth century. He saw man constructing methods and means of organizing his existence that would place him in a cage, constrained, deprived of his potentialities, and deformed in his spirit.

Coe's (1970:236) description of the differences between early Christian hospitals in the Middle Ages and those found in secularized Renaissance hospitals confirms Weber's fear. Coe declares:

> The service in-the-name-of-salvation motif which characterized the medieval hospital at its best had become transmuted to a duty of welfare care, grudgingly accepted by the state and community.

### He Is Lord

The Christian sociologist, as well as those working in health and social services, must resist such contemporary tendencies by an explicit commitment to Jesus Christ as Savior and Lord. We must strive to harmonize our sociological and professional thinking with the eternal Word of God, whether of method or explanation. By doing this we will proclaim the central objective of the sociology of health, and all other human enterprise, to be the lifting up of Jesus as Lord and Savior of all creation.

## Discussion Questions

1. What sociological constructs refer to the separation between man and God? Which of these have importance for the sociology of health? Why?

2. In what ways do a biblical perspective highlight the false optimism found in secular-humanist assumptions about health and illness?

3. Consider the health care-giving system in your community. In what ways does this system express our Lord's concern for the healing of the whole person? In what ways does it not?

4. Do you believe sociological research is possible on the spiritual aspects of health and illness? Why? Why not?

5. Choose a medical problem with sociological dimensions. Can you see new aspects of this problem: causes, correlates, and consequences by using a biblical perspective with Jesus at the center? How might you change the socially approved interventions for this medical problem from a biblical perspective?

6. In what specific health problems is the relation between sin and illness or disease relatively easy to discern? In which is it more difficult? Can you account for the differences in ease or difficulty of identification?

7. How does the call to be a sacralist and not a secular-humanist present itself in your current life situation, especially in the study of sociology and other academic subjects?

8. Where would you begin to "take the roof off" in the sociology of health to effectively bring the Good News to health care workers? How would you as a health care worker do this in your work?

9. How does Frank's idea of man's demoralization tie in with the biblical perspective of man's natural condition? How does the Gospel speak to man's need?

10. What are the problems and advantages in reconceptualizing health primarily in terms of man's reconciliation to God through the new birth and growth in Christ through active participation in a Christian community?

# References

Adams, Jay
> 1973 *The Christian Counselor's Manual*. Nutley, N.J.: Presbyterian and Reformed Publishing Co.

Berger, Peter L.
> 1967 *The Sacred Canopy*. New York: Doubleday.

Coe, Rodney
> 1970 *Sociology of Medicine*. New York: McGraw-Hill.

Dubos, Rene
> 1961 *Mirage of Health*. New York: Doubleday.

Ellul, Jacques
> 1973 *Hope in Time of Abandonment*. New York: Seabury Press.

Frank, Jerome
> 1974 "Psychotherapy: The Restoration of Morale." *American Journal of Psychiatry*, 131, pp. 271-274.

Freeman, Howard E., Sol Levine, and Leo G. Reeder (eds.)
> 1963 "Present Status of Medical Sociology," in *Handbook of Medical Sociology*. Englewood Cliffs, N.J.: Prentice-Hall, pp. 479-484.

Freud, Sigmund
> 1975 *The Future of an Illusion*. New York: W. W. Norton.

Jackson, Joan K. and Thomas H. Holmes
> 1960 "Alcoholism and Tuberculosis" (ed. by Dorrian Apple) in *Sociological Studies of Health and Sickness*. New York: McGraw-Hill, pp. 179-185.

Jones, R. K. and P. A. Jones
> 1975 *Sociology in Medicine,* New York: Wiley.

Kelsey, Morton T.
> 1973 *Healing and Christianity: In Ancient Thought and Modern · Times*. New York: Harper and Row.

Lewis, C. S.
> 1945 *The Problem of Pain*. New York: Macmillan.

MacNutt, Francis
> 1974 *Healing*. Notre Dame, Ind.: Ave Maria.

McKay, Donald M.
> 1974 *The Clockwork Image: A Christian Perspective on Science*. Downers Grove, Ill.: InterVarsity Press.

Mechanic, David
> 1968 *Medical Sociology: A Selective View*. New York: Free Press.

Muggeridge, Malcolm
> 1971 *Something Beautiful for God: Mother Teresa of Calcutta*. New York: Ballantine Books.

Schaeffer, Francis A.
> 1968 *The God Who Is There*. Downers Grove, Ill.: InterVarsity Press.

Simmons, Leo W. and Harold G. Wolff
    1954 *Social Science in Medicine.* New York: Russell Sage.
Sorokin, Pitirim A.
    1956 *Fads and Foibles in Modern Sociology and Related Sciences.*
        Chicago, Ill.: Regnery.
Tournier, Paul
    1965 *The Healing of Persons.* New York: Harper and Row, 1965.
Weber, Max
    1958 "Science as a Vocation" (ed. by H. H. Gerth and C. Wright
        Mills), in *From Max Weber: Essays in Sociology.* New York:
        Oxford University Press, pp. 129-156.

# PART VII

# SOCIAL CHANGE

# SOCIAL CHANGE

Is it "change and decay in all around I see," or "change with its challenge all around I see"? Is change a near constant, a near absolute? It is a fact of human experience and history that change is inevitable. No society, however "primitive" or "static," is exempt from it. This is evident to all who are even superficially familiar with biblical and secular history. Two popular books that deal with past and future change would help you see this more clearly. (1) In his brief, insightful book, *The Ordeal of Change*, Eric Hoffer gives a historical overview of the significant material and ideological innovations that have influenced the course of human history. (2) In a somewhat longer, but equally fascinating book, *Future Shock*, Alvin Toffler authenticates the fact that most of the phenomenal changes have really occurred during this century—and there is every indication that the rate of change will continue.

Of course, as a student living in the last quarter of the twentieth century, you are undoubtedly aware of many of these changes. In the previous sections of this reader we have really been dealing with this fact as it touches many aspects of human interaction and culture. For example, many writers have referred to Marx's ideas. One of the criticisms of Marx is that he ignored the very dialectical method of interpreting history that he employed. He expected the so-called dictatorship of the proletariat to usher in a classless society that would also produce a new man—free, humane, unalienated, and cooperative. Man would be free of his competitive and conflicting spirit. Once he progressed to this level man would live harmoniously. But if Marx had been consistent with his dialectic method, he would have envisioned his "utopian" state being surpassed. In actuality, his thought has been modified in many ways. Revisionism is inevitable, despite the protestations of orthodoxy. In a very real sense, change is a constant—we are always in the process of becoming.

Unfortunately religion has often been a reactionary conservative force in society. In many ways this has been functional, as many changes are premature and precipitous. As Alfred North Whitehead said, "All change is not necessarily progress." Nonetheless, for the most part the rear guard action of religion has been dysfunctional to the realization of social and economic justice. Too often this has meant a defense of unscrupulous and unethical political and economic practices that have been used to oppress and exploit people. Too often the church has taken a stand or position that proved to be diametrically opposite to that of the Old Testament prophets and Christ. Several authors in this reader have suggested religious groups that have identified with Christ's teachings by taking a stand for social and economic justice. (If you are a practicing religious person, you know of programs your denomination has undertaken in this area of service.) Donald Kraybill, you may recall, insists that Christ's ministry was specifically directed toward the needs of the poor. Therefore, to identify with Christ is to identify with all those forces that work constructively for justice.

In this last section David Lyon examines in some detail the concept of social change by evaluating three prominent theories: the *modernization theory* of Daniel Lerner, the *class-conflict theory* of Karl Marx, and the *postindustrial theory* of Daniel Bell. While he sees each possessing valid insights into the factors or variables that bring about change, he finds them all wanting. In addition to his careful, incisive critique, he raises questions and makes suggestions that should enable the Christian student to formulate basic principles to evaluate other theories of social change.

C. Emory Burton points up the inevitability of social change. From a biblical perspective he presents God as one who reveals his nature through his activity in history—through change. Furthermore, the kingdom of God that Christ inaugurated is always in the process of becoming. Christians have the privilege and responsibility of allowing God to rule through them—*i.e.*, work through them to bring the kingdom in.

William H. Swatos' article deals with "Violence, Revolution, and the Christian." He discusses the positions the church has taken toward violence, as well as the fact that the church has often perpetrated violence. Because of man's fallen nature, he sees violence as something humans must live with, but also as something which can be restrained. He sees man's hope for the present and the future in the redemption that Christ has provided. Violence and revolution seldom achieve the intended goal. The alternative is to practice justice and make them unnecessary.

# 38
# Social Change and Utopia: Evaluating Modernization, Marxism, and Post-Industrialism[1]

*David Lyon*

In the contemporary world, history has overtaken itself, and people strain to look into the future. E. H. Carr put it like this: "Modern man peers eagerly back into the twilight out of which he has come, in the hope that its faint beams will illuminate the obscurity into which he is going" (1951:2). Social change in the nineteenth century appeared to be so rapid that history, the previously used means of accounting for it, could not cope: sociology had to be invented. One of its major inventors, Auguste Comte, was clear about the purpose of the new discipline. It was *voir pour prévoir* (to see in order to foresee) and *prévoir prévenir* (to foresee in order to anticipate).

Sociology, for Comte, had both a cognitive and a normative purpose. That is, he believed that an accurate understanding of the times ought to be yoked with a desire to anticipate and actively influence the future. Even though this worthy aim was not realized by Comte, it has not diminished sociologists' zeal to attempt similar projects. Today, and from a very different perspective from Comte, critical theorists also attempt a marriage between social analysis and some conception of the good society (Connerton, 1976).[2]

**David Lyon**
*Senior Lecturer*
*Ilkley College, Yorkshire, England*
Although David Lyon has lectured at Wilfrid Laurier University in Ontario (1976-77), he is an English sociologist with degrees in history literature (BSc) and sociology/history (PhD) from the University of Bradford. The author has written in the areas of Marxism and Christianity. His interests also include secularization theories, social change, and the Christian understanding of religion. Mr. Lyon is an elder in the Pollard Park Evangelical Church, a non-denominational congregation.

We shall argue here that such a procedure is not only inevitable, but necessary and desirable from a Christian point of view. The analysis of social change, which is our specific topic, always involves evaluation. The criteria of evaluation are derived from the sociologist's view of the good society. And even if the ideal society is located in the past,[3] it is often assumed that features of that society may be incorporated in the society of the future. But something else is going on at the same time. The sociologist is also weighing empirical evidence in order to ascertain whether or not *change* has in fact occurred. Both these issues—the empirical adequacy of change theories and the nature of their inbuilt "utopias"—are discussed here.

We shall examine three kinds of change theory. They also relate to different *stages* of history. They are as follows: (1) modernization (a variant of industrialization) which focuses on the shift from "traditional" (preindustrial) to "modern" society; (2) Marxism, which highlights the nature and crises of capitalist society; (3) and lastly, postindustrialism, the idea that advanced societies are entering a new phase—the service society. With each, we ask questions about both the consistency and use of evidence and the plausibility of the theory, as well as its future orientation or utopia. But our preliminary task is the justification of our own criteria.

### Issachar and History

The idea that the Christian community ought to know the significance of what is going on in public affairs finds firm rooting in the Scriptures. The need to understand history, which includes social change, is a common biblical theme. At the crucial moment at which David, king of Israel, took over the throne from Saul we are told of the men of Issachar. These men within his court "understood the times, with a knowledge of what Israel should do."[4]

The whole Christian message is grounded in history, and in a sense of history. Knowledge of the causes, channels, and consequences of change serve as a guide to worthwhile action. The Hebrew passover, for example, was not only a reenactment of past events, but also a guide to modes of action. The memory of the course of change was bound up with action in the present. Because the Israelites, who were aliens in Egypt, were liberated from oppression, they were commanded to treat aliens within their borders in a nonoppressive way (Exodus 23:9). Likewise, the Lord's Supper allows believers to participate in a historical event which looks back to the cross and points forward to the coming of the fullness of the kingdom. This interim meal reminds Christians of the ongoing presence of the living Christ, motivates action, and instills fresh hope of things to come. Past, present, and future all have strong significance for Christian commitment.

But how does the Christian scholar discern the times, especially when there is such a range of apparently plausible sociologies of change available? Nicholas Wolterstorff (1976) argues that the belief-content of authentic Christian commitment ought to be allowed to guide[5] the weighing or assessing, and devising of theories. The Christian scholar is a Christ-follower, living in a community of fellow-believers whose everyday life and world-view is shaped by the authoritative Word of God. Christians are, among other things, witnesses of the biblical teaching that events are the activities of God, agents of the coming kingdom, and evidences of what life in the new order might be like. Thus all change is seen as something that has meaning external to it; that is, in relation to God and his kingdom. It is a process in which Christians are involved as participants in each generation.

### History: A Christian View

Thus there are views of history, and social change in particular, that are quite compatible with Christian believing. Others are either less compatible or quite inconsistent. One Christian historian has argued that elements in a Christian understanding of history might include the following: time as past-present-future, periodization, history as a directional process of events, the universality of history, human beings as its makers, and its meaningfulness (MacIntire, 1974). These are useful tools with which to evaluate theories of social change.

The very concept of social change must involve some historical judgment that things social have come to be what they previously were not. To speak of social change at all, the past-present-future scheme must be assumed. The Greek notion of timeless permanence as the backdrop to the human context of change is not compatible with Christian beliefs. The Christian scheme involves past events (like the Last Supper) as different from present events (like the church celebrating the Lord's Supper) and from future events ("the marriage supper of the Lamb"). But this does not mean that Christians believe in the inevitability of progress. Some things may improve, others may get worse. For example, general human progress, as Herbert Spencer envisaged it, is another notion incompatible with Christian commitment. The directional process towards the *eschaton* ("last things"—the final triumph of God in Christ) in no way implies human progress is automatic. Moreover, there is nothing in the historical process itself which determines the future. Historicism asserts that the meaning of history resides in the historical process itself; either in the triumphant destiny of human knowledge (Comte) or the liberation of the proletariat (Marx). This absolutising of history, as Dooyeweerd (1960) might describe it, denies that there is meaning given external to history, denies that absolute truth is possible, and provides an alternative to Christian belief. Thus the Christian rejects the idea that social change is part of a predetermined pattern of events outside human control.

There is, of course, a strong sense in which God is both the sovereign controller of history and the one who gives it meaning. But this is at the same time an affirmation of human responsibility before God. For human beings have been given the task of both opening up the creation (Genesis 1:28) and proclaiming and acting upon the Gospel of the kingdom (Matthew 28:18-20; 22:39). They are responsible to God to make history in a manner consistent with the creation, the kingdom, and the work of the Lord Jesus Christ. Nor is this task limited to one section of humanity. All ethnic, sexual, and economic barriers have been in principle broken down in Christ. Any theory of social change which discriminates or militates against the full development of the whole world, in all social sectors and for both sexes, cannot be reconciled with Christian beliefs. This Good News is for all creation (Mark 16:15).

Thus, we may sketch some of the parameters of the Christian understanding of social change. It occurs in time, refers to historical events, and has to do with (social) movements which result in different patterns (of social behavior) from before. All is not flux, neither is all persistence. Some things persist, others change. A working definition of social change, that seems compatible with what we have said about history, has been provided by Anthony Smith (1976:13): "a succession of events which produce over time a modification or replacement of particular patterns or units by other novel ones." But this is merely a definition of social change. Our task is to evaluate theories of social change. For this, Smith's definition must be fleshed out with reference to particular theorists. But first, we glance at the question of a guiding ethic, or utopia.

**Where There Is No Vision . . .**

We have said that an accurate understanding of the times ought to be yoked to some conception of the good society. In Christian terms, this utopian vision[6] may be summed up in the biblical word *shalom*. The proverb asserts that "where there is no vision, the people perish" (Proverbs 29:18, KJV). The reference is to viewing the future in the perspective of God's revealed lifeways for humankind. Without this, all simply do what is right in their own eyes. *Shalom* is the biblical vision of wholeness of relationships—both between God and persons, and between persons. The creation account, as much as the future kingdom, gives indications of its nature (Lyon, 1979b). It is the direction in which the whole creation is finally heading—the full realization of the kingdom of God.

One important warning. *Shalom* as a sociopolitical utopian vision differs from other utopias in at least two important respects. For one thing, it is not brought about by unaided human effort: rather, it can be realized only as people cooperate in God's purposes. Second, because *shalom* is an eschatological expectation, it is "realizable only imperfectibly in the here and now" (Gillett, 1976:84). The turn-of-the-century advocates of the "social gospel" made the fatal mistake of identifying the kingdom of God (shalom) with some humanly perfectible society. This is no different from the Marxist hope of ushering in "human" society by means of revolution. It is constrained, and doomed never to be realized because of human finitude and sinfulness.

It may be objected that social change theories imply no utopia, no future vision. But we shall argue that this argument is difficult to sustain. For sociologists are themselves inescapably bound up in the process of social change. They are both molded by it and desire particular directions for it. Our ideas of what ought to happen are intertwined with assumptions about what has, will, and can happen. Whether or not it is acknowledged, social research serves certain ends. This becomes all the more evident with regard to anticipating social change (Winthrop, 1968). Thus it is important to isolate the purposes guiding the thought of each social theorist, including our own. (Strasser (1976) has called these the "guiding interests of cognition.") This is what it means to be "reflexive," for a sociology to be "self-conscious."

True, there once was a time (epitomized in the intended contrasts of Engels' book title, *Socialism: Utopian and Scientific*) when science and utopia were thought to be incommensurate. But that age of epistemological innocence is almost past. As Tom Kitwood has argued, "The consequence need not be a despair of science, or a relapse into sub-jectivism, but simply the recognition that all theories, even those which are highly effective or intuitively satisfying or complete, are not strictly determined by empirical data . . . theories are not so much 'true' in an absolute sense, as effective, for certain purposes" (1978). All theories are directed inescapably towards certain purposes.

## Utopian Imagination

What then might Christian commitment contribute to a utopian imagination? José Míguez Bonino (following Gutierrez) has argued that faith stirs utopian imagination by pushing towards the kingdom of peace and justice. The vision of a truly human society is put before us, which human scientists may analyze and project in concrete ways. A genuine basis for hope is given in the promises of God and the resurrec-tion of Christ. But there is also a sober expectation of conflict: the kingdom cannot be fully realized until finally ushered in by Christ. One consequence of this is that there can be no "suspension of ethics"—no human class, group, or generation can be considered as merely instru-mental in the struggle for a new society (Míguez, 1976:129). To these aspects one might add that the creation patterns are also highly rele-vant to the utopian vision. The kingdom is, in a significant sense, the realization of creation possibilities (Lyon, 1979b).

All this is nothing new. Turn-of-the-century Dutch Christian leader Abraham Kuyper, for example, was engaged in a very similar exercise. One of his central thoughts was the notion of "architectonic criticism." He was an astute social critic who perceived that certain evils were structural to society. He worked towards social reformation, based on biblical insights. He took note of the class-struggle, and the connection between capitalism and colonialism. Assumptions from his faith-commitment informed his vision of what ought to be, and he worked through social analysis and political action towards those ends.

In fact, some of Kuyper's agenda items could still be ours today. Conflict between interest groups, such as classes, continue to vitiate hopes of harmony and human fulfillment. This is linked to the unequal distribution of resources and opportunities, both within and between societies. As B. Goudzwaard (1972:49) neatly puts it, "The West in its prosperity structure is oriented solely towards itself." We must also examine scientific and technological aspects of social life which have done so much to shape the modern world. To what purposes are they put? How can the power of commercial interests over them be weakened? What *is* the family? These are all questions which cry out for biblical reappraisal in the modern world. The Christian ought to work for participatory and cooperative structures for industry. He or she should also work for the reformation of the bourgeois Western family, restoring a truly interdependent and truthful set of relationships as originally intended.[7]

But it must be stressed once again that this agenda is couched in a Christian context. The hope of utopia is not in the future society itself, but in the God who reveals his way for mankind. For it is easy to slip into the comforting mindset of so many who propose and work for utopias—namely, that salvation is to be found in the new world. As Tony Walter, following a Bergerian analysis, has shown, movements like popular utopian ecology can be seen as responses to modern homelessness, which has its roots in a much deeper alienation of man from his Maker (Walter, 1978).

And Andrew Kirk maintains that accompanying such a utopian method must always be "the unique message of the Gospel which freely offers complete liberation" (Kirk, 1976:93). This Christian utopianism is a product of faith, but is not coextensive with that faith. This marks the difference between it and other utopias.

### Three Sociologies of Change

We have seen that social change theories all have some connection with an ideal society or utopia, and they all relate to actual historical events or movements—or they should. We have also sketched the beginnings of a Christian understanding of change and utopia. It is in terms of these two criteria—the empirical adequacy seen in Christian perspective and utopian vision in terms of *shalom* or the kingdom of God—that we try to assess three theories: modernization, Marxism, and postindustrialism. We start with modernization.

### *The Grocer of Balgat—Modernization*

The passing of traditional society is epitomized, for Daniel Lerner, in the grocer of Balgat. Balgat was a tiny, unheard-of village just south of Ankara, Turkey, where the grocer and the chief were the prominent figures. But it was the grocer, with his connections with the city and his exposure to the media, who was the prophet of modernity. The chief represented traditional values—the wisdom of age and the inferiority of women. The grocer was a marginal person, in transition from one world to the next, but not quite at home in either. While the chief was content and thanked God for his lack of suffering, his children, his headship of the village, and his strength of brain and body at age 63, the grocer was not. Restlessly, he declared his ambitions: "I have told you I want better things. I would have liked to have had a bigger grocery shop in the city, have a nice house there, dress in nice civilian clothes."

What then is the process of change which Lerner discerns in Balgat? He characterizes it as the infusion of a rational and positivist spirit in a traditional society—a shift in the modes of communicating ideas and attitudes. In particular, Lerner focuses upon new media, such as radio and film, and their impact in the change process. The grocer well illustrates Lerner's thesis, for the emphasis of this modernization theory is on the personal meaning of social change, "the transformations worked in the daily lifeways of individuals of these large historical forces."

The Western model gives clues for the general sequence of events from which the Middle East deviates only in particulars, though sometimes as deliberate policy. Lerner repudiates the charge of ethnocentrism in his interpretation by asserting that this is a universal process. Everywhere increasing urbanization leads to increasing literacy and more media exposure in general, which in turn is associated with increasing economic and political participation.

The key features of Lerner's theory of social change are as follows. First, he sees the "mobile personality" and "empathy" as prerequisites to modernization. People need to learn new roles, and see themselves as others see them. The empathizer tends to be a film viewer, the voter, and the consumer. Lerner hypothesizes that high empathetic capacity is predominant only in modern society, which is distinctively industrial, urban, literate, and participant.

Second, the mass media are seen as the "mobility multiplier." Just as geographical mobility (exploration) opened up new worlds and gave way to social mobility, so social mobility has given way to *psychic* mobility in the modern age. This experience which is mediated through mass communication makes an artificial, vicarious universe which at once simplifies perception (what is seen) and complicates response (what is to be done). Media discipline the empathetic skills which produce modernity.

But third, Lerner would argue that the media only spread psychic mobility among those who are already socially and geographically mobile. Modernity is a *system* of interlocking parts. He continues by suggesting that the direction of change is always from the oral (face-to-face communication which tends to be prescriptive) to the media (which tends to be descriptive). Because modernity is a system, this means that it can be "out of phase." For example, he maintains that modernity may overproduce people who have one foot in the old world and the other in the new. This can lead to intense frustration and political extremism.

For Lerner, the crucial issue is not whether, but how the transition from traditional to modern should be made. The big psychological need in the Middle East is for "a massive growth in *imaginativeness* about alternatives to their present lifeways, and a simultaneous growth of institutional means for handling these alternative lifeways" (410). People participate in modern society (their participation makes the society modern) by having opinions. They receive their opinions largely from the media. Thus the media teach participation. The kind of empathy achieved by the media and its consumers determines the quality of participation, and thus the prospects for the society.

What kind of theory is Lerner's? As we have seen, it is a theory of the mechanism of change, where innovation and its channels are the key. It is a kind of diffusionism, and as such holds that changes originate mainly outside a given unit or pattern, and that the task for research is to locate the channels through which change makes its impact (Smith, 1976:70). Communications theory is the most popular version of diffusionism, through the "marginal man" and "social movements" orientations are also important.

*Towards a Critique*

For all his disclaimers, Lerner's theory touches off some of the warning bells wired up to our guiding beliefs. For the dichotomy between restrictive traditional and open participant society is nothing if not deterministic and ethnocentric. There is an inevitability about the way he describes the "system" of modernity, and the way that this may be "out of phase," that is, ultimately, out of phase with the so-called Western sequence. Moreover, the actual dynamics of his theory have to do with psychological variables—empathy and psychic mobility. But beyond this, his "guiding interests" may be discerned in the direction of his determinism and the locus of his ethnocentrism. For Lerner's theory may happily be married with other neo-evolutionary and systemic[9] approaches to social change. In fact, to a certain extent his theory may be said to implicitly depend on them (Smith, 1976:77). For his conclusion about the "prospects for the modernizing society," one detects a desire to produce a theory of orderly growth and suggestions for overcoming difficulties. The progression to modernity is based on Western experience. Diversions along this route are temporary, for modernization seems to be the major example of general historical trends towards complexity, flexibility, and increasing participation.

A more original contribution to the diffusionist understanding of the mechanisms of social change has been provided by Berger, *et. al.* in *The Homeless Mind* (1974). They use the term "modernization" with reluctance, being extremely critical of modernization theories in sociology. For Berger, *et. al.* (hereafter referred to as "Berger") modernization consists of the growth and diffusion of a set of institutions rooted in the transformation of the economy by means of technology. Following Weber, Berger sees technological production and the bureaucracy as the primary agents of social change. But there are also secondary carriers in the city and in sociocultural pluralism. However, institutional modernization is only half the story. There is a dialectical relationship between that and consciousness-transformation. Berger is much more interested than Lerner in the impact of events, and the role of human decisions at critical times. He is not concerned simply with the behavioristic "culture and values" question, or with the Marxist notion of modernization as the imposition of infrastructures of domination, where consciousness is a dependent variable. He is concerned with the possible alternatives to modernization, the parameters of choice as set by both institutions and consciousness. Thus they attempt to avoid the problems of the Lerner-type theory, which sees modernization as progress-following-the-Western-pattern.

Perhaps Berger's key point is that modernization is not an inevitable and irreversible process. While he is skeptical about the "greening" of modern society, he still maintains that modernization cannot continue indefinitely. In fact, he urges us to think of modernization, de-modernization, and counter-modernization as *concurrent* processes. (1974:169). Let me elaborate on this. As far as the developed countries go, there are limits to de-modernization, however desirable this may appear to be. Death and suffering on an unimaginable scale would follow the destruction of the technological and bureaucratic structures. Certain "packages" cannot be taken apart. What opportunity there may be for de-modernization depends upon freedom and affluence which can support a tolerant pluralism. As for the developing nations, the possibilities for counter-modernization are somewhat more remote—since they cannot afford pluralism. The de-modernizing hopes in those places center on the success of the quest for metaphysical homes while modernization erodes the old certainties. Such homes may be found in some form of nativism (backward-looking) or socialism (forward-looking).

With the focus still on the channels or carriers of change and on consciousness, Berger has a tendency to underplay other issues, such as power and conflict. But he does provide some important correctives within the "modernization" thesis to Lerner's model. While his skepticism about the possibilities of de-modernization are probably well-founded, he nevertheless does not embrace the kind of determinism which characterizes Lerner's work. When he comes to the "political possibilities" he complains that "the social sciences seem to be haunted by the opposing images of B. F. Skinner and Che Guevara." Either there is the pedantic scientism which either has no utopian imagination (or whose utopia makes the blood curdle), or there is the messianic utopianism "with the heady rhetoric of revolution and violence." Berger's ambition is to contribute to neither of those, but to a modest utopianism. The obverse is that the grocer of Balgat need not be the final prophet, and sole exemplar of change.

### The History of Class-Struggles—Marxism

Many Marxists would take a very different view of modernization from both Berger and Lerner. This stems from their different understandings of social change. Fundamental to this is the notion of class-struggle. In the developing nations, for example, André Gunder Frank speaks of the "development of underdevelopment" by Western societies. Inequality must be the starting point for understanding social change. However, it can be argued that studies of development, revolution, and neocapitalism are beginning to stimulate theory of a nonorthodox kind within Marxism. That is, both in relation to modernization and postindustrialism, Marxism is taking a new significance (Bottomore, 1975).

We shall not discuss here the Marxism which follows the line of

Frederick Engels, particularly over historical change and its dynamic. It was Engels who invented the term "historical materialism," and this only made reference to one aspect of Marx's work. Anthony Giddens has succinctly described what happened. Referring to Engels' *Anti-Duhring* he notes that "Engels obscured the most essential element of Marx's work, which was the dialectical relationship of subject and object in the historical process." In doing so, Engels helped to stimulate the notion that ideas simply "reflect material reality" (Giddens, 1970:304). The German Social Democratic Party (whose Marxism Weber was to virulently oppose) took up Engels' view, as did the orthodox Marxism which became fossilized in the Soviet Union. This served to inhibit sociological research on social change in a Marxist perspective for several decades.

The "Marx-interpretation industry" which has flourished over the past ten years or so has focused on the question of the unity of the Marx corpus. The *Grundrisse*[10] in particular has persuaded many scholars that certain guiding threads run throughout Marx's work, uniting the "early writings" with *capital* (e.g. Walton and Gamble, 1972). This is the view taken here. Moreover, the key thread is the fundamental concept of human labor in a historical perspective; the developing interchange between persons and nature, creating and transforming social structure and forms of consciousness, and a close relationship between the type of society and the mode of production.

The self-creation of persons through labor was the beginning of Marx's view of social change. This is what he meant by the "materialist conception of history." Matter is *not* all that there is according to Marx. In the *Theses of Feuerbach* Marx wrote that "the materialist doctrine concerning the changing of circumstances and upbringing forgets that circumstances are made by men and the educator must himself be educated." The materialist concept concerns labor, and labor is associated with economic life: Marx believed that economic life was the key to understanding social life in general. In their social production, according to Marx, men enter into certain relationships which correspond to the stage of development of production forces. This is the economic structure, which has its corresponding forms of consciousness. At a certain time, however, the forces of production will be seen as a constraint on the relations of production (property relations under capitalism), and social revolution is likely to ensue.

While Marx certainly opened himself up to the charge that he was a kind of determinist, such a view of historical change as that just mentioned is not enough to substantiate the charge. All he would say is that technological change is a necessary but not a sufficient condition of social change. He was far more flexible in this than many of his subsequent interpreters. He also gave weight to noneconomic forces in social change. Though probably less important, he believed that what he called "ideology" was a significant means whereby, for example, class rule was perpetuated. Moreover, as more than one commentator has noted, Marx's view of the role of ideology in society is quite compatible with the more detailed studies undertaken by Weber of the sociology of religion (Birnbaum, 1953, Giddens, 1970).

Persons making themselves in social context—this is the essence of Marx's understanding of social change. As he wrote: "Men make their own history, but they do not make it just as they please; they do not make it under circumstances chosen by themselves, but under circumstances directly encountered, given, and transmitted from the past." The concept of class unites objective and subjective sides of the dialectics of labor. Social change occurs when classes conflict, and as the economic substructure develops. In general, Marx held to a two-class model (appropriate to the Victorian Britain which was the focus of his observations), though he acknowledged the existence of others. The division between the classes was basically along the lines of the ownership of the means of production, and he predicted that the gap between them would widen as capitalism developed. The class of destiny, of course, was to be the proletariat—the class "with radical chains" which should be the maker of revolution. But this was not an automatic process.

Class-consciousness was the subjective side of the coin. This had to be developed through unionism and, naturally, through the use of Marx's own ideas in the overcoming of alienated consciousness. But Marx always held the two aspects—objective conditions and subjective consciousness—in dialectical tension. Though as is well known, he had an ambivalence about actual future trends which left open the possibility for more than one prediction or prescription. On a day-to-day basis, under capitalism, there is alienation and an intensification of class-struggle. But when "practical consciousness" (praxis) comprehends the situation, significant social change may take place.

Marx did not, however, develop his theory in a vacuum. It was yoked with historical events, in particular, the development of capitalism itself. He highlighted the role of the expropriation of the peasantry (in a long drawn-out process starting in the 11th century), the enclosures, and the primary development of entrepreneurial industrialism in the cities. (Again, this is not incompatible with Weber's emphasis on the Protestant Ethic). Marx follows his own dictum about the economic law of motion of society, while Weber gives weight to other contingent features of social life, not intrinsically economic.

## Structural Inequalities

The debate over the correctness of Marx's historical analysis will probably continue for a long time. But one thing is certain, it is not as crude as it might appear from the Weberian critique, which was a critique of Marx's interpreters. However, Marx does pinpoint alleged inequities and conflict-sources—the contradiction between the alienative impoverishment of the individual and the huge self-fulfilling potential of modern industry. What bearing, therefore, does this have upon the anticipation of future change? Marx was not dogmatic about the increasing misery of the proletariat, but he did believe that the gap between different economic classes would be maintained and widened while capitalism prevailed. This seems to be true, at least in the British context (Westergaard and Resler, 1976). But it is possible that it is also true in the wider, global context, as theorists such as André Gunder Frank would maintain. He argues that contemporary underdevelopment is in large part the historical product of relationships between advanced and non-advanced societies. It is in the interest of the advanced societies to "underdevelop" others (Cockcroft, *et. al.*, 1972:3). At this fundamental level, Marxism points to the inequalities of the capitalist system, and also reveals its purpose-commitment, a new kind of society.

On the other hand, Weber had a more exogenous understanding of social change (that is, change originating *outside* the unit being considered), and he emphasized voluntarism and the role of ideas. Thus, some would argue that he demonstrated his freedom from determinism and from utopian vision. Actually, he remained a pessimist about the possibilities of ever breaking out of the bureaucratic cage of rationalization and disenchantment—he held out no rosy hopes for mankind. But this in itself is a kind of determinism, that allows no scope for human creativity which might eventually find freedom from the inhuman process of rationalization. Whereas for Marx, his intrinsic view of the future included the idea that the contradictions of capitalism could be overcome, and that people would become truly human.

Marxism as sociology (or, better, political economy) shows itself to be a self-confessed committed science, that sees socialism as the ideal form of social relations. It is this which guides research to significant topics. For, as Marx himself argued, in the final thesis on Feuerbach, "The philosophers have only *interpreted* the world in different ways; the point is to change it." But this raises a major problem. Change the world into what? Eduard Bernstein, the first important follower of Marx's basic ideas, who also had the nerve to question details of Marx's analysis was extremely concerned about this. He pointed out that "peasants do not sink; middle class does not disappear; crises do not grow ever larger; misery and serfdom do not increase. . . ." (quoted in Bottomore, 1975:20). Although he himself never made a significant contribution to the task of defining what the new world should be like, he believed that an ethical theory of socialism is essential. Socialism may be a noble ideal, but are violent revolution and political repression justified as a means to that end?

Marxism may be a moral science, but in the end one could argue that it is lacking the *basis* for that morality (though writers such as Kolakowski, 1969, and Stojanovic, 1973, have made strides in this direction in our day). The Marxist sociology of change focuses attention upon, and tends to absolutize, the economic structure of society. It is historical (event-related), and it especially highlights inequalities and perceived injustices with regard to the distribution of both opportunities and resources. It does not allow us to ignore the role of ideology in legitimating and perpetuating control. But while it may help us to foresee possible changes, and may also catalyse revolutionary action, it offers no guarantee whatsoever that one form of domination will not simply be replaced by another. The transcendence of state-capitalism with its inherent inequities, rather than the *nature* of that transcendance (that is, the proposed alternative), tends to become a goal in itself.

### The Knowledge Society—Postindustrialism

Thus far, we have examined two kinds of theories of social change, modernization, which focuses on the channels through which change is diffused, and Marxism, which focuses on the origin and foundations of change. Both are concerned with the major process which has characterized Western society over the past two hundred years—the application of calculative rationality to the productive order (Giddens,

1973:262). This is industrialism. Postindustrialism is the idea that Western societies are entering a definitively different phase from either preindustrialism or industrialism.

To recap, Lerner's modernization theory is exogenous and has to do with the *mechanisms* of change. It is rather deterministic and ethnocentric. Lerner assumes that modernization is a process accompanied by an increasing degree of participation. The only conflict is between the old and the new life ways. Berger, writing about modernization, but in opposition to this kind of theory, argues for a greater awareness of consciousness, and the possibilities of choice which help determine the direction of change.

Neither Lerner nor Berger, however, concern themselves overmuch with the possibility that the direction of change or the ability to make choices is severely limited by one's social position. This is where Marxism becomes relevant. Marxism focuses on the *origin* of change from the point of view of the development of labor, and in terms of a socialist future. There is inherent conflict over ownership of the means of production, and thus the Marxist would argue that the meaningfulness of one's participation in modern society is determined by class-position. However, Marxism has a tendency to be interpreted deterministically, and has no future ethic. Weber's more voluntaristic approach to the origin of change is complementary to Marxism, with more detailed work on ideas, but is ultimately more pessimistic.

Daniel Bell, who is taken to be the foremost exponent of the postindustrial idea, takes a neo-evolutionary stance. He focuses on the *form* of change, the consequences of specific processes which he discerns in Western society. In some ways Bell's work is compatible with that of Lerner, though it is broader. It is more in the Weberian tradition, in that rationality is the key to change: theoretical knowledge is the "axial principle" of postindustrial society. However, the burden of other change theories looked at here has been the transition from industrial to postindustrial society. Just as Marx and Weber in one era, and Lerner in another, were convinced that a qualitatively new kind of society was coming into being, so Bell is convinced that another is being born.

Daniel Bell thought that he saw the "end of ideology" in the late 1950s, and this is written into his postindustrial society, where conflict is minimized. In *The Cultural Contradictions of Capitalism* he expressed his hope for the future in terms of applied knowledge:

"Within limits, men can remake themselves and society, but the knowledge of power must coexist with the knowledge of its limits" (Bell, 1976:282). His "guiding interests of cognition," therefore, have to do with his liberal vision of a rosy future, where knowledge rules and conflict has been reduced to a minimum within a pluralist democratic structure.

## Social Forecast: A Rosy Future

Bell follows the tradition in sociology which sees the coming future as being one with the present; his is "a venture in social forecasting." Moreover, he obliges sociologists to rethink the tired categories of industrial society, and to evaluate them in the light of contemporary evidence. He asks, what kind of world do we presently inhabit, and what can we expect to happen in the next few decades? In addition, he is concerned to anticipate change in the light of past changes, and to help ensure a better future for mankind.

In his description of the dimensions of postindustrial society, Bell locates the particular changes with which he is concerned in the "social structure." He makes an analytical distinction between social structure, culture, and polity. Social structure refers to the economy, technology, and the occupational system. He stresses that he is dealing with the meaning and consequences of certain tendencies in Western society (epitomized in the USA). Five are crucially important: (1) In the economic sector, according to Bell, there has been a decisive shift from goods-producing to a service economy. The USA is the world's first service economy, where by 1980, 70 percent of occupations will be in this tertiary sector. (2) At the same time, the actual distribution of occupations within that sector are weighted towards professional and technical groups. Scientists and engineers are the key group in the postindustrial society. (3) Above all this, however, is the axial principle of the centrality of theoretical knowledge as the source of innovation and policy-formation. This is symbolized in R & D (research and development) which unites science, technology, and economics in the postindustrialized world. (4) But the postindustrial society has a distinctive future orientation: technology is consciously planned in order to obviate the more disastrous of its consequences. (5) Lastly, there is a new intellectual technology for decision-making. Intuitive judgments may at last be replaced by problem-solving rules.

Bell concludes that all this adds up to a new, integrated society, where there is more conscious and informed decision-making. Welfare choices are guided and limited by knowledge, and ideological conflict becomes far less prominent. The new value system of society is determined by attitudes to scientific knowledge. It would seem that there are no limits to the potential expansion of postindustrial society, except those inherent in the state of knowledge itself.

But how secure are the empirical grounds for Bell's optimistic forecasting? Does his work indicate a change compatible with Smith's definition of social change? (i.e., "a succession of events which produce over time a modification or replacement of particular patterns or units by other novel ones"). Of course, many of the changes which Bell highlights have taken place. But does this mean that there is a new social order about which we must ask a whole new agenda of questions? For all his emphasis upon the meaning of these changes, it is by no means clear that Bell himself has probed too deeply their meaning. In fact all too often he relies on surface appearances—a phenomenon not unknown among those who share his guiding interests of cognition.

Krishan Kumar (1976) for example, has pinpointed the way in which Bell uses statistical "evidence" to make his case for a postindustrial society. First, Bell's assertion that the shift to a service economy is a new departure is not supported by historical evidence. For the increasing emphasis on services as against the primary sector is a process as old as industrialism itself. It happens because of the more rapid growth of demand for services than for goods, and the fact that the pace of growth in manufacturing output per capita leaves "spare" labor to be used in services. Second, Bell sees greater humanization of work within the white-collar service industries. But here again, there are difficulties. The giant corporation still dominates Western society, and even in smaller enterprises the ethos of the giant corporation prevails. One need only think of contemporary social work to realize that systems theory has conquered even the "caring" services. But Bell is also wrong in equating white collar with "services." How many cleaners, transport workers, and garage mechanics wear white collars? In short, "the evidence suggests that work in the service sector is less skilled, lower paid, less unionized, less educated, and less secure than manufacturing" (Kumar, 1976:450).

Furthermore, might not the larger number of professionals be due to the relabeling of occupations than a real increase in the old-fashioned professional class? ("Sanitary engineers" must be within

Bell's professionals!) And what of the knowledge explosion? We may be living through one, but as Kumar points out, this tells us nothing about the uses to which it is put, whether it has any use at all, or has any profound effect upon social life. Bell cites R & D expenditure as evidence, but this is not conclusive. How much so-called R & D money in fact goes on stationery or marketing? And how much leads to innovation? Evidence from innovations shows that the majority of innovations come from outside R & D! And last, the connection between R & D and human welfare is far from obvious. The majority is still devoted to destructive (war) purposes, or goods with built in obsolescence, or medical research geared to those who can afford treatment. And 99 percent of the knowledge effort of industrial societies is devoted to the developed world. Welfare is certainly not a global concept.

## Old Questions

The questions raised by Bell's alleged postindustrial society are all too familiar. Who and what is this knowledge for? Who controls and who is thereby alienated from the system? The competitive struggle for power and profit still exists. Is the social structure really separable from the polity, as Bell argues? Bell has taken Weber's thesis of relentlessly encroaching rationalization (though not his pessimism about it) and made it the rationale for his underlying view of social change. While there is evidence for some far-reaching changes in the social structure of advanced societies, it is doubtful whether this spells a new social order. Kumar suggests that some of the confusion arises because we have not properly understood the nature of industrialism, which contains all the basic features of Bell's putative new world. But he agrees that we need to concentrate sociological research upon the undergrowth of society, where these semi-hidden changes are taking place.

Others have been more sympathetic to the postindustrial idea, but have seen a different future in it. In fact, some of the "old questions" have been raised about it, especially by Alain Touraine (1971). He sees in the postindustrial society a new form of class conflict. Where Bell sees social divisions largely overcome, the domination of technically competent elites widely accepted, and the general course of social development determined by economic growth, with no widespread basis for dissent, Touraine sees the opposite. For Touraine, the old divisions between labor and capital have become less important; his post-

Marxist theory suggests that knowledge-control is the new basis of division. The political events of May 1968 in France illustrate this conflict.

But a post-Marxist theory does not have a monopoly of all the "old questions." The class-struggle might continue along different lines. Furthermore, if we accept the class struggle as the most important feature to be examined, we shall miss other possible questions. Some proponents of a postindustrial idea think not of an affluent technological service society, but of a decentralized agrarian economy following in the wake of the failure of industrialism (Marien, 1977; Kumar, 1978:301 f.). The possibilities are still wide open.

### Christianity and Culture

The intention of this paper is to search for a Christian evaluation of sociologies of change. We have seen that an adequate theory of change has to take account of many factors, including the origins, mechanisms, and forms of change. It should not be deterministic or ethnocentric. Moreover, it is clear that empirical and historical evidence must be used with honesty and understanding, beyond the comprehension of surface phenomena. But we have also argued that evidence will always be used in the context of particular world-views and visions of the future.

Bell's work on the postindustrial idea is of major significance to those of us who live in the West. For he has tried to discern the pervasive and distinctive signs of the times in what he thinks of as the leading countries of the world. It is also important because he is concerned about the shape of the future. But what of his world-view? How does he evaluate change?

Bell reveals himself as a humane Western liberal, who holds a high view of religion as a source of values, though he only gives religion a place *within* culture. He even believes that there will be a "great instauration" or renewal of religion and culture in the postindustrial age (1976:146-171). This is because religion is "a constitutive part of man's consciousness: the cognitive search for the pattern of the 'general order' of existence . . ." (1976:196). According to Bell, orthodox religion has declined partly because "its view of man as Homo Duplex, the murderous aggression and the search for harmony, is too bleak a view for the utopianism that has burnished modern culture" (1976:167). He says that what we need now is a sense of the sacred, otherwise we shall be left with "the shambles of appetite and self-interest, and the destruction of the moral circle which engirdles mankind."

Bell has a keen sense of some of the things that are wrong with the modern world, and some lofty ideals of what should be. But they are essentially conservative ideals, where religion plays the part of a curb on passion and the excesses associated with the quest for self-realization. And they are ideals which exclude others: his notion of welfare, for example, does not have much to say about global justice. In fact, as Bernard Zylstra has boldly put it: "This neo-conservatism is not an authentic spiritual quest for the normative transcendent sources of political authority, social order, and cultural standards. Neo-conservatism remains confined within the immanent horizon of modernity. Beyond that horizon lies the source of justice and equity, personhood and harmony, loyalty and love" (Zylstra, 1977).

### Beyond the Horizon

Daniel Bell contrasts orthodox religion with utopianism. Zylstra's comments suggests that the two are not incompatible. This is the position taken here. Bell admits the urgent need for utopia, but maintains that "the ladder to the city of heaven can no longer be a 'faith ladder' but an empirical one" (1960:405). Now, if all Bell is saying is that orthodox religion (Judaism or Christianity) is incompatible with humanistic optimism, then he is right. For that kind of utopianism is bred from the idea of humanity as self-directing and autonomous. But if he is saying that Christians may not have a hope of *shalom* and the kingdom of God, which connects vitally with empirical reality and social change, then we must differ. In fact, those who believe in the adequacy of any "empirical ladder" alone are deluded. The very source of human hope is indeed beyond the horizon.

But that hope-source, Jesus Christ, has shown his intimate and urgent concern for what is within the horizon by his incarnation. Through the work of his life and death on the cross, not only his people, but the whole creation may be set free (Romans 8:3, 21). As hymn-writer Isaac Watts neatly phrased it: "He comes to make his blessings flow/Far as the curse is found." He who is the Alpha and the Omega (beginning and end) is also concerned for the history and social change in between.

If there is to be a Christian evaluation of social change theories, which inevitably have a bearing on future change, then some idea of what might be a desirable future is essential. Christian hope can contribute to an explicitly purposive sociology of change. And as we interact with other change theories, a Christian perspective may be worked out. We shall draw one or two threads together in conclusion.

Perhaps one characteristic of Christian thought in this field ought to be the refusal to be limited to one kind of explanation of social change. Of all areas, this has been one bedeviled by all-encompassing explanations in terms of one over-riding factor. The only overriding factor in history is the activity of God—other alternatives are distorting parodies of this truth. History is a richly woven tapestry, impossible to encompass in terms of one theme or impetus. Moreover, the implication of Anthony Smith's argument (1976:122) is that theories of the monocausal type tend to focus on only one aspect of change—origin, mechanism, or form. Thus other aspects tend to be relatively neglected. Marx and Weber focus mainly upon the impetus and origin of change, Lerner and Berger mainly upon the channels, and Bell upon the forms and consequences—though there are of course overlaps with all three.

### Critically Using Change Theories

Each theory may have its uses. The endogenous neo-evolutionism of Bell may highlight some important trends in industrial societies, but this may need to be supplemented with the diffusionism of a Lerner, which is exogenous and gives a central role to intrusions which break open existing patterns. Beyond this, it would take someone working in a more Marxian tradition to point out the role of conflict between groups struggling for power in changing situations, plus a Weber perhaps to enlarge on the role of ideas. On their own, though, they tend to determinism, ethnocentrism, or just sheer inadequacy.

But as was suggested at the outset, one way in which Christian beliefs could potentially direct emphases is by focusing on the anticipation of change. In a sense, this is the very justification for studying social change. All theories of change are in the end underdetermined in relation to the available evidence, and all reveal their effectiveness only in relation to certain purposes. It has been argued that authentic Christian commitment may be realized by making explicit the purposes in view, in a kind of modest utopian method or sociological ethic. If analyzed with an eye to their latent utopianism, theories of social change which have been glanced at here are seriously deficient. There is a certain naiveté about Lerner's anticipated future, in which the inexorable forces working especially through the media produce something like a Western-style participatory democracy. Bell's optimism about the hyper-expansionist postindustrial society is one which ignores the role of the developing nations in maintaining such an economy in advanced countries. And Marxism, while it is sensitive to the issues of underdeveloped, is deficient in that it fails to specify *how* suffering and class-conflict may be overcome.

So we may say, then, that while the Christian evaluation of theories of social change may be guided by an understanding of a Christian philosophy of history, a utopian method is called for to enhance this evaluation as it relates to the *anticipation* of change. Other matters, such as the belief in the openness of history, a desire for theories which adequately deal with the different foci (origins, channels, and consequences of change), and the sensitive use of interpretive understanding of empirical evidence, are assumed to be centrally important. But it is the historical and utopian framework which will contribute to a distinctively Christian weighing and devising of theories of social change.

## Discussion Questions

1. How far do you agree with Comte's stated purpose of sociology?

2. In what ways is Christianity grounded in historical events?

3. Is the idea of "progress" compatible with Christian believing?

4. Discuss the differences between "Utopian imagination" and "blueprints for society."

5. Is "Christian utopianism possible"?

6. What are the main criticisms that may be leveled at David Lerner's understanding of "modernization"?

7. Is Marx's socialism "utopian" or "scientific," and what difference does this make to the Christian assessment of Marxism?

8. In what ways is Bell's theory similar to nineteenth-century evolutionists? What might Christians say about such a theory?

9. According to this paper, is it *sociologists* or *sociology* itself that is inherently critical/purposive/value-laden?

10. Following from question nine, is it therefore possible (as Wolterstorff and others contend) that Christian guiding beliefs may function *internally* to scholarship as well as externally (i.e., in the personal life of the sociologist)?

## Notes

1. This paper was originally read at a conference arranged by the Institute

for Advanced Christian Studies at Wheaton College, Illinois, July 1978. It has been modified in the light of helpful discussions with colleagues there, and also the comments of Dr. Howard Davis of the University of Kent at Canterbury.

2. The understanding of social change has not grown steadily with the development of sociology, however. A trenchant criticism of functionalism is that it cannot adequately cope with social change. The area of sociological ethics, with respect to the anticipation of future change, is another underdeveloped field.

3. I am thinking here of those, such as T. S. Eliot, who see medieval Europe as a golden age.

4. The refernece is 1 Chronicles 12:32 (NASB). Of course, one would not wish to press single references, but it is arguable that this is a common theme, especially in the wisdom and prophetic literature.

5. Wolterstorff in fact speaks of "control-beliefs," but this has restrictive connotations which might suggest a foreclosing of possibilities. Maybe "controlling *and* guiding beliefs" would be a better formulation.

6. The word "utopia" is, of course, controversial. I use it in a similar sense to Bauman 1976; it criticizes the present, and projects a desired alternative. Beyond Bauman I would say that people cooperate within God's purposes to bring it about (Matthew 6:10). For a useful discussion see Levitas 1979, and for a Christian perspective Kirk 1976.

7. See, for example, the perceptive work of Olthuis 1975, Walter 1979, and Storkey 1979.

8. Why these three? They are all popular, internationally known, and sociologically sophisticated (although see the criticisms which I make of them). Modernization is chosen rather than the more helpful "industrialization" because it is better known in North America. Both are umbrella terms which beg many other questions. The three theories have different (though complementary) foci, and overlap with each other. They are also, to a certain extent, in competition with each other. This comes out in the argument.

9. "Neo-evolutionary" refers to the late twentieth-century versions of the evolutionary doctrines which were current in the nineteenth century. They stress that change is an outgrowth in an organic sense from some social unit. Change is intrinsic to the unit (endogenous). "Systemic" refers to those theories which assert that social life is a system, like a human body: each part is interrelated and change in one part leads to change (adaptation, etc.) in another.

10. *Grundrisse* means "general outline." This book is central to an understanding of Marx's work. See Lyon 1979.

11. See also the very valuable discussion of industrialism in Kumar, 1978.

## Resources

Bauman, Z.
    1976 *Socialism: The Active Utopia*. London: Routledge.

Bell, Daniel
    1960 *The End of Ideology*. New York: Free Press.
    1974 *The Coming of Post-Industrial Society*. Harmondsworth: Penguin.
    1976 *The Cultural Contradictions of Capitalism*. New York: Basic Books.
Berger, Peter L., Brigitte Berger, and Hansfried Kellner
    1974 *The Homeless Mind*. Harmondsworth: Penguin.
Birnbaum, N.
    1953 "Conflicting Interpretations of the Rise of Capitalism: Marx and Weber." *British Journal of Sociology*, 4, pp. 129-141.
Bottomore, Tom
    1975 *Marxist Sociology*. London: Macmillan.
Carr, E. H.
    1951 *The New Society*. London: Macmillan
Cockroft, James D., André Gunder Frank, and Dale L. Johnson
    1972 *Dependence and Underdevelopment*. New York: Anchor.
Connerton, Paul (ed.)
    1976 *Critical Sociology*. Harmondsworth: Penguin.
Dooyeweerd, Herman
    1960 *In the Twilight of Western Thought*. Nutley, N.J.: Presbyterian and Reformed Publishing Co.
Giddens, Anthony
    1970 "Marx, Weber, and the Development of Capitalism." *Sociology*. 4, pp. 289-310.
    1973 *The Class Structure of Advanced Societies*. London: Hutchinson University Library.
Gillett, D.
    1976 "Shalom: Content for a Slogan," *Themelios*, 1:3, pp. 80-84.
Goudzwaard, B.
    1972 *A Christian Political Option*. Toronto: Wedge.
Kirk, A.
    1976 "The Meaning of Man in the Debate Between Christianity and Marxism." *Themelios*, 1:3, pp. 85-93.
Kitwood, Tom
    1978 " 'Utopia' and 'Science' in the Anticipation of Social Change." *Alternative Futures*.
Kolakowski, L.
    *1969 Marxism and Beyond*. London: Pall Mall Press.
Kumar, Krishan
    1976 "Industrialism and Post-Industrialism: Reflections on a Putative Transition." *Sociological Review*, 24, 3, pp. 439-478.
    1978 *Prophecy and Progress: The Sociology of Industrial and Post-Industrial Society*. Harmondsworth: Penguin.
Levitas, Ruth
    1979 "Sociology and Utopia." *Sociology*, January.

Lerner, Daniel
1958 *The Passing of Traditional Society.* Glencoe: Free Press.
Lyon, David
1979a *Karl Marx: A Christian Appreciation of His Life and Thought.* Tring, England: Lion Publishing
1979b "The Challenge of Marxism" in D. Wright (ed.) *Essays in Evangelical Social Ethics.* Exeter: Paternoster.
MacIntire, C.T.
1974 *The Ongoing Task of Christian Historiography,* Institute for Christian Studies, Toronto.
Marien, M.
1977 "Post-Industrial Society." *Futures* (October) pp. 415-431.
Miguez-Bonino, J.
1976 *Christians and Marxists: The Mutual Challenge to Revolution.* Grand Rapids: Eerdmans.
Olthuis, T.
1975 *I Pledge You My Troth: A Christian View of Marriage, Family, Friendship.* New York: Harper and Row.
Smith, Anthony
1976 *Social Change.* London: Longman.
Stojanovic, S.
1973 *Between Ideals and Reality.* London: Oxford University Press.
Strasser, H.
1976 *The Normative Structure of Sociology.* London: (Routledge & Kegan Paul).
Touraine, A.
1971 *The Post-Industrial Society.* New York: Random House.
Walter, J.A.
1978 "Home or Castle?" *Third Way.* 2, pp. 1, 3-6.
1979 *A Long Way from Home,* Exeter: Paternoster.
Walton, Paul, and Andrew Gamble
1972 *From Alienation to Surplus Value.* London: Sheed and Ward.
Westergaard, T. and R. Resler
1976 *Class in Capitalist Society.* Harmondsworth: Penguin.
Winthrop, H.
1968 "The Sociologist and the Study of the Future." *American Sociologist,* 3, pp. 136-145.
Wolterstorff, Nicholas
1976 *Reason Within the Bounds of Religion.* Grand Rapids: Eerdmans.
Zylstra, Bernard
1977 "A Neo-Conservative Critique of Modernity." *Christian Scholars' Review.*

# 39
# Social Change and Christian Responsibility

*C. Emory Burton*

When we compare the world we know today with the world of twenty or thirty years ago, we are struck with vast and profound changes in the way we live. Technological advances, for example, have given us new appliances, computers, and new forms of transportation and communication. Changes in family life and overall life-style point to less tangible but just as real changes in social norms and values. We have witnessed social movements that have sought to change the existing structure on behalf of equality for blacks, women, and other oppressed peoples.

In a widely read book on social change, Alvin Toffler says, "Change sweeps through the highly industrialized countries with waves of ever accelerating speed and unprecedented impact" (Toffler, 1970:9). Change seems built into the very structure of the universe. Twentieth-century persons see the world they have come to know becoming a different world—strange, and often frightening—right before their eyes (Brockway, 1970:16).

## Change Inevitable, But . . .

Social change may be defined as a succession of differences in time within a persisting identity (Nisbet and Perrin, 1977:266). It refers especially to activities that affect the structural form of the society. Studies of social change begin with *concrete* social behavior occurring in time and place, and in relation to circumstances or conditions.

**C. Emory Burton**
*Assistant Professor of Sociology and Chairman of the Department*
*The University of Alabama in Huntsville*
Emory Burton received his PhD from the University of Tennessee. He also earned a BD from Garrett-Evangelical Theological Seminary. Mr. Burton specializes in mass behavior and urban sociology. The author is an ordained minister in the United Methodist Church and preaches occasionally.

Almost all authorities agree that the contemporary world is changing more rapidly than at any time in human history (Moore, 1963:2; Toffler, 1970:22). There is widespread agreement that many social processes are speeding up—strikingly, even spectacularly. The present is characterized by a much greater degree of change than was true in the past, and some of the changes are of such great magnitude as to suggest changes in kind.

Furthermore, the proportion of contemporary change that is either *planned* or the secondary consequences of deliberate innovations is much higher than in former times (Moore, 1963:5). This means that the rapidity of social change cannot be interpreted as evolutionary or impersonal change.

Many theories have been proposed to explain or account for social change. One of the best known is Marxism, which stresses the priority of economic forces as determinants of all changes. That economic factors are crucial for many kinds of changes is generally conceded, but most authorities believe that Marx overstates the point. Max Weber, writing partly in reaction to Marx, found noneconomic changes (including religion) vital to an understanding of economic change. Weber's view that social change can only be understood by reference to time, place, and circumstance, is generally accepted today.°

Despite some theories that stress the inevitability of change, it seems more correct to state that change is *contingent* and not necessary. This means that its occurrence has a chance-like or often random quality which cannot be separated from the particularities and unpredictabilities of concrete situations. Social change, then, is not logically necessary or inevitable. As far as the scientific or critical understanding of change is concerned, no necessity or ironclad determinism is found (Nisbet and Perrin, 1977:288). In fact, most significant changes, rather than being the outcome of predictable evolutionary trends, seem to be directly related to events that provoke *crises*.

It should also be noted that even in the midst of profound change, there is an underlying basis of persistence and regularity. Without some continuing *sameness*, some identity, the very conceptualization of change is impossible (Moore, 1963:6; Nisbet and Perrin, 1977:269).

---

°A full discussion of theories of social change would take us beyond the scope of this chapter. See Moore (1963), Nisbet and Perrin (1977), or a chapter on social change in any good introductory sociology text.

Sociologists have commented on the sheer power of persistence, inertia, or fixity in human behavior (Nisbet and Perrin, 1977:271). Persistence and fixity are very powerful realities. Habit, custom, adaptation (even to the absurd and potentially lethal), and sheer inertia are strongly built into the socialization process. This may explain why basic change for most of us is an ordeal, an agony—something frequently resisted at all costs.

No matter how extreme the need is to change our old ways, we adopt, in effect, various fictions through which we convince ourselves that a change of behavior is *not* needed. We try to rationalize, claiming that the old and cherished, if properly understood, can continue despite all overt evidence of its unsuitability (Nisbet and Perrin, 1977:281). So most of us tend to spend most of our lives, after a certain age, in repeating what we know, and in finding more extensions or adaptations of what we learned earlier in life. The consequence is that few of us can be said to welcome change—at least in those primary spheres where we feel most deeply identified. Toffler (1970:20) even claims that the majority of people find the idea of change so threatening that they attempt to deny its existence.

### The Biblical Understanding of Change

When the Christian seeks to understand the significance of change, particularly social change, he starts with the biblical perspective. Theologians say that the nature of God is revealed in historical events; it is possible to interpret these acts of God as social change (Cox, 1965:105). The action of God has a dynamic, historical character. The Hebrew people interpreted many events that brought about social change, such as their deliverance from bondage in Egypt, as acts of God. For the Hebrews, God was alive in the midst of her history, in her involvement in political crises and complex social and cultural problems. Indeed, when the Jews were undergoing dramatic social changes they seem to have been closest to fulfilling their calling. Talcott Parsons (1960:295) says that the most creative periods of religious development tend to be times of social turmoil rather than settled peace.

The Bible presents us with a God who is creator and ruler of all spheres, including the world of nature and of human society. They are established to serve God's purpose for man.° Therefore it logically

---

° In this chapter "man" refers to all mankind without regard to sex.

follows that they must be used and changed in line with that purpose. Throughout the Bible, there is a strong teleological emphasis, which stresses the dynamic nature of God and the fact that his action in history is moving toward a goal.

In a sense, creation is never complete, but is moving toward a goal. Harvey Cox (1965:76) believes that man has a crucial part to play in the creation of the world. Something of this idea is conveyed in the words of the apostle Paul: "For the creation waits with eager longing for the revealing of the sons of God" (Romans 8:19).

Paul H. Lehmann (1963) contends that it is only in Christianity that history is understood as a compound of stability and change, decay and fulfillment. Thus, change is seen as the prelude to authentic stability, and decay as the occasion for fulfillment. When Moses asked God what name he should reveal to the people of Israel, God revealed himself as "I will be who I will be." Therefore, his action must be understood by looking to the future more than to the past. Lehmann goes on to say that God is creating the conditions for human fulfillment in interrelatedness in the world.

According to Richard Shaull (1967:33), God's action in the world aims at its transformation, and the coming of Christ and the work of the Holy Spirit release new and disturbing forces in history that affect the process itself. Those who participate in God's work cannot seek refuge in old ways, nor draw back from the front lines. It is in this struggle that the battle for the future of man is being waged.

### Jesus and Change

Whatever else we may say about the ministry of Jesus, it involved change. Everywhere Jesus ministered, men were changed: blind men began to see; lame men began to walk; deaf men began to hear; persons possessed of demons were set free; hungry men were fed. Jesus came with a summons that demanded a response. Peter and John left their fishing nets (their occupation); the sick through faith got well; the rich young man was challenged to sell his property and give away the proceeds. No one who met Jesus could doubt that something momentous had occurred, or that having an encounter with Jesus did not call for some kind of response.

Furthermore, the sayings and actions that got Jesus into the most trouble were those that challenged the traditions of the past or the status quo, such as his claim that the Sabbath was made for man, and not man for the Sabbath (Mark 2:27). He accused the Pharisees of making void the word of God through their rigid adherance to tradition (Mark 7:13). His parable of the wineskins (Luke 5:36-39) suggested the need for new forms for new ideas. As Brockway (1970:104-105) says, Jesus seemed to be indicating that God was present in the activity of change every bit as much as he was in the maintenance of the valid traditions.

The word used in the New Testament for change (normally translated "conversion") is metanoia, "a very radical change." The former self dies and a new self is born. It is a total change for the person involved: "all things become new." *Metanoia* involves a sweeping change in one's perception of self and the world. As Cox (1965:118-119) says, it results in a life in which one is now able to see, hear, walk, and leap for joy.

## The Kingdom of God

Probably the most significant biblical concept relevant to social change is the kingdom of God, which was the very heart of Jesus' message (see Perrin, 1963). The *kingdom* refers to the sovereign rule of God over the whole range of human life. The dynamic nature of the kingdom is illustrated by Jesus' comparing it to a grain of mustard seed which grows into a tree, and to leaven at work in the meal (Matthew 13:31-33).

The coming of the kingdom presented itself in the form of claims requiring the renunciation of certain things and the acceptance of a new discipline of discipleship. The new way of life entailed a radical break with the past. Those responding to the appearance of the kingdom were expected to sever all past ties and set aside all past values to enter into the new activities and responsibilities required by the kingdom.

When Jesus began his ministry, he proclaimed, "The kingdom of God is at hand; repent, and believe in the gospel" (Mark 1:15). The good news of the Gospel is that the kingdom of God was inaugurated by the first Christ event. The kingdom came in Jesus when God's doing something wholly new coincided with man's laying aside previous values and loyalties, and freely entering the new reality. In short, man is summoned to discard the old and take up something different.

Long debates have taken place over whether the kingdom of God is a present reality or strictly a future event. New Testament scholars tell us that neither is a correct understanding, for the kingdom is that reign of God which is *in process*—i.e., it is in the process of unfolding itself in history. The kingdom of God is always just arriving; it is always "coming," the new reality which is beginning to appear. If this is true, then we live in a world where the coming of the kingdom is a continuous process. The Christian is called to discern the "signs" of the kingdom and to respond appropriately.

The view of some, that we are called to *build* the kingdom through *our own* efforts, as though a *perfect* kingdom could be realized historically, is unrealistic and unbiblical. But it is nonetheless true that the elements of divine initiative and human response are inseparable. In the gospels, Jesus personifies the kingdom of God (Matthew 12:28), and that kingdom, concentrated in the life and ministry of Jesus, represents the partnership of God and man in history.

It is therefore possible to interpret God's action as calling men to cooperate in his kingdom. Our call, then, is to discern the action of God in the world and to join in his work. Cox (1965:125) would interpret this as working for the liberation of man to freedom and responsibility. When we are faithful to the call of the kingdom, we will join our efforts with God's, working for human deliverance and fulfillment.

### The Coming New Age

The New Testament has an interesting contrast between "this age" and "the age to come," between the world as it now is, and the world as it will be when God's purpose is consummated. The whole tenor of the New Testament is to look *forward* to a better age. Paul urges his listeners not to be "conformed to this world" (Romans 12:2); the Christian is never completely at home in the present world. As Cox (1965:118) puts it, those who continue to live in "this dying age" suffer from a deformed and distorted vision of themselves and of reality as a whole. The true Christian is one who has "tasted the . . . powers of the age to come" (Hebrews 6:5).

The distinction between "the present age" and "the age to come" is not the same as that between "heaven" and "earth." The biblical promise is a new heaven *and* a new earth (Revelation 21:1). The whole idea suggests the renewal or restoration of *all* things.

Paul says the form *(schema)* of this world is passing away. God's purpose is that creation itself may be "set free from its bondage to decay" (Romans 8:21). God does not call Christians to escape *from* history, but to commit themselves to a radical transformation *of* history (Robinson, 1960:16). We could say that the new age is breaking in wherever men are summoned to dignity and accountability, where defeat and resignation give way to freedom and responsibility (Cox, 1965:143).

## Christian Change Includes Social Change

Some Christians have said that the change the Gospel calls for is strictly an individual matter, without direct relevance to the social situation in which man finds himself. Such an interpretation not only misreads the message of the Bible, as we have tried to show, but fails to understand what sociology tells us about people.

Our self-concepts, attitudes, motivations, and our very perception of reality influence our social behavior in our personal careers, our social location, the job we hold, etc. Therefore our changed lives will be reflected in our social interaction, and in the changing of social, political, economic, and religious structures that are unjust. The summons men hear must occur within the matrix of a new social situation, a new objective context. This insight is a commonplace in sociology, but it is one which the church has too often overlooked.

Most religions, including Christianity, have traditionally given a sacral (sacred, unchanging) character to its institutions (the status quo). In fact religion has been a major factor in preserving them against the forces of major social change. To a point, this is commendable: it has promoted the preservation of much that is of value in our society and culture. But when faced with dynamic social changes and revolutionary upheavals, this function can become a barrier to needed change. Indeed, the great temptation facing the church is that it becomes the rallying point of all who fear change (Shaull, 1967:31). And as Parsons (1960:295) points out, religion in most societies tends to be mainly a conservative force, preventing society from departing from the established ways.

But Parsons (1960:297) goes on to say:

> The very fact of the association of religion with the areas of strain and tension in human life on the deepest emotional levels means that it is likely to be one of the main areas in which responses to such situations are creative rather than traditional.

The Protestant movement known as Calvinism interpreted the

concept of the kingdom of God as a *present reality* on earth (as well as a future hope). It was the duty of man to create by divine ordinance. This whole idea of mastery has oriented man to the control of the world in which he lives as distinct from a fatalistic "acceptance" of things as they are (Parsons, 1960:297; Cox, 1965).

John E. Nordskog (1960:293) shows that the closest logical relation exists between religion and progress because both words express a process of evaluation. Religion denotes the whole-hearted response that a human being makes to life and to the universe. Unfortunately, this relation has too seldom been understood in history.

Parsons (1960:297) has spoken of religious attempts to make over the world by active intervention, in the service of human goals. Cox (1965:117) interprets the Gospel as a summons to leave behind the society and symbols of a dying era and to assume responsibility for devising new ones.

As Shaull (1967:27) puts it: "All orders of society are losing their sacral character and are now open toward the future, to be shaped as man wills." A. Van Leeuwen finds a growing tendency toward the emergence of messianic movements dedicated to the liberation of man from all that enslaves and dehumanizes him.

Given the fluidity of a dynamic society, we should now be witnessing gradual progress toward the shaping of new social structures, which would offer a greater degree of justice and well-being to the depressed classes of the world. As Shaull (1967:28) says, this has not happened to a significant extent as yet, but there are signs that Christians are awakening to this responsibility.

Today, the Gospel summons man to frame with his neighbor a common life suitable to God's kingdom. He responds by leaving behind familiar patterns of life that are no longer appropriate, and by setting out to invent new ones. Man must be ready to develop new ways of dealing with the emerging realities of history.

The "social gospel" movement, begun in the last century, was a needed corrective within the church (despite certain over-simplifications). This movement, within both Protestant and Catholic branches, sought economic and social reform in the spirit of a Jesus who had given himself to the poor and who had been denounced as agitator and revolutionary. Today almost all major Christian bodies take open stands on social issues in their concern for racial equality, economic justice, and a world at peace.

A concern for social justice in the name of God is not a recent idea; it goes back at least to Hebrew prophets such as Isaiah and Amos. The Hebrews were interested in a righteous society and established a set of laws to ensure it. And the New Testament speaks of a God of love who is ultimately concerned for every man. Christians, then, must be committed to play a healing, reconciling role in the social and political struggles of man.

Even the most controversial of social issues—political change—is included in God's concerns. Political change refers to change in the way the society as a whole orders itself. Paul was very concerned about the Christian's life in society, and even urged the church at Ephesus to come to grips with the powers and rulers of this age (Ephesians 6:12). Especially in our time, society orders itself through governments, and the Christian is called to have a deep interest in the role of governments in such areas as meeting the needs of impoverished peoples.°

Some of the areas of need Christians are concerned about today include help for the poor and disadvantaged, food for the hungry, unemployment, the environment, mass transit, housing, prison conditions, the reduction of arms, minority rights, women's concerns, and civil liberties.

As brief examples of the involvement of churches in social change, the World Council of Churches has awarded grants to thirty-seven groups to fight racism. Its general secretary recommends a setting up of an advisory group to monitor "human rights." The National Association of Evangelicals and Fundamentalist churches have also adopted resolutions calling for vigorous social action (Coffin, 1977).

## The Christian and Revolution

An important, though controversial aspect of this subject is yet to be discussed—the Christian and revolution. Wilbert E. Moore (1963:33) defines a "true" revolution as a rapid and fundamental alteration in the institutions or normative codes of a society and of its power distribution. Allan R. Brockway (1970:41) speaks of revolutionary change as rapid change with little continuity with the past. He adds that it demands a response from us in a way that cannot be

---

°See Anthony Campolo's chapter, "Politics and Principalities and Powers." For an excellent book on the Christian in politics from a Protestant point of view, see Miller (1958).

avoided. Revolution, then, is a decisive break with the past, a change to a radically different stance.

In a very real sense, therefore, the early Christians were revolutionaries. They lived, of course, in a society dominated by Rome. Allegiance to the state was proved by public obedience to a state-approved religion. When Christians declared themselves unwilling to serve a state religion they became revolutionaries. Rejection of official religion meant that Rome itself was rejected, that a new social and political order was being advocated and practiced (Brockway, 1970:43-45).

Today, Christians and many others are upset and confused when confronted with the reality of revolution. They see certain injustices round them and want to work for reasonable and gradual changes in society. But they may not understand the dynamic process going on around them.

It should be remembered, as Shaull (1967:39) points out, that a crisis in any social structure does not necessarily endanger the well-being of those who live in it. It is more likely to be a new opportunity for a richer life, especially for those groups whose well-being has been ignored.

Some of us have lived through what could be called a revolution in the area of civil rights. I can recall the status of the black man in my home state of Alabama in the 1950s. Many whites felt very threatened by the movement of blacks toward freedom in the late fifties and sixties. But enormous changes have taken place, and the whole society is much the better for it. (Of course, many changes in this area are still needed.)

As Shaull says, "The God who is tearing down old structures in order to create the conditions for a more human existence is himself in the midst of the struggle" (Shaull, 1967:37). God has taken human form in the concreteness of historical life and has called us to follow this path if we are to be the salt of the earth and the light of the world (Matthew 5:13-14). In this involvement we can perceive what God is doing, understand how the struggle for humanization is being defined, and serve as agents of reconciliation.

For Christians, revolution which is of God is to be received as good; revolution that is not of God is evil (Brockway, 1970:45). It is not an easy matter, of course, to determine which are of God. Brockway suggests that God could very well support a revolution if it were designed to bring about harmonious social relationships.

In Latin America today, Christians find themselves swept along by a seething social upheaval. Many Christians there see no meaningful hope for their countries apart from revolution. The Roman Catholic Church, especially through some of its younger priests, is fighting oppression and a feudal system. This can be seen in El Salvador where Jesuit priests are working with the poor (Coffin, 1977). Religious leaders are confronting government leadership and defying repression. A majority of Catholic bishops in Latin America have called for a conference on human rights as a step in their campaign for the poor, the dispossessed, and the neglected on the continent.°

Two concerns for many Christians are the sharp division of the world between the rich and the poor nations, and the tremendous concentration of economic and political power in a few hands. With this in mind, Shaull (1967:28) even believes that social revolution is the primary fact with which our generation will have to come to terms.

> If we hope to preserve the most important elements of our cultural, moral and religious heritage and to contribute to the shaping of the future, we cannot remain outside the revolutionary struggle or withdraw from it (Shaull, 1967:29).

Shaull reminds us that God tore down in order to build up (Jeremiah 1:10), and that he broke the power of the oppressor in order to establish his justice (1 Samuel 2:1-10; Psalms 9 and 146). The righteousness of God, according to the psalmists and the prophets, means that he lifts up those who are bowed down and humiliates the oppressor.

A contemporary theological movement of a semirevolutionary type is "liberation theology," which condemns economic injustice and insists that it is the Christian's duty to fight oppression. Adherents quote Jesus' words in Luke 4:18: "The Spirit of the Lord is upon me, because he has anointed me to preach good news to the poor. He has sent me to proclaim release to the captives and recovering of sight to the blind, to set at liberty those who are oppressed." They see God acting with man in a cooperative process of liberating humanity and the world (Coffin, 1977). Though we may not agree with all aspects of this

---

°This has brought the church into interaction with Marxists. The relation between Christians and Marxists is a complex subject, see Ogletree (1968). See "Coming to Terms with Karl Marx," Chapter 13.

movement, we should appreciate the urgency of responding to God's call to identify with the underprivileged in our world. °

In the Christian perspective, the revolutionary process is a reality that we dare not ignore, but it loses its character of determinism and inevitability. The Christian is free to attempt to understand what is happening by analyzing the concrete social, economic, and political realities, while remaining sensitive to the direction in which things seem to be moving. As Shaull (1967:38) says, the dynamics of the process is actually determined not by some inevitable law of history, but by the interworking of God's pressure for change and man's response to it.

Shaull (1967:39) gives some needed caution about making an idol out of revolution. The overthrow of the old order will *not* automatically bring about a more just society. This can come only as we work to shape the new out of the concrete material given in a specific situation. Those who seek to replace an unjust order with a new one should remember that in the long run, the new order will be an instrument of humanization only if it, too, is open to change. And finally, while revolutions today are basically struggles for justice, in God's world justice and *reconciliation* belong together.

## Summary and Conclusion

Thus far we have noted the accelerated rate of social change in our time; found that the Bible speaks of a God who is revealed in social change (or historical events); noted that the message of Jesus calls for change, especially in the message of a kingdom of God that is being realized; and that the New Testament contrasts this "present age" and the "age to come," and sees creation as moving toward a goal. God's concern for man includes social and political justice, even perhaps to the point of favoring revolutionary movements.

We have seen that the emphasis of the Bible, particularly the New Testament, supports social change. The Christian is called to leave the powers of "this age" and seek a new one. God demands change in his creation, and he is present in the changes that take place around and within us. Brockway (1970:170) says that freedom from fear of change

---

°In his 1979 visit to Latin America, Pope John Paul II appeared to reject "liberation theology," but he reaffirmed the church's commitment to human rights and social justice.

is the life-giving Word in Jesus Christ. It is freedom to receive change as a good gift.

We have, then, the responsibility to examine changes as they occur in order that we might not blindly accept, condone, refuse, or reject them.

Since the Christian is open to change and to the future, this means, as Cox (1965:121) says, that antiquity is no longer a mark of authenticity. What one has accepted must be constantly tested in the light of God's Word and of a world which never stops changing. The past is celebrated and appreciated, but it can never be allowed to determine the present or the future. In a dynamic world, the past can be preserved only as it is constantly being transformed.

A cautionary note would remind us of the danger of "giving our blessing" to causes indiscriminately, or elevating political programs into holy crusades. We should avoid the temptation to trust in the power of man to build a completely new order and to solve all problems that may arise. The kingdom of God demands that we promote changes, but we must accept the fact that they will never be fully realized in history.

As even Shaull (1967:36) concedes, the Christian looks for stability on the other side of change; he is therefore free to be fully involved in dynamic changes, even revolution; but at the same time, his understanding of what is going on obliges him to work constantly for reconciliation.

Christians are called, says Brockway (1970:178), to serve the Lord of change, not change itself or any agent of change or any result of change. To apply Christian principles to a rapidly changing world is a difficult and demanding task—but Christians who live by grace are called to follow a God who "makes all things new."

### Discussion Questions

1. Name some ways American society has changed over the past twenty years or so in such areas as social norms, social attitudes, and lifestyle. How has the church changed?

2. Nisbet and Perrin say that few of us can be said to welcome change. Do you agree, and is that a problem as far as Christian faith is concerned?

3. If you agree that God is revealed in social change, what are some events of our time in which God may be found?

4. Does the phrase "the kingdom of God" carry implications for our lives today, or is it something to come only in the future?

5. What part, if any, do men and women play in the kingdom of God?

6. Religion has tended to be a conservative force in society. Is this good or bad? To what extent can it also be a challenging or transforming force?

7. When the church takes stands on social issues, is this part of its essential mission or is it somewhat marginal to its primary task?

8. Which of the areas of needed social change do you feel are the most important as far as Christians are concerned?

9. Do you believe Christians should ever support revolutions? If so, in what manner? If not, why not?

10. In what ways can Christians work for peace and reconciliation in a world such as ours?

## References

Abrecht, Paul
　　1961 *The Churches and Rapid Social Change*. Garden City, N.Y.: Doubleday.
Brockway, Allan R.
　　1970 *Uncertain Men and Certain Change*. Nashville: Graded Press.
Burton, C. Emory
　　1968 "Christian Liberalism." *Engage*, 1:5 (November 15).
Coffin, Tristam
　　1977 "An Extraordinarily Hopeful Ferment." *The Washington Spectator and Between the Lines*, Vol. 3:15 (August 15).
Cox, Harvey
　　1965 *The Secular City*. New York: Macmillan.
de Vries, Egbert
　　1961 *Man in Rapid Social Change*. Garden City, N.Y.: Doubleday.
Lehmann, Paul H.
　　1963 *Ethics in a Christian Context*. New York: Harper & Row.
Miller, William Lee
　　1958 *The Protestant and Politics*. Philadelphia: Westminster Press.
Moore, Wilbert E.
　　1963 *Social Change*. Englewood Cliffs, N.J.: Prentice-Hall.
Nisbet, Robert, and Robert G. Perrin
　　1977 *The Social Bond*, second edition, ch. 10. New York: Alfred A. Knopf.
Nordskog, John Eric (ed.)
　　1960 *Social Change*. New York: McGraw-Hill.

Ogletree, Thomas W. (ed.)
  1968 *Opening for Marxist-Christian Dialogue.* Nashville: Abingdon Press.
Parsons, Talcott
  1960 "Religion as a Source of Creative Innovation," in John Eric Nordskog (ed.), *Social Change.* New York: McGraw-Hill, pp. 295-298.
Perrin, Norman
  1963 *The Kingdom of God in the Teaching of Jesus.* Philadelphia: Westminster Press.
Robinson, John A.T.
  1960 *On Being the Church in the World.* Philadelphia: Westminster Press.
Shaull, Richard
  1967 "Revolutionary Change in Theological Perspective," in Harvey Cox (ed.), *The Church Amid Revolution.* New York: Association Press, pp. 27-47.
Toffler, Alvin
  1970 *Future Shock.* New York: Random House.

# 40
# Violence, Revolution, and the Christian

*William H. Swatos, Jr.*

The debate over the proper stance for a Christian to take with regard to revolutionary violence has existed from the days of Christ's ministry to the present—sometimes the arguments have been strong and passionate, at other times weak and formal. While we will take a brief look at both the biblical and theological bases for the various positions that have been defended at one time or another, our primary interests in this chapter is in the exploration of revolutionary violence as a sociological phenomenon within the context of a Christian commitment.

This is a complicated issue. Nevertheless, I hope to offer a few insights as a sociological perspective can bring to an understanding of the questions involved. In the final analysis, however, the student must think things through for himself and formulate his own philosophy towards revolutionary violence.

First, let us define a few terms to give us common ground. By *violence*, I mean an act or acts of human or nonhuman origin that inflict either psychological or physical pain upon a person or a group of persons. Such violence may be direct (e.g., a shooting or knifing), or indirect (e.g., a loss of property that causes psychological stress, hunger, or disease). Here we will use *revolution* in only one of its several meanings; namely, a conscious effort on the part of a small or large group within a society to alter its mode of government outside of legitimate

**William H. Swatos, Jr.**
*Associate Professor of Sociology and Department Chairman*
*King College (Tennessee)*
Mr. Swatos is an active member of professional organizations related to his fields of interest which include the sociology of religion, sex roles, sociological theory, and the history of sociology. He has written numerous articles in his discipline. An ordained Episcopal priest, he has taught at the Episcopal Theological Seminary in Kentucky before coming to King College. He earned his PhD from the University of Kentucky.

channels. By this definition, we exclude both the duly elected leader whose views may radically diverge from those of the existing power structure, and also those kinds of massive social change that are the generally unintended and unforseen consequences of technological advances (e.g., the Industrial Revolution or the Atomic Revolution). By limiting our definition to violent revolutions, we also exclude from consideration the relatively innocuous palace coup that has become a standard manner for changing government in some countries, though not formally legitimated.

## Biblical and Historical Perspectives
### The Old Testament

One way of looking at Old Testament history is as the continuing saga of revolution by and among the Israelites. From Moses to Gideon, David to Jeroboam, Jehu to Judas Maccabeus, revolution is a perennial theme. In some cases it is at God's direct command, while in others one senses that God is using the revolution to effect his ultimate purpose and vindicate his righteousness.

Although one may read prophetic announcements of a coming day of "peace on earth, good will towards men," the history of the chosen people is, throughout, one of violence. From a sociological viewpoint, I find one of the most interesting accounts of the futility of pacifism in the second chapter of 1 Maccabees: A group of devout Jews fled to the dessert to escape ritual religious pollution at the hands of the soldiers of Antiochus IV Epiphanes. The persecutors, however, merely followed them, waited until the Sabbath, and when the Jews refused to flee because they did not want to profane the Sabbath day, they killed them all.

> When Mattathias [Judas Maccabeus' father] and his friends heard of it, they mourned deeply for them. "If we all do as our kinsmen have done," they said to one another, "and do not fight against the Gentiles for our lives and our traditions, they will soon destroy us from the earth." On that day they came to this decision: "Let us fight against anyone who attacks us on the sabbath, so that we may not all die as our kinsmen died in the hiding places" (1 Maccabeus 2:39-41, NAB°).

---

°Quotations in this chapter are from *The New American Bible*, unless otherwise stated.

## The New Testament

When we come to the New Testament, however, a strikingly different picture emerges. Nonviolence and obedience to civil authority are predominant themes. Before Pilate, Jesus replies:

> My kingdom does not belong to this world. If my kingdom were of this world, my subjects would be fighting to save me. . . . As it is, my kingdom is not here (John 18:36).

Paul, in the thirteenth chapter of his letter to the Romans, claims that all authority comes from God alone and opposes revolution in the strongest possible terms. The revolutionary opposes not only the temporal ruler, but God himself. The epistles of Peter echo the same tone. Only in the Book of Revelation, the Apocalypse, is there an opening provided for the possibility of resistance, although it is questionable whether one should regard the highly symbolic nature of this book in any literal sense (Garrett, 1976, 1977).

### Christian History

Historically the attitude of Christians toward revolutionary violence has been generally negative, particularly during those periods and in those places where the church became an arm of the state. Even before Constantine, however, Justin Martyr was writing of the church's concern for, and support of the pagan emperor. The record is replete with accounts of Christians willingly dying for their faith, rather than resisting evil by the use of force. Tertullian, one of the early church fathers, was particularly strong in his pacifism, but he ended his life with the Montanist "heretics." A century or so later, however, Augustine, concerned about the spread of Pelagianism, elaborated what has since become known as the "just war" doctrine—a theological justification for the Christian's participation in military combat. As centuries passed, violence was increasingly used, and the state church gave its blessings to the use of force in order that the state might maintain its position or conquer other peoples. As church and state were fused into one, many saw the biblical position "compromised" (see Troeltsch, 1931).

Although Luther particularly condemned the Peasants' Revolt, there were considerable Christian revolutionary outbreaks during the Reformation period and the years that followed in its wake. Certainly the English (Puritan) Revolution of the 1640s must be seen as one strongly motivated by the apocalyptic visions of the Antichrist, of the angel of darkness appearing as an angel of light, and of the trials and tortures of the righteous by satanic forces (Hill, 1971). And just as certainly, this revolution, more than any other, paved the way for the development of "modern" society. However, as Max Weber has shown in his definitive essay *The Protestant Ethic and the Spirit of Capitalism,* the faith and piety that was the integrating factor in life and motivated this uprising was itself soon left behind.

Occasionally Christians have also engaged in nationalistic revolutions, attempting to free a given national/ethnic group from the domination of a larger, more powerful state. These rebellions were generally given the greatest degree of church support when a Christian subgroup was fighting against a dominant that was not Christian. Much rarer are the cases in which Christian believers actively supported the overthrow of even a nominally Christian power structure. Two of the most well-known are the American and Irish revolutions, and both of these rebellions are post-1650 and British in background. To that extent I would urge that they must be seen as rooted in the rather unique Puritan revolution mentioned earlier.

Much more typical of the church's general attitude, however, was the extremely weak support provided to those Christians dedicated to the destruction of German Nazism, particularly Hitler and his cohorts, prior to and during World War II. For the most part, Christians within a society have been reluctant to engage in battles against this-worldly oppression out of religious conviction. Generally, they have supported standing armies, colonialism, imperialism, and a status quo that places religion second to politics and economics.

## Contemporary Society

In the modern world there are two areas of immediate concern for the Christian sociologist with respect to revolutionary violence. One is Africa; the other is Latin America. Both are difficult for the modern North American/European Christian to comprehend fully. Both are underdeveloped continents with developing social systems. In Latin America the church and the powerful leaders of government have generally been in league. Yet over the past two decades a growing concern for the poor and powerless has led many of the clergy and laypersons within the church to engage in sociopolitical action to restructure the social order. While Dom Helder Camara calls for a *Revolution Through Peace*, the Christians for Socialism in Latin America and elsewhere have developed a "theology of liberation" (see Gutiérrez, 1974). In this liberation theology, Jesus appears as "the subversive of Nazareth" and the Gospel "is subversive toward all powers of death; it is a source and force of liberation." Thus, "revolutionary praxis comes to be recognized as the matrix that will generate a new theological creativity." Although never explicitly championing violence, in their various national organizations Christians for Socialism make it very clear that they do not reject violent revolution in the cause of "liberation" (Eagleson, 1975).

The African situation parallels that of Latin America, but it is further complicated by racism and, in some areas, competition between Christianity and Islam. Both black and white Christians have been martyred in considerable numbers in sub-Sahara Africa. Some claim that more Christians have been killed there in this century than in first-century Rome, although this is difficult, if not impossible, to document accurately. The *apartheid* policies of South Africa and the terrifying dictators of newly independent black nations (of which Idi Amin was the most well-known, but not unique) have served to produce a "theology of violence" there as well.

In response to these developments, a British professor of theology, J.G. Davies (1976), has recently written a book in which he has developed a doctrine of a "just revolution," quite akin to Augustine's concept of a "just war." T.J. Nossiter (1976:59) has summarized his argument well:

> . . .A Christian may and should engage in revolutionary violence on the grounds that *(a)* it is the strange work of love to destroy what is against love ["Our God is a consuming fire"—Heb. 12:25]; *(b)* that ultimately there comes a point when the physical—or psychological—violence of society against its members reaches a level which justifies resistance in much the same way as we would oppose foreign invasion or personal assault; *(c)* that the Bible and Christian history are full of precedents; *(d)* that ends *sometimes* justify means; *(e)* and that, finally, though violence is never "good," it may be "right."

Jacques Ellul (1969, 1971, 1972), on the other hand, an equally distinguished French theologian, has consistently denounced all such justifications of violence as contrary to the very core of Christian living, to the work and person of Jesus Christ, and to the expression of his Spirit. In the light of these conflicting views, how is a decision to be made?

## Sociological Concepts and Insights

*Social Control*

Social control is a basic sociological concept. It refers to society's mechanisms for keeping its members in line, and for calling those who get out of line to account for their behavior. All societies have mechanisms for social control; no society could exist without it. On the one hand, the social control mechanisms used most often in society are nonviolent in nature, and usually involve informal sanctions imposed by peers or other primary group members. On the other hand, if all nonviolent means of control fail, all societies have violent social control mechanisms that are then put into action. It is critically important that we recognize that this is as true of free democratic societies as it is for totalitarian regimes. And, unfortunately, whenever the church has wielded political power, it has resorted to violent means just as much as "secular" rulers. We need only recall the Inquisition, the persecutions on both sides during the Reformation, the religious wars that followed, and the trials of "heretics," "witches," and other "wicked people" that took place in the "holy commonwealth" of Puritan New England.

*Official Violence*

A second concept that is critically important is that of official violence. Through their study and elaboration of social control, many sociologists believe that violence is endemic to the human condition, and that the maintenance of social order ultimately rests upon the state's ability to use force to suppress disorder. Violence, then, is not something done by the "bad guys"; rather, it is believed to be a constituent part of the lives of everyone of us. In the final analysis, we believe that our lives and property will be "safe" because we trust the legitimate authorities within society to maintain order, even if this means using violence. For the Christian, this is but a simple extension of the doctrine of original sin and the fallen world. Therefore, by our very nature, as sinful and sinning human beings, we are all involved in violence as members of society. For those of us who live in a democratic society, the problem becomes even more acute. Provided that elections are held fairly and honestly, we are ultimately responsible for the way violence is exercised in the name of the state. We are thus not merely involved in violence, but we are also the perpetrators of it. Official violence is exercised not in the name of the king, but of the people. From this perspective, the question then becomes: What is the proper exercise of violence?

*Legitimation*

The voluntary acceptance of governmental power by a people or society is called legitimate power. Legitimation "explains" or "justifies" its actions, making what it does both meaningful and ethical. A fairly conservative reading of the New Testament, for example, suggests that those in power are there because God put them there. Because they are there at his behest, they have the right to use force to punish evil. Even if the ruler uses his power wrongly and punishes good, the Christian is not to rebel. Instead, he should bear the suffering gladly, uniting himself to Christ. From this viewpoint official violence is always legitimate and never to be actively opposed.

In matters of conscience, one may resist official decrees (i.e., if Christianity is outlawed, one may continue to hold and practice the Christian faith), but one is to accept whatever punishment is meted out for civil disobedience. To act in this way is to take up Christ's cross— and follow him to Calvary, if need be—in the sure and certain hope of the resurrection of the dead. Such a reading of Scripture was clearly held by many early Christians who died for their faith. Indeed, it was upon the graves of martyred saints that the church was built. Furthermore, it remains the motivating principle for many contemporary Christians, and for classical Christian pacifism as well.

A broader reading of the Bible, however, has lead many Christians, at least from the time of Augustine onward, to feel that more is involved in Christian witness than martyrdom. They believe that Christians in government—whether as officials, advisers to rulers, or citizens in a democracy—have a responsibility to work for the creation of a just social order consistent with God's revealed will. This understanding of the Christian's social vocation is based in part on an implicit recognition that the New Testament was written in the first century when most Christians expected Christ's return to come quickly. As time passed, the imminent return seemed less and less likely. Over the next two centuries, however, the church grew both in numbers and influence. As the church became a social power, some means of maintaining social control had to be implemented. The result was, in effect, the develop-

ment of a "political theology" to legitimize the fact of Christian participation in official violence.

These two interpretations of church-state relations are actually
ideal types. They have been interwoven in specific historical configura-
tions to form the dominant theme in the question of church-state relations: (1) The Christian should advance the cause of Christ's kingdom
on earth as he has opportunity and (2) the Christian should suffer
passively when circumstances do not permit him to effect change
"within the system." In neither case is he to engage in activity consciously intended to overthrow the prevailing social order.

### *"Christian" Revolution?*

The apocalyptic theme, however, never fully disappeared from
Christianity. As the second of these two interpretations came to
dominate Western Christendom, questions began to be raised about
"Christian" rulers whose administration departed totally from the
"plain word of Scripture," making a mockery of the claim to be "Christian." Could this, in fact, be the Antichrist? Speculations about unjust
"Christian" rulers, in both church and state during the Reformation
period (particularly in seventeenth-century England), resulted in the
development of a theology of revolution. Were there circumstances
under which it was right to remove a ruler from office forcibly and/or
overthrow a government? Some Christians held that there were indeed
limits to be placed on official violence, and that the people or society
that was being oppressed could rise up against the government. Paul
reminds us that Satan himself may appear as an angel of light and "his
ministers disguise themselves as ministers of the justice of God" (2
Corinthians 11:14-15). Therefore, any attempt by rulers for the loyalty
of their subjects, apart from a life in concert with the Gospel, deserved
no special recognition in a Christian commonwealth. The Puritans and
their continental counterparts were attempting to turn the established
"state church" structure on its head and create a "church state."

One curious element in these arguments was the extent to which
they minimized the role of leadership figures. Resistance, rebellion, or
revolution was seen as legitimate only when it arose spontaneously, out
of common consent. Contemporary sociologists would seriously question the possibility of this leaderless revolution actually occurring. Although crowds, mobs, or other "leaderless groups" might gather
to protest particular governmental policies or actions, even they

eventually "give birth" to a leader. And the sustained effort necessary to effect a revolution takes much more careful planning and organization than lesser forms of collective behavior—in revolutions one expects leaders and a chain of command.

### Church-Sect Typology and the Response to "Evil"

What we find here, then, is a kind of dialectic. On the one hand, the church has no social power base and is persecuted. On the other hand, as the church gains a power base, it finds it necessary to exercise some form of control over recalcitrant members in order to maintain social order (often identified with "God's plan"). Because of this, Christians, as the church, tend to become both *in* and *of* the world. The inevitable result of this is conflict between Christians and non-Christians, and among Christians themselves. Christian theologians would associate this conflict with human pride and its sinfulness. Sociologists, however, would be more likely to see conflict in terms of ideological power struggles for control over the development of the social structure and the use of its products.

Thus, when one religious group confronts another, both have certain economic or power interests. Before long one group is without a power base and persecuted by the other group (which sees its interests threatened), or the two groups are at war with each other for eventual domination. Problems such as these are usually dealt with in sociology by use of the church-sect typology. The "Christians for Socialism" and similar groups can be likened to a sect: minority radical elements in their respective societies protesting against the dominant religiosocial group—i.e., the church (see Swatos, 1975).

### Optimism, Pessimism, and Realism

This understanding of the problem leads us in several directions: First, it can generate a certain amount of optimism. Throughout history the perpetration of official violence has had limits. At some point the ruthless pursuit of violence by one power group has always been checked by the opposition of others who rise in protest. Thus, although violence does seem endemic to human society, this has always been mitigated by some sense of justice. We hope that the future will bring a narrowing of the limits of official violence. Certainly we can work toward this end. At the same time we ought to be able to take some consolation in the history of revolutions that form so much of our past.

As our understanding generates optimism, it also generates an equal amount of pessimism. Sociologists do little to dispel the old adage that corruption comes with power. Whatever optimism we may have about the possibility of overthrowing oppressive regimes must be balanced by the pessimistic recognition that new oppression is likely to follow as new power elites settle into place. Only continuous revolution could avert this. But continuous revolution eventually destroys the basic fabric of any society. It prohibits the stability that is necessary for cultural development and economic self-sufficiency.

These perspectives, in turn, ought to create in us a sense of realism and healthy skepticism about the promises of revolutionaries. Sociology ought to make us less concerned about rhetoric and material promises, and more aware of structure, checks-and-balances, and of compassion and rehabilitation, rather than punitive "revolutionary justice." On the one hand we should recognize that no human system of government is flawless, incorruptible, or nonviolent, including those that claim divine inspiration. On the other hand, we ought to seek from any revolutionary group mechanisms for change, recall, open debate, and the honesty of trial-and-error. And in all of this realism demands that we recognize that injustice can never be eradicated as long as the human condition persists. While violence is never "just," it apparently is a part of the human condition. In short, we must live with both eyes open, no questions answered (no "final solutions"), always skeptical, and yet forever hopeful.

### The Christian's Faith and Hope

Finally, our little sociological adventure ought to confirm our Christian faith. Man's sinfulness, his need for redemption, his inability to save himself, the otherness of God, and the glory that shall be revealed as the whole earth groans and travails, are all very much a part of the struggles of contemporary society. Christianity may not make our plight any "better," but it does make it more bearable. Likewise, the concept of a "Christian society" must be seen more as a goal worth pursuing, than as an empirical reality man can achieve. Christ's claim to have a kingdom "not of this world" and his call of people "from" this world must be realistically balanced by his own activism *and* the price he paid for it. Though Christ immersed himself in the needs of everyday people and lashed out against oppression and official hypocrisy, his reward was the cross and not a seat on the Sanhedrin.

Christ's life and death, like the relationship between the world and the church or the revolutionary and the established power in a society, is an empirically irresolvable paradox. For the Christian that paradox is resolved in the resurrection, which is victory over death. Ultimately, it will be resolved at the parousia that initiates a new world order and the triumph of the power of God over all powers and principalities of this world. We thus bear the charge to "redeem the time," knowing that Christ has gone before us.

God's Word informs our conscience through the power of the Spirit. We serve God and Christ as we reach out through the church to serve humanity, establishing a just society. Christ is our Emmanuel. He must be our motivation. The end, however, is his, not ours. It is in this hope that we claim the high calling angels cannot share.

## Discussion Questions

1. Using the books of Samuel and Kings, find a revolution recorded there and discuss its meaning for biblical history.

2. Several of the gospels record the story of Jesus casting the moneychangers out of the temple and in one case he is even described as using whips in this process. Elsewhere he claims not to bring peace on earth, but a sword. How do you reconcile these images with those of love, forgiveness, and the suffering Savior?

3. What other New Testament examples can you find in which violence or disobedience to authority is explicitly practiced or sanctioned by Jesus and/or the apostles?

4. Do you feel that the modern church as an organization works to support or to question the political status quo? On what do you base your answer?

5. Are there times when you would say, because of the *situation*, that the "end justifies the means"?

6. Davies says that though violence is never "good," it may be "right." What does he mean by that? Do you agree?

7. To what extent do you believe that the statement "might makes right" is an accurate reflection of morality-in-practice by any people at any point in time? On what do you base your answer?

8. If social order is impossible without violence, how is the proper exercise of violence to be determined and by whom?

9. "A pacifistic society is a sociological impossibility." Discuss.

10. People sometimes speak of themselves or others as "innocent bystanders" to a particular occurrence. To what extent is the use of this concept morally and/or sociologically justified? To what extent is it not?

# References

Berger, Peter L.
  1963 *Invitation to Sociology*. Garden City, N.Y.: Doubleday.
  1969 *The Sacred Canopy*. Garden City, N.Y.: Doubleday/Anchor.
  1970 *A Rumor of Angels*. Garden City, N.Y.: Doubleday/Anchor.
  Berger, Peter L., and Thomas Luckmann
  1967 *The Social Construction of Reality*. Garden City, N.Y.: Doubleday/Anchor. Berger, Peter L., and Richard J. Neuhaus.
  1970 *Movement and Revolution*. Garden City, N.Y.: Doubleday.
Camara, Helder
  1971 *Revolution through Peace*. New York: Harper and Row.
Cell, Edward
  1967 *Religion and Contemporary Western Culture*. Nashville: Abingdon.
Davies, J. G.
  1976 *Christians, Politics and Violent Revolution*. London: SCM.
Eagleson, John
  1975 *Christians and Socialism*. New York: Orbis.
Ellul, Jacques
  1969 *Violence*. New York: Seabury.
  1971 *Autopsy of Revolution*. New York: Knopf.
  1972 *The Politics of God and the Politics of Man*. Grand Rapids: Eerdmans.
Garrett, James Leo, Jr.
  1976 "The Dialectic of Romans 13:1-7 and Revelation 13: Part One." *Journal of Church and State*, 18, pp. 433-442.
  1977 "The Dialectic of Romans 13:1-7 and Revelation 13: Part Two." *Journal of Church and State*, 19, pp. 5-20.
Gutiérrez, Gustavo
  1974 *A Theology of Liberation*. London: SCM.
Hill, Christopher
  1971 *Antichrist in Seventeenth-Century England*. London: Oxford.
Martin, David
  1966 *Pacifism*. New York: Schocken.
Nossiter, T. J.
  1976 "Just Revolutions." *Expository Times*, 88, p. 59.
Swatos, William H., Jr.
  1975 "Monopolism, Pluralism, Acceptance, and Rejection." *Review of Religious Research*, 16, pp. 174-185.
Troeltsch, Ernst
  1931 *The Social Teachings of the Christian Church*. New York: Macmillan.
Weber, Max
  1930 *The Protestant Ethic and the Spirit of Capitalism*. New York: Scribners.

# SUBJECT INDEX

# NAME INDEX